LETTERS TO EVA
1969–1983

Letters to Eva

1969–1983

A. J. P. Taylor

edited by Eva Haraszti Taylor

Century
London   Sydney   Auckland   Johannesburg

Copyright © 1991 A. J. P. Taylor and Eva Taylor
All rights reserved

First published in 1991 by Century
Random Century Ltd
20 Vauxhall Bridge Road, London SW1V 2SA

Century Hutchinson Australia (Pty) Ltd
20 Alfred Street, Milsons Point, Sydney, NSW 2061, Australia

Century Hutchinson New Zealand Ltd
9–11 Rothwell Avenue, Albany, Auckland 10, New Zealand

Century Hutchinson South Africa (Pty) Ltd
PO Box 337, Bergvlei 2012, South Africa

A. J. P. Taylor's right to be identified as the
author of this work has been asserted by him in accordance
with the Copyright, Designs and Patents Act, 1988.

Set in 11pt Linotron Baskerville

Printed and bound in Great Britain by
Mackays of Chatham, Chatham, Kent

British Library Cataloguing in Publication Data
Taylor, A. J. P. (Alan John Percivale) 1906–1990
Letters to Eva: 1969–1983
1. Historiography. Taylor, A. J. P. (Alan John Percivale),
1906–1990. Interpersonal relationships with Taylor, Eva Haraszti
I. Title   II. Taylor, Eva
907.2024

ISBN 0-7126-4634-5

Contents

Introduction	vii
1969	1
1970	7
1971	31
1972	63
1973	119
1974	175
1975	235
1976	297
1977	345
1978	401
1979	427
1980	455
1981	463
1982	481
1983	491
Epilogue	499

Introduction

I first met Alan in 1960. He was part of an English academic delegation visiting the Institute of Historical Research of the Hungarian Academy of Sciences in Budapest. As my special field was nineteenth- and twentieth-century English History I was assigned to be his companion. I was delighted; I had always been a great admirer of his.

We spent a great deal of that short time together and, while sitting on the banks of the Danube, Alan began to tell me of his life and his troubles with his first and second marriages. Margaret, his first wife, had deeply wounded him by her infatuations and his second marriage, to Eve, was proving to be no happier. Despite our growing mutual attraction, we both felt we had too many commitments to be able to take our tenuous friendship further.

In 1969 I came to London for a month on a scholarship as a guest of the British Academy. Alan and I renewed our friendship. He had left his second wife, Eve, and returned to live with Margaret. However this was simply to be for their mutual convenience, and not to resume their marriage. We spent many happy days together; I worked hard in the PRO and then Alan took me out in the evenings, once even to the Connaught, and showed me Blenheim and Oxford. But I soon received news that my husband was very ill and in hospital and returned to Hungary.

My husband had been ill for a good many years. Once I returned, we had a chance to spend some time together, but shortly afterwards he died. I do not remember too much about the days and months that followed. I survived because I had to. Alan began to write to me and his letters became a great comfort to me.

To begin with, our correspondence was clandestine. Alan did not wish to upset Eve in any way. We were, however, able to see each other occasionally. In 1970 Alan and I met at the annual conference of the Ranke Gesellschaft; I had brought with me a small statuette of a bearded old man to give to Alan. 'I shall wait for you until you are as old as this man,' I whispered. Despite our commitment to each other, I had no desire to be Alan's mistress. I longed for a relationship in which both partners could be absolutely free; cheating and illicit liaisons were never to my taste.

In 1971 when we met in Salzburg, our relationship had developed to a new closeness.

We continued to correspond, and met every six months or so for the next five years. In 1976 I was given another scholarship to go to Britain for three months. Alan was now divorced from Eve, and it was during this time that we began to consider seriously the possibility of getting married. At the end of my three months' stay I went back to Hungary to make preparations for our marriage.

Once married we continued to live apart until 1978, when, with great sorrow and apprehension, I left my now grown-up sons and my beloved Budapest, to begin a new life in London with Alan.

Our life was not always easy; Alan still had very strong commitments to Margaret, his first wife, and his children from that marriage, and also to his children from his second marriage. I found being a foreigner somewhat difficult – in my country I was a respected academic. I did not want to upset Alan, but I found it tiresome when he spent the majority of his weekends and an evening a week with Margaret. They had a lot to talk about, and had known each other for over fifty years, but I found it hard not to resent her and not to be lonely when he left me on my own. But, despite these difficulties, we had a very happy marriage. I continued to see my sons, and we had an arrangement that I would spend every Christmas with them, and also a few weeks in the summer. At these times, Alan continued to write to me.

After the last entry in July 1983 Alan and I did not part again until November 1987, when he had to go into a rest home. He needed twenty-four-hour supervision and care as his Parkinson's disease had taken over his body. His mind was still working but not the delivery. In one of his best hours he whispered to me: 'The next time you can't do something, not to worry, just draw the curtains . . .'

I kept Alan's letters because I like them. I believe they testify to a humane, generous and original human being. They are period pieces which reflect the values, the culture and the priorities of an English radical, of an English socialist in the second half of the twentieth century. Alan's genius made him not only a distinguished historian of his age both at home and abroad, but a very popular one as well. As he used to say, he was always on the side of the lads. His simple, original and witty style reflected his thoughts and he was not ashamed to declare proudly that he learnt his way of expressing himself from the great orators and

INTRODUCTION

writers of the past. His letters add a great deal to the understanding of how his mind worked, his values, his method of working and his personal habits. They make for a better appreciation of him as a historian and as a person.

Regrettably, Alan destroyed all the letters I wrote to him. His life during this period was overshadowed by marital problems, and for a long time our correspondence was kept very quiet. I have omitted passages of a very personal nature, and out of consideration for other people's feelings, but have not indicated where, as this would spoil the flow of the narrative.

Eva Haraszti Taylor

1969

5 May 1969

Dear Eva,

Many thanks for sending me the offprint of your article. I have long thought that there should be studies of the influence which the Anti-Corn Law League had in Europe, and your article is a most useful contribution. I went to Vienna with the idea of pursuing this subject in 1928, but somehow never got around to it.

When I was in Budapest, you suggested that I should send a spare copy of my *Origins of the Second World War*, in German translation, for the Institute of Historical Research. This I now gladly do. You will see that there is also a special German preface by me, and a rather funny comment by a German professor who can't decide whether my book is pro-German or anti-German (it is neither). Some copies of my *Bismarck* in German translation had also turned up, so I send one of these for the Institute also.

I managed to talk about Michael Károlyi* on Southern Television, but failed to get an article about my visit to Hungary into the *Sunday Express*. When are you coming to England?**

Regards to Tibor,

  Yours sincerely,
  Alan Taylor

24 November

My dear one,

What a strange cool letter to receive from you, and yet one I expected. No gesture of friendship – not even my name at the beginning. A most formal business letter. I laughed very much. You cannot rub out our time together. You will go on remembering it, and so will I, though

---

* First president of Hungarian Republic, 1918. Károlyi was for some years an émigré in England, and became a close friend of Alan's.
** Between May and September Eva came to London for a month, to research in the Public Record Office.

no doubt when we next meet – if ever we do – I shall fail to recognize you.

I am not going to keep bothering you by saying I love you. You know it and don't need reminding. My divorce will go through next year. Thereafter, if you are ever free and want to marry me, I shall be waiting. Or if you are even free for a shorter time, I am available. I am going to Rome for the first week in May. Any hope you can meet me? Or, if you come to England, I can take the place of the British Council for as long as you want to stay. But don't think I shall be sad if we don't meet or come together. I have the happy confidence that all is well with our feelings for each other.

Now for more important news. There is a very long and unconsciously funny book on *Peterloo* by Walmsley, arguing that it was all a mistake and that the governing classes, especially the magistrates, were most kind, well-meaning men. On the other hand (a phrase you have heard before), he has one good point. He has discovered that most of the newspaper reporters who wrote up the story of the massacre were not there at all and made up the story afterwards. This is the way reporters behave.

There is an article in *Past and Present* on 'Chartism in London', arguing it went on for a long time after the 10 April meeting, and a long book-review article on *Labour History* in the *Journal of Modern History* – much what you would expect. On quite a different theme, the *Vierteljahresheft für Zeitgeschichte* has an article showing that Esler, the carpenter, arranged the bomb attempt of November 1939 against Hitler all on his own (just like van der Lubbe with the Reichstag fire). You can imagine that this gave me great pleasure. There is a new high-flown attempt to prove that van der Lubbe had Nazi accomplices, but no evidence has been produced.

On your subject, nothing much new in book. Be sure to look at the life of Baldwin by Middlemas and Barnes. A very bad book, but with much important material on British foreign policy in the Thirties, particularly the peace ballot, Abyssinia, and the Anglo-German naval pact as preliminary to modifying Locarno. One day I shall shake your views on the naval pact. When at Cambridge recently, visiting Churchill College (where I saw the Hankey papers), I met a young man on leave from the Navy, who is doing a thesis on the Anglo-German naval pact principally from the Admiralty records. He is called Macell, and I shall arrange for him to write to you in the New Year. You may have questions you can put from afar, or even better here is an excuse to come again. We were quite mad not to spend every minute of the time together.

How exasperating it is to think that you were living in London twenty years ago. If we had met then, we could have had all our lives together. Probably you would have found me unsatisfactory, as my two wives have done. Now I really am improved and good value. Please come back to me when you can. I need your love very much. If you can't come you know what to send me, as I send it to you.

X
Alan
X

I shall write again in time
unless you tell me to stop.

11 December

My very dearest one,

My first impulse, when I had your letter, was to fly out to Budapest for a few days.* I wanted only to express my sympathy and to sustain you by my affection. On reflection I decided you would not want to be bothered with me just now. It is better that you should carry your grief alone among friends, and not with an almost stranger to trouble you. Later I will write about the many problems which I see ahead for us. Now I only want to say how deeply I sympathize. You had a good married life for twenty years and can always look back to it with contentment. You have two boys who need you, and I know how much you love them. Help them to grow up, affectionate and yet free. You will find lots of happiness in this, even though you'll miss something of what made you happy in the past. As to you and me, I'll not stir it just now, except to say this. I think I can contribute something to your life and happiness. I know you can to mine. We must somehow find a way of doing it.

Now to turn to what you call illuminating topics. My views on the naval pact are not precise and certainly not so informed as yours. The principal motive on the British side was, I think, to prepare for the general naval conference which they expected in 1936. If Germany were already satisfied, then it might be easier to settle Italian and French wishes also. This looks far-fetched, because in fact the naval conference never came off. But the British were not to know this at the time. I am

---

* Eva's husband died at the age of 44 following an operation for stomach cancer.

pretty sure that the impulse for it came from the Admiralty, though the Foreign Office was quite pleased to do something which, it thought, would appease the Germans without in fact giving anything real away. There was here a basic and genuine misunderstanding between the two sides. The British thought they had made a concession in accepting a modification of the Versailles rules. The Germans thought they had made a concession in agreeing not to build a great navy. According to a recent German book, *Vom Politik zu Weltpolitik* (800 boring pages), Hitler until this time had no interest in colonies or, in consequence, in the navy. He supposed that the British, being given by him the rest of the world, would give him eastern Europe. When the British were not persuaded by the naval pact to renounce eastern Europe, Hitler took up both colonies and a great navy in order to blackmail them into giving up Europe. Finally, by 1937, he became keen on an African empire for its own sake, deciding that he would conquer the west before he conquered the east. All a bit far-fetched, but I think the naval pact greatly helped Anglo-German misunderstanding! I'd tell you more about this German book and about another one, describing the German attempt to influence British public opinion, only I know you don't read German and, even for love of you, I am not going to summarize two books each of over 800 pages. On top of this Fritz Fischer has written yet another long German book, discussing Germany's imperialist and aggressive aims before the First World War. I doubt whether German wickedness explains the whole of modern history, though it no doubt explains quite a lot.

I have got *Beaverbrook* to 1943 and am beginning to think that I shall finish it before I die. I am going to lecture on him in Oxford next term. Television asked me to take part in a series, called 'Heroes' – talk on someone I admired for half an hour. I considered all sorts of conventional answers – Cromwell, John Bright, Tom Paine. Suddenly I had the right idea: Captain Swing (name used by the agricultural labourers in the revolt of 1830). I don't think the BBC liked this. At any rate I have heard nothing.

With very deep love which one day will come true.

X
Alan
X

1970

23 January 1970

My sweetheart,

    Your letter distressed me very much. I ought to be able to help you and do not know how to do it. When you feel lost and sad in the world, remember that someone loves you, enjoys your company and has you constantly in mind. Now listen to this delivered in a solemn elderly way. Children don't go on living in sorrow – after all, all children nearly lose their parents – and they need cheerful people around them. This is what you can give to their lives. But it is also very important that you don't make them the only centre of your life and only source of happiness. You have to treat them in such a way that they gradually grow away from you and become independent without upsetting either you or themselves. I know this is very difficult. I have had a very bad personal life for thirty years past, as you know, and throughout my unhappiness – which still goes on – I've relied on my children for happiness and fun. But I think I've also managed not to be too much with them, so that now they still enjoy my company greatly and yet, the grown-up ones, have a very active life of their own. That is what you have to do, and one of the ways of doing it is to have other sources of contentment, if not of happiness, so that they will know you will be all right when they go off. And that is what I can offer you occasionally, though how long I shall be here or worth offering is difficult to tell.

    I forget whether I told you the full titles of the two German books I mentioned. They are *Das Ringen um England* by D. Aigner and *Vom Reich zum Weltreich* by Klaus Hildebrand. They are both much too long, but so are all German books.

    Captain Swing never existed. I think it derives from swing meaning hang (as death punishment). The implication was that Captain Swing would hang all the rich landowners, though he was more likely to get hanged himself.

    I am giving six lectures on Beaverbrook in Oxford this term. Very difficult, most interesting for me, but for anyone else? I have to work very hard to keep the attention of the audience.

    I think of you with much love and hope that our dreams – or at any rate mine – will come true. Send me a kiss next time, as I do.

                  xxxxxxxxxxx   Alan xxxxxxx
                                   x

3 March
                                   Your letter was adorable.

Dearly Beloved,

You can be sure of my feelings. I needed no encouragement from you. I knew I was right in caring for you as soon as I saw you again (this does not alter the fact that I have already forgotten again what you look like). And there is no need to fear that I merely turned to you because I had experienced failure before and wanted to compensate for it. I'm quite content with my past efforts even if they went wrong in the end, and I'm quite content now to be on my own. If I had not met you again I should never have looked at another woman in all my life. Now I don't need a wife, but I would like to have you as a person.

Now here are some bits of news. *English History 1914–1945* is coming out here as a Penguin paperback and as some different paperback in America. I read through the text again very carefully and found still many many mistakes. Now I hope I have put them right. The Penguin edition of the *Communist Manifesto* with my introduction has reached its fourth edition. Soon everyone will learn about Marx from me, and I am afraid that my views on him are rather frivolous – but then nearly all my views are. And on top of this *The Habsburg Monarchy* has reached another edition in paperback. I read this carefully also. I thought it rather good, though too mechanical – names of political tendencies instead of anything about people. It is history written in a sort of shorthand, just giving the headings so that anyone can write the whole book for himself. I also found a number of mistakes. Oh dear, how careless I am, or perhaps how careless English printers are.

There were some special lectures in Oxford, named after William of Waynflete, the founder of Magdalen College. The man who was set down to deliver them – some frightful American sociologist – failed to come at the last moment. So I said: what about me? I did them for nothing, since I could hardly propose that I should be paid. This was the first time I had lectured in Oxford for seven years and I don't suppose that I shall lecture again. Guess what I lectured on: 'Max Aitken, Lord Beaverbrook.' Six whole lectures on him. They went with a bang. Never less than 350 in the audience and I gave them a wonderfully gay turn, assisted of course by Beaverbrook who was himself a very gay man. The quotations from him were a great success. Some of the lectures were quite serious history as well, but you know I can't be serious for long.

I've got the Life to the end of the Second World War. In a sense the big story is over. Beaverbrook was out of politics for ever after that. I'll have to get away from narrative and describe the things he was doing in a general picture – running his papers, writing his books and so on. It is very moving. When well over 70 he took up the writing of history again and devoted most of his time to it. The result was two marvellous books.

I'll send you a book about history by a young historian soon. It was a present from him to me and now is a present from me to you. It's not very good, but it has some funny pages devoted to me, and they will amuse you. Here is a confession: I never read contemporary novels. I stopped with Evelyn Waugh, but I shall try and find *The Raging Moon*. H.E. Bates, I am sure, is no good except perhaps for foreigners (in the way they admire Byron and Oscar Wilde?). My only relaxations are chamber concerts and the cinema – usually Westerns. I can't stand serious film or serious theatre. So perhaps we aren't suited?

Don't worry. I love you and I think you love me. Write to me as quickly as you can and say you are coming to Rome. Or if you can't come to Rome, never mind. We shall still go on caring for each other. So write to me in any case.

Very much love, my darling

Alan
XXXXXX

23 April

Darling One,

I ought to have replied to your letter of 31 March earlier. It was sweet and right in every point. I am more sentimental but you feel more deeply. We will arrange the future when it comes. Till then we will write as very good and loving friends, though I hope you will send me a kiss now and then. After all, no one else does, and I grow hungry for them. I know you will not change your mind about coming to Rome. But if you do I shall be at the Hotel Inghilterra, via Bocca di Leone, from 3 to 10 May, busy addressing American businessmen only on Ascension Day. So change your mind.

Venice was a great success. My two boys and I walked I should think down every street, entered every church and noticed at least the name of every picture. It is easy to visit the capital of a dead Empire, it is just like London and in a sense Budapest also. Ichabod, ichabod, the glory has departed (quote from the Bible. Do you know the Bible or were you brought up a Roman Catholic?).

I did a rather shocking thing. I got a cyclostyled letter in Russian, and as I can't read Russian except with difficulty threw it away. Then an angry man rang from the Soviet Embassy to ask whether I was going to some conference in Moscow. I had to invent excuses that I had been away in Italy, but of course I could not go in any case since they were not proposing to pay for me. Foreign scholars get supported by their governments. We do not. But I suppose I missed a chance of seeing you.

I have been asked to some sort of historical conference in West Germany from 16 to 19 September, where they will pay my expenses. Are you going? Or shall I perhaps ask them to invite you. It is a three-day discussion on the background of the Second World War. Good for your history as well as being good to see me. So enquire into it or get me to stir them up. You really would have something to contribute, as I will emphasize to them. I have given your address to a Cambridge researcher who is working on the Anglo-German naval treaty, while on leave from the Navy. Be kind to him if he writes. He is much better looking and much younger than I am.

I am rather stuck over Beaverbrook. I have got him to the end of the Second World War when he left active politics. But he had another nineteen years to live, running his papers, writing books, keeping up with events. There is plenty of material but it no longer falls into tidy chronological divisions, and I am only good when handling narrative. I'll have to do all the research before trying to write any of this. I'd like to write at some length and thus safely turn my book into two volumes. Meanwhile I worry a little and get bored with these endless files.

Nicolson is very interesting but not very reliable. I do not believe he wrote his account of the pre-Munich debate at the time, and I am sure he inserted Boothby's name into the 2 September debate very late. Nicolson was a very attractive man. Yet curiously he gets less attractive as one reads more of his Diary. Vita was a very pronounced lesbian, and Harold had a softness for little boys, so their marriage worked best when they were apart. There is a new book by Rhodes James called *Churchill. A Study in Failure*. It is stimulating though there is little new in it.

I miss you very much. I miss your voice and I miss your hair. I should like very much to put my arms round you or to be again having lunch in the inn at Burford, talking about the Levellers and the Chartists. Next time too we shall go to Newport, even if there is nothing to see. I hold out my hands to you in imagination and send across the continent many loving kisses.

xxxx my Darling, Alan

1970

12 May

My Dearest,

You will no doubt have laughed at the telegram I sent you. I knew there was no chance of your coming to Rome but thought I had better warn you off all the same. I behaved in my usual impulsive manner. As the time drew near I began to feel that I could not bear to be in Rome for a week without you when I had planned that we should meet. I further reflected that I should get little pleasure from addressing successful American businessmen and their wives. Finally Rome seemed unattractive when gripped by strikes of garbage men and public transport. By this time I was angry with myself for ever having agreed to go at all. So I wired cancelling my visit. The organizers then became very agitated and urged me by telephone to come if only for a couple of days, which I ended by doing. It was not much fun – rain, cold, and all these American businessmen. I suppose you will be interested to know that even these representatives of American capitalism are all violently against Nixon and applauded me when I said America had no business in Vietnam. Of course they belong to the class of independent capitalist adventurers for whom war is highly expensive, apart from the fact that their sons are liable to be called up.

The other thing I learnt from them was that over 50% of children of high-school age are drug-takers. They treated this as normal, though of course highly worrying and unwelcome. I suppose a similar figure in England is 5%. This makes America a totally bewildering country.

Now I have another project which no doubt you will also reject, as you do all my ideas. From 16 to 19 September I am going by invitation to Königswinter, somewhere on the Rhine, to a conference of historians organized by the Ranke Gesellschaft, which is a very reputable body. They are going to concentrate on the international situation in the years 1933–35. I shall talk about England and France. Some German will talk about Germany, and there are various other papers. I have suggested that, as you know more about the Anglo-German naval treaty than anyone else, you should be invited. So you will understand their invitation if it arrives. Your presence will inspire me. Of course I shall spend all my time talking to you instead of to the other professors, but I find professors boring in any case and might fall into the clutches of some Fraülein if you are not there. Do please come. It will be much better than going to Moscow, which I fear you may be planning. I can help with your fare if you happen to be short of money or can't get it from your Institute. Seriously, it would be good for your history and for the historical standing of Hungary.

Funny story. Recently St Antony's, Oxford, noticed that they had never had a Bulgarian and asked for three nominations from the Bulgarian government. The Bulgarians answered with one, who on arrival turned out to be the daughter of the prime minister – a Mme Zhikova who actually brought her husband with her. She gave a talk on Bulgaria's cultural heritage. Afterwards one of the audience said: 'You emphasized Okhrid as part of Bulgaria's cultural heritage. I can't find it on my map of Bulgaria.' The representative of the embassy said quickly: 'Mme Zhikova is tired now and cannot answer any more questions.' You will enjoy this story if you know Balkan affairs as well as I do.

I love you very much and think of you most of the time when I am not working. I wonder if you ever think of me.

    Many kisses, xxxxxxxxxx
    Alan

June–July

My Darling,
 I am writing this in my rooms in Oxford and think of the happy time we had together here last year. I went to Blackwell, the booksellers, today, and there I saw a book on the Chartist land settlements by Alice Hadfield (published strangely enough by a firm in Newton Abbot). It had maps and photographs of Charterville allotments and descriptions of other settlements in Hertfordshire and Gloucestershire – most interesting.

I have been carrying your letter with me for the last two weeks and have thought of it all the time. Like you I have so much to say. But first I must deal with some practical points. I heard from the director of the Ranke Gesellschaft that he had invited you to the conference. Has he sent the invitation in the right formal way? Is there any more I need do – such as tell him to write to you differently? Or is all well? So long as you can get a visa (why is the English word visa and the Hungarian or central European visum? Who is bad at Latin, you or me?), there is no other problem. I will bring plenty of money so that I can provide for us both, and maybe we could have a day or so on our own after the conference, even if it will be in Germany. At any rate, say if there is anything more I must do.

About Moscow, I do not share at all the attitude of the British

1970

historians. It is idiotic to refuse to go to Moscow because of what the Russians did to protect their overlordship of Czechoslovakia. Particularly when the very same high-minded British historians do not refuse to go to the United States despite American crimes in Vietnam. I attacked the British historians for going as individuals, which of course they can. I committed myself to going. Then I changed round. The public reason I gave was the arrest of a visiting British lecturer Grey who was arrested in Moscow and accused of anti-Soviet propaganda. I declared in the *Sunday Express* that this made Soviet Russia or any Iron Curtain country unsafe – because after all I was sure to make some anti-Soviet remark in Moscow, just as I make anti-British remarks in London and would make anti-American remarks in America if I were ever fool enough to go there. My real reasons for not going to Moscow are two. Firstly all international historical conferences bore me. I can't stand listening to other people's papers, usually in translation. I don't believe the discussion has the slightest value. I know how to score points and defend myself but this does not advance the cause of truth. I am not much interested in meeting other historians except the few I know already. I've tried an international conference once at Vienna. Of course that was all right because Vienna is almost my second home town. But the conference part was a complete failure, no doubt from my own fault. I met a number of British historians whom I often meet in England. I did not meet you, which was the only reason I decided to go. So I said never again. The second reason for not going to Moscow is that I can't stand the Russian hours. I can't wait until 3 p.m. for my main meal and I like to go to bed soon after ten in the evening. This is the real reason why I have not been to Russia since 1925. Maybe I was not so rigid then, being a teenager, but I remember that even then I thought the meal-times sheer hell and had some awful rows because I wanted to go to bed and the Russians wanted to sit up. The same rule applies to Spain, which has dinner at ten in the evening – too late for me. I would not go to Spain (except maybe for one day of rejoicing), even if Franco fell and the republic were restored.

Other practical points. Your young people are right about *Oh, What a Lovely War!* The film version was soft and romantic, trying to make us sorry for the chaps in the trenches. The stage version was really hard and far more effective. My friend Len Deighton, the crime-story writer, put up the money for the film. When he saw the soft way it was going he took his name off the credits, though he is still very wisely taking 25% of the profits.

The American edition of *English History 1914–1945* is not abbreviated. It has just come out in American paperback. Would you like a copy? What I said on television about the original landing on the Moon is that it was the least interesting event since the death of George III. (That is an English 'in' joke. He died after being mad for 11 years. I suppose the Hungarian equivalent would be the death of Ferdinand der Trottel which was I think about 1867. I know he was alive in 1866 because when the Prussians occupied Prague he said, 'Even I could have done as well as this.').

The Bible is one of the most staggering books ever written, particularly when read in the English of James I's time. It is, as you know, one of the greatest prose works in the English language. The early books are fascinating for their mixture of legend and reality. I think the histories get rather boring after David. Those Jewish kings are a dreary lot. Then the prophets liven things up again. Some are very grand, some are mad, which is also enjoyable. The New Testament is extraordinarily different. Whereas the Old Testament is in glittering grandiose prose, the New is obviously the work of simple almost illiterate fishermen. I don't find Jesus a very interesting character, though he was obviously a good man. I don't like Paul at all and have difficulty in reading his Epistles. But I once read the whole Bible (except for the genealogical tables) to my daughters.

I am still loyal to Beaverbrook and work on him nearly every day. I have written, though not finally, up to 1946 when he opposed the American loan. I have also gone through his remaining papers until his death in 1964. Then I must write this story also. That is difficult. There is no obvious way of dividing into chapters, just the story of a busy journalist and historian. Aged 83, he wrote: 'Writing good books, that's my passion now.' I wonder whether I shall write the same. And why do you think he started writing again? Because I praised one of his books in a review. This was before I knew him and it gave me great pleasure.

So as ever I put my arm around you and feel you close to me. In imagination I am successful. In reality I don't expect to be. Even when we are in bed together we shall only lie and talk. Maybe.

Much love and many kisses,

xxxxxxxxxx
Alan

I shall write again when I have anything to say, whether you write or not.

1970

16 July

My dear sweet Girl,

My letters anger you, or nearly, and your letters delight me. You write so well from the heart and with an emotional reality that comes straight to me. You write firmly and so will I. When we meet in Germany, if we do, I shall be very pleased to see you, and I think you will be pleased to see me. That is all I expect and all I want. What happens in the future is a matter of daydreaming and does not affect the fact that we are fond of each other. Never doubt that your company always makes me happy and I expect always will. But as a good intellectual there is also a lot of my mind always busy on other things. A writer can never give all of himself because his typewriter is really his first love.

You think that like most intellectuals I am afraid of real doings. No. I am merely rather bored with them. If something important comes up – like the Campaign for Nuclear Disarmament or freedom in the universities – I have great moral courage. This isn't boasting. It just happens. Once in a political fight I am the hardest man in the business, quite indifferent to what people say or to my own position. But I always wish I were not involved, and I drop out as soon as the particular question runs down. Years ago when I was trying to get an academic job, the head of the College said disapprovingly: 'I hear you have strong political views.' I replied: 'No. Extreme views, weakly held.' Now I hope never to be drawn into public battles any more. But of course if there were something which set me alight – in this country probably the colour question – I'd risk everything all over again.

My way of life has nothing to do with being an intellectual. It is, as you say, a matter of taste. My father, who had the best proletarian outlook of anyone I ever knew, also liked going to bed early. I don't like conferences and smoke-filled rooms. I like country walks, sunbathing, and swimming every warm afternoon. I like driving a big car very fast, though nowadays it makes me stiff. I like looking at churches and listening to quartets. That's about the lot. I like making love with someone I love. Otherwise I am not much concerned with women as women, though I certainly prefer women's society to that of men. English society is nearly always masculine. That is why I don't have much social life.

My Italian friend and translator, Lucia, told me that the best friendships are between men and women, and I am sure she is right. She has a funny life. She is very intelligent, sophisticated and likes literary society. Her husband, though the top medical professor in Rome, only likes going on safari (hunting big game) in Africa, and is actually proposing to settle in Kenya for good, running a medical mission and going on safari. She will give up Rome for his sake, but not without regrets.

About the German conference, I think you should be ready to say something about the naval treaty during the discussion after my talk. But there will only be two hours altogether. I suppose all the other speakers will read their address from a prepared paper. I shall make my talk up as I go along, and then I shall be in difficulties if they want to publish it afterwards. I imagine you will have other opportunities to raise your subject, and you will certainly establish your position as an authority on it. I suppose there will be many German professors in the audience, and I shall have to improve my German if I am to hold my own.

I have read the Hadfield book now and greatly enjoyed it, though you have to know the districts to get real satisfaction from it. She does not make the essential point that what really killed Chartism was the cheap emigrant ships to America. The workers in the North of England towns wished to escape from industry and dirt, as O'Connor's land schemes showed. But there was no free land in England. There was in America, and all the toughest Chartists went there. The emigrants were not the really poor. They were skilled craftsmen who took their tools and their skill with them. No doubt their descendants are all strong Republicans and supporters of Nixon, if not of Agnew. Incidentally, Lloyd George was in some ways a throwback to the Chartists. He was for ever producing land schemes which were quite inappropriate in our industrialized society, where agriculture is one of the most mechanized industries – producing an enormous amount with a very small labour force.

I went to York and got an honorary degree, which pleased me because I had been at school in York for five years. Otherwise it was rather silly, as such ceremonies always are. The University Orator praised *The Struggle for Mastery in Europe*, which is the dullest of my books. *English History 1914–1945* is now a paperback in Penguin, costing only 12/-. I suppose you have a copy. Otherwise I'll send you a copy of the American paperback, which is in rather larger type. *Beaverbrook* is getting along well. I begin to think that I shall have written the first draft by the end of the year. I shall really be at a loss how to spend my life if I once finish the book altogether. No doubt something will turn up. Somehow I cannot imagine myself idle for long. I have also got the Diary of Lady Lloyd-George ready for publication. I think I told you about her. She was his mistress and secretary for thirty years and put up with every sort of humiliation because she loved him – also of course because he introduced her to high life and the inside of politics. I suppose the truth is that every woman gives and every man takes. Then he is angry, as no doubt I have been, when the woman tries to reverse the situation. I've always tried to play fair – giving as much as I took. I now think from experience that women don't really like this. They want a master, not an equal partner. But I could never be that. Maybe this is merely the echo of a past situation. The young seem to be partners successfully. The funny thing is that the young are both harder and softer than me at the same time. They behave as partners, but they are also much more ruthless to each other and to themselves. I've no doubt they are a better generation. When Beaverbrook at 85 was asked what he had done in life, he replied: 'Well, there's my son. He is a much nicer man than me.' I feel the same about my children.

It is a wonderful thought that we may meet soon. I have just booked my flight to Bonn and must soon begin to think what I shall say.

Darling, I love you very much. I put my arm around you and send you a big big X.

Alan

13 August

Darling,
You will be on holiday and far from any thought of writing to me. I am shortly going to Pembroke for a fortnight, and like you will be occupied with other things than writing letters. So this is a good opportunity to say that I shall be glad to see you at Königswinter. I haven't thought what line to take in my talk. Indeed, on reflection I can't see what is particularly significant in the years 1933–36. Nothing was happening. I suppose this was the significant thing. Give me a bright idea to hold my talk together.

Another milestone passed. I have gone through all the relevant Beaverbrook files right up to the end of his life. Now I must settle down and write the chapters on his last twenty years. You know how it feels when a stage of one's work is passed – glad it is over and yet missing it. I can't imagine coming down here [Beaverbrook Library] every day and not pulling boxes from the shelves. And whatever will become of me when I have finished even writing the Life? Fortunately I shall still find plenty to revise. What I am really dreading is that I shall live long enough to face the task of rewriting *English History 1914–1945*, as it ought to be rewritten now that the archives are being opened. Another gloomy task faces me. That stodgy book of mine, *The Struggle for Mastery in Europe*, is coming out in paperback and I think I ought to compile a supplementary bibliography of all the books which have come out since 1954. But I'm not sure that I shall. I've lost interest in most of the subject. The nineteenth century now seems very far from me.

Art news. There is a bad historical film about Cromwell. There is a nude show called *Oh, Calcutta*, which is an obscene joke in French. Not a show for me. Crossman has become editor of the *New Statesman* and at once persuaded me to start reviewing for the paper again. I was too weak to refuse. I told him the return of all us old writers was like the return of the Napoleonic prefects to office in 1830, when Louis Philippe became King. I don't think he took the point that he was Louis Philippe to Kingsley Martin's Napoleon. But it is true. We are all buttoning ourselves into intellectual clothes which are now fifteen years old and correspondingly tight.

I had many other things to tell you but can't remember what they were, except the one thing I remember which is that I love you. So many and a warm embrace.

xxxx
Alan

9 October

Darling, My own dearly and truly Beloved,

Your letter moved me deeply. It was so full of love and of sincerity. It gave me such hope and at the same time filled me with regret that we were not together. I sat here in my room and cried and cried, but it was as much with happiness as anything else. I kick against the situation. We are wasting our lives, though we both think it is right to do as we do. But it is sad all the same. I wonder whether you will really love me when you know me better and see more of me. I am not so keen on people as you are. I like being with a few intimate friends occasionally and then, I am afraid, I am glad to see them go. What I want from life is to be alone with you and really no one else around. I like young people as far as I like anyone, but I feel that with them it is a one-way affair. We give to them and do so gladly. There is really nothing they can give to us.

The reason why this letter is such a mess is that I am learning to use an electric typewriter. I am sure it will be easier and much better for my work once I can manage it, but it is like an untamed beast and runs away with me. You have only to wave a finger anywhere near the keys and off the machine goes. It is even more frightening than learning to drive a car, when you have the same feeling that the machine has taken control. At the moment I find that it is a great nervous strain to be precise and accurate all the time. Once I overcome this, I shall be writing much faster than before. So think of me sitting down like a little girl to improve my typing.

I had a short tour to the North of England, lecturing to branches of the Historical Association. At Doncaster the headmistress of the Girls' High School fainted in the middle of my speech, though I don't think this was because I was so exciting. At Brimsby they took a picture of me which I send. I don't like it much and my hair is untidy. The other photograph is better and funnier. It was taken seven years ago when I was visiting Beaverbrook in the South of France. He bought the little stone pavilion in England, complete with cherub, and set it up in Place Beaverbrook, Cap d'Ail, where he was an honorary citizen of the commune. I was rather good-looking in those days, at least better than I am now. You will also be interested to hear that the jacket I am wearing in the photograph is now still in use as my second-best, used on all but the smartest occasions. Indeed, I now reckon I have so stocked up my wardrobe that I do not need to buy any more clothes as long as I live.

I went to dinner with Sir Oswald Mosley the other night, which I expect shocks you very much. However, there is nothing to it. He is now an old man, forgotten and without influence. He still has illusions of grandeur. He is proposing to visit China, and is sure that if he does so Mao-tse-Tung will take his advice how to make peace with the West. Alternatively he feels that the world economy, East and West, will one day break down, and that then everyone will send for Mosley as saviour. The only interesting thing about the dinner is that it was at the Ritz, and that is a better place to eat in than the Stegerwaldhaus. I think there I had the worst food I have ever had in my life. Poor Germans, so rich and so badly fed!

In the October number of the *American Historical Review* there is an article by A. J. Marder on the British Admiralty and the Abyssinian crisis. As you know, I think Marder is right at the top of historians, and this article is very good. Of course he is a bit soft on the admirals. Though he is an American, for some reason he is in love with the British

Navy, and our admirals are lucky to have him as their historian. The article will be useful to you, though you will probably be less sympathetic than Marder to the admirals.

There is a great long boring *History of the Second World War* by Liddell Hart. I don't recommend it. Wars, like the rest of history, are interesting only when they are presented as being about people. Battles without humanity are no more interesting than chess, and I've never been a chess player.

I hear the British Council are bringing a Hungarian here to study Michael Károlyi. I suppose he is one of your colleagues. I shall be discreet, just saying that I know you and asking how you are. Otherwise my historical news is slight. I have begun to write the last chapters of *Beaverbrook* and hope to get on quite quickly unless this typewriter reduces me to a nervous wreck. I seem to have been enslaved to that old man for ever.

The other day I went to look at the flats which the City of London is putting up not far from here. I thought it might do for us one day. But the flats are like prison cells in a mediaeval castle and, to make things worse, they are furnished with highly up-to-date 'trendy' furniture. If you are here soon, we'll go and look at them. The thought of life there will make you laugh. I hope that *Chips** made you laugh too. It is a most ridiculous book, but very revealing about one sort of politician.

Darling, never forget that I love you very much with a sort of ache. You are rarely out of my mind except when I am working.

Oh, my Darling, I long to see you and feel close to you.

xxxxx
Alan

2 November

My dearly Beloved,

That was by far the most beautiful letter I ever had from anyone in all my life. Can you wonder that I love you so much? I have found the perfect wife – late in life and under almost impossible circumstances, but very great luck all the same. There are two other things I must tell you. You ask whether our relationship as it is now is the maximum. No, a

---

* *Chips: The Diaries of Sir Henry Channon*. London, 1967.

thousand times no. Maybe it will be all we can get. But if ever we had the chance to come together it would be even better.

Here to amuse you are some faults of mine. Unlike you I fuss over my meals, or rather over one meal a day. I'd rather sit down over a good meal than go to the theatre, and I get thrown out if I don't have an evening meal at a fairly regular time. I like old comfortable clothes and hate dressing up, though I like to see my womenfolk smart. I don't like people much except when we have something interesting to talk about, and even then I often disturb things because I can't keep serious for long. I am very frivolous at heart, unable to take any principles or activities seriously. I write mainly for fun, though it would not be fun if I were not a conscientious historian at the same time. I don't like the theatre. I rarely like modern films. I like opera and chamber music, so long as they are at times which do not interfere with my meals. I have always lived on the fringes of the capitalist world, despite my socialist principles, and therefore like to have a substantial capital in the bank. I have no objection to making money by speculation as long as capitalism lasts. Indeed there are many things I would give up gladly if everyone else would – money, smoking, private cars, rich eating. But as long as others do these things, I do, and I am beginning to think they will last my time. I'll tell you some more another day.

Meeting Mosley is typical of my faults. I first met him in order to discuss his autobiography. I was asked to push him into being franker about his Fascist time – how he strayed so far. This was worth doing. But I suppose he thought I liked hearing him talk, though he is a vain arrogant man. He is lonely, isolated, an insignificant figure. So I accept his invitations because I am sorry for him, even though I am bored when we meet and I expect show it. There is another reason. He asks me to the Ritz and I like going there not from snobbery but because it is a perfectly preserved luxury hotel of 70 years ago. Not a single article of furniture has been changed. At any rate I expect that Chips, who is fun to read about, would be equally dull to meet.

I have admired Marder's work for a very long time and was even more impressed when I met him recently. I said to him: 'It is good to meet an equal.' He said: 'It does not happen enough and I feel the same.' He has the quiet confidence of a great scholar without being in the slightest degree arrogant. Now, alas, he has gone back to the United States.

Now I'll tell you how my life goes so that you will know that when I say I am busy I am really doing many foolish things. I took Crispin* to see *Traviata*, which he enjoyed very much. I went to a party to

---

* First son of Alan's second marriage to Eve Crosland.

celebrate a new book by Asa Briggs on the BBC, and drank a great deal of champagne. I went all the way to Colchester to take part in an oyster feast, given by the town council. I had 24 oysters and made a speech which the audience rightly thought was amusing but also slightly shocking and irresponsible.

I am having some worries. Max Aitken is beginning to feel that he may not agree with all I write in his father's Life, and wants to lay down that the book cannot come out without his permission. Of course I can't allow my book to be censored and it is silly of him to fuss, seeing that I loved his father so much. But it may lead to a row which I should not like at all.

Colour of hair? Well, here is a picture taken in 1961, which shows my hair at any rate darker than it is now – darkish mouse-coloured. The woman talking to me is Lady Dunn, now Lady Beaverbrook.

I hope this letter brings you a little pleasure and a little love. I think of you all the time and wonder about your sons.

And I wonder whether I should treat you badly when we set up together. I am very selfish and very weak. But love makes a difference, and I have never loved anyone as I love you and have done for ten years past. Oh yes, there was one. I loved Beaverbrook as much or even more, but it was a different sort of affection – a mixture of admiration, excitement, gratitude and sadness at his essential loneliness.

At any rate, I love you very much and wish I could feel my arms around you. Don't bother to write in a hurry. I know you are thinking of me and even love me – just a little bit.

Oh, I have forgotten one thing from the past. When we were at Königswinter we made a great mistake not to visit Trier and to see the 20 Romanesque churches in Cologne. Next time, if there is one, we should plan to spend a week together after the conference – or 8 days in all if that is what you are allowed.

Longing thoughts and love,

Alan

I love you very much, so much that it hurts.

xxxx

1970

Friday, 6 November

My dearest Love,

No sooner have I written to you than I must write again, this time for a different reason. All I want to send is my pleasure in reading Neville Masterman's review of your book.* I know you now say that you are not interested in the Chartists. I am sure all the same that you will welcome a good review by an Englishman who actually reads Hungarian. And I at last have some idea of what your book was about. But what is this I read in a footnote of 'the distinguished bourgeois historian'? Of course it is always nice to be called distinguished. But bourgeois? Little did you know, when you wrote that footnote, how much I should count in your life and how much trouble I should ultimately cause you. At least, I often fear that that is how things will work out.

If you are not too bored by the Chartists, could you not translate it into English? I could then put your English right. Or perhaps you had better keep this task until you are living in England, when you will need something to occupy you while I am away running this Library or lecturing in the far parts of the country. It is strange to think that my first idea on going to Vienna in 1928 was to study the relationships between English and Austrian radicals, so our minds have always been working on the same lines.

As I am writing to you, I would like to put a problem before you, or at least ask you to think about something. You always tell me not to think ahead, but it was a good thing I did or we should not have gone to Königswinter, and in that case we should not now be married, as the old phrase has it, in the sight of God. Well, we should be looking towards next year. I'm sure it is essential that we spend some time together clear of other people, to see whether each of us really is what the other thinks. I'm confident we shall love each other more, the more we are together. But we must make sure. So set your mind to it, and I'll try on my side.

Here I have only room to say that I love you very much, and in any case it is all I wanted to say. I make myself unhappy with longing every time I write to you, and of course happy with love at the same time. Tell me sometime that you truly love me and have some hope that we shall be happy together.

Love and love and love,

Alan

* *Chartism*, published in Hungary in 1967.

Friday, 27 November

My Darling and Beloved Wife,

    This is not a real letter. It is only a message for you to receive before you go to Moscow, if you are going. I will write you a much longer letter before Christmas, so again you will get two lettters in exchange for one, and you deserve them – your letters are so much more interesting and more human than mine. I really have become a dehydrated scholar, knowing no one, seeing no one. I think I was always like this by nature, with a few close friends but not caring much for society. My troubles have made me worse.

    However, be sure that I am not turning to you so that you will console me for someone else. I want you for your own sake, and still more I'd like to make you happy – though I often doubt whether I am capable of it. I'll warn you of the dangers in good time.

    I am very distressed when you say I was determined to leave Königswinter on the Sunday. I wanted to stay. You said you wanted to be alone, and I believed you. I'll also admit that I hate telephoning, but I'd have done it if you had encouraged me. Let us in future be honest without reserve. I'll say I hate telephoning or whatever it is, and you'll say you want me when you do. At the next Ranke Gesellschaft conference, which I hope we shall both go to, I shall plan to stay eight days or as many as you have free, and I shall have money for us both. I also think we ought to meet somewhere for a week together, say in May. I have a lot of money in Italy due to me, but I'll suggest other places if you don't like Italy. It is quite true as you say that we may discover after a week that we don't love each other as much as we thought we did. But that is a reason for trying it out. Actually, I'm not very afraid of this, though it could happen. I am afraid that we may find the practical difficulties too great. If you come here we can plan to take a trip together for as long or as short as you like, or – if you think it improper to go away with me – we can go around in London. Morally you are the bourgeois, not me. I can't face the States, I really can't. So please think about meeting in Venice or Ljubljana or somewhere like that. These are only preliminary thoughts.

    Do not be unhappy or hurt about me. Think how good it is to love and be loved. This often cheers me when I am depressed, and I often am just now. I feel I've gone downhill a good deal this autumn, but it may be imagination. At any rate my love for you is not imaginary. I'll write again quite soon, and I think of you always. Deepest love, my dear.

                                 Alan

1970

4 December

My dearest Love,

You are quite right. Our letters are too intense, I suppose because we have so few opportunities to express our love. So this time I am going to write a friendly letter without intense feelings. I will make only one personal remark at the beginning and one at the end, and then get on with practical things. Here is the one at the beginning: you are a very lovely woman.

I suppose I ought to have read Speer's memoirs, but somehow I could not face his apologetics and half-hearted admission of guilt. His book is full of lies. He sings the usual tune: 'I didn't know and I ought to have known.' In fact he knew. His economic organization was based on slave labour, and Speer controlled this himself. So I don't think I'll bother with him. The only interesting Nazi in my opinion, in the sense of having original ideas and making a difference to events, was Hitler himself – utterly loathsome, but important. All the others were unimportant like the epigones of Lenin and Stalin. I do not know precisely who writes the reviews on the *Economist*. At one time I thought that I must have written them since they so often expressed my opinions. Then I watched carefully and saw that the *Economist* review always followed one by me elsewhere. So I evidently have an admirer. Some of them are written by a woman on the staff. Some are by James Joll. Perhaps they are both other versions of me.

Roskill's second volume will not be out for some time. He is bringing out the second volume of his life of Hankey quite soon. Then he'll go back to his own work, and he is a quick though rather boring writer. Did you ever read *Former Naval Person* by Peter Gretton? It is a study of Churchill and the Navy in both wars, and I thought it very good indeed. Gretton is a professional sailor who rose to be Third Sea Lord and then had to leave the Navy from ill-health. Now he is at University College, Oxford, and is a most attractive man as well as a really good scholar. But I expect you know all this.

Like you, I get absorbed in my books so that I hardly notice what is going on in real life. On Thursdays when the editor of the *Sunday Express* rings up and wants an article for the coming Sunday, I am always most surprised at the things he tells me are in the newspapers. I quickly have to read them all over again, or sometimes I am too lazy and just make them up. When I am sleepless at night, as I occasionally am, I always go over what I have written the day before and think how I can improve it the next day. Perhaps it makes us bad companions. Perhaps it helped to ruin both my marriages. I don't understand how it should affect you.

You are always lively and sympathetic in society, and no one can feel you are buried in your books.

I don't regard many of my books with affection once I have finished them. I have to keep up with *The Origins of the Second World War* because people are always arguing and asking about it. It seems to me very sensible and simple but not very exciting. I like *English History 1914–1945*, though I now see many passages which I should do differently. I suppose I am condemned to rewriting the whole book when I get a bit older. *The Struggle for Mastery* seems to me boring though ingenious, like a sort of crossword puzzle. My favourite child is *The Troublemakers*. My unfavourite, as too clever and showy, *The Course of German History*. It puzzles me that I ever knew enough to write most of these books. It also puzzles me that I should ever have wanted to write most of them. Do you know the story of Swift re-reading *The Tale of a Tub* in his old age and saying: 'What a genius I had in those days.' I feel like that about *The Troublemakers* and not about much else. I don't know what I'll ever think about *Beaverbrook*. I am getting a little weary with it and shall be glad when it is finished, fun though it has been. I said to Max Aitken: 'For your father's sake neither of us can afford to quarrel over this book,' and he agreed. But of course he'll use this to try to make me give way and not the other way round. I don't worry about it. Or rather I worried for a couple of days and then got over it. That is always how I go on. At a certain point I close the curtains – say over unhappiness in life.

A practical request, please. I have a student who is writing a thesis on the Austrian Army in 1848 from the social and political point of view. He has already learnt German and spent a year working in the Kriegsarchiv in Vienna. Now he is learning Hungarian and would like to come to Budapest for a similar purpose, though not for so long. Now first he would like to know if any Hungarian scholar is working on this subject or anything like it. So please send me the name and address of the head of your Institute. You will not come into it at all. I shall not even say I got the information from you. Secondly, do you think your Institute or the Academy has some fund with which they could help the boy while he is in Hungary? He can travel there on his own resources, but it would be nice if he had something to live on while he was there, and he deserves it. He has a very good subject, and is attractive as well. However, he can find this out for himself once he is in contact with the Institute.

This reminds me. You tell me much about your present and nothing of your past. I'd like to think that you had a happy life, if only because it would give me more confidence that perhaps I could give you a sort of happiness also. At any rate, always write to me about everything.

1970

Here is some terrible news. Yesterday I received from the Ministry of Social Security a reminder that I should shortly reach the age of 65, and asking me whether I proposed to retire, as I would then get a pension. There was a space for 'Yes' or 'No'. So I wrote 'No' and sent the form back. No pension for me until 70. Then I get one, a higher one, and can go on working. I was shocked at even the most distant prospect of retiring, when I am working better than ever and one day will write a good book of history.

The other day I went down Houghton Street outside the London School of Economics. There was a crowd of students, shouting, blocking the road and demonstrating. I said to them: 'Excuse me, I want to go through.' So they stopped shouting, made way for me and even recognized me. Then I came to a double row of policemen with linked arms and an inspector directing them. I said again: 'Excuse me, I want to go through.' The policemen broke arms, stood aside in their turn, and I went on my way. The demonstrators went on demonstrating, the police went on pushing and arresting. A very English story, don't you think?

Here is my second message: I love you very much and would like to feel you in my arms. Please go on loving me.

xxxxxxxxx
Alan

1971

9 January 1971

My Darling and dearest Love,

Your letter from Moscow rejoiced me. It was somehow very Russian in feeling, as though part of a Russian novel. Even the paper you wrote on had a Russian air. You tell me so much of yourself. This moves and delights me. When I try to do the same I always find myself writing about my reactions to other people. I've often tried to be interested in myself, if only as an observer, and have never succeeded. I suppose this is what makes me a good historian. I never reflect on how my writing makes me appear and am surprised when critics make personal attacks on me. I think – what has He (that is how I see myself) got to do with it? When I wrote *The Origins of the Second World War* it never occurred to me to bring in my own attitudes before the war, and so I received the ridiculous accusation of having been an appeaser.

Now here are some fragments of historical news. Ian Colvin has summarized the Cabinet proceedings for 1937–39 in a book called *Chamberlain's Cabinet*. Chamberlain comes out of it far worse than we could ever expect, Halifax badly also, strangely enough Hoare goes up. The idea that they ever wanted a Soviet alliance is dead for good. You must get it. Colvin is no historian and exaggerates Chamberlain's ignoring of the Cabinet. All prime ministers do this. Then there is a Macmillan paperback called surprisingly *The Origins of the Second World War*. I've protested against their stealing my title. The editor Esmonde Robertson is quite a sensible man. His book is an anthology, mostly attacks on me, with an occasional defence from me which is quite out of tune with the rest of the book. They are all involved polemicists. I keep saying – this is now a purely historical problem, and they don't understand what I mean.

I'm on edge and disturbed at the moment for a purely professional reason. I have only the last chapter of *Beaverbrook* to write, from 1955 to 1964, and I want to bring out his amazing achievement in becoming an historian, and a very good one, when he was over 75. This is the chapter in which I really must do him justice and also bring out his personal impact on myself. But I hate talking about myself and don't know how to do it. So I'm excited and yet worried. After that, I'll revise and cut and try to make the book livelier. One distant day there will be no more to write. But I know from experience that something else will turn up. At least I hope so.

This letter is too much about me. I think about you every day and puzzle over our future relations. We must discover each other deeply and truly and then see what happens. It will be interesting at all events!

Life here has its troubled side, what with electricity strikes and inflation. Politics too will have their interesting events, though probably unwelcome ones; we have the first really Tory government since the nineteenth century.

I'll write a proper letter soon.

More love than I can express,

xxxx   Alan   xx

7 February

My Darling,

I thought I should never be able to communicate with you again. The Post Office strike seems to be with us for ever. It really is most extraordinary. Neither side negotiates. The government do nothing. The end of the Roman empire must have been just like this – posts stopping, news drying up, until you felt that life was really coming to an end. However, I have broken out. On Monday I am going to Brussels to give a lecture to the senior staff of International Telegraph and Telephone, a huge American concern, on of all things 'The Cold War'. When there I will post this letter to you – that is if I remember. At any rate, I can just tell you that I am still alive and think of you all the time. I can hardly believe that you still exist. But I know that when we meet, if ever we do, you will still mean everything to me.

I remember you once mentioned to me a book called *The Raging Moon*. I looked at it and thought it was not for me. You are a sentimental, emotional person. I am troubled by feelings and yet hard on others. I like cleverness, not emotional scenes. Well, the book has now been made into a film, which I am sure is also not for me. But maybe it is for you, so you had better look out for it. Here in London we have nothing but films about sex, and not emotional films either. Straight technical films, apparently explaining how to do it. Strange, are all English people, and for that matter Danes and Swedes and Germans, no good in bed? I think it is part of the tendency of modern times that people like watching instead of doing. They watch television about the country and mountains instead of going for walks. They go in vast crowds to football matches instead of playing any game. Or maybe they do both. Perhaps all those who watch sex films are really better in their technique afterwards. But I doubt it. However, if you like I'll go to a few to get some new ideas in case we ever meet again. This is a joke, so do not be angry or upset about it.

Somehow I have been very busy with rather useless things: telling Dutch television why decimal coinage is bad, telling English viewers why I think the Moon shot is utterly silly, lecturing here and there on subjects which the audience do not understand anything about, even the revolutions of 1848. I have spent much time being miserable about my life – mistakes all the time, much unhappiness to others, and nothing to show for myself. I need you badly to pull me into a better frame of mind, but I can't believe you need me. I have less than nothing to offer. However, I love you very much. Think of me sometimes. Maybe even write if the strike ever ends.

xxxxxxxxxxxxxxxxxxxx
Alan

19 March

My dearest Love,

I wrote you a hasty letter the other day, and as soon as I had sent it realized that you would not like it – all about practical things and my own troubles, nothing about you. Have no doubt. You are in my mind all the time. You should tell me more of your activities. You speak of your book and don't tell me whether it is published. If it appears in German, then I can translate it. There is an extraordinary market for books about the Second World War and its background, and yours would easily find a publisher. Even I think of lecturing about 'The Coming of the War' again, but now I would emphasize the real World War which began in December 1941, not the little European episode of 1939. We historians must stop treating Europe as if it were all that mattered in the world.

You never tell me anything of your boys. How is their work progressing? What are their future plans? And how are they doing with girl-friends? When will they take to long hair and beards? Or has this habit not reached Hungary yet? You ought to realize how much I should like to share your interest in them as in everything else.

Now back to me in the hope that this amuses you. My relations with Max Aitken have taken a new turn. I went to see Lord Goodman, Max's solicitor, and he was entirely on my side. He said: 'Of course the biography is entirely yours and Max has no right to censor it. But he must read it and I am sure you will listen sympathetically to his comments.' Goodman wrote this to Max also. The difficulty is that Max cannot read anything beyond the headlines in a newspaper. So he is in trouble and doesn't know what to do. He has retreated into silence. I have told him the book, or nearly all of it, is ready for him to see. He doesn't answer. Of course I shall get my own way in the end. It is a very funny situation.

I am taking the boys to Paris for a week after Easter. I don't think it will be as much fun as Venice, because we shall spend so much time dodging the traffic. But I suppose Paris is a great experience for young people. Daniel* complains that he will miss a Chelsea football match, but there is a price for everything in this world, at any rate under the ethics of capitalism. Crispin has become an opera enthusiast. He and I are going to the *Entfuhring* – foolishly called the *Seraglio* in England – next week. This week he is taking a minor part in the school *Hamlet*, and I am going to see him tonight.

We have one strike after another and a terrible government, I really think the worst government since Lord Liverpool's. It is a truly Tory government, which we have never had since the Reform Bill. There is a new history of British society edited by Hobsbawm. Look out for it. The two Victorian volumes by Harrison and Best are very fine indeed. *The Nineteen Thirties* by two silly women is atrocious – straight Communist propaganda. Maybe you will think it is all true.

Next Thursday I shall be 65, what a frightful age to be. I shall go on pretending that I am just over 50. How long we have known each other. Do you remember that Monday morning in 1960 when we sat by the Danube and you asked me why I looked so unhappy? I have loved you ever since, even when I thought I had forgotten you. By now you have probably forgotten me. Much love from me all the same,

        xxxxxxxxxxxxxxxxxxxxxx   Alan

* Second son of Alan's second marriage.

8 April

My Darling,

I have a lovely long letter from you full of kind thoughts and good advice. I am on the last pages of *Beaverbrook*, so I can safely lay them aside to write you a letter before I go off for Paris at Eastertime. This is really a troubled country. No sooner do we get over the post strike than we have a go-slow on the railways. I begin to wonder how much we shall be delayed on the train to Dover. Coming back will be worse, for by then all the railwaymen threaten to strike or go-slow, and maybe I and the boys will be at Dover for days. However, I do not worry much about this.

I have a feeling from your letter that you are beginning to think that the love between us should diminish into a good warm friendship because anything else would be too difficult. These feelings are bound to come up sometimes when we do not see each other much. I deliberately do not suggest that we should meet more often. For each time we get deeper into love, or at any rate I do, and the partings become increasingly painful. Maybe we shall really lose our love while we wait in this way. I doubt it. The difficulties are great, and again we may decide they are too great when we sit down some time next year and talk about them. I doubt this also. I am always very hesitant in action beforehand, imagining even more difficulties than there are. At a certain point I become not merely courageous but foolhardy, rushing into something with blind resolution. Of course I hesitate again later, but you can rely on me still to take a big jump some time. So even if you too hesitate, go on loving me and believe that something will come of it. I need you. You need me.

Forget the last paragraph if you like. I know you believe in waiting on the future without impatience. So I turn to news.

The new books seem to be all about newspapers. David Ayerst has written a history of the *Manchester Guardian*. Donald MacLachlan has written a life of Barrington-Ward, editor of *The Times* after Dawson. There is plenty about appeasement, but not much new. I think now we have to look into the Cabinet records and not take so much notice of what the papers were saying. We need to break up the pre-war period more. The first stretch ends with the reoccupation of the Rhineland when Versailles was finished. Everyone then thought they were back with old-style diplomacy and had plenty of time. Even Hitler, I think, was surprised when events went so quickly. Far more interesting is, what did the Americans think they were doing about Japan? Did they really believe they could stop Japan without a war? And why did they want to stop her? I am quite in the dark.

I am looking forward to not having to write something every day. Of course there will be much to revise, and I shall have to write around to many people asking for permission to use their letters. But the book is finished as a design. I am entirely pleased with it, though I doubt whether anyone else will be. It is history, not biography. I know what Beaverbrook would have said about it: 'It weighs too much.' This is all he said about the life of Lord Northcliffe. But this time he can't answer back. Whenever I caught him out, he used to say: 'Ah, you're a clever fellow.' I wonder.

You never send me a kiss. This does not stop me sending you plenty. That is how I feel, my love.

xxxxxxxxxxxxxxxxxxxxxxxxxxxxxx
Alan

19 May

My Beloved Darling,

Oh, how glad I was to get your letter. I know you have many things to do, and that in any case it is silly writing to each other too often. All the same I imagined things – perhaps you were ill, perhaps you had (very wisely) fallen in love with a Hungarian, or maybe had gone to some other country. Now I promise not to worry again, and you too need not worry if I am slow in writing. And here is something very serious I must say to you. Do not ever have the idea that I want, as you put it, to close our relationship. Yes, there will be difficulties, and it will need our joint action to overcome them. There is the special difficulty that, however confident in each other's love, we must learn to know each other better before we do anything decisive. I must tell you too that I have good reason to be worried on my side. For me our coming together would be pure gain. I should have you with me in England, I should go on with my work, I should live in my usual surroundings, such as they are. You will have to leave your country, get used to new things, maybe be bored or with nothing to do. It is a big risk, and we must think hard about it next year or whenever we see a chance of action. Then again I must ensure your financial future. I have a few years to live, you have many. We do not need to talk about these problems now. They make me hesitate. But my feelings for you are not likely to change. Write this in your heart: I Love You.

Now here is a practical question or maybe two. We must meet some time this year. I have got myself tied up for July and August, and I expect you have. After that comes the question of the Ranke Gesellschaft. Hauser tells me they want new speakers each year, quite rightly, and they have asked Martin Gilbert. I shall be welcome if I go, but I do not need to go and am not anxious to do so. What is your position? Will Hauser pay for you to go to Ulm? I would like to make two suggestions, and you must decide between them:

1. We should not go to Ulm at all, but should use that week (end of September) as a good time to meet – a sort of excuse. We could pretend even to ourselves that we were at Ulm and we should be somewhere else. Where would you like to go? I favour Venice. From the point of view of money it is much the best place for me, since my publisher can help me. It is a marvellous place which, I think, you have never seen. I know it well and have in mind an attractive, simple place to stop. We can talk, go around together, and make excursions. I can pay your fare, either by sending money to Budapest or when we meet. Also I will reserve single rooms so that your high moral principles will not be disturbed. But maybe you would like to go somewhere else. I'll go anywhere you like.

2. You may feel it your duty to go to Ulm, or maybe you are anxious to meet historians which, I know, gives you pleasure. In that case, let us meet somewhere on the way three or four days before the conference meets. I have not looked properly at a map, but surely we can meet somewhere in Austria on your way to Ulm. I think it would be more fun in Austria than in Germany. On the map Linz stares at me, but it is not a very exciting place. Please write and tell me what you think. I know you don't like making plans beforehand. So far accidents have worked out all right for us. But we can't expect this to go on. We have to do things more consciously and deliberately than you would like. We shall not meet unless we plan to meet, and I at any rate worry that we have not much time. Despite my apparent energy and youth, I shall perhaps not last all that long. So please cooperate that we should meet towards the end of September and, if that turns us into lovers more seriously, so much the better.

There is an end of my planning activities. Now I'll tell you what news I have. First, because you like news of history, there is a book on *The Anti-Appeasers* by V. Thompson (Oxford) – about the Conservative

1971

rebels, showing that they were a confused lot, even Churchill. Not much original material. Two books about newspapers: *The Guardian* by David Ayerst – very good though brief account of how W. P. Crozier, the editor, set the paper firmly against appeasement; *In the Chair* by Donald MacLachlan, about Barrington-Ward who was assistant editor under Dawson – appeasement as a highly moral course, allegedly abandoned immediately after the occupation of Prague, also a very funny account of how B-W made *The Times* as pro-Soviet as it had once been pro-Nazi, or more so. In my opinion we have had about enough of the appeasement question. There is not much left to say about it. The appeasers wanted to avoid a war: they were not pro-Nazi, they were simply living under the cloud of the First World War. In any case the alternative, it seems, was to push on with rearmament and not have a policy at all. We really have to face this: the French were determined not to fight, and I fear that the Soviet government was in much the same position.

More seriously, there is a detailed book on the foreign policy of Hitler's Germany from 1933 to 1936 by G. L. Weinberg, who wrote earlier books about Germany and Soviet Russia – you'll remember them. For this book he has done a lot of detailed work on the microfilms of German records which are in Washington. Some interesting and new results: Putsch in Austria. I don't think he initiated or inspired it. It was simply that when any Nazi crackpot put up a scheme, Hitler rubbed his hands and said: 'Fine.' He made absolutely no preparations to exploit the Putsch or alternatively to protect himself against its failure. He simply encouraged his followers to throw fireworks in all directions in the hope that some of them would go off. Now here is the central question I'd like to put to you, which Weinberg has not grasped at all. In *Mein Kampf*, and in plenty of other places, Hitler laid down a clear policy, a much more coherent one than *Lebensraum*: alliance with England and Italy in order to end the hegemony of France. Now when he came to power he made absolutely no effort to achieve either of these alliances. He allowed German diplomats and some Nazis too to try for them, but he did not bestir himself at all. He was pushed into going to Venice, but he attached so little importance to this that he had authorized the anti-Dollfuss Putsch. In the end he got the Italian alliance. But not at all by his scheming. The Abyssinian affair and then the Spanish Civil War pushed Mussolini into his arms.

Similarly Hitler did absolutely nothing to get a British alliance. Rosenberg tried. Maybe Ribbentrop tried. Hitler did nothing. Here again events pushed the British towards him. The naval treaty was their idea, not Hitler's nor even Ribbentrop's. Am I right on this? You are the only one who knows. If these two paragraphs are right, and I think they are, two alternative questions follow. Was Hitler simply a lazy fellow who hoped that something would work out in his favour? Or did he calculate with extreme subtlety that holding back was the way to pull over both England and Italy? Either way, it confirms my view that Hitler had no fixed plan of action. Even so, I don't understand why he made such little effort to win over the British government. If there was one thing which seemed a certainty in the early nineteen-thirties, it was some sort of Anglo-German front against Soviet Russia. Why did it not come off? This is very much your subject and you alone know the answer. It will give us enough to talk about for a whole week in Venice.

Beaverbrook is really finished except for a long introduction explaining why anyone should be interested in him now that he is dead. As I read my book over and over, looking for mistakes, I get to like it more, but I still doubt whether others will. However, Max Aitken has now approved the bits about his mother and about old Max's love affairs with other women, so I have no personal difficulties to overcome. I have even got approval from the second, present Lady Beaverbrook, and that was no small achievement.

I forgot almost my other bit of news. I have been invited to go to Denmark for a week early in September and lecture at three universities there about 'The Origins of the Second World War'. It should be fun, even though I shall not have time to visit the Danish sex shops or study the Danish permissive society.

Up to here, the letter was written in Oxford while I was on my weekly visit. Now I am back at the Beaverbrook Library and reading my manuscript over and over again. Each time I find some new joke or remark to put in. Occasionally I notice something to leave out.

Paris was a great success, though walking round the streets there has not the fascination of Venice. There is a great deal old about it, but it has no feel of being an old city – less even than London. The old buildings, churches or mansions are stuck there like islands in a modern sea. The oddest place we visited was the Victor Hugo Museum – still widely visited and yet surely no one reads Hugo any more. Flaubert, yes. Stendhal, certainly. But I am sure Hugo is dead, much more so even than Scott. Perhaps this is an insular Englishman's judgement. The boys enjoyed it, I think. I am now hoping that I shall walk at any rate some of the Offa's Dyke path on the border between England and Wales when it is opened in July.

I was wretchedly ill with a head cold which dragged on for weeks and weeks. Now I think I am returning to the land of the living. My thoughts turn to you every day and for much of every day. I wonder whether you ever think of me. Send me at least two kisses next time.

Deep love,

xxxxxxxxxxxxxxxxxxxxxxxx
Alan
x

8 June

My Darling, My Beloved Girl,

Oh dear, how I want to be with you. This is a practical letter written in a hurry about our autumn plans. I think it would be a mistake to try to fit in Venice and Ulm. Venice is a whole day or more from Ulm by train. Also it would be a shame to rush through Venice in two or three days. As well – and please don't be cross with me for saying this – I should feel very much out of things if you were with friends. Even though they left us alone, you would be embarrassed by my always wanting to go off together and I should be embarrassed when you talked Hungarian as you are bound to do.

I suggest you and I should meet in Salzburg, say on 29 September. Salzburg is on the direct line for you to Ulm, and we can be in Ulm in two or three hours on the Sunday. Also it is a lovely place which I have not seen for 35 years. I am more at home in Austria than in Germany. Of course it may rain all the time, but this is the only objection. Let me know about this as soon as you can and I will book two rooms. I have plenty of money (with £15,000 to come for the Beaverbrook book!) and can pay all the bills. Do say yes.

I know what is in your mind. You think you ought to have a chaperone. You can trust me absolutely to do and be whatever you want. We are both grown-up people. Even you are no longer a romantic girl. So things will go just as you want them to and not otherwise.

Here now is a confession. I can't come earlier because I have promised to lecture in Denmark in mid-September. So I shall only be free towards the end.

Does this make sense? Selfishly I want you for a few days on our own, just to be together and to grow to know each other more. Think of this and throw your love for me into the balance.

I've lots more things to tell you and will write again a letter full of news and very few endearments. I love you and believe that you love me.

xxxxxxxxxxxxxxxx
Alan

19 June

My Darling,

    This is a letter merely to give you pleasure. I was wondering to myself why I loved you so much. It started with the colour of your eyes and the spirit which lay behind them. Then you not only listen to what I say. You are actually interested in it, or seem so. You give out sympathy instead of demanding it all the time. I feel I have someone to rest on. What I don't understand is why you love me. Perhaps it is less serious with you. I am often jealous at the thought that you are giving out your warm personality when I want it for myself. But of course I would not have it otherwise. I try very hard to deserve your love, though I can't help being a selfish solitary person for much of the time.

    The other day a young man from *The Times* came to write a sketch about me. He said, 'Of course you were an only child', and recognized this because he had been one also. It makes you depend on yourself. I even write books just to please myself. At the same time one wants intimate friends and lovers, not acquaintances – to make up for the brothers and sisters one never had. I expect he is right.

    I must tell you about Offa's Dyke, which is my project for July. Offa was King of Mercia – English Midlands – in the eighth century. He built a great ditch all the way along the frontier of his kingdom with Wales. It ran from the Severn to the coast of North Wales. Much of it has been ploughed up or turned into roads, but on the hills it still runs for miles often to a depth of six feet. Altogether the distance is 170 miles, with the Dyke visible for about half the way. The country is empty, a true frontier area to this day with hardly any villages. The path has only just been delineated, and I expect we shall often have difficulty in finding it. So I do not think we shall make fast progress. But it should be a wonderful experience. The Dyke itself is a great creation in what we mistakenly call the Dark Ages.

    I have not written much about Beaverbrook's love-life. He destroyed most of the records and his girl-friends would not be much more than a list of names. He ran after girls from the time he came to England and had one very serious affair while his first wife – she died in 1927 – was still alive. This affair lasted ten years. His mistress was married, so Beaverbrook could always send her back to her children when he was busy with other things. He also complained if she went on holiday with her children when he wanted her to go on holiday with him. Then he took up with a Viennese ballet dancer and asked her to marry him. She decided he was too old and married someone else. After that he had a rich art expert and then a lively young Jewish girl.

Lady Dunn, who became the second Lady Beaverbrook, cleared them all out. All his girls were sophisticated, gay, devoted to him. He gave them much money and sometimes attention. I don't think he ever gave his heart except to the first of them. By ordinary standards, he was in his relations with women a bad man. Even though he was the fifth child in a family of nine, he too always behaved like an only child. I don't understand this, but so it was.

Now there are some tales until I write to you again. Think much of my proposal to meet in Salzburg and write to me soon what you decide.

I love you dearly,

xxxxxxxxxxxx
Alan

9 July

My Darling,

I had your sweet postcard and was very amused by it. I can see you are a bit nervous about our next meeting, and think it will be more harmless if you mention it casually at the end of a postcard. Don't worry. It will be fun and will give us a taste of happiness which we shall remember for life. Once having persuaded you, I thought everything would be easy. I chose an hotel at Salzburg from the 198 hotels on the list. Surely Salzburg should be empty at the end of September. Not at all. The hotel I wrote to was full. I have now written more anxiously to the Travel Bureau in Salzburg, asking for two rooms almost anywhere. I'll let you know the results in good time. I suppose Salzburg is rather like Stratford-on-Avon, or for that matter Oxford – a place where coach tours run all the year round. The one thing certain is that we shall not hear a word of German spoken. Nothing but American, with every now and then an Austrian using a very strong *Wienerisch* accent. I can understand what they say in Salzburg, whereas Tyrolese is quite beyond me.

The last time I spent a few nights in Salzburg was in 1932, when I attended an early Festival. Then I went again in 1936 and attended a much better Festival with Toscanini conducting *Falstaff*. We had a house on the nearest lake and drove into Salzburg for the performances. I'm not tough enough to do that nowadays. I am beginning to find that driving a car tires me, particularly as I insist on driving very fast under all circumstances. Some time in the fairly near future I shall give up my car and rely on public transport, which is more restful. I don't suppose I'll slow up in other ways.

This is not a real letter, only a message to say that I have got arrangements in hand even if not successfully so far. Also, there is a more important message: I love you very much and am desperately anxious to meet you. Don't be shy when we meet. We shall waste precious time if we have to get used to each other all over again. I wonder whether you'll recognize me? And even if you do, you may find that you don't love me any more. My darling, I count the days till we meet.

xx
Alan

15 July

My Darling Sweetheart,

I'm glad you're content about Salzburg. I have just heard from another hotel which has got us rooms from 29 September to 3 October. If I understand your card of 9 July properly, you could come before 29 September, and so could I – say 27 September. I'm greedy for every day with you I can have. I'll tell Veronica* to ask you about this and, if you agree to 27 September, I'll get her to try to book rooms for the extra two nights. I hope all goes well with Hauser. Even if it doesn't, you must come to Salzburg in any case. I can pay all your expenses and I'll bring

---

* Veronica was Alan's secretary at the Beaverbrook Library. Eva invited her for a holiday in Hungary.

1971

money to cover your fare as well if we meet. I thought of sending the money with Veronica but feared you might be embarrassed. In any case, come somehow. I am desperate to be with you and only fear you will be disappointed in me.

I seem to have lots to do. *Beaverbrook* is finished. On Monday next I go to Offa's Dyke for a week with Crispin and Daniel and Giles* and Janet, his wife – quite a party. Then on 30 July I am going to Yarmouth in the Isle of Wight** for a week with my grown-up family, or some of them. Later in August I am going to the Lake District for a fortnight with the young ones. Early in September I am going to lecture in Denmark. And yet I say I hate travel. Salzburg is the only place I really want to go to. We have had a fortnight of very hot weather and I have been bathing every day. I feared it would be too hot to walk on Offa's Dyke, but it is now cooler so we must be all right. The sun gives me skin trouble and this makes me sulky. I shall have recovered by September.

Next winter I think I'll write my life just for you. Maybe you'll make money out of it after I am dead, or maybe you'll find it too uninteresting to publish. Being a good historian I am curious about other people, but not about myself. Indeed, whenever I think of my own life I become very gloomy.

I could not have managed things worse if I had tried. You are my one bit of good luck and never forget it.

xxxxxxxxxxxxxx

That's for love,

Alan

10 August

My Darling,

Veronica has come back full of sun and happiness. It made me envious that she had been with you and had seen so much with you that I had not. The truth is that I am a lazy creature who does not make enough effort to run after happiness either for himself or for others. I ought to have arranged a meeting long ago. Instead I have drifted,

---

* First son of Alan's fist marriage to Margaret Adams.
** The Mill, the Taylor family home there.

waiting for some easy opportunity. Well, now we have one. I have just received the invitation from Hauser and I expect you have received one also. But you must come to Salzburg, even if you do not intend to go on to Ulm. Veronica has, I think, explained to you that I can try and change the date of our hotel reservations only when I hear from you. So let me know as soon as you can. She will organize the change of dates even if I am away.

    I had a splendid time walking Offa's Dyke. I managed to cover fifteen miles every day for a week and suffered only from blisters, not from weariness. The border between England and Wales is the most beautiful country, middle-sized hills, and no one in sight all day. I am anxious to get back there for a second week next year. Soon, on 20 August to be precise, I am going to the Lake District for a fortnight with my two boys. But I expect I'll hear from you before then. I get depressed and lonely sitting alone in this Library when everyone else has gone home. It upsets me that we are missing life together. But what else can we do? Whenever I think of you, and that is often, I love you very much. Do you love me too? If so we shall somehow find happiness together, although we shall no doubt also have lots of troubles.

    Much love, my Dearest,

                              Alan

19 August

My Darling,

    I think of you nearly all the time and imagine the good holidays you are having with your boys. By now you will have acquired your car and perhaps even learnt to drive it. Do not come to any harm, at any rate until we have had our meeting at Salzburg. To me, this is more important than the meeting of Napoleon III and Franz Joseph at Salzburg in 1867.

    Rosemary Brooks, the archivist here whom you no doubt remember, died suddenly yesterday. I depended on her very much and she was kind to me during my many troubles. Now I feel very lost. As you can imagine Veronica is very upset too. I put my arm round her for the first time in a comforting fatherly way. It makes a great hole in one's life when someone goes who has played such a big part in it.

1971

I am relieved in a way that I am going to the Lake District tomorrow with the boys.

What I want very much is that we shall really build up our affection when we are together on our own. Life has given us so few opportunities of sharing happiness. We must make sure that when it comes we take it with both hands.

This is a message of deep love.

xxxxxxxxxxxxxxxxx
Alan

25 August   Lake District

Oh, my Sweetheart, you are a very unpredictable girl. I suppose misunderstandings are easy when we think in different languages and belong to different civilizations. I'm sorry that I wrote anything which shocked you. I did not mean to. It is not a crime for a man to find a woman physically attractive. I often used to do so. But concerning you it is all of you, not just your body, which attracts me, and I'll always do my best to make you feel this. You seem to think I have some wicked designs on you. Well, I have two designs. The first is to make you feel for me some of the love I feel for you. The second is that, if we become truly assured of our love, we should marry at some time in the future. To speak very frankly, I can't see how our marriage can be arranged, what with our respective families and the problem of providing for you after I am dead.

I worry about these things. I walk round London and consider where we should live if we ever got married. So I take you too much for granted and say things which are not in tune with you. Please understand and forgive my faults where you cannot forget them.

I shall be at the Hotel Traube, Linzergasse 4, Salzburg on 29 September. If you come we shall have a good, friendly time. Maybe we shall learn to love each other more, maybe we shall change our opinions. Never judge people by what they write, only by what they are. So love until we meet – if we do.

Alan

7 September

My Darling,

I was excited when I got your letter. First I thought: Hell no, I won't go, it won't be a success. Then I thought: Success or not, it is one chance of happiness in a lifetime. So I sent a telegram to the hotel in Salzburg cancelling the cancellation which I sent yesterday. And I renewed my air reservation which I had also cancelled. In fact, whether you change your mind again or you don't I shall be at Salzburg from 29 September till 3 October.

I don't think I shall go to Ulm. Last year was interesting as an experience. It would be tedious to hear the same voices all over again, especially when two of the voices will be English people whom I should not bother to listen to in England.

But please do come. Your last letter was so loving that my heart filled with pleasure. I need some cheerfulness. I am sad at the loss of Rosemary (she died suddenly of a fit of asthma). I am sad at ending *Beaverbrook*.

This time it is real that we are going to meet. I won't say a word to spoil it. And I'll try not to do anything to spoil it when we do meet. I get to Salzburg about midday on the Wednesday and will wait around for you at the hotel, unless you can tell me the time your train arrives when I'll meet you at the station. Don't be alarmed if I don't reply immediately to any future letters. I am going to Denmark and shall be away all week. All the love I have to offer,

xxxxxxxxxxxxx
Alan

4 October

My Darling, My Beloved,

This letter will, I hope, greet you on your return to Budapest. I have just had the best three days in my life. Crispin and Daniel both met me at the airport. Crispin asked me whether I had had a good time. I said to him: 'If ever in life you have as good a time as I have had these last few days, you will know that a miracle has happened.' I did not tell him where I had been, and he did not enquire.

You know that from now on I shall always tell you what is in my

1971

mind with complete frankness. If you do not like something, you must say so. But you must never be angry (I'm sure you will be all the same). Now here is the important thing I want to say in this letter. Somehow we MUST make a future together. I do not know quite how we can do it or even when. But we MUST. It would be utter madness to throw away all that brings us together. Having said this, I feel I ought to say the opposite (on the other hand). For me our coming together has only practical problems. Otherwise it is sheer gain. For you, on any detached view, it would be far better if you took up with someone in Hungary where you belong and where your future is secure. If you fell in love with or married an Hungarian I should be very, very happy for your sake. Never doubt that. As it is, I feel selfish in encouraging you to love me. Please understand my contradictions.

It would be very wrong to fill all our letters with academic discussions about the future. But I have to write about them while my mind is full. As I see it, there are two obstacles. One is the purely practical question of arrangements. It is no joke to start life all over again as though we were both in our twenties – a house to buy and equip, everything to be decided from scratch. But I am sure we can overcome this if we join together strongly enough. The other obstacle is more serious. I keep coming back to it. You are 15 years younger than me.* You will outlast me by 20 years or more. An ordinary husband provides for his wife's old age. But I am starting very late and have two earlier wives to keep. Somehow you must hold on to your existing security in Hungary. I can't see any answer at present, but maybe you have friends you can discuss it with if only in an academic way.

The only thing we can decide for sure is that we will meet next year more or less about this time. We'll start maybe at Ljubljana and go on to Venice and Ravenna. The most important thing is to be together. During the interval I expect our present enthusiasm will run down. I wasn't sure before I saw you in Salzburg whether we had been wise to meet. I wasn't sure also whether I should recognize you. In the dark on the station I almost passed you by. Perhaps you had doubts also? Probably we shall again. But now we know that they disappear when we meet. I've never had before someone I could trust completely, so that I know I can talk about my difficulties without ever offending you. Your only fault is that you don't talk about yourself enough. You encourage me to talk and I enjoy doing it. But equally I'd like to know what goes on in your mind and how you have experienced life. Once I start talking I never stop voluntarily. So you must fight for attention. You must shout

* Eva was actually 17 years younger.

out: 'Now it is my turn. Please be interested in me for a change.' You see, I *am* interested in you, but I forget to say so when I start talking about myself. Perhaps once I have written my autobiography for you I shall be bored with myself and thankful to hear about anyone else.

This is the end of sombre and futile reflections about the future. Now I will tell you news in the way that people write to each other. First, do you realize how near to death I have been? There are two planes a week to Salzburg – one on Wednesday, one on Saturday. The Wednesday plane conveyed me safely. The Saturday plane killed everyone in it. Probably it was sabotaged by Irish republicans who could as easily have operated three days earlier. I can't say that I should have been worried if I had been killed, and no doubt the opportunity to worry would not have arisen. But it was a near thing. Next time it will be some danger which I shall not escape. On top of this I nearly did not get back to England. When I arrived at the airport I was told that there was fog in London and that no planes would go there that day. However, we went off after a short delay. I hated being back, hated being on my own, thought of so many things which I ought to have said to you and did not, recalled exactly how you looked.

Veronica says she is better. I shall send her off for a fortnight's holiday as soon as I have less work for her to do here. I fear I have lost interest in this Library now that *Beaverbrook* is finished. I am restless and discontented, but I can't settle to anything new until I have done the index for *Beaverbrook*, a laborious task which will use up months of my time. Also, I am on edge with everybody because I can't share my experiences and say that my feeling about life has changed. You know how sulky and depressed I can be when I have nothing settled with which to occupy my mind.

I have taken your lighter to Dunhill. They will not only repair it. They will also give you (free) an entirely new internal mechanism, since yours is apparently out of date. So if I can ever get it to you, you will be able to light your cigarettes most efficiently. Last night I smoked one of your cigars and thought about you. I thought of our day at St Wolfgang and of the concert, and of how we sat in the courtyard of the castle. It is damnable that happiness has come to us so late. You can pretend that I am still young, but I have the historian's awareness that old age is just round the corner. Even so, nothing will destroy the memory of our three days together.

I have finished Martin Gilbert's third volume of *Churchill*. It now lies on my mind as a great indigestible lump of cake lies on the stomach. Somehow I must write a long review of it, when I have really lost interest in the Gallipoli affair. When you get back, read my review of the life of G. D. H. Cole in the *New Statesman*. Igoe, who hands out the documents here, told me that it was the best book review he had ever read. So my powers have not waned altogether. If you can't find the review I'll send it to you.

Beautiful weather, I hope for you also. I am reading Butler's autobiography – dreary rubbish. Send me a full account of the conference, complete with flattering remarks how everyone missed me.

Now I send you a very important message:
I Love You.

x
Alan

22 October

My Beloved, my Darling,

When I got your letter I was intoxicated, I wanted to reply at once, I thought of nothing else and kept reading it over and over – just like a lovesick schoolboy. If we are not going to consume all our activity in writing letters, we must limit it to once a fortnight or so. Remember then that I don't expect you to answer this letter straight away, and similarly I shall let a week or so pass before I reply to your next letter. I can't believe you will ever write me such a marvellous letter as your last one. In any case it is not necessary. Like you I feel secure, serene and quietly happy. I know that future difficulties will arise from the external world and not between ourselves. I'd always tell you what I thought or wanted, and I'd be sure that you would agree or disagree with equal confidence. I suppose one only learns slowly from life how to put complete trust in someone else. Or maybe we are specially suited to each other.

Here is an explanation. 'My feeling about life has changed.' I feel there really is something which inspires me and fills my mind even when I don't see you or even consciously think about you. And something to explain on your side. You say: 'Perhaps I have some more 5 years.' Is this a bit of romantic melancholy? Or have you a real reason to think you will not live all that long? I must say I should hate the idea of living into extreme old age. Indeed I'd be glad to go at seventy, which is not so long now. But the normal thing is that you would outlive me by twenty or thirty years. That is one of the reasons why I see such difficulty in setting up together. Another is that even in the next few years I shall probably be less fit and therefore need more care than now. However, these are problems for the future.

I have been too busy to call [at Dunhills] this week. In any case there is little chance of your getting the lighter until we meet at Ljubljana or Venice or somewhere next year. What luck that Hauser is having yet another conference, and that we are not going to it.

On a practical question about an index. Professional index-makers go through the proofs with a pencil, underlining every word that should be in the index, and then go back picking the words out. I don't bother. I rely on my eye being quick enough to notice the words on each page. You need a large pile of cards, rather larger than playing cards. You give each topic or person a separate card (this sounds a lot, but it is far better to make too many cards than too few). Then you spread the cards in alphabetical order round the table in front of you, leaving just enough space to work on. Each time you find a word to be indexed you pick out the card, and as soon as you have made the entry put it back. As I am only indexing my own books, which I know well, I cheat a bit. Where I come across a man or topic which I know is not going to come in again, I put it on a card with others. At the end you arrange each letter of the alphabet separately and do one letter at a time, if necessary shuffling the cards which have more than one entry on them. It is all simpler than it sounds. Space is the most important thing – a big empty table-top.

Now I wonder what I can tell you about myself, apart from the fact that I love you and think of you at every spare moment? I went to Birmingham and gave a lecture on, of all subjects, the governing élite in Austria-Hungary. I enjoyed very much this return to old themes, and the audience of some 200 were very pleased too. Then a professor and two lecturers took me out to dinner. The company was agreeable, but the host delayed a long time ordering any wine and when it came it was white. You know how impatient I am to have a drink with my dinner. The one bottle between six went in no time. We had finished our meat before he said he would order some more, and again it was going to be white – sweet this time. I struck. I said: 'I must have red wine,' using the excuse that I was eating cheese. So I got something, though not very much.

I am having a really terrible time with the proofs of *Beaverbrook*. I sent precise instructions to the printer that, while in my text very few capitals should be used, in the quotations which are many they must follow exactly what was typed. Instead they killed all Beaverbrook's capitals. Now I have had to put them all back on something like 700 pages. The printer will have to correct all this. Then I must read it again, and only after make the index. Veronica is loyally reading the proofs also. I miss Rosemary Brooks, who had a better eye than either of us for proof-reading.

I have been reviewing a lot of books, none perhaps that would interest you very much. My review of *Churchill* is written. I have reviewed two rather popular books – one on Napoleon, presenting him as a kind family man; the other on Wellington, presenting him as a super-human hero. I don't know which is the sillier.

X
Alan

P.S. I love you.

8 November

I have some book news for you. The diaries of Sir Alec Cadogan have just been published, 800 pages of them. Interesting before the War when he opposed the Vansittart line, only to switch around and support the Polish guarantee. During the War nothing except complaints against everyone else. I am also reviewing an enormous German book on economic appeasement by a German called Wendt, a pupil of Fritz Fisher's. He argues that there was early economic antagonism from January 1933 until November 1934, when the Anglo-German payments agreement satisfied both the City and British exporters. He ties this in with the Anglo-Naval treaty as ending the hostility towards Germany. From that time on Germany was regarded as a good economic partner, and the economic negotiators were still looking for new agreements in the summer of 1939. He says firmly, there was never a breach after November 1934, and the political conflicts were regarded as a nuisance. I am sure this is right. Never was a war less desired on either side. We anti-Fascists who agitated for war scored an unusual sort of victory and at a high price.

We have had a most marvellous autumn. Until a few days ago I was wearing summer clothes and sitting in the sun at lunch-time. On Sundays Crispin and Giles and I have been walking the Pilgrims' Way, a prehistoric road which runs from Winchester to Canterbury. We do about 12 miles each Sunday, and shall go on doing so until the weather turns against us. Some of it has become modern road, but very often we are pushing across fields or cutting our way through undergrowth. Crispin refuses to let either of us see the map and then blames us when he goes wrong. Crispin and Giles stride ahead of me, talking all the time, and I plod along by myself. I tried to persuade Daniel to come also in order to have some company, but he is always at football on a Saturday and has his homework to do on a Sunday. You can imagine I enjoy myself very much.

We had another go at admitting women into Magdalen. This time we got 32 in favour and 17 against. But it needs a two-thirds majority so, as you can work out if your mathematics are good, we were one short. I begin to think I shall not see women in Magdalen in my lifetime. Not that I care one way or the other. It is merely fun for me.

I hope this letter will not be too bulky to reach you. Somehow I must make you feel across the great gap that I love you and have you in mind all the time. If you ever receive any letters from me, write to me. But I shall go on with complete confidence even if I don't receive any letters. At least I'll try to. Oh, Darling, I long for you so much.

xxxxxxxxxxxxxxxxxxxx
Alan

Next letter will be written on 22 November.

22 November

My Darling,

I was enormously relieved to get your letter. Despite my instructions to you not to worry, I worried a great deal. I imagined that you were ill or cross with me, as you were before we met at Salzburg. I wondered whether I should send you a telegram. In the end I was patient, and rightly. Like you, I will not worry again. I will write once a fortnight, and you do not need to write at all unless you feel like it. My feelings are just the same as yours. You are always with me. I think over things I want to tell you and see you all the time listening to me, only too much. I must train myself not to talk all the time and to let you have your share. I see you beside me in bed.

Now here are some replies to your letter.

Explanations: A tall poppy is a classical allusion. Some ancient king wanted advice how to run his kingdom. The wise man took him into the garden and struck off the heads of the tall poppies. Moral: strike down over-mighty subject. A shadow cabinet means the leading members of the Opposition party, each of them allotted a particular subject and

1971

meeting to discuss general policy. Nowadays it is almost a formal institution, with appointments made to it as though it were real. The editor of the *New Statesman* is Dick Crossman, who was Minister of Health and then Leader of the House of Commons in the last Labour government. He has decided to leave politics, though he is still an MP, and so can be thoroughly irresponsible when writing in the *New Statesman*. My brother-in-law is Anthony Crosland, a more moderate character, Minister of Education at one time and then Minister for Trade. He is hardly a Socialist at all, moves in high society such as Princess Margaret, and is now out of favour with the party, since he did not vote either for or against the Common Market.

I have been too busy to visit Frances.* She is, with all her apparent simplicity, a very devious character, rightly called Pussy. I think she decided that once she had accepted Lloyd George on his terms she would stick to her bargain, and always did so in the period covered by the Diary. But I suspect that they had troubles later on. However she has won now and, I am sure, imagines in recollection that their relations were always perfect. How can you say that I lay down conditions just as Lloyd George did? I offer all I have, but am also thinking of your future and know that I cannot be of use to you for long. What I love in you is your independent spirit, so go on standing up to me when you feel like it.

I am overwhelmed with work. I am again reading the proofs of *Beaverbrook* and preparing to make the index. I must write an introduction for a *Dictionary of History* which I helped to edit. I must write 5,000 words on Lloyd George for a silly collective volume on *Great Men*. I am still struggling through Wendt's book, which has over 600 pages. He has gone all through the economic papers of the time and shows that businessmen, especially industrial exporters, were keen on association with Germany right up to the end. In April 1939 they were planning a joint economic campaign against the United States in South America. This is not exactly new, but it has been overlooked by those who stuck to the Foreign Office papers. I shall give the book a long review in the *English Historical Review*.

But even with all this work you are never out of my mind. Carry the thought of me with you each day. We are tied together even though a continent divides us. Whatever else happens I intend to go on living until next September, when we shall see Venice just before it sinks beneath the waves. I already imagine every minute of it. Now I must go to the BBC and make a programme on Beaverbrook for sound radio.

* First David Lloyd George's mistress, then wife.

Max Aitken said my book was the finest biography he had ever read (not much tribute – I don't believe he has read any other). I replied: 'If so, it is thanks to the subject.'

Here is a bit of news for you. I hear that Catherine Károlyi recently found Michael's early letters. They were all about his love affairs, long before she knew him or was even born, and also showed his political naïvety. She therefore destroyed them all. I can't believe this is true, but you never know with Katus.*

I love you very much and for ever,

xxxxxxxxxxxxxxx
Alan

6 December

My Darling, my Sweetheart,

I count the days impatiently until I am due to write once more. Of course it is right that I should ration my letter-writing, just like sex, but I get very restless for the next time all the same. This morning I had your brief letter. I will get the full details of Wendt's book this evening and add them before I send you the letter tomorrow. And of course I shall send the book itself as soon as I have written my review. I was planning to write the review over the Christmas holiday, when I had nothing else to do, but I'll try my best to do it sooner. It is the burden of making an index which weighs on me.

As to the book, I guess that he did the research here a few years ago when the archives were open only until 1937 or 1938. He has used the Board of Trade papers a good deal for the earlier years. Later he relies on newspapers and particularly economic journals – *Financial Times, Financial News, Economist* – as representing business opinion. At first the bankers and businessmen were tougher against Germany than the diplomats. Once they got a payments agreement in November 1934 they were anxious to build on this and kept at it despite political difficulties. Most of them imagined that Germany had adopted autarchy solely because she had to. They hoped and expected that she would go back to a free world market if she got the chance. Wendt ought to have looked at what went on on the German side, but he hasn't. For instance, did Hitler

---

* Hungarian for Catherine.

1971

like autarchy for its own sake? Probably. The English also had the illusion that there was a 'moderate' party led by Goering, and 'extremists' represented by Ribbentrop and apparently Himmler. I think this was all a fantasy, fed to them by Schacht who was cheating both sides. By the time he gets to 1939 Wendt is merely using the well-known material about Wohltat and Wilson. We do not learn much by being given Dirksen's reports all over again. In fact the story was by no means new to me. I knew businessmen wanted to share out world markets, particularly if worked against America. I hope that helps for the time being. I'll send the book as soon as I can. Never hesitate to ask me for this or for anything else. You are the only person I care for in the world, and there is nothing I would not do for you.

Don't be depressed because someone else has written on a subject related to yours. This is always happening, and there is always room for other studies with a different approach. You have got the naval agreement as your strong point, and Wendt does not really touch on politics at all.

I can't explain Grantham childhood. Who said this? Give the context or page reference. Grantham is a town in the Midlands, which I often go through when driving to Yorkshire. But it has no other significance for me.

I have been very busy correcting proofs and making the index. Sir Max says he is going to sell the serial rights to the *Observer* or *The Sunday Times* for an enormous sum, which will come to me. I think he is optimistic. The book seems to me too boring for newspaper readers. It has come to 681 pages – too long, as Beaverbrook would say. But I still find it fun though I do not expect anyone else to.

My one piece of news is that Poland now wants to establish relations with the British Academy. The council of the Academy said that with my experience of similar trips to Hungary and Bulgaria I was the right person to make the first exchange. So I hope for ten days in Poland, perhaps next May. Perhaps I shall be lucky again and find some Polish girl as bewitching as you. That is a joke which will not even tease you. Do not worry. I am tied to you forever and ever and never have the slightest desire to look at any other girl. I fear that Poland will be rather boring, though the Poles themselves are lively enough. Cracow is the only ancient city left. All the others were destroyed during the war, though Warsaw has been carefully rebuilt. However, Cracow is one of the few places I still want to see, so I shall get some profit out of the visit.

I gave your address to Sophia* with the warning that she should write to you if ever I fell ill or had a car accident. She said [that] being

---

* Second-daughter of Alan's first marriage.

so happily in love herself, she knew that it was worth any sacrifice. You should also get someone trustworthy to whom you can give my address in the same way. We all go on thinking that nothing can ever happen to us, but some time it does.

Now here is the information you want. Bernd Jürgen Wendt: Economic Appeasement. *Handel und Finanz in der Britischen Deutschland-Politik 1933–1939.* Published by Bertelsmann Universitätsverlag, Dusseldorf. There is no price marked on the book. It is one of a series edited from Hamburg by Fischer and others.

Did I ever tell you I loved you?

xxxxxxxxxxxxxxxxxxxxxxxx
Alan

28 December

Dearest and Beloved,

I am a day late with my letter. Monday was a holiday here, to make up for Sunday which would have been, so I did not come to the Library. I had a wonderful letter from you, like all your letters. I read them again and again, particularly the words I can't decipher – that's the historian's training. Here are some replies. Do not worry that I may change or find you less attractive. Of course I am bound to grow old and then will lose spirit. This can happen suddenly. I've no illusions about you. It is your companionship and spirit that counts, and that won't change. I shall go on needing you and rejoicing in you. You on your side must follow your own rule. If you lose interest in me, you must say so. I think we'll go on being close for a long time.

Next, how do I manage as a historian? Here is a secret: I know my faults. I work very thoroughly and patiently. Then I make up my mind. I take a risk. Ninety-nine times out of a hundred it comes off. The hundredth time I make a mistake. I get a reputation for being slightly careless, but this is deliberate. If you wait until every detail is right, you will produce nothing. I have a neat mind that likes to see results. Sometimes I make patterns too precise, but that is better than drifting in a fog. I drive a car the same way, usually a bit too fast rather than too slow. So far the risk has not caught up on me.

Here is my day, so that you'll be able to go along with me. I wake up between four and five. I read a little and then sleep again until 6.30.

I get up, shave – with a cut-throat open razor – and have a cold bath. When I am dressed I come down, grind the coffee and drip it on a cafetière. One day I have bacon and egg, the next I have a kipper. I wash up, I make my bed, I clean my shoes. As I also have *The Times* and the *Daily Express* to read, this takes me well over an hour and it is nearly nine o'clock before I am ready to depart. Then I walk through Regent's Park to a tube station, and from there I am in Fleet Street within ten minutes. I give Veronica a nice smile, read my letters, dictate some answers and then work all the morning – correcting proofs or reading a book I have to review, or talking with some student who wants my advice. You can imagine all that well enough, and you can imagine even better the biscuits and cheese I eat at lunch-time. After lunch I go for a walk round Lincoln's Inn Fields or through the City. The other day I went to look at the new flats which the Corporation of London has built at the Barbican. I don't think this would do for us – too much like a fearsome mediaeval prison, but it was worth examining. I shall have to start thinking about the size of what we want – two rooms, three rooms, four rooms. It all depends on you and on when we create anything. We must talk about this and not write.

Well, now I have got myself to the afternoon and there I will stop, so that you will have all the excitement of a serial. Next letter you shall learn what hapens to me in the evenings. Do not fear: I never lay hands on a girl. I hope very much that you really understand me as much as you think you do. Remember – and this is really important, truly and lovingly – I can never be serious for long. I am serious about loving you, but all the rest is jokes for your benefit. You must never worry if I say things which seem to you frivolous or even alarming. It is only the way my mind runs. When I remember to be serious, I am settled on you – a most extraordinary thing. I never thought after my various unhappy experiences with women that I should be wholly and absolutely committed to a woman. I know I can say and do anything with you and you'll accept it.

Instead of going on about my day, I will tell you about my Christmas which was not particularly gay. I have never liked Christmas much. I suppose it is the Quaker in me: I hate feast days. I like to give people presents, but it seems to be silly to give them on a special day. However, what happened at Christmas was this. I saw most of my older family before Christmas. I distributed presents to my grandchildren and some of my children gave presents to me, though I can't remember what they were. Oh yes, they also took me out to dinner at a Chinese restaurant, not the finest of foods.

I walked on Hampstead Heath. Then very foolishly I looked at the proofs of *Beaverbrook*, which I thought were fully corrected, and discovered many new mistakes. From that moment I have been reading hard, hoping that I will get the proofs really right this time. So instead of having a holiday I am depressed and overworked.

Important: I sent you a little extra Christmas present simply because I was having a photograph taken for publicity purposes and it seemed to me a very good one. Also, Veronica telephoned me after I left the Library before Christmas that there is a present from you waiting for me. Oh, Darling, how good you are to me. Do not believe in me too much. I want to love you, I want to make something of our love, but I know how weak and unsuccessful I have been in the past. I can't help doubting whether at this late stage in my life I can really put things right. This is an untidy letter. I meant it to be so careful and well designed. Then I discovered that I had still too much work to do on *Beaverbrook*. So all I can say systematically is

    LOVE   LOVE   XXXXXXXXXXXXXXX   Alan
                                                                          Xmas kisses

1972

10 January 1972

My Darling, my dearest Beloved,

There, you, see, I am right up to date, writing on a Monday. As a matter of fact I nearly didn't. I have been working on my index every day for the last fortnight. Today there was the last stretch. I feared that if I started on the index I should not have time to write to you. But I finished before lunch-time, all of it over. So now I have all afternoon to write to you and think about you. Like you, I begin to imagine things. Perhaps you have already had a car accident, or the illnesses of the winter have caught up with you. But do not worry. This is only a joke. I shall never worry about you, only think happily. Long stretches of every day are filled with you. I wonder if you will find something to be angry about, as you did before you came to Salzburg. I am sure at some time to do something wrong and you will write me a stern letter. Oh dear, I love you so much.

I see there is a conference of some sort at Salzburg. Were you ever there? I spent the happiest three days of my life there. It was with a girl. Now that I think more, it was with you. There are things I am ashamed of about Salzburg. I hurried you around too much. When going to St Wolfgang I relied, as I always do, on my ability to find the way, and wandered in back streets to nowhere. We ought to have got off the bus at St Gilgen and gone both ways by boat. This is a terrible weakness of mine: I will never ask the way or for guidance. You must be firm with me. Partly it is timidity, partly it is independence, not wanting to seek help from others, though of course that is what information offices are for.

It seems far longer than a fortnight since I wrote to you. Nothing has happened, but it makes the days very long to be compiling an index from morning to night. What shall I do now? I can't face starting a short history of the Second World War straight away. So I must try to write an autobiography for you. I am frightened of this. I don't think I have the gifts. I can't even remember most of the time. What I can remember makes me unhappy and resentful. Either I made other people unhappy or they made me unhappy. I've had an empty frivolous life and not done much that I wanted to do, writing in the void without any real belief in anything. You'll understand when it comes out. I don't like other people much. Here is another great fault. I'm soft-hearted about other people and yet can't sink myself in them. Both Margaret and Eve treated me badly in one way or another. I should either have accepted it all without complaining or I should have walked out altogether. Instead, I have broken away and yet gone back to care for them, which probably does more harm than good. I end by resenting them both. Forget this dreary subject.

Not much book news. A second volume about Hankey is coming out. As it only goes from 1918 to 1931 it is not much use to you. But there is a good theme which runs all through British policy from the making of the Entente. The Navy basically always wanted to rely on sea power and keeping out of Europe. The Army was absolutely set on sending an army to France from the moment the Entente was made. This argument goes on throughout the inter-war period, as you have no doubt discovered. In the Second World War it was an argument between the Navy and the Air Force. Volume III of the *Official History of the Second World War: Grand Strategy* has just come out; very good about the confusions over the Mediterranean and the Second Front. Churchill, for once, comes out well. In 1943 he felt deeply that he had promised a Second Front to Stalin and criticized the Chiefs of Staff very hard when they hung back. The records show that he was far less an opponent of the Second Front than is usually made out. This makes me feel again that I shall have to revise *English History 1914–1945*. There is also a silly book called *Munich to Dunkirk*, which takes a first run through the newly-opened archives. I fear we shall have a lot of this half-baked stuff, spoiling the field for more serious and more competent researchers. Actually I have been wasting my time reviewing three very fat books on spying for the *New York Review of Books*.

Here is some more of my life for you. After I've had lunch I go for a walk in Lincoln's Inn Fields or through the City. Some days I walk over to the Festival Hall and buy tickets for a concert. Then I come back to the Library, write letters to the various girls I am having love affairs with (another joke, don't fear) and read books I have to review. I wait till the rush hour is over. Then I walk through deserted back streets all the way to Camden Town, which takes just under the hour. Usually Margaret cooks an evening meal for me. Sometimes, when she is loyally attending a Labour Party meeting, I cook it myself. One or two evenings a week I go to the Beefsteak Club – a dining club for journalists, writers and politicians (mostly Conservatives) where I get an old-fashioned English meal. I drink half a bottle of wine and smoke a cigar. If at home, I occasionally watch television or more often play chamber music on the gramophone. Soon after ten o'clock I go to bed. I don't go out much. I have no friends left in London and neglect the few I have. Also, if I go out, I get tired soon after ten and have to leave the party just as it is beginning. But here is news to make you jealous. The other evening I went to a reception at the British Academy and there among other Fellows present was Professor Kathleen Tillotson, a very distinguished literary scholar who is editing the novels and letters of Dickens. She was my first girl-friend, purely intellectually, almost fifty years ago. Now she is on the point of retirement. She was pleased to see me and said: 'Have you regrets about you and me?' I said: 'No, we were on parallel tracks and could never meet.' She said: 'I feel the same.' I liked her very very much, but there was no sexual attraction. Strange. Here is important news. I love you very very much and I know that you feel the same. My Darling,

Write me a little note one day

Alan

24 January

My Dearest,

I had a most lovely letter from you. I have read it so often that I hardly had time for any work. It was not so much anything you said, but the feeling and understanding in the whole. Now here is what I have learnt from it. I won't worry about the future. Something will happen some time and we will work out what is best for us and for others. Maybe the future will never come. Perhaps even now the atom bomb is blowing up somewhere. *Carpe diem*, which I believe is Latin for enjoy here and now. I won't get depressed about the future, or if I do I shan't tell you about it. Together or apart we give each other happiness. At least you make all the difference to me and I seem to do it for you, I can't think why. After all, to the eye of the detached observer I am a selfish elderly man with the spark of life dwindling to embers – a phrase more literary than true.

So here instead is general talk, as if we were sitting side by side and running over our interests with only a very occasional sensual contact one way or another. All the same I wish I felt you by me physically. Your body is rarely out of my sight, however much I try to keep our relations on an intellectual level. Bartók: My great love in music is for chamber music. I have Bartók's quartets and play them often on the gramophone. I go to a concert whenever I am offered one of his quartets.

Like everyone else I enjoy the Concerto for Orchestra and the Music for Percussion and Celeste. I don't like *The Miraculous Mandarin*. Vaughan Williams had something in common – interest in folk music, for example, and in later life VW tried to write symphonies of social significance, one of them specifically about the Spanish Civil War. I used to like his works very much. Now I don't bother about them. Elgar is a much greater composer. If I want modern music I prefer Stravinsky and even Schönberg. Webern is very good. I can't understand Boulez, let alone Stockhausen.

I have done well musically just recently, mainly because Crispin has started going to chamber concerts with me. The other day I heard Schubert's Octet, a work I could hear over and over again. He and I also went to *Orpheus in the Underworld* by Offenbach, which is a piece of Second Empire foolery. Sadlers Wells which is, as you probably know, our *Volksoper*, is gradually putting on *The Ring* in English. I never thought I should go to that again, but Crispin is taking me to *Rheingold* next month. That is not so bad. It starts at the civilized hour of half-past seven. But what shall I feel like when he insists on going to the *Valkyrie*, which starts at five? So you see there are stormy times ahead.

I have not been to a cinema for a long time except to see revivals of films made in the Thirties and Forties. Recently I saw *The Big Sleep*, a Raymond Chandler thriller. I can't stand modern thrillers, which are much too brutal for me. *Easy Rider* was certainly not my cup of tea (English idiom). Losey is another of my dislikes. I saw *The Servant*, which seemed to me pretty unpleasant. I also saw his film about Oxford, which had pretty pictures and a silly story. I have kept away from *The Go-Between*, which I am told is again lovely to look at and affected in presentation. Did you read the book? I thought it was a skilful work of art though very mannered and artificial. But I am hopeless on fiction. I shall try to go to *Gumshoe*, a parody of the old thrillers, and probably to *The Anderson Tapes* which is highly spoken of. And of course there is a new James Bond film, the old rubbish and as enjoyable as ever.

I have had some good reading. The best was the latest instalment of Boswell's original *Journal*, covering 1776 to 1778. I suspect Boswell is a purely English taste. I enjoy it perhaps more than any other book. There is a very comical book by Goronwy Rees called *A Chapter of Accidents*. This is about his relations with Guy Burgess, the chap who defected, and of how they ruined his life. Maybe it won't be allowed in your country. It really has no political significance and is purely a fun piece. After all, poor Burgess did not know any secrets worth revealing. I have just written a long piece for the *New York Review of Books*, not out yet, on a batch of spy books, saying what nonsense they all are. The one thing I learnt of any interest is that the pro-Soviet spy ring in Germany, Rote Kapelle, never passed on any information of the slightest importance.

I have finished my index and am catching up on other work. First I must write an essay on Lloyd George for a volume of essays on great men. Then I will edit interviews which Crozier of the *Manchester Guardian* recorded during the Second World War. After that I can see that I am going to be pushed into writing a short history of the Second World War, though I can't yet see the theme which will hold the book together. Maybe I am too much influenced by my recollections, unreliable of course, and that is bad for a historian.

I have drunk all your wine. It was very enjoyable, the more so of course because it came from you. On my side too: Thanks. Thanks even more for existing and for loving me and for being so patient. Nothing can express all the happiness you have given me. I have to say it again and again because my heart is so full. If you write a novel, do not put me in it. No one will believe that such a character existed.

Do not trouble to write when you don't feel like it. I shall write again in a fortnight's time because I always want to, and in between I shall think of you every day.

Love
XXX   Alan

7 February

My Dearest,

How easy it is across a continent and different languages to create a misunderstanding. You are quite, quite wrong to think that I ever do not want letters from you, long letters all about yourself or about anything that comes into your head, just as long as they are letters. I don't want you to feel that you have to write, and I suppose I said that too strongly. I want you to write when you feel like it. But remember every letter is a joy to me. I know that you have many other things to occupy your mind, and I'm confident that you are thinking about me whether you write or not. So put the idea of my not rejoicing in your letters out of your mind.

On my side I know you like hearing about my activities such as they are, and I put down words on paper without plan or calculation. Here are some words. I've been very upset over the events in Northern

Ireland – 13 civilians killed last Sunday, the worst killing of civilians here since the Gordon Riots. I have been looking round for some way of protest, but the old method of speeches by indignant intellectuals does not work any more. People have become bored with politics even when wicked things are being done. I even tried to enlist other elderly men who would go to Northern Ireland and march at the head of a procession so as to be killed first. This was a romantic idea which met with no response. And of course, as soon as I look at it as a historian, I see that there are rights and wrongs on both sides. The Protestants, however mistakenly, do not want to go into an Ireland dominated by Roman Catholics.

I have a more practical worry, quite apart from morality. I was planning to take the boys to Ireland for their summer holiday. Now I wonder whether it would be safe. If you have a GB car you cannot carry a sign saying: 'I am on your side.' It would not be pleasant to have stones thrown at the car. I think we shall have to find somewhere else and I can't think where. Holidays have always been a great worry to me. Really I don't like them. I get bored if I haven't enough to read, and am not good at being lazy.

Here is another and more important point about holiday plans. When would you like to meet in Venice? It would suit me to come towards the end of September. This would be a good time to close the Library for a week or so, and I shall have finished with my earlier holidays. I expect you will have settled your boys for the autumn also. Would 25 September be a good day to start? We can then have a week together and part the following Monday or Tuesday. Don't think I am dictating. I can come earlier, though not much later. Also, the weather goes to pieces after the end of September. I believe we shall have a wonderful time.

I have managed to write an essay on Lloyd George, with the theme that he was a dynamic force who never fixed himself on anything. He believed in action for its own sake and was too much of an individual to work with others. It has made a good piece. Now I am beginning to look at the records of interviews which Crozier of the *Manchester Guardian* kept. They are fascinating. Personal pictures of Baldwin, Churchill and all the other great men. Talk about the background of events before and during the War. It will make a good book, I think, and it will be a good exercise for me to edit it so that I shall have to look up precisely what was going on at the time. Even I, with my wonderful memory, forget things. One thing I don't forget is sitting by the Danube with you so many years ago.

Last week I went to the seminar Alistair Parker is running. He talked about the Abyssinian crisis, quite interesting though he is by no

1972

means a good speaker: too many Ums and Aws. The British Cabinet were dominated by the idea that they must get France committed, because of their worries about the Mediterranean fleet. I expect you have realized this. I had not. Even the Hoare-Laval plan was done for this reason. If it were accepted, the war would be over. If it failed, France would be committed to the oil sanction and heaven knows what. I meant to go again this week, but the room was full and I thought I should not take the place of some student who would get more benefit from it.

On public affairs again. We have now had a miners' strike for over a month. A miner has been killed while picketing. Soon the electricity stations will run short of coal, and we shall have electricity cuts. As even our central heating works by electricity nowadays, we shall be sitting in the dark in our overcoats. A jolly prospect.

I don't seem to have written much of importance. It is just the pleasure of talking to you and thinking about you. When you feel like it, do the same. Only don't feel you have to. Each of us is firm and confident in the other.

Very much love,

xxxxxxxxxxxxxxxxxxxxx
Alan

20 February

Darling,

Well, you are not as good a correspondent as I am. Perhaps it is because you do not have an electric typewriter which does all the work of itself. However, don't worry. I don't expect you to write except when you feel like it.

We have been going through a rough time, fortunately not with cold weather to make it worse. The electricity goes off for six or nine hours most days, and this stops the central heating as well as the light. So there we sit in the cold with candles. Fortunately the Library is on the same circuit as the newspapers, which have their private generator, so during the day I have lived in warmth and comfort. The worst time is in the evenings when there is nothing to do, not even watch the television. And of course few theatres and no concerts. I suppose it will gradually get better now that the strike is likely to be over.

Not that I am complaining. I was on the side of the miners during the great strikes of 1921 and 1926, and I'm on their side now. I'm trying to formulate a letter to *The Times* saying that 19 February will long be remembered as a glorious day in the history of the Labour movement. And of course this is only a beginning. I think we shall see a challenge to the entire economic policy of the government on the part of all workers in the public services. I daresay it will hit well-off people like me, but I can't say that I care about my individual future compared to that of the working class.

On Thursday I went to Brighton and lectured at Sussex University on 'The Left in the Thirties'. I had an enormous audience. After telling of our old battles where we tried hard and did not do very well, I was carried away by excitement and said: 'We did not succeed then. Now I rejoice that I have lived to see the day when I can say to you – ladies and gentlemen, the miners have won.' It brought the house down. Still, the class war is easier to be romantic about than to live through, which is what is likely to happen. How lucky you are to live a quiet life.

I seem to have had a busy time. On Monday I went to Woodford over in Essex and talked about Churchill. Tuesday I went to Oxford where we had no electricity and dined by candlelight, a great improvement. Wednesday I talked to overseas students about the decline of Europe, such as it is. And Thursday I went to Brighton. This coming week I am going to Canterbury to lecture about Beaverbrook as a historian. All of a sudden I have come alive again. I don't suppose it will last. Indeed, until the miners won I was very depressed and hopeless about everything. I can well understand that I am not a cheerful person to write to. On top of it all I have lost a book belonging to the London Library, a most careless thing to have done.

I think about you a lot. Indeed, I could not keep going at all were it not for the memories of what we have done together and the thought of what we shall do. But I don't see what there is in it for you. Every now and then I start to worry that the barriers of space and language between us are too great for us to overcome. So do not forget me altogether.

Working on the Crozier interviews, I have been thinking again about the nineteen-thirties. It seems to me that the German problem, which now seems to us so large, was eclipsed at the time by all other sorts of problems, so that people went on thinking that it would go away of itself. The statesmen were a poor lot. Now, with Heath, we have come near to wanting Baldwin back.

My publisher is now trying to push me into writing a history of the Second World War. I have told you about this before, but then my news such as it is does not change. It would be very good to treat the War as a historical subject, but I don't know that I am capable of doing it. Admirers tell me that I am the greatest living historian, but I have too much sense to believe it.

I've written this letter a day early because it is Crispin's half-term, so I shall take him to Cambridge on Monday and he can decide which College he would like to go to in eighteen months' time. In any case it will be an excuse for a day off.

The only bit of cultural news is that Brecht's *Threepenny Opera* is being played in the West End. Have you ever seen it? It is a wonderfully anarchic piece, too hard even for the young of the present day. I think the present performance has softened it up, but I shall take the boys as soon as the lights go on. It will make them realize that we were quite tough in our young days. Crispin wants to add to his musical education by hearing some Mahler and some Schoenberg. I'm quite keen on the second but not on the first.

What else would you like to know? The government is still marching into Europe, whatever that means. I can't get excited about it, though I think it is a foolish thing to do. President Nixon is in Peking, which is certainly a sensation in its own way. Did you notice one funny piece of news, perhaps not interesting in Hungary? The Yugoslav radio denounced the IRA as clerical Fascists, just like the Croat Ustachi. In a way it makes sense. Nationalist sentiment does not fit into the Marxist analysis, but it is the force which has kept European history going. I think there will be real bad trouble in Yugoslavia when Tito dies, if not before. They have nothing to hold them together except memories of the partisan war, and that was a long time ago.

There is something else you may like to know, or which in any case I want to tell you. That is that I love you and miss you every day. I hope this still means something to you. When you write, tell me about your boys. I like to think of you with them. My Italian friend, whom you disapproved of, is very worried because her daughter has become a socialist revolutionary. I told her this was a very good thing to happen in a capitalist society. So she is resigned to it.

Love now and all the time,

xxxxxxxxxxxxxxxxxxxxxxx
Alan

4 March

Darling Eva,

 I am lucky. I had two letters from you: one quite short but full of kind things, and the other yesterday very long and even fuller. I didn't mean to push you into writing unless you felt like it, only some sign that you are alive and think of me occasionally. There are some immediate points to reply to in your letter. Did I say that you should not count on me too much? I didn't mean emotionally. I am just as attached to you as you are to me and think of you nearly all the time. But I am burdened with things. I suppose I am at a loss now that I am not living with *Beaverbrook* every day. I don't see my way clearly. I have accepted the responsibility of running the Library and could do it easily when I was writing Beaverbrook's life. Now I need to go to other libraries, to say nothing of the PRO,* and the Library has become a bit of a burden. Much worse, I am weighed down by my failure of two marriages. I have two women on my hands, both grasping at me all the time, blaming me for everything that has gone wrong. I don't have any faith in my ability to make anyone else happy. So I merely say: don't build me up as a strong and resolute person when I have created for all those around me a life of muddle and dissatisfaction. You imagine a lot about me which does not exist.

 More practical and more urgent. Of course I can change the time of our meeting at Venice. My timetable is this. On 4 September we return from Ireland. I ought to have a week or ten days in London, seeing that the Library is all right and sending the boys back to school. How would it be to go to Venice on 14 September and stay until 21 or 22 September? At the other end I have a lecturing date on 12 October, so we could go to Venice from 2 or 3 October until 10 October. In the earlier period Venice will still be rather full still with tourists; in the later one the weather may easily have gone damp and cold. So I favour the earlier dates. Will they suit you? Please write and tell me the exact dates when you must be at this conference. You might miss the first day or so and it would still be all right. I can't be more precise about dates until I know yours. There is another argument for the earlier dates. I shall probably close the Library for the second half of September. So it will be quite in order for me to be away then. By October it will start again and I ought to be there. Let me know as soon as you can. I know an attractive *pension* away from the crowded areas where I think we can be happy. Of

---

* Public Record Office.

course we could go somewhere else than Venice, but you ought to see it once in a lifetime.

I have had a terribly busy time since I last wrote to you, made worse by the power cuts which are now over. One evening I took the chair for a man called Broszat, talking on the sociology of the Nazis. He said it was all the fault of the Protestant middle classes, formerly Liberals, who resented the loss of their position. Not a profound analysis. Plenty of the Nazis from Hitler down were former Catholics, and the appeal was more to the lower middle class than to the high bourgeoisie. He was also a boring lecturer and the heat was off. So I closed the meeting without there being any questions. Then I went to the University of Kent at Canterbury and talked about Beaverbrook as a historian. This was a great success, though I doubt whether the young people will read any of his books. I have also had a round of entertainments. I took the boys to a film called *Gumshoe*, which is a sort of echo of the films Bogart used to make. As such it was quite funny, though the thriller part was not very convincing. And last night I went of all things to the theatre, not my favourite form of entertainment. Daniel was keen to see *The Caretaker*, Pinter's first success. Have you seen it or the film that was made of it? It is all about a ghastly old man who moves in with two strange brothers and ruins their lives. It was quite funny except that it was exactly the same for two and a half hours. It could have gone on for ten hours or stopped after half an hour. As it was, it ended at a quarter to eleven and I go dead soon after ten o'clock. This is another reason why I am not good to live with. I drop into bed, then wake up at four in the morning and lie awake worrying until it is time to get up. On Monday I go to Wolverhampton to lecture about the Second Front. Then my round of duties will be over.

I also heard Alistair Parker talk about the outbreak of War. Not many surprises. Halifax dithered until the last moment. Parker claims that Chamberlain did not. I wonder. One thing strikes me about the Crozier papers I am working on now. Before the war people, at any rate English people, had so many things to worry about, they hardly noticed Hitler much of the time. Rearmament was a professional affair, interesting to those who wrote official papers so they now have an impact on us. But Crozier, as a newspaper editor, asked far more questions about the Spanish Civil War and Mussolini's intentions in the Mediterranean, to say nothing of Ireland and India. We get it all wrong when we see intelligent people or even the government obsessed with Hitler, at any rate until Munich or perhaps even until after the occupation of Prague. I think that even Hitler himself did not expect big things to happen until

1942 or 1943. Parker says Germany was in a desperate economic state in 1939. I doubt this, but you can discover evidence for any theory.

They tell me the climate of our continent is changing. It is getting warmer everywhere, something to do with the melting of the ice caps at the North Pole. England will soon have a Mediterranean climate. On the other hand, the level of the sea will rise and we shall all be drowned. So no more skiing in Hungary.

I think of you so much. And love you

xxxxxxxxxxxxxxxxxxxx
Alan

20 March

Darling,

I am really very selfish. I write to you always about my affairs and forget yours. I ought to have said what good news that you have passed your driving test and have your car. It shows that you are very clever to become a driver at your quite advanced age. I am sure that I should not pass the test so easily despite all my experience. When I started to drive forty-nine years ago, no test was necessary, and I have never had to take one since. We old drivers who held licences before tests were introduced in 1934 are a dying race. Talking of age, I read in a newspaper the other day that John Betjeman was described as 'the venerable poet'. He is a year younger than me, so clearly I shall soon be described as 'the venerable historian'.

I also failed to answer your enquiry about Sophia. I wonder why she alone of my children excites your curiosity. She has recovered from her car accident which I think I told you about. She is very active in the International Socialists, who are the present and most popular form of Trotskyites. I don't know what they stand for except Trotsky's old idea of permanent revolution. In real life Sophia is a devoted schoolteacher, wearing herself out for the girls she teaches. Daniel has also become a Trotskyite. At least he went to an all-day demonstration of a rival faction, but it turned out that what really attracted him were the pop groups which played all day. His school rebellion has now faded away. Wisely, he thought that it was too much trouble. He refused to take my advice that he could only defeat the headmaster by understanding the rules better and being more persistent in demanding that they should be changed. In that case, he said, by the time we have changed the rules I shall have left school. Giles's wife is expecting her first baby any time now. She will thus provide a future head of the family, if such a thing can be imagined nowadays.

I went to Wolverhampton immediately after writing to you last. It was a very exhausting time. Rain all the way there and all the way back to Oxford. I stopped with some people in an old-fashioned country house. I had almost forgotten the conditions we lived under until quite recently. No central heating, cold passages, and the sitting room with a log fire which was lit only when we went into it. On top of this I had for once a disappointing audience – not many people and the few did not seem interested. However, I was just as interested in what I was saying. At Oxford we had a College meeting. The students asked to be allowed to attend our business meetings. I spoke up for them but was defeated by 30 to 15. I heard all the arguments that were used two hundred years ago against parliamentary reform. The people (i.e. the students) did not really want to be represented. It was all the work of a few agitators. In any case the students were virtually represented already – by their teachers, who knew better than the students what was good for them. Besides, how should we know that elected representatives really represented the students? Also it would hamper freedom of debate – just like the arguments against publishing the proceedings of Parliament. I enjoyed the arguments very much. Of course the students will go on making this demand, and of course it will be agreed to in time when all the good effect of agreeing to it will have been lost. I am an old-fashioned Radical who believes in making concessions ahead of what is demanded.

I am increasingly cheerful and excited about the Crozier material. Yesterday I visited Mary Crozier at Kew and collected a further set, including some very good ones with Beaverbrook. The work on them is very laborious. I have to identify unimportant people and look up forgotten events which no one cares about. But if I didn't explain everything critics would complain, and rightly so. It is fun to be doing something which is research, and pedantic at that. I had quite forgotten the pleasures of serious history. Not that it will occupy me for long. Then I shall have to start worrying about the Second World War and, as I have told you already, I can't see my way into it. I was talking yesterday with an old pupil of mine who was a bomber pilot throughout the war and he said the war was neither exciting nor routine. It was just a regular job that we went on with conscientiously. There is not much for a historian in a war that nobody questioned. At least it seems to me like that in recollection. That reminds me, *I've promised you to write an autobiography just for you.* Every time I think of it, it depresses me and I put it off. I have enjoyed the isolated incidents of my life very much, but when I consider the general pattern it has been awful: thirty years of living from day to day. I run over with resentment against all that went wrong. Resentment most of all against myself for not breaking away from the past and starting all over again. Yet each time when I consider the children of both marriages I don't see what else I could have done. So I fear that it will be an unhappy frustrated book.

Sorry at that outburst. With you happiness came back when I thought I had finished with it for ever. I saw some pictures of Salzburg the other day and every moment of it came back into my mind. The next time seems a long time in coming, but remember each day it is one day nearer. Quick, quick, shall go the days. And quick, quick, you must write and tell me exactly what dates suit you best. Here's another thing. No news or reply from Poland. I'm sure they have not forgiven me for my behaviour at Wroclaw over twenty years ago. I am rather relieved. Unlike you, I hate travelling about and making conversations in bad French with strangers.

The Sunday Times are going to serialize *Beaverbrook* early in June. At the end of June it will come out. Praise flows in to me already. Though this is pleasant, I know the book's faults and am not really impressed.

Yesterday I went out all day with Crispin.

As usual a selfish letter.

Love and love again.

                           Alan

28 March

My dear one,

How sweet you are to send me those lovely records. I have not played them yet. My only good outlet is a stereo gramophone and radio which I gave to the boys, so I have to go round to them and persuade Crispin to play Bartók rather than Haydn. I don't suppose I shall get through your records until I get back from Rome. Lovely as they are, I'm not sure that I like this celebration of my birthday. Sixty-six is too old for anyone to have much hope from life. I am running down, though I don't feel like it.

I had a catastrophic celebration of my birthday here. I took Crispin to a performance of *Rheingold* in English – by no means my favourite opera, but very good for him to hear and not too long. In the afternoon we went for a walk, and I changed my jacket for a windcheater as I usually do. Then we went for a quick Italian meal before the opera. When we had finished, I felt in my pocket and realized that I had left my wallet in my windcheater. Fortunately Crispin had enough money to pay with. I still did not appreciate the full extent of the disaster. Only when I got to the theatre did it dawn on me that I had not got the tickets. They too were in my wallet. We grabbed the car and hurried back. I collected my wallet, but by the time we got back *Rheingold* had started. It has no interval so of course we could not go in. By half-past eight we were sadly at home playing dominoes. As I told Crispin, he has another sixty years to hear *Rheingold* in. Actually we can go next season, probably in the autumn. But it was sad. He was more philosophical about it than I was.

Now two professional points about the Anglo-German naval agreement. I had a visit from an Italian girl called Brundu who has just done a thesis on it. She seemed intelligent, though I did not discover what sources she had used. I told her to write to you with her questions, so if she does you will know what to expect. I also told her my own view, perhaps not very well informed, that on the English side it was intended to remove an obstacle to the forthcoming naval conference, and was mainly inspired by the Admiralty. You must tell her why you think this is wrong. Now for my own problem. There are references to these naval problems in the Crozier interviews, and I shall have to explain the situation in my introductory notes. I'm clear about the Anglo-German agreement and I know that there was no general agreement in 1936. Was there a conference at all which broke down? Or was the idea of a conference abandoned when it became clear that the Japanese would not agree to any limitation? If you can tell me this, it will save my looking it up for myself.

My work on the Crozier interviews is going well. They fall into distinct sections. They begin with the old world which still sprang from the peace settlement. A lot about the disarmament conference – in one sense dead stuff, but with everyone saying that Hitler is more sensible than the French. This section ends with the Abyssinian crisis, and Crozier believing that Hoare was going to be the saviour of the League. After this there is a break until 1938, when Crozier and the people he talked to were all imagining that the Czech crisis was purely an affair of finding a solution which would satisfy the Sudeten Germans. Another break and so nothing on the outbreak of war. But a great deal on the long pause between the conquest of Poland and the campaign in France. Finland becomes the favourite topic. Shall we help Finland? How can we do it? What will Sweden do? The real war with Germany is quite forgotten. It is important to be reminded how far the British and French governments were from reality. These sections make the first part of the book.

Suddenly Crozier arrives at the Battle of Britain and the year after it when we were on our own. The tone is much more personal. There are splendid scenes with Churchill, and even better with Beaverbrook. At one of these Citrine of the TUC was both exasperated and delighted by Beaverbook and said to Crozier in a whisper: 'He is a bugger, isn't he?' He *is* a bugger. Then there are all the people who think they are going to overthrow Churchill and either run the war better or make peace. There was much more political intrigue behind the scenes than anyone knew at the time. The final passages on the real World War I have not gone on to yet. Crozier died early in 1944, so the book ends in the air and is all the better for doing so. You can see I am having fun. But it is very hard work. During the war Crozier got the secrecy bug like everyone else and kept the records in his own difficult handwriting. I can't trust Veronica to decipher this, so I have to do all the typing myself.

On Tuesday the boys and I are off to Rome. Address: Hotel d'Inghilterra, via Bocca di Leone, Roma. I'll try to send you a postcard if our schedule of sightseeing gives me a moment. We are faced by a preliminary trouble. The BEA pilots are starting a work-to-rule which will mean great delays, so I have no idea when we shall get to Rome. And they say it will be even worse getting back. All such problems solve themselves in time.

Yet again a selfish letter, all about myself. Our weather is bad for Easter. Yours may be better. I think of you taking your car into the country and displaying your new skills as a driver. Here there are ten million cars on the road, and the sensible drivers like me leave their cars at home. I think about you a lot and wonder what you are doing. When am I going to be able to translate your book from German into English? It will give me an excuse for postponing my book on the Second World War. Also, I badly want to do it.

It seems that I shall be going to Poland after all. I'm not looking forward to it. When are you going to Latvia? And above all, when is the best time for you to come to Venice? The thought of this is the one thing which keeps me cheerful. So much love is in my heart. Send me a sign that you are alive.

Much love and even more than that,

xxxxxxxxxxxxxxxxx
Alan

1972

16 April

Darling,

I came back from Rome two days ago and at once went down to the Library to see whether there was a letter from you. Sure enough there was. You are too good and patient with me. At the moment I am weary and good for nothing. Rome was, I think, a success, though we had occasional quarrels.

However we saw everything – every early Christian church, all the Roman remains, nearly every art gallery. I now know Rome much better than most Romans do. We walked along the Appian Way, the boys climbed up the dome of St Peter's; we even went, not very successfully, to a football match. The crowd was too great and we saw very little. Still it was fun.

We saw much of my Italian friend Lucia Biocca and her family. You would not approve. They are Communists or nearly so – at least will vote Communist. Signor Biocca was a resistance fighter and is now the top surgeon in Rome. She researches into mice. Good people, no doubt. I said – let the children go their own way, it is useless to make them different or suddenly wise. But I don't think my words have any effect. It is much easier to be sensible about other people's children than about your own.

Here are wise words about your boys. Once they have got the feeling that they are independent, they will discover for themselves that they still need you and will rely on you more than ever. Like most things, independence seems desirable only until you get it. Then you want support as well. So do not imagine that the real need for you is over.

I was so weary of foreign travel when I came back from Rome that I decided I could not face going to Poland. So I cancelled my visit. I know it is very bad of me to refuse to go when they had invited me and no doubt made preparations. But I get bored talking ceaselessly to historians. I only want to see Cracow, and the price of having to see everything else is too great. So I shall stay quietly in England. Advancing years are a good excuse for not doing what you do not want to do.

However, have no fear. I shall not feel too tired to come to Venice. I will at once enquire about a *pension* and arrange my journey, starting probably on 15 September. Now here is an important question. Are you sure you would prefer Venice to anywhere else? It is a lovely place and you ought to see it once. The only defect is that there are few places where we can just sit in the sun, if there is any. Still we shall be together. I think a *pension* is better than an hotel, because it is a labour to have to go out every night and the restaurants are not particularly exciting. I will arrange *demi-pension*, which will leave us free. I hope also we may fit in a visit to Ravenna. Mainly I think of our being together. My confidence in you will make things easy.

I can't tell you about England. It too seems foreign after I have been away. We are threatened with a railway strike which I don't think will happen. The Labour Party is in confusion over the Common Market. Perhaps my old friend Michael Foot will become deputy leader, but I fear this will make him respectable instead of the rebel and radical he used to be. My boys tease me and say I am not much of a rebel myself. This is partly true. I am ready to leave the future to the young and feel that I have played my part, insignificant as it has been. You'll be able to judge when I write it all down.

As to *Beaverbrook*, there are some faults. Often I have written about subjects at length because they interested me as a historian and not because they added to the picture of him as a man. I fear that ordinary readers may be bored by such things as the Empire Crusade or the explanation why he was an isolationist. Then I have often been too soft on him. I have told the truth, but I have not underlined how tyrannical he could be or how he could always put the blame on to other people. He was thoroughly mischievous and I can understand why people did not trust him. However, the reviewers can find all this out for themselves. Despite the faults, I have tried my best and maybe it is my best book. After all, I don't believe that history has any vital message. If a book interests people and gives them a feeling of life, I can't want more.

I'll have to start work again tomorrow. I see the Second World War gradually turning into an interesting subject, but it worries me that I know so little about it. I am very good at thinking of questions, but I am not at all sure that I shall find the answers. And there is a real problem: how to make young people realize that the war was worthwhile. They are now all so sceptical about it.

Family news for what it is worth. Janet, Giles's wife, is now ten days overdue with her baby and hence enormous and very tired. One day I suppose she will produce a new head of the Taylor family. Sophia is still very happy with her man. Crispin seems very confident that he will do well in his mathematics examinations, and I am confident with him. I have begun playing the Bartók quartets. They are marvellous. Thank you again.

1972

You have just sold the American *Beaverbrook** to a Book Club, which will bring in lots of money! I'll write a better letter soon.

Very much love, and loving thoughts

xxxxxxxxxxxxxxxxxxxxxxxxxx
Alan
xx

1 May

My Darling,

How lovely it was to get a long letter from you and to have such a rich exchange of ideas. You understand me better than I understand myself. It did not occur to me that I should not go to Poland until I contemplated the practical arrangements. Then I realized that I could not go around acting the great Academic for a whole fortnight.

I answer your practical points. You can certainly write to the agency that handles your money. There seems no reason why it should not hand over some to your boy, particularly as there will be more coming in soon from the American Book Club. There may be some difficulty about British income tax, but the agency will tell you. I am delighted to hear that your book is being considered for English translation. Is there anything I can do to help? Unfortunately, I can't express an opinion about it until I can read it in English, and by then the decision will have been taken. It will be fun if I disagree with it, but I promise not to do so deliberately. As to my activities, *Beaverbrook* comes out here on 26 June (a little later in the States). The Crozier interviews are working out well. I am too occupied with them to start on my autobiography. I went to the annual dinner of the British Academy the other night. The President made a reactionary speech in which he said that the universities were destroying all academic standards by trying to keep up with modern ideas. I shouted 'Nonsense' very loudly, at which all the professors and civil servants were considerably shocked. It is hard to go on being a left-winger when you are elderly and a senior academic figure. Indeed, I have got used to

* Alan made over the royalties of the American edition to Eva.

being described as the doyen of English historians, or the most distinguished historian in the English-speaking world. They would have done better to say this when I was still having an active university career. I suppose they only say good things about me or anyone else when I am dead.

I knew (for once a bit of foreknowledge on my part, not yours) that learning to drive was harder than you thought. It takes years of experience. I am only getting to be a really good driver now, just as I am learning how to handle society and the world. One day, if I can find time, I will write a really good book about something, though I am not sure what. The only thing on which I go on having original and changing ideas is about the background of the Second World War, and my earlier book rather spoils me for writing it again.

The Library is in good shape. Veronica seems very well.

Giles's wife, Janet, had a daughter last week. She had to have a caesarian birth, apparently because the baby's heart had stopped beating. However, mother and daughter are both now well. If it had been a boy they would have called it Calvin, so there is general relief in the family at the harmless name Alison. I'll lay in some icons as a coming-of-age present for her when I am gone.

My thoughts are constantly on Venice. It ought to be the best time of year, though I've known the rain to fall very heavily. I hope you'll overcome your dislike of flying and come straight by air. Then we can meet at the airport, whichever arrives first waiting for the other.

But maybe you have forgotten how I look, and when we meet you may decide that you are not keen on me any more. I am sure you've built me up in your imagination as more and better than I am. That can't happen the other way round, because you are even better in reality than in imagination. At any rate, don't be shy when we meet. One thing you cannot imagine is the pleasure of walking around Venice, particularly in the districts where few tourists go. It is a fantasy city even if it is slowly dying.

I am reading a fascinating book, in Italian, about Italy in the First World War. The harsh conditions under which the soldiers lived is extraordinary, far worse than on the Western Front. And so is the savagery. Decimation was a common practice. Any company that retreated or protested had one man in ten or even five shot at random. I suppose the Italians have been a cruel people since the days of Rome. I'm also reading a thesis by a man called Barcsay about the Károlyi revolution of 1918–19. Competent but rather unsympathetic. Did I tell you Katus has destroyed a lot of his correspondence because it was too pro-Communist?

Oh dear, I want to see you and love you very much.

xxxxxxxxxxxxxxxxxxxxxxxxx X
Alan

15 May

Dear One,
How delightful it is to think that, ever since writing my last letter to you, I might have been in Poland and that I have not been. Not that there has been much here of any cheer. The weather has been cold for the last fortnight. We are back with all the troubles of a go-slow on the railways. I am on edge waiting for *Beaverbrook* to come out. And what a long time to wait – until 26 June. They say producing a book is like having a baby. But at least an expectant mother is involved until the last moment, whereas an author finishes his labours and then stands helplessly by while the book is being ruined by the printers. Two preliminary opinions: one by my old friend Keith Kyle, a TV commentator, who was fascinated by every line, and the other by a *Guardian* reporter who found much of it rather too detailed and wondered why I had spent five years of my life on an unimportant man. The reporter is going to write me up in the *Guardian*, I hope more penetratingly than the man in *The Times* did.

Your last letter spoilt me. I had almost forgotten that you could write one so long, and it is too soon for me to expect another. Maybe you will send me a little note sometime that you are alive and well. I don't worry when you don't write because I know that you are thinking about me – perhaps too much. So never write unless you feel like it.

I seem to be reviving all my old girl-friends. I told you, I think, that I had met Kathleen Tillotson, whom I knew when I was a schoolboy. She is now a retired professor of English literature and wrote a very good book which you should read called *Novelists of the Eighteen Forties*. Then last week in Oxford I was taken out to dinner by Betty Kemp, an eighteenth-century historian, who was a pupil of mine in Manchester before the Second World War and is now trying to become a professor. I gave her what support I could, though I fear that male prejudice will be too strong for her.

I have failed in my attempt to get Magdalen to admit women. The university takes the line that it would injure the woman's colleges if men's colleges went mixed, so they are not going to allow it. A real die-hard argument. I expect my younger colleagues will try to revolt, but it looks as though the battle has been lost for my academic lifetime.

Crozier gets on well, though very laboriously. I am not sure it is interesting enough to find a publisher. There is a new and rather dreary life of Metternich by Alan Palmer, but then he was a dreary man – none of the redeeming personal characteristics of Bismarck. However, I must write something about it for the *Observer*. The *Sunday Express* seems to have forgotten me. I have not written anything for it for the last two months. The truth is that Max Aitken has become entirely Tory and does not want radical articles any more. The *Sunday Express* is now all for killing all the gunmen in Ulster and fighting the unions in England. It is even supporting the Americans in Vietnam. For this and other reasons I am gloomy. This old country seemed to have been getting better and more enlightened in a slow sort of way. Now everything is going to the bad again. No fighting spirit on the Left and no belief in anything. All people want is to get out in their cars on crowded roads. Our prices have gone quite mad. All at once things cost twice what they did last year. Even I shall soon be a poor man, not that I worry about that. But it is all a sad contrast with a few years ago. The Labour government caused all the trouble by not trying to practise some socialist principles.

Here is a funny story to show how mad the world is. A TV producer in Los Angeles rang me up to say that he was producing a programme in Stockholm discussing the problems of economic growth, and would I go to Stockholm to take part in it? Fortunately I could honestly say that I knew nothing about economic growth and cared less. But what an extraordinary idea: taking expensive people all the way to Stockholm, so that he could tell viewers in Los Angeles that that was where they were talking.

I have settled on 14 September for the time we shall meet in Venice and found an attractive *pension* where we can have a room and a bath. If it rains we can dine at the *pension*, and when we want to go out in the evening we can take our midday meal there. I hope you approve. Do you need money for your fare? If you do, I'll send you some. In any case I can supply you with Italian money when we meet. A man in Milan, as maybe I told you, wants me to write an article on the history of England, so I shall be well supplied. Actually he promised to send me a contract and he hasn't, so I am not yet sure that I have landed this particular fish. But I shall pull in lots of money when

1972

Beaverbrook comes out. It is to be serialized in *The Sunday Times*, so you will be able to read bits that you will recognize.

Daniel tells me that he is on strike at school against having to wear school uniform (which he rarely does in any case). I said he ought to follow constitutional methods of protest, but if he doesn't I shall not condemn him. Crispin strongly disapproves. He is Clerk of the School Parliament at his school and is very stern against anyone who breaks the rules. My little grand-daughter is now making progress, and Giles is behaving as though no one had ever been a father before. That is all my family news.

The only other news is that I think of you every day and am counting the days until we are in each other's arms. Do you ever think of me?

Love to you with much warmth,

xxxxxxxxxxxxxxx   Alan

28 May

Oh My Dear,

You seem to be a long way away. Often I wonder how we managed to overcome the obstacles of distance and language even enough to have one happy time together. As the months pass my memories of Salzburg fade into the distance until I can hardly believe that it happened. Of course, what I am really saying is that I don't want you to write when you don't feel like it or are too busy, and yet I miss your letters when they don't come. However, it is really not all that far until the middle of September which should put everything right.

I have been rather gloomy for quite different reasons. I have had what is called in English a cold in the head: a thickness that makes me feel quite stupid. Then I have anxieties about the appearance of *Beaverbrook*. I hope you got your copy by the way. It is far too big and everyone says so. The publisher would have done better to bring it out in two volumes, but nowadays this is never done. I don't worry for myself. What people say about me does not interest me much. Besides, I know both the merits and the defects of the book better than anyone else does. But I worry what they will say about Beaverbrook. I fear I have been too honest about him. Even those who have read the book ask: Was he worth it? What did he do in life – as though that mattered. People are surprised that I, a supposedly serious historian, should have spent five years on writing the life of a rather unimportant man. I try to explain that I did it out of curiosity – his own motive – just to find out about him. Of course I did it also because I loved him, but that memory fades too. Now I often remember the times when I found him exasperating and wondered why I ever wasted my time in his company. Our worlds were miles away from each other, a thing that I appreciated and which I am sure he did not. It never occurred to him that there could be any worlds but his. However, it will all be over soon. The book will come out. The reviewers will misunderstand it as they always do, and I hope people will buy it. I told the *Observer* that I was the only person qualified to review it, but this was not an idea that appealed to them. I hear the book has caused a row on the *New Statesman*. It has been given for review to Tom Driberg who wrote an unsatisfactory life of Beaverbook years ago, and Paul Johnson who regards himself as a great authority on historical biography wanted to do it. The only one certain to praise it will be Michael Foot, who of course thinks it is wonderful.

Then I have had worries with Daniel. He has been campaigning at his school against school uniform (does such a thing exist in Hungary?). The headmaster is a reactionary fellow. He called a meeting of parents. Of course only the conventional ones turned up and voted unanimously for keeping school uniform. On top of this the headmaster announced that as the boys had organized a petition against school uniform he was abolishing all the school committees on the grounds that petitioning and committees were incompatible. This seems to me nonsense. I could not go to the meeting and wish I had, so that I could protest. I advise Daniel to use the constitutional machinery, but of course he is too impatient and takes it out of the school by doing no work. I should like to move him to another school but this can't be done in the middle of his course. Maybe I'll move him for his last two years. I suppose the young must fight their own battles, but one can't help wishing one could show them from experience how to do it.

There is yet another book on Chamberlain's dealings with Germany: *The Diplomacy of Illusion* by Keith Middlemas who wrote a rather bad book on Baldwin. This is better if only because he has used the Cabinet and other papers more thoroughly than anyone else has done. But he starts off with his mind made up. He thinks Hitler was determined on a great war and that therefore Chamberlain was wasting his time. I'd rather start out with my mind a blank and let the story tell itself without saying all the time what a blockhead Chamberlain was. Still, you will need to get the book and you will recognize all your old friends at the Admiralty. The fascination of this period is curious. Every time a historian comes along with the claim that he has really found the explanation and gets no nearer than before. I think Munich and its background should be forgotten for a while so that we can get on to other more important things.

Public affairs are also gloomy. After all the delays and evasions by the government we shall end up with a railway strike or something like it. And in the end the railwaymen will get their increased wages and our travel will cost more. It is I fear the failure of the Labour government that has got us into this mess.

The only other news is that the Duke of Windsor has died, and as an authority on his period I have been pronouncing about the abdication on the radio. I had a ponderous discussion whether it could happen nowadays, a subject to me of the most profound unimportance. But the monarchy is something people like to talk about.

You must write to me about your son's visit to England. And if you can you must write to me about yourself, if only to let me be sure that you are still alive and still occasionally thinking of me.

The weather is very bad. I have quite forgotten what it is like to lie in the sun or to bathe at Highgate Ponds. I gave four lectures at University College London on Europe in the twentieth century, which I found very exciting and very tiring. The young people were interested and also I think rather puzzled. Next year I shall start lecturing again at Oxford, just to show that I can still do it.

My mind is always on Venice, sometimes with excitement and often with anxiety. I am sure I shall turn out to be for you less than I was or what you expected of me. So we must both wish that time should go quickly.

All my thoughts are with you and all my love,

xxxxxxxxxxxxxxxxxxxxxxxxx
Alan

15 June

Dearest Love,

Our letters crossed, I suppose because the last Monday in May is our national spring holiday, and letters are delayed.

I have arranged about Venice. We shall stop at the Pension Dinesen, San Vio, 628. I shall arrive about midday and can wait for you at the airport or go to the *pension*, whichever suits you. I shall have money for us both, so you will only need enough to pay for getting to the *pension*. My next activity is to write an article about English history for an Italian encyclopaedia, so there will be a nice present waiting for us. No doubt I shall think of other instructions as the time approaches.

I am still recovering from my cold and don't feel very gay, except when I think about you. The weather has been very bad. It is a good thing you don't live in England. Either it is cold or it rains. I haven't been out walking all day for weeks. Unless things change I shall go to Offa's Dyke untrained and shall soon get footsore. However, so will my companions, Giles and Crispin. The latter is just nerving himself for his final school examinations, when we shall find out just how good he is as a mathematician. He is the best at his school, but now he will be judged on a national standard.

Daniel is still in trouble at school for organizing a peaceful petition against school uniform. What is worse, the headmaster blames it on me. He wrote me a quite hysterical letter, saying that I was behind all the opposition to him. I sent a conciliatory answer, but it had no effect. I should like to move Daniel to another school, but that is not easy in the middle of a course.

Crozier is causing me some anxiety. I have practically finished the work on it and am now not confident of finding a publisher. The Lady Lloyd-George diaries which I thought should be a best-seller only sold some three thousand copies, and this will not tempt a publisher to try with another set of diaries. Maybe a university publisher will be ready to undertake it. I don't want any money for myself out of this, so long as I can see the Crozier interviews as a book.

The publicity for *Beaverbrook* is building up. I made a long radio talk with Michael Foot on Beaverbrook, which is going out next Tuesday. I have two television programmes on it, and another when I shall be shown off as a personality. After being away from the television screen for so long this is quite exciting, though also very tiring. For once I have to wear my best clothes instead of looking rather disreputable. You will no doubt be glad of this change.

1972

The other evening I went to a great public dinner, given by Max Aitken in honour of Lord Thomson, who owns *The Times*. It was a pretty dreary affair, with speakers trying to make out that Lord Thomson was a great man simply because he has lots of money. They did not succeed. In ten days' time Hamish Hamilton is giving a party to launch *Beaverbrook*, which should be a bit gayer. But I get rather weary of explaining why I like Beaverbook and wrote his life. I am tempted to reply that I can't remember. It seemed right at the time and is now a long way away. I can't live in the past as I suppose historians ought to do. By the way, did you get the copy of *Beaverbrook* I sent you? It is so heavy that perhaps it disrupted the postal system.

That is the end of my activities. I am beginning to think about the Second World War and how to write about it. It really is an extraordinary subject. The First War is easy to explain. After all, it grew out of the existing system and followed on previous history. It was just another war. But in the Second War everyone went mad. If you look at Germans nowadays, you can't understand, at least I can't, how they did such atrocious things. And consider how we went on in England – certain that we should destroy the Nazis even when we were alone and ready to destroy ourselves and all Europe to do it. It is really impossible to explain to young people what we thought we were up to. What will the future make of us? Now we are living in a relatively sane world, and that makes the Second War all the more mysterious.

The Library is now full of summer researchers from America. They must surely find European affairs even stranger than I do. But they toil devotedly away.

At Oxford we are still fussing over the admission of women to men's colleges. The University has now ruled that no more colleges can go mixed for five years, so it looks as though Magdalen has missed its chance, at any rate while I am there. I have only four years more. Maybe I shall be glad to retire by then, though I doubt it.

This is a dull letter, partly because nothing is happening and partly because I am depressed by so many things private and otherwise. The one important thing is that I am counting the days until we are together in Venice, and I know that you are counting them too. It is extraordinary to be a lover at my age, but then life goes on being extraordinary and unexpected.

Here is lots of love and ceaseless thoughts about you,

xxxxxxxxxxxxxxxxxx
Alan

24 June

Beloved,

You write such sweet letters. I don't know what I have done to deserve them. Believe me, I will never worry about you, and I know you won't worry about me. I wish that I could be with you more, but that's a different thing. If I really count in your life, that's satisfaction enough for me. My worries come from other people, not from you, people who make demands on me when I don't want to be concerned with them. But no one can shake off the legacy of his past actions and mistakes.

I asked Frances Lloyd-George's daughter whether she minded the publicity about her mother's love life, and she said: 'It is impossible to realize that one's parents were once human.' I expect your son feels the same about us.

On the other practical point, I have sent you the book about the Chartist land settlements and also the one by Middlemas. They are both little presents to you. There are still more books coming out derived from the Cabinet papers before the war. They don't get any further. By now the story is, I think, clear and we ought to get on to something else. There will be a review of Middlemas by me in the *Observer* on Sunday, and one on an enormous war book the week after. Incidentally, I got an invitation from Hauser to this year's conference. How glad I am that we are not going.

Beaverbook comes out on Monday. I am not very pleased with the prospective reviewers. Muggeridge is doing it in the *Observer* – a man who knows no history and also built up Beaverbrook as evil personified. Robert Blake in *The Sunday Times* will be better. He is a good historian, though of course having written the life of Bonar Law he is marked as Beaverbrook's man. Tom Driberg will do it in next week's *New Statesman*. He will be concerned to show that his biography is better than mine, which it isn't. However, Paul Johnson is angry that he was not asked to do it in the *New Statesman*, so he is going to do a second review a few weeks later. David Farrer, who was once Beaverbrook's secretary, is going to say it is marvellous in the *Daily Telegraph* on Monday. Having lived with the book so much I have now lost interest in it. Indeed, I can hardly remember why I once liked the old boy so much. His impact has faded from my mind.

Hamish Hamilton gave a party for the book the other night. It was not very exciting, mostly booksellers who had to be told that the book will be a best-seller. I have also done two radio talks about it and two television shows, with Boothby claiming to know more about

1972

Beaverbrook than I did. It keeps me in a whirl of activity, and Veronica enjoys keeping a record of my engagements.

I am against your coming to Venice by car. It is a long way and very tiring. The joy of Venice is to be free from cars and to go everywhere on foot or on the water. Also I think Florence is too far. It is better to get to know one place really well. We can keep Florence for another year. If we go anywhere let it be to Ravenna, which is small enough to see in a day, or a day and a night.

As to my own plans, boring as they are, I am going to walk Offa's Dyke with Crispin and Giles for a week beginning on 15 July. It will be an odd party but they get on very well. I only fear that we may have the one hot week of the year and that it will be too hot to walk. On 15 August I go to Ireland for three weeks. The country will be marvellous. After that I am going to Venice to meet a girl I know. This is the only date I am really looking forward to.

Crispin is in the midst of his mathematics exams. I asked him how he had done and he said: 'I think I have passed.' When I then asked what this meant, he said: 'Oh, I think 35%.' I daresay he is right. He has decided to go to Christ's College, Cambridge, a college I know nothing about but it sounds delightful. He has chosen a college that neither I nor his mathematics master recommended, which shows he knows his own mind. Daniel has at last started to work hard, as I knew he would. He is still on bad terms with his headmaster; Daniel needs no inspiration from me to be a rebel, but it is no good arguing with a silly old man. Still it is hard that the children should have to carry the sins of the father. For that matter, my reputation as a rebel is largely undeserved.

The weather is still cold beyond description. The longest day is past, and I have not bathed once or even sat out reading. The central heating is still on, and the sun never shines. It must be due to the Tory government, who incidentally are in a fine mess. All their policies are in ruins. The other day I went to a high-class lunch party (present among others the Duke of Bedford) and they were all saying that it was just like Weimar before Hitler.

I told them not to be silly, which actually cheered them up.

Love and love and love,

xxxxxxxxxxxxxxxxxx
Alan

8 July

My Darling, Oh my Beloved,

What marvellous letters you write to me. I don't deserve the half of them. Indeed every time I get a letter from you, I feel how unworthy I am and how useless to you. Things will get better in time.

Now let me talk selfishly about my own affairs. *Beaverbrook* had lots of reviews, most of them more about him than about the book. Nearly all the reviewers were newspaper men, not historians, and to them his career as a newspaper proprietor was all-important. Robert Blake treated the book historically and was very flattering. Muggeridge was very bad, merely repeating stories against Beaverbrook that he had told a hundred times before. Dick Crossman in the *Sunday Telegraph* wrote a review full of mistakes. I wrote an answer pointing out some of them. I don't think he read half the book. The *Guardian* also had a silly review by Brian Inglis repeating the slanders about Beaverbrook's finances. And Arthur Marwick, one of the few historians who reviewed the book, thought that much of it was very boring. The *Listener* was oddest of all. It sent the book to a poet Roy Fuller who didn't know what to make of it. Cameron Hazelhurst, a pupil of mine, said in *The Times* that I ought to have used the PRO records of Beaverbrook's ministries. I felt that I had too much material already. I wanted to get it all into one volume, though it is really too big as it is. The great thing is that there were lots of reviews so I hope the book will sell. As you say, I think of both Beaverbrook and Károlyi with affection, but it is in the past, something that is over and done with. I can't really recall the emotions I once felt.

To amuse you, I have begun my autobiography and will bring the first chapters to Venice. As I expected, I am more interested in other people than in myself. I go on writing about my family background and can't visualize the little boy living in it. Also it is turning out very matter-of-fact, dates of when my parents were born and how much money my father made. But I have difficulty recreating them as people. Also I am so distressed and upset by the many mistakes I made and the humiliations I suffered. I have got in a good sex bit at the age of five with a young servant-maid. The Freudians will like that. Maybe you'll be shocked and want me to take it out. Or maybe you'll laugh. I had quite forgotten it until I came to write. Being a historian I can't help reading later significance into events that at the time were probably not like that at all. Still, it gives me something to do.

How strange to be interested in Boothby. He is very well and has,

I think, escaped the alarm he felt when his wife, who is thirty years younger than he is, wanted to start a family. That was never to Bob's taste. He is steadily building up a reputation that he was a great and important statesman in the nineteen-thirties, when in fact he did not count for anything. Now he is talking his way into the history books. All the students go to see him and write in their books what he tells them.

The weather continues very bad. We have not had a single warm day. I hope that it will continue like this next week when we are walking on Offa's Dyke. Instead I expect it will be the one hot week of the year. In two months' time we shall be together. I really don't think of anything else, just live from day to day and wait for the time to go by. Never fear that I shall embarrass you or worry you in any way. I shall just take your hand and say 'Hello, Love'. That's all for now.

Love as strong as ever,

x x x
Alan

24 July

Dearest Love,

Though it is a fortnight since I wrote to you time has gone by so quickly that nothing seems to have happened. This is only another way of saying that physical activity such as walking takes up more time and energy than intellectual activity, if that is what I can suppose to be doing usually. Well, what have I done? The weather has improved for one thing and we have had some hot days, with their usual consequence so far as I am concerned: outbreaks of skin irritation on my hands, arms and even – after I was foolish enough to wear shorts – on my legs. It really is a curse which grows worse with the years. One day of sun, especially by the sea or when I am sweating and therefore salty, and there are these tiresome outbreaks all around. There seems to be no remedy except to keep out of the sun which I am reluctant to do. Doctors can only advise that I should get it over: if I go in the sun enough my skin will get hardened. It never does. Your love for the sun would not suit me at all.

As an additional ailment I have developed a stiff shoulder and painful upper arm, I think from not sitting quite right when driving my car, or maybe it is pulling to the left and unconsciously I keep adjusting my body to this. It must be a sign of old age. It is bearable in the daytime but becomes a nuisance at night when I get wakened up by pain unless I take one particular position. I must also report, as an end to my physical ills, that I am developing the wrinkled stomach skin of an old man. It has nothing to do with being fat, which I am not, but simply it falls into folds. As I so often think and say to you, it is very annoying to begin to look like an old man when I feel physically like a young one. As to mental age, that too does not seem to get any greater.

Now for some more cheerful news. Offa's Dyke was a great success. The weather, though sunny, was not too hot, and there was a fresh breeze most of the time. So we managed fifteen miles a day over very rough country. Giles and Crispin get on wonderfully. Indeed Crispin said to me: 'I am very worried. I am getting to talk like Giles and even to think like him.' They both enjoy reading maps and tracing the path. They are both organizers, though Crispin throws in a moral element as well. A generation divides them – Giles is 35, Crispin 16 – yet they seem exactly the same. I don't know why. Neither of them resembles me in disposition, and yet as they have different mothers, they cannot derive their characters from them. We took an old friend of mine from Oxford with us, I suppose in his late forties. As he had done no walking since last autumn, he was almost dead after the first day though he loyally struggled along each day thereafter. As you may imagine I was secretly pleased with myself to do so much better. We had one good dinner at a country hotel in the hills. Otherwise rather dull food. All English hotels are corrupted by abandoning English cooking and trying to imitate foreign cooking unsuccessfully. After five days the weather turned too hot, and we spent the day bathing in the Severn. Then it rained, so Crispin and I toured the Welsh castles, built by Edward I to hold down the conquered Welsh. They are models of military architecture and exactly like British posts you would find on the North-West frontier of India or French posts in the Atlas Mountains. Coming back from Wales in the evening we found an endless stream of holiday traffic. I said to Crispin: 'I'll now show you how I used to drive. You'll never again deny that I am a good, safe and fast driver.' Then I overtook one car after another all the way back to our hotel. Crispin confessed that he had never seen driving like it. I suppose I was excited by the air and the mountains.

What a boring letter this must be for you. But I have no news except these trivialities. The reviews of *Beaverbrook* have dried up until the American ones start in August. Though it has had great publicity I doubt whether it will have really big sales. People will only buy the biography of a prime minister or a general, however dull. I am sure they feel, perhaps rightly, that Beaverbrook had no historical significance. I am already beginning to forget the subject. Instead I brood on the Second World War. I suppose I shall start writing it in the autumn. I wish I was well enough equipped to do it as a series of separate histories – Poland in the war, Germany in the war, France in the war, England in the war, and leave the reader to add them all together. After all there was no such thing as the Second World War in the abstract. There was a war in relation to each country, and each of these wars was different.

Politics are in a very bad state, and I should be distressed if I worried about public affairs any more. The Protestants and the Catholics are killing each other in Northern Ireland, or rather the IRA who are not Catholics at all are killing on behalf of the Catholics. Class war is raging at home. Of course I'm on the side of the dockers against the government. Yet what the dockers are defending is not the working class but their own right to monopolize a particular sort of job, and that this job must be kept going for ever even when it is no longer needed. The handloom weavers all over again.

I hope you were pleased with my last letter and its little apology. All my loving thoughts go to you.

xxxxxxxxxxxxxxxxxxxxxx
Alan

7 August

Darling,

The fact that I can write August as the date means that we have only a month before we meet. I want to see you very much and am becoming very impatient. As I am going to Ireland very soon and do not know when I shall write again, I write now about practical questions. First, have you enough money for your fare? I can send some if you need it but shall not have much time on getting back to London. So I hope you can manage. As I think I told you, I arrive at Venice airport at 13.35 on 14 September. What would you like me to do? If you are coming by air about that time, I can wait at the airport or you can wait for me, and we can go into Venice together. If you are coming by train I can meet you at the station, so long as I have time to get there or rather to leave my luggage at the Pension Dinesen and then get back to the station.

If neither of these is possible, I will go to the pension and wait for you. You take a porter from the station or the air terminal and he will accompany you by water bus (*vaporetto*) to the pension. He has a fixed charge. You also have to pay for luggage on the *vaporetto* as well as for yourself. You'll need money for this and, if you are coming by air, for the fare from the airport to the air terminal. Otherwise you will need no money at all. I have plenty of Italian money and will give you a good portion of it as soon as we meet. You will be able to buy yourself some nice clothes, though Venice is an unnecessarily expensive place. I hope this does not sound too complicated. It is simple really. You have only to tell me what to do and where to be and I will do it.

I have no instructions for you except to come and be yourself. You have probably forgotten what I look like. I am very tall with curly black hair and a most distinguished figure. I am so handsome that people turn round in the street and look after me. So now you will recognize me easily.

As to clothes, it is a difficult time of year. It can still be quite hot or it may rain. I shall remember to bring a pullover this time so I shall not need to buy one. The one we bought in Salzburg by the way is very impractical. It is too light in colour and so shows all the marks when I spill food or tobacco on it, as I often do. Venetian food is not very rich, so you will not have any stomach upset. There is a very good spirit called grappa which you will find too strong; beer is at any rate better than French, wine rather uninteresting. There is a lot of fancy fish, mostly such silly things as octopus and scampi. I prefer to stick to meat, though it too is rather boring.

I am busy making some more lira. The Italian encyclopaedia people decided that my article for them was not long enough so I am rewriting the whole thing – laborious but profitable. As long as I have some reason to sit at my typewriter I don't complain. I shall have a good piece of autobiography to show you, all my youth. When I try to remember it, I can only remember the books I read, beginning with *Pilgrim's Progress*. But there are some quite funny passages. I shall stop that chapter with the First World War or just before it. You may find it so uninteresting that I shall not write any more.

Back to Venice, this time on a literary theme. You surely know *Farewell to Arms*, the early novel that Hemingway wrote about the Italian front in the First World War. It is very good though sentimental. At the end of the Second World War Hemingway went back to Venice, this

1972

time as a senior American officer, and wrote another novel called *Across the River and into the Trees*. It is not a good novel, but for people in Venice interesting. The central figure is an elderly American officer like Hemingway and he tries to recapture his experiences of the First World War by having a love affair with a young Italian girl. She treats him as a father and he dies of a heart attack. Is this a warning for me? At any rate, it is a curiosity as a second time round.

I am still struggling through long books, the latest of them a ridiculous history of England by Paul Johnson. It is a prolonged attack on the Common Market and, what is even stranger seeing that Johnson is a Roman Catholic, on the Roman Catholic Church, which he says is quite as dangerous as international Communism. I laughed a lot at his wild remarks. You will see my review in the *Observer* when it comes out in September.

As to my movements, I go to Ireland on 15 August and shall be back in London on 5 September. We shall be moving around in Ireland so I will not bother you with any addresses. If you have any urgent messages, write to the Library and I shall find them when I get back. Veronica is going to Brittany for a fortnight, but, though she talks of 'we', I still can't discover whether she has a boy-friend. I think she met your boy recently. At any rate he rang up and chatted with her.

What are you doing? I hope you are away in the country and having sunny weather. The sun recently appeared in London. I hurried off to Highgate Ponds with the intention of lying in the sun and then swimming. While I was half-asleep naked, it began to rain and I had to go into the water in order not to get wet. Now we are back with cold weather. Daniel is still away at Youth Hostels in the Lake District. Miraculously I have not had a telephone call from him saying that he is in trouble, so maybe he will get home by his own endeavours after all. Next Thursday he will be fifteen.

I think I am a bit fatter than I was last year. This is another way of recognizing me. Oh Darling, do hurry to Venice and do be excited to see me. I think of our meeting all the time.

Love,

xxxxxxxxxxxx
Alan

13 August

Dear One,

I am not really due to write a letter for another week, but I wanted to answer your questions and to say all sorts of thank-yous. First, thank you for the ornamental fruits and the lovely red wine. I thought I had to eat the fruit but Veronica explained it was for decoration only. I don't expect to keep the wine for decoration also. And thank you much more for the lovely letter. I like it when you sit down and let your pen run without reflecting what you are going to say. In this way I feel nearer to you. Little correction of English. When something is going to happen, like our meeting in Venice, you write 'When'. 'If' is a hypothesis which may happen or may not. The German *wenn* which means 'if' causes confusion.

Here are some answers about *Beaverbrook*. Beatrice Lillie was a very good comic actress, almost a clown in fact. She still is, though she does not appear often nowadays. She married a descendant of Sir Robert Peel. The marriage did not stick. Foul weather. There is a recognized English expression that so-and-so is a fair-weather friend, meaning that he only sticks by you when things are going well. Churchill reversed the expression and said that Beaverbrook was a foul-weather friend because he always turned up and supported you when the weather was bad and things were going badly. Max was always inclined to criticize you when things were going well and even to run little stories that made you seem slightly absurd. As soon as you were in trouble no effort was too great for him.

Corelli Barnett's book is not much good, though it makes lively reading. It is really half a dozen books rolled into one. He starts with a denunciation of the public schools as making the English governing class pious and soft so that they were incapable of holding the Empire with a strong hand. Then it occurred to him that the Empire was a great waste of effort anyway so he denounces that. Next back to the decline in English leadership by a demonstration that their industrial system was incapable of meeting the demands of the First World War. After that the Empire comes back into his mind and he shows all the nonsense of pretending that the Commonwealth was a real unity between the wars. At this moment news reached him that the official records were open for the pre-war period, so he hurried off and wrote yet another account of Chamberlain's diplomacy. This is not bad, but we have recently had it two or three times already. I must confess with regret that Middlemas's book is the best of the set. He is rather pompous and arrogant, but he has done his work. Now I have cleared my conscience.

Daniel came home cheerfully having survived his fortnight in Youth

1972

Hostels. He announces that next year he is going to cover all the Youth Hostels in France. But the youth of nowadays put up with hardship and discomfort that I should have found intolerable. I have always believed in travelling by the Blue Train, to use an expression that is now out of date. There are no Blue Trains any more.

Crispin is reading *Principia Mathematica* by Bertrand Russell and Whitehead. Russell said that the book was so intellectual that he never recovered from writing it. Crispin seems to take it in his stride.

The weather is as dull as ever. Do you know, I have only bathed twice this year instead of being at Highgate Ponds every day.

That's all, except to say lots of love. As to Venice, it is a case of when we meet, not as you write if.

Love again,
x
Alan

6 September

Dear Heart,
At 10 p.m. next Thursday I shall be waiting for the train from Trieste by the engine, or whatever they call the substitute for an engine which pulls the train nowadays. I wish I had realized earlier that you were bound to come via Trieste. Then I might have met you on the way after visiting Porec on the Istrian coast. However, we will perhaps meet there in the spring. I hope you will not be tired. I am sure to be, so late at night. I am gloomy with life after finishing *Beaverbrook* and cannot see what lies ahead of me. Also I am not as marvellous in any way as you think I am.

Ireland was far more successful than I expected, though it is a strain being with a person for whom one is indifferent. Two things made an improvement. We had a schoolfriend of Daniel's with us whose own holiday plans had gone wrong. Second, the weather was beyond description – unbroken sunshine day after day as though it were the Mediterranean. Empty beaches, sea warmed at any rate a little by the sun. I went to the beach entirely alone and turned brown.

I shall have lost it by next week. Though sometimes bored by Ireland, I benefited from doing nothing for three weeks and feel easier in mind, though maybe not younger in body.

If anything goes wrong, you know where to go: Pension Dinesen. But I shall not fail.

Love,
Alan

When I think of our meeting, I tremble and feel quite weak.

30 September

Darling,

    I can't find words to say how happy I was in Venice and how I rejoice that you were happy too. I worried, as usual, that you were upset towards the end, and so was greatly relieved when I received your little letter from Venice (only yesterday – I suppose the chaos at the Venice post office). I simply do not have a feeling of life without you. Somehow we must arrange to be together. I have been thinking on wrong lines. I thought of all the reasons why it would be a mistake to marry me, and believe me, there are many reasons. I ought to have been thinking whether I wanted to marry you, and of course I do. The arranging of this will not be easy, and you must be patient. Indeed, if you go off and marry someone else, or merely lose interest in me, I shall not complain. I shall actually be glad for your sake because I think I am a bad bargain. Now I will not discuss this until I have something more constructive to say.

    I wasn't at all well when I got to Turin. Too much good food perhaps in Venice and even more in Turin, where Venturi took me out for the day and gave me mushrooms for lunch. I had a terrible tummy upset and stayed in bed for a day while things blew over. Apart from that I had an interesting time. Venturi, now the professor of modern history, was a partisan during the war. Afterwards he was cultural attaché at Moscow and used the opportunity to learn Russian, which enabled him to write a very good book on the Populists. I suspect he was a Communist during the war and was disillusioned by his time in Moscow. His wife, also a partisan, is still a Communist, having escaped the experience of Moscow. He told me an interesting historical thing. Thanks to the difficulty about Trotsky, who is still a non-person, not only is there no proper history of the Bolshevik revolution in Russian, there is not even a life of Lenin, and of course there is no good life of

1972

Lenin in any Western language. How extraordinary. He also told me that he had met an elderly scholar who had been instructed to investigate Lenin's family background. He discovered that Lenin's maternal grandfather was a German Jew. When he revealed this he was sent to Siberia, and the story is lost. I rather doubt whether it is true. In any case it is of no importance. Curious all the same.

Turin is impressive. A planned eighteenth-century city with fantastic baroque churches and palaces. I saw a very good museum of the Risorgimento, full of praise for Cavour and Victor Emanuel, with Garibaldi kept well in the background. I had a very good time, apart from being ill, and was very glad to get back to England. Since then I have been all alone in the Library, waiting for Veronica to come back on Monday. I have reviewed *Queen Victoria* and am now working on *Lady Astor*, who is a very unattractive character to those who did not know her. She was a bully as only very rich people can be. I will send you both books when I have finished with them. Reading them will remind you of me and of our time in Venice. How funny that you should think me cold on our last day at the Lido when I was feeling so content and secure. It shows how easily people can misunderstand each other even when they are in love.

Roger Louis, my old pupil, now a professor in Texas, has put together a book all about *The Origins of the Second World War*, and its critics. They do not come out of it well – almost hysterical and evidently unable to read. Now it seems a not very important book, wrong only in failing to make its real subject clear. All it said was that, even if Hitler had ideas of world conquest, which I think he had, the Polish war was not an essential part of his plans and was indeed a mistake. Whatever else he wanted he did not want a war with England, at any rate not until he had conquered Russia. But of course when I wrote it I thought the outbreak of war in 1939 was the really important event. It wasn't. The really important event was the transformation of a small European war into a world war by Hitler's attack on Russia and the Japanese attack on the United States. This is what I shall try to say in my history of the Second World War, though I shall have to remember that readers want events, so that they can look at the pictures. I seem so busy with other things that I can't imagine myself ever settling down to writing another book. Looking back, I ask myself how did I ever find time to write *Beaverbrook*? It must have been some other person.

Last night I went to Sutton and gave the first of four lectures on Great Britain in the twentieth century. A good subject and a full house. I have not been to the boys yet, but shall try to persuade Crispin and perhaps Daniel as well to come on a long walk tomorrow while the weather is still fine. Despite my still troubled tummy I feel very energetic and refreshed by our wonderful time. Next week I shall find out about Ljubljana and Porec and tell you what can be arranged for next April, if you still want to come. It is also cheering news that I have found a publisher for the Crozier interviews, though it will mean a lot more work on the proofs and the index. It will not bring in much money.

I saw a portrait of Maria Theresa in Turin. She looked very satisfied, so Francis I had evidently found the right point. Joseph II on the other hand looked as though he could not find it with anyone. As to Victor Emanuel, he evidently thought of nothing else. I think of the same topic quite a lot and hope you do also. Be a good and loving girl. Do not write unless you feel like it. I shall keep to my routine of once a fortnight and shall think of you every day in between.

Love, just as strong as when I was with you.

Alan

14 October

Beloved,

I had your beautiful letter. It filled me again with memories of Venice.

You may count certainly on our being in Ljubljana on 6 April. I have found that there is a plane only on Fridays from London. So I suggest two nights in Ljubljana and three in Porec, which is a delightful seaside resort as well as having a sixth-century basilica. For our last night we might go to Kopor near Trieste, so that I can depart for Florence the next morning. If you feel like coming by car, this will make our movements easier. But it is a long way and you should use your car only if you are certain that it will not tire you. We can get about easily by public transport, and I don't want you to be tired as you were in Venice. Not that I mind what happens so long as we are together.

Do not worry about your work. I expect that you are stuck because you have finished one job and cannot settle to another. I am exactly in the same state. Far from working steadily as you imagine, I am occupying my time with trivialities. I know I ought to get going on the history of the Second World War, but I can't think how to start. The ideas go round my head instead of sorting themselves out. In the long run this is a good thing. It is better to have the book half arranged in my head before I start to write. Then one day I shall begin turning out my routines of a thousand words each day. As regards your own work, ought I not to see your book in English before it is published? I don't trust any foreigner, however skilful, to write perfect English, and I could surely make some corrections. I did a good job on Nancy Astor which will appear unsigned in *The Times Literary Supplement*. The more I wrote, the more I disliked her. What was she? An arrogant, rude woman who got away with her rudeness because she was very rich. I'm glad I did not know her. *Beaverbrook* is out in the United States, and you ought to receive some more money. I haven't had any reviews yet but no doubt shall. My other project, rather foolish, is to agree to edit a series of short illustrated books about English Prime Ministers. I fear that I shall have much worry making the contributors write good history instead of personal anecdotes. As to Crozier, I am revising the manuscript for the last time before it goes to the printer. Then I shall try to sell it also as a serial in one of the Sunday papers. So you see I find plenty of excuses for not settling down to the Second World War.

Here is a little confession. I was asked to a party at the Hungarian legation next Tuesday, but this clashed with another at the Turkish embassy that I had already accepted so I had to refuse. I hope your friends will not be disappointed. But I truly was committed already. This week I start in Oxford and must think of something really interesting to say about history in general. Maybe after all these years of silence in Oxford I shall have forgotten how to give good lectures.

Another letter all about me. I think about you all the time. The thought keeps me going all the time. My memories of the Lido are exceptionally vivid. It is very sad that you should have been in doubt about me that day, when I was more content than usual. It just shows as you say that people easily misunderstand each other. But don't think that we failed to communicate in Venice. We said much to each other and I felt that we were knowing each other better all the time. Of course we slip back when we are not together, but we start again on a higher level. I can't express what a wonderful experience it all was. The only drawback is that your absence makes me irritable with other people. I really cannot be bothered with anyone else, however much it is my duty to do so.

Veronica is very well and the Library still very busy. I keep telling her that she ought to get a more active job but she only smiles and says how she likes the Library. We are surrounded by buildings that are being knocked down. The dust and noise are almost unbearable. I suppose it will be years before the new buildings are up, and then they will be hideous. Yet another book to review: the second volume of

Wellington by Elizabeth Longford, not interesting enough to bother you with it. I am also expecting at last Hauser's book on Anglo-German relations 1933–36, truly the work of a lifetime. One other event: I had an interview – in German – with German television on the Hitler boom in England. Apparently there is a film about him and two long BBC series. I said no one was interested in Hitler as a political figure but that he was *ratselhaft*.* I think that is right. Forgive this boring letter. I am much better except for a cold. I never go to doctors!

All the love in the world,

Alan

30 October

Beloved,

I am worried about you. I am sure you are committed to what you call your little operation, and I shall not be at ease until I hear that it has been successful. These things are always a trouble until they are over. I say this without experience, never having had an operation in my life. The worst that happened to me was the removal of a splinter from under my thumb by a doctor in Rome. And of course I had my gums cut about every week for a year. So get well quickly and write to me that all is well.

I won't bother you with my troubles that are tiny in comparison to anything that might happen to you. I am still drifting mentally, thinking about the Second World War without seeing a clear picture. I don't know what impression I want to make. Do I want to show that the war was a terribly muddled affair, as all wars are, or do I want to say that after all it was that unique thing – a just war that was worth fighting despite all the suffering it caused? What will future historians say? Will they understand, as we do, that Fascism had to be destroyed? Or will they lump the Second World War into the same class of European follies as the Napoleonic Wars or the First World War? I don't know what to think.

My review of *Nancy Astor* came out in *The Times Literary Supplement*, and its editor sent me a special line of congratulation. Christopher Sykes was not so pleased. I also had great fun reading the second volume of Elizabeth Longford's life of Wellington. He was a silly old goose, constantly expecting the social roof to fall in and doom to arrive. But he

* puzzling

1972

was also a very funny eccentric man. His love affairs reach a high level of comedy. On a slightly more serious plane, I am working through Hauser's book on Anglo-German relations between 1933 and 1936. It looks as though he wrote it solely on the basis of the published documents and then, late in the day, inserted a few scraps he had found in the PRO. But he has not worked systematically through the Cabinet papers, though these are much more informative than the FO stuff. Also he got hold of Wendt's book on economic appeasement and used some information from it, without realizing or making clear that Wendt really transforms the entire story. Altogether not a remarkable accomplishment for a man who was past the German age of retirement.

I have got more use from a rather journalistic book by Bethell called *The War Hitler Won*. This is simply about the Polish war. The good material in it is the new story of how the British went on negotiating through Dahlerus well into November 1939. They dreamt that Goering was ready to supersede Hitler and be content with the German territories of Poland. This is good 'dirt' as we say in the trade. You must get hold of it. If you can't, I will send it to you.

I have just been to the Peak District with Daniel and Crispin for a couple of days. We tried to climb Kinder Scout, the local mountain, and were caught in rain and mist, so much so that the Mountain Rescue Team came out to find us. I wisely had already turned back and was able to show that we knew what we were doing. The next day was beautifully fine and we went for a less alarming walk in Dovedale. So we had a very good time.

We are in the midst of yet another economic crisis, as we shall go on being as long as successive governments, even Labour ones, and the trade unions shy away from the fact that Liberal capitalism will not work any longer. We are moving into Socialism backwards, a very bad way to do it effectively. Meanwhile prices go up. New strikes are threatened. The electricity will be again turned off. A sort of modified Fascism is quite a possibility. And on top of that the Common Market will add to our troubles, pushing up prices further and causing unemployment. I think that everyone except me must be mad.

I heard the Prague Quartet the other night. They are very good. Do not miss them if they come to Budapest. They played a Mozart quartet, the second quartet of Janáček, and the Dvorak American quartet. Beautiful easy music, played magically. Otherwise no event of any significance. You will be glad to hear that I have been re-elected a Fellow of Magdalen for another three years, which will be my retiring age. So I have one point of refuge. Tomorrow I shall give a public lecture at University College on 'Stalin Twenty Years After'. I can't imagine what I shall make of the old monster, the most powerful figure of the twentieth century.

Oh, how I love you and how I miss you. The thought of you is always with me. Like you, I go over our time together and recapture the joys of every moment. I must say over and over again: it really was a wonderful time.

Every letter I write is an effort to show my feelings and my thoughts. All the love in the world,

xx
Alan

Enclosure: me as a male model in the *Observer*.

xx

11 November

Beloved,

This is the day we used to celebrate as Armistice Day 1918, the day of 'No more War'. Now we remember on Sunday, and then not very seriously except for the old soldiers. I got your beautiful letter immediately after posting my own and wanted to write at once. But I controlled myself. There are two practical points I must deal with first. The arrangement with the American Book of the Month Club is made by the American publisher and does not concern either you or me directly. It only means that there will be a larger royalty figure, though whether that will ever cover the advance you have already had I much doubt. The American reviews that are now coming in are very weak, badly written and most of them saying that I was wrong to write a biography of someone I loved. They all took it for granted that I could not tell the truth. Also they wanted a book of anecdote, not of history. So I am gloomy about large American sales.

Money. Yes, I am very hesitant. Even apart from money it seems to me very rash to take you away from your own country where you have two sons and a position.* You would like it at first but perhaps then

* Eva was a research fellow at the Institute for Historical Research of the Hungarian Academy of Sciences.

you would become homesick. However, money is a great obstacle. At present the inflation here is going at such a rate that I cannot see into the future. As you say, even a flat would be very expensive. Sophia has to pay £20 a week and possibly more for three rooms. On top of that we should have to start from nothing with the furniture. I have virtually nothing except what is in my two rooms in Oxford. And then I wonder how I could keep you. Margaret and Eve each cost me £1,500 a year, quite apart from their household expenses. Coming up is Crispin at Cambridge, and after him Daniel at some more modern university that will be equally expensive. At the moment I am well off with the returns from my books and the serialization of *Beaverbrook* on top of it. Against this I have lost my contract with the *Sunday Express*, because it has become too right-wing to employ me, a loss of over £2,000 a year. And I don't seem to get television work any more, which used to bring in another £2,000. I used to think I could always make lots of money if I needed to. Now I am beginning to realize that as I get older people want me less. I get forgotten just because I have been around so long. Newspapers and television are always on the lookout for new writers and new faces. I am an old one. I would not write this to anyone except you. There is something even more difficult. I might be able to provide for us both while I was alive. How long will that be? It would never do for you to be here without me and your present security in Hungary lost. I don't think these are problems we can overcome by letter. Better for us to talk about them when we meet. Then we can either overcome them or accept that they are insoluble. I have plenty of other problems but these are enough for the moment. Too old, too old, rings in my head all the time. Please be patient with me and understanding. It would be the final blow if I felt that I had only succeeded in making you unhappy. Together or apart we love each other.

I shan't write about these things again unless you want me to answer some particular question. I'd rather tell you about my life. I have had a very busy time, too much so – it has left me tired and rather despairing. On Monday I went to Cambridge and gave a lecture before a large audience on Nazi foreign policy and its relationship to German society. This was a good theme that I had not worked out before. I was pleased with myself and was glad to give a good impression on Cambridge professors as well as on students. One of them said to me: 'After such a lecture I can't understand why you are not a professor in Oxford.' Neither can I. I suppose I never pushed myself enough. On Wednesday I was in Oxford for a College meeting and once again tried to get the admission of women. Very annoyingly my supporters failed to turn up and I only got 24 votes against 14, when I needed a two-thirds majority. Now I shall leave the question alone until my last College meeting, which will be in June 1976. Perhaps the obstinate old men will be spared this threat by my being dead before that date. Apart from you, I hope so.

Then on Thursday I went to Bangor by train, a wearisome four-hour journey. Quite a good lecture on Beaverbrook as a historian, a subject not chosen by me. I was not happy about it. I felt that this was a subject I had finished with and could not return to. I ought to have talked about some future work, not about what was in the past. Fortunately in north-east England, where I am going next week, I am talking about the Second World War and its origins, so I should feel more at home. One other lecture: 'Stalin' at University College. This was a great success also, though I think I was too kind to him. It is very easy to say that he made Russia a great power. Ought one not also to say that for the Russian people the price was too high? I never am sure whether this is a right thought for historians.

The photograph will amuse you. It is three Taylor men on Offa's Dyke. Crispin in a very characteristic attitude, Giles with his Buddha-like stomach, and me in my Italian peasant's hat. You will observe that they made me carry the rucksack. No doubt a father's duty. Crispin and I have now finished the Pilgrim's Way as far as Canterbury. The weather has at last turned cold and I doubt whether we shall get any more walking until the New Year.

I have been too busy to go to any concerts except for the Prague Quartet that I told you about. Covent Garden are shortly doing *Tristan and Isolde*, and I fear I must take Crispin despite its length. I am more cheered by the thought that the Coliseum are putting on *The Merry Widow* for Christmas. This was Hitler's favourite opera and almost mine. A favourite in any case, as it must be with anyone.

I have finished Hauser's book. It improves towards the end when he gets to the reoccupation of the Rhineland. Some English historian ought to have done this already from the English records instead of leaving it to a visiting German. But all our historians are still busy on Munich and the outbreak of war – dead themes. When I have reviewed Hauser, I shall really have to start writing my own next book. So no more autobiography for the moment.

That's all for now except for the thoughts about you which are always in my mind. There are still so many things that we should say to each other and do together.

All-embracing love,
Alan

1972

24 November

Beloved,

    You have caught up on me. I have now had two letters to my one. While you are in hospital you will not want to write so maybe I shall redress the balance. After I sent my last letter I feared it was too pessimistic and negative. It is crazy for us not to be together. I feel that as much as you do. But I also see difficulties and pour them out to you when they come up. If only you were here, things would be much easier. We could consider both your money position and mine. We could also consider the practical problems involved. As it is, I think as though I were the only one in existence and can't carry things all on my own. Probably it is better not to write about these questions. We must discuss them unemotionally when we meet. Financially it is very annoying that the *Sunday Express* has no further use for me. When the New Year comes I shall enquire whether some other paper would like to have me – maybe the *Sunday Mirror*, which is where I started as a feature writer over twenty years ago. Otherwise I shall have to write more books. What weighs on me is that it all depends on my keeping fit and, more difficult perhaps, keeping talented. If I stop writing my income stops, or most of it. Then I have two women to keep.

    Here are some questions and some answers. Did I send you Middlemas's book *The Diplomacy of Illusion*? Another copy has come to me from America and I can send it to you if you have not got it already. I have often wondered who writes in the *Economist* so exactly like me. I think it must be James Joll, certainly on general history. But on Victoria and Albert it may just be some woman on the staff. This is a puzzle to which we shall never know the answer. Christopher Sykes is a literary man who writes about the Middle East and about people's lives. As to Muggeridge's autobiography (which I have not read) it is awful. We were close friends in Manchester forty years ago. I shared with him many of the experiences he writes about and know that they were not as he says at all. The *Manchester Guardian* and its editor were endlessly kind and patient with him, though he was far from conscientious in his work. He imagined then that he was a left-wing Socialist though he had never been to a party meeting of any kind or done any practical work. I warned him again and again that he would be disillusioned about Soviet Russia if he went there expecting to find Utopia. He refused to listen to me. On his return he denounced me as a friend of Soviet Russia, as I was and am. Some of the events he described did not happen. Many present him in far too favourable a light. In those days he used to make out that his was a 'permissive' marriage and acted on this doctrine, though Kitty got great unhappiness from it. Now he has lost his sexual powers he pretends he never had them. In journalism too, no man has been more unscrupulous in getting stories and in seeking well-paid employments for himself.

At least he was never a male model. I did it for fun. Also I like the limelight whether it be television or a fashion photographer's camera. The lecture at University College was a great success, perhaps too favourable to Stalin because he made Russia great. What a dreary thing to do! I also had a wonderful time in the north-east. A lecture at Middlesborough, one at Newcastle-on-Tyne, one at Durham. They liked my performances so much that on my return they sent me a book token for £10. Wasn't that nice of them? It has never happened to me before. The visit also had its disadvantage. I did not take warm enough clothes and got chilled to my bones. Ever since I came back I have been racked with aches and pains, unable to lift my arm for pains in the shoulder. I thought these pains came from driving the car. As it is, I have not driven the car for a fortnight and yet I ache all over. However, I am now wearing all my winter clothes, including a vest – a garment I try to avoid until deep snow falls.

I have started on *The Second World War* so I am ahead of you. But even though I have started writing I can't get to the war. I feel that unlike the First World War, where I started on 28 June 1914, I must explain the background – Fascism, economic rivalries and so on. About Hitler you are partly right and partly wrong. He wanted to make Germany a great power, indeed a world power. He was on the move and nothing would have turned him into a peaceful, harmless statesman. But he did not want a world war. On the contrary he was convinced that Germany would and must lose if it came to a world war. He aimed at successes without war, or with small wars. Then Germany would suddenly step into the ranks of the world powers by surprise. Therefore the question is not: why did Hitler go to war? But why did he slip into wars that he did not want, and why did he undertake certain wars and not others? Also, why did the other powers not resist him? If they had resisted him earlier, he would never have got going at all. If they had resisted later, he might have become too strong. Arising from this, a confession. I used to say we could never trust the Germans. Now I am becoming soft towards them. Considering the past they really have done well to support Willy Brandt, who after all fought against Germany and came back as a Norwegian citizen. Maybe the memories of the Second World War really are beginning to fade after all.

The *Observer* colour supplement had a long piece the other day about the lost crown of St Stephen and what happened to it after the war. I don't suppose anyone in Hungary is deeply interested in this but it makes an entertaining story. Tito is in trouble, all the old problems that historians write about and that the Yugoslavs claimed had been forgotten – Croats versus Slavs, soon no doubt Bulgarian agitation in Macedonia. Let us hope very urgently that Tito lives until next April so that we shall not arrive there in the middle of a revolution. I have just written another article for that Italian encyclopaedia and arranged that the fee, a smaller one, should be sent to Florence. This is surely inviting fresh trouble, as in Venice. How deeply the events of those days are fixed in my mind.

Darling, my loving thoughts are with you. Do not trouble to write until you feel like it.

xx   Alan   xx

10 December

Beloved,

Thanks for the lovely books. I liked both the sculpture and the herdsmen and have displayed them to the readers in the Library. Last time I forgot to sympathize with you over bumping into someone else in your car. These things happen and afterwards, looking back, one cannot understand why. The instinctive reaction to avoid a crisis takes years to acquire. I have not had a bump for over ten years, but I still do foolish things such as backing into a lamp-post. And even driving well does not preserve one's car. Mine is scratched in many places by other drivers rubbing into it when it is parked.

I have been rather miserable and unwell. The aches that I brought back from the north-east have got worse and now turned, I suppose, into rheumatism. Tomorrow I shall go to a doctor and commit myself to a course of massage or other treatment. The truth is that old age is creeping on, reinforced by this climate of ours which has been at its damp worst. Last Wednesday when I drove to Oxford I had a thoroughly enjoyable time, being diverted from main roads by flooding, drains overflowing and so on. But it was not good for my shoulder.

Apart from this I have no stirring news. The other night I went to dinner with the Skinners' Company, a city company going back to the Middle Ages. It was a typical English fancy-dress affair. None of the present Skinners has ever skinned an animal or would recognize a skin if they saw one. They are prosperous stockbrokers, bankers and lawyers, pretending to maintain a traditional way of life. There were boring speeches about the merits of their company, five courses of very good food, and the band of the Welsh Guards playing throughout dinner. I had to go once for the experience, but it will be a long time before I go to such a thing again. The Company is of course enormously rich, spends much of the money on enjoying itself and the rest on maintaining an expensive school at Tonbridge. An odd aspect of English life.

I tried to start *The Second World War* by going off with a bang at the first shooting. Then I decided that I couldn't present the Second War like the First as just an event. I must give the feel and the atmosphere. Even when you put down all the causes from the great Depression to Fascism, you are still left with the feeling that the Second War was totally mad. That is why people retreat into the explanation that Hitler was mad and that it was all due to him. But why should a madman (if he were one) have exercised such influence and attained such power? It all seemed straightforward while it was on. Now I am bewildered and my historical techniques seem quite useless.

I didn't expect to hear from you, knowing that you were just off to hospital. I hope it was not a troublesome affair and that you will be happily back with your boys for Christmas. I sent you a little gift, not possessing your art of knowing something unusual to send. See the boys use some of it usefully. Incidentally, I'd be glad to know some time how much you have received from *Beaverbrook*. The company who handle it for you tell me nothing, and I'm curious how it is selling in America. There have been a few American reviews – all bad. Most of them treated Beaverbrook purely as a newspaper proprietor, and all of them said I liked him too much to tell the truth about him. Really only someone who liked him could tell the truth about him. He seems a long way from me now – not only dead, but after writing it all down, very distant so that I am no longer interested in him. At any rate, whatever I do in the future I shall never write another biography, it is not my sort of thing at all.

I heard the Bartók Quartet the other day. They played Bartók No. 4 and a Mendelssohn quartet, both perfect. I think they are the best quartet going around today. I hope they do not have such success in western Europe that they are never in Hungary. Otherwise I have done nothing. All the films nowadays are about sex or violence, neither of them concerning me any more. I think about you a lot, indeed being kept awake by pain I think of you most of the night. Have a good

Christmas after which I shall write to you again – perhaps more cheerfully.

Enough love to go round the world,

Alan

20 December

Beloved,

It is useless for you to tell me not to think of you any more. I think of you all the time except when I am working. It is just one of the facts of the situation. It would be far more sense for me to tell you not to think about me. I am truly a trouble to you, just as I have brought trouble to two previous wives. I have no confidence that I can be a different person now. However, there it is. We think of each other. We shall go on doing so. And therefore we must accept this with all its consequences. I told you I should not discuss such serious things until we meet in April. In any case I must see Porec.

You are a little sentimental in telling me to have a good time at Christmas. I detest Christmas and always have. Unmeaning exchanges of wishes with people you never give a thought to otherwise, and festive eating of not particularly interesting food. When the boys were younger they had the excitement of receiving and even giving Christmas presents. Now they are bored with such things. It is all a routine. Nor am I likely to have a wonderful New Year apart from you. Sometimes interesting things happen to me, and there is always curiosity in opening a new book. But I'd be glad to have done with the whole affair. I've written as much as any reasonable man should. I've practically got both my families on their own feet.

Don't take this too seriously. I am very gloomy at the moment for a variety of reasons. First, I can't get it [*The Second World War*] moving properly. I restarted with a short chapter drawing the contrasts between the First War and the Second, quite good but perhaps unsuited to an illustrated popular history. And I've started the run-up to war in 1936. But I have done this three times – in *The Origins*, in *English History 1914–1945*, and now trying it again. I can't say something different each time and yet I can't copy from my previous books. So I am very much on edge, dreading each morning when I must sit down and type, rewriting much of what I wrote the previous day, exasperated with my mind for not running smoothly into a straight narrative. No doubt things will get easier when I am really in the war, though I am not sure. At present I feel like a woman who is having an illegitimate baby and can't tell anyone about it. I am irritated with others for not realizing that I am at a deadlock, and yet of course there is no reason why they should know anything about it.

Secondly I still have rheumatism, aches in arms and shoulders. I've started rubbing in embrocation but so far with no effect. I suppose I shall have to discover a masseur who may rub my pain away. But my doctor was not encouraging. 'Lucky you have nothing worse at your age' was all he said. As well, maybe because I was worried by my work or maybe because I am generally depressed, I have been thoroughly exhausted and sometimes dizzy. I don't like feeling ill – never have been ill in my adult life and don't want to start now. So I kick against my surroundings. I should not tell all this to anyone except you. And you must not be worried by it. It is good for me to pour my feelings out to you, however selfish this may be. So be patient and listen without reproaching me.

The world is enough to make anyone gloomy. It shows one should always expect the worst. I said before the American elections that Nixon was only playing with peace in Vietnam until the elections were over. As time went on I could not believe my own cynicism. I thought peace was really here. Now it turns out that peace was a fraud all along. But I don't believe (this is perhaps my kind-heartedness) that Nixon and Kissinger consciously cheated the American people or the world. I think they cheated themselves. They persuaded themselves that the Vietcong were anxious to give up and would settle on almost any terms. In fact Vietcong and the North Vietnamese are a hard people. They have been living with war for over twenty years and they will stick at it until they achieve total victory – i.e. a united country with no foreign influence. The Americans, though not hard, are pigheaded. They still won't admit that they have been wrong all the time. A bad outlook.

These thoughts run through my head because on New Year's Eve I have to appear on television and survey the events of the year in FIVE minutes. What a terrifying prospect. After that, other pundits will criticize or denounce my remarks. And then a variety show will present: 'Fanfare for Europe'. You really would think that all English people are running round embracing each other and saying – Hurrah, on first January next we shall be Europeans.

What cheerful news can I give the besotted viewers? The best I can do is the recognition of the Oder–Neisse line and the discovery that there is after all a Good German – Willi Brandt. I daresay I'll name him as the man of the year. Oh, there is one other thing. The idiocy of voyages to the Moon has come to an end. That is something to be thankful for.

This is not a regular letter, or at least it is a few days early. I'll get through Christmas, take the boys on a sightseeing trip to Norwich for a couple of days, and then write to you again immediately the New Year arrives.

If you are wise, don't think of me any more. But be sure I shall be thinking of you.

                xxxxxxxxxxxxxxxxxxx   Love   xxxxxx
                                    Alan

1973

6 January 1973

Beloved,

Oh, how very much I love you. You should not worry about me. It is I who should worry about you. When I review the failures of my past life with bitterness, I think: how can I have the folly of involving any fresh person in it? Of course what really weighs with me are the practical difficulties. If only you were here for a long time, we could clear up all our problems and make all our arrangements. So I say as I have said before. These are things that we must face when we meet. Writing about them only upsets us both and leaves us full of worries. So don't worry. I promise I will not. In no time at all we shall be together and ready to think about what concerns us.

I have been lazy about my rheumatism. I must get a masseur but the Christmas holidays have stood in the way, and I go on thinking that perhaps it will clear up of itself. I have sent you a couple of books that you may find interesting. One is a rather absurd collection of essays in which economic historians explain what a splendid experience the Industrial Revolution was for everyone concerned. It will make you laugh. I particularly enjoyed Hartwell's surprise that the benefit for the working classes was so long delayed. Then there is the usual attempt to discredit Engels. The other is a routine history of Austro-Hungarian foreign policy. There is nothing wrong with it and not much right with it either. I had read it all long ago. And what is the point of publishing again documents that every scholar knows already? The writer is evidently an admirer of mine. At any rate he sent me a copy when the book was published and now another (which I have sent to you). I suppose he hopes that I shall review it, but it did not come to me from any paper and I am relieved not to have to do it.

I got through Christmas somehow, mainly by going on with my autobiography. I have now finished with my first boarding school. It gets politically more interesting with the impact of the Bolshevik revolution and my parents' conversion to a sort of Communism. I suppose that, far from being a heretic, I merely trailed behind them. My parents seem to me much more interesting than I was or am. But that is the defect of the historian who has to be interested all the time in other people. I'll try to write some more before we meet.

I'm glad to report that *The Second World War* is moving, though very

1973

slowly. I have now got to the outbreak of the Polish war, so am at last clear from the origins of the Second World War which I have written about so often already. I daresay the book will now become more lively as a result.

On New Year's Eve I was on a television show organized by David Frost. There were all kinds of show business people, most of them very old like Ethel Merman (*Call Me Madam*). In the middle of this noise and hullaballoo I came on, also very elderly, and gave a straight lecture for five minutes about the events of 1972: principally the recognition of China and East Germany. I felt greatly out of place, but plenty of people told me afterwards what a relief it was to have a bit of serious talking. So I was happy even though I did not get to bed until one o'clock in the morning. I was looked after by a lovely black girl, slim and elegant. She gave me a kiss for the New Year and I discovered by exploration that she was not wearing a girdle. She said no one did nowadays – they made you flabby. Cheer up. Don't be jealous. I did not even learn her name and shall never see her again.

Tomorrow I am discussing with Dick Crossman on television for forty minutes. He has set the theme: 'Most political history is fiction'. This seems to me merely silly. But I don't know how I can explain this to Dick, still less to the audience. History is a version of events. The fact that there are other versions does not make any one of them wrong. It is just like taking different views about a human being.

I have also seen a two-hour film about the last days of Hitler, to be shown on television tomorrow. Quite good drama, but historically all wrong. No dramatist and no actor can reproduce the hypnotic power that Hitler exercised over those around him right to the end. I started by making a list of the mistakes and then gave up. I might just as well list the mistakes in Shakespeare's *Henry V*.

After Christmas I took Crispin and Daniel to Norwich for a night. The Cathedral is marvellous, almost the best I have seen. Early Norman in a grand continental way. The city is also very good. It has closed most of the central streets to traffic. You can walk about just as men did in the Middle Ages. As well there are 32 mediaeval parish churches, only one or two really distinguished but again giving the feel of what a city ought to be. Unfortunately the next day there was thick fog. I had to drive back to London using headlights and never getting into top gear. I reflected how wise you were to sell your car. It can often be a heavy burden.

Did I tell you that my contract with the *Sunday Express* ran out at the end of the year? I assumed that as it had become very right-wing the editor did not want me at all. So I wrote him a letter of farewell. Then he rang up, said he could not bear to part with me and agreed to take fewer articles but at a higher fee. So I shall get £1,200 or so instead of £2,000. With my books I shall easily make up the balance. So financially I am no longer worrying for the moment. Of course we are all worrying at the effects of inflation. This has now taken the place of unemployment as the main disease of the capitalist world.

I took the boys to *Hair*. I found the show unobjectionable though I did not particularly enjoy it. The nude scene was entirely harmless, much more so than many played partly dressed. Young girls' bodies are sweet but to me completely sexless, just like boys despite the tiny firm breasts. Later this month I am taking Crispin to *Carmen* which everyone ought to see once in a lifetime.

I almost forgot the best thing I've seen: *The Great Dictator*, Chaplin's film about Hitler and also Mussolini. It is much the best picture of Hitler, certainly better than the ambitious TV film. Did it ever reach Hungary? Or maybe you saw it in England.

Think of me a lot, always without worry and just of what sort of person I am.

Darling, my love to you always and just as ever,

Alan

20 January

Beloved,

You must never be afraid to meet me or be with me. I am sorry that I put things at Venice in the wrong way. I've always judged situations from someone else's standpoint instead of my own, and it does not really help. I truly try to be frank. But I have a complicated mind. I no sooner begin one argument than I see some other and get confused. I know quite clearly that I want to be with you. I also know there are difficulties, and throughout life I've seen the difficulties more clearly than the way out. That is why I need to talk to you if I can do it in a way that makes sense to you. No more of this now.

Now about your questions. I will send you the Bethell book, but you must send it back after you have read it because I have already entered it in the Library catalogue. And I'd like the Wendt book some time if it is not too much trouble. As to the Chartists, what does the Academy want? Would they like a British publisher to agree to take, say,

500 copies? I could ask David and Charles, who published the book on the Chartist land settlements. And I'll enquire about possible London publishers. But I need some details, or if possible the book in English. Tell me roughly the length in English, what is new in it, how far it uses English sources or Hungarian. You know the sort of thing. I'll do the best I can. I am seeing my literary agent on Monday and will ask his advice. Preface by me??

Before I go any further there is a problem about my typewriter. The ribbon is half blue and half red. I don't like red but the blue is running thin. So don't be startled if next time you get a letter all in red. It will not be a sign that I have changed my political beliefs. Incidentally I have just got to them in my autobiography. Starry-eyed Marxist idealism in a little boy. Belief that the revolution was coming tomorrow and so on. I'm sorry we had an awful little room at Venice. I knew the *pension* would not be grand, but thought rightly that it was much more agreeable than living across the Grand Canal. So there was an explanation.

I had a bad time on television with Richard Crossman a fortnight ago. It was his programme. He was supposed to interview me and to discuss how a historian worked. I wanted to explain the mixture of firm information and creative imagination which the historian has to use. And I thought that, as it was his programme, I must cooperate with him and not fight as I usually do on television. To my surprise he started off on Beaverbrook, a subject I had almost forgotten about, and repeated all the silly stories against Beaverbrook that I had dismissed. I ought to have hit back and didn't. Instead Crossman talked practically all the time. There was no meeting of minds. He was politician pure and simple. I refused to accept his standards and could not develop my own. He thought it was a good show because he had had things all his own way. Nearly everyone else thought it was very bad. They did not blame me. But of course I blamed myself. If the other man won't cooperate one must take the offensive however much you don't want to. So I was miserable and feared that I had lost my television gifts.

My aches and pains go up and down. Keeping away from the car does not seem to make them better. Driving it does not seem to make them worse. I suppose I must wait in patience until the weather gets warmer. In other ways too I go up and down. *The Second World War* is moving at last. I have got to the French campaign of 1940 and that should come out really fast. Then I shall have to do a lot of thinking. But I am beginning to have confidence that I shall get to the end some time this year. So far it has been quite fun though very hard work. After that I have thought of a task for next year. We have the love letters exchanged between Lloyd George and Frances Stevenson. Now that she is dead there can be no harm in publishing them. I daresay it will cause trouble. Lloyd George's letters are very passionate. Of course this was to console Frances because they were together so little. In the nineteen-thirties they both strayed and then came together again. A very human story. I must ask Frances's daughter whether she minds the letters coming out. Otherwise I can go ahead – with the aid of a new secretary!*

Next week I start lecturing at Oxford on the Second World War, always a good way of learning a subject. If you lecture more on Hungarian politics you will come to understand them too. I can't say that I do. I only know that Michael [Károlyi] was a dangerous guide. He did not understand them at all. That was his virtue. He was too good for this world, especially for Hungary.

You say I think of you a bit. Why, I think of you all the time. I wonder what you are doing. As I walk down a street or look at a church, I think: Eva ought to see this. I have just seen an exhibition called 'The Impressionists in England'. Endless versions by Monet of what he saw of the Thames from a window in the Savoy Hotel. It was quite fascinating. Angus Wilson is not my favourite writer. He is very clever but it is all spoilt by his homosexual outlook which produces a sort of sniggering. He is not interested in human feelings, only in making fun of them. But then I am a bad judge. I hardly ever read modern novels, having given up with Evelyn Waugh. Instead I am reading *Little Dorrit*, not the best of Dickens but better than anything they do nowadays. And at night I am reading the Pepys diary which is coming out with a complete text. Rather boring and at the same time irresistible. I prefer Boswell.

Write to me about your book. Now I am going to think about you a lot more. After that I will do a bit about my schooldays. It is strange how little I have changed. I don't seem to have developed at all. I suppose it seems so because I am less interested in myself than in other people.

Darling, your letters are marvellous. I wish I could write as well. As it is I can only love you.

xxxxxxxxxxxxxxxxxxxxx
Alan
LOVE

* Veronica, Alan's secretary, was leaving.

1973

1 February

Dear Heart,

I hope all's well. I don't expect you to write except when you feel like it and I know you would let me know if anything went wrong – if you decided I was a bad bargain or that you are tied up with work. I am a creature of habit and must write once a fortnight for my own sake as well as yours. Do you remember Tristram Shandy's father who always wound up the clock and had sex with his wife on the first Sunday in each month? One Sunday she interrupted his activities by asking whether he had wound up the clock, and this is how things went wrong with Tristram from the moment he was conceived. I'm like that except that I think I am beyond sex. Don't take this seriously.

I have been enquiring further about your book. The most promising London publisher is Allen and Unwin. But they are sure to want to see the book in English before they agree to take it. Maybe the promise of an introduction by me would help. But I too must see the book first. I might disagree with it! I still favour David and Charles down at Newton Abbot in Devonshire, partly because they are more enterprising and partly because they like the subject. Let me know when you have something to show.

I have had a good task this week. The *Times Literary Supplement* wants to discuss how far history and fiction correspond. Do historians guess when the facts run out? A historical novelist is going to write an article on History and Fiction. I have written one on Fiction and History. Most people misunderstand how historians work. They think we invent things. Actually we interpret them. In the phrase you so much liked, history is a version of events. Do you see the *Times Literary Supplement*? Otherwise I'll send you a copy of my article when it comes out. Writing it has kept me off *The Second World War*. The autobiography goes on reasonably well. As I think back I am amazed how solitary I was – not a single friend while I was growing up, just reading all the time. As I expected, I am much better writing about other people than about myself. I have plenty to say about my parents, this curious couple who combined being wealthy and working in the Socialist movement. My father really turned himself into a working man except that he did not work. My mother became a near Communist in the way that she had previously been a Methodist. I don't think she knew the difference between the two. All the same I don't think it is worth writing. It gets less and less interesting for anyone except me – and perhaps except for you.

Aches and pains somewhat less. Other troubles rather more. I get dizzy, perhaps as a form of tiredness and general worry. I suppose age is catching up with me. I am patiently teaching Crispin to drive. Or rather I take him out for practice every Sunday and leave him to get the tricks of driving from a professional teacher. He is coming on well, very steady and clear about what he is doing. He sticks firmly to the rules, always observing the speed limit. I have never known anyone who is so orderly. Now as a hobby he is reading law and begins to wish he had decided to be a lawyer. But he will fall in love with mathematics again when he goes to Cambridge. Daniel threatens to become an intellectual despite his wild ways. He is reading *War and Peace* and has also discovered the merits of dictatorship. I try to defend democracy with all its faults. Young people go wrong because they always assume that they will do the dictating. I have always expected to be one of those dictated to, and that makes me wary.

I have been reading the love letters between Lloyd George and Frances Stevenson that we have in the Library and think I will edit them next year. I am sure I told you this before, which must make my letters boring. I must keep a notebook, ticking off the subjects I mention in each letter so that you will not hear them all over again. However, there is one subject that bears repetition. This is how much I think of you. All day long I have ideas that I want to share with you and wish I could put my arms round you. Lloyd George called Frances 'Pussy', and Churchill called his wife 'Cat'. I once had a cat called Colette. In character and behaviour she was just like the writer.

We are having a miraculously mild winter. No snow and quite high temperatures. They say the climate is changing: wetter winters and wetter summers also. Have you had any snow? In Austria, I read, the ski resorts are in a bad way with no snow and few visitors. Our economic troubles go on, prices still rising, and the trade unions restless. We have a Conservative government operating Socialist policies very badly, and a Labour opposition that does not believe in Socialism at all. A gloomy outlook.

A dull letter, I am afraid. I only wanted to tell you that I was alive and that I love you very much. Think of me a little and think too that we shall be meeting very soon.

All the love I have in me goes to you,

xxxxxxxxxxxxxxxxxxxxx
Alan

1973

18 February

Oh, my Darling,

I had just fallen into a rather gloomy mood and almost decided that I could not write this weekend when I got your bewitching letter. It almost made me cry with love. I feel now so warm towards you, so longing to see you, and also so convinced that you will find me disappointing. You are angelic. Don't think however that I have any illusions about you.

The *Listener* version of my Crossman ordeal was nothing like as bad as the original. It cut out a great deal of what he said and did its best for me. On reflection, I behaved wrongly. I felt, as I told you, an obligation to him. I thought that it was his show and that if he wanted to talk all the time he was entitled to do so. I ought to have reflected that my overriding obligation was to the viewers, and that I must stand up for myself even if Crossman would be put out. A lesson for the future. Never lower my guard when I am on television. And perhaps not anywhere else. Many people said they had enjoyed it and were surprised when I said how bad it was. I suppose they were being polite.

I first read *Fanny Hill* when I was a schoolboy and was I think then shocked. Then about ten years ago it was for a short time legal and in every newspaper shop. I read it again with amusement, I am afraid not with admiration. You must of course read the unexpurgated edition. Otherwise there is nothing in it. I don't think it was meant to be charming. Cleveland, the author, was a dissolute clergyman who wrote it to make money. The book was as pornographic as he could make it. It is not a genuine attempt to describe what a girl feels. It is a man's fantasy of what he wants a girl to feel and of the prodigious sexual feats he could perform. Men in the eighteenth century, and perhaps many of them now, like to think that they possess a gigantic penis, very red and always erect. This enormous instrument is to be thrust into a woman who gets enjoyment the nearer it is to rape. Sex is domination: the man forcing himself on to and into the woman and she rejoicing at the exquisite pain.

I think it is all rubbish. Nowadays at any rate man and woman are partners. Certainly as far as I am concerned I want my partner to get pleasure, not pain. The important thing, which of course also excites me, is that she should have a satisfactory orgasm thanks to my cooperation. Indeed she ought to have many, one after another. That is the woman's contribution if she is fully involved. It is her good fortune that she is not finished with one orgasm but all the readier for the next. So there should be quite the opposite of the situation as Cleveland pretends it is. The woman, because she takes longer to get going, should be forthcoming and should let herself go. The man should hold back because once he has had an orgasm it is all over with him. Maybe this is only my opinion. They tell me some men can have one orgasm after another. I can't. After one I'm finished for a week or so. Of course there is bound to be some male domination however equal the partners feel. He has to be on top – at least I have never found any other position half as satisfactory. Also he has to be active. A woman need only open her legs. A man must have an erection. If he loses it, as I often do, there is nothing to be done. I hope you aren't shocked at all this. I always write to you in love and complete confidence, knowing that if you don't like anything I say you'll forget it. In one way I am handicapped as a sexual performer. I can't stop thinking even at the best moments. I am the observer from outside even when I am engaged. This is the price of being an intellectual.

Lady Chatterley's Lover, though also rather a silly book, is much better in one way. Lawrence wanted to write about a woman's enjoyment as well as his own. He overdid it and romanticized it. But I think he did a great work. More women nowadays have orgasms than ever before. And men make sure they do. Indeed, I expect that women find *Lady Chatterley* very old-fashioned. Its work is done. But it needed to be done once.

Turning to more practical matters, I'll invite Ránki to dinner one night and had already thought of doing so. I'll keep off the subject of you, but not so obviously that he'll feel I am avoiding it. Some people wrote to me that they wanted to set up a Tibor Szamuely memorial prize and would I support them. I wrote back that though I had often had fun in his company I didn't think he had contributed enough to justify a prize. I hear he left a history of Russia almost completed, so perhaps he will turn out to have produced something after all.

My best experience has been to hear the Smetana Quartet from Prague. They were out of this world. They played with such intimacy. It was like four extremely civilized men having a quiet conversation with each other. They passed the melody from one to another and created a feeling of unity and intimacy so that the audience seemed almost to be intruding. At the moment I put them at the top of any quartet I have heard since the war. They are very good musicians as well as being such beautiful ones. Now I can't see any good music coming for months on end.

The Second World War is moving slowly. A new burden has fallen on me. *English History 1914–1945* is due for a new edition, and the Oxford Press wants me to bring the bibliography up to date. I shall rewrite it entirely. This is work I always enjoy but it will be quite laborious, particularly as I have not kept my list of books up to date. But as you know I am a fast worker. I have had a bad cold, awake half the night because I could not breathe properly. It is blowing over – literally. My rheumatism on the other hand is better and I have even enjoyed driving my car. We are in the midst of industrial disputes. Everyone asks me what is the answer and when I say Socialism, they think I am being impractical. The only practical effect is that the gas pressure is down and that it takes longer to cook. I don't worry much about such things.

Please feel warm about me as I do about you. Just think of our being together. LOVE.

xxxxxxxxxxxxxxxxxxxxxxxxxxxxxx
Alan

3 March

Darling,
It is hard to realize that in just over a month we shall be seeing each other. This time I do not think I have forgotten what you look like. And I? Will you see in me a decrepit old man whose charms, such as they were, have vanished? I should guess not. On a more practical level, I had better tell you where to go. We have a room at the Grand Hotel Union, Miklosiceva Cesta 1, Ljubljana from 6 to 8 April. The telephone number by the way is 20707, though I don't suppose you'll need it. My plane is due to arrive at half-past four, which means that I should be at the hotel about six. I hope very much that you will arrive before me this time. One important bit of advice. Be sure to get out at the right station. If you don't you will arrive in the middle of the night as you did before. I have mislaid the name of the hotel at Porec and will send it next time I write.

My present feelings are gloomy. I badly need your company to cheer me up and feel more hopeful both about myself and about the world. Foolish though it is, I get depressed by public affairs. We have now a government that has completely lost control of events and a Labour opposition that is equally bewildered. It is a very bad thing to live in a country that thinks rightly or wrongly that it is going downhill. We have a half-hearted gas strike which does not have any effect so far, but with the possibility hanging over us all the time that the gas will be cut off, in which case we shall be cold and have no means of cooking. I am not looking forward to going to a restaurant for all my meals. Then we have sporadic rail strikes when most of the staff cannot get to the Library. And all my shares are falling on the Stock Exchange.

Yesterday I parted from Veronica. I gave her a handbag and the staff gave her a cream cake which she insisted we should all eat – very bad for my figure. When it came to the actual parting it was undramatic. I said: 'Goodbye, I shall miss you very much.' She said: 'I don't want to go but I think I ought to.' I kissed her half-heartedly, which I don't think she welcomed. She was a very welcome figure to have around, so cheering to look at and generally reassuring. My new girl [Della] promises to be efficient but rather too eager – maybe a form of shyness that will wear off. I am depressed about the Library in another way. Readers have dwindled to almost nothing. I think it is merely a change of fashion. Students are now moving towards the Second World War and there is not much about that in the Lloyd George papers. I always expected that the interest in him would decline sooner or later, and I suppose he will recover. All the same, I can't help feeling that the Library won't last for ever, even in the sense of for ever for me. Max Aitken is over sixty. When he goes his successors will not be interested in the memory of Lord Beaverbrook and will grudge what the Library cost. Perhaps I shall be too old to care.

My cold has gone. To balance this I cut my finger on my razor and have to go around with it wrapped up. Also I am bored with life. I've made a poor show of my life. *The Second World War* is moving rather faster than it did, but I can't persuade myself that it is any good. I am sure it is without the speed and zest that my book on the First World War had. Too many ideas and not enough order in putting them down.

You will be astonished to hear that I have actually been to the cinema. I saw Buñuel's new film, *The Discreet Charm of the Bourgeoisie*. See it if it comes your way. It is very funny though quite pointless and I could not understand it half the time. Typical modern film, with real life and dreams all mixed up. I prefer the old days when films told a story. Otherwise all the films are either full of violence or of simulated sex. Very strange. As someone once told D. H. Lawrence, much to his rage, the sex act when looked at from outside is merely funny – two people tangled together and displaying emotions that the onlooker does not share.

What shall we do all the time in Yugoslavia? We shall not have such a full programme of sightseeing as we had in Venice. I enjoyed every minute there. I have a feeling that you did not enjoy it as much and were not quite at your ease in my company. Would you like to tell me why? If not I must try to work it out for myself. Or maybe I must simply be loving and happy and hope you will be too. We should treasure every moment and make sure that our time together is perfect.

Have you found any reading to follow *Fanny Hill?* I doubt it. *Fanny Hill* is a book all on its own, or maybe such books were common in the eighteenth century and not written now. Here is an interesting bit of information. A smart woman's magazine asked men what they thought women found attractive in them. Then they asked the same question of women. The men all thought women liked he-men with great muscles and pronounced chests. A good many thought women liked tight trousers with the hint of a powerful penis. So men are all trying to look like heavyweight boxers. In fact what women put first were slender buttocks. They wanted a slim, elegant figure with no muscles showing. And of course the penis did not occur to them at all.

Here is a little question that might enable me to get a tiny mention of Hungary into *The Second World War*. What is the truth, or at any rate the now-agreed version about the bombing of Kassa. At the time it was alleged to be Soviet planes – that certainly wasn't true. Then the Germans were blamed as a way of pushing Hungary into the war. Or perhaps the Hungarians did it themselves. I seem to have read somewhere that a Slovak plane has been suggested. I'm sure I have read something but I can't remember what.

Did I tell you that I had been asked to give the Creighton Lecture at London University, which has been their top historical lecture ever since 1907? I said Yes and immediately afterwards was asked to give the Neale Lecture at University College London, which is their top historical lecture. I thought this would be too like monopoly so said No. However, it looks as though I were coming back into fame. These things go in waves.

All I wanted to say in this rambling letter is that I count the days until we are together, just as when a boy I counted the days until the end of term. I shall have two chapters of autobiography for you to read, right up to the end of my schooldays. It is mainly the history of an intellectual who did not intend to be one.

Darling, how lovely love is.

xxx
Alan

16 March

Darling,

I hope you have had my letters and I hope you are well and happy. I won't say more because I don't want you to write if you don't feel in the mood or are too busy. Maybe you have been off on some foreign jaunt, perhaps to China or Outer Mongolia. As long as you arrive safely and enthusiastically in Ljubljana – I can't spell the place properly – I shall be content. Don't have last-minute thoughts of not coming. Remember we nearly missed Salzburg, and what a lovely experience it turned out to be.

I am glad to report that my rheumatism has practically disappeared, though as soon as I write this I imagine that another ache is starting. I can't say that the weather helps, being still cold and grey. This very night we put on the clocks and start Summer Time, though it does not seem like it. I had a good trip last week. I went to York to talk to the Historical Association there about the Second World War. It was greatly appreciated. Every time I give this lecture more ideas come into my head and I feel that I must rewrite everything I have written. I went early in the day so that I could walk around York on my own. I passed the front of Bootham School but did not go inside – no nostalgia for me. Instead I went to the Minster, which has been lavishly restored and is now so bright that you hardly need street lighting at night. After that I looked at the churches I remember as a boy and found them either shut or destroyed for the sake of the traffic. But York is still a lovely place.

Last Sunday I took Crispin out in the car all day. He had never driven such a long distance before and did very well. He is very precise in observing the speed limits which makes me impatient, and he won't overtake even when I tell him exactly how to do it. He keeps saying in his orderly way that he is not interested at present in learning to drive well; he is only interested in passing his test. This is logical but mistaken. The better you drive, the more likely you are to pass your test. We went to Chichester and looked at the Cathedral which I had never seen before. It is very modest and beautifully unspoilt.

Last week I was sitting alone in the Library when there was a tremendous bang. A bomb, planted no doubt by the Irish, had gone off in the next street outside the Old Bailey. Every window in the street was blown out, and as one of the buildings had over two hundred windows you can imagine that there was plenty of broken glass. Over two hundred people were taken to hospital. The injuries were caused by a muddle between Scotland Yard, the police centre for most of London, and the police in the City of London who are an independent force. The Irish, as

1973

usual, gave warning that a bomb had been planted so that there would be plenty of time to clear the buildings. But the City police did not get the message from Scotland Yard in time and 200 people paid the price for the fact that we still have mediaeval institutions. Yesterday we had a bomb alarm at the Library and we all moved out. But it was a false alarm. Nothing happened. There is, so far as I can see, no solution to the problem of Northern Ireland, so these bombs will go on for ever.

Our other troubles are better. The engine drivers have gone back to work, so the Library staff will be able to come in. This past week Katherine, the archivist, has been taking two hours to get to the Library and then has to rush off to feed her baby. On the other hand, we are threatened by another miners' strike and that will mean no electricity, so we shall be cold and living with candles in the evenings. However, I am all for the working classes asserting themselves though it is a great nuisance as well.

I haven't read much of interest, only a life of Field Marshal Alexander who was a dull character – perfect soldier, perfect gentleman, but never gave offence to anyone not even the enemy. I have also read two very dull books on the Liberal Party before the First World War – a party that could never win mass support and was always searching for a policy that would have a popular appeal and yet be harmless. Such policies are not to be found easily and the Liberals never succeeded in finding one.

Next Sunday I shall be sixty-seven, the age when professors retire but not me. I shall then have been driving a car for precisely fifty years and never lost my licence. I suppose it is time I gave up, but at the moment I am feeling pretty young. Surely I must grow old some time?

I saw Veronica the other day. She is obviously happy in her new job and has to work harder. As a result she is more alive and looks years younger. I'll take her out to dinner some time soon, though not to the Connaught. I also met my old girl-friend Kathleen Tillotson the other day. But she was still young in spirit and we had fun talking. As I was never attracted to her sexually, even when she was young, I did not expect to be now and surely enough I was not. We listened to a very boring lecture by Sir John Summerson on 'Building in London in the Eighteen-Sixties', a subject that I did not expect to find boring. I did not even manage to go to sleep.

Is there anything you want me to bring to Yugoslavia? I shall bring my bathing trunks, but I know from experience that the sea will be too cold to bathe in even if the sun is very hot. We shall just have to sit and talk. Or maybe we will just sit. I hope to collect some money for the Slovene translation of *The Habsburg Monarchy*.

I have no more to say this week except that I am counting the days until we meet and am thinking of all the things we can do together. The hotels will be grander than the *pension* at Venice, at least I hope so. Send me a postcard to say that everything is in order and that you'll be there as lovingly as you have always been. Oh, dear, it is a puzzling thing to be in love.

All my love, darling,

xxxx
Alan   x

25 March

Dear Heart, My Love,

My birthday. I am 67, feeling pretty young and even more so next week. Veronica: the kissing was half-hearted on both sides, more on hers than mine. I think she was shocked that I kissed her at all, and when I pulled her face round and kissed her distantly on the lips she was very remote. This is just her nature. I'll take her out to dinner when I come back and tell her nice things about you.

I'll be quite glad to have Wendt, though I do not attach much importance to it. Do not bring it if it is a burden, and don't bring any other things that will weigh down my luggage. You see how unromantic I am. I can't think of anything to bring for you except myself and that is hardly a romantic package.

This is not a proper letter, just to say that I got your letter and enjoyed it. I have my air tickets, and the hotel reservations are in order. I see we are threatened with rainy weather but maybe it will be fine on the Adriatic. Like you I am so dominated by the thought of seeing you and holding your hand, kissing you, feeling you near me, that I can't write a whole lot of rubbish as I usually do. So I only say I want you as a person very much and count the days.

With love and love and love,

Alan

I shall not write again unless any problem comes out. Don't be alarmed if I am late. The plane is sure to be delayed.

1973

March

Darling:

Just to say Thank you. How silly you are to think of me.

I shall have plenty of money so don't bring more than small change in dinar.

There are strikes on the airlines and I may be delayed for that reason also.

Sunday Times mentioned my birthday and added descriptive: 'Controversial historian and about the best thing ever discovered by television.'

Love, Alan

22 April

My Dearest Love,

How I miss you. It seemed so natural and right that you should be beside me, as though we had belonged to each other for ages. I think this last was the best time for us and the best time I had in my life. Certainly not the surroundings. I cannot imagine drearier walks even in an industrial city. But it did not matter because we were together. Of course you would do better to marry someone younger. Being nearly twenty years older than you, I am bound to leave you alone after a few years. So have no qualms if you find someone suitable. Otherwise you will find you have only got me.

I was glad I took a taxi. Even so the traffic in Trieste was enough to make the journey last a full hour. I had a fine fast train, met the boys and had a good hotel – more lavish than anything Porec could provide. Florence gave us plenty to see, but we did not like it as much as either Rome or Venice. In comparison it is a provincial town, full of good pictures but lacking in the grandeur of a capital city. The Medicis were not much more than local princes, very rich and ostentatious but without the sense of power you get in Venice and Rome. The tourists are everywhere, far worse than in the big cities, coach-load after coach-load. You can't get near the pictures because of the conducted tours. You can hardly move in the streets. You hear nothing but German and American. Food better than Venice. The weather was very good. I see now there is snow in Florence, so we just left in time. We went to Fiesole, which is attractive, and to San Gimignano which is a rather pretentious over-preserved mediaeval town. I came back still with lots of lire, so we shall have money to go to Italy again when you are free to do so. The political situation is very acute, violence from both Left and Right, with the papers solemnly discussing whether Fascism will come again. I don't think there is much danger of this. The capitalists have learnt that Fascism is not pleasant even for them. Also they get plenty of wealth without all the trouble of enlisting Blackshirts. Most of all, Fascism needs nationalistic grievances such as the Italians had or imagined they had in 1922. Nothing like this exists now.

Here is another thought that crossed my mind when in Florence. The city was full of Germans, many of them elderly. They looked so orderly, civilized, restrained. Yet they must have been in the prime of life under Hitler and most of them must have been Nazis. You think one man is a quiet distinguished scholar; perhaps he was once a German officer, massacring prisoners-of-war in Russia. And that grey-haired lady. She was no doubt a Hitler *mädchen* and after that a guard in a concentration camp. How could such ordinary people have been so surpassingly barbarous? It is beyond my understanding.

My review of Kingsley appeared in the *TLS*. It seemed to me better than most of the reviews, partly because it was anonymous, so that I did not, as others did, air my own memories of him. I will send it to you. In fact tomorrow when I go to the Library I will arrange a regular subscription to the *TLS* for you, so that you will get it every week. I hope this meets with your approval. It is the only way of really knowing what is being written in England and what it is worth.

Bad news. I developed rheumatism again in Florence, probably because the window was just over my bed. My shoulder has been agonizing, so that for the last few nights I have hardly been able to sleep. Now I am taking a new cure which it is promised will cure me. It better had. I have also got catarrh, which has spread to my ears so that I am partly deaf. On top of this the weather is terribly cold. Altogether a sad picture. I shall be all right in a few days so don't worry about me. Also, I will write next time with more news. At the moment I am still suspended, having almost forgotten what the Library or my work is like.

I tried to show how I loved you and I know you feel the same. The happiness we had together will go on sustaining me through all my difficulties. You didn't say much about my autobiography. Send me some criticisms.

Love and love and love.

xxxxxxxxxxxx
Alan xx

1973

5 May

My much Loved One,

Your letter brought tears to my eyes. I really do not understand what I have done to deserve such love. It is wonderful that I can bring a little happiness to someone. And I feel just the same, always happy and secure when I am with you and even happy to think about you when we are apart. Of course you have always seen me in favourable circumstances – no other commitments, hotel servants to provide for us, free to be together all day long. In ordinary life you may find me irritable, harassed by other people, and neglecting you. It is a risk I often think about. I have no such fears about you on my side, though I expect I shall be a bit sulky if you show too much interest in other people. After weeks or months without rain we are now having a sort of monsoon. I have never seen heavier rain, so much so that often I cannot go out.

I have fixed up Ránki for dinner on 23 May. Naturally I shall not mention you, except to enquire perhaps what you are doing now. I don't suppose he will attach any significance to it, at any rate you can rely on me. I liked being in Oxford, particularly at the thought that all my colleagues of my age must retire in the autumn whereas I go on for another three years. I am on the last stretch with Crozier, correcting the proofs and making the index. Very laborious work which I shall be glad to see the end of next week. After that I must bring the bibliography of *English History 1914–1945* up to date before returning to *The Second World War*. I have had a lucrative offer from a publisher to do a very short *English History* to go along with illustrations – something to occupy my time in 1975 or thereabouts.

I hope the *TLS* reaches you all right. In the number of 13 April, as well as my review of Kingsley, there is another review of mine on two books about the Liberal Party. And next week the front page will be taken up with an article of mine on Roger Casement who was hanged for Ireland. He was a blatant homosexual but that did not make him any the less a hero. The *TLS* does not pay well, but it gives me the chance to write really long and rather good pieces. Actually I lose money by it because it prevents my reviewing the same books for the *New York Review* which pays much better. Still money is not everything, though it is quite something.

Michael Howard on the Continental Commitment does not concern you a great deal. It contains the Ford lectures which he gave in Oxford a few years ago. He intended to argue that England practised 'Splendid Isolation' until the beginning of the twentieth century and then got drawn more and more into Europe. He found to his surprise that it was not like that at all. British involvement in the First World War was meant to be a once-for-all affair. After it British policy was 'Never Again' – withdrawal from Europe and concentration on the Empire. Hence Neville Chamberlain's policy, far more concerned with the Far East than with Hitler. But he only deals with this in a single lecture, and that very sketchily. The sudden switch back to Europe was quite unexpected, and even then it was only to secure France, not to protect central Europe. The conversion to Europe, which has now happened, came years after the Second World War and was not a continuous process. I don't think that Howard, a committed European, understands this properly. I don't understand it either, but at least I appreciate that it was not intended. It makes things more interesting when they are illogical and unexpected. I will try to lecture about this at Oxford at some time in the future.

I was amused to hear that Neville Masterman disapproved of me, or at any rate of *The Origins of the Second World War*. The truth is that English historians have not read my book or, if they have, have not thought about it properly. They learn from others that it is a book apologizing for Hitler. It isn't that at all. All it says about Hitler is that he was an opportunist, as every practical statesman is, taking gains where he could. But of course he always aimed at German domination of Europe. The real point of it is that England and France went to war by mistake, hoping till the last moment that Hitler would get his domination of Europe in an orderly manner. Both England and France were quite happy to abdicate as European powers and were ruined by getting into the war. However, I shall never live down the misunderstandings and don't care about it any more.

I at last went to a film the other day – *Cabaret* with Liza Minelli – Judy Garland's daughter. She is not as good as her mother. The film is taken rather remotely from *Sally Bowles* by Christopher Isherwood. Minelli did at any rate what she was supposed to do: be a very second-rate singer trying to become something more. I don't think it was worth going to, but one has to try occasionally. Hitler is having a boom here. A new biography by Colin Cross (nothing much in it except on his early life); a film on *The Last Ten Days of Hitler* with Alec Guinness, and another film on the same subject to come. I can't think why people get so interested in this. Hitler is interesting as a public man, not as a private person. I tried to persuade the boys to go with me to see *Misalliance* by Shaw, but they showed no interest.

My aches and pains are still troublesome. I fear that driving the car and working the typewriter both make them worse. They will get better when it stops raining. Think of me wriggling about with pain at night when my arm hurts.

Darling, it is wonderful that you love me. You ought not to, but I'm not going to argue against it. I love you too, and am happy just to be writing to you. Whenever you think of me, remember always that I love you too.

Love, Dearly Beloved, much much love,

Alan
xxxxxxxxxxxxxxxxxx

18 May

Dear Heart,

You say I must not write to you. I have to, so that you don't get things wrong. I thought I had said enough at Porec to show that everything can be arranged in time. I didn't perhaps speak clearly enough – when I am talking to you I forget that there is always a little barrier of language between us. And, being always apprehensive, I feel that I must not be too confident because so many things might go wrong. However, here are some firm things I tried to say at Porec. After I have been to Ireland with the boys, I shall start a divorce from Eve.

Once I am divorced, there are only practical difficulties. I have already put down my name for a flat in the City. There is a waiting list for at least a year, so that might come at the right time. Maybe I talked too much about the difficulties and not enough about the hopes. You think I am strong. I am not. I am soft and easily upset. But I can go forward all the same. You also think I am fit. So I am at the moment. But it is no good pretending that I am a young man. I am 67, an age when both my parents were dead. If I fall ill and lose my power to make money, then I have not enough resources for a new life. My own idea is that, when I am free, you must somehow come here and see for yourself. I can end my old life unaided. But I can't even start a new one without help from you.

All this is very unsatisfactory for you. So many things might go wrong. So long a time of waiting is inevitable. I have always said that I am a bad bargain for you. Even at the best we shall have only a few years together. Then you will be left even more solitary than before. If I were really strong I should pretend not to care for you any more and so make you really free. I am too selfish to do that. On my side I want you. For your sake I wish I didn't.

I think what we had better do is this. I will go on writing you friendly letters. You do not need to answer them or even to read them.

For my sake, if for no other, you will lead a good and happy life, not worrying about the future and making sure that you will have a good life even if I can't summon you here. All I can promise you is that I will try. I can't promise you I will succeed. If you think this is not enough, then indeed I must stop writing to you. But I shall still go on with my divorce and see what happens. Surely it is better you should know what I am doing than to live in ignorance, imagining that all sorts of things are going wrong.

I have had great happiness with you and hope to have more. For your sake I bitterly regret that I ever started running after you and tried to involve you in my life. You would have been far better off without me. Now I can't help having visions for the future. I had better not write any more now. Otherwise I shall argue myself into final despair, which isn't yet necessary. So just tell me either to stop writing or to write friendly letters which will still give us a knowledge that we exist and think of each other. Of course, if you marry someone else, that is much the best for you. You will stay in Hungary and you will have a better future. I shall be no worse off than I am now.

I am more overburdened with work than I have been for years. The new bibliography is terribly hard work, and I have four great big books to review, two theses to examine. I am not enjoying life.

I send you a little bit of love and a good deal of gloom.

Alan x

1 June

Beloved,

I had such a beautiful letter from you. I can only say to you what you said to me – I didn't mean to upset you. Like you I go up and down, sometimes confident about the future, sometimes fearing that the difficulties created either by other people or by money will be too great. But I will have a real good try in the autumn when Daniel will be sixteen and able to look after himself.

The other night I took Amelia,* who was on her own, out to dinner. She told me her troubles with her husband. To cheer her up I

---

* First daughter of Alan's first marriage.

told her my past experiences with two wives and then said, all the same I am going to try again shortly. I did not of course say who you were. She said – how can you be so sure and confident that you will get on when you have only seen each other for a few days here and there? It certainly looks rather strange to others. I could only say I was absolutely sure. I wonder whether you are. No use writing more just now about a hypothetical future.

I had Ránki to dinner as you proposed. He was very friendly, but I must confess he is not very interesting. I daresay he still finds England and especially Oxford rather strange. On the other hand he is obviously skilful at arranging jobs and missions for himself – not only his time in England but trips to the United States. He knows how to organize his life well if that is the sort of life he likes. I was rung up the other day from the University of California and offered a highly paid job there for the whole of next year. As you no doubt guess I did not hesitate to refuse it. It is bad enough going to Oxford every week. I certainly could not go further.

Then I have had a long talk with the young colleague of yours who is working on Michael and who delivered the bottle of Tokay. Perhaps, as it was meant to be a parting present, I should send it back? (This is a joke only. I could never part with a bottle of Tokay. Oh I do love you. I hope you do not mind this change of colour. I must use the other half of the ribbon sometimes.) I told him some stories about Michael and Katus but, as I explained, I never keep letters and had none of theirs. On reflection I do not think that Michael ever wrote me a line. Katus may have sent an occasional message that she was coming to London or something like that. And when she was writing first Michael's memoirs and then her own book, she used to instruct me how to influence the newspapers and get good reviews for her. Of course I never took any notice. Your young friend casually mentioned your name. I did not respond even to ask how you were, only an enquiry whether you too were working on the Károlyi papers. In fact you can be sure that I was completely and absolutely discreet.

Now bad news about myself. Having just got rid of the rheumatism with all its pains, I am in fresh trouble. Last Saturday I went out all day with Crispin to give him driving practice. It was a sunny spring day. As he was driving I did not wear my driving gloves and took no precautions. Result: a flaming outbreak of dermatitis on the fingers of both hands. The scars are like raw burns, turning into blisters. I put on Betnovate, the latest remedy, night and day. This eases the irritation and pain but so far does not cure it. Also the trouble makes me nervous and irritable. The complaint is quite unpredictable. Last year I went round in the sun a great deal and had no trouble at all. This year I get caught before the summer has properly started. I suspect that haze in the air acts like a magnifying glass. Once it has cleared off I shall take good care to wear gloves and of course a straw hat. It worries me because I know how you enjoy the sun and I really dare not go to hot places. This may be a problem between us some day. On the other hand (my favourite phrase, do you remember?) I can't blame it on old age. It started twenty years ago, and the worst attack I ever had was in 1964 when I really thought I should die, I felt so ill. I am not proposing to die just now, but I am not in a good mood and have great difficulty in working. This is why I am writing to you on a weekday instead of waiting until the weekend. Today I could not face sitting in the Library and toiling over the bibliography of *English History 1914–1945*. So I merely dictated the few letters that needed dealing with and then left. This also explains why this letter is a bit dull and gloomy. For once my gloom has nothing to do with you but is caused solely by the state of my hands. Damn. Another spot has just broken out half-way up my arm. (Not only did I not wear gloves, I wore a shirt with short sleeves and am now paying the penalty.)

Here are odd bits of news about my work. I have finished the index for Crozier and the book will be published in July. I'll send you a copy of course. I have nearly finished the bibliography. Then I am faced with a new biography of Macaulay by an American professor of literature, perfectly competent and rather dull. After that I have got a new biography of H. G. Wells, also competent and rather dull. His own autobiographical works (and that means all his novels) are a good deal more interesting than someone else writing about him. Wells worried about the world, hoped for Utopia and thought everything might go wrong. He also had Woman trouble – two wives, four long-term mistresses – and never got it really right with any of them. Too selfish? I think not. Too hopeful. Every time he thought it would be perfect and it never was. Maybe I shall find the answer when I have read a bit further into the book.

Please report that the *TLS* is arriving safely. The last few numbers have been very boring, which is another way of saying that I have not written anything. Perhaps next week with a clever article by Trevor-Roper will be better. You will see that he is a beautiful essay writer. No brilliance of individual sentences or epigrams, but a smoothness that carries you irresistibly on.

I have just made £750 by speculating on the Stock Exchange. This is not something to do every day and perhaps shocks you a bit. I do it more for fun than for the money. We have just had a great political scandal because two ministers went with prostitutes and had orgies. One of the ministers appeared on television and explained that he liked variety. Very strange. Forgive me that I can't write any more. I'm not in a good state. I shall be when I write next.

Please try that the thought of me makes you happy and does not upset you. I need your help.

Loving thoughts and kisses,

Alan
x

16 June

My Dearest,

I am not feeling like a serious letter today. We have fine summer weather at last and, though I sunbathe and swim, it also upsets me. I am always afraid of getting more skin trouble, and I suppose this makes me nervous so that I become depressed. In fact it is now my turn to worry about the future. If only we were in the same country how easy everything would be. As it is I miss your sweet presence and constant loyalty. It makes life empty to be without you. But I do not intend to write about it.

Instead I will entertain you with my intellectual activities, such as they are. Are you receiving the *TLS* regularly? Let me know about this if you can ever bring yourself to write. You never told me what you thought of Kingsley, or for that matter of my review. It was a rather silly book that did not do him justice. With all his confusions he came up with the right answer (that is, the Left answer) in the end. I have had a lot more reviewing. First there was the life of H. G. Wells, all about his muddles and his mistresses. Though his two wives are dead, his four long-term mistresses are alive and all four talked frankly about their life with H.G. They are all still fond of his memory, though they found him impossible to live with. What was missing in the book was any hint that often he was a very good writer. His novels always go to pieces in the end, but they are very good for most of the time.

Then I have had a life of Macaulay by a solemn American who started as a German. He thinks he has discovered the great secret that Macaulay was hostile to his father. Repressing this, he was incapable of married life and was therefore in love with his sisters. I had fun showing how ridiculous this was. Macaulay was simply a very clever man with all that that implies. All he suffered from was brains in the head.

There is also a new life, or rather the beginning in the first of five volumes, of Lloyd George by John Grigg. You will be able to read this review at any rate in the *New Statesman*. His secret too is easy: intense ambition. He sacrificed his women and himself to this. Did I tell you about his daughter Jennifer? I visited her and showed her the letters between Lloyd George and Frances Stevenson. Until she saw them she had no firm idea who her parents were. Frances never told her whether she was adopted or a real child. She said to me: 'I did not know whether I was my mother's daughter, and I was pretty sure I wasn't my father's. Now I have no doubt. It has changed my whole life.' A touching story. Forgive me if I have told you this before.

On a more serious level, I have read a book on *German Strategy Towards Russia 1939–41* by a Canadian called Leach. It is very good though dull, much the same ground as Hillgruber's book but not so long and, I think, clearer. I have now come to the conclusion that all the explanations of Hitler are right. He was a Fascist, an anti-Bolshevik, with a long-term plan to conquer Russia. At the same time he was an opportunist who took advantages as they came. In 1941 he attacked Russia because this had been in his head for a long time. But he also attacked Russia because it was the convenient thing to do at that particular moment. He failed not because he made mistakes, but because Germany was not strong enough to conquer the world and his cleverness had its limits. I don't know how to put all this into my book. But that is how it is, a muddle like most history.

Here is a curious little coincidence. A hundred years ago my grandfather James Taylor started to make a fortune on the Manchester Cotton Exchange. Now the cotton trade is ruined, and the Royal Cotton Exchange has been turned into a repertory. Amelia is now acting where once her great-grandfather dealt in cotton cloth. So the wheels of time go round.

There is trouble at Magdalen. The President, Griffith, whom you did not meet, always drank a good deal. He has had a severe attack of delirium tremens. He has lost his grasp, but he thinks he is cured and refused to resign or even to take a long holiday. Unless he breaks up altogether we are stuck with him for another eight years. I feel a sort of loyalty to him, but fear that the younger Fellows will become impatient and that there will be a row. As Colleges are self-governing, there is no way of getting him out without a formal enquiry that would be too painful to contemplate. As you can imagine, this is upsetting for me as Griffith is a very old colleague of mine and, in his way, an old friend. I wish he would have a second attack and be carried off. But it is not a pleasant prospect.

1973

I had a laborious time writing a revised bibliography for *English History 1914–1945*. Now it is done and I am not looking forward to rewriting the entire book. But I think it will have to be done when my other tasks are completed.

Crispin and I are still going out on driving lessons whenever he is free. Incidentally, he has taught me how to back round a corner which I could never do before. So there are some compensations. As we go out in the car every weekend there is no opportunity to walk all day, and I am fearful that when we go to the Lake District next month I shall not be in good condition to climb mountains.

If you ever write to me, tell me what you are doing and how your boys are getting on. Your life seems so remote from mine. I find it difficult to imagine what happens to you from morning to night, and am weighed down by missing you. What are you going to do this summer? If I feel better by late September I'd like to propose something, but I don't know what to propose. See if you can make some suggestion. Yet meet we must.

Now I must start rubbing myself with cream to keep off the ultraviolet rays. This afternoon I shall swim half a mile and then sleep in the sun, hoping that I have rubbed myself everywhere. Nowadays I even dream of you. That is a way of being nearer you.

Oh dear, I wish I could see you and make everything easy between us. As it is I can only send much love and the assurance that I am the same person I always was. I have drunk nearly all the Tokay. By the way, if ever you have a friend coming to England please return the guide to Venice. The boys want to go there again.

My darling, I love you,

xxxxxxxxxxxx
Alan

26 June

My Darling, my Dearest Dear,

What marvellous news. I haven't been so cheered up since I finished *Beaverbrook*. At any rate it is marvellous. A week in Paris and at just the right time. I say Paris rather than London for a number of reasons. We may not have another chance of Paris, whereas if all goes well we shall see plenty of London. Also it is better you don't come to England (or me to Hungary) until our relations are firmly established. I love Paris. I shall enjoy showing it to you, except that I have forgotten so much. Have you been there for any length of time? Of course if you prefer I will bring my car over and we can tour France a bit. But frankly I shall find that rather tiring, and I think you will get tired changing hotels every night.

Now as to time. I shall close the Library for the last two weeks in September, so can be free at any part of that time. I must be back before 5 October when I have to take Crispin to Cambridge, and thereafter I don't have a full free week until mid-December, what with lecturing in Oxford and lectures elsewhere. Can you be in Paris by the second half of September? In that case I'll come on Monday 24 September and stay until Monday 1 October. We can go to Chartres for the day and anywhere else you like. I am not keen on Versailles, but there are plenty of better things to see.

If you approve I'll book an hotel for us both. This is better than my coming to wherever you are stopping, as it will create embarrassment when I depart again. I know a quite attractive hotel on the Left Bank not far from Notre Dame called the Mont Blanc. I was there with the boys in 1971 a few months before we met in Salzburg. Please let me know as soon as possible whether these dates are right. Then I will go ahead and book. After that you do not need to write again unless you feel like it. Oh dear, the prospect has quite changed my life. Before your letter came I was very down: the weather too hot, the difficulty of writing *The Second World War* too great. Now all is well.

Here are comments on the rest of your letter. Flucinor: not received. I will gladly try it for your sake, but I don't believe in it. I have Betnovate, which is probably another version of the same thing. In any case Flucinor is, I notice, produced by ICI, so presumably it is available in England if it is any good.

My former pupil: this is the one word in your letter I could not read. Is it Michael Lewis? In that case I must say I can remember no Michael Lewis. Possibly he heard me lecture in Oxford. At any rate I'd like to hear more of him. Also it would be a good idea to send the Venice book back with him. As you say, he won't draw any conclusion from it. If he is an Oxford man, he can leave it at Magdalen whenever it suits him.

I think that is all in your letter that requires an answer, at any rate it is all I can read. As for my own news, *The Second World War* is again creeping slowly forward. I'll get half of it written before I go to Ireland. The weather has been very sunny with fresh breezes, so that swimming has been delightful. I wish I had learnt to swim better when I was young – to dive and crawl as well as do breast-stroke. As it is, all I can do is to swim two hundred yards in one direction and then turn round and swim two hundred yards back again.

I am just making a new will. I have left the copyright of my books and of my unpublished writings to you. You can decide what to bring out and also which books to keep in print. You'll also get the money. Maybe in ten, twenty, thirty years, whenever I am dead, my books will not sell as well as they do now.

This is a letter out of series as they say. I won't write this coming weekend. I will the weekend after, just before I go to the Lake District.

Marvellous news, marvellous time to look forward to.

I love you!!

Amazing.

xx   xx   xx
Alan

8 July

My Dearest,

I am now as gloomy as last time I wrote to you I was elated. I am fearful that we are not going to meet in Paris as easily as I hoped. The reason is this. The other day I had a letter from our old friend Hauser asking me to address the Ranke Gesellschaft in the middle of September (as an added temptation, he said he had invited you also). Of course I shall not go. I suggested two other English historians for Hauser, both more suitable than I am. But then Hauser went on to suggest that I should go on for a visit to Austria and then meet him again at Budapest for a conference on, I think, 24 to 27 September. At once I saw the ruin of my plans. You will surely want to stay in Budapest until the conference is over, and it will be October before you arrive in Paris. Now all this may be a false alarm, so if you have already written anything different disregard what follows.

I have to be back in England by 3 October in order to take Crispin to Cambridge on Friday 5 October. The following week I have a date at Harlow on 9 October and at Liverpool on 12 October. After that the term starts both in London and in Oxford. I have a class in London every Tuesday afternoon and a lecture in Oxford every Thursday morning. I don't think I could suspend either of them for a week, though I can't tell this until the term begins. In other words, I could only come to Paris from a Thursday afternoon until very early on a Tuesday morning. I shall not be free again until the beginning of December. By then you may have gone back to Budapest, and in any case Paris is not such fun in December as it will be in September. So you see my troubles.

The best of course will be if you go off to Paris without waiting for the conference at Budapest. I don't even know what the conference is about, and whether it is the kind of thing that interests you. For my part I hope never to go to a conference again. After all, I only went last time in order to meet you. Perhaps it would be a good idea for you to go to Hauser's conference. Then you could use this as an argument for going on to Paris straight away. If these suggestions are not any good, then you must just tell me when you intend to be in Paris and for how long. I will then fit in as best I can. By writing only about my difficulties I seem to be dictating to you what you should do. It isn't that at all. Of course I must fit in with you as much as you do with me. But I can only see my side of things. If only I had had the sense to retire, I would be completely free and could come to meet you anywhere. But you would not like me half so much.

Please come to Paris on 24 September, or about then, if you can. If you can't, it can't be helped. We'll manage something. My other cause of worry is the financial situation, with the pound going to pieces and prices roaring up. I have enough foreign money for a week in Paris, so I am not worrying about that. But the future prospects of this country make me feel that it will not be a good place for you to live in. We'll solve that difficulty when it comes. I wish I were nearer to you. We could arrange anything in a few minutes' talk. As it is, you seem as far off as the Moon.

Now I won't continue these gloomy topics any more. On Tuesday I go to the Lake District for eight days with three of my sons. So I shall not receive any letter from you, even if you write, until 19 July. Do not expect therefore to get an early reply. I look forward to the Lake District with some fear. Down here in London it has been hot and sunny for the last fortnight, and I think too hot for climbing hills. Even if it is cooler in the Lake District, as I think it will be, I have much doubt whether I am in good condition. Instead of going a long walk every Sunday I have been taking Crispin out for driving practice, and I am sure I have lost the use of my legs. However, there could not be a finer death than to fall down on a mountain. I'll send you a postcard as soon as I go up a mountain successfully.

Thanks for the *Companion Guide* to Venice. It arrived in Oxford by an unknown hand. At any rate there was no card with it. I am still at a loss who Michael Lewis can be. No doubt it will turn out to be someone

1973

I have known all my life. We had a good Old Boys' party at Magdalen. President Griffith got through his speech without difficulty. At present he is being very virtuous and drinking only water. But I wonder how long his good resolutions will last.

I have got through all my reviews. Wells came out in the *Observer* and so did Macaulay. Lloyd George came out in the *New Statesman*. On reading them again I felt I had been too soft on all three books. I am so anxious not to get (or retain) the reputation of being a savage reviewer that I now lean over on the other side.

I have at last been to the cinema. Yesterday afternoon I saw the Czech film *Closely Observed Trains*. Have you seen it? About a youngster who works at a little railway station. He is unsuccessful with girls and tries to kill himself. An experienced woman initiates him. He is cheerful, blows up a German ammunition train and is shot by a German guard. All told in a gentle Czech undertone. In a way very boring, but also extremely charming and convincing.

I have been swimming a lot. I have skin trouble still, but not as bad as it was. On Wednesday Crispin drove me to the South Coast near Eastbourne (Karl Marx's favourite resort). We went to look at Pevensey Castle, a big fort on the Saxon shore built by the Romans. Most of the Roman walls are still standing. Then a mediaeval castle was built inside the Roman walls. And, most extraordinary, in 1940 the Army revived Pevensey as a strongpoint and put disguised machine-gun posts in the Roman towers. As it was three miles from the sea where the Germans were expected to land, I can't believe that it would have been much use. But it makes a romantic story.

Forgive all the trouble I am causing you. I'll make arrangements about Paris as soon as I hear from you and know what is going to happen. Even if things go wrong, here is the same message as always:

Love and Kisses
x x
x   Alan
x

21 July

Dear Heart,

You do not need to fear that this time my letter will be gloomy. On the contrary I am again cheerful that Paris will work out somehow. I will make a provisional booking at the hotel for 24 September. If you can't be there by then, I will come later though for a shorter time. Despite your love of my profile I shall not bring my car. We shall have a better time in Paris than going round the country, and a car in Paris is quite impossible. So you will have to sit sideways in a restaurant when you want to get excited over my profile. We will go to Chartres one day and I am also anxious to see St Denis, outside Paris, which I missed last time because I foolishly went on a Sunday.

Talking of books, I sent Crozier off to you yesterday. You will see that it is a very handsome volume. The editorial work I did also appears impressive. It will be published in a week's time and I have already promises of some fine reviews. So it will sell better than I expected and my reputation, already high, will rise higher still. Not that I care. On the other hand, I wrote a piece on Hitler's strategy for a magazine and the editor says it is too dull to publish. Really he did not like my argument that Hitler was a brilliant strategist in an unorthodox way. He wanted me to say that Hitler made nothing but blunders.

Our week in the Lake District was a great success except for the weather. It did not rain much, but there was cloud on the hills and whenever we got above 2,000 feet we were walking in thick mist. So we did not see much and once nearly got lost. Crispin saved us with fine work with a compass. We went up four mountains, all over 1,000 metres high, quite a feat for an elderly man, and I never had trouble except slight sores on my feet which I always covered up in time. Indeed I think I am tougher on the mountains than I was fifty years ago. I grew up in the Lake District, so it was specially enjoyable for me. The boys got on very well with each other.

The only defect is that I had trouble with my car. First the exhaust manifold went and the car made a noise like a racing motor bicycle. Then on the way home the silencer jammed the engine. We were stranded on the motorway late at night, had to leave the car at a garage and arrived home at midnight, having had nothing to eat all day. These are the occasions when I regret that the car was ever invented. I shall recover it tomorrow and hope that its deficiencies have all been remedied.

I got the Flucinar the other day. I now know what it is. It is sold in

1973

England as Sylanar and is a cortisone compound. English doctors are now afraid of cortisone and prescribe Betnovate instead. But I shall loyally use it if my skin breaks out again. Recently we have had little sun, so I have recovered for the time being. Ireland, where we go on 15 August, is sure to be wet and rainy so again I shall have no trouble. I have met another acquaintance of yours, sent to me by Neville Masterman, a fellow called Arday. He is now working in the Library. I don't think his subject is very rewarding. There was no British policy towards Hungary between the wars. I am moving slowly with the *Second World War*, not seeing clearly how I ought to treat it. I shall be glad when the book is finished and I can get on with the love letters between Frances Stevenson and Lloyd George.

Your last letter inspired me. It makes me love you more than ever. But don't worry about me. We shall get things right somehow though the problems seem very difficult. The thing I am most anxious about is money. Prices have nearly doubled during the last year, and my income has not doubled with them. It is the one problem that is really going to get in the way. But don't think about it until it happens.

Lots of love, and lots of thoughts,

xxxxx   xxxxxxxx   xxxxxx
Alan[x]

4 August

Dear Heart,

59 years since the outbreak of the First World War. No one, I see, has remarked on it, and a good thing too. That war has departed into history and even the Germans don't care if their government started it. I had a little book containing thoughts on the outbreak of war by Eulenburg and Lichnowsky. Not much in it though quite a good introduction, longer than the book, by the editor. However there was another foreword, of which I wrote: 'Professor Trevor-Roper, an authority on English history in the seventeenth century, also contributes a foreword.' That was a joke that I had been wanting to make for a long time. It is the sort of thing which makes more solemn historians regard me as a playboy.

I look forward every day to hearing from you about Paris. But of course I realize that you can't write until you hear from others, and you are not likely to hear while you are enjoying the sun at your Danube cottage. So I must be patient. I have arranged everything I can on my side. I have provisionally reserved a double room in a Paris hotel. I have enough francs for a week. And the Library will be closed at that time so that I can get away with a few days' notice. If you can't be in Paris until the beginning of October, it can't be helped. I'll come as soon as I can, though it is not an easy time for me. Still, let me know when you get some news. I shall be at the Library until 14 August. Then I shall be in Ireland for a fortnight, and back on 31 August.

I will write to you again before I leave, but probably not from Ireland where I am always kept busy one way and another. Oh, I do so hope our Paris meeting will come off.

I have just had a great disappointment and I don't know when I have been so depressed. It concerns Crispin more than me. I had taken him out day after day in the car. He drove very well. He knew every trick. He could reverse perfectly round a corner, start uphill, knew when to stop. Last Thursday I took him for his test. I was perfectly confident he would pass and sat peacefully waiting for him. He came back very upset. He had failed for a lack of control of the clutch. He said: 'I think there is something wrong with the clutch, I could not hold the car.' When I went to the car, I found the clutch had broken down. I could not drive the car at all and had to be towed back to the garage. Poor boy, it was not his fault at all. A mechanical failure which could not be foreseen and could have happened at any time. I think the examiner should have seen that there was something wrong with the car and stopped the test. But of course Crispin could not have passed with a faulty car. He is very brave about it. I feel I have let him down, particularly as he will have to wait for months before he can take another test. No doubt absurdly, I feel that I have failed all my children in not providing them with a stable family life. I thought at the time that it was not my fault. But I ought somehow to have mastered my difficulties and got things right. As it is, I have been a bad father, not fit to have children. It seems a wasted life, devoted to my children and yet not good enough for them. Now even the two boys are growing up. They won't need me any more and won't bother about me. I say to myself: it was bad luck. But I keep feeling: it was bad management on my part. Sorry to pour all this out to you, but there is no one else I can tell it to. I hate to think of my past record, and have at the moment no faith in the future.

I sent you a book on the German invasion of Russia. I thought it rather good and gave it a big review in the *Observer*. But I must also confess that I sent the book to you simply because I had two copies. The other book of really great interest I cannot send to you, because I have only one copy. It is the third volume of Ullman's book on Anglo-Soviet relations 1917–1921. This volume finishes the story of how Lloyd George made the Anglo-Soviet trade agreement and thus tried to end the Cold War. There are some marvellous stories in it. The British government had broken the Russian codes and intercepted all the messages between Moscow and the delegation in London. Of course the intercepts are not in the PRO but Ullman, who is a brilliant researcher, found them elsewhere. It is one of the best discoveries in research for a long time. Another very funny thing is that all the senior ministers opposed the settlement with Russia and tried to stop Lloyd George. When they first met Krasin, Curzon refused to shake hands with him until Lloyd George said: 'Curzon, be a gentleman', and Curzon reluctantly took Krasin's hand. Even better, Sir Henry Wilson, Chief of the Imperial General Staff, decided that Lloyd George was himself a Bolshevik and tried to organize a military rebellion against him. Churchill was to lead it. But of course Lloyd George outwitted them all. The book cheered me up during my great depression.

I have at last got *The Second World War* moving, and begin to think that I shall finish it by the end of the year. I have got to Pearl Harbor and the German failure to take Moscow, so the real war is about to begin. I am looking forward to what will happen next. In a curious way, whenever I write even about something I know really well, I don't know what is going to happen until I have written it down. Writing books is a way of teaching myself and discovering ideas that I had never thought of before. I suppose that is why other people think that my books are too clever by half.

I'm sure that you do not want to hear all this. What you want to know is how much I love you. I miss you very much. I want to hear your voice and feel your presence instead of merely sitting at my typewriter.

Deep thoughts, my darling, and love as ever.

x Alan

11 August

Dearest One,

How wonderful the post is nowadays. You wrote last Saturday and your letter was already with me on Tuesday. So I have been able to carry it about and think about it for days on end. I wish you were on the Danube. You should not stay dutifully at home, where you can be later when the sun does not shine. I long all the time to hear that you will be in Paris at the end of September. This is not only selfishness on my part. I am so much tied up after October begins, and it seems so silly that I cannot come to Paris for a long stretch when you are there. Sometimes things have worked out well for us, and maybe it will be so in this case. There is a worrying difference between us. You have behind you twenty years of a happy married life, and so are accustomed to happiness. I have behind me now thirty years of unhappiness, and it has become a habit. I often wonder whether I can ever settle into happiness again. It is like not walking or swimming for a long time. You get so that you can't do it. I've come to accept trouble and estrangement as normal. Truly I can hardly remember when I was happy except with you. A few years before the war when we lived in the north of England. After that, nothing.

I think very highly of Graham Greene as a writer. Indeed he is the best novelist we have. But I don't really like his serious books. His soul-searching doesn't interest me. I enjoy what he calls his entertainments – his thrillers. *Gun for Sale* and *The Confidential Agent* are very good of their kind. The work of genius is *The Quiet American*, which tells everything about American policy in Vietnam. *Our Man in Havana* is very good too. His latest book is *Travels with my Aunt*. This is very funny in a lazy sort of way. Characteristically, Graham thinks the funniest part is that he has given the names of friends and acquaintances to various characters in the book – a childish prank. *The Power and the Glory* is his masterpiece, but I can't read it. Muggeridge said recently that he himself was a sinner trying to be a saint and Graham was a saint trying to be a sinner. Graham was very angry at the suggestion that Muggeridge was a sinner. He claimed that category for himself and practically no one else. I have known Graham off and on for years. At lunch or dinner he constantly looks over his shoulder because he is convinced that someone is spying on him. To his disappointment, no one ever is.

You will be amused to hear that I rang up your boy and that he is coming to see me on Monday morning. I shall try to talk to him in

1973

German. He will get a shock when he sees how old I am. Remember that you see me through the eyes of love and so don't see the reality.

I've not much news. I have begun to write on the real World War after Pearl Harbor and begin to think that I shall finish the book one day. But I get so many interruptions at the Library. Yesterday an American woman talked to me about her ideas on the Genoa conference, a thing I could hardly remember. Then an English woman talked to me for another hour about an exhibition of cartoons that she was planning. Neither of them, you will be sorry or perhaps glad to hear, was attractive.

We are having scandals in England quite as good as the American Watergate. First we had a sex scandal with Cabinet Ministers resigning because they went with prostitutes. Then we had a financial scandal over building contracts which smears leading members of the Labour Party. Now we have a spy scandal with the British government employing convicted criminals to infiltrate the IRA and carry out sham bomb attempts in the Irish Republic. It certainly makes an agreeable summer.

Economics are in a fine mess. Prices go up and up. I think we shall have a financial crisis, and the government will have to cut down its spending. Then we shall have mass unemployment and industrial unrest. These are troubles from which your country is free. It is the price of capitalism when people no longer accept its ethic.

The Crozier book had very good reviews. Whether it will sell is a different matter. I expect I shall settle for *Darling Pussy* if I ever get down to preparing the book.

Write to me soon that you are going to Paris in September. The thought of it seems too good to be true.

So with much and longing love, desperately anxious to feel as well as to see you. I can't believe it will really happen.

      Love,
       Alan
   x

1 September

Dear Heart,

    I am waiting anxiously to hear from you. The room I have booked in Paris will be reserved for us until 15 September. After that we shall lose it. So it is very important that I should hear from you before then. The moment you know when you can be in Paris, send me a telegram to the Library. Then I will either confirm the room or cancel it for a later date. Of course I understand that you cannot act until you hear from the French authorities. But stir things up as much as you can. It is easy for me to come to Paris on 24 September and will be less easy afterwards. Also I am going away for a few days on 17 September. So Friday 14 September is the last day when I can arrange things for Paris on 24 September. I hope this is clear. Also, I hope oh so much that everything will work out all right.

    I have thought of something I should very much like to do when we meet. I can't write to you about it except to say that it concerns you and should give you pleasure. You must think also of something you very much want to do, and I will do my best to join in whatever it is. I daresay you can guess some of it, but not exactly what I have in mind. It will make you laugh, I hope. Then you will say: 'What a lovely idea.'

    I got back from Ireland on Thursday. Some of the time there was very enjoyable, some of it not so good. We had two days of very heavy rain when we foolishly drove all day in the rain looking at ancient Irish churches and getting very wet in the process. Then we had lovely weather and swam in beautiful warm sea with just enough waves to lift us up and down and sometimes big enough to knock us over. The boys are growing up and will not want the company of their quarrelling parents much longer. I feel rather sad, as though life were coming to an end. I have spent 25 years principally with my children, from 1937 when Giles was born until now. And now it's over. I have almost forgotten what grown-up society is like except with you. You will understand because your boys have given you the same company and the same pleasure and are beginning to live their own lives. In October Crispin will go to Cambridge – the first time away from home – and I shall have no one to go walking in the country with on a Sunday. I shall try to interest Daniel in the same activity, but he is less enthusiastic. I am glad to report that he passed, not very well, in all his 6 'O' levels, so he can now go on to more advanced work and has already announced his intention of going to Oxford or Cambridge. He has not the same clear purpose as Crispin, but he is very intelligent and will end up as a journalist or some other form of writer.

1973

While in Ireland I read an enormous biography of Sir Walter Scott – twelve hundred pages. Not the sort of book I should ever read except on a holiday. I remember you asked me who Sir Henry Raeburn was – I can't imagine why. He was a Scotch portrait painter of the late eighteenth century, in much the same style as Reynolds or Romney. He painted Scott among other people, a famous portrait. Otherwise I know nothing about him and am puzzled that you ever heard his name.

I've told you, I think, that your boy came to see me. I liked him very much. By now he will have hitchhiked all round Scotland and perhaps be back at home with you. Give him my greetings. I hope he approved of me as much as I approved of him.

I am now writing about 1942 and hope to finish the last Axis victories before I come to Paris. The pattern works out very satisfactorily: Japanese and German victories until the summer of 1942 – then a halt in all spheres and Allied victories beginning in the autumn. I fear I shall be criticized for emphasizing Hitler's ability as a military commander. He nearly won the war for Germany. Yet people like to think he was no good and that the German generals would have done much better – a most foolish view. There were few good German generals and as to the Allies – Zhukov and Montgomery perhaps. All the rest were administrators.

I think about you a great deal. I want very much to hold your hand and to put my arms round you. Often I wonder whether it is all imagination. Can we really love each other when we know so little about each other? So telegraph or write quickly, quickly.

And take a big kiss from me.
Much love,

Alan
x

7 September

Darling,

I wait anxiously for your telegram or other news. Meanwhile it has crossed my mind that you may be able to come to Paris and not know where we are to meet. So here it is. Hotel du Mont Blanc, 28 rue de la Huchette, Paris 5. It is on the south bank just near the Pont Neuf. I shall arrive there about six o'clock on 24 September and wait for you. I intend to stop for a week. But of course I shall not come unless I hear from you that all is well.

As to communicating with me, I shall be working here every day until 14 September. That day I must cancel the room if I don't hear from you. The following week I shall be in the Isle of Wight. But I shall come to the Library on 21 September and see whether there is any letter from you. But it will be too late for me to arrange to come to Paris. What a nuisance it is that we are so far away from each other. The space between us seems to be limitless, as though you were in another planet.

We are having the most fantastic weather, the hottest and sunniest September on record. Every day I break off my work at lunch-time and go to Highgate Ponds for the afternoon. I lie in the sun, suitably guarded by skin cream, and swim in the lovely fresh water. It is not as good as the sea at Glenbeigh.

I won't write any more. I want you so much and it only makes me unhappy to write about it. Never mind, we shall meet in Paris later even if for a shorter time.

All the love and all the kisses in the world.

x Alan

4 October

Darling Girl,

This is a letter out of series, just to say that it was the best week I ever spent in my life. Of course we ought to have gone to a concert or to more cinemas. Still it was, as my boys say, *smashing*.

I had a dreadful journey. Very agreeable to Boulogne where I was to take the hovercraft, hardly anyone in the carriage. At Boulogne I was told that the sea was too rough and that the hovercraft could not operate. So back to the train and on to Calais, where an enormous crowd emerged from the train in order to cross by boat (and a car ferry at that). A solid mass pushing forward over the quays and up the one gangway, me heaving my heavy suitcase for a good half-hour. On the boat every seat taken, with me perching on the edge of a life-belt chest. At the bar no tea, only beer. Fortunately an Irish chap stationed in Germany recognized me and drew me into conversation. We stood at the bar for an hour and a half while the ship went up and down and the women were seasick. He drank whisky, I drank beer. At Folkestone more pushing in the crowd, and a train to Victoria with every seat again taken. Back in London at half-past eight instead of half-past six. A warning against relying on a hovercraft. But boats are far worse, and aircraft worst of all. What shall I do next time?

The Second World War is rolling forward. As a result of Paris I feel better than I have done for years, despite a looseness of the bowels that still continues. I think of you every minute of the day and much of the night too. No more. I am off to dinner at the Beefsteak Club.

I love you so much,

Alan

13 October

My Darling,

I get very impatient waiting for Saturday so that I can write to you, and now here it is. How much I enjoyed our telephone conversation. I could do it every day, but we should soon have nothing to say to each other except mutual love.

Now here are a few important topics. First a confession. You made two suggestions about my autobiography. The first was to put in something about the primitive conditions at Oxford, and that I have done. The second was something about my life either in London or Vienna, and I cannot remember what it was. Please remember on your side and tell me what to do. I have started another chapter on Manchester – at present very taken up with university details, but it will get more political and more personal later. I have also got moving with *The Second World War*. I've stopped the Germans at Stalingrad, beaten them at El Alamein, and landed in North Africa. Now I am preparing for 1943, a year of ups and downs. After being gloomy about my progress I am now beginning to think that I shall finish by the end of the year. Second point. I have sent two books to Ferencz and will send the third next week. I have no new books of importance to report. A life of Hitler by Maser, or rather a collection of details such as his enormous reading. But I think I told you that before.

Bruce Lockhart's diaries are coming out soon: nothing of importance except on British internal politics and gossip about who was sleeping with whom. As they are now all sleeping in the grave, the subject is of no great interest.

I have been rushing about a good deal. On Tuesday I went to Harlow and lectured on the Second World War. It is a new town in Essex. They have a community theatre but no company to play in it, so they fill it with lectures and other forms of entertainment. Yesterday I went to Liverpool on a similar errand. Enormous audience. Whether they understood what I was trying to say I have no idea. The trains are now so fast that I was able to come back the same evening after the lecture and had rather a bad meal on the train. Next week will be more peaceful except for a journey to Oxford. I think I might be able to come to Paris for the night of 8 November, a Thursday. Let me know whether you would like this. I'll let you know whether the aeroplane is really practicable. Of course I may have to call it off if the weather is bad. But I can always telephone at the last minute!

On Thursday I met a colleague from pre-war days. He went on an economic mission to Washington during the war, never came back, and is now economic adviser to the Mexican government. After parting from his wife 25 years ago, he married a glamorous Mexican girl at the age of 70 and is even fitter than I am. He still plays tennis. All this was a great encouragement to me. I didn't ask him how good he was in bed, but to judge from the satisfied condition of his wife he does not do badly. He is deaf in one ear. So at least I have one lead on him.

I have bought a new jacket for the autumn. Very smart and, what is more important, very warm. The weather has broken and I expect it has in Paris too. Are you warm in the hostel? Is there anything you need? Are you eating proper meals? Do not work too hard. It does no good.

I took Crispin to Cambridge and left him with a sad heart. But he will enjoy life very much and I rejoice for him. Daniel is trying to read half a dozen books a week. As he also insists on leading a full social life – going to a cinema once a week and also to a pop concert – I do not think he will succeed.

The news in the great world is gloomy. I do not think we are in sight of a world war, but there are plenty of other troubles. We are sure to have petrol rationing here soon which will be a nuisance for my car, though I can get an extra allowance as a journalist. I think the Israelis are in the wrong but I can't help hoping that they will win, simply because they have no other way of survival. It is the Crusader states all over again.

In imagination I am constantly back at our delightful room at the Mont Blanc. What I particularly liked was to wake up in the morning.

Somehow things will never go wrong between us. We seem made for each other. This is very strange and a great stroke of luck.

Now I must collect my summer clothes which have actually gone to the cleaners. I shall be so smart next time we meet that you will not recognize me. And with that much love and thoughts.

Oh, so much love,

Alan

27 October

My Darling,

What a wonderful thought that we shall be together a week on Thursday. At least I assume that the Mont Blanc is all right though I have not yet heard from you. And be sure to insist on a room at the back. I am lecturing at Oxford at nine o'clock in the morning. Then I shall catch a train to London, take train and plane to Paris, and should be with you between six and seven. If possible, let me know the telephone number of the Mont Blanc so that if there is fog or other delay I can ring you there. There is fog this week so it will probably be raining by then, and that makes safe travelling weather. It is very important that we should go out to dinner first. I shall have to leave about midday on Friday, so we shall have a good time together.

Here is another question. If you get another month in Paris you will need more money. How much? Maybe you can get permission to stay longer and no money, in which case I can provide. Shall I bring 2,000 francs with me just in case you need it? You have only to instruct me.

I have had a wearisome week, mostly from eating too much. On Wednesday night a very nice girl called Betty Kemp, an eighteenth-century historian who was my pupil at Manchester before the war, took me out to dinner at the best Oxford restaurant. It cost her £12, which shows you that English restaurants are even more expensive than French, and not such good value. On Thursday I attended the Restoration Dinner at Magdalen, again too much to eat. We celebrate each year the restoration of the Fellows and President in 1688 after James II had turned them out for refusing to elect a Roman Catholic as President. Boring speeches in a smoke-filled room. Yesterday I had to go to a lunch to celebrate the publication of Nelson's *Dictionary of World History*, of which I was advisory editor. It contains over three million words. Too much food once more.

I have one disturbing bit of news for you. There is a new volume in the *Documents on British Foreign Policy*. It is on naval affairs from 1934 to 1936 and shows, among other things, that the Treasury wanted to abandon the United States in favour of Japan, so as to save money. There was a battle between Chamberlain and Simon, with the Foreign Office winning. The naval treaty with Germany was to clear the way for the naval conference. Japan apparently was prepared to agree to a greater naval strength for Great Britain, but insisted on parity with the United States which ruined everything. The volume is too expensive for me to get for you, but I'll try to borrow it somewhere. I suppose it is what you always expected.

I reviewed a book on Hitler for the *New Statesman*, and have also done a biography of Baldwin by Montgomery Hyde for next week's *Observer*. Did you know Mrs Baldwin's answer when asked how she could endure sexual relations: 'I closed my eyes and thought of England.' And here is Churchill's remark when he heard that Baldwin was still alive: 'What, is the candle still guttering in that old turnip?' The latest literary sensation is a life of Harold Nicolson and Vita Sackville-West, his wife, by Nigel Nicolson, their son. She had a passionate love affair with a woman called Violet Trefusis (daughter of Edward VII), which she described in physical detail. Harold, who was vaguely homosexual himself, went on loving her though they never had sexual relations after the birth of their children. I don't think this strange story should be told, but times have changed.

The world is in a high state of excitement. I missed the evening news on Thursday, so did not know that the nuclear weapons were about to go off. By the time I looked at the papers on Friday morning the crisis was over. Of course the position in the Middle East is insoluble. The Arabs are determined to destroy Israel altogether, and the Jews are determined to keep it as an exclusively Jewish state. It is the story of the Crusades all over again. In the end the Crusaders were driven out, and I expect the Jews will be also. But maybe not in my time. As some Frenchman said: 'It is only the provisional that lasts.'

What goes on in Paris? Have there been lots of strikes? Has there been lovely weather? I expect we shall have petrol rationing soon, but as a journalist I can get extra petrol so have little reason to worry. It was very wrong of you not to go to any of the Crouzet receptions. It is good for you and for any historian to meet other historians, though they usually turn out to be very dull. I fear I am as bad about this as you are. I see that my Turin friend Venturi is in Oxford this year, so I shall invite him to dinner and expect that he will turn out better company than Ránki. At Easter I hope to take the boys to Venice. Can you be free exactly at Easter weekend? If so we could meet at Split or somewhere else in Yugoslavia. We must remember to discuss this.

Crispin was summoned to see the chaplain of his College. He said firmly: 'I think I am an atheist,' and the chaplain got no further with him. Crispin is a rigid unbeliever, and is refusing to go even to the service commemorating the past benefactors of the College. Good for him, though I have always been weaker about such things. How are your boys surviving without you? And thank you for the bottle that Veronica at last delivered. It is not as good as grappa, but very good all the same. I drink it out of the bottle before going home in the evenings.

Now think often of the things we shall do together, and answer my questions if you can find time to do so. I am happy at the thought of your existence, as you are at that of mine.

Love a thousand times,

Alan

29 October

Dearly Beloved,

This is just a brief note to tell you that all is well. On Thursday, 8 November, I shall arrive at the Gare du Nord from Le Touquet at 17.44. I shall come straight to the Mont Blanc unless you tell me otherwise. And on Friday I shall leave the Gare du Nord at 13.20, so we shall have a free morning together. I hope the weather is better than it is now – fog in the mornings and cold sun in the afternoons.

Be sure to let me know about your need of money, if any. I shall go to Oxford on Wednesday 7 November, so must know about money the day before. How eagerly I think about our little room.

I am now going to the Turkish Embassy to celebrate the 50th anniversary of the Turkish republic. Is that anything to celebrate?

Deep love,

Alan

At lunch today I was told that *The Go-Between* by L. P. Hartley was a very erotic novel. Do you agree?

5 November

My Sweetheart,

This is just to confirm that I shall come to the Hotel de la Bretonnerie as soon as I arrive in Paris. As I don't know where it is, I shall probably take a taxi. Of course you could meet the 17.44 from Le Touquet at the Gare du Nord, but this is risky. We are sure to miss each other. So I shall take a quick look round and then away to the hotel. It would have been rather fun and an adventure to spend the night in your room. But it would have been very uncomfortable. And for dinner? I should quite like to go to the Restaurant Vagenerde in boulevard St Germain, which we couldn't visit last time because of our tickets. I'll bring some money. I'll try to find Hauser's book, though I think it has little of interest. I shall not bring Nicolson's book, which I do not possess and which in any case will not answer your question. I think two lesbians rub hard against each other until they have an orgasm. Lydia Lopokova, the ballet dancer, was as mystified as you. She said: 'I can understand two men. There is something to get hold of. But how do two insides make love?' Lucky you and lucky me not to have to worry about such things.

I went to Cambridge on Saturday to see Crispin. He has never been so happy in all his life. Amelia is in very bad trouble, more over money than over heartache. I'm in bad trouble too at the thought of all the difficulties ahead of us.

No time for more,

Love,
Alan

11 November

Beloved,

My electric typewriter has broken down and I am back at my old manual. I had an easy, relaxed return. It really is the perfect way to travel from Paris to London – special train, empty airports at Le Touquet and Gatwick, all complete in four hours. I was even able to put in a couple of hours at the Library. As always, I was happy at every minute in your company. Everything was good, even my cutting myself when shaving.

The moment I hear you can stay until the end of the week in December, I will book my flight for 12 December and we will go to the Bretonnerie again.

You cannot imagine how relieved and happy I am to have started divorce proceedings. You do not need to worry that I shall ever reproach myself. In my opinion the formality of a divorce can no more prevent two people being friendly than the formality of a marriage can compel them to love each other. I'll be glad when it is over and all that behind me. Already I feel great relief.

Some time, presumably when you get back to Hungary, you must get clear the legal position on your side. Are you quite sure that you can keep Hungarian nationality when you marry me and have British nationality? Will you really be able to come and go freely? And are you sure that you will keep your pension rights when you have British nationality and perhaps have been living in England for years? Of course you may decide that you would rather not marry me, and I'll think you are right. You could marry me so as to have freedom of movement and yet not settle in England. In Crispin's favourite phrase: 'We shall see.'

My stiffness of neck and shoulder is still bad. Hot bath in the evening drives it off, but it comes back the next day. We shall have petrol rationing soon and I keep my tank full. In any case, as a freelance journalist I can get unlimited petrol. You will be thinking of me tomorrow afternoon. I'll write to you about it next weekend, though no doubt it will turn out very much like any other lecture. I read my draft chapters of *The Second World War* yesterday and am cheered about them. They are better than I thought.

This is not a proper letter, only to say that I am safe back and LOVE you.

X
Alan

19 November

My Dearest Love,

You may certainly count on me to come over on 12 December if you are able to stop in Paris that long. So reserve our delightful room at the Bretonnerie as soon as you know. In any case, I have remembered that the first seminar is to be held on the Thursday afternoon, so I must come back that day. The only obstacle is a possible petrol shortage with a cut in air services. We should know long before then.

I delayed writing until Monday in the thought that there might be a letter from you. I can always write again if necessary.

You sound as if you have been having a worse time in Paris than we are having here – a strike by greengrocers, and restaurants closed for lack of food. I hope you are not starving. Here we have alarms rather than real troubles. The electricity has not yet been cut off. There is no petrol rationing and there is even Sunday motoring. As to the great economic crisis, it is still all talk. Intellectually, in my head as it were, I believe that there is a terrible crash coming with millions of unemployed, and in that case England will be no fit place to live in, certainly not for you. On the whole the worst has a way of not happening, but anything is possible with this government, or maybe capitalism has become unworkable. We have lost the capitalist ethic and found no new one. The Labour Party seems even more helpless than the Conservatives. I am theoretically gloomy and cheerful in my day-to-day affairs, apart from having rheumatism now and then.

The Creighton lecture was, I think, a success. There was a great crowd, so much so that I had to use a microphone much to my annoyance. Len Deighton, the thriller writer, came specially from Ireland to hear me. Even Daniel, who had never heard me before, was impressed. But I was not altogether happy with it, perhaps because I had given it two or three times before and no longer had the excitement of discovering new ideas while I was talking. Kathleen Constable, now Tillotson, came. With my head full of my autobiography, I reminded her how we often met for tea when we were at Oxford. She replied that we met once during the three years, and I daresay she was right. I have a feeling that she was in love with me, when I was not with her. She asked me whether I had any regrets. I gave an evasive answer.

I have been trying to find the volume of British documents on naval affairs and have not yet succeeded. I will report to you when I do. *The Second World War* is moving along. I have finished with 1943, and am now writing to you partly in order to put off starting 1944.

I have sent in the petition for divorce. What is the point of prolonging a marriage that has broken down, particularly when I should like to be married to someone else?

What news from Russia? Clearly you must go if you can, even though there is no hope of my seeing you there. I could not face Russia, really I could not. But wherever you are I shall go on loving you. Now I must do some work.

All the love in the world,

Alan

21 November

My Beloved,
I received your letter of 14 November with its marvellous news only yesterday. Book our room for 12 December. Also look around for an agreeable restaurant nearby. I shall arrive at the Gare du Nord, probably at platform 8, at 17.44, and go to the Silver Arrow counter on platform 1 to check my return the next day. If you are not there I shall proceed at once to the hotel by Métro. So do not worry to come to the station if it is a trouble.

The approaching divorce depresses me. I can't believe that I ever brought anything but unhappiness to her. Perhaps I asked too much. But it is terrible to think that I wasted twenty years of my life or, to count the years of unhappiness with Margaret, thirty. Still, I have had uninterrupted happiness with you. We must treasure every minute. I'll write again soon.

Loving thoughts,

Alan

I rang you on Monday – in vain. Will ring again. X.

28 November

Sweetheart, Beloved,

Your letter of 22 November to hand, as they say in business correspondence. Here is the answer to your urgent practical query. Eden announced the staff talks to the House of Commons on 25 March 1936 (my birthday) and Lloyd George criticized them. The British government had chosen the exact words used by Grey in 1912, i.e. the talks were not a commitment. Lloyd George said that a guarantee to France was quite in order but that no pledge such as staff talks should be made, which said how the guarantee was to be carried out. He drew the parallel with August 1914 when the BEF had to go to the French left and had no choice. I'll look up the precise references in *Hansard* for you.

I've got the British document volume on the naval talks. But what am I to do? It is very heavy and it ought not to leave the Library. I'll tell you what I can when I come. I've read the Anglo-Jap material with a very anti-American paper by Warren Fisher. So far I've not found much of interest on the Anglo-German side.

Here is a remark about the future which you will find typically male, or maybe you will think it nonsensical. I want to marry as much as you do, but I have to think of the practical side. You must face it that you will live for twenty years or so longer than me, and yet I can't provide properly for these twenty years as I could if you were my first wife ever. Quite apart from this – and again you'll laugh – I am terrified by the present British economic situation. It is quite possible that we shall have this winter a total economic collapse – no oil, no coal, no heat, no light, millions of unemployed. All my resources are in stocks and shares. If the stock market collapses, as it well may, I shall be quite poor instead of being quite rich. The last time this happened – in the Great Depression – I was young, I had a job, and in fact my shares did quite well too. This time it might be more difficult. I tell you, my sweet, what I would not tell anyone else: I'm frightened. Of course it is no good worrying. I am much better off than most people and have a long way to go before I starve. But you know what happened to old people all over central Europe in previous periods of inflation: all their savings were lost and they became paupers. The only skill I have is writing in journalism or books, and that will not keep me in a crisis. So until I can see an end to the present troubles, with some prospect of my investments recovering, I can't say what I want to say: 'Marry me if you please, Mrs Smith.' I have absolute confidence you will understand. After all the crisis cannot go on for ever. I suppose I have been expecting the collapse of British capitalism all my life. Now that it comes I am rather annoyed. You are lucky to be in a Communist country and safe from such things. I won't write any more about this. But just be clear about this. My anxieties may be foolish but they are solely about money and economics. I haven't the slightest doubt that we should be happy together and somehow we must do it. But I've always remembered that life and even love don't work without money.

So far our troubles are theoretical except for the rise in prices. There is no shortage of petrol, and drivers are beginning to drive fast again after being asked to go slow for patriotic reasons. We have had no electricity cuts, though they are sure to come. It has started to snow though not heavily. Yesterday night was colder than any night last year. I am very fit as a result. Cold weather never did me harm. Last night I went to a chamber concert with Daniel – the first time he had been to any sort of classical concert (he goes to plenty of pop concerts).

Did I tell you that I was described by a reviewer in *History* as 'our greatest living historian'? Too kind, as Florence Nightingale said when receiving the Order of Merit on her death-bed. What a beautiful letter you wrote me. But you too must not worry. You are not a problem. The situation is a problem but that is something different. It would be easier if we could be together more so that we could solve the problem together. Never mind.

This letter is out of turn. I wanted to tell you about the staff talks and will write again next week. I have booked my flight.

Love in handfuls,

Alan

2 December

My Darling,

This will not be a real or even interesting letter. I am too depressed. Silly no doubt to be depressed by such a little thing as shortage of petrol. But it is the coming economic collapse that worries me. Soon I shall have to live on a pension instead of earning, and pensions do not go up with inflation. Perhaps in a year's time the storms will have blown over and we shall laugh at my anxieties. They are the penalty for too much intelligence.

I have a new worry. There is now a threat of a rail strike, and I need the railway to get to Gatwick next Tuesday. If the railway fails and

I can get petrol, I will go to Gatwick by car. Otherwise I may be stuck. So here is my intention. If I cannot come I will telephone you at six o'clock on Tuesday evening, 11 December. If I do not ring by half-past six you will know I am coming. I can't think of anything better. Of course, if there is better news before then I will let you know by telephone or letter. The maddening thing is that it is all apprehension. At present we still have full heating. I can buy petrol so long as I don't try at the weekend. The trains are running. Ministers say the economy is still booming. Over it all I feel the approaching hurricane. Useless to say to myself: Things never turn out as bad or as good as they are expected to be.

More cheerful, I'll have some autobiography for you, completing my chapter on early life at Manchester. It is quite funny, but as with other chapters I feel there is not enough of me in it. I can't help it. I am interested in other people and not in myself. There seems so little to tell. One day soon I will show what I have written to Isaiah Berlin, and perhaps he will tell me what I ought to have written. I am so depressed that I cannot go on with *The Second World War*. Otherwise I am well and longing to be with you. I dread the future. Please forgive me. I hate to lose spirit when we need each other so much.

Love and hope for our being together,

Alan

x x x

16 December

My darling,

My journey was fairly easy. A good train to Le Touquet. There the bar was open and I had another glass of beer which carried me through the afternoon. At Gatwick I did not have to wait long for a train, but it was then very slow and I did not get to London until after five o'clock instead of at four. So I was too late for the seminar at the Library. This was no great loss.

Our night at Paris was wonderful. We are closer than we have ever been and I am more confident about the future – apart from money. What has always worried me is that I should have to arrange things all on my own. If in 1975 we can be together, then the difficulties will disappear. In Crispin's phrase, we shall see. No more about this except to express my complete security in you, and I know you have it in me.

Our industrial troubles are tiresome. The government are like Houdini. They have tied themselves into knots. Unlike Houdini, they are unable to undo the knots. Yet the answer is so simple. We need a more egalitarian society and most of our troubles would disappear. If I have to give up my car, that will not worry me as long as everyone else does the same. I must also report that at present my nails are very clean. *The Second World War* is getting on at a great rate. Soon the Russians will be besieging Budapest. Next month Hitler and Mussolini will both be dead. And I am also writing a glowing tribute to Namier, though also quoting Beaverbrook's remark (in his case about Bonar Law and Churchill): 'I have had two masters and one of them betrayed me.'

Next week I shall send you *Germany's First Bid for Colonies* as a little Christmas present instead of money. Let me know as soon as you can about Split. I think I shall be able to afford it. And for your own sake don't go to Russia. A year alone is too long. A proper letter next week.

All the love in the world,

Alan
x x x

22 December

My Beloved, The One and Only,

It has been raining heavily and that reminded me of our day in Chartres. Despite the rain and despite the fact that we could see practically nothing in the Cathedral, what a wonderful day that was, a day that will always live in my mind. Whenever I am depressed I think of it and of our whole week in Paris. It was the best week in my life, when I was happy again after so many years and confident that I had found someone who would always bring happiness to me. All our times together have been good, even during the rain at Porec, but Paris was the best. Venice does not come back so well to me. Strangely my happiest time was on the Lido, when you were least happy. I suppose I was too content to show it and merely became lazy. Always I say Thank You for every moment we have been together. I hope I have made you happy too.

This will be a letter merely telling my silly news such as it is. No peerings into the future and no complaints. Conditions are not bad at present despite the economic crisis that looms over us. The Library is on the *Daily Express* generator, so we have light and heat all the time, even over the weekend. I have no trouble with tube or bus and can always walk if anything goes wrong. Katherine Wheeler, our archivist, has to rely on the train and so takes two or three hours to get into work. I gave her and Della a bottle of champagne each, which I hope you approve. They are both too serious to welcome perfume. So far we have had no electricity cuts in the home and I don't think they will start until after Christmas. In any case we cook by gas, so if necessary we can eat by candle-light. I am well off for petrol at the moment and intend to go on an all-day walk tomorrow unless it is raining too hard. As to the crisis in the great world, I don't see at the moment what will be the way out. The miners are working a regular week so they can't be accused of striking, and they will not work overtime until they get higher wages. The government will not give them higher wages and threatens to put all industry on a three-day week. Sooner or later someone has to give way, and I don't think it will be the miners. But how this will be arranged is a mystery. Heath deserves a prize as the worst prime minister this country has ever had. Harold Wilson also deserves a prize of some sort for failing to offer any convincing alternative. So perhaps we will see the crisis of capitalism after all.

Now as to my work, I have finished the year 1944 with the Russians at the gates of Budapest. I shall stop for a little while so that I can form a clear picture of the final year . What is to be the moral of it all? How do I say goodbye to the Second World War? I think my book will be condemned as becoming too pro-Russian towards the end. The Western powers never treated Russia as an equal and brought much trouble on us all. I wrote a savage paragraph on British intervention in Greece, and I don't see how I can avoid condemning the British also over Trieste. I have to say what I think right.

London University wants to publish my Creighton lecture. So I will break off my book and try to turn the first chapter into something that looks slightly different. They wanted to publish it without paying me anything. But I thought it was enough to give the lecture for nothing and held firm. Not that the published lecture will produce much.

'Mrs Simpson' was not well received by the *Daily Express*. They want something more dramatic, and particularly they want something about the social world in which she and the King moved. I am not good on this sort of thing. Really I do not care about Mrs Simpson at all and am writing on her solely for the money it will bring. It is terrible the things I am not interested in – the monarchy, football, religion. Perhaps I am not human at all.

1973

We had a paper on the Peace Pledge Union the other night at our Library seminar. The young man presented an academic piece. Having lived through it, I wanted to say that it wasn't like that at all. People can't understand how it was possible to be strongly against Hitler and against the British government at the same time. But of course the government wanted to keep Hitler in power, if only he would be a little more moderate and leave the West alone. I doubt whether historians will ever get it right. This is a warning to us that we are probably also wrong about earlier periods. Perhaps history is not a version of events but a distortion of them, an imaginary creation that has little connection with what really happened.

My family are scattered. Giles and Janet have gone to her parents in Sussex, where Giles will be able to go shooting pheasants. Sebastian* and Mary have gone to her parents in Lancaster, where Sebastian will be able to go on the Lake District mountains if it is fine. I think he is mad to go so far when the petrol supply is uncertain, but he is a gambler in everything, taking risks and confident that he will find a way out. Sophia and Rob have gone to his parents, and Amelia has gone with them since she cannot go to Tim's. They see us all the year round so it is quite fair that they should go off for Christmas. I shall sit quietly at home on Christmas Day, and very glad I shall be. I hate all the artificial jollity and over-eating. First I did it to please my parents and then to please my children. Now I am free to please myself and do nothing.

I shall give the boys your *Larousse* as a Christmas present. I shall also give Daniel the *Dictionary of World History* that I helped to produce. And I shall give Crispin a book about the National Trust properties that he and I can go and look at later. I suppose I ought to have given him a book about Lloyd George now that he has become a Liberal. That won't last, at least I hope not. Janet had me and the boys to dinner the other night. I left at ten and they, I hear, stayed until midnight. They clearly do not keep my hours.

Well, my love, that is all for now. In a fortnight's time I shall be taking the boys to York for the weekend, so my next letter may be a little delayed. But it will come. Be sure of that. Write when you feel like it and never otherwise. And let me know as soon as you can whether Split will be possible. I'll send you the money for the fare. Love to your boys. Tell me if the books arrive for Ferencz.

I love you so much, my dear,

Alan

* Second son of Alan's first marriage.

1974

3 January

My Dearest Love,

I had a card from you full of love, written on 22 December. You ought by now to have had two letters from me – one telling you that I had arrived safe though rather late from Paris and the other just talking about this and that. Our posts are very delayed over Christmas, but you are sure to have had both letters by now.

Is there any difficulty about your owning property in England and receiving the money from it? I ask because I have just made a new will and have left to you the copyrights of all my books. This will be quite a good revenue for some time – two or three thousand pounds a year. Then it occurred to me that perhaps you would not be allowed to be a property owner even of books, and I don't want my literary earnings to be confiscated by the Hungarian state. Of course it will be quite simple if you are by then living in England. And of course the question may never arise as you are so convinced that you will die before I do. How are you? No more dizziness and fainting fits I hope. I am pretty well at the moment except when I work too hard and am too tired to sleep.

Life here is rather troublesome at the moment, though not really bad. Before Christmas with the oil shortage we had a petrol panic, with people going from one petrol station to another. The main cause of the shortage seems to have been that everyone kept their tanks full all the time. Now the shortage seems to have blown over, but the price of petrol has gone up greatly. Then the trains are tiresome. For instance, there are no trains at all on a Sunday. So the boys and I will have to stay in York until Monday morning even though Daniel is supposed to be back at school that day. But as I do not go on many train journeys the situation does not worry me much. The worst hit are the people who live outside London and come in by train every day. There again it does not affect me.

The go-slow in the coal mines has compelled a three-day week in the factories, and I suppose that all the companies I have shares in will go bankrupt one of these days. Otherwise I don't notice the effects. The Library is on the *Express* generators so we have heat and light all the time. The situation is quite mad. The government are determined to ruin the country rather than reach a sensible agreement with the miners. I think most people are on the miners' side, but I am not a good judge

1974

of public opinion. The Labour Party is too frightened to say anything. I reflect on the collapse of capitalism which I have foreseen so often, and think that this time it might really happen. But somehow it seems unlikely.

When the crisis started we had really sensible reactions from people, everyone saying that we had lived too lavishly and that we should stop eating up the natural resources of the planet within a generation. No more oil, no more plastics, less paper and so on. Now the alarm has been forgotten and the crisis is regarded as a temporary accident. I should be happy if motor cars really disappeared. But the streets are crowded once more.

I am busy. I have finished my chapter on my life at Disley outside Manchester with lots about my political activities, which still seem to me quite sensible. Now I must describe Oxford in wartime, an interesting story I suppose but all mixed up with the beginnings of my great unhappiness. Until I met you my good life ended when I was thirty-five, only half as old as I am now. Then I have a final chapter on *The Second World War* to do, rather difficult also because I can't turn it into a propaganda chapter in favour of the Russians. On top of this the proof of *Beaverbrook* has arrived and I must correct 900 pages of the Penguin edition within ten days.

I am looking forward to York. Let me know quickly and soon about Split. I want to book the hotel there as soon as possible. Absurdly enough, despite our economic crisis the pound is now appreciating and I shall get 40 dinars to the pound. Let me know how much you want for your fare. I thought I had a lot of other things to ask and tell you but they have gone out of my head. But my love for you hasn't. Greetings to your boys.

Much love, and even more,

Alan
x x x

20 January

My Own Darling,

A long, a very long silence from you. No complaint from me. I hope it means you have too much work. I hope it does not mean that you have been in any way ill. I know it does not mean that you have forgotten me, and am sure that you think about me for much of every day just as I think about you. How many places are now indissolubly linked with you – Venice, Paris, Chartres. Paris was the best, I think. I remember every little thing about it, even that extraordinary film.

I have booked everything for Split. If for any reason – going to the Soviet Union or family ties – you can't come, I can easily cancel it so don't worry. Otherwise here it is. We go to Split on 29 March and stay until 4 April. I can't come earlier because I have a meeting at the British Academy on 28 March, and I can't come later because I must give the boys a week in Italy before Easter. I fly to Zagreb and from there there is a local plane to Split at 16.30. You should be able to get to Zagreb in plenty of time for that plane so we can fly on together. Coming back I have to leave Split at 7.50 (when you can come too), fly from Zagreb to Rome because there is no direct plane and then fly back to Venice. There the boys will meet me and I shall go on with them to Ravenna by train. Quite a day. Let me know as soon as you can if this is in order for you, even if you do not write about anything else. The weather may be very hot in Split, as it was when I was there in 1929, or very cold as it was in Porec. An insoluble problem.

End of practical arrangements. Our weekend in York was a great success. We stopped in a grand railway hotel built in the middle of the nineteenth century with vast corridors and high ceilings. We saw the Minster and St Mary's Abbey and the Roman walls. We visited I can't think how many parish churches and the hall of the merchant adventurers. On Crispin's insistence we went out to the new University and saw ultra-modern buildings also. Unfortunately the effect is rather spoilt by squatters' huts which have been put up to house married graduates. We lunched in a pub where I was recognized and we were all given too much beer. I also called at Bootham, my old school, and met the headmaster. It looked as uncomfortable as ever, a really Victorian establishment. I was able to show the boys my name on the roll of honour as a distinguished scholar. The old city is being ruthlessly pulled down so that motor cars can go even faster, just when the petrol is running out. But there is still plenty to see.

Daniel announced that he was not coming to Venice because Crispin and I talked to each other all the time. However, he agreed to come on condition that he was free to go on his own whenever he felt like it. I accepted this bargain, and all will be well. Crispin has now departed for Cambridge. I miss him but know he is happier there than at home.

The Second World War is finished, except that I shall have to revise and rewrite a lot of it. But that goes faster than thinking what to say. I am already looking at the Lloyd George letters and realize they will take

1974

a lot of work. My own life story has got to the move from Manchester to Oxford. The next chapter, if I ever write it, will deal with the beginning of my misfortunes. They went on until I met you. Now I don't worry about life and only theoretically about the future. Somehow we shall come together. Make sure that you can keep your Hungarian nationality even if you have a British passport.

The political and economic world is still in trouble. The ordinary citizen does not suffer except from the shortage of suburban trains. But the economy is running down thanks to the government's determination to beat the miners. I don't think they will succeed. But I don't see what future there can be for this country. No one, no one at all, offers a constructive alternative, certainly not the Labour Party. Yet the answer of a Socialist community is so obvious. Alas, no one believes in it or takes it seriously. So I expect we shall all be ruined sooner or later.

I have had a good run on television after being forgotten for so long. On Friday I was on English television and debated the idiotic topic as to whether there was still a class struggle in this country. What else? I got in the last word by saying that, if the present wages were really good enough for the miners, then why not make that the top limit for everyone else? Then a few days earlier I did a piece for Dutch television, so contemptuous of the government that the camera crew cheered. And tomorrow I do two reminiscent talks for North German television about the year 1934. I can't remember what happened then, but no doubt something did. I only remember it as the year when I first grew climbing French beans. Altogether a good run.

I am glad to report that I am very well, with no rheumatism and no other complaints. I have walked a lot, though Daniel is less enthusiastic than Crispin for all-day walks. This week I start lecturing again at Oxford – on the Second World War, which should be easy enough. No books for you at present. The only one I have read was a life of Jackie Fisher, all about the Navy before the First World War which is hardly your field. There is a film about Hitler made from Eva Braun's home movies. I don't think I shall bother to see it. I know only too well what Hitler looked like.

What a boring letter, but it is full of love for you. Write to me when you can spare a moment. And never never forget me.

All sorts of love,

Alan

2 February

My Darling, my Beloved,

What splendid news that you can come to Split. We shall have five, no six, good days together. I answer at once the only practical point in your letter. It is better that you should get your own ticket all the way to Split (i) because you can then book all the way through and be sure of a place on the Split plane, (ii) if anything goes wrong and we miss each other you can go on to the hotel at Split and wait for me, or vice versa. In any case I'll send you the money for the fare as soon as you let me know what it is. So find out quickly. The Split hotel and the Italian ones too are very slow in replying. I think I shall have to get a travel agency to telephone to them. The posts generally are very erratic. Your letter of 12 January only arrived on 19 January, that of 26 January arrived on 29 January. You can imagine my delight at the second when it came so quickly and was full of such good things. I have been puzzled all my life what women have seen in me, and you most of all. But you? With your different background, a happy home life for so many years. What can I give you except a few flashes before old age knocks me out and makes me merely a burden? However, I take my good fortune while it lasts.

Our economic situation goes on worrying me. Outwardly nothing has changed. We don't have any fuel or light cuts. There are no serious shortages in the shops and petrol is again easy to find. But there is the endless uncertainty. Will there be a miners' strike? If so, will all investments go to nothing? I had counted on them as security and even comfort for my old age when I could not earn any more. What will happen to my pension? Will it become worthless too? Previously I could always write more books or speculate on the Stock Exchange. Now publishers are not keen on books and there is no opening for speculation – at least I can see none. I dread the future, but of course it has a way of turning out less bad than one expected. Look at the Second World War, which did not inflict hardships on me at all. Instead it was fun and full of exciting experiences.

Now for my labours. *The Second World War*, though finished, is still full of work. I have to choose the maps and illustrations, always a difficult thing for me to do. I have to remove the most obvious mistakes which Michael Howard and Len Deighton are discovering for me – the first as a professional historian, the second as an expert in the techniques of war. After that there will be proofs and the making of the index. As for the Lloyd George letters, I am a little worried now that I begin to transcribe them. Taken as a whole they make a fascinating story, but in detail each one is not very interesting. Always the same story, Lloyd

George for ever writing that he wants to see Frances and making no effort to do so. I wonder whether she was really taken in. Certainly Lloyd George loved her, I think because she was so acquiescent and also because she was obviously very sexual. But he had no intention of ever leaving his family, and made out to her that he found them very tiresome when really he enjoyed life with them in the country.

How fortunate you are to be reading *Karamazov* for the first time. It is as you say one of the greatest books in the world, quite different from *War and Peace* but on the same scale. I have no great books left to read, so I might as well be going. At present I am reading Gibbon in bed and Macaulay during the day. Macaulay is very entertaining and very superficial. Gibbon is far better, but he wrote before the great historical discovery that the past is different from the present. I think I will start reading Balzac all over again. He wrote no perfect book but they add up to something tremendous, a great improvement on Proust. No new books on history are coming out. Hauser sent me the lectures given the year I was at the Ranke Gesellschaft, and the year after when you were there. Not bad, but not creating any uniform impression. He wrote how he had missed you last autumn.

I'll hope to have all the plans fully arranged before I write again. All you need to do is to get to Split somehow on 29 March and I shall do the same. I shall have plenty of money whatever troubles the future brings. I have sent two books to Ferencz. Let me know when they arrive.

A special very intimate caress,

Love and love,
Alan

4 February

Dearest,

This is not a real letter, only a supplement to the last one when I forgot some things and left them out. First your emissary arrived this morning with the bottle of Tokay and the lovely picture. It must be quite near the Hôtel de la Bretonnerie. I shall start drinking the Tokay in a few minutes' time. Secondly, your writing is not at all difficult for me to read. Indeed it is much better than mine. The boys say they cannot read it at all. That is why I always type my letters. One day I will send you a handwritten letter and you will not be able to read a word of it. But I can tell you that Lloyd George writing in pencil is also pretty difficult.

Thirdly, I was fascinated with your news about Baroness Hatvani. I think she is called Lotsi, or was that the Baron? Did you know that he was one of the great lovers of the age – three wives and I don't know how many mistresses? Give her my warmest greetings if you go and see her again. She can tell you many stories, slightly malicious, about Katus. I'd also like to hear her on my two wives. Perhaps she imagined she did, or perhaps the Hatvanis stayed longer in Oxford than I thought. It would especially interest me to know whether someone as shrewd as the Baroness diagnosed how badly things had gone wrong with Margaret. Did you hint anything to her of our relations? They would give her great pleasure. To Katus, on the other hand, never a word.

Well, that is all I had to say. I am copying Lloyd George's letters all day long so my head is full of endearments, so many I can hardly believe Frances believed them.

But you can believe mine.

Loving thoughts,

Alan
x x x

17 February

My Beloved,

I cannot write 'Beloved Girl' because it does not sound right in Hungarian. Lloyd George used to write 'My Girl' or 'My own Girl'. He also called Frances sweet or sweetheart, which I don't like much. Perhaps Beloved Lass, which is good North Country, would do. At any rate you are My Lass as much as Frances was Lloyd George's Girl, or even more so. The letters are curious. He was certainly cheating her – telling her how wearisome it was to be with his family when he was really enjoying himself. Was she sometimes cheating him? I think she deliberately aimed to keep him jealous and maybe, being a flirt, she did not have to try. It is difficult to imagine Frances, whom I only knew when she was over eighty, as a flighty and extremely sexual young woman.

Paris is always in my mind. Somehow it was different from everything that went before, more intimate, more secure. We had excursions that were perfect even when it rained. I go over our outing to

1974

St Denis – a rather squalid industrial town but a wonderful place to be in. The Cathedral had everything right for us – the wedding, the tombs of the kings, the slight confusion of it all. And do you remember that strange Moroccan restaurant where we had lunch? I remember it better than any other meal we ever had. Chartres ought to have been a failure with the ceaseless rain and the Cathedral too dark to see properly, to say nothing of being driven out of one restaurant because it would not give us a simple meal. Yet Chartres too was memorable for ever. One day we must go there again, see the Cathedral properly and think of the two bewitched lovers who walked there so happily in the rain. Sometimes one has luck in life, for me not often and so the more precious. So a special Thank You for those days.

It will not be long now before we are together – less than six weeks. Surely the weather in Yugoslavia will be fine this time. And Split is one of the best show places in the world. There is enough to see to keep us busy all week. The first hotel I wrote to did not answer. I have written to two more, one sounding rather luxurious which I think it would be fun to stop at just for a few days. I have one worry.

I am still going over *The Second World War*. Michael Howard did not find many faults except on small technical points. But I worry over the end. I want to explain why the Americans used the atom bombs without making too much of the idea that this was in part a gesture against Russia. And I am worried too about the origins of the Cold War. I am sure the sole motive of Russian policy was defensive, but they were also difficult people to negotiate with. On the other side, I think the Americans were assertive without knowing clearly how far they intended to go. They had a vision that the Russians could somehow be pushed back without war and had no idea how to do it. All this really needs a different book, but I can't leave events hanging in the air. I'll take my time and go on thinking, an unusual occupation for me. I am more accustomed to let the record speak for itself and merely write from one event to the next.

Our troubles go on. There is a general impression that the miners will be bought off after the election, but I think this will not be as easy as most people imagine. At the moment Heath looks likely to win. We shall have increasing inflation and as a consequence increasing unrest. Then world prices will begin to fall. There will be a new short-lived boom and the whole cycle will be repeated. It is generally thought that Wilson will retire from politics if he loses the election, and at present he is not making any impression. He seems to have lost his gifts if he ever had any. There is also a strange idea that we are the only people in trouble, when really Germany and Italy are in as bad a state, perhaps more so. Every country has its own reaction to crisis. The French always make a revolution. We have a general election and, if things are bad enough, a coalition government. The Germans and Italians have a dictator. I wonder if they will this time? Not a cheerful lookout.

The crisis has done me a lot of good. I have been interviewed by German, Dutch and Canadian television. The Dutch paid least but gave me a bottle of gin which I have drunk. The Canadians wanted to interview me in front of a lion, so I had to go to the Victoria Memorial outside Buckingham Palace and talk in a howling gale. The Canadian girl asked me at the end: 'What do you think of the monarchy?' I reflected and answered: 'I am afraid I never think about it at all.' She did not expect that answer. The Queen is somewhere in the Pacific – the first time I think a monarch has been out of the country during a general election.

Daniel has gone skiing in Switzerland for a week. I have to go for solitary walks. He departed in confusion, having mislaid half the things he needed for his holiday. Crispin tells me he has so much work to do that he never has time to think. He also tells me that a surprising number of people at Cambridge are interested in Christianity. At Magdalen our students are planning a sit-in to protest against the cost of their meals. So the whole world is on the move.

Tell me how your boys are doing and whether the books arrived. I expect they will take weeks and weeks. I also expect that your next letter will take a long time to come. That does not matter. We shall feel each other quite soon. Do not imagine the sea will be warm enough to swim in. It will look marvellous, but the looks are deceptive.

Lloyd George finished with loving messages in Welsh. I have to make do with English but the meaning is the same. It is just Love all the time.

Love all the time,

Guess who this letter is from

x

1974

18 February

Dearest,

I have your two cards of 9 and 12 February. We are in danger of getting into confusion about our travels. I had assumed that you would be coming by air. Sleeper to Zagreb may be more restful. But my recollection (from forty years ago) is that the train journey to Split is very wearisome. Would it not be more fun for us to fly together from Zagreb to Split? If all goes well I arrive at Zagreb airport at 13.50. There is an internal flight to Split at 16.10 and, if I miss that, another at 19.30. If you met my plane we should be together that much sooner. I can't get tickets or booking on the local plane here, but I should think you could. I'll pay whatever it costs. Just let me know. I can't tell you yet the name of the hotel in Split. None has replied. The Yugoslav agency here said they would all be empty in late March and that I did not need to book (which I am trying to do). This is another reason for meeting at Zagreb. Returning, I have to leave Split at 7.50 so maybe you'd do better to go by train. I hope this is not all too confusing.

Do not bring Wendt. *Captain Swing* I have already. I can't remember why I did not take a shower the last morning in Paris. Indeed I thought I did. Perhaps I couldn't find a towel. Or perhaps I decided I hated showers in comparison to a bath. In my last letter I forgot to tell you that, thinking about Paris, I want you so much that I call out to myself – Eva, Eva, with tears in my eyes. What a nuisance love is. Did you enjoy our telephone call Oxford–Budapest last week? The operator must have thought it was two lovesick youngsters.

Love, love, love,

Alan

28 February

Darling,

I answer your last letter of 21 February straight away, even though this is election day and I shall not know the results until tomorrow. Arrangements good. I'll expect you at Zagreb airport. If you fail to turn up (or I fail), the one who is there must go on to Split by the 19.30 plane. I'll let you know the name of the hotel as soon as I receive it. I'll send you £40 on Monday, a bit more than the fare in case you need it.

Of course I shall come to Split. We can't tell what will happen by September.

As to your other questions, I like *The Woodlanders* quite a lot and think *The Mayor of Casterbridge* one of the great novels of the world, much better than *Tess* or *Jude*. Do you know when the subscription to the *TLS* runs out? If not I will find out and renew it. It is a strange erratic journal, often very good and with some terrible highbrow rubbish. I am not a Magyarphobe and never have been. I was against the Magyar governing class, which is quite another thing. The proof is not only you but Michael.

Sophia is very well. Officially she stopped work on 19 February, but she invited her sixth form to her flat and is teaching them there. That is real devotion. She should have her baby in about a fortnight. She is also busy electioneering for a Trotskyite or something of the kind. Mary Taylor, Sebastian's wife, is also expecting a baby. She decided she must either go back to work as a secretary or have a third child, and it was pretty obvious which she preferred. I hope I've answered all your questions. I'll write again on 10 March or thereabouts unless some problem comes up earlier. Soon I shan't need to write at all. Think of kissing each other.

XX   Alan   xxxx

4 March

My Darling,

It is beginning to look as though I shall have to write to you every day between now and 29 March. I don't suppose you will object, nor shall I. Here is the new situation. I went today to book a single ticket from Zagreb to Split. The Yugoslav air office here answered that both flights on 29 March were fully booked, though they have put you on a reserved list. Now what shall we do? Can you perhaps discuss this with the Yugoslav air people in Budapest or telephone their office in Zagreb? If I hear of anything at this end I will inform you at once. Meanwhile, I have one air ticket but no seat for you. I think that unless we can get more certainty you had better go from Zagreb to Split by train. You can always get the money back for the ticket if you don't use it. I have sent you £40 so you will have enough money.

Therefore: (1) I assume that you will go by train unless you decide to risk it; (2) I will let you know at once if I get a seat for you; (3) the hotel at Split is the Marjan. We will meet there. (It looks rather grand and vulgar; if I hear from a more modest hotel I will let you know.) It was stupid of me not to get an air ticket for you originally. Like you it did not occur to me that the plane might be full. That's all of importance. If you decide firmly and finally to go by train, I'll cancel the air ticket I've booked. After all, the important thing is for us both to get to Split that evening. Let me know at once.

I'll try to telephone you about 10 p.m. on 13 March, and if necessary on 23 March (risky this, I shall probably have had too much to drink at a College dinner).

Oh, my darling, I long to be with you.

LOVE x x Alan

6 March

Darling,
Disregard my last letter. I have now heard from the travel agency that there is a place for you on the aircraft to Split. We'll hope to catch the 16.10. Otherwise we'll go on the 19.30. All you have to do is to go to the airport and wait for me to arrive at 13.50, or if not at 15.30. I'll know more precisely next week. In any case I shall have your ticket so there is nothing you can do except wait. I expect you'll recognize me – a bent, shuffling old man, probably in a wheelchair.

Love as ever,

Alan

16 March

Dearest Heart,
I have really nothing new to say after our telephone conversation on Wednesday evening. Everything is now arranged and we shall not need to change or discuss any more plans. I shall not telephone you next Saturday night, if only because, as I told you, I shall have had too much

to drink. I got an answer from a cheaper hotel at Split, but I thought it would be nice to have a few days of luxury. I hope it will not be too showy and without a Yugoslav character. The Dalmatian coast is more Italian than Yugoslav except in language. Even the food is Italian but better. I was thinking how agreeable it would be to swim in the covered bath in the afternoon and then go upstairs. Does the idea sound attractive to you? Particularly if it is sea water, and you will taste of salt.

I have written a lot more of my autiobiography. I've finished the chapter on my life in Manchester and Disley and have departed for Oxford. That chapter cheered me because I had liked Disley so much. The next chapter on my beginnings at Oxford and the collapse of my private life was horrible. It made me feel I wasn't fit for life any more and destroyed my self-confidence. I suppose the feeling will pass but at present I am in a melancholic mood, looking back at thirty years of a wasted, unhappy life. It really was bad luck that this should happen to me. I shall not be depressed when I arrive at Split.

I collected Crispin from Cambridge yesterday. He is growing up fast, already quite different from the schoolboy I took to Cambridge six months ago. I'm glad to say he voted Labour after threatening at one time to vote Liberal. He is going on a student visit to Russia in September, so perhaps you will meet him. Daniel claims to have a girl-friend, which is good news also.

That's all. I shall not write again, and I hope there will be nothing to telephone about. I expect I shall have no dinars on me, so will be glad of a few until I can cash my cheques. I hope you got £40 from me. It is a wonder that sterling still has any value.

With very much LOVE,

        Alan

15 April

My Dearly Beloved Darling,

 Never before have I felt so completely empty and barren as when I left you. Except for you there is nothing in life that interests me. Without you I am incomplete, not properly a person. Somehow we must come together. As you well know, I see all the difficulties and they often overwhelm me. But we must overcome them. It is no good writing about these problems. You will only misunderstand and think that I am making excuses to do nothing. On the contrary, I want to clear them out of the way. I think that while I am alive I can manage for us both. What worries is what will happen to you afterwards. You will laugh at this and say it does not matter. But it does. You must somehow keep a Hungarian life going and yet we must be more together. Please think over these things. Don't write about them. We will talk them over and solve them when I come to Hungary in September. If you don't feel like writing or lose faith in me, don't bother. I shall go on writing and in time we shall find a way out.

Now no more about us except to say that every minute with you was precious. My subsequent adventures were rather ridiculous. I had an easy flight to Zagreb and on to Rome. There no one even mentioned the question of money, so I had worried quite unnecessarily. Then things went wrong. Our plane to Venice was delayed for nearly two hours. In fact it never arrived. A reserve plane was brought into service and it too proved faulty for another hour. As a result I arrived in Venice airport at six o'clock instead of at three. I seized a taxi and arrived at Mestre with one minute to spare. I climbed into a first-class compartment and walked up and down the train looking for the boys. They were not there! I was in despair. I thought something bad had happened in England, or that their aeroplane had crashed. I changed at Ferrara, and had a very inadequate meal in the station buffet, and went to the right platform for my train to Ravenna. There was some announcement over the loudspeaker that I did not understand. Timidly I enquired and was told the Ravenna train had been moved to another platform. I arrived there just in time to see it going out. I was again in despair. I felt I must get to Ravenna, where an urgent message from the boys would surely be waiting for me. So I took a taxi which cost me 14,000 lire, say £10. At Ravenna no message and no boys. I went to bed suffering from indigestion after eating nothing but bread all day long. At midnight Crispin knocked at my door. Their plane too had been late, but they had the sense to catch the last train. So all ended well, with me feeling as though I had been through an ordeal.

Ravenna was marvellous, one Byzantine church after another. The boys enjoyed it as much as I did. We moved on to Venice, where we stopped in a *pension* in the next street to ours. The food was much better, indeed the best food I have had in Venice. Living conditions not so good. No shower or bath, and I kept myself clean for ten days solely with a bidet. It works all right and proved that baths are unnecessary. The boys enjoyed Venice very much. They are now old enough to appreciate it, and they remembered just enough from their last visit to feel at home. Daniel went off on his own whenever he felt like it.

There is no need to tell you what we saw. We went to the Correr gallery and saw the Carpaccio. We went to the icon gallery. Santa Maria dei Miracoli has now been marvellously restored with, I think, English money. The Romanesque church which you and I failed to get into has now been restored also. Very good, one of the best things in Venice and a relief after so much bad Gothic and Baroque. Ca'Oro is still of course closed for repairs. I don't suppose it will open in my lifetime. One day we made a trip to see Grado and Aquileia, two great basilicas. We had a row over where to eat lunch. We also had to wait until half-past seven for a train back and it was desperately cold. But worth the trip. Italy is very expensive, much more than Yugoslavia. I still have some Italian money left, but my next trip there, if it ever comes, will be my last. I drank much grappa, also met what the boys called two 'trendy Hampstead intellectuals'.

Good journey back. I've finished the book on Stalin, and also the one by Hingley, which is awful. I am now reading yet a third by Ulam, which is much the best though also much the longest. All three are absurdly anti-Bolshevik, though of course it is difficult to write sympathetically or even impartially about Stalin when you think of the Terror and the purges. Yet he was more than just a tyrant. If he went mad before the end, it was because of the terrible problems he had had to face. In a way he is in the end a rather sad and even endearing character, truly trying to do his best and driven wild by his temper which he couldn't control. Still he made Great Russia.

Tomorrow I shall go to the Library and send you the photocopy of Hauser and also the little guide to the Library. Next week I am going to St Andrews to lecture on 'The Coming of the Second World War'. In other ways I am rather gloomy.

Other news. Sophia is well but not yet delivered of her baby. What I want is you. Whenever I am really black and miserable, I think of you and of all the things I meant to do and say and it cheers me up. So you do the same. Remember how badly I need you.

I'll write again in a fortnight's time and report on St Andrews.

Much love and much longing,

Alan

1974

28 April

Dearly Beloved,

    The postal service must be improving. At any rate I got your letter on Friday when I returned from St Andrews. And what a lovely letter it was. It consoles me a little when you write that you are happy, and I know that it is partly due to me. I am the same. Often miserable at the bad way my life has turned out, and then reflecting that I have had at least one stroke of luck. I suppose, as you can see from my autobiography, I never had any ambition and so am not cheered up by my own success. Indeed I now despise most of my books, though not all. Even the ones that are reasonably good don't seem to me any longer worth writing. I'd like to be remembered for *The Troublemakers* and *English History 1914–1945*. I don't care about the others. I even rather resent having spent so much time on *Beaverbrook*. I had to get him out of my system, but now I don't think he was worth it. Lady Beaverbrook has now arrived in England and threatens to take me to the races, a prospect I do not like at all. I suppose I shall have to go some time, otherwise she will think I dislike her as most people do. I don't dislike her, I am merely sorry for her and so have to be kind to her reluctantly.

    I spent the whole of the week after I had written to you reading the three books on Stalin, as I told you I would. You will find a review of them in today's *Observer*, which I will cut out for you if I remember. They are all three far too long and stuffed with silly Cold War ideas. I criticized them, but at least I read them conscientiously. The book in German by Doherty is not worth sending to you. It merely recapitulates what we know from the British archives. The argument, not altogether unsound, is that the British government dropped appeasement after Prague, or at any rate pushed it into the background, and instead tried to stop Hitler by giving guarantees to all the east European countries. The absurd idea was that if these countries got British guarantees they would resist Hitler and thus Great Britain would not need to fight. Did you ever hear anything madder? I'll only give the book a few lines in the *English Historical Review*. I am writing a long review of the Fischer *Festschrift** for the *Journal of Modern History*, but there is not much more I can do than catalogue the pieces. There is a very good piece on the Russian bogey by an old boy called Epstein, otherwise nothing of great value. I expect the book will reach your Institute. If it doesn't, I will send it to you. I suppose Hauser's book better come back to me, seeing

---

* Publication on occasion of a celebration or in honour of a person.

that I gave it to the Library. But I don't think anyone in the Library will ever read it, so keep it as long as you like or even for ever.

Now for my expedition to St Andrews. I had a delicious journey in a first-class sleeper, a form of travel I always enjoy but can only use when paid for by others. I had a good hotel. In the evening they gave me dinner – not a good one. Then we went to the lecture. I said, How big an audience? Oh, a hundred students and twenty or thirty staff. As we approached the lecture hall we saw a queue stretching as far as eye could see. All the arrangements had to be changed. They moved to another hall which held 1,500 instead of 200, and even then they only just got them in. The move took half an hour, which effectively killed the idea of questions afterwards.

Earlier in the day three students took me out to lunch. One of them, who had read *The Origins of the Second World War* (another book I'm not particularly proud of), said to me: 'Why are you lecturing on a subject which you fully covered fifteen years ago?' I said: 'Wait until tonight and you will find not one sentence is the same.' So it proved. I explained that my book had the wrong title. It was really only about the origins of a minor war in Europe, a war that ended in June 1940. That is when the origins of the real World War began. I greatly enjoyed myself, mainly because I was working this idea out fully for the first time. It makes a very good lecture. Someone should do a book on it. But it needs, I think, a knowledge of both Russian and Japanese and I can manage neither. As I argued it out, I was struck very forcibly by the fact that Hitler's long-term anti-Bolshevism was a sham. His concern was to pretend to be an anti-Bolshevik so as to cheat the West. He made no preparations for war with Russia until late in 1940, and I think his main idea was to eliminate Russia so that England would give in. He didn't attack Russia because she was great or dangerous but because he thought it would be easy. And of course the Japanese never wanted war with America – nor America with them. It made a splendid lecture, maybe the best I have ever given. But it is all too easy. I am like a tennis player who goes on the court knowing that he is going to win. Of course I have to try hard all the same. More than one person said to me afterwards: 'I have never heard a lecture like that in my life before.' And I said: 'And you never will again.' A very satisfactory visit, and I never noticed how tired I was until I got back to London.

Now here is an odd story. If you remember my autobiography at all – and why should you? – you may remember a school friend I had called George Clazy who killed himself for love of a girl. I tried to play older brother to Bob, George's younger brother. He too had matrimonial troubles and got himself deliberately killed during the war because his

1974

wife had betrayed him in some way. He left a small son. Coming down by train from St Andrews, a smart middle-aged businessman got in opposite me. He worked on his papers for some time and then said: 'Excuse me, are you———?' I thought he had recognized me from television and said: 'Yes, I am Alan Taylor.' He then told me he was Michael Clazy, Bob's son, and had always known that I was his father's best friend. So I said: 'Now you have found a godfather.' Wasn't that touching? He got out at Edinburgh and I read Doherty's boring book all the way to London.

On Tuesday night when I left for St Andrews, Sophia was going to motor me to the station. But she failed me by going off to hospital the same morning and had her baby half an hour before I caught my train. A girl whom she has called Rosa. You can no doubt guess why, though hardly anyone in England has ever heard of Rosa Luxembourg. Sophia is very well. Rosa has got jaundice, which I am told is common with newly-born babies though I have never heard of it before. I shall buy Rosa an icon which she can receive as a present when she grows up. The girls Sophia teaches like her so much that they have already been to see her in hospital. I am sorry to say she has weakened on her principles. She calls herself McGibbon, which is the name of her former husand. She lives with Rob Howard and now, though not married to him, she is agreed that Rosa shall be called Howard too. I said I thought she should be called Rosa Taylor, but this idea met with no support.

Crispin has departed to Cambridge, where he says everything is very boring. Daniel is reading *The Sound and the Fury* by Faulkner, which I do not envy at all. Politics have been quiet over Easter but there is plenty of trouble to come. Prices are going up faster than ever. The motor industry is approaching collapse. Michael Foot is having a great success with the unions, but one day his Menshevik charms will be exhausted. I am as gloomy as ever about the future but have decided not to worry about it. The only future that matters is ours, and we must settle it when I come out in September. One thing I do not understand. Things will get progressively worse and the Conservatives naturally are deliberately keeping Labour in office. But why does Labour cling to office when disaster clearly lies ahead? Why don't they provoke a crisis and force the Conservatives to turn them out? I am at a loss. The French presidential election is very funny. I don't think de Gaulle foresaw that his own constitution might one day be used to bring a Communist-Socialist coalition to power. And what price Willy Brandt with an East German spy as his closest adviser?

Oh dear, I have gone on and on just because I wanted to talk to you. I hope my talk has not bored you. You know the other things I want to say. I love you. I miss you. I am incomplete without you. And I count on your love as something that will hold us together for ever. By the way, tell your boys that their notecase enabled me to smuggle lire into Italy, though the smuggling turned out to be unnecessary. Give them my greeting.

Love, Love, Love and Love,
Alan

6 May

Darling,

You will be surprised perhaps to get a letter from me so early. I spent the entire weekend reading *The Treaty Breakers** and now write while it is all fresh in my mind. It is a really competent professional job. You explain exactly how the proposal for a 35% limit came up on either side, how it was discussed and what followed from it. Now, having said your book is technically faultless, I will start arguing with your general approach. As you may remember I (who know much less on the subject than you) attributed the Anglo-German treaty to two motives, which were inter-connected: (i) anxiety about the Far East and desire to free the fleet for action against Japan; (ii) desire to clear the way for the 1936 conference. You give plenty of evidence regarding the first. You hardly mention the second. Did it really not come up at all? Or is it that you were not interested?

Your book makes the story clearer and simpler. The Germans wanted to separate England from the Stresa front. They therefore offered the 35% limit. The British jumped at this, and that's the whole story. Now here is a point where I disagree with you. You repeatedly ascribe the treaty to appeasement, and of course the British themselves often said that it was silly to go on imposing Versailles on the Germans. But was the treaty all that appeasing? It was the Germans who proposed it, which you might call appeasement on their side. The British accepted it as a good bargain. This seems to me sensible. If the Germans stuck to their word for good and all, then the treaty was a great gain for the British. Even if the Germans only kept their word for a few years, the British gained. The British were not at all deceived. Indeed, as far as I

---

* Eva's book on the Anglo-German Naval Aggreement of 1935.

1974

can see from your book they did not slow down their building programme at all because of the treaty. Of course the same is true of the Germans. Hitler had already decided not to build a battle fleet and not to bother much about submarines. Presumably he would have done this without the treaty. In fact both parties behaved exactly as they would have done without the treaty. If the British had surrendered Austria for instance, in exchange for the treaty, that would have been appeasement. But they didn't. Before the First World War the Germans refused an armaments agreement unless (i) the British limited their fleet; also (ii) the British made a political agreement as well. Hitler did not make either condition. I don't say the treaty made much difference. But as far as it made a difference it brought gain to the British. All this I deduce from the evidence in your book.

Here are two criticisms. I should have liked you to carry the statements about the size of the German and British fleets further. It would be interesting to have the exact figures at the outbreak of war. If, as I think, the Germans were behindhand with their building, this would show that they had observed the treaty limits. The deficiency in submarines was surely very grave and could be said to have lost Germany the war. Something has gone wrong with your account of the Japanese navy on p. 79. You say that nine out of her ten battleships were sunk already in December 1941. This should surely be December 1944 or something like that. On the next line it should read *Yamamoto* (sunk in a last desperate attempt to relieve Iwo Jima). It really would have been a help to have the figures for all three navies, and maybe the French. I thought you rather skipped over the American side, but perhaps there is not much material.

Second criticism. You accept contemporary left-wing gossip too much. Sir John Simon was supposed to have betrayed the League over Manchuria. You'll find if you look that he had operated very skilfully and actually brought the fighting to an end. Simon was not second rate or failing in health. He had a cold, unattractive personality, but he was very able. I don't understand the reference in the footnote bracket on p. 41 that Halifax succeeded Simon, or maybe I have misunderstood it. I don't think that Hoare was a tired or ageing man when he became Foreign Secretary. That was a story put over to excuse the Hoare-Laval plan. Like Simon, Hoare was very able though without a strong personality. In 1939 he was the only one to press really hard for the Soviet alliance. You overrate Eden, who was a poor soft creature as everyone now recognizes. People no longer believe in the Cliveden set. It was invented by Claud Cockburn as a joke (like most of *The Week**). Genuine analysis of the visitors to Cliveden shows that they were of all

---

* Satirical magazine, edited by Cockburn in the 1930s.

sorts. The main feature of the Cliveden weekends was not agreement on appeasement, but argument over everything. Don't attach too much importance to Vansittart's opinions. They were hot air. And in general, before dismissing the appeasers of 1935 so firmly, surely you should ask – what else could they do or should they have done? The Germans were going to break the disarmament clauses of Versailles. No one was going to compel them to observe them, the British public least of all. The British Admiralty wanted to avoid an arms race. Bullying the Germans had been tried by the French. It had failed. Negotiating was the alternative. This would have been a mistake only if it had led the British to cut down their rearmament, and I don't think it did. One other thing I'd have liked: after the various papers on defence requirements, I'd have liked to know how far the proposals were carried out – e.g. how many battleships when war broke out, Singapore, etc. You ought to have sent the book to me to correct the English. On p. 23 'deception' should be 'disappointment'. Dill was John, not Jack. Altogether a very fine achievement.

I'll write again soon.

x
Love
Alan

12 May

My Dearest and Only Love,

The posts are improving. I got your letter of 6 May on 9 May, only three days later, and it was a joy. Now let me answer your questions. St Andrews is on the coast of Fife, about forty miles north of Edinburgh and fifteen south of Dundee. It is the oldest university in Scotland, with a cathedral which was destroyed at the Reformation. The Reformers, led by John Knox, hanged the archbishop from the walls of his own castle. Before the war it had 10,000 inhabitants and 600 students. Now it has 11,000 inhabitants and 6,000 students, so you can imagine the townsfolk feel rather eclipsed. I, too, heard from Hauser and said I couldn't come. Besides, I don't want to meet historians any more. I've learnt all I can from them.

I have done nothing, seen nothing, been to no concerts – mainly because Daniel could not make up his mind until too late whether he

1974

wanted to go or not. The weather has been fine but cold, until today when it is mild and rainy. The petrol shortage is over, though petrol had doubled in price. I shall have to give up my car soon, partly because it is too expensive, partly because I am getting old.

I have started on the Lloyd George letters and am gloomy about them also. I can't see that they will make a readable book, but there is no way of finding out except to put them together with explanations and see what they look like. But I dislike the idea of probably wasting my time. Veronica called at the Library the other day. She was as elegant as ever – no make-up incidentally – and also as uncommunicative. When I asked what she had been doing, she only said she had been very busy.

The economic situation is still bad and likely to go worse. Prices rise faster than ever and industry is slowing down. Of course history never repeats itself, but there are many signs that we are approaching a crisis on the level of the nineteen-thirties. What happens to capitalism and unending prosperity if we have another Depression with millions of unemployed? We all thought Fascism was dead. But will it stay dead? Sebastian tells me the storm will really blow in the autumn and that it will take at least four years for the capitalist world to recover. Of course he is guessing like everyone else. By a strange chance every leading figure in the Western world is discredited. Nixon is nearly finished, Brandt is out, here we have financial scandals which are going to hit some high-placed Labour men, no certain President in France, Italy near to chaos. In fact Italy is bankrupt. With import controls her economy will run down. And then what? I have still lots of lire and would like to spend them before it is too late. But I can see no way of doing it unless by any chance you can come to Italy, which I know you can't.

So are you surprised that I can't plan about the future? We really must see more clearly first. But be overwhelmingly sure about one thing. I love you all the time, think about you much of the time, count on your love as my inspiration. I am weak and hesitant whatever you may think to the contrary, but that does not alter my love for you. It is not just theory. I think about every little episode of our life together, silly little things which you have forgotten, but which make me laugh and feel happy. I could tell you so many things I noticed about you in Paris or at Split. I also remember our silly and unnecessary walk to the bus terminus and the seat at Trogir where we sat out and looked at the sea.

My last letter about your book was an extra one. I will send a copy to Marder when it arrives. And I shall write again in a fortnight's time. I need you very much, oh so much. So pray for the recovery of capitalism, and keep your fingers crossed (English expression).

Love now and always,

Alan

25 May

Darling,

I can't remember whether I am due to write this weekend or next. Never mind: maybe you will get an extra letter. I tried to telephone last Wednesday evening and actually got through to Budapest. But you were engaged, or so the operator said. I will try again in a few days' time – nothing to say except that I want to hear your voice. At present you seem far away and I feel utterly lost. I wish my life would come to an end. The economic situation here is terrible. Prices go up every day, and soon the pound will be almost worthless. It is all right for workers and such-like who can push up their wages, but it is ruin for those with fixed incomes. I can't see at all what is going to happen to me, and I am too old to discover new ways of earning a living. The only consolation is that there are many thousands in the same position.

I am beginning to think about coming to Hungary. The situation has become a little complicated. I am a little frightened about coming. I shall feel very lost not knowing a word of the language, and I shall be embarrassed if I meet any of your friends – that does not apply to your boys of course. Will it not lead to gossip and scandal if we are together on the Danube? You know best. If you think it will cause no trouble, of course I'll come. But if you have any hesitations we must think of something else. My money will still be worth something, though not for long. So we could make an expedition somewhere if you thought that better – maybe somewhere in Hungary or back to Yugoslavia. You will know what to decide. But we must meet somehow.

One thing puzzles me. Do you have no inflation in Hungary? Oil prices have gone up all over the world. Surely that affects your transport charges and the factories that use oil. There must be many things you import from the Western world and that must push prices up also. I do all the shopping and I am staggered to notice how much prices go up between one weekend and the next. There seems no reason why this should ever stop. I wish you were with me. All these troubles would seem less if we were together. How delicious it would be if you were still in Paris and I could come over to see you. We arranged things very badly not to be more together when it was possible. But it seemed safe then to put things off for the future.

No letter from you. I don't expect one in the ordinary way, but I am anxious to know that you are not cross with my remarks on your book. You can see how carefully I read it and how I appreciated it. My one academic activity was to give a talk to a seminar in Oxford last week on 'The Soviet Problem in British Policy', going right back to the Bolshevik revolution. It is a very interesting subject in which Great Power rivalries, fears of international revolution and anxiety about Communism at home are all mixed up. Someone should write a really detached book about it – not like those dreadful American books about Stalin. I can't understand why the Americans have been so much more anti-Communist than anyone else since the very earliest days. I suppose it is anger that someone else has eclipsed them as the truly democratic state. Also of course a system of individual liberty soon allows the class struggle to develop until it is quite out of hand. However, it is too late in life for me to learn about the Americans.

Last Tuesday I had dinner with Lord Coleraine, the only surviving son of Bonar Law who, as you may remember, was Prime Minister after Lloyd George and died in 1922. The son too seems to have died in 1922 in a sort of way. Life stopped for him when he ceased to be the son of a prime minister, and he has drifted through life constantly thinking and talking about the days when he thought himself important. A strange fate.

I have read nothing except for a book in French about the Third Reich and Switzerland. Very interesting in its way. The Swiss managed to combine conciliation and obstinacy. They gave in over supplying Germany, but they never weakened over their defence of the free press and they firmly suppressed any Nazi organizations in Switzerland. The most curious point of the story is that all the plans for getting Switzerland under German control – whether economic or political or even military – came from subordinate officials acting on their own. You get the impression that Nazi Germany for all its apparent dictatorship was an anarchy with all kinds of officials playing their separate games. As a further curiosity, whenever on rare occasions these plans against Switzerland came to Hitler's notice he rejected them and said – leave Switzerland alone.

Evidently his passions were not engaged and he took a completely realistic line. For Hitler there were no practical gains to be made by conquering Switzerland, and it was silly in wartime to fuss over the idea of bringing the Swiss back to German nationalism. Also he was afraid that the Italians would grab too much!

Politics are frightening and also funny. Northern Ireland is in a state of anarchy, with all the schemes for a better future destroyed. I can see no policy except for the British troops to withdraw and let the Protestants and Catholics fight it out. I think the Protestants will win. Harold Wilson has made his secretary a peeress, just to show that he cares nothing for public opinion. I can't think of any previous case and it brings the House of Lords even more into contempt than it is already. It is sad that the Left did not win in France, but I don't suppose it would have made much difference. As to poor Willie Brandt, women have been his ruin. Take warning. I am hard at work on Lloyd George with something of the same idea in mind.

I miss you very much. You are all I have in life now that my children are grown up. So I am feeling depressed that you are so far away. Think of me occasionally and let me know what you think about September.

All the love in the world,

Alan

9 June

Darling of my Heart,

It cheered me greatly to hear your voice the other night. I had begun to think that you were ill or that you had forgotten me. But there is no need to write when you don't feel like it. I am a systematic person and write regularly. Also I count the days until the second Sunday comes round and I can sit at my typewriter. As I told you I have been depressed, but there is nothing to be done about it.

I am also depressed about public affairs. Inflation gets worse every week, and my income is beginning to run down as I get older and work less or have fewer ideas. Some authorities expect a world slump by the autumn, though of course they pretend it will not be severe. I think it will be worse than the Depression of the Thirties. Then I was young and could face it. Now I can't. The only thing I live for is to see you in September. That is not far off now.

1974

The most interesting thing for you is that Alistair Parker, whom you no doubt remember, has written an article in the April *English Historical Review* on the Abyssinian crisis of 1935–36. He has a certain amount from the Admiralty papers about the situation in the Mediterranean, though he does not add anything to what we know from Marder. But he has a lot more on negotiations with the French. The British government thought France was essential as a counterweight against Germany, and so could not threaten Laval. Similarly Laval needed British support against Germany and yet would not go against Italy. So they all cheated. The Hoare-Laval plan, or something like it, was discussed in the Cabinet before Hoare went to Paris, and everyone approved it including Eden. After it had been made, the Cabinet again approved though they thought Hoare had gone rather far. They ran away purely because of public opinion and made Hoare take the blame. The funniest bit of information is that the most stalwart supporter of the League and collective security was Sir John Simon. Now you did not expect that, did you? There is less about 1936. The British experts said there was no chance of Mussolini's conquering Abyssinia before the rains came, and therefore he would have to compromise. The League was going to triumph after all. Final news: when sanctions were called off, Eden was just as strongly in favour of doing this as any other member of the Cabinet, and it was pure accident that Neville Chamberlain, not Eden, first announced it in public. Of all undeserved reputations, Eden's is the worst.

After the countless lives of Hitler and Stalin, the lives of Churchill are now beginning, especially as it is his centenary year. There is nothing new in them. The more historians look at the official records, the lower Churchill's reputation appears. He had great gifts of inspiration and driving people, but he had no judgement. Marder quotes Roosevelt as saying: 'Winston has a hundred ideas every day and four of them are right.' I have also read a life of Bukharin by an American called Cohen. It is not really a life, but an analysis of his ideas particularly when he was Stalin's partner between 1925 and 1928. He invented the idea of a genuine alliance between peasants and workers, much as I suppose now operates in China, and this made him of course the advocate of producing consumer goods. When Russian industry failed at this, the peasants became discontented and the kulak war began. But the alliance between peasants and workers comes up again whenever Communism takes a less extreme line. In fact Cohen ends by presenting Bukharin as the truly wise Communist. I wonder? A curious thing about Bukharin is that he never did any work except write newspaper articles. He never held an executive post even when he was No. 2, or even equal top, in the Politburo. I can understand why Stalin became impatient with him, though there is still no explanation why he was killed. You get the impression that it happened automatically.

Here is a reason for cheerfulness. In August I am coming back to television in a weekly discussion programme after fifteen years of absence. The others are not very exciting: Enoch Powell; Lord George-Brown; and Woodrow Wyatt. Powell, though very clever, will I think be too pompous and slow for quick argument. George-Brown may well drink too much, even though the performance is at midday. [Journalist] Woodrow Wyatt, whom you have probably never heard of, is a former Labour MP who has gone Right. He will be quite lively but superficial. Maybe there is no one better. The reason for the revival is funny also. The television companies have been told that, unless they raise the intellectual level of their programmes, their contracts will not be renewed. So we are being put on purely as window-dressing. Once they get their contracts, I expect the show will be killed. So I had better make the most of it.

I haven't had a letter from you yet so can't comment on any of your news. There will be more to say when I get your letter. Our postal service is chaotic. Letters take two or three days even in England, and often weeks abroad. I had a visit from Lucia Biocca the other day. A letter I wrote to her in Rome had taken six weeks to reach her. Her daughter is no longer a Buddhist. Her elder son who is studying psychology is now running into psychological difficulties himself. This often happens. It is a good thing we do not live in Italy, where things are worse even than they are here.

Events in Northern Ireland prove what I have always known, that two communities cannot live together once they become conscious of their separate existence. Different religions, like different nationalities, have to be sorted out. Opinion here is coming round to this view.

This is a dull letter, but it shows I am thinking of you constantly. The memories of Split grow upon me and I am now beginning to think that it was the best time we had. But then all our times have been good, except that you were less happy at Venice than I thought you were. Be happy at the thought of me and of our common memories. And be sure that I shall go on loving you.

Love and love and love,
x
x   Alan
x

1974

22 June

My Darling,

What a miraculous thing the telephone is. One moment I was sitting in my room in Oxford, and the next was transported to you in Budapest. It was nice for once to hear your boy's voice. I hope they teased you a little afterward: 'Your lover is on the 'phone.' Did they say something like that? Our little talk has, I hope, fixed our plans. I shall have enough money to come by plane and I'll bring some with me as well, unless of course there is a complete financial crash in this country by then, as there may be. If money still holds out, we will go to Okhrid in the spring. I've provisionally fixed in my mind to come on 10 September and to stay for ten days. Would that be all right for you? Perhaps, if I have money enough, we could go to an hotel in the mountains for two or three days just to be by ourselves. I'm nervous about coming, not because I am worried about your boys, but because I shall feel so strange in Hungary. But don't worry, I shall come. Don't arrange for me to meet people except for Mme Hatvani, whom I should like to see. You are quite wrong that I like arranging things. I don't. I do it on holiday because I want to think of things that will amuse us both. But I'd much rather be peaceful with you and not have to decide what we should do the next day.

Things here are in a very bad state. Prices are going up faster than ever, and wages with them. But what is the good of that to me who do not live on wages? I can't push up my fees, and the money simply vanishes away. We are going to have a terrible crisis from which I can see no way out. There will be a slump, great unemployment, and then some sort of National government with a reactionary programme. Will there be riots or revolution? I do not know. But however much one wants revolution in theory, it is no fun when you are old. Like everyone else I have saved for my old age, but my savings and my pension will be worthless. I dread the thought that I may be driven to go to America just to keep alive. Truly I'd rather be dead. Perhaps some of these terrible things will never happen. And after all, there are many people much worse off than I am. So let's forget about it and think only of September.

I am still slaving away on Lloyd George's letters and begin to think they will take some sort of shape. Perhaps they will make a new fortune for me. Today I am going on television to talk about the paperback of *Beaverbrook* and I hope that will push up the sales. Tomorrow I am going to a concert to hear Verdi's *Te Deum* and a Berlioz symphony. Crispin got a first class in the first part of his mathematics examination. It looks as though he really is good at it.

There is a long and very boring life of Churchill by Henry Pelling, always a dull writer. You would not think he could make Churchill dull, but he has. I am going to call my review 'No Warts'. You know what Cromwell said when someone was going to paint his portrait: 'Show me warts and all' (his face was covered with them). Well, Pelling has managed to describe Churchill with no faults and no failures. Not a Churchill I remember. I wrote a long article about Fritz Fischer for the *Journal of Modern History*, and as the editor had some justified criticisms I wrote it all over again. Now I am really pleased with it. The First World War and its origins has a new boom, mainly because of interest in Fischer's works. I have picked it up and am lecturing about it as a change from lecturing always about the Second. It is really much more difficult and I suppose was more decisive. That was the time that finished European civilization, and we have been waiting for the crash ever since.

I took the boys to see *Pygmalion* last week. I had forgotten what a bad play it was – clever things by Shaw of course. But he was hopeless on the relations between men and women, and so could not decide what Higgins and Eliza really felt, if they felt anything. He meant *Pygmalion* to be his *Doll's House*, but there was no passion in it and no tension. Or perhaps it is that I don't like the theatre.

Here's a funny story. A Scotch girl I met in Vienna in 1930 sent me a long letter of abuse, saying how I had trifled with her affections and what an evil man I was. I only met her a couple of times, had no interest in her, and had long forgotten that she existed. And she had been storing up her resentment all these years, or else she has gone slightly mad as old women sometimes do. At that time I was in love with Else Sieberg, the Viennese girl I told you about, and had no thought for anyone else. I tore up the Scotch girl's letter and hope I shan't hear from her again. But it is a warning that one's past can suddenly catch up with you – not that I have the slightest reason to feel guilty in this case.

We have had some fine weather at last. I have been swimming and sunbathing at Highgate Ponds every day and really prefer it to going away on holiday. What is more it is free, so I don't have to worry about inflation.

I nearly forgot one bit of news for you. As well as Alistair Parker's article on the Abyssinian crisis, there is a new book on it by Frank Hardie, not as good as Parker's article but more systematic. Hardie has still the contemporary delusion that the League could have saved Abyssinia and so prevented the Second World War. I don't take that view as you know. Stopping Mussolini would not have stopped Hitler, and making an alliance with Mussolini would also not have stopped him.

September will soon be here and we can talk of these things. We can enjoy each other's company. These are the thoughts that keep me going.

And here is all my love, my dear,

Alan

12 July

My Darling, My Dearly Beloved,

Your adorable letter came yesterday and I am writing before the weekend so that you should get my letter all that earlier. I love you so much. Now here are my practical arrangements. I shall come to Budapest on Monday 23 September, arriving by British Airways at 14.15. I shall go to the air terminal in Budapest and wait for you there. I have to bring £30 in florint vouchers with me, which I suppose I use in hotels or perhaps can give to you. I'll also bring £100 in travellers' cheques if I can manage it. Now that is all the practical side.

You told me not to talk or write about the future, and now you have done it instead. Or at any rate you have written about my not marrying you. When we were last together I tried to explain the insuperable economic difficulties. When I talked originally about the future, I foresaw an increasing prosperity both for myself and for this country. You can't realize how near we are to catastrophe. Many serious judges think that all our banks may close their doors in a few months' time. Prices have doubled within the year and are going up faster than ever. My income does not go up. Indeed, it gradually goes down as I write less. The *Sunday Express* does not use me any more. My pension and my insurance policies which will start in two years' time are calculated according to the pounds I paid in the past, and these are now worth only a few shillings. You must remember a time in Hungary when all pensioners, including even professors, were starving or very near it, and we may come to that soon. I can't plan a future until I can see some chance of a more secure one. I know I worry too much. But I assure you many people worry more. Nearly everyone except the wealthy capitalists and the industrial workers are frightened out of their wits. And I've only described the lesser dangers. We might have civil war and Fascism, or some other form of dictatorship. At any rate the crisis is far worse than 1931 and we know what that led to.

I hate our separation as much as you do. Apart from you I have no one to care for. Of course I have Crispin and Daniel, but I am increasingly cut off from them. And now guess what worse thing has happened? I was planning to go to the Lake District with them on 22 July, and now there is a strike at the refineries which has cut off the supply of petrol in the north of England. If it lasts we can't go. You can't understand how deeply unhappy I am, hating life apart from you, resentful that things should have gone so wrong for me. Why me, I keep asking? I have truly had a ghastly life for more than thirty years. Writing my autobiography after the Second War, I hated it so much I could not get on with it. You are the only woman I have really genuinely loved. I love you. Tell me how to solve the economical problems of western Europe and we can marry straight away. We shall discuss this when we meet.

Now I must stop this soul-searching and answer your questions. If your boys go to Bulgaria, I know a very nice historian called Bogidar who took me round some years ago. I'll try and find his address. Poor fellow, he was writing a thesis on the Congress of Berlin – could anything be drearier? Daniel cannot start driving lessons until he is seventeen on 10 August.

I'd like to meet your friends when I come to Budapest, though I shall be shy and embarrassed. I'm not keen to meet historians. You see, I am not really interested in history any more except when I am writing it. Also I don't want my visit to get around to Katus, who would make mischief out of it. My holiday plans: 22 July to 3 August in the Lake District if the petrol is there. 16 to 27 August in the Isle of Wight with my grown-up family and all their brood (including four step-children of Sophia's).

No, I don't think I shall write anything on Churchill. There are too many already. However, I am to deliver a centenary oration on him at Leeds University in the autumn. As to the television series, it is a great event. Years ago, from 1950 to 1959, I took part with three others in a weekly programme called first 'In The News' and then 'Free Speech' when we sat round a table and argued about current affairs. It was finally killed by political pressure because the politicians were jealous of it. Now one of the television companies has decided to revive it. I am the only survivor of the original four. (W. J. Brown is dead; Boothby has become too garrulous; Michael Foot is out as a minister.) It looks as if I shall be the only Left speaker, and I'm not very reliable in that role. If all goes well, the series after running for eight Sundays will start again in the autumn and might run for years. At any rate it is very important that I should be there all eight Sundays so that I can re-establish myself as a television personality. Maybe I shall be no good. Pray for me on 4 August at 12.30 p.m.

The Lloyd George love letters are going well. I have transcribed about half of them. I have put them in their historical setting and explained enough to keep the readers happy. You ask what is in them? Why, love of course. Passionate longings. Emotional memories. He must have been a rather violent lover. His letters are full of threats: I shall squeeze you, crush you, you must be strong when I return. You will need all your strength and energy. Alas, I was never like that.

Still, I think I have written you quite a good love letter. Why don't I go to America? Because there are no good buildings to see and no good food to eat. Also their inflation is running at 20% – more than ours. You can't imagine how awful it is when prices go up every day. But I mustn't start on that again. I shall write before I go to the Lake District – if I go.

Devotion, Love, Longing, and thoughts for our wonderful coming time together.

XXX
Alan

20 July

Darling,

This is not a real letter, only a message to say that I am alive and reasonably well. Actually I feel not at all well today. I think I have been working too hard, or perhaps am merely weighed down by the troubles of the world. Our economic problems are now eclipsed by the war in Cyprus. What a blessing that we are no longer a great Mediterranean power automatically involved in war whenever anything happens there. I am also glad that I am not on holiday in Cyprus. Of course you never know when trouble may start somewhere else.

I already have glowing praise for *The Second World War*. A Dutch publisher who saw it said that it was the greatest book since *All Quiet on the Western Front*, a comparison that had not occurred to me. An Italian publisher has also taken it. Also I have nearly finished Lloyd George's love letters. As I go on I find them very depressing. By the nineteen-thirties the repeated protestations of love no longer ring true. Frances was having an affair with someone else and yet wrote as gushingly as ever. Lloyd George knew what was happening and somehow curbed his jealousy. But I keep thinking – do all expressions of love grow false in the end? I worry so much that in one way or another we shall lose interest, and yet I need you so much. I have really been very upset all week, silly as it sounds.

I got one of the books for Pisti and sent it by post. The other had to be ordered and will take about three weeks. So I will probably bring it with me. My air passage is booked, but I have heard nothing about my visa. It would be tiresome if I was not let in to Hungary. In that case we should have to go to Ohrid. But I expect it is just bureaucracy.

I go to the Lake District on Monday. The alarm about petrol has now I think blown over, but instead I am worried that my back brakes need renewing, and I don't see when I can get them done. However, I shall drive all the more carefully. I shall come back to London on Saturday, 3 August, and appear on television the following day. I will write to you immediately thereafter and tell you how I got on. I have not complete faith that I shall be as good as I was fifteen years ago. Maybe climbing mountains will help.

I won't write any more except to say that I love you deeply and am impatient to see you.

XXXXX
Alan

7 August

Darling Heart,

I received your beautiful letter and should have written before, but have been so busy. I have my visa and also £30 of vouchers for florints. I will also bring £100 in travellers' cheques with me. Will that be enough? Get in some wine so that we can drink every night. There is one important thing I must tell you so that perhaps you will worry and suffer less. I SHALL LOVE YOU TILL I DIE. There will never be any change on my side and I expect not on yours. We have still plenty to find out about each other, but I don't think either of us is likely to be disappointed.

1974

Now I'll tell you such news as I have. The fortnight in the Lake District began badly. The oil pump in my car collapsed on the motorway and we had to spend the night in an hotel in Wolverhampton while a new one was fitted. Thereafter all went well. The weather was good nearly every day, and there was usually no cloud on the hills. The first day I went up Helvellyn (3,200 feet) with Crispin and Daniel. They did a second mountain while I walked sedately home. Giles and Sebastian joined us in Borrowdale and we did two more mountains. Then Sebastian left. We went on to Coniston and did three more mountains. I was amazed how easily I climbed. I am really fitter than I was fifty years ago when I started up these mountains, a little short of breath but then I always was. Despite streams of cars on the roads the Lake District is still deserted as soon as you get on to the field paths. Often we walked all day without meeting anyone. I wish I lived there always, but that is not a practical proposition. My only complaint is that it was never warm enough to bathe.

It was very good being with the boys for a whole fortnight. And then suddenly, when we are back in London, I see them no more.

My TV show, 'Free Speech', was not as successful as it should have been. We duly met. We decided to discuss whether democracy in this country was doomed – I of course saying that democracy had never been stronger, particularly when the unions were doing so well. My antagonists, particularly Malcolm Muggeridge, seem to forget that trade unionists are people, indeed the most democratic people there are. We did our half hour with a lot of lively though ragged debate. Afterwards the producer said: 'Splendid, could not have been better' (I thought it could). Then he added: 'I have one little disappointment for you. The show did not go out.' Apparently, as it was being relayed all over the country, it had to go over the Post Office lines. The Post Office engineers objected that they were having to operate with members of a different union and, just as the show started, they pulled the switch. We were told that the show will go out some time during the week, but I doubt it. Let us hope that we shall have better luck next Sunday. However, we got paid (£100 a show) which is the most important thing.

Now I am wildly busy. I spent all yesterday choosing the illustrations for *The Second World War*. I have a very good editorial assistant at the publishers, a girl called Penny (Penelope), very young, very attractive, very resolute rather in the way Veronica is. Don't worry: (a) she is married; (b) I love someone else. I haven't had time to get back to Lloyd George. While away I read *Emma* by Jane Austen and found it very boring. To show you the pace of inflation, our hotels cost each of us £8 a night with dinner and breakfast. A bottle of wine in an hotel now costs at least £2. I shall soon be ruined. What a dull, silly letter. It is just to show you I am alive and thinking always of 23 September.

Now much love,

Alan

15 August

Dear Heart,

It occurred to me that, once I get to the Isle of Wight, I might be busy, particularly if the sun shines and I want to lie on the beach. So I am writing to you a little ahead of schedule. Also I am always anxious to write after I have had a telephone conversation with you. We shall be together in little more than a month. I am glad you are going to the Ranke Gesellschaft; it will make a change for you. If we had known you were to be out of Hungary, perhaps we should have met somewhere. But I would rather see your home. My pupil Alan Sked will also be there. He is a most attractive boy, so much so that Della is in love with him, much to his embarrassment. So beware. He teaches the nineteenth century, which is neglected nowadays as though it were the Middle Ages. He spent some time in Budapest, knows some Hungarian and wants to know more, and has a very good knowledge of the Habsburg monarchy. He and I are the only people who ever worked on the Vienna files about Italy in 1848 – the subject of his thesis. So you will find him rewarding historically and I expect you will succumb to his charm as well.

I am still not confident I shall be able to come. I cannot believe that our economic difficulties can go on much longer without a real crisis. Then foreign travel may be stopped. Alternatively airlines may close down. You know how I always look on the black side and expect the worst. My motto is all right so far, as the man who fell from the top of a skyscraper said as he passed the tenth storey.

That's all for now.

Very much love,

xxxxxxx Alan

1974

31 August

Beloved,

It was wonderful to hear your voice the other night. It made me long to be with you, and I shall be soon. You know when I am arriving: 14.15 on 23 September. If anything goes wrong I will telephone, but I don't see what should except of course the English revolution. I have also got money, discovering to my surprise that anyone can take £400 every time he goes out of the country. Surely far too much? It won't last.

I had a good time in the Isle of Wight, the finest weather I can remember. I spent most days on the beach and got brown at the price of a few dermatitis spots on my hands. Unfortunately the tide was low in the early mornings so that I could not bathe before breakfast.

I took down two dozen bottles of Yugoslav wine and we drank them all in ten days. I found this wine, red at that, rather good. But then the best Yugoslav white wine, such as we drank at Split, never leaves the country. I'm keen to go to Ohrid next spring. You had better find how you go from Budapest, via Belgrade I expect. We might spend a night there, but it is not an interesting place except that I have friends there. Crispin is off to Russia on Monday. I am glad to report that he has had his hair cut in honour of the occasion. Sebastian has also had his hair cut – very short, because he says he can only afford to have it done twice a year.

'Free Speech' is getting on agreeably. I enjoyed our discussion on private armies last Sunday, though we got on to a false trail by discussing trade unions instead, when I said they were an essential part of democracy. We can't go on discussing the economic situation every week, so I fear we shall be rather stuck for a subject tomorrow morning. Did I tell you that, in order to get round the ban from the Post Office engineers' union, we have to record at eight in the morning, after which the tapes are taken by car to Birmingham where they can be sent out on TV lines? This means getting up about six, which is no hardship to me or to Malcolm Muggeridge who says he always gets up then. He has become benign and our old friendship has been restored. In the intervals of recording we chat about Manchester in 1930. You know all about that from my autobiography.

I've written a good deal more for you to see, including my post-war visits to Czechoslovakia and Yugoslavia and Margaret's infatuation with Dylan Thomas, which really brought us to disaster. I have done everything on *The Second World War* except make the index and have nearly finished Lloyd George's letters, including the period when Frances was unfaithful to him. I have not yet found a publisher and sometimes doubt whether I shall. Who cares now whether Lloyd George had a mistress? Indeed, who remembers him? Royal romances, such as Edward VIII, are always good selling stuff, but you can't say the same of prime ministers.

I am reading a book by H. C. Deutsch, an American, on the way Hitler got rid of Blomberg and Fritsch, not a topic that interests me. It only goes to show that generals are very silly people the world over. Then I have a long history of the British Army in India and a work by an American on the battle of Arnhem, one of the great failures of the war. Finally there is a life of Massingham who edited the radical weekly, the *Nation*, during the First World War. It surprises me that I have any time to write my own books.

I am thinking of you in your little country cottage and looking forward to going there with you. Let me have a full report of the Ranke Gesellschaft, especially whether Alan Sked was any good. You can give my regards to Hauser, though not too enthusiastically. I expect he has a good idea of our relationship and probably thinks he arranged it all, which is true to some extent. Maybe we should never have met again if I had not suggested inviting you to Königswinter. But Salzburg really settled things. I wish we could go to Austria again, but I am told that it is now one of the most expensive places in Europe. News from Italy. Lucia's daughter has now finished school and is going to the University of Urbino in order to study Aesthetics, to which Lucia added: 'My God!' Alan Sked, who visited the Bioccas when he was in Rome, says that they are Communists although very rich and living with lots of servants. I suppose Communism is a luxury which only the rich can afford.

Our economic conditions go rocketing on. As prices go higher, I buy less, including driving my car slower in order to save petrol. In fact I can't say that my economic circumstances are much changed. I have lost a lot of money on the Stock Exchange. Two years ago my shares were worth nearly £100,000. Now they are worth less than £20,000. But I was only holding them as security against my old age, and their going down only means that I shall have to go on working which will be very good for me. This must all be very boring for you, but I haven't much news after being away on holiday.

I still love you very much, which I hope will be welcome news to you. I miss very much being near you. You know how it is. We love each other and have perfect peace only when we are together. Do you think

1974

we shall ever have a row? Perhaps we were near it at Venice. We shan't be any more.

    Much love, my darling.

Alan

Your letter is still wandering somewhere between London and Budapest.

8 September

Lovey (that's the way to spell it),

    I only just got your letter of 22 August and don't expect I shall get another. Indeed, the way the posts are going we shall soon have to write one year if the letter is to get there the next. Now here are the answers to your practical remarks. You are not to worry about anything. I shall worry until the actual moment when I find you waiting for me at the air terminal. I always worry on a journey in case things go wrong, and I shall worry all the time I am in Hungary because I cannot speak the language. But there is no need for you to worry. We shall get on happily all the time. If I want anything I shall ask you for it, and if there is something wrong I shall tell you. It is possible that I shall be bored if I haven't enough to read, but I can always read books on architecture. I have got Pisti's other book and will bring it with me. You and I will drink at least a bottle of wine every night, and if the boys drink too we may need more. I expect we shall get through a dozen bottles, but you don't need to get them all in advance. It will give me something to do. Besides, we must go out to a restaurant occasionally. I should very much like to go away for a few days, either to the hills or to the place where you were brought up. Balaton will have lost its charms by this time in the year. I am curious to see how you will fit me into your flat. I don't need much except a hard bed, and of course don't forget that I often have to get up in the night. Shall I follow my English system and eat an egg for breakfast, or shall I admit that I am on the continent and eat something for lunch? We shall see. But the most important thing is that you are not to worry. I shall be just as eager as you are that our time together should be happy. I am not in the habit of complaining, and certainly not to you. So instead of worrying, just think what a good time we are going to have.

I have been so busy that I am quite bewildered in my head. I got back from the Isle of Wight, pushed on with Lloyd George's letters, and then had all my time taken up with *The Second World War*. First I had to choose the pictures, then I had to invent captions for them, and now I am making the index. I average 25 pages a day and there are 234 pages, so you will see that I shall be fully occupied until I come to Hungary. In a way it is fun making an index, because you see for the first time how the book is shaped. But it is a great labour as well, and the work seems to be endless. On Friday I had a wild time, just as if I were a real working journalist. First, early in the morning, the editor of the *Daily Express* rang up wanting an article for Saturday, discussing what we should do about rival marches, Left and Right, every weekend, which lead to street fighting. My answer: sensible people should keep away and go for a walk on Hampstead Heath instead. It made quite a good piece. Then I went to a ridiculous lunch arranged by *Time-Life*, the American magazine, at which four so-called experts talked about the state of the nation. It was all taken down and edited for publication. The other three were all from *The Times* and unbelievably right-wing. They kept lamenting that extremists had now got control of the trade unions. I said: 'Is it extreme to think that the rich should be paid less and the poor more?' They could not understand at all. I had a hard row with one of them. 'On the other hand', they don't grasp that this country might run into measureless difficulties without there being a general collapse of capitalism. One of them, when asked when the real crisis would arrive, replied – 1980 or 1984. That does not interest me very much. I hope to be on the move by then. Very silly, but it earned me 300 dollars. Wisely, I did not drink any wine and did not eat much.

A good thing too, for when I got back to the Library the editor of the *Sunday Express* rang up and explained that a half-page advertisement had fallen out so he needed an article to fill the space, he did not mind much on what. So at five o'clock I had to press the button on my electric typewriter once more and turn out a thousand words saying that public opinion polls were a danger at election time. Now that's the way to be busy. But if every day were like that I should never get any books written. Not bad to earn $300 in one day, not so good when you reflect that after paying income tax I only have £60 of it left, and depreciated pounds at that.

I have just spent an exhausting two hours initiating Daniel into driving. No doubt he will succeed in the end. Everyone does. 'Free Speech' is still running on television, though I expect it will be suspended if and when we have a general election. One looks certain for 3, or 10 October, so I shall be back in nice time to discuss the results. My impression is that they will be much as before – a Labour government without strong support. I'm not sure that is a bad thing. The personal problem is that Harold Wilson is failing physically. He has lost his drive and his speeches, though clever, have become mechanical. But, like most people in his position, he does not realize that he is going downhill. Perhaps I am also not what I was. Do you think so? To myself I seem as good as ever both mentally and physically, but others probably notice a difference. You must tell me. Of course the election is really too early. The crisis has not yet come home to people and so they aren't looking for a remedy. This winter we shall have great unemployment and British exports, like everyone else's, will dry up. The situation gets more and more like 1931 except that there are neither Fascists nor Communists wanting to take over. There is just an emptiness. A situation without parallel.

I almost forgot to answer one point in your letter. You must not be cross that I destroyed your letter. I always destroy letters as soon as I have answered. If I kept every letter of yours I should get confused as to which I had answered. I am not sentimental about material things, except a little perhaps about that little red bear which you gave me in 1960. I am sentimental about you. I think of you all my free time. I think about the words and thoughts in your letters. But the physical side of the letter – the ink that it is written with and the paper it is written on – means nothing to me. In any case you should not keep my letters. As it is, you can look up a previous letter and find I have made the same joke or told the same story. Much better that every letter should be a surprise. Also, if you destroy my letters, you will not be able to quote them against me!

A year ago I was just getting ready to go to Paris. I think of that time with great sentiment. The nights were the best we have had and some of the days were good too. We must go again, if only to visit Chartres when it is not raining.

I shall bring £100 in travellers' cheques and £100 in marks. Have I said this before? I shall not write again: 23 September at 14.15 on a BEA plane.

What a splendid thought.
    Love to Lovey,

                        Alan

5 October

My Darling,

    I can't really wait a week to tell you how much our time in Budapest meant to me. I have never felt so close to you, so convinced that we were made for each other and that we should never quarrel or drift apart. We seemed so secure together, as though we understood everything without needing to talk about it. But you must never never do things just because I say so. I am sure you are back at making coffee your way, and quite right too. You sometimes say I cheated you. Not so. Life has cheated us. If British capitalism had gone on being prosperous we should have arranged things by now somehow. In this atmosphere of impending catastrophe, we can't do anything except wait for the crisis and see what happens afterwards. Perhaps the crisis won't happen, but I can't see how it can be avoided. And yet the streets seem more prosperous than they have ever been. It is like the conviction that it will rain tomorrow. This does not make you wet today!

    I have sent you two books: *The Habsburg Monarchy* and *The First World War*. You will find to your surprise that I am quite a good historian. You may also notice that, though *The Habsburg Monarchy* is a good book, I wrote better by the time I got to *The First World War* and I hope that I write even better now. I still can't help being too clever every now and then. This is what shocks people about my books. The flight back was most agreeable. The plane was punctual to the minute. In fact I was back in London by half-past three. As I told you in a note in one of the books, we got a choice of red and white wine, and two glasses at that. The lunch was less fancy than the British one and much better: just a vast plate of all kinds of salami. No cheese, but then Hungarian cheese is not much good. As soon as I was back I was in for a busy time. Dutch television wanted me at once and set up their cameras as soon as they could lay hands on me. As a reward I got a bottle of Dutch gin. Then the *Express* wanted an article from me. BBC television fixed me up for next Friday. In fact the telephone at the Library did not stop ringing all Friday. It reminded me of Németvölgyi 70/72,* where also there is a perpetual telephone.

    I don't suppose you want to hear anything about the election. All the leaders keep saying that there is a grave crisis and then failing to make any suggestion for solving it or even for making it a little better. Instead they make promises for a better future that can never be fulfilled. What a strange thing is human psychology. You would think that in the

---

* Eva's address in Budapest.

present situation any politician, unless he really had a vision, would be anxious to escape responsibility. Yet here they all are, fighting to get into office when they know that they will discredit themselves by doing so. Perhaps Wilson is now so mad with vanity that he thinks he will somehow solve our troubles, or maybe he is so stupid he doesn't know there is a crisis. The whole situation baffles me and I try not to think about it.

Alan Sked called on Friday. He does not know that you and I are especially connected. At any rate he only mentioned you casually, saying you had met. But no indication that you had any conversation together. The Ranke Gesellschaft gave him rather a surprise. It did not occur to him that even elderly German professors could be so German-centred. He said that when he spoke of Great Britain's world policy, they asked: 'But what about her German policy?' He was also surprised that they still took for granted the most extreme version of the Cold War, none of them questioning that it was entirely Russia's fault. If we really go next year, we shall have a difficult time, you on the rising, me on Suez. I'd be quite glad to go to Salzburg again afterwards – or perhaps to Ischl, where we could eat the rich cakes. We shall see when we get to Ohrid. Maybe there will be exchange control by then and I shan't be able to move. So let us just hope and not worry.

I returned to find Daniel canvassing hard for the Labour Party. I don't think the Labour Party much good, but still I am very glad a son of mine is working for it, just like his half-brothers. In fact Giles and Daniel have been out canvassing together. Crispin of course thinks such political activities ridiculous and will not even say who he is going to vote for, which he is quite entitled to do. He went by train to Lincoln all on his own and spent something like four hours looking at the Cathedral. He said that he was able to understand and study it more than if I had been there, and is therefore convinced that in future we should go on separate holidays. This makes sense though I regret it. Crispin suffers from being too rational. Tomorrow I take him by car to Cambridge, and shall not see him until he comes up to London to see *Cosi Fan Tutte* on 29 October. I told him about the frightening unanimimous way audiences clap in Budapest, and he said it was the same in Moscow. I said it was the mindless mass; he said they were merely asking for an encore.

I have got through most of the book on Engels. It is extremely sympathetic and ingenious, but written in a sort of American jargon which I find difficult to understand. Maybe I shall do better with the life of Edward VIII that I must review next.

It is really true, Lovey, that I think of you all the time. I have become so involved in your existence that everything is empty without you. I smile constantly at little memories of the funny little things we did together. For instance, our trip to Szentendre (spelling?) was somehow a very funny day, wandering around in the struggle to get into churches and then suddenly everything was simple. Life together seemed so simple, so natural. I have had more exciting times with you, but none where we seemed to fit in so well physically and mentally. You are not the first woman I have been to bed with, but you will be the last.

I am tied to you for ever and ever.

Now I really will not write for a fortnight if I can restrain myself. My Love, my Dearest, my Lovey, I love you very much and for ever.

Alan

18 October

Lovey Mine,

I have just got your letter. It is raining and I can't go out to do some necessary shopping. So instead I write to you. I love you just as much as you love me. I feel now that we are well and truly married, absolutely one body and soul. To tell you the truth, when I got your letter I cried a bit, just at missing you. I hate to live without you and yet there is no escaping fate. I get more and more frightened about the future, but there is no point in going on about that. I think British finances may hold out well enough for us to meet at Ohrid in the spring. On the other hand, I have lost faith in Italian finances and have sold my lire. Unless the pound sterling collapses I can always get more if we go to Italy, and I'm not keen to do that. Rome is the one place worth going to except for Venice, and it is very expensive and very crowded. So we may have to do without that.

The Library has been occupying all my thoughts. Max's announcement knocked me over. I was so upset I came back here at once and rang you up. That consoled me. I am quite sure no one will rescue the Library in its present form. Beaverbrook is already too forgotten, and if his own family abandon him what hope is there elsewhere? I am also pretty sure that, even if there were more money from the newspapers, Max's financial advisers are saying that the Library is a waste of space which could be used as offices for journalists. So I am lost. I am negotiating with the Department of Manuscripts at the British Museum, which is keen on principle to take the papers and then starts financial difficulties also. As they will have no vacant room until April 1976, they have not enough staff and can't get a grant for any more, all the papers will have to be bound so that they can't be stolen and so on. I am also approaching University College London. One difficulty is that owing to staff shortage the Post Office that handles mail for WC1 and WC2 (where both the British Museum and University College are) has broken down and is submerged in piles of mail weeks old. However, I am counting on Max's statement that he can keep the Library going until 1976. If he agrees I will write to Lady Beaverbrook, a very wealthy woman, and see if she will put up the money. But I am afraid the family want to be rid of the concern.

It is perfectly simple why I don't want to go to the USA. There is nothing there to interest me, and the food and drink have no attractions. I can think of nothing more ghastly than to teach American students. I gave up teaching Oxford undergraduates ten years ago. Why should I start again with inferior material? I like lecturing but not teaching. I have also run out of ideas for books. I have got two to carry me on until 1976. First, while the Library keeps going I'll try to finish my autobiography. Then, as I think I told you, I will write a short history of Great Britain from 1901 to 1975. Some of this is a total blank in my mind, but I suppose I'll be able to fill it in time. Please note: I am neither a Russell nor a Toynbee. I am not a prophet, a pundit. I can't tell the young how to run their lives. I have no message except a private message for you. I am desperate to have some time with you before I die.

Now I get to your page 2. Your English is very good, both when you write and when you talk. Far from being bored by your talk, I am absolutely enchanted by it. Sometimes I am afraid I seem rude, because instead of listening to what you say and following your arguments I am ravished by the sound of your voice. I could listen for ever. It is sensual, like having a hot bath and what happens afterwards. But surely nothing did. I'll try to insist on it for Ohrid. Everything is right and perfect with you except that you don't make coffee the proper way.

Now here is the news of my doings. On Wednesday October 9 I went to lecture at Leamington. I was met by a nice young schoolteacher who took me to his home and gave me dinner. On the table were three cups. His wife said, 'Would you like some tea?' I said, 'No thank you' and she took the cups away. In the middle of dinner she said, 'Oh, I forgot, would you like something to drink?' I, having seen three wine-bottles on the sideboard – one of them opened – said, 'Oh, yes please.'

She went out to the kitchen and produced three glasses of water. That was all. I had to go straight to the lecture; when I got to the station to go back to Oxford, the refreshment room was closed; so it was half-past ten before I got to a pub in Oxford and had half a pint of beer. Can you imagine anything like it?

The day after the election kept me busy. I went on television about nine in the morning to generalize about the results, and then did a long run for American television, explaining that we were not on the brink of revolution or civil war. The Americans were most surprised. Monday I did another show discussing whether Hitler wanted to make the Duke of Windsor head of a Vichyite England in 1940. The story has just come out in a sensational book, otherwise worthless. The people on television were most surprised when I told them that all this about Windsor and Hitler had come out in the German documents years ago. Wednesday 16 October I was in Oxford again, renewing acquaintance with my colleagues. When I remarked to John Stoye that I had been in Hungary, he said: 'I suppose with that nice historian who came to dinner?' So I suppose that our love showed even then. Magdalen College is spending too much. £50,000 last year and probably £100,000 this. As a measure of economy one of my colleagues proposed that we should reduce dinner in Hall from four courses to three: total savings in a year, £700. I suppose it is useless to give them an elementary economics lesson. In my opinion, in a period of inflation one should spend as much as one can before money loses its value altogether.

This week I am going to the Isle of Wight, where I am president of the local branch of the Historical Association. So I shall be driving round a lot. I keep resolving to give up my car and then get fun out of driving it. But it is really becoming impractically expensive. I can't tell you how flattered I was by Pisti's remark. I should have been unhappy to upset the boys and was fairly confident I hadn't, but Pisti says more than I deserve. Perhaps they are content that there is someone who will take their mother off their hands some time and make her happy. At any rate it was a very nice thing to say. Give them both my affectionate greetings and say they must let me know when there are more English books they need.

That reminds me I have just sent off *Bismarck* and *The Struggle for Mastery in Europe*. *Bismarck* makes good reading and is I think reasonably sound in its psychology. It is strange that the Germans have not translated it, perhaps it is not respectful enough. *The Struggle for Mastery* is very scholarly, very learned, with a very good bibliography, but boring to the last degree. I can't think how anyone reads through it. Is there

1974

any other book of mine that you want? All the titles are opposite the title page of *Beaverbrook*.

Oh, Lovey, I want you so badly, I love you so much. Before I came to Budapest I wasn't sure we should get on in your home. Now we are sure of each other for ever.

I love you almost too much.

Damn, I'm crying again.

                xx   Alan

28 October

Dearest Love,

I can't remember whether I ought to be writing this weekend, but I want to in any case and there is no stopping me. Now first I must write very seriously. You must realize that I am no longer a rich man. The economic crisis has hit me very badly. Sometimes I wonder whether I shall be able to afford ever to see you again. My heart is set on Ohrid so I must save for that, and there is no way in which I could afford to come to you for Christmas also. What happens after Ohrid no one can tell. It is possible that things may get easier next year. It is more likely that this country will go bankrupt and that all foreign travel will be forbidden. If you told me that you could not live alone any more and that you were going to marry to set up with someone else, I should understand and even be glad that you would be happy. So do not feel tied to me unless, like me, you are tied by love. I am even sorry that I thrust my love on you. I don't think I should have done if I had foreseen the catastrophe that would fall on this country. But I just could not help it. So please be patient and think of me always even when we cannot meet.

I am very curious to hear about The Lady from Tapolca.* Was that her husband all the time? Or was she, like you, lucky enough to have a lover? You can share your secrets with her as with no one else, just because your paths in life will otherwise never cross. I do hope they were together on the same basis as we were. I am curious also to hear that you have received some more books I sent you and what you think

---

* A mysterious woman Alan and Eva had seen on their holiday in Eastern Hungary.

of them. At least my letters reach you, which they would not do if you lived in Italy. I think that in the spring before I come to you I shall take the boys to France, not to Italy, which will be cheaper and easier to arrange. We shall see.

The British Museum has agreed to take the contents of the Beaverbrook Library and I am going to negotiate the details later this morning. It is miserable for me, like being sentenced to death and waiting for the inevitable day of execution. No doubt I shall get used to it. All my work has fallen behind. I reviewed the book on Engels as you will see in the *TLS*, a better piece at any rate than Richard Cobb's. Lloyd George has got stuck because I have had so many other things to do. Last week I seemed to be motoring ceaselessly. On Wednesday I went to Oxford. On Thursday I gave a lecture, very satisfactorily. Then I drove to the Isle of Wight and addressed the local branch of the Historical Association. Crowded house and praise of 'the greatest living historian' – meaning poor me. Friday back again to Oxford for a College feast. Maybe it will be the last as the College money is running out. They say that next autumn all the universities except Oxford and Cambridge will have to close down. I wish the country would stop private motoring instead. Yesterday was a fine day. Sebastian and I went for an all-day walk, as his two children were away with their grandparents and he was free for once. The weather is fine and very cold. Soon no doubt coal will run short and the heating will go off. In Glasgow civilized life has already come to an end. An interesting period to live in, but not a pleasant one.

I must stop and rush out. But my thoughts are with you all the time. You are my mate, my own girl.

Much love,
Alan

3 November

My Dearest Love, My Dear Wife,

You must know from your great experience how it is with men. When things are going well they hardly think of their women at all, and then when things go wrong, they start to cry out – Comfort me, comfort me. Well, I am a bit like that now. The killing of the Beaverbrook Library on top of my money worries and general political apprehensions has been almost too much for me. I had counted so much on the Library. After the many setbacks I've had in life – not being made a professor, not even being kept on properly at Oxford – I thought: now I really have arrived. Sentimentally, it was good to be doing something for my old friend's memory. Now I feel I have been made a fool of. It is obvious that Max Aitken does not care in the slightest about his father's memory and nor does anyone else. Why should I alone have to try to keep him sacred? Max is cheating me in another way. The story that the Foundation has no money is window-dressing. The truth is that Max wants the floor space to turn into offices and now regards the Library as a waste of space and money. In that case, why did he ever ask me to take it on and devote my life to it? The moral is that you can never trust rich men. I'd like to show I resent his treatment of me. But I can't. I deserved it by trusting him and I can't complain at my own stupidity.

I don't see my future at all. The British Museum people are very keen to have the papers, but it all depends on their building plans being executed by April 1976 and in the present economic climate I have great doubts whether they will be. I'm also now preparing to talk to Ede at the Public Record Office, but he too depends on the building plans at Kew being carried out. If I can't get something sensible settled by the end of next year, perhaps I shall fly into a temper and recommend Max to sell the whole lot to Texas. Why should I devote my life to something no one else cares about? Every time I survey the problem and the way I have been treated, my anger rises higher. Now I am working my temper off on you. After all, I have no one else whom I can pour my troubles out to and will listen.

Now what can I tell you that is more cheerful? Yesterday Daniel was praised by his instructor and told that his driving was very good. So perhaps he will pass after all. More cheerful again: Crispin and I went to *Cosi Fan Tutte* last Tuesday. It was lyrically beautiful even though the two girls were well into their fifties and the two men lovers looked like middle-aged business-men.

I have lots of books to review, amusing but not important: Edward VIII, Brendan Bracken, the pre-1914 Radicals. Now I have got a collection of long essays by Arthur Marder, as good as ever: 'The Dardanelles', 'Churchill at the Admiralty in World War II', the sinking of the French ships at Oran, and one that will interest you on the Royal Navy in the Mediterranean during the Abyssinian crisis. Alistair Parker has done most of this already, but Marder writes so much better. I will send you the book when I have written about it. I have also thought of a little Christmas present for you which I will bring to Ohrid if we get there. Did you see the one bit of good news for us that the dinar has been devalued by 7%? So things will be a little cheaper.

First we had very cold weather. Now it is very wet. It is a good thing I am not going for an all-day walk this Sunday. Instead I just sit here and think of you. What wonderful happiness we have had together in our brief meetings.

Very, very much love until I write again.

Alan

8 November

Lovey Dovey,

Guess what. The little card you wrote to me on Tuesday full of love arrived here this morning only three days later. It was a ray of light in the general gloom surrounding me. Things go from bad to worse. Now Max says he meant April 1975, not April 1976, so the Library will be wound up in a few months' time and I shall have no refuge. It seems useless to protest. Instead I shall loyally cooperate to kill the Library. I went to see Ede and decided that I preferred the PRO to the British Museum, so I shall recommend that it gets the papers. Their new building at Kew will not be ready until some time in 1976, but they have plenty of storage room at Ashridge and the papers can be buried there for a year, just forgotten. I might as well be buried too.

Now about your longer letter. It was foolish. If by breaking you mean that we should forget each other, well we can't. We exist for each other whether we write or not, and there is no escape. Perhaps it was unfortunate our love ever happened, but now it can't be wished away. As I told you, if you became attracted to someone else who could marry you and give you a shared life, I should be *very* happy for you and not particularly cast down about myself because I would know you were happy, which is what I care most about. But until something like that happens we must go on having short stretches of happiness unless or until capitalism recovers.

So you don't need to be angry with me. Some of your questions are natural. Others bewilder me. How could you think I was snobbish in any way? I am the only academic historian who can talk naturally to ordinary people on television or at trade union meetings. Taxi-men give me a cry of 'How are you doing, Alan?' That pleases me much more than praise from some professor. I have two rules: I am no better than anyone else, and no one else is better than me. That makes me aggressive towards the vain and arrogant, and friendly towards the simple and straightforward. Maybe I am intellectually arrogant with fellow intellectuals.

Of course I don't mind my friends knowing about you. Indeed, perhaps I talk about you too much. The story seems too strange for them to believe – except John Stoye, who has met you. But Katus is a gossip who goes about stirring people up and making mischief. I would never trust her not to use stories against me just out of malice. Money. No, I am not rich any more. Indeed I was never rich in any serious sense. I earned quite a lot from my books and other writings, but I didn't have a private fortune. Now my best days are over financially. The investments I had have shrunk to practically nothing. They don't even cover the loan I have at the bank, so I don't know how I shall ever pay it off. My book earnings are going down because my books were all published a long time ago. My best score was with *Beaverbrook* which I shared with you, and I shall get no more from it. *The Second World War* is too small to be really profitable. I reckon I'll get £1,000 a year for six years from it, which will not compensate me for the ending of the *Beaverbrook* sales. In not much over a year I have to retire at Magdalen, and now I am on the point of losing my position and expense account here. I should say I have about the income of a university professor, and have to work much harder for it. From now on my income will be going downhill when prices are going up. I shall have to keep Crispin for three more years and Daniel for four. Maybe you should disapprove of me that I am a bourgeois intellectual believing in all sorts of bourgeois things such as freedom of expression and thought, freedom of movement. But I'd sacrifice them all if it were really necessary for the well-being of the working class. Seeing you have confessed something unimportant about your mother, I'll confess something important about mine though you know it already. She was a bitch, and I fear I have inherited some of her characteristics. Maybe I should also confess what you also know: that my father, though the most angelic man in the world, was devious and a dodger. But I am not ashamed to have inherited even his less admirable characteristics. At any rate no more of this nonsense, please.

Answers to questions. I read *The Masters* and enjoyed it. But I don't think most Colleges are like that. At Magdalen we fight over things like the election of a president, but no one takes it seriously and, far from there being passionate ambitions, we have great difficulty in finding anyone who will take the office. Zeldin is a former pupil of mine who now teaches at St Antony's. He contributed two volumes on France

1848–1945 in the *Oxford History of Modern Europe*. It is clever, but a ragbag of information arranged under such headings as Trade Unions, Sex, Radicalism, Art. I like history to be chronological.

I am exploring further about Ohrid. Maybe we could both fly to Skopje and then take a motor-coach to Ohrid. There are apparently no package tours and the regular fare from here is £170. Also, I can't give you a date because of the uncertainty as to when the ending of the Library will take place. So we might meet in April or we might meet in May. But we'll meet for certain unless there is exchange control. The current talk is that there will be an annual limit of £75 that one can take out, and as I bring £200 every time I come to you that would be awkward. Please be patient and loving and don't get romantic or fanciful. Remember we are just two middle-aged people who are fond of each other.

A whole afternoon spent in the pleasure of writing to you instead of in work,

LOVE
Alan

17 November

Lovey Mine,

I rang you on Friday just to hear your voice and was too early to find you in. I shall try to ring again on Wednesday, but cannot be always sure of getting through, so do not be disappointed if I don't. It was foolish of me to fix a day in advance as we can never be sure it will work. I won't do this again, but I hope it was some evidence I was thinking of you.

The affairs of the Library go from bad to worse. Max Aitken sent me an abrupt message that we must be out in April next, but so far has refused to see me and I can't go ahead without more information. I don't even know whether the Foundation is entitled to give its papers away. As the [Beaverbrook] Newspapers lost a million and a half last year, I can understand his difficulties, but I wish he would understand mine. One particular anxiety is that if we have to close in April this may ruin my plan for an April holiday. In this case I shall try to meet somewhere in May. Please, please be patient. I am doing my best but am in great trouble.

1974

I am enquiring whether there is any chance of a package holiday which would take me to Ohrid more cheaply. There is also a winter weekend holiday of four days in Vienna for £55 which might enable us to meet. But everyone tells me that Austria is terribly expensive apart from the travel. You might find out on your side how much it would cost you to get to Ohrid. Probably it will be too expensive for you too. Healey's budget did not put any limit on foreign exchange, but there will be another budget in March and this may do so. Trouble, trouble everywhere. Our civilization may crash and all we shall have left is love at a distance. Please keep it alive whatever happens.

The lastest scientific alarm is that a new Ice Age is approaching and that Britain will soon be covered with ice a mile deep. Perhaps not in my lifetime. Actually we are having very mild weather though not as good, according to the weather reports, as you are having in Budapest.

I will send you Marder's book in a few days' time. It is very good. The one on the Navy and the Mediterranean in 1935 you know already, but he has added to it. He also has a furious battle with Roskill over Winston at the Admiralty. Peter Gretton told me he was so angry with Roskill's article (*Royal United Services Institute Journal*, 1972) that he tore it up. These admirals are certainly formidable combatants in retrospect.

Now I am reviewing a book called *Treaty-Breakers or Realpolitiker* for the *Hungarian Quarterly*! Will it be all right if I tell the editor to pay the fee to you? It will be something for us to spend when I come next September. But perhaps you would rather not reveal our acquaintanceship. Let me know.

The Lloyd George letters have gone to my agent, who will now find a publisher. I am curious to learn whether they will really bring in a lot of money. *The Second World War* is timed to come out next May, just thirty years after the end of the war. I am confident that it at least will do well.

Tomorrow I am going to Leeds to lecture on Winston Churchill. I wonder what I can find new to say on this old war-horse? I am also writing an article on him for a Dutch newspaper, so he is turning in some money for me, and I think I will keep my Dutch fee in Holland.

My letters are getting out of step. This time I shall really not write for a fortnight, but I shall be thinking of you all the time.

So many Kisses and all my Love,

Alan

1 December

Lovey Dovey,

Yes, I like that name best also. Or if you like me to use your name more: Lovey Dovey Eva. You see I have stopped myself writing to you until today, though I often want to so desperately. Nothing but gloomy news. I have tried to find a tour which would take me to Ohrid more cheaply than the regular fare. No luck so far. The air fare to Vienna is now £130, only £20 less than the fare to Ohrid. There are the weekend trips to Vienna costing only £55 with the hotel included. We could manage this all right so long as you can get a visa, but it is only for three nights. I'll look for a five-night tour. Otherwise we must put up with three. I can't say when it will be until I know when the Library is to be disbanded.

That is the second bit of gloomy news. I simply cannot get to see Max. I think he is going crazy and others think so too. Economic difficulties have got him down. He says we must close the Library next April. But neither the Record Office nor the British Library will take the papers except as a gift, and the Beaverbrook Foundation, being a charity, cannot give its assets away. I have implored Max to get legal advice. No answer. So I am in great anxiety and despair. Once the crisis is passed, if it ever is, I shall make a new life somehow. But I am not as resilient as I used to be. Perhaps like Max I cannot handle the economic difficulties that are coming. We are in for total social collapse and that is no fun for someone who is old and cannot fight for himself ever more. So you must just be patient and think of me in my trials.

I sent you Marder's book. I can't send you the one on Edward VIII because I have sold it. In any case it is not worth reading. Did you ever read *The Making of the British Working Class* by E. P. Thompson? It is just your kind of book and you should get it from a library as I have done. It is first about the period of the French revolution and then about the eighteen-twenties, before your Chartists. Thompson is very much on the radical side, though I think he tells anecdotes instead of being a true scholar. However, you must read it if you have not done so already. I expect you read it years ago.

So far as my work goes, I am marking time after sending Lloyd George's letters off to find a publisher. I suppose I had better get on with my autobiography, of which I have not written a line since I came back from Budapest. The thought of writing the miseries of my life depresses me and I can't face writing about it. You are the only person who puts life into me and you are so far away. So please think about me and all the happy times we had together. We shall have many more when the present dark days are over.

Nothing is happening in the world. I went to a marvellous concert when Brendel played Schubert. He is our best living pianist, dominating the piano world as Horowitz once did and with less showmanship. Now the concerts are running down for Christmas. There will be nothing worth hearing until the New Year. Only endless performances of Handel's *Messiah* and the *St Matthew Passion* by Bach, neither of them my favourites though the *Messiah* once was. I also cannot find any play that I can take the boys to at Christmas, though as you know I am not an enthusiast for the theatre in any case. Crispin comes home next weekend. I shall be glad to see him as far as I am allowed to. I got him *Fidelio* for Christmas, and have given Daniel some trendy shirts. Give something from me to your boys from the money I left with you. I shall bring a present for you when we meet. How badly I wish that it would be soon.

Sorry to be so gloomy. I don't seem to have any cheerful news to bite on. I must try to have a little holiday over Christmas, but where? I shall write again in a fortnight's time and will then be more cheerful.

All the love in the world,

Alan

13 December

Lovey Dovey,

Now this time I must really not write you a depressing letter, however gloomy I feel. Instead I will tell you that I have been thinking of the past and of our times together. I can't imagine a life without you in my thoughts. We have had difficulties and misunderstandings, and perhaps we shall have more. But they will not cause real trouble, especially if you don't have any wild idea of breaking. And this is a good opportunity to thank you for everything. Thank you for every little moment together. Thank you for making it so clear that you are really interested in me. I am just as interested in you, even though you complain that I do not show it.

Well, that is a paragraph that should make you happy as it has made me happy writing it. I won't bother you with public affairs except to remark that I think the pound sterling is in for a bad time, perhaps a total collapse with our money valueless and inflation running wild.

Indeed, being always inclined to look on the gloomy side, I am surprised that the collapse has not come already. However, there is nothing to be done until it does come except to go on with one's work and other activities. As a result I have been doing more book-reviewing and television than ever. No appearances in the *TLS*, I am afraid. Here is a comic little situation. You get the *TLS* every week. But the Beaverbrook Foundation is now so poor that it has cancelled the Library subscription for the *TLS*, so that I do not see it at all. You will have to draw my attention to articles in it instead of the other way round. Now I remember that I did have one little piece in it – what I read as a child. I hope you enjoyed it. I was amazed that no one else, even of my generation, read *Pilgrim's Progress*. I hope also that you enjoyed Roskill on Marder. Very funny.

The dissolution of this Library is now in full swing. Strangely enough, after my preliminary upset I am rather relieved. I am not by training or inclination an archivist. I have really neglected the papers and got on with my own work. Now I shall still have a room, though not such a grand one, a telephone and Della as secretary. So I shall have an easier time, free to get on with my own work. Did I tell you that I had found a perfect home for the papers? The House of Lords Record Office. It will take the papers on deposit, so there will be no problem of ownership and whether the Foundation can give them away. It is a delightful archive situated in the Victoria Tower. The Clerk of the Record Office, Maurice Bond, is an accomplished scholar who is his own boss rather like me. He has been coveting modern political papers for a long time, and now he has got more than he ever dreamt of.

Christmas is rather a frightening prospect. Giles and Janet are going to her parents who have a farm in Sussex. All the rest are staying in London for the first time for years. So we shall have six grown-ups and six grandchildren (two of them little babies of course) for dinner on Christmas night. It will be quite like old times when I had all the children living at home, often with their wives, lovers or mistresses. On the other hand, I see Crispin and Daniel less and less. However, we are to make a trip to Worcester and Gloucester immediately after Christmas when we shall look at cathedrals and enjoy ourselves.

All my love,
Alan

1974

16 December

I have just received your letter of 8 December, quite the most adorable letter that even you have ever written. It makes me love you more than ever. I give first practical answers to your questions. Daniel's exam is not until next summer. I can think of nothing more dreary than to go to the Canary Islands. In any case it is too expensive. I have started on my autobiography again. I certainly shall not leave out a moment with you. I shall try to come to Budapest for three days in March unless the affairs of ending the Library keep me too busy. A weekend trip is far cheaper than the ordinary flight. I can't stand Osborne's plays. I hope to see *The Birthday Party* by Pinter soon at the Shaw Theatre. I am going to the Bartók Quartet on 12 January, nothing until then. I sent your book to Mrs Goldfinger. Alan Sked got his doctorate. I was so depressed I asked Alan to stop it, but he refused and now I am glad.* Bergmann I also cannot stand. See how difficult I am. *Brideshead Revisited* is not Evelyn's best book. He knew this and later said it had been written by Ludovic (character in *Sword of Honour*, which is his masterpiece).

Here is a confession that I hope will not upset you. The only thing I want in life is one day to call you my Wife. It seems as though it will never happen but I still want it. Lots of good wishes for Christmas. I shall write again before then, my Beloved.

Love and Love,
Alan

22 December

Lovey Dovey,

I told you I would write again before Christmas, if only to send you a special greeting of love for the New Year. Also, there were some things I forgot to write about in my last letter. I went to see my doctor lately and complained that my back passage itched. He decided that I had cancer of the bowel and put me through all sorts of tests. Result: no cancer of the bowel. He then suspected I had diabetes and gave me further tests. Result: no diabetes. In fact there is nothing wrong with me,

* Alan Sked was working on a volume to celebrate Alan's 70th birthday, *Crisis and Controversy, Essays in Honour of A. J. P. Taylor.*

not even blood pressure and no sign of enlargement of the prostate, the usual failing of old men. To complete my examination I went to an optician and had my eyes tested. Result: they have not changed for ten years. One thing I learnt from my optician. Once a week you should put your glasses in warm water with detergent and leave them for the night. Next morning you scrub them with a nail-brush. It sounds tough but it works wonders.

Now as to our spring meeting. I am still enquiring about Vienna. Is it certain you can get a visa for Austria and, if you do, will this mean that you will not be allowed to go abroad on holiday for another three years? It would be silly to sacrifice your chance of a visa merely for a three-day holiday. However, I'll find out the cost of three days in both Budapest and Vienna and decide later. It is also possible that there are cheap flights to Budapest quite apart from the regular three-day tours. There certainly were last autumn when my flight cost only £50. The rest was a compulsory purchase of forints which I should have needed anyway. I shall also make further enquiries about a cheap trip to Ohrid, but I think that with the moving of the Library and all its contents coming on I can only be away for a few days. So we should perhaps save up Ohrid for the autumn. Every time I am tempted to add: so long as sterling survives. I expect it to crash any moment, but as you will remember I was equally pessimistic when we met in Paris more than a year ago. What a good time that was.

I had a good trip to Durham last Wednesday. Very sensibly I went by train – more restful and also cheaper now that petrol costs 74p (15/-) a gallon. I gave a lecture on 'Churchill during the Second World War' which was much appreciated – not praise, but serious historical estimate. Then I was entertained to dinner by the businessman who had paid for the lecture. He was very fat and asked me how I kept my figure. I said, no bread or potatoes. He put this down in a notebook. Next morning I spent two hours in the Cathedral and saw it more thoroughly than ever before. I appreciated for the first time that at Durham there are rib-vaults a hundred and fifty years before Gothic is supposed to have invented them, rather as complete Gothic appears at St Denis long before it should. This is probably too technical for you, but I'll explain it when we meet and if I can understand it properly myself.

At Durham station I had a fright. I put down my bag near a seat and went for a walk along the platform. When I came back my bag had gone. I asked at the office. I asked all the porters. No one had seen or touched it, or so they said. As a last despairing move I looked in the parcels office. There it was, off on a voyage to nowhere. I recovered my bag and my nerve just in time for the train.

1974

Yesterday I drove down with Daniel to visit Jennifer, Frances's daughter. She was attractive. Daniel is now driving quite well, but too fast and too fiercely. He has definitely decided not to go to a university next year. He says he wants to go and work abroad. I have grave doubts whether this can be arranged, but we shall see! I'd like to send him to you for a bit.

There, that's all my bits of news. I'll write after the New Year.

Special kisses for Christmas, my Darling,

XX   Alan   XX

1975

7 January 1975

Lovey Dovey, My Sweetest Girl,

I rang you up last night. You weren't there. I was sad, angry at the foolish situation that keeps us apart. There truly is one thing only I want from life and that is to be with you. I go on believing that all will come right in the end, but it is a long time coming. I miss you so very much. I want to hear you talk and I want to tease you about worrying over our relations. They will never change and we shall never lose faith in each other. That is for sure. Of course you may decide to marry someone in Hungary so as to have companionship in your old age. Even that would not alter my feelings for you or, I think, yours for me. We are stuck with these feelings whether we like them or not.

Here is the practical news I wanted to tell you last night. There are cheap flights to Budapest every weekend, arriving Friday, going back Monday, and I don't even need to pay for an hotel room. I can just be with you. The cost is only £50 and £9 in forint cheques, which is really very cheap. So it looks as though the weekend of 23 March would be fine. However, there is one other course. I shall find out also about Vienna. If it is just as cheap, if you can get a visa without losing your claim to another one, and if you would like three days in Vienna, we shall go there. But it is essential that you should let me know as soon as possible about whether you want to go to Vienna and whether you can get a visa. At any rate we'll be together one way or the other.

Economic gloom continues. Prices go up in the most unexpected ways. Companies go bankrupt or have to be rescued by the government, which I expect to go bankrupt in its turn. We shall certainly have mass unemployment this year, simply because there is no demand. The car industry is going bankrupt all over the world. If the government really goes bankrupt, as is likely, sterling will lose all value. I shan't be able to come and see you (cheer up, this won't happen until after April) and, unless some kind foreign country takes pity on us, we shall all starve to death. That is what I am expecting for 1975. But if there is once an upturn, credit will revive and we shall have another boom even madder than the last.

Here is a confession: I can't remember when I last wrote to you. This shows that, like all old people, I am losing my memory. At any rate here is some news, some of which I must have told you already. We had

1975

an enormous family party on Christmas Day – all of them except Giles and Janet, who were with her parents in the country. Two days after Christmas I went with Crispin and Daniel to the Midlands where we saw Worcester and Gloucester Cathedrals. This was a great success. Both Cathedrals were very good, though not in the same class as Durham. We did not have any difficulties with parking, which is always my worry when I go anywhere. We stopped at Tewkesbury for the night. Hotel not very good, perhaps being worn out by the Christmas festivities.

I am getting on with the closing of the Library. Among other things I shall sell most of my own books. Is there anything you would specially want? I'll try to pick something out for you – anything on diplomacy pre-war, for instance. I am also furiously writing my autobiography so as to have something to show when we meet. I have now got to 1956, so I shall reach you soon. I shall not be too flattering about you all at once.

Darling Heart, I am flattering about you now. I love you. I long for you. Be patient. Let us love when we can. There is difficulty nowadays in telephoning from the Library. So you must be patient about that too.

Love and Longing,

  And Kisses,
      Alan

17 January

Lovey Dovey, Eva Darling,

I have just received your letter of 5 January. What a long time some of your letters take, and how erratic they are. Sometimes here in six days, some in ten. However, we spoke on the telephone the other night so we know each of us is alive. I was a little distressed by our last conversation, distressed and puzzled. What could I have written to upset you? I cannot remember in the slightest what I wrote, but whatever it was was written in love. If you can remember, write and rebuke me.

Now let me get one thing clear. I have tried to do it before and you won't listen. I am on quite good terms with Margaret, and we get on well mainly because we are mutually tolerant. But I can't forget that she ruined my life and never gave me a proper chance to make a new life with Eve. Now I live with her because it is the easiest thing to do after the storms I've been through. But nothing on earth would ever induce me to marry her. On the contrary, she is the last person I would marry.

She may call herself my wife. I can't contemplate such a thing. There's only one way I could ever be happy again, and that is to marry you. I know it is impossible unless economic circumstances change, and you told me never to mention it again. But now it was you who brought it up. Believe me, I am a one-girl man. I shall not return to this subject and I hope you also will not – unless you decided to marry someone else. I think we are locked together come hell and high water, as the English saying is.

I'll arrange to come to Budapest the weekend before Easter. It is short but it can't be helped. Actually I don't think I shall get much other holiday this Easter because I shall have to supervise the moving of the papers to the House of Lords. Purely as a matter of theory and not because I have any plans at the moment, surely your last absence from Hungary as a tourist was in 1972 when we went to Venice. So you are due for another time of permission to go abroad. Something might work out in the autumn, though I am not confident. We must discuss this when we meet. In fact we shall have so much to discuss that we shall never stop talking. Of course if you go to Paris I can let you have some money, unless we have a tight exchange control by then which is more than possible.

I will bring *Sword of Honour* with me. Evelyn gave it to me himself, as I may have told you, because I mentioned it in my bibliography of *English History 1914–1945* as the only great English novel of the Second World War. I will also get the Snow book and might even read it. I expect you have read *Sword of Honour* when it was three separate books. It is not much changed except to be harder and more tightly written. I suppose reconstructing it was the last thing Evelyn did.

I am working hard on my autobiography so as to have something to show when we meet. Also I have just made a will leaving the autobiography to you. It might make some money. In any case you are the only person who can decide whether it should be published.

Poor you. Poor you. Poor you. You must have had a bad time over Christmas. I only hope everything is now going well. We are threatened that winter will arrive here some time. Up to now we have had only mild spring weather, but there is plenty of time for February to be cold and snowy. Perhaps everyone will have flu then. I hope not me. I am a bad invalid.

I expect I told you most of my news in my last letter. Here it is again in case I left anything out. Worcester and Gloucester were a great success. Crispin drove his friends to Edinburgh and back without mishap. I am glad I let him have the car while I still own one. Now he has returned to Cambridge, where he is far happier than in London.

1975

Daniel has become a keen Labour Party worker. He has been made membership secretary of his ward and has now been put on the GMC (general management committee) of the constituency. There he will find Giles established as the most powerful figure. The two get on wonderfully well together. Certainly there is no feud in the younger generation.

Unlike Crispin, Daniel is also keen on the theatre. He and I are going to *The Birthday Party* by Pinter. If it is anything like *The Caretaker* it will be a success. Last Sunday I heard the Bartók Quartet playing miraculously. Of course I thought of the last time I heard them. On Monday I am going to Glastonbury to lecture. Then I shall hear the Smetana Quartet playing Beethoven. They are the Bartók's only rivals. Maybe too I shall hear the Berlioz *Messe des Morts*, though Daniel refuses to go to this with me. He certainly knows what he likes and what he doesn't. That is about all my activities, except that I shall start lecturing in Oxford next week. Rebecca West has recovered her affection for me and has asked me to have dinner with her. Probably she has forgotten why she ever took offence.

Politics are in a sad state. No one knows how to treat our economic troubles and we are in for bad labour troubles. I think the entire Western world is approaching breakdown, with this country almost the first to go.

I shall never be evasive with you. And on your side, never think that my letters are teasing. It is only that you perhaps misunderstand them. One other thing. I try to be cheerful but the closing of the Library is a terrible blow to me. So I need your love.

And here is mine,

Love,
Alan XXXX

31 January

Darling Heart, Lovey Eva,

Here is some news that will, I hope, please you. At 14.15 hours on 21 March next, all being well or as the old-fashioned say DV, I shall step from the British Airways plane at Budapest Airport and shall be with you until 15.30 on the following Monday. I am sorry it is so short but the cheap trips only work for three days. While we are together we must make better plans for the autumn. We should, I think, go straight to the police so that I can register. I shall probably be able to get money changed at the airport. Let me know as soon as you can whether this is all convenient.

I will bring you *Sword of Honour* and a Penguin of *The Conscience of the Rich*. Della and Bill Igoe persuaded me that I had got it wrong and that what you really wanted was *In Their Wisdom*, so I have got that too. I will bring some elegant tea and also a little joke present I have got for you. Where did I get to with my autobiography? I think to the breakdown of my first marriage, in which case I shall have two more completed chapters to show you. Indeed, with any luck I might have more. Anything else you would like me to bring? We must also discuss what if anything to do about the Ranke Gesellschaft. I am not keen to go firstly because I think we should be embarrassed if we were together under the eyes of elderly German professors, and secondly because if I go they will surely want me to talk about Suez and I surely will not want to.

You told me that I should never be evasive with you, and so I won't be. The truth is that closing the Library has been a great blow to me and has left me rather depressed. What is worse, I myself have to direct the dispersal, which is like burying someone you love as well as seeing him or her die. Papers to the House of Lords; cartoons to the University of Kent; Canadian papers to the University of New Brunswick; original letters to be sold, and so on. Of course I shall get over it but things will never be quite the same again. In a way I have lost my purpose in life – no doubt an unimportant purpose, but a purpose all the same. So you must be a little patient with me and, if it is not too much trouble, very loving. Perhaps that is no difficulty. It will all be over the week after I return from Budapest, and the sooner it is done with the better.

No sensational news. I made a trip to Glastonbury to lecture to their Historical Association. Agreeable to be able to drive quite a long way and to know that someone else is paying for it. Good and very large audience. For once the Historical Association charged for admission, so I think they made a profit out of it. Disappointing the next morning. I had hoped to spend an hour or two looking at the Abbey ruins (where Joseph of Aramathea is supposed to have planted the Holy Thorn). But the ruins are in the open and there was a very cold wind blowing, so I got into my car and drove back to Oxford. That has been my only public activity.

I heard the Smetana Quartet playing two late Beethoven quartets, and am going again on Sunday to hear them play the Janáček quartet. In their way they are as good as the Bartók Quartet, beautifully restrained playing so that you feel that they are playing to each other and not thinking about the audience at all. I also heard a rather absurd combination of instruments playing ragtime, including Scott Joplin and others. Has the craze for ragtime (which is different from jazz) reached Budapest? Ferencz will probably know if you do not.

Last night Daniel and I went to see *The Birthday Party*, Pinter's first play. Have you ever seen it?

Peculiar, to say the least. Not as good as *The Caretaker*, but fascinating all the same. It is said that the two intruders come from some gang and that Stanley has been a traitor to it. I think everything much more mysterious than that. Fortunately Daniel was very amused. Good news. He has passed his test at the first go. Now of course he wants to drive mine. Bad news. He and some friends were caught gambling (playing cards for money) when they ought to have been at Assembly singing hymns. A foolish thing to do, as I told him. But there is no virtue in standing by someone who is not foolish and in trouble. The time to do it is when he is, so I shall have to fight the headmaster on this rather weak ground.

By a pure stroke of luck I am involved in post-war history. I have written a long piece for an Italian magazine *Storia Illustrata* on Yalta. Now I have a book on Potsdam for a long piece in *Harpers*. The embarrassing thing is that the historical verdict, as I see it, comes out so very strongly pro-Russian. And the harder I try to be impartial the more pro-Russian it turns out. At Yalta there was agreement because the British and Americans treated the Russians as equals. At Potsdam they did not. Hence all the troubles in the world from that day to this. I'll try and bring copies of both articles.

My typing is very bad today. I fear my nerves are in a bad state. At any rate I am not doing it deliberately. You are the only bright spot in my dreary world. Think of me and love me as I love you.

    Kisses, my Darling,
     x
      x   Alan
     x
    x

10 February

Dearest Eva (just to show I remember your name),

I had a sweet letter from you dated 30 January and write back with love. I understand your problems so well. Indeed, I worry that you are so lonely except for your two boys. I reproach myself that I entered your life. If we had not encountered decisively at Salzburg you might now be happily married. Perhaps I should give you up as you so often threaten to do with me? Otherwise I will give you as much happiness as I can. That reminds me about my coming visit. We shall not have much time. Therefore you must be used to me straight away. No reserves, no shyness, no getting used to each other. We must just be perfect together from the beginning as we were last September.

On a practical basis, what sort of weather do you expect? Here we have not had a single winter's day. It has been mild all the time. The grass continues to grow. Not one flake of snow. How is it with you? Of course we could have really cold weather in March, so I had better come well prepared. I have today sent off to you *The Conscience of the Rich* and *In Their Wisdom*, so that I shall have less to carry. I shall bring *Sword of Honour* and also *The Second World War*, advance copies of which have just come out. Did I tell you that I was on a new task: picking out all my essays on English history and putting them into a single volume for Penguin. If I am not careful I shall have no less than three books in one year. Perhaps a grand finale to my career.

About Rebecca, I got to know her when she published *Black Lamb and Grey Falcon* and I praised it. I used to go often to her house and liked her husband Henry Andrews even more than I liked her. Occasionally they spent Christmas with us. Rebecca was quick, perceptive, exciting. I thought she often overdid things, seeing mysteries and conspiracies where there were none. I also thought she wrote far too much about traitors after the war. Henry was a much more level-headed character. Indeed I think she is an overrated writer, writing all the time about very rich and very unimportant people. After Henry's death we continued very friendly until as a sort of birthday present I sent her an old telegram from her to Beaverbrook describing H. G. Wells as a bore. She never answered and cut me off altogether for some years. The other day unexpectedly she wrote rather sadly that she was solitary and would like to see me. I wrote back eagerly. But she has not answered. I fear she is breaking up and has probably forgotten that she ever wrote to me. She also said she was almost blind – cataract I suppose. If I were you I should not waste time reading any of her books.

And here is what has been happening to me. I went yet again to the

Smetana Quartet when they played the two Janáček quartets. I gave a very good lunch-time lecture at University College on 'The Origins of the First World War'. See, I am moving backwards. I talked all about Fritz Fischer and found more to say than on the Second War. Then I went to the Berlioz *Grande Messe des Morts*, by the Birmingham Symphonic – very well done and very exciting.

Daniel asked whether he could use my car on his own. I said Yes, but not in the evenings. Janet remarked it was like telling a girl that she could go out on her own but must be back at ten. So I agreed for the evening also, on condition that he did not drink. I think that was fair. Daniel now spends most of his time distributing Labour pamphlets and attending ward meetings. I am very pleased, and so is Giles who goes along with him.

I'll write again soon. All the love in the world,

X
Alan
X

15 February

Darling Lovey,

This is quite ridiculous. I wrote to you only last Tuesday, and here I am already answering your letter of 6 February. Like you, I know I shall let a long time pass unless I write to you at once. Also, I like writing and am unable to deny myself the pleasure. First I must tell you that you are not old for me and never will be. You remember what the Commander says in *Man and Superman*. He told every woman he met: 'One white hair of the woman I love will always mean more to me than that of any girl.' Tanner was shocked, but I mean it. One gets weary of other people. I don't think we shall ever weary of each other. That should be some consolation for you.

Now as to your queries. DV means God willing – *Deo volente*. Old-fashioned people still put it on the dates of their future appointments. I sensed that you were a little embarrassed about what the two boys would think of us. Well, I can tell you, knowing many young people. They accept without question that we have our own lives to lead. I am sure that your boys were not a bit troubled. Otherwise Pisti would not have said that the sooner I came again the better.

As you say, you are greedy. The obstacle to bringing all the books you want is that books are heavy, too heavy for me to carry in a weekend case. I shall bring *Sword of Honour, Portrait of a Marriage* which has just come out in paperback, and *The Second World War: an Illustrated History*. That is all I can manage. You have romantic tastes. The correspondence between Rebecca and H. G. is rather silly, nothing like as good as *Darling Pussy* which you will get in the autumn. I have also resolved that in future I will cut out the reviews I write for the *Observer* and the *New Statesman* and send them to you. At the moment I am reviewing nothing, but there is plenty to come.

I am in rather a distressful state. The central heating in our house went wrong and we have had to keep warm with the occasional electric radiator and gas fire. Of course the weather turned cold and I have felt wretched except in the warmth of the Library. The break-up of the Library is now on the move. The cartoons have gone to Canterbury. Tomorrow a bookseller is coming to look at the books and will, I hope, carry them away. If he gives me a lot of money I shall have something to spend when we meet for a longer time in September. But the ending of the Library makes me sad as it comes nearer. It is no good saying I shall still have a good room and a secretary. It won't be the same when I have no real reason to be down in Fleet Street at all. This time I feel my life is really finishing. However, there is also good news. University College London has renewed my lectureship there for another year, and as it is an unofficial one there is every chance that I shall go on when I have passed the official retiring age of seventy. That as you know is coming fast.

We had great fun watching the election of Margaret Thatcher to the leadership of the Conservative Party. I don't care who leads the Conservative Party. They can have an orang-utang if they like, as Peacock once suggested in a novel. The orang-utang was elected for a rotten borough under the title of Sir Oran Haut-ton. Have you ever read any Peacock? He is very funny, though you need to know a lot of early nineteenth-century literature and politics to enjoy his novels. There are good satirical portraits of Shelley, Byron, Brougham, James Mill and other intellectuals. When I was young I read him constantly. Unfortunately there is no good collected edition in one volume, otherwise I would get it for you. I am reading *Dombey and Son*. It has some good things, but on the whole is very bad. I told Kathleen Tillotson this when we last met. She answered that I had told her exactly the same twenty years ago. Alas, I forget my old conversations with her, though I forget none with you. In my autobiography I have just got to 1958 when I visited Budapest and met a girl who sat by the Danube with me and bewitched me for ever. Who could have foreseen that a romantic dream would come true? It has brought me the only happiness in life after many sorrows.

Darling Pussy has gone to the printers and will be ready in the autumn. I am hoping that it will also be serialized in either the *Sunday Express* or the *Sunday Times*. Now I am deep in my old essays, preparing them for a collected volume. When Swift read in old age *The Tale of a Tub*, his first work, he said: 'What a genius I had in those days.' I feel the same about my essays. I don't think I have the same gifts now, though perhaps I have others.

I am glad to report that Daniel is still deep in Labour Party work. He uses my car now when he goes to the cinema, but has promised never to drive it when he is likely to drink. His gambling escapade passed over with a stern warning. He is turning into an intellectual, very Left and very dogmatic. He has no patience with my gloomy views. All the same, our economic position is very bad. Inflation running at 20 per cent and vast debts abroad so that I really fear we may go bankrupt. I can't see freedom of movement going on much longer. My stockbroker asked me whether I should like to buy £2,000 worth of gold coins. I refused to confess things were as bad as that, but perhaps they are.

Deep and abiding love, even if you are old,

Alan
XXX

5 March

Lovey Mine,

Don't be alarmed. This is not a letter saying that I am not coming. I wrote you a letter on Sunday. Then I found I had no stamp so took it to Edinburgh, where I bought a stamp and posted it to you. As I told you, I decided that this should be my last letter. But then yesterday when I returned from Edinburgh I found your letter of 25 February waiting for me and felt, like you, that I wanted to talk to you. So here is yet another letter which shall really be my last.

I have nothing to report. I had a very agreeable journey to Edinburgh by sleeper, the best form of travel. I examined a boy for his Ph.D. which I gave him. I gave a very good lecture on 'The Coming of the Second World War' to an enormous audience. There was a reception for me and then a quiet dinner. After that three historians spent some time talking to me. My host Paul Addison was very good. At half-past ten he said: 'Alan likes to go to bed at this time, so out you go.' Easy journey back on Tuesday, except that the pork pies had run out at the train buffet. Now weighed down by 500 pages of a biography of Mosley which the *Observer* wants to run as a very long front-page article. I shall have to be brutal to him. He comes out very badly – not merely wicked, but totally lacking in judgement. That is my news. I am very well except that I have arthritis in my left thumb and can hardly hold a razor to shave with. Would you like me with a grizzled grey-white beard? I should not like myself.

The Library is beginning to disperse. I have sold my books for £375. This should pay for a holiday for us in September. Something to look forward to. You find your feelings for me mysterious and puzzling. There is really no difficulty: we are married except that circumstances keep us apart. No worse than if I were a nineteenth-century civil servant in India and you had to live in Europe. I can't remember what I wanted to say in Hatvanyv* Street, perhaps what a rise in the world after his living in a flat in Oxford. Michael would have laughed. He never took Hatvanyv seriously, and no doubt this was why Hatvanyv was malicious about him. You are right that the *TLS* has deteriorated. Its job is to cover all the important books as they come out, and it is not doing that job any more. Instead there are whole numbers devoted to subjects that do not interest me at all – philosophy and mysticism and far-fetched literary themes.

Future lecture plans. I shall give four lectures at University College in the autumn on 'History in General'. I do this each year for the beginners. And next January I shall give three lectures at the Senate House on two wars and a peace – 1914–45. I didn't choose this. It is part of a series. I shall also be lecturing in Oxford for the last time, I don't know on what. Then I shall abandon my Oxford rooms and probably my car. Sebastian is very contemptuous of this. He says my car won't fetch much money and that I should therefore hang on to it until it drops.

When next in Oxford I shall search whether there is a paperback of all Peacock's novels. If there is, I shall bring it with me. I have discovered that apples – home-grown too – are cheaper in Oxford than in London, so come back loaded every week. I went to a boring party last night for the opening of a special Penguin room at Foyle's. The invitation said: 'Champagne Buffet'. There was champagne, but I assumed buffet meant

---

* Baron Hatvanyv – a Hungarian émigré living in England.

enough food to count as my dinner. It didn't, so I had to leave the party and go to the Beefsteak Club which was also boring.

I now firmly resolve not to write to you again. I think a lot about you as you tell me to. Oh, one thing I forgot. With so short a time I'd rather be with you than go to a concert or to friends. But you decide.

Loving thoughts which make me restless.

X   Alan   X

30 March

Eva, Lovey,

I simply must write to you although I had resolved to wait a fortnight. Like the girl with Malcolm, I really only want to say thank you a thousand times over. In all the gloom that surrounds me, the thought of you, and of course still more being with you alone, makes me happy. I don't care what happens to me or in the world as long as I can go on seeing you. And let my love make you happy also. Oh, I love you so much.

I shall certainly meet you in September for at least ten days. Find out, when you can, how you stand with being able to go abroad. The most sensible thing it seems to me is that we should meet by going towards each other, not by going still further to Ohrid. Would you rather go to Italy or to France? We could meet in Verona, which is not a difficult journey for you or for me. Perhaps even I could pick up some money in Milan. Or we could go to Burgundy, which would mean meeting in Paris. If you can't cross the frontier I shall come to Budapest and we can go away together. By the way, the Paris hotel was the Mont Blanc. We shall not go there again – rather the Bretonnière, if that was its name.

I have had a busy time. On Wednesday I spent five hours making a television programme for Canada, of course for a suitably high reward. It was all shot in the open air and, as it was raining most of the time, this was no great fun. I stood outside the Bank of England and talked, then the Stock Exchange, then St Paul's. Then we moved to the Houses of Parliament. After lunch we went to New Scotland Yard, to talk about violence; to 10 Downing Street, to talk about prime ministers; and finally to a house T. E. Lawrence once lived in, to talk about English eccentrics. It was certainly a hard day.

Apart from that I have made a radio talk about *The Second World War* and have five more to come, all in the hope that they will sell the book. In any case it keeps my thoughts off the closing of the Library. It is being literally torn to pieces. The shelves have gone. The books have gone. Soon the tables and chairs will go, and there will be nothing left except an empty floor. The bosses cannot find a new room for me, so Della and I will just stay where we are, which suits me fine. Maybe they will forget about me and I shall stay indefinitely. But it is a miserable business, just when I thought I was settled for life.

I have read all the six books on Edward VII, becoming increasingly bored with his love life as I read each one. What on earth is there to say about a man who was Prince of Wales until he was sixty, except that he amused himself somehow? Of course it is all the fault of television – thirteen programmes on him as Prince of Wales, and now another thirteen threatened on him as King. I think I'll write my review solely judging him as a telestar, a subject which I ought to know well. There is after all no serious point in the subject. Bagehot called him 'an unemployed youth' and so he was, making activity for himself. I wonder how any woman could love him when he was so fat. He must surely have had to use some unusual positions to get over this.

No serious news. I have two reviews in the new *History*, neither of them important. Alan Sked came round and showed his usual easy charm. Crispin has arranged to go to Dijon for the whole of July. We went for a long walk yesterday. Daniel set off for Blackpool on Friday in a snowstorm. But he was determined to go and since I have not heard that he has crashed I suppose he is all right. Tomorrow I am going to Eastbourne in order to meet Giles for a day on the South Downs way. Twenty miles at a stretch, when I have not walked so far since last summer!

The next thing I must do is to write my intellectual biography for the *Review of Modern History*. I can't think what to say. As you know, I can only write about the women in my life. Thank goodness one of them came right even if a bit late. That is why I love you.

        Alan   XXXXXXX
      Love, Love, Love
              X

1975

8 April

Eva Lovey,

The time must be coming when I shall receive a letter from you. I always worry a little when no letter comes. I begin to think that you have grown impatient with me or feel that I am not worth bothering about. But then I reflect that you often don't feel in a mood for writing, and of course I don't want you to write if you don't feel like it.

The Library has now been stripped to its foundations. The documents have gone to the House of Lords. The stacks have been torn down. The furniture has been removed. Even the carpet in the lobby has been pulled up. All that remains is the portrait of Lord Beaverbrook surveying an empty floor. At present no room can be found for Della and me, so we are going to stay where we are indefinitely. There will be knockings and disturbance while rooms are being constructed inside the Library floor, but I shall not mind that. I am not sure, however, that I shall be able to stand it when the advertising department moves in. I have now learnt why the Library was killed, and it has nothing to do with shortage of money. Apparently they are installing new machinery on the floor below the advertising department and did not allow for the fact that the machinery was too tall to be accommodated on a single floor. In fact, the machinery stuck up into the offices above. New space was needed for the advertising offices. None could be found so they simply grabbed the Library. Sad, but it can't be helped.

Fortunately I have been too busy to have time to be miserable. I wrote a front-page review of Skidelsky's biography of Mosley for the *Observer*. You will be angry that I should write at all about such a wicked man, but if you ever read the piece you will see that I have not treated him in any favourable spirit. I can't send you the review because I am going to use it in my collected essays, but you'll see it later. Next I am struggling with a book about British prime ministers – short essays of no great value, but I suppose I can have some fun with it. I am also reading a fascinating book about the Channel Islands under German Occupation, showing how the British government neglected the Channel Islands. Towards the end, when food was running short there, Churchill insisted on intensifying the blockade and said of the German soldiers: 'Let them rot.' Someone pointed out that the inhabitants were also starving, at which he said more or less: 'Then they must rot too.' I have also read a book about the Danish Resistance, a most honourable record. Out of 7,000 Jews the Danes got all but 400 away to Sweden, an operation in which the whole nation cooperated.

My other activity is preparing for a burst of publicity over *The Second*

World War: an Illustrated History. It comes out next Monday and I will send you the reviews as they come in. I am going to talk about it on radio and on television, and I am going to autograph copies at bookshops. I shall be running around wildly. You did not give me your opinion of it. Perhaps you did not read it while I was with you. Oh, how lovely that was. The only other bit of news is that on the Monday after Easter I walked sixteen miles along the South Downs way along with Giles, Crispin, Amelia and her chap, quite a family party. I am glad to report that I was totally untired, unlike Amelia who thought it a bit much!

I read in *The Times* every day that you are having marvellous weather. We are having a belated winter, snow, sleet, bitterly cold wind. I am wearing a vest for the first time. My doctor has again decided to fear that I have cancer of the bowel, but I am sure I haven't. I'll tell you about it when I have any news. I'll also tell you next time of my summer plans, which are very few. This is really just a letter to say I am alive and loving you, my dearest.

XXXXXXXXXXXXXXXXXXXX
Alan

18 April

My Beloved Darling,

I am somewhat anxious at not having heard from you. Perhaps your letter has gone astray, as mine did from Edinburgh (did you ever receive it?). Perhaps you are ill. Perhaps you have taken up with someone else. Or perhaps you are angry with me for not spending more time with you. More likely, knowing you, you are just not in the mood to write and, if you are in that mood or lack of it, I don't want you to write. You know how I need you, and you also know that I don't deserve you. So you do things the way you want.

I have had a troublesome time. First, it was very fortunate that I did not try to go away anywhere for Easter The weather has been unpleasant to a degree with cold, snow and rain. But now it is spring. All my summer clothes are in Oxford and I am not going there for another fortnight, so I suffer from my clothes being too warm.

The Library is being literally knocked down, men smashing down the walls with great hammers and the electricity wires being torn from the walls. However, I have just learnt that a very agreeable two rooms are waiting for me at the front, and Della and I will move there soon. You can write to me, if you ever write at all, at the same address, and I'll let you have a new one when I get it. Meanwhile I am working hard. I have got *Darling Pussy* off to the printers. I have gone through my essays and prepared a good Penguin for the autumn. All I need is a title. 'Essays on English History' sounds so boring. I'll have to think up something like 'Men and Events' or 'Policies and Politicians' with 'Essays in English History' as a sub-title.

The Second World War came out last Monday. I have been hard at work on publicity. I have done altogether six radio programmes. They all ask the same questions: Why do I say the Second World War was a good war? I am tempted to answer because I wrote a good book about it. Then they say what mysteries are there still about the Second World War? To which the answer is – why did people ever fight such a mad war? But that will not do either. Today I am going to be interviewed by Finnish television and Canadian. On Wednesday I was interviewed by Southern Television, and I only just escaped going all the way to Glasgow in order to have a discussion with Oswald Mosley. I'll be glad when the storm of activity subsides. Only two reviews so far, both excellent, but both in serious papers and by friends of mine. I'd like to have some in the popular press so that there will really be mass sales.

My two boys seem useless for any summer holiday. Daniel refuses to go to the Lake District and Crispin will be away in Dijon. I am firm in my own plans. Somehow I will spend a fortnight with you if you'll have me. I will send you £350, which is the most I am allowed to send you. Be sure to save it up and not spend it on other things. It is for your fare to Italy or France, or for our expenses in Hungary. I'll not send it yet awhile to make sure you don't spend it. In any case we must get our plans clearer. I hope you don't go to the Ranke Gesellschaft, much better to spend the time with me. But I wanted to begin thinking about it now. Otherwise I should go mad. Every moment of the day I think how we could be doing this or that. It is a catastrophe that we cannot be together all the time, but there it is. The economic situation here is much worse, prices doubling every couple of months. I don't know how any of us on fixed incomes are going to survive. But I mean to survive somehow until September. Please write and go on loving me.

Rather unhappy, but still loving you as much as ever.

Alan

22 April

Darling Loved One,

    I had a feeling that there really was something wrong with you this time. I worried and worried. Yesterday I rang you up and got no reply, but maybe I rang a little early. Then this morning I got your lovely letter (because you always write lovely letters) and worried no more. Of course I am distressed you have been ill, but now you are slowly getting better. Do not start work again too soon. Rest and enjoy the sunshine, which I hope like us at last you are getting. I can only write back what you write to me: do not leave me, do not die. I have no intention of having cancer. I am not unhappy so long as I can think of you, though sad not to be with you. The end of the Library was a blow, but now I am relieved not to have the responsibility. Tomorrow I move to a big office in the front building and so start as it were anew. Letters will reach me at the old address, but the new one is simply 121 Fleet Street, London EC4. However, you don't need to write for some time now that I know that you are all right.

    Answer to your wicked thoughts. Della cuts open the envelope of your letter but does not remove the contents and would never dream of doing so. I wonder about everything, but never doubt that I need you. I change many of my opinions because of further thought and new ways of seeing things. Sometimes I change because of new evidence. The Mosley quotation which offended you was torn from its context. It was taken from a review of his autobiography where I said that in his early Socialist days he promised to become a superb political thinker etc. He or his publisher has used it as though it applied to Mosley now. In last week's *Observer*, or the one before, you will find a whole page by me on Mosley. Some people have said that I ought not to write about Mosley at all. I think I took the right course. I praised his early career and then emphasized how he had gone wrong especially over anti-semitism. You will see from the most recent issue of the *Observer* (20 April) that Mosley himself is angry because I went over his past record instead of praising what he does now. So having given disaffection on both sides, I think I must have been about right. In a way it is a new version on a smaller scale of the trouble I had over *The Origins of the Second World War*. I am firmly and unshakably against Fascism, as my record shows. I also think that Fascism and even anti-semitism should be treated in a scientific, academic way, discussing its ideas and showing how they were perversions of good ones. After all everyone writes books about Hitler, and I think quite an interesting one could be written about the ideas underlying *Mein Kampf*, which is not only anti-semitic. I myself am quite willing to say, as I have in *The Second World War*, that Hitler was often a brilliant strategist and that there were many good things in his economic policy. I think the destruction of Hitler and his system was the best thing that happened in my lifetime. But I don't think he was the only wicked force in the world. What about the Americans who dropped the atomic bombs on Japan, or for that matter the politicians and scientists in more than one country who are preparing for a nuclear war on a vast scale? In fact, if we did not write about wicked men we should not be able to write history at all. I am so clear that they were wicked that I don't bother to say it. My job is to get the record straight. So do not hesitate to write to me your wicked thoughts, as you call them. Some of them are misunderstandings, as for instance your disapproval of what I said to Baroness Hatvani, or that Della opens your letters. Others are a genuine difference of point of view. I hope we shall always differ over many scholarly questions. That is what academic life is about. You ask why I change my views. Because I put my conscience as a scholar above everything else, or even above anyone else. I may often be wrong, but if so I err honestly and for no calculating reason. A cynic? How can I not be when I have spent my life writing history?

Don't exaggerate the advantages in my life. I see Daniel for two hours on a Sunday afternoon. I don't see Crispin when he is at Cambridge, otherwise for one hour on a Saturday afternoon. I see the others about once a month, not that I complain but they are hardly companions for me any more. Margaret is no companion for me. She cooperates in the house, as I do, but we have no common interests. When I go out I go alone, and the same with her except when she wants to use my name and reputation.

Back to my book. Rather bad reviews in the *New Statesman* and the *Economist* – not hostile, but short and rather uninteresting. In the *NS* the reviewer merely said he had tried to write a book like mine and had failed. On your questions, Hess was important only as a stand-in for Hitler, making rabble-rousing speeches. He never attended meetings of the top men and after 1936 had little idea what was going on. Yes, Gamelin was as silly and pretentious as I make him out to be. Churchill said: 'more a professor than a general'. Here is another review for you. I will send some interesting ones if they ever come in.

My Darling Pussy has just gone to press. My *Essays on English History* go to Penguin tomorrow. So I have time to breathe. On Thursday I go to the annual dinner of the British Academy. There will be no brown-eyed girl sitting opposite me as there once was at the dinner of the Hungarian Institute of Historical Research.

Never doubt me. I shall stay in love with you till I die. Let me know as soon as you can whether you will be able to come abroad in September. If so we'll meet in Milan. If not I'll come to Budapest. Now I regard your home as mine and I like coming home.

LOVE   LOVE   LOVE
Alan

6 May

Beloved or (if you prefer) Lovey Dovey,

I received your letter of 23 April. Maybe you have sent another one since then which will no doubt arrive in time. It is only when letters are sent from Edinburgh that they go wrong. So this will be a cheerful letter as far as our relations are concerned.

I have now finally left the Library building, and it is being knocked about preparatory to housing the advertising department. But I shall never enter it again nor want to. I have made my peace with the closing of the Library and it has become simply part of my past life. After all, I have had many disappointments and setbacks in my career and have never harked back to them after. I have an enormous room in the newspaper building, a room that previously housed the managing director. Sebastian has a theory that many rivals are quarrelling to get the room and so the managing director's succession, so they gave the room to me and so kept all the rivals out. It has no air-conditioning and will be very hot when the sun shines. But I shan't care. I shall simply retire to Highgate Ponds.

I have no urgent work. I have no responsibilities. I am waiting for the proofs of *Darling Pussy* and meanwhile relax a little. Somehow we shall certainly meet in September. My only worry is external – the deterioration of the British economic position and the likelihood of devaluation or possibly of restrictions on foreign travel. I wanted to send you some money, so as to make certain that I could come to you in September or that you would have the fare to come to me. But of course if you really can't control your spending habits and would simply run through the money, there is no good sending it. Have another think and consider whether for my sake you could lock the money firmly away in your bank until I come. When people, especially women, say they don't know how to manage money, I suspect that they are proud of it and feel it somehow emphasizes their feminine charm. Don't fear that I shall ever be cross with you about this. I'll simply take care. But I repeat: it would be better for us both if I could send the money.

I've had lots more reviews, mostly rather poor ones. I don't mean hostile, merely feeble. One reviewer said the text was merely a commentary on the illustrations. How could it be when the entire text was written before the illustrations were chosen? Of course some foolish reviewers have said that I made too much of Russia's part in the war, as if that were possible. But these things are of no importance. I attach importance to reviews if they make real criticisms or put new ideas into my head. I also welcome them if they help to sell the book. Now the sales are running hard of themselves, so I do not need to bother. There will be another lot of reviews when the book comes out in the States. Then I am sure there will be much more indignation that I am a pro-Russian or even a pro-Communist propagandist. To set against this Daniel asked me the other day why I had such a reputation as an anti-Communist. I said I did not know I had, but he said among the Young Socialists I was regarded as a puzzle, being very Left and yet not going with the Communists. I tried to explain but am not sure that I succeeded. In any case Daniel told me that British Communists are now reformists, far to the right of such revolutionary Socialists as himself.

I went to North Shields on Friday to lecture on Hitler. I can't remember now what led me to choose the subject. The lecture went all right but I kept thinking what a dull, uninteresting man he was. Talking of Fascists, I reviewed the biography of Mosley on the front page of the *Observer* and said that his purpose in creating the Blackshirts was to create disturbance and then seize power. Whereupon he threatened the *Observer* with an action for libel. In the end he was satisfied with their publishing a letter from him, in which strangely enough he did not deny the charge but merely said it was libellous. I think I shall not be bothered with his invitations to dinner again.

I have read a long book about Roosevelt last year and about how he revived the love affair of his youth. The last thing he saw before he suddenly fell unconscious was Lucy Mercer's smiling face – a really beautiful story. Otherwise there is the usual nonsense about how he was deceived by Stalin and about how Poland was betrayed to Russia by the Western powers. It is extraordinary how ignorant people are in regard to Poland, or about Hungary for that matter. They write about the Polish territory which was torn from Poland by Russia in 1945, whereas it was Russian territory that the Poles had stolen from Russia in 1921. There is no catching up on such errors.

Now I have started on volume IV of Martin Gilbert's *Churchill*. This is all on the Lloyd George time from 1917 to 1922, vast number of subjects but I am not sure they are worth writing about at such length. They don't add to our knowledge of Churchill or of history. There are two hundred pages on Churchill's war of intervention in Russia and all so monotonous, the same thing over and over again. Churchill putting forward all sorts of arguments and cutting down the British forces, Churchill putting forward the same arguments all over again. He managed to spend a great deal of money and caused the death of thousands of Russians, all for a political dogma that the Bolsheviks were wicked and uncivilized, when he knew absolutely nothing about either the Bolsheviks or Russia. It is far more discreditable than the Dardanelles. Then there are hundreds of pages on the Middle East, with Churchill telling the Arabs that the Jews will never be allowed to seize their lands and at the same time encouraging the Jews to go ahead. This time I think Churchill was the deceived, not the deceiver. I can't understand how Lloyd George put up with him or why.

I am going to Oxford for a couple of days in order to sit on a committee to choose a tutor in Politics. Soon I shall be at an end in Oxford and shall lose my lovely rooms, another epoch in my life closing. I am sorry to say democracy is breaking into College. Until now I had breakfast almost alone in the elegance of the Senior Common Room. Now I have to have it in Hall among the undergraduates. Revolution is knocking at the door. It is most alarming.

A cheerful trivial letter, but that is what I meant it to be.

With very deep and very lasting love which we must both just accept and make the best of.

Alan

15 May

Deepest Beloved,

This letter will make you slightly dizzy if it arrives as quickly as yours did to me. You wrote last Sunday and your letter only took four days to come here. It was a beautiful letter, the most beautiful letter you have written me. So I thought I would repay you by answering at once. Also I have been out to lunch with Dan Davin, the head of Oxford University Press, and am feeling too sleepy to do any work – not that I ever work in the afternoons. With any luck this letter should reach you next Tuesday. Do not feel that there is any obligation on you to answer

1975

at the same speed. However, it is a delight to write to you this rather gloomy May afternoon.

Here is some practical chat. Some time soon I will send £200 to you. This should pay all right for any fares you may have to spend or our common expenses. As you know, I am allowed to send £350 in a year and so should keep some in reserve in case you go to France. Of course there may soon be a ban on foreign travel here if the financial crisis explodes, but we can go on planning that it won't. I should like to come to Budapest in September and will plan to do so – say in about the second week in the month. I hope we can go away together for a few days. My scheme for getting money in Milan does not seem like coming off. If it does we can think again. I'll collect some money in Milan and meet you in Venice or Verona. If you come to Venice do not get off at Mestre. Seriously, however, it will be Budapest. Later perhaps I could come to Paris for a few days if you are there. But Paris we could certainly do.

My other plans for the summer are these. I thought I would have no companion to go to the Lake District with me: Giles and Sebastian are too tied with their children, Daniel is bored with the Lake District. Crispin and I, however, are going for the last week in June before he goes to Dijon. Daniel says he would like to go to the family home in the Isle of Wight, so I am going also for the first part of July and again for the first part of August (it is let in between, in order to pay some of the expenses).

My other commitment is that the television discussion programme 'Free Speech' is to return for six weeks from the end of June. As I enjoy my appearances and get £100 for each one, I had better stay in England until they are over. I have had some other TV performances recently, and tomorrow I am going to give a half-hour lecture on Britain and Europe: 'Half In, Half Out'. Really I shall ramble over the history of unity and disunity, ending up with the unhelpful remark that history gives us no guidance one way or the other. As to your enquiries, I have called my essays at present *Policies and Politicians: Essays in English History*. I can't use a title containing anything about Europe because (a) the essays are not about Europe; (b) my other volume of essays is strictly Europe. My autobiography is stuck at present. I shall write a lot in the Isle of Wight when I shall have nothing else to do. Do not worry about your own part in it. You have read the account of our first meeting and can judge for yourself. When it gets more on to you, you will appear as the heroine of the book. I have had a miserable life which would have ended in unhappiness and failure if you had not come along. As it is, I have nothing in life to moan about. I hate the way our society has developed, ending in catastrophe or something like it. I don't much like the way my own career is ending. The closure of the Beaverbrook Library really was an undeserved bit of bad luck. However, I have forgotten about the Library already. I live from day to day, writing reviews, meeting people, preparing to write my intellectual biography during the summer. I think my position here may end at any moment and that I shall be thrown out. But let things come as and when they will.

I will bring the reviews of *The Second World War* when I come, also my review of Mosley which most people said was too favourable but which Mosley himself complained of. The British Academy dinner was very boring – Harold made a dreary speech. Dickens is head of the Institute of Historical Research: a commercial traveller in history, vain and full of his own importance, but I get on with him quite well. The English translation of your book (or books) should be shown to me before it is published so that I can make the translation idiomatic. In your Chartist book you ought to add a short account of our visit to Charterville! Did you get the Penguin volume about Lytton Strachey that I sent you? It is even more ludicrous than the story of the Nicolsons. Is there anything else you want? What I want apart from your kisses are your comments on *The Second World War*. Or perhaps you are overawed and bewitched by its brilliance. *The Times* reviewer this morning described me as 'our outstanding old-fashioned historian', a strange fate and quite true.

I can't write such a lovely ending of my letter as yours is. I can only say I love you and want you, and that my wants are physical as well as intellectual.

Alan

24 May

Dear Heart,

Our last telephone conversation distressed me. You must never be angry with me. You must just say what you want and I'll accept it.

There is one other thing I must mention to you. For the first time I begin to feel that I am getting older. This is not meant to be melodramatic, simply a fact that I notice nearly every day. Do not count on me always for the future. I shall not be there. My machine is running down.

1975

I have to make an effort to do things. Of course, with the Library gone I am in a very discouraged state. I seem to be leading a pointless existence and don't want to go on. Also, of course, I have lost faith in the future. I have spent a lifetime believing in Socialism and now I see that nobody wants it. Until recently we were a progressive people. Now what people want is to get back to the past and, if they can't do that, then they would rather go nowhere. I see more and more clearly how inflation destroys the spirit of a nation. Certainly this nation has lost heart, or perhaps it is only me. At any rate I fear the future – my own and the world's. Maybe nuclear weapons will solve all our problems by rubbing us out. Here I end my laments.

I have finished Erickson on the Soviet-German war to Stalingrad and have given it a glowing review. The details are very boring, but they add up to a splendid picture. The relations between Stalin and his generals are very interesting. He could be very rude to them and then calmed them down with a glass of tea. He did not learn caution until after Stalingrad. Thereafter he ran things very well. I have also read an absurd book by Michael Pearson called *The Sealed Train*. It is all about Lenin's return to Russia and how he was in the pay of the Germans. The train story is true, as everyone knows. The rest is manufacture by Kremlinologists in the West. Even Pearson describes it as 'speculation', 'logical speculation', 'conjecture' and so on. My own view is that Parvus made off with the money. If Lenin had taken money from the Allies no one would have objected, and Lenin held that they were all imperialist brigands.

I have landed an interesting though laborious commission. A television and film producer called Jack Le Vien wants to make six ninety-minute films, or rather plays, about Churchill in wartime. He obviously does not know the details and so has brought me in. I can surely draft six scenarios and then a professional playwright will do the rest under my supervision. I should make quite a bit of money if Le Vien can find an American backer. Otherwise we shall be left hanging in the air. Otherwise I am gloomily contemplating the prospect that I must revise *English History 1914–1945*, a job I'd rather leave to the younger generation.

I read in *The Times* that you have been having hot weather. Here it is savagely cold and we have the central heating on all the time. Sophia's little girl Rosa has got measles. I have nothing worse than arthritis in my thumbs which gets more and more painful. Tiresome. I won't write any more except that I am impatient for September.

Now here's love and a kiss or two.

XxXxXxXx
Alan

4 June

Darling, dearest, Lovey dovey, and all the other nice things you wrote in your letter,

I am certainly not depressed or distressed now that I have your lovey-dovey letter of 28 May. I am up in the heavens with love and fond anticipation. We had a marvellous time when I was in Budapest last September. We shall have a marvellous time again. I'll probably come about 8 September and stay for ten days or two weeks. Of course, if after all you change your mind or your plans and want to go somewhere abroad, I can arrange that too. But with the depreciation of the pound, foreign countries are now very expensive for me, and things will be much easier in Budapest where we can spend the money you have already got. If there are any historians around, I might do some advertising of *The Second World War* as well. I'll make fixed plans a little later when I see what other commitments I have. Just think how nice it will be when we are together and I put my arms around you. Like you, my wants are now very simple. Just to be with you and to feel you next me.

My life goes rolling on. I have written scenarios for five of the six Churchill plays and will do the sixth tomorrow. Do you remember when we visited his grave at Bladon? To me every moment of that trip is still vivid. I don't think the producers will really like the plays I have designed – too historical, and also emphasizing that Churchill became a less significant figure as the war went on, so that at the end Stalin and Roosevelt took hardly any notice of him. The producers want to end with him on the balcony on VE Day. I shall try to end with Churchill brooding that he has not been much of a success to judge by what came after. However, the scenarios have been an interesting break from other work even if they come to nothing. Now I face the black shadow of writing my intellectual autobiography for the *Journal of Modern History*. The truth is that I am bad at introspection, particularly intellectual introspection. I simply can't make out what my books are like, except that I wrote them to tell a story. I read *The Course of German History* the other day. It is pretty bad, too clever by half. *The Habsburg Monarchy* is better because less controversial. And *The Struggle for Mastery in Europe* is really unreadable. I think that with *Bismarck* I turned the corner. All my books after that are more human. What do you think? Give me any impressions you have that I could use in the article, not that I promise to do so!

Last night I went to a Lord Mayor's Banquet at the Mansion House. It was very glittery. I had to wear a tail coat (hired), white waistcoat, white tie. There were Beefeaters and men in red uniform.

Trumpets when we went into dinner and a band playing between the courses. Food very ordinary, much as you could get at Lyons. Drink better and cigars very good. I gave one of the only two speeches in a thoroughly irresponsible manner. It was much appreciated and people said it made the dinner worth coming to. A very absurd affair, but it was interesting to see inside the Mansion House for once. Tonight I go to the annual dinner of the History Department at University College, which will be much less ambitious, and I shan't have to make a speech.

Crispin will be home this weekend, I am glad to say. Daniel has his exams coming on and is not cheerful as to the results. He may do better than he expects but, as he told me, he is trying to do two years' work in six weeks, having been persistently idle until now. Incidentally, you are quite wrong to think that I am happy with Margaret. She is a great burden on me and I lament it constantly. She is by no means rational, getting into all sorts of anxiety about herself and about her children and grandchildren. She also exploits me, making plans that suit her and then suddenly springing them on me. Certainly she is sensible she wants to keep hold of me and therefore avoids rows. Also she has the virtue of liking to cook, and prepares meals that are too elaborate. But I can never forget the past, and I don't think she cares for me at all. So you don't need to feel that you have a rival.

Why do you not tell me more of your own work? I know you are busy all the time, and yet have little idea what you are doing in detail. As for me, I have reviewed the fourth volume of *Churchill* and gave a big write-up of Erickson's book on the Road to Stalingrad. Now my desk is actually clear for once. My mind is only half on my work. It is always too full of you and, when I have had enough of thinking about you, I think of our various times together. There were some beautiful episodes. I do hope we can have a few more foreign excursions before I die or before capitalism collapses.

I have had to go over to a black ribbon. I do not like it so much but it produces better results.

Much love, very much love,

Alan

16 June

Sweetheart Mine, Lovey Eva,

What a speed letters go at nowadays. I was just sitting down to write this letter when yours of 12 June arrived – marvellous letter, full of love and of interesting things. I shall never manage to answer all of it. Last Wednesday (11 June) I tried to telephone you, and three times about ten o'clock you were engaged. You use the telephone too much! I shall try again this Wednesday when I am in Oxford.

Now for the only practical thing in this letter. I will come definitely on 10 (not 8) September, if this is all right for you. This fits in better with me. I will stay 12 days or perhaps a fortnight. We shall see. I shall go happily with you to Balaton or anywhere else. Let me know also definitely that 10 September is all right. You ought to have received the money by now. I am fearful of money problems by then. The pound is depreciating all the time at a terrible rate, and I am fearful that by September there will be strict exchange control or perhaps even a ban on foreign travel. I always expect the worst, as you know. Yes, yes, yes, do get Ránki or the Institute to invite me to lecture just before I go back to England. An Hungarian translation will give me money for another visit, even if the pound has sunk to nothing. If I reach you by telephone on Wednesday, I'll settle the dates once and for all.

Now I start on your letter. You will I fear never get the Edinburgh letter. I have just realized that I did not send Martin's book, so it is not surprising that you did not get it. You will.

No other reviews of *The Second World War* have come along, a little to my disappointment. I suppose I must wait now for the academic periodicals. Good news is that Penguin has bought the paperback rights so the book will go on for years and be my best protection against inflation. When does your subscription to the *TLS* run out? Let me know so that I can renew it. Incidentally, the *TLS* has not reviewed *The Second World War* yet, so there is still that to look forward to.

What you should know about the Mansion House is that, as you say, the Lord Mayor lives there during his term of office. It is a lavish eighteenth-century structure, more like a palace than a house. In November the new Lord Mayor gives a banquet to the Prime Minister and other great figures, and the Prime Minister makes a speech laying down his policy if he has one, which Wilson hasn't. Whoever told you that Boom was coming in 1976? Surely it is very un-Marxist to expect capitalism to recover, however temporarily. The real dilemma is this. The capitalist remedy for our crisis is deflation and mass unemployment. The organized workers won't have this and are strong enough to resist

1975

it. But the alternative is a planned and controlled economy run for and by the working class. But there is no one willing to do this. The old excecutive class will refuse to run anything except deflation. There is no effective Communist Party, and the leaders of the Labour Party certainly have not the courage to lead a revolution, however peaceful. As well, the workers themselves reject responsibility. They are still at the stage of saying that someone else must do it for them. The crisis will have to go far deeper before the workers are driven to act in their own despite. I should not be at all surprised at a Fascist right-wing attempt which will be defeated. Then we shall have a modified Communist economic system, introduced by democratic methods. But of course the capitalist world may be frightened of this and come to our rescue – a humiliating thought. As to the Common Market, it does not matter one way or the other. It certainly will not save us from ruin, and if we became prosperous we should not need it in any case. By the way, I am gambling on the Stock Exchange in a share involved in North Sea oil and hope to turn £900 into £10,000. Crispin is very disapproving, and quite right too.

I purposely avoided reviewing Sylvester's diary so as not to spoil the market for *Darling Pussy*. Also, it would be unfair to him when I knew so much more of the story than he did. All the reviewers have been very critical of his mean spirit. No, I certainly did not enjoy bigamy*. I hated it. My life has been a misery ever since Margaret took the wrong turning, until I met you. You surely realize, and this is no pretence, that I never really loved anyone until I met you. I seem all my life to have been waiting. Finally I found what I had been waiting for when I had given up all hope.

Jack Le Vien is a freelance maker of films and television programmes. He did a very successful or at any rate profitable series on Churchill's life, and now wants to do Churchill at war. I shall get quite a good cut of the profits if the new series comes off, but I am beginning to think that people are now bored with Churchill and that there is no longer much money in him. However, I have plenty of other things to do.

I have got my autobiography up to our meeting at Königswinter. As you can imagine, it gets more and more centred on you. Since that time nothing seems to have happened in my life apart from our meetings, especially from Salzburg onwards. I have had no exciting political experiences and no book to show except for *Beaverbrook*, which is really irrelevant to my serious work. I have also started my intellectual autobiography though I cannot tell how it will work out. It seems to me

---

* Not used in the literal sense.

that as a scholar I was always solitary, a 'loner', having to work everything out for myself. Also, I discovered that in writing history I was more interested in writing than in the history. In other words I suppose I am more an artist than a scholar, though I happen to be a good scholar as well. Yes, you are right. Writing *Bismarck* taught me to think about people as well as about facts, even though it is not a very good biography. As to prejudices, I have none except a dislike of bad scholarship. I have no loyalties except to historical truth. You might say I was a Communist fellow traveller, an anti-Communist fellow traveller and my own traveller all at the same time. I see everyone's point of view, I am afraid, even Hitler's. And I don't think my own point of view when things were happening in the past has any relevance for now.

Here are my plans. On Friday 20 June I go to Buttermere in the Lake District with Crispin, and return 27 June. On 1 July I go to the Isle of Wight for ten days with Daniel and some friends to the house that belongs to my first children. You can write there if you like: The Mill, Yarmouth, Isle of Wight. 9 July I return to London and shall be here until 4 August when I go to Yarmouth again.

I am beginning to make typing mistakes. I must be getting tired. So I will stop and go to the old-fashioned upper-class Beefsteak Club.

With adoration and love and affection and longing. Put your arms around me soon.

Alan

2 July

My Sweetheart,

I have been neglecting you for more physical pleasures such as swimming and climbing mountains. The first thing I did when I got to Buttermere was to send you a postcard, but I expect it will take at least a couple of months to reach you or perhaps never arrive at all, like the letter from Edinburgh. At any rate I was thinking of you a lot. I had a very good holiday as I will tell you in a moment, but it would have been better if you had been there. Everywhere you go in the country you see young people or sometimes quite middle-aged ones walking around holding hands or sometimes stopping to kiss and embrace. It is disturbing. In London and when I am working I do not think much of you or any other woman. It is on holiday I really need a companion. Crispin was very good, always interested in things and prepared to talk about anything. But it is not the same. For years and years I have had to make do with the companionship of my children for want of anything better. Now I shall not have them much longer – they will be doing other things. But just think it is more than thirty years, a whole generation, since I had a proper marriage. Ever since then I have been either solitary or on edge. Do you wonder that I am so anxious to be with you? At any rate, that was what I was thinking as I walked on the hills.

Now as to these hills we had a good time. The weather was perfect: fresh early summer air, one day sunny and the next cloudy enough to walk, though the tops of the hills were always clear. Indeed I have never seen the Lake District mountains clearer. When it was hot we sunbathed by the lake and swam in it. Buttermere Lake was rather cold, so we went to the next valley where the river was as fresh but somehow less cold. Even Crispin, who has set his face against swimming for some years past, suddenly developed an enthusiasm for it again. The first day we went straight up the side of a mountain called Robinson (no relation to Crusoe). I sweated a great deal and totally lost my breath. My heart beat violently. I thought maybe I should die. After about half an hour I recovered and not only that – never got short-winded or exhausted again, though of course I sweated. Later Crispin found a mountain called Pillar that we particularly wanted to climb, but our guidebook said: strictly only for strong walkers. We climbed up the pass and looked across to the other side of the valley where Pillar went steeply up three thousand feet. I was sure it was quite beyond me. However we started on our way, with some terrifying paths, or traverses as they are called, across the rock face. At one point I got quite frightened and called for Crispin who had disappeared. I heaved myself over a ledge and there unexpectedly I was at the top, having beaten the guidebook time by nearly an hour. I was not even a bit tired. Really I am becoming young again – perhaps an Indian Summer, if you know the expression. I had another symptom of youth which I'll tell you about some time.

Now I have just arrived in the Isle of Wight where the weather is equally good, and this time I have my typewriter with me so that I can write you a letter instead of sending you a postcard. I received the *New Hungarian Quarterly* with my review of you in it. I thought, reading it again in print, that it was very fair and also sensible. Tell me if you don't think so. But as you know very well, I had to review the book just as I would that of a stranger. I can assure you there was no flattery in it. Noting the review of Ránki's book, it occurred to me that he ought to review mine, as I would his if it came out in English. Also, he might really feel that it would be worth while for me to give some talks at the Institute when I am with you. I foresee that with our mounting economic crisis it will soon be impossible to leave this country without some official invitation, just like you. So the sooner I establish a reputation in Hungary the better. Make some tactful enquiry if there is any opportunity for me between 10 and 22 September. I'll soon be writing to you with details about my visit to you.

There were articles in the *Observer* about the way children do not welcome a new man coming into their mother's life, and still more into theirs. I really don't think this is true of Ferencz and Pisti. They seemed friendly to me from the first moment, and I think they were glad you had found someone to love and be loved by. However, it crossed my mind that we should not be ashamed or worried about it, rather on the contrary show them we are glad that they are glad. In my experience a new person coming into a family resents the family much more than they resent her.

I am overwhelmed with work even on holiday. I have to rewrite, or rather to expand, the six play scenarios I did on Churchill. I have an index to make for *Darling Pussy*. I have three books to review, including a very funny one on British policy in the Balkans during the Second World War, pro-Communist in Yugoslavia and anti-Communist in Greece, quite crazy. I was asked to perform as a literary lion at the Edinburgh Festival, in a feature called 'Meet The Writer'. I would make a little speech about my book and then people would consult me about how to write books like mine. I said No. Do you approve? It is bad enough writing my intellectual autobiography for the *Journal of Modern History*. Incidentally, do you still receive the *Times Literary Supplement*? You can't receive it every week because it has been interrupted by strike action.

I am also back on television discussion every Sunday with the same old crew – George Brown, Malcolm Muggeridge and Peregrine Worsthorne. We have to go all the way to Birmingham to do it. Last Friday I drove 320 miles from the Lake District to London; on Saturday 60 miles to Oxford; on Sunday 60 miles to Birmingham and 120 back to London, and today (Tuesday) 100 miles from London to Yarmouth. Quite like old times when I thought nothing of driving two or three hundred miles a day. Yet another sign of returning youth. I expect it will end in my dropping dead just as I have recovered all my youthful powers.

Oh darling, I do love you so. You can't imagine how delightful it is to be talking to you indirectly by letter and soon we shall be talking in reality. What do you want – Martin's book, anything else? Vol. IV of *Churchill* is not worth struggling through, and also it is too heavy.

Much, oh so much Love,

                Alan   XXXX

14 July

Sweetheart and Beloved,

Your letter of 7 July came just before the weekend. It was very good, full of love and made me full of love also.

Now here are some practical points. I shall get Hamish Hamilton to send a copy of *The Second World War* to Ránki with a note that is sent for review. Perhaps he would also arrange a translation which would give me a lot of Hungarian money. (I intend to write to Mashkin* and ask how much money I have in Russia, but every time my heart sinks at the boredom of talking to historians I don't know.) I shall be very sad if your essay is not used in my *Festschrift*. I refused to have anything to do with the preparations, but what happened I think was this. Alan Sked started it and got into a muddle, not asking a number of people I had suggested. Then a more efficient man called Chris Cook took it over, and he never consulted me at all. I tried to ring one or other up to see whether it was too late to ask you: Alan is in Austria or somewhere else in Central Europe, Chris is in America. So it seems there is nothing to be done. You ought to go over *The Appeasers* when I am in Budapest. I might be able to add something, or alternatively I could disagree with you and we could have a quarrel which would make our subsequent reconciliation in bed all the more delightful. Actually I never manage to quarrel with you or even want to.

Julia Namier on Namier is not at all about the Namier I knew. For one thing he was great fun, which her Namier was not. Malcolm said the same thing to me the other day. Also I knew Clara, the first Mrs Namier, and liked her very much. She was kind, wise, fascinating and very humble, not a bit like Julia. Julia sees herself as a great writer with profound insight, and I think she made Lewis profound to suit her taste. He was getting old; he had never had a home in England, and he was

* M. N. Mashkin, a Soviet historian, who wrote the introduction to the Russian edition of Alan's book *The Struggle for Mastery in Europe*.

grateful for her company. So he conformed to the picture she had drawn. I refused to have anything to do with the book – partly because I did not want to be identified with it, partly because he had ceased to be the Lewis I knew.

I am delighted to give a lecture at the Institute. What on? I suppose 'The Coming of the Second World War' would be the best. It has been a great success here. I am also running 'The (British) Left in the Thirties,' but I think that would be too remote a theme for Hungarians. I'm not keen on lecturing at the University. Surely it won't have reopened then? Few people would understand me and I don't know what I could say to them. But you decide. I should like to meet the *New Hungarian Quarterly* people, especially as I am now one of them. I am less keen on a party. But you decide. I'm always glad to do what you want. I have booked my flight for 10 September and shall return on 24 September. Ferencz will find England much more expensive than last year. I shall be again at Yarmouth Mill from 4 to 18 August. Then back here, so perhaps Ferencz can give me a ring. They have cut off all private phones in Beaverbrook Newspapers (which means I can't telephone you until I am back at Oxford).

I recently wrote when describing one of our meetings: 'No two lovers ever took longer to come together!'

I had a very good time in the Isle of Wight. The weather was marvellous – sun all the time and yet not too hot. I swam a great deal, and quite long swims for me, sometimes quite out to sea. It was a great pleasure having Daniel with me – the first time since I left his house. He and his friends went out looking for girls – in my car. They did not succeed until the last day when they brought home three attractive waitresses. All went well until the boys revealed they were 17: the girls were in their mid-twenties and not inclined to go around with babies. Daniel has not the slightest idea what he is going to do. I think he is waiting for his exam results. Then he will know whether he has any chance of going to a university. No doubt he will find something. He has certainly grown up a lot.

Television yesterday was very successful. We discussed the crisis and got lots of calls afterwards that it was the best discussion we had done, and also the best discussion there had been anywhere on the subject. I took up a line that was sometimes extreme Right and sometimes extreme Left, but perhaps they are the same thing. I have reviewed Stephen Koss's book on the Nonconformists and am preparing to review Cowling's new book which is quite mad. I have written an article for *Die Welt* saying that democracy is quite safe in Western Europe so long as it becomes economic as well as political democracy. I'll keep it for you if they accept it. Tomorrow I am going to Henley to lecture at

1975

the Administrative Staff College on Lloyd George. So at the moment I have too much to do, most of it rather pointless. In fact I must stop now in order to write some business letters.

Love all day long.

Love
Alan

23 July

Darling,

I write quickly back as you do to me. On 31 July I have to go to Lancaster to give a lecture. I shall be back here the following afternoon, and Ferencz can ring me here if he is free. But do not let him bother if he is busy; I shall see him in September. On Saturday 2 August I go to Birmingham for television, and then straight to the Isle of Wight where I shall be until 18 August.

Now Wales. The most interesting thing is the castles in North Wales put up by Edward I to hold down the Welsh – Conway, Carnarvon, Beaumaris, Harlech. There are also pre-Edwardian castles in the hills. Then there is Telford's bridge over the Menai Straits. North Wales is overrun with people. There is also Chirk Castle, an enormous 'Norman' castle put up in the nineteenth century. In South Wales there is St David's Cathedral, a magnificent sight, and there is a Roman amphitheatre at Caerleon near Cardiff. I prefer South Wales, though of course there are no great mountains. Inland there is beautiful country, though with less to see in the way of buildings. Robert Owen came from Newtown (different from Newport, which I must warn you with the new motorway is not worth visiting. Perhaps we shall go there one day all the same). How much of my autobiography did you read? I have finished it, though not to my satisfaction. I'll bring the final chapter (1965–75) and any earlier chapters you have not read. Apart from you, my life seems to have tailed off and I can't keep saying: 'I love Eva Haraszti.' Maybe you'll think I have told too much, but it is all alive in my memory.

I'll write a proper letter next week.

Eternal Love,

Alan

1 August

Well, My Darling,

Here I am in the middle of a heat-wave. I see from *The Times* that you are having even hotter weather than I am, but of course you are used to it and like it, which I emphatically do not. Fortunately my room here is air-conditioned and I have been to Highgate Ponds nearly every afternoon. It is now Friday. On Monday I shall go to the Isle of Wight where I can bathe in the sea. This sounds delightful, but the Isle of Wight can be even hotter than London. I shall be here for the day on 11 August and then back for good (until I come to see you) on 18 August. If you want to write to me in the Isle of Wight, the address is simply The Mill, Yarmouth, Isle of Wight. Perhaps the drought means that the world is coming to an end. It makes me feel like it.

I have finished my intellectual autobiography and shall bring it with me. It certainly demonstrates that my life has been determined by accidents. It also shows, I fear, that I am incurably frivolous. I am sure American historians will be shocked by it. However, I can't change my spirit at seventy.

I had your Hungarian chap here and had an interesting talk, though I don't think I was much use to him. For one thing the period is a bit early for me. More importantly, the real answer to his question – what did English opinion think of Hungary before 1914 – is that it didn't think at all. I kept wanting to say this to him and then reflected that he is stuck with the subject so I must not discourage him. This universal system of young people showing their abilities by researching on pointless topics is terribly futile, though I can't think of a better one. I have also had a phone call from Lotsi* and shall try to see her when I get back. Otherwise we must go and see her in Budapest.

I forget if I discussed what I should lecture on. I find that 'The Coming of the War' goes down well. It might also amuse the Institute for me to talk on 'The British Left in the Thirties'. Keep a careful eye on the *TLS* for me. I do not see it every week and may miss a review of *The Second World War*, though of course they may have decided not to review it. It seems absurd that you should have to watch the *TLS* for me, but so it is. When we meet I want to discuss the future a little. I always say this and never get around to it. However, this is for you to think over. Sterling, as you know, is depreciating badly. Every year it loses value and maybe I shall be too poor to arrange any foreign trip. So if we could have one good holiday together before it is too late, we should consider

* Baroness Hatvanyv.

our plans. Perhaps your American trip will rule this out for next year. But perhaps you could come through England or France. In England there is no currency problem. We could go somewhere such as the Lake District as man and wife. Think it over and remember to talk about it.

The English papers were not keen on Heller's new book in comparison with *Catch-22*. But I shall no doubt read it when I come to you. Of course you are tolerant and read everything. How can you bear to read that terrible bore Snow? In my opinion he is a non-writer.

A new task has come up. *Ten Days That Shook the World*, which was controlled by the Communist Party, has run out of copyright, so now Penguin will be able to reprint it with my introduction which the Communist Party previously banned. I wrote it ten years ago and now I think I can do it better. At any rate I shall tackle it at Yarmouth. So I shall not be as bored as I expected. What weighs with me is that there will be some twenty other people at The Mill, most of them children, and I'm not sure I can stand it. If it is fine I can spend most of the day in the sea or on the beach.

Dear Heart, I love you very much. I can't believe that you will go on loving me much longer. I get so old and so dull. One day you will look at me and think – whatever did I see in him? Did I tell you that Malcolm Muggeridge told me to take cider vinegar for my arthritis? He says it cured Kitty. I am drinking it assiduously. It is no worse than some *vin ordinaire*. Crispin returns on Saturday. Daniel has got a job in a light engineering factory.

Lots of lovely warm feelings.

Alan
X

14 August

Darling,

I have altogether forgotten when I last wrote to you. In any case I am weary of trying to write a long contribution on the Battle of Britain for a Spanish encyclopaedia of history, and escape it by writing to you. Also it is splendid to think that there is now less than a month before we meet. You will know the time of the plane arrival even if I forget to send it to you, so we shall meet in our usual slightly embarrassed way at the airport. I become increasingly impatient as the time goes by. I expect you do too. Think of our being close to each other. It never loses its wonderful joy.

I have no news except heat. I suppose you are used to it in Hungary. We have never had a summer like it, except perhaps 1911 when there was the Agadir crisis and the temperature was unbearably high when the House of Lords debated whether to pass the Parliament Act. I am not hardened to hot weather as you are. Fortunately I have been in the Isle of Wight most of the time, so could spend my time in the sea which is as warm as the South of France. I float on the waves and bob up and down. Apart from that I groan at the heat and rejoice every time there is a thunderstorm. I suppose I shall be equally dissatisfied when it turns cold. On Monday next, 18 August, I go back to London and shall remain there until I come to you.

I suppose you know John Reed's book, *Ten Days That Shook the World*? I have rewritten my introduction and I hope improved it. I don't expect you will approve of it. It does not conform to the version of the revolution built up later. But that is how it seems to me. Writing it gave me something to do in the hot weather. Now there is only this wretched Spanish contribution to labour on.

There was an alarm that the *Observer* would close down because of labour troubles. The paper is overmanned and the unions refuse to agree to any reductions. Now there seems to be a compromise, and I shall be able to go on writing for the *Observer* until the next crisis. I shall be sorry to lose it, partly because it brings me in some money and more because I get the books I am interested in. In the latest number of the *TLS* you will find a review of Tibor's book*, and also a review by Ignotus of a collective history of Hungary. I thought Tibor's book sounded pretty foolish, and that the review by Ignotus was foolish too – more about himself than about the book. Be sure to remind me when the *TLS* runs out and I will renew it.

Crispin had a good time – though very hot – in Dijon. Now he says that he is better at French than he thought and should have taken a higher course. However, he refused to speak French to me. Daniel has got a job in a light engineering factory and earns £38 a week. He says that, constantly speaking for the workers in the Labour Party, he wanted to find out what workers were really like, and is delighted with the result. I am proud of both of them – at last doing something enterprising and not merely staying at home. On the other hand Daniel has caused two bumps on my car. As he is now rich, or fairly so, I shall make him pay for them. The house here is swarming with my daughters and their

---

* Tibor Szamuely's book, *The Russian Tradition*.

children and their friends' children, so it is not as peaceful as it might be. But I don't complain. It is good to have them around.

My former pupil Roger Louis wrote and told me that I must put into my autobiography how much influence I have had on younger historians. I don't see how I can do this, which is for others to say. But it is pleasing all the same. It never occurred to me that I had influenced anybody. Nor is it important to me. The only important thing in my life is our love. Now I must go and swim.

Love, love, love.

Alan

24 August

Dear Heart,

Oh Lord, it does seem a long time until 10 September. I get increasingly impatient and desperate to see you. However, there is no way of making the days move faster. I need some advice if you have time to write to me before I leave. What clothes shall I bring? Shall we be going somewhere cold? I'll bring the Salzburg pullover of course (I never wear it except with you), but I suppose I ought to have a warm jacket. As I am going to talk at the Institute, I will bring a dark suit and for once look respectable. I have received the photographs that Ferencz left for me. I will also bring the Joplin record if I remember and 'Oh, What A Lovely War', if I can extract it from Crispin. And I really must remember this time to bring the gas-lighter. My only instruction for you is to lay in plenty of wine. You know I am next door to an alcoholic.

I met the other day the acquaintance who was in Budapest last time I was there, and learnt that the British Minister is John Wilson who wrote an excellent life of Campbell-Bannerman. So he would be pleased to see me and we must try to arrange something. But of course in September he is sure to be away, recovering from the strain of entertaining Jim Callaghan.

Here is some agreeable news. Daniel in his school-leaving exam got A in History, C in Economics and C in English. He used to make out that he was interested in economics, not history. Now he confesses that he was really interested in history but was afraid he was not good enough. He wants to go to a university to read history, and with an A he should get in easily. I am delighted to have a son who shares my interests. Not that he does. His history is Marxist and social. He regards me as old-fashioned. So I am, and proud of it. He will not go to a university until October 1976. With unemployment so high here he will have difficulty getting a job, but something will turn up. Crispin, who is as you know very high-minded, has also failed to get a paid vacation job and is working for Oxfam for nothing. This charity is the one thing he believes in. Daniel of course doesn't. He thinks charity silly and revolution the only moral course. I am on Daniel's side, though with some scepticism.

I had very good weather in the Isle of Wight till the end and have never been in the sea so often or for so long. Strangely enough, I had no skin trouble all the time I was at Yarmouth despite the constant hot sun. Now, back in London with no sun, I have come out in sores on my hands. Curious. I am trying to cure my arthritis by taking cider vinegar as recommended by Malcolm Muggeridge. I really think it is making my thumbs easier, even though as a remedy it is an old wives' tale. As with most remedies, if you believe in it, it works. I am trying very hard to believe.

Most of the time I am very bored with no book to write. I am writing some contributions to a Spanish collective work on the Second World War.

I have lots of things for you to read.

Love, and I'll soon show you how much,

Alan

1 September

Lovey Dovey,

I have just received your letter of 23 August. Do not worry about the future, at least don't worry more than you can help. Everything will come right in the end. The only thing I want in life is to marry you, and I am prevented only by the obstacles in the way. If there is ever an economic recovery we shall see things differently. At present, as you say, don't talk or even think about it.

My important practical news is that I arrive at 12.50 next Wednesday. I expect they will give me some sort of meal on the train, so don't wait to eat until I arrive. It will probably be two o'clock before I am through customs. There is one very worrying thing. Heathrow Airport is in chaos with road improvements. Hence it sometimes takes four hours to get to the plane. If I am not on the plane do not worry. Make quite sure the plane from London has arrived and then go off, unless you like to enquire when I am likely to arrive. When I do finally come I shall telephone you from the airport and take a taxi. None of this is likely to happen, but I wanted to warn you just in case.

I rang you on Saturday evening and you were no doubt out enjoying yourself. Never mind. You will soon see me as well as hear my voice and that will be better for both of us. I shall bring my intellectual autobiography where I badly need a last sentence. I will also bring chapter XV of my autobiography, though from references in your letter you must have read some of it already. The Braudel number of *JMH** was in 1972. You will be amused by the contrast between his contribution and mine. Maybe I'll be dead by the time it comes out. I will also bring Martin's book. I don't think there is anything else worth reading but something may turn up. There are no new sensational accounts of people's private lives. No doubt we get them all straight away in the newspapers. I sent Antonia Fraser a letter of good wishes and had a sweet note back. Strange for a woman of 43 with six children to be running off with another man, but then I am seventy as nearly as makes no difference.

Henri Michel's book on the Second World War has been translated into English. It has everything very nearly, including too much about France. But it is rather boring all the same. I will bring the new Penguin edition of *English History 1914–1945*, which has an up-to-date bibliography including a mention of you. When you read it you will kiss me. The *Observer* is saved for the moment, though its long-term future is still gloomy. It will be tiresome to find another outlet when I shall be so old. Incidentally, how miserable the *TLS* was not to review my *Second World War*. I suppose they thought it was just a picture book. But everyone else gave it long reviews. However, it is still selling satisfactorily. I am hoping I shall get a proof copy of *Darling Pussy* in time to bring it with me, but can't be sure. That will be the great sensation of the autumn.

Daniel has now admitted that with an A in History he will have to go to a university. But where? He has turned down Oxford and Cambridge, and I know little about the rest. Crispin says he is beginning to doubt whether he wants to be a mathematician for the rest of his life, in which case he will become a chartered accountant – I am going to La Belle Hélène with him on Tuesday night just before I come to you. I wish you could be with us. Sebastian's house was flooded with seven feet of water after a thunderstorm, and in Hampstead at that.

Love and excitement soon.

Alan

* *Journal of Modern History.*

26 September

My Beloved,

I think the last fortnight was the best time I had in my life. Of course we have always been happy together – or nearly always. But this time it was better than ever before. It seemed so natural. Now away from you seems totally unnatural and very hard to bear. There is suddenly an emptiness when before life was full. However, I shall not write about that. Nor will I write about your coming to England until you have made definite plans. I will wait patiently for your instructions.

Easy flight. It took me longer to get from Heathrow to St Mark's Crescent* than from Budapest to London. No sensations while I was away. I did not enquire further. I have not seen any of my children or heard from them. Indeed, the only event has been a long letter of a very friendly nature from Bernard Martin, raising some points about my review of his book. I was so pleased that I wrote a long letter back. If he goes on to a second volume he will have to do more serious work on the British side.

Literary sensations are few. The book by Norman Stone on the Eastern Front in the First World War is just coming out. So is Paul Addison's on *The Road to 1945*. There is not much in this for you. It is really about the development of social policy during the war, and how Labour inherited some of the war spirit – and then threw it away. *My Darling Pussy* comes out next week. It has just been serialized in the *Sunday Times*. I had two invitations to go to Canada and turned them both down. If you go to America you will have to go alone.

Politics: Mrs Thatcher has been advertising herself in America and Canada. If she were offered for sale I should not buy her. The latest talk is that we are at the bottom of the recession and that boom will soon be here. I have heard this talk often and do not believe it. More bombs have gone off in London and neighbourhood, but none yet at the *Express*. As my room is entirely surrounded by windows, I shall have to take shelter quickly or be showered by flying glass. A medical expert has announced that sex keeps people young and that one should never give up. One old lady of seventy told him that she and her husband still had very good sexual relations and had no intention of stopping. Another old lady said it was disgusting for anyone to have such relations after the age of fifty.

I agree with the first lady.

* Where Alan and Margaret lived.

1975

I haven't found yet any of the paperbacks you want, but have only tried one shop. I shall go elsewhere next week and am sure to find some of the books then. Also, I shall have more news for you. This letter is merely to say that I am safe and sound and that I love you so much, more and more every day. My love will go on and on and in the end everything will come right.

It is very cold and yesterday it rained hard all day. I went to the Beefsteak Club and had a very boring dinner. Give my greetings very affectionately to the boys. I shall not forget about Romanesque architecture.

Deep Love,

Alan

1 October

Dearest Love,

This is not a real letter, merely something to accompany the cookbook. This is the only one of your requests that I can cover. *I Claudius*, *Girl, 20* and *The Pursuit of Love* are out of print. I will keep looking out for them and send them or store them until you come. As you have no doubt noticed, I forgot to bring the Scott Joplin and Tom Lehrer records back with me, so they have become a little present for your boys. I shall buy the Scott Joplin records again for myself when I can find them. Tom Lehrer is now out of date, funny to listen to once and very good for your English, but not worth acquiring again. At any rate, don't worry about it.

I notice every day that you are still having high temperatures in Budapest. I hope you are at the Lucacs bath every day and wish I were. Somehow we must arrange things better. I don't know how and I don't know when, but it is the only thing that counts in my life. I hope your scholarship money is not in English pounds. Sterling goes down every day and prices go up. Of course pounds still buy something but not all that much. However, I can provide what you need if you do come.

I am frightened about the future and also feeling rather ill. I can't settle to any new work and have got through most of my old work, so I am bored as well as miserable. I'll write you a more cheerful letter next time. As a matter of fact, writing you even so gloomily cheers me up quite a lot.

I love you as much as ever I did,

Alan

7 October

Dearest of all women (you see how I learn from you),

This is my last day in my present room. Men are already packing and I am busy stowing my belongings in drawers. Meanwhile I take time off to write to you. You can still write to this address, though I am going across the road to the *Evening Standard* building, smaller, noisier and inferior in equipment. This will give me an excuse for being there less.

You are very foolish to think you lose my love simply when I am silent. Often I have nothing to say and I can't go on saying I love you, I love you. Often it is when I am silent that I love you most, as happened that day on the Lido. So never fear again. I feel just like you about Kőszeg.

I don't understand your remark about how madly you behaved on the last morning. I thought we were just happy together, but perhaps I have forgotten something. You know how unobservant I am. It is more important to behave madly on the first morning when we meet again. We shall surely have many good times together. I have already told you, I think, not to worry about the Joplin records. You must play them often and often. How fascinating about the water we drank. But no mineral water any more.

I am having a troubled time apart from having to move rooms. There was a threat that Lloyd George's grandson would claim copyright in the *Letters* and try to prevent publication. But I think we have beaten him off. I have promised to write a little book on Great Britain this century, 1901–1975. At the moment I can't think how to do it. However, I sent off my little piece on the General Strike which was much appreciated and I am turning out more pieces for the *Spanish History of the War* – rather a boring task. On Saturday I took Crispin to Cambridge. He had forgotten to warn the College he was coming and found his room covered with paint-pots and everything sticky. Daniel keeps close to the revolutionary path. He now reads a paper called *Militant* and actually expects a Socialist revolution in this country. I told him I had been expecting one for fifty years and had now given up.

Shaw's *Black Girl* is poor stuff. His best writing is in his prefaces. Next Wednesday I shall be in Oxford and shall try to ring you up. If not, the following week. No more now except of course:

Love,
Alan

17 October

Dearest Heart,

No. It is impossible. We mean everything to each other. We cannot live without belonging to each other. It will make things no easier if you break with me. You will still be thinking of me all the time, as I think of you. Whether I am with you or not, you are the only thing in my mind. In my present difficulties and worries I truly could not go on without the thought of you. We can't fight over this at a distance. It isn't fair, truly it isn't.

If we are going to change things you must help me. I can't do everything on my own. The burdens on me are also burdens on you, and we must carry them together.

You can break with me if you think that best. I shall go on writing to you and not expect an answer. You can tear my letters up. But I can't get you out of my mind, and I think you will be unhappier if you know I am unhappy than the reverse. After all things can't go worse between us, unless I become too poor to come to Hungary. They can possibly go better. But in any case, if a complete change in my life is essential to you we must consider in practice how to do it. I think of you always as my wife and this won't change. You can't insist on my casting you off. At any rate I beg you to decide, if you are determined, only when we meet and can settle things together without all the strangeness which distance brings. I write no more on this question except to say this: I fully understand why the situation makes you unhappy, and if you finally resolve that there is no way except to break both our loves I shall never complain or criticize you.

The *New Hungarian Quarterly* puts me in a difficulty. I really have no effective answer to this question. Perhaps say this or something like it: I read the *NHQ* with interest and admiration every quarter, and particularly admire the balance it maintains between political and literary articles. I rarely understand the articles on economics and am sometimes out of sympathy with the political ones. I incline to suggest that articles by official persons are not impressive for the English reader, who distrusts all articles by officials and ministers. We could do with more about the practical problems of Hungarian life – anything from the routine of housekeeping to family relations. Do Hungarian men help with the washing up? Who decides where to go on holiday, and where in fact do you go? The literary and artistic articles are the ones that set their mark on the *NHQ*. They are the most welcome. I have no advice except this on how to broaden the *NHQ*'s appeal. The truth is that all sponsored [publications] from other countries encounter a certain amount of suspicion. I expect the same is true of British Council publications in Hungary. Pass this on in your own words or if you think it not worth saying, tell the *NHQ* that I had really nothing to reply except admiration for their excellent publication.

What a score to have a second review of your book by Hauser. He and I seem to have taken much the same line. Perhaps he expresses his admiration more clearly. I meant to do so, but was a bit embarrassed by the feeling that I might be influenced by our relations. Hauser confirms what I felt, that this was a first-rate enterprise in diplomatic history. However, he also confirms my opinion that the naval treaty did not express full-blooded appeasement. You can't bully me into not disagreeing with you occasionally, however hard you try.

I am having a miserable time. The full impact of the loss of the Library is only beginning to dawn on me. And it isn't only that. I had a very active time writing books – *Second World War*, *Darling Pussy*, intellectual autobiography and so on. Now my life is totally empty. I can't settle to anything. I come here every day. There are virtually no letters. I have nothing to do. I try to read, but again to no purpose. It is really the worst time I have had for years. When I was younger I could pull up the spirit to overcome my difficulties. Now I am overwhelmed by them. You don't judge me properly. You see me when I am lyrically happy and uplifted. You can't imagine how black and blank I feel when I am not with you. Unlike you, I do not get gloomy. I hate life actively. I am bad-tempered with everyone, and particularly with everything that happened to me. I truly see no way out. When you get to seventy and feel your life is a failure, you can't help feeling that it is too late to begin again. This is not a plea for sympathy or consideration. It is just a statement of fact. I dread the day beginning. I dislike it while it is on.

And I am glad when each day is over. I am sorry to have written this, but it goes on in my mind all the time.

Darling Pussy had very good reviews. No claim for infringement of copyright has yet appeared, but I fear one will. I have done nothing of the least pleasure or importance except to go briefly to Oxford. This is now also a source of unhappiness because I am conscious it is coming to an end.

Please hesitate before throwing me away. I wish I didn't love you but there is no escape.

Alan
X

28 October

My Darling,

Your letter tortured me. It is a catastrophe that I make you unhappy. I understand exactly how you feel and I reproach myself every day that I ever thrust myself upon you. I love you and shall always love you. You can be sure of that and should need no reassurance. But you don't understand how weak and irresolute I am. I have had so much unhappiness and upheaval in my life, and I fear any more. On a practical basis I shrink from the practical problems involved. I am useless at finding somewhere to live or equipping it.

Now we can see things better when we are together. Please don't fight with me by letter. It only makes us both unhappy. Please, if you love me, be brave. Accept our difficulties and make the best of them. Things will change. Of course I may die, though I don't feel like it. If I don't, you know I shall be thinking of you all the time. I am in fact as miserable as you are, wanting your company and wanting the feel of you. But you romanticize a bit. Please, please, think of me as weak, not as a hero. When we meet and talk I'll try to do better. Write and say the thought of me makes you happy. I can't bear it if you don't.

Stephen Koss is a very good historian from New York who does a lot of reviewing for English papers. He is a very good friend of mine, perhaps the best I've got. Peter Slansky is also an American historian. I have never seen Rex Harrison except in *My Fair Lady*. He is a society light comedian, not in the sort of vein I am interested in.

I spent four days by myself in Oxford. It was a great escape from

London and I enjoyed every minute of it. I wasn't sure that I should telephone you after your previous letter, but I shall now. Or rather when I go to Oxford tomorrow. I went to dinner with Pat and Mary Thompson. When you are in England we can go to them for the night. They will be delighted. And I am dreaming of a week or so when we go on holiday together. You must reflect where you would like to go. But perhaps you will despise me for my timidity and not want my company. I fear the future. I fear that I may lose you. Oh, please don't turn against me or let yourself be unhappy. Altogether I am in a black mood. On Friday I am going to Canterbury to speak on 'The Left in the Thirties'. That will restore my spirits. *My Darling Pussy* is doing very well, though some reviewers said that the letters were too trivial to be published and I rather agree with them.

As you say, maybe I have been spoilt by too much success, everything going right, and I have no courage when they go wrong. You must fight against unhappiness and so must I. Your boys admire me too much, but I appreciate it. Like you, they don't realize how weak I am. Give them my love and tell them to keep the drain clean.

Think always of me and of my love.

All my love now,

Alan

9 November

Darling Heart,

I expect you are cross or disappointed by my last letter. You don't need to be. When I contemplate future problems, my head goes round and round and I don't know how to solve them. But once they are there I manage to find a way somehow. We can't settle our personal problems until we are together and then we can. I have been thinking a lot, and I feel more and more that it is nonsense for us not to be together somehow. We ought to put down the difficulties in a row and then cross them off one by one as we decide on answers to them. At any rate, it is pointless to write about these things. We can only find our way when we are together. So I shan't write any more about them unless you want me to.

Now here is my news, such as it is. The thing which occupies most of my mind at the moment is that I cut myself shaving this morning and

1975

I keep worrying whether it has started to bleed again. As usual, I can't think how it happened. My hand was not shaking and I was taking as much care as I usually do. But first I cut my lip and then to my surprise I cut my throat. Perhaps it was a death wish. If so, it did not succeed. All that happened is that I have got blood all over my collar.

Last Friday I went to Canterbury to take part in the opening of the cartoon exhibition. It was very well done and made me envious to see how much better they displayed the cartoons than I had ever been able to do. In many ways it was really a stroke of good fortune that the Beaverbrook Library was closed. It was impossibly amateurish. All the same I feel cheated when I learn that this year Beaverbrook Newspapers, far from being in financial difficulties, have made a profit of two million pounds and paid a dividend of 10 per cent. Tom Driberg came with us to Canterbury in order to write the exhibition up for the *New Statesman*. You'll find his account this week in the 'London Diary' that he writes. He was much impressed by my lecture which he described as an astonishing *tour de force*, particularly because I did not use any notes. So he can never have heard me lecture before. I certainly gave a good lecture and much enjoyed myself. Tom is only my age, but the hand of death is on him. He is unsteady on his feet, he has angina and his face has suddenly become that of a very old man. People who didn't know were astonished that we were the same age and said Tom looked ten years older. Distressing in a way, except that he keeps his spirits absolutely undimmed.

I had another remarkable encounter at Canterbury. You may remember from my autobiography that my father had a girl-friend called 'Little Dolly' who consoled him for my mother being so tiresome. Before my lecture a little elderly woman came up (partly I think because the hall was full and she couldn't get a seat) and introduced herself. It was 'Little Dolly' with her husband. She was still very pretty and very well-preserved, with a young woman's face. Remembering what she had meant to my father, I kissed her and told her husband – 'I have always regarded Dolly as my stepmother.' Both of them were very pleased at this. Dolly told me: 'My friendship with your father was the most wonderful thing that ever happened to me in my life.' A curious little thing that hadn't occurred to me before, but which I noticed when she spoke of him, is that in all their relations over a good ten years she always called him Mr Taylor and never by his Christian name. A moving little story. I shall try to see her again.

Canterbury has been my main event. I lectured in Oxford on Thursday for the last time this term. Indeed I shall never give the lectures on 'History in General' in Oxford again. I am not sorry. My audience began big and soon ran down to very few. I don't know whether it was because my lectures didn't interest them or because they didn't like getting up at nine o'clock. Either way I don't care. If people don't want to come to my lectures I certainly don't want to give them. London audiences are much more faithful. Next term I shall lecture in Oxford on 'How Wars Begin' and then my Oxford career will be over. But as my London post is a special one I shall be able to go on lecturing for years and years and I think that, having no Oxford commitment in future, I will offer to do more lecturing in University College, London, without asking for any more pay.

Eric Hobsbawm has written a somewhat pretentious book called *The Age of Capital*, which apparently ran from 1848 until 1875. I thought we were still living in a capitalist world, but I suppose he was stuck for a title. I learnt some miscellaneous information, as I always do when reading economic history. Did you know that Thomas Brassey, the railway contractor, employed at one time 80,000 men? There is a good deal in the book about those two profound old gentlemen Marx and Engels, but mostly to say that they had despaired of revolution coming in their lifetime or perhaps for ever. I don't really like these books on a period which so obviously belong to a series and have nothing original to say, even though I suppose my book on Great Britain in the twentieth century, if I ever write it, will be much the same. I am already reading some English history and also going back into the nineteenth for an essay on Europe that I must write to accompany some photographs.

German radio wants an hour's interview with me in German on my career and outlook. I don't think my German is good enough, even though they are offering £200. I sent my intellectual autobiography to the *Journal of Modern History* and the editor said it was delightful, which was not my intention. He has chosen lamentable people to write articles: D. C. Watt from England, an American called John Borley who is apparently interested in German and Austrian history, which I ceased to be thirty years ago, and some German I have never heard of. I had offered him excellent names, but I suspect he wants to get articles hostile to me. I was angry at his letter and nearly wrote calling the whole thing off. Then I thought: all I care about is to get my piece published, and if the editor chooses inadequate people to write about me that is his affair. So I made no complaint.

Crispin has firmly decided that he cannot face a lifetime devoted to mathematics and is set upon becoming a chartered accountant. I am sorry he won't stay in university life, but it is his life he has to live, not mine. He is even considering becoming an income tax inspector. I can't make him be something he does not want to be. Daniel, I am sure, will be a Labour MP in no time. He is not merely interested in politics. He has drive and the personality to get things done. I never thought it of him.

I will write again if I hear from you or even if I don't.

Love to my Beloved,

Alan

11 November

Dearly Beloved,

I just got your letter of 5 November and write at once because it is so sweet and loving. I hope you remembered that 5 November is Guy Fawkes Day, when the Houses of Parliament were nearly blown up. I shall never write a gloomy letter again. It is not fair on you and does not help either of us. In any case, I am now much more clear-headed and cheerful. Of course I know it was wrong of me ever to take up with you. You are a woman who deeply needs a man's company. If I had not run after you, you would have found by now a good Hungarian man to share life in your later years. As it is, I spoil you for others and yet can't give you what you need. The strange thing is that I am desperately miserable in my present life even though I have difficulty in escaping from it. For years the company of my children saved me from complete unhappiness. Now they don't count in my life any more, being too busy with their own. The older ones are friendly when we meet, but I can see I shall never have holidays with them, and now my holidays with Crispin are fading away. Next year Daniel will go to Manchester University and I shall lose him also. So there will be nobody to keep me from you or to be your rival.

It would be wrong to say that I am depressed about my work: It has somehow just stopped and I don't know how to start it again. I have lost all idea how to write a book. I write reviews. I advise my few pupils, but I am getting out of touch with new historical work. It was madness to sell nearly all my books when the Library closed. At that time I could not see any future for myself as an historian and just wanted to wind everything up. So I drift from day to day without creating anything or thinking about anything. Also, I was discouraged last week when my lecture audience faded away, though I know quite well that it is my persistence in lecturing at nine o'clock, not any fault in what I say, that leads to the falling off.

All the same I deny that I am moody, depressed or wordless when I am with you. I am happiest when I am silent; I just lie on the grass and enjoy life. This is the one way in which you misunderstand me. I know that again and again you have worried that I am bored or depressed because I don't speak. You see, I do so much talking and thinking. With you I am at peace and don't need to do either. So never accuse me again of being wordless or moody.

On practical points, I'll leave you to decide where you want to live in London. Like you, I think a flat alone would make you unhappy and resentful when I could not be always there. We can always change things when you come. Get your visa or residence permit here for a good long time. You don't need to stay for as long as the permit says, but it would be very annoying if it expired before you wanted to go back. Money is no difficulty. I can provide for you whenever you want, or indeed all the time you are here. You must not argue about this. You must take my money because I like giving it to you and it is the least I can do.

I'll take you to Dorset, though not to Max Gate which is a dull house (not on show) that Hardy built for himself. His birthplace is a little cottage on Egdon Heath, or whatever it is called in real life. I'll also take you to Newport, though as I have told you there is nothing to see. I have a string of Historical Association meetings to fit in, including one to Cambridge. When we go to Goole (near Hull) we can go on to York. What researches have you to do in Oxford? It did not occur to me that there were any important papers there for your work. I think it is bound to become common knowledge that we are going around together. This will provoke the problem and perhaps a solution. At any rate something will happen.

Answers to questions. As to Lloyd George not going to Washington, certainly the doctor said 'No' and was right to do so, as Lloyd George well knew. All the same, he liked to think he was really fit enough to go and therefore built up the story that he was against Churchill's conduct of the war. I suspect that he was never really fit after his prostate operation, at any rate not fit enough to hold office. I don't think anyone wrote to me after *My Darling Pussy* had been serialized. A number of reviewers said that the letters were too trivial to be published, but most of them said they were important for Lloyd George's later political career and some said they were interesting as love letters, though they didn't think much of Frances as a letter writer. Women liked the book more than men did. A few women have stopped me in the street and said how they enjoyed it. It is the same with Della and Veronica, who worked on it. They were more moved by it than I was.

I go to Oxford tomorrow though not to lecture. On Thursday I go to *Reading Historical Association* to talk on 'The Coming of the Second World War'. I am bored by the subject but have no other.

Deep love,

Alan
X

21 November

Darling Mine,

You see I am keeping up to date with your requirements. I thought *Girl, 20* was very funny and I hope you will also. I have not read his latest about old people sinking together into the grave, and shall not do so. It will remind me too much of my own future. What else shall I send you? I am on the look-out for *I Claudius* and fear it must be out of print. Tell me any other paperbacks you want and I'll send them. I charge the postage to Beaverbrook Foundation.

I have had a little piece of news that will not however benefit you. Robert Skidelsky, who advises an American university at Bologna, has invited me to go and lecture there for a few days. Bologna is one of the places in Italy that I have not seen and want to see, so I shall arrange something in the spring. I shall only be there for three days, and in any case it will be in May when I suppose you will have gone home again. But I wish you could come with me. I shall collect a modest sum in dollars and handsome expenses.

It is extraordinary how emancipation is now becoming a commonplace. The *Daily Express* is running a serial on the pleasures of sex, explaining that it is much better when you love each other and are entwined out of bed as well as in. There was a section on the value and pleasure of just touching each other and not worrying what would happen, if anything. All very sensible, but it would never have happened in Lord Beaverbrook's time. He did not like sex talk at all. It is said that in his old age he liked fellatio, but this is not something I should ever enquire into. Then the *Daily Express* had an article on its main page by a woman writer, saying that in the last ten years or so religion has died completely and that fifteen years ago when she was young of course she went to bed with a fellow student, though they did not talk about it to others. No paper would have published such an article ten years ago. Now it is merely a relief from the news of all our economic difficulties.

I am reading as industriously as I can Dick Crossman's *Diary* as a cabinet minister – less than two years in 700 pages. Much of it is about his work as Minister for Housing, very important I am sure but totally uninteresting for anyone except experts in housing. Truly Dick was an innocent. He bounced into the Housing Ministry knowing nothing of his subject and confronted civil servants who had been on the same sort of work for twenty years. And then he expected them to change all their methods and aims overnight. When they didn't, he complained that they were dictating to him and that the Minister was powerless. There are some funny accounts of Cabinet meetings, with Harold Wilson always playing tactics and never putting forward a policy of his own. In lots of ways Wilson is like Asquith or Baldwin, but you feel that he believes in even less. For him the game of politics is all that matters. Well, I like the game of history but it becomes rather a hard game when I have to read 700 pages of routine stuff. And Dick did not even write it: he dictated it on to tape late at night. A publisher called William Armstrong has unearthed a great stock of late nineteenth-century photographs and has enlisted me to write an introduction on *The Last of Old Europe*. As you can imagine there are lots of pictures of old Hungary – peasants in traditional costume on the Puszta, magnates in court uniform, early steamers on the Danube. I shall make a contrast between the peasants or the village pedlars and the railways and streets of the modern towns. It is all pretty obvious, but I suppose it will make a book of sorts. At any rate it is something to do.

I have just remembered that I must rebuke you about one thing you wrote. You must not hero-worship me. I am not a hero, I am an ordinary human being who – except for you – has been unlucky in life. See me as I am, not as you imagine I am. So beware not to have illusions and then you won't be disillusioned.

I have felt rather ill recently and am often dizzy. My digestion and bowels are not working as well as they used to. As my doctor said, the machine is wearing out here and there, and there is nothing to do about it. I certainly don't worry but it is a nuisance.

I need very much to hear the sound of your voice and to feel the pressure of your hands. I have many other things to write and no time to write them now.

You can see from this letter how much I love you.

     Alan XXX
          X

1975

28 November

My Own Darling,

    What a shame you were in the mountains when I rang up the other night. I will try again next week. But we must face the fact that the telephone is becoming too expensive. It now costs me £2 just to say 'Hello' and 'How are you?' Economic conditions here are becoming very bad. We are constantly told that inflation will slow down. So far it hasn't. Every time I buy anything I am astonished how much it has gone up since the previous week. I used to think I was well off. Now I do without all sorts of things and still seem to be in difficulties. Unemployment is now as bad as it was between the wars, and I don't see why it should not go much higher. We are within sight of a financial collapse in this country, though I don't think the capitalist system has yet reached its end. There is more gloom for you, though in fact I have ceased to worry about such things.

    Daniel has not yet been summoned to an interview at Manchester, but I am sure he will be accepted. I have no idea at all how he will spend his life. I don't see him as a university teacher or as a journalist. Perhaps he will go straight into politics, though maybe there will be no future for a Left Socialist by then.

    Other news. Tom Driberg has had a heart attack while attending the World Council of Churches at Nairobi, an extraordinary thing to do. He is said to be 'satisfactory', whatever that means. As to the Beaverbrook Library, Max Aitken closed it simply because he wanted the floor space for the advertising department. But I suppose he had lost interest in it as well. At any rate, it has gone and there's an end of it. I never give it a thought except to reflect how well the papers are now looked after. I am sure 'Little Dolly' always called my father Mr Taylor and always thought of him like that. Remember he was as old as her dead father would have been. He was a new father to her, and she was the daughter he had lost. Neither of them ever understood that they were in love, and they never wanted it any different.

    How splendid you are writing your autobiography. It will be in Hungarian, so I shall never be able to read it. You will have to read it to me, translating it into English. I suppose it is true that for people who are not self-centred an autobiography seems uninteresting, though it is interesting to others. Mine seems very uninteresting to me, but you liked it and it was written for you. Pat and Mary Thompson liked it though they want more on the recent periods, which I can't remember half so well. I seem to have done nothing except write books and count the days as they go by. I only come alive when I am with you, and then you are uneasy when I am silent with happiness. Do not worry. I expect you to grow older like everyone else, but it is you I love, not just your physical appearance. All the same, I hope your physical responses will grow ever livelier.

My interview in German will come off early in January. Tomorrow I am going to be interviewed by Swiss radio on the plans for devolution, to me a totally uninteresting subject. I should have liked Arthur Marder to write about me. Instead he is going to do a book on the naval war between England and Japan, a topic no one has treated. I have just read Dick Crossman's diary as a Cabinet Minister from 1964 to 1966, very boring on the whole but with some funny passages. I have reviewed it in the *Observer* next week (December 7). Perhaps you will see it. I am writing on 'Europe 1848 to 1914' for a collection of photographs. The sort of article that writes itself but is quite a labour all the same, even at ten thousand words. I have written a contribution to a Spanish history of the Second World War and will get $1,250, but it won't make me rich any more.

On a more practical level, we have 37 candidates for one research fellowship at Magdalen, seven of them historians. Next week I shall go to Magdalen for two days and read three long theses. Strangely, I still feel more at home in Oxford than I do in London. I have had rooms in Magdalen for twenty years and till recently I spent more time there than anywhere else. Also, my life in London was first unhappy and now tedious. As usual I have written a dull letter all about myself. But I can't go on writing: I love you, I love you. It is true all the same. Never doubt it despite our problems and worries. I worry a bit physically, but not very much and expect I'll live a few more years.

All my love for ever,

Alan

11 December

My Sweetheart,

I have had your sweet beautiful letter of 1 December. We will surely get tired of telling each other how beautiful our letters are. But they really are, you know, so what can we do? I have just bought fresh copies of the Joplin records, so the ones I left with you have now officially become your Christmas present. This year's best-selling novel is *The*

1975

History Man by Malcolm Bradbury. When it goes into paperback I will get it for you unless you have been able to get it from a library. The subject will no doubt appeal to you.

Now let me see what you say in your letter. What a funny story of your visit to the mountains and of Elizabeth's* going off in a huff. I should much like to go unless it creates embarrassment among your academic colleagues. Why did you not go with the man who offered to take you home in his car? Surely he would not have managed to seduce you while on the journey, and you could jump out when you got back. But I am glad you have some male company. For one thing you need it; for another it teaches you how much better I am than any other man (joke).

The review of *Darling Pussy* by George Malcolm Thomson was very foolish. The Jennifer mystery is as you say solved and not worth writing about. G. M. Thomson was for many years one of Beaverbrook's secretaries and ghost writers. Now he is very old and I think must be losing his wits – he never had many. *Darling Pussy* is selling very well, which is all that matters. Did I tell you that the Lloyd George family tried to stop publication by claiming that they owned half-copyright? I told them to fuck off (English idiom), though not exactly in those words. Thereafter silence. They were merely trying to bluff. I wrote Jennifer a Christmas letter of greeting. No reply. Perhaps she is offended too, but I don't care. To tell you the truth, I have had enough of Lloyd George after doing first the Stevenson diaries and then the love letters. However there is no escaping him. The BBC are preparing a ¾ hour radio programme about him and also an hour television programme, in both of which I shall take part. More cheerful television news is that the BBC have agreed to take six television lectures called 'The War Lords' some time next summer. Five are easy: Mussolini, Hitler, Churchill, Stalin, Roosevelt (do you think that is the right order?). But what am I to do about the Japs? They played a big part in the war but had no obvious war lord. I must read again Butow's book on Tojo and the coming of the war. Until I get all these programmes out of the way I shall not start on my new English history book. I can't say I am sorry. I can't see how to shape the book or what new things I have to say. So maybe I shall never do it.** I have plenty of other things to occupy me. I told you now about my visit to Reading. Yesterday I went to Mold in North Wales, again on the Second World War. Good appreciative audience, but most of them rather elderly. Lavish Welsh hospitality, really rich food and very good. I stopped with a Welsh-speaking household, nothing artificial about it.

---

* The wife of the late György Ránki, a colleague of Eva's.
** Alan only ever completed one chapter.

They are all pleased to have got devolution, whatever that may mean, but they don't want independence. They want their own language and the economic benefits of being joined to England. They were delightful people, except that I see the shadow of Dylan in every Welshman.

Next week I have a lecture to the Central London branch of the Historical Association, and Crispin and I go to *Valkyrie*. I had a long and friendly talk about his future. It makes sense that he does not want to spend his entire life doing pure mathematics, and if he can study accountancy it will be a good and profitable profession. If he can't get into a firm he will go on at Cambridge for another year and then think again. All really seems well with him except for the worry all young people have in our country – will they be able to get a job? Daniel, who cares nothing about the past, has now become my favourite son, particularly as he uses all the Marxist arguments I used fifty years ago.

I don't understand why my bowels worked so well at Budapest. Food? Raw paprikas? Or psychological content? At any rate they are very irregular now. My doctor says I am totally fit despite this. Deep love, I'll write again before Christmas.

    XXXX Alan
     X

22 December

My Sweetheart,

I had your card with its message of love and send you mine in return. I am at the moment rather gloomy. My work is not progressing. I feel more and more I shall never write another book. Most of all, Christmas always gets me down. I have never liked all the fuss over decorating the house and eating a large Christmas dinner. This year only Giles and Janet have gone to her family, so all the rest will be sitting down to roast beef on Christmas night. They have something to rejoice over. I haven't. Every day reminds me how badly my life has gone in the past, and I lose confidence in the future. It is wrong of me to tell you all this. In your company I cheer up and perhaps I shall again.

Here are some more interesting topics. I have read and reviewed a book on *British Public Opinion and Abyssinia*, which I will keep for you. A bit thin, but some interesting points. When MPs said they had received 'shoals' of letters protesting against the Hoare-Laval plan, on investigation 'shoals' turns out to be three or four. Waley says that at a meeting of protest at Manchester University 'one of the speakers was a history lecturer called A. J. P. Taylor'. This was no doubt meant as a joke. I wrote to him: 'You are wrong. I was the sole speaker.' Not of course that I believed in collective security or the League of Nations as you do. I merely wanted to discredit Baldwin. And of course the outcry did no good. It killed the Hoare-Laval plan, but we did not get the oil sanction and the Emperor of Abyssinia lost all his country instead of losing two-thirds.

I am also reading a very good book on the British military campaign in Ireland after the First World War – a topic strangely enough that has never been written before. It is a wonderful tangle of confusions, with the British government wanting to restore order and doing this by indiscriminate reprisals. In fact it was British policy or lack of it that made Ireland a nation, as happened also in other countries. Finally, I have read the first volume of Malcolm Muggeridge's autobiography. There is far more about his feelings, or what he now thinks were his feelings, than about what happened. And he is unbelievably hypocritical. He goes on about love for others and self-sacrifice. Yet no man has been more self-centred and cruel towards others. As to his denunciations of sensuality, he has been promiscuous all his life until his powers failed. I read it with great pleasure as a work of fiction and fantasy. I did not believe any of it. But then I have never believed anything Malcolm said. I have enjoyed his company, well knowing that he would say malicious things about me as soon as we parted. If you once write people off because they are hypocritical or unreliable, you end with no friends at all.

The only event in my life is that I went with Crispin to *Valkyrie*. He enjoyed it very much and so did I, though Wagner is not at all to my taste. *The Ring* is really dreadful rubbish. How can people sit through it time after time when they could go to operas about real people such as *Othello* or *Falstaff*? Still, I am glad to have seen *Valkyrie* after a gap of over forty years. I am not at all sure I shall be as glad to see *Siegfried* if it ever comes round. We had a rich supper in the interval, which made things more bearable. Crispin is still set on becoming a chartered accountant and, as he seems to know what he is doing, I have ceased to argue with him. Daniel has been interviewed at Leeds University and is going to be at Manchester University. Both would like to have him, so he will now have to make up his mind. Both are good universities and I shall be pleased whichever he goes to.

I expect you are off skiing. Give my love to the boys and to yourself. Indeed for you lots and lots of love,
    Love,

                        Alan
                         X

1976

7 January 1976

Beloved of my Heart,

    I can't believe I have written you three unanswered letters. I seem only to write when I hear from you, but perhaps I miscalculate. I don't mind as long as I can keep writing to you. I have been very ill. Margaret exhausted herself over Christmas and took to her bed altogether. I had to do everything and became exhausted in my turn. After that I caught some virus and for once went to bed also. Now, apart from a constant cough, I am without fever but I feel weak and good for nothing. I am not good at being an invalid and get impatient with myself.

    I have great difficulty with my work. I think I have done enough illustrated books and don't want to get known merely as a man who writes the text for illustrations. So I ought to revise *English History 1914–1945*, but it is a daunting task. I have made a mistake, one of the worst in my life, when I sold most of my books. First I sold most of my books in Oxford when I had to move from three rooms to two. Then I sold the rest when the Library closed. I thought I should never need them again. Now I need them and Daniel, whom I never thought would be an historian, needs them also. And I have none. Last year when the Library closed I was in despair and thought my life ended. Instead it goes on and I have to fill up time because I have nothing to work on. I truly do not see a way out, not that I am any longer unhappy or depressed. I am just empty.

    I am glad you liked *Girl, 20*. I think it is his best book, so funny and yet so understanding. I am reading of all things *Nana* by Emile Zola – the story of a dissolute life under the Second Empire. Really there is nothing dissolute about it in our times. Then it was only actresses who went to bed with everyone they met whom they liked. Now everyone does, or so they say. There was a girl on television the other night who said of course she was promiscuous just like men. *Nana* is a straightforward romantic novel except that she shows her passing affections by fucking instead of holding hands. I don't suppose it matters. She ends badly by dying of smallpox, which is pure accident and not what she particularly deserved.

    Arthur Waley, author of the book on Abyssinia, was a professor at LSE and is now Keeper of Manuscripts at the British Museum. In the *Historical Journal* there is an interesting review of another book on

Abyssinia by Frank Hardie. James Robertson, the reviewer, says that the British were planning to grab Abyssinia for themselves and this drove Mussolini to get in first. This is what I said at the time, but it was pure guesswork and afterwards I thought I must have been wrong. Apparently I was right after all – green fingers again. There is also a book on the Dominions and USA as influences on appeasement by Ovendale (unknown to me). He shows that Chamberlain was not pushed by the Dominions but only used them as an excuse. One minor point. I have always wondered why the British government took such an alarm in February 1939 – expecting a German invasion of Holland and suchlike. Answer: merely a speculative piece by Vansittart suggesting what the Germans might do. Van was a very dangerous and foolish man.

Daniel visits Manchester next week and is also going to Sheffield, purely out of curiosity. Any of them will take him, so he will have to decide for himself. I am impartial between Manchester and Leeds, so he will do well in either case.

Crispin has been offered a place by two firms of chartered accountants and will certainly settle for one of them. I am now quite reconciled to it because it is clearly what he wants to do. But first he proposes to go off on Voluntary Service Overseas for two years. If he does I don't suppose I shall see him again, but that can't be helped.

Be sure to get permission to be here for as long as you want, as I have told you before. I can supply you with plenty of money. I have lectures at Portsmouth, Goole, Bournemouth and Cambridge, to all of which we can go together. England being more conventional than Hungary, you will have to be Mrs Taylor unless you have objections. I also have half a dozen lectures in London. It is the one thing I can still do well.

You will never lose me. Do not ever contemplate such an idea. Now I will try to get better before I write to you again.

With my love which you will never lose,

Alan

20 January

Darling Beloved,

Your letter of 14 January quite alarmed me. I tried to think what I had written that offended you. Perhaps, I thought, I had written something wrong when I had a high fever. Then I decided you were

1976

imagining it. You must not do this. You must not worry. I shall not change my feelings about you, though I may change my feelings about myself. I am in great gloom. But I shall not write about it. I'll talk and perhaps be encouraged when you come. I am still not at all well. I can go out and walk quite a long way. But my head is full of cold and my chest full of cough. I suppose I am a bad invalid. But these feelings make it hard for me to work. In the end, after thinking over this project and that, I am sure I shall settle for rewriting *English History 1914–1945*. There are interesting things to do there. But then I stop myself and ask – why spoil a good book? Perhaps a revised edition will destroy the spirit. When I wrote *English History 1914–1945* I still had great hopes for the future. Now I have none. But I have told you all this before.

Practical arrangements for the future are very important. I cannot be sure that I shall be in London when you arrive. I have lectures in Oxford and also some visits to distant Historical Associations. So I may not be able to say in advance whether I can meet you or not. Please let me know the following: where you arrive (railway station or airport) and at what time. If you come by air I shall not meet you at the airport, because traffic conditions are impossible, so take the coach to the air terminal in Gloucester Road. If you come by train I shall try to be at the station. If I am not at the air terminal or station, take a taxi to wherever you are living. There you will find a letter from me saying when I am coming to meet you. So be sure to send me your London address. If by any chance I don't get your London address and there is no letter from me, ring Della or me the next morning: 353-8000, extension 3460. I am sure something will go wrong, but I don't see why it should. Once we meet we will settle everything. Early in March I have to go to Goole on the Humber. We can go up a day early and spend the night in York. This will enable us to see the Minster. Or we could go to Lincoln if you preferred. A little later I have to go to Bournemouth, and this will take us near Thomas Hardy's birthplace. Then I think that before Easter we could take a week's holiday and go to the Lake District – or anywhere else you liked. I must not take you away from your research too much, but after all it is more important to be together than to work. We will also talk about our practical problems if I feel well enough. At present I can't imagine any future.

Of course I am working quite hard despite all this self-pity. There is an enormous new life of Lloyd George by Peter Rowland, competent in a boring way but not exciting. Marder has produced a whole book on the Dakar Affair, very good of course but I do not believe Dakar deserves so much attention. Then I have to review a German book about Spain in the Second World War, also a rather unexciting subject. What really keeps me busy is reading the proofs of and making an index for my *Essays on English History*, very laborious but very enjoyable. Reading some of my essays, I think like Swift when he re-read *The Tale of a Tub*, 'What a genius I had in those days.' Then sometimes I think I could do it much better nowadays. On the whole I am quite pleased with my intellectual powers.

Others points from your letter. I lost my big sitting room in College some years ago, not long I think after you were there. Now I have my bedroom and the smaller sitting room with my desk in it. But not many book-shelves. So I sold my books, which was quite mad. Then I could not imagine where I could put my books from the Beaverbrook Library, so I sold those also. Of course I ought to have kept them. *Sword of Honour* is yours. If I want to read it that will be a good reason for coming to Budapest (joke). But remember that Evelyn Waugh gave it to me so it has a sentimental value. Usually I think it is silly for people to write in books, but I wish Evelyn had written in this one. However, he can't sign it now. Daniel has decided to go to Leeds. He will study International History and Politics. He was quite surprised when I told him I was the top international historian. Or perhaps he was teasing me. Now send practical answers quickly.

Lots of love and longings to be with you,

Alan

2 February

Darling,
Here is a practical letter about my future engagements and plans in case you come to England. But perhaps you have run into difficulties. As you know I go to Oxford every Wednesday and usually spend the night there. These are my other dates:

16 February: midday lecture at the Senate House, London University.
17 February: lecture to Historical Association, Portsmouth.
23 February: lecture at Senate House, also on 1 March.
3 March: If you are here by then we will both go for the night to Pat and Mary Thompson in Oxford. On 4 March we will go to York just for pleasure and to look around.
5 March: Historical Association lecture at Goole, a place I have never

been to. If you won't be here by 3 March, let me know so that I can put off our visit to Pat and Mary until later. They are almost my only friends.
12 March: we might go to Dorset or Salisbury for the night, so that you could visit Thomas Hardy's birthplace.
13 March: Historical Association at Bournemouth. We can stop the night somewhere, though preferably not at Bournemouth.
19 March: Historical Association lecture at Surbiton, which is a suburb of London. You will probably have wearied of my lectures by then, except that the Surbiton one will be on the General Strike.

After this I thought we might go to the Lake District for a week or so, either early in April, say 8 to 15 April, or later on if the weather is bad. From 3 to 7 May I am going to Bologna, where you will not be able to accompany me. If you had rather, I'll cancel my visit and go another year. I have a few other dates later in May, but will be free to go away some of the time.

Let me know what you think of these suggestions. If you approve, bring strong shoes for when we go up mountains. There may be other places you'd prefer to go to. I'll go anywhere to be with you.

That is the end of my practical letter. We are having miserable weather, very cold with damp sleet, and even in the house it feels cold and raw. My room in Fleet Street is so cold that I have struck. I go down to open and answer my letters. Then I leave, usually before lunchtime. I also insist on Della going home early. Poor girl, she has had a misfortune. One day she forgot to buy an Underground ticket. At the exit she offered to pay, but the collector refused her money and she had to go to court. She has now been fined £25. Even so she did not do too badly. Most of the other offenders were fined £50 and some even more. I am sure she was innocent, or at least did not forget deliberately. But it is a warning to us all, except that I can travel free by bus during the day.

I have just written a reasonably long review of Marder's book about Dakar. The book is technically perfect as usual, but I wonder whether Dakar is worth writing about – a badly planned enterprise which miscarried after three days. I don't think it had much effect on the war one way or the other. I don't know what I shall get for review next. And here let me give you a warning. Do not read *The History Man* by Malcolm Bradbury, which is hailed as the best novel of 1975. Apart from finding it unreadable, I thought it was nonsense and pretentious nonsense at that. He is showing off his cleverness, not trying to create real people. I have also finished *Nana* by Zola, entertaining in its way but pretty bad as a novel. Malcolm Muggeridge's latest enthusiasm is for Kierkegaard. He announced that he had had a message from the spirit world that

Kierkegaard like himself disliked television. Or so it is reported. I only heard the story at second hand.

I forgot one date. My young admirers intend to give me a dinner on or about 25 March and you will be expected to be there. I dislike the whole idea. I am not pleased to become 70. I am not pleased with my life. I have no message for the young and I can't understand why they admire me so much. I am merely a very ordinary historian who is clever with words, but not I think with ideas. If you stay until the summer, there will some sort of party for me in Oxford also.

I am still not very well. The cold weather has set me back and I don't feel like attempting anything. I shall be better when you come. So let me know your plans as soon as you can.

Much and much Love,

Alan

13 February

Dear Heart,

I wrote you a long letter this morning saying that I was waiting patiently to hear from you. Just as I had finished, your letter arrived (with one stamp too many, which I return) so I tore up my letter and started again. Since then I have done a show for German television, so I am not sure that I shall catch Friday's post. There are many practical things to write about. I must be in Oxford from 24 to 26 February, and shall probably not be back in time to meet you. Telephone Della (surname: Hilton) as soon as you can and give your address. She will know where I am and will get a message to me. Maybe we might go out to dinner that evening, but I can't be sure. At any rate, whatever day you come ring Della as soon as you can. She knows all about us, as I suspect Veronica does. I see that Pinter refers to Antonia Fraser as his paramour. Would you like that instead of mistress? Or do you prefer partner, as I do?

I have warned Pat and Mary that you may not be here in time for the visit of 3 March. In any case we go again on 29 April when I have to speak to Pat's seminar. He is a good modern historian – Liberal Party, English trade unions etc. – but is very lazy and has never produced a proper book. She is a lovely person. As a young woman she witnessed all my troubles with Margaret and was much on my side. When she and

1976

Pat first came to stop with us, unmarried of course, I said: 'Two rooms or one?' She said firmly, 'One.' The other day she asked me the same question and I gave the same answer. Goole is slightly troublesome. They want me to spend the night with the headmaster of the local grammar school. I daren't introduce you as my wife for a whole evening: they would ask too many questions. So I shall explain you are a Hungarian historian wanting to see the Historical Association, and we had better go to an hotel with different rooms. We can discuss this.

There is now a new project. The BBC are opening new premises at Manchester and want to do an hour of television on Manchester's history, all introduced by me – Peterloo, the Chartists, the Anti-Corn Laws, Engels, and so on. It will take at least three days to make or maybe even more. I suggest we should go up together early in April and explore Lancashire when I am not working on the set. We might even get a weekend off. I shall get this planned before you come.

The trip to Dorset and Bournemouth will present no difficulty. I have also to make six programmes on 'The War Lords', but they will be done in London and not until the end of May. But probably there will be other television programmes. I'd like you to see me as the King Pundit of the studios. I have also committed us to go to dinner with Terry Kilmartin, literary editor of the *Observer*. I love his wife Joanna, though she is no rival to you. There is no trouble about your being seen everywhere with me. There will be no scandal and I do not care in the slightest if there is. As a matter of fact I am too old to be suspected of any scandal, certainly not with an attractive woman who could have far better men for the asking. All I put forward now are practical problems and answers. More general problems can be dealt with when you are here. I do not know all the answers to these, but we must find them together.

General advice of a practical nature. It will probably still be very cold, though not so cold as I see it has been in Budapest. But remember our houses are not so well heated. Bring some heavy walking shoes if you have room. We might get to the Lake District after all. If not, we can walk in the Peak District. You can buy all the cosmetics you want in England, but I don't guarantee French perfume. You will discover most English restaurants are now very expensive. Drink is still cheaper than elsewhere. I have plenty of money waiting for you. I will provide £20 a week and more whenever you want it. With all this television I am well off. Also I have made money speculating on the Stock Exchange. So have no qualms.

I must hurry to post this letter. Let me know precisely as soon as you can so that I can tell Pat and Mary whether to expect us. I have much more love to write but no time to write it in. So all you get is just

Love,
Alan

21 February

Dear Heart,
No letter from you yet. The post takes longer than you think. However, I am assuming that your arrival is fixed for 18 March. I shall be in London that day. I will find out when your plane arrives and shall be waiting at Gloucester Road air terminal precisely one hour after that. I shall wait patiently until you arrive. If by any fate I am not there, you should wait patiently in your turn in the arrival lounge. I will take you to wherever you are proposing to live and then we can have dinner together. The next day I go to Wimbledon to talk about the General Strike, and hope you will come with me. Otherwise my only plans are for Manchester. It looks fairly certain that they will come off early in April. We can go together for some days. With luck we shall have a free weekend when we can go to the Peak District if the Lakes seem too far. I'll try to settle this in advance. Later we will make other excursions, interrupted only by my tiresome trip to Bologna. The young people may hold a party for me on 25 March, and of course you'll come. A couple of days before we might go somewhere for the night – Canterbury, or anywhere else you'd like to see. That is all of a practical nature.

I had a trying time just before I telephoned you. On Tuesday evening I went to Portsmouth to lecture. I was given dinner of a sort at the College of Further Education. On the table were only tumblers. Sure enough I was offered a choice only of water and orange squash. I chose water and gave a good lecture. As I reached the railway station for my return journey it was nine o'clock and the bar closed. At Waterloo, which I reached at eleven o'clock, the bar also closed precisely on my arrival. No drink the whole evening. I had a committee meeting at eleven o'clock in the morning at Oxford. So despite my later return, I rose very early and was in my car soon after eight o'clock. Then the clutch failed. I managed to get the car back to the garage, but of course going to Oxford by train I was too late for my committee meeting. Altogether most exhausting. I am only just recovering from it all.

1976

To add to my troubles, Daniel has flu. I can't go to see him and he can't spend Sunday afternoon with me as he usually does. Sebastian also has flu and so could not come to lunch with me on Friday. I shall be solitary all the weekend. However, I have some good news for my future activity, alas not with you. The Edinburgh Festival has literary as well as musical and theatrical events, and this year the main literary event will be a seminar on War – whatever that means – conducted by Len Deighton and me. We shall sign copies of our books, make short addresses and I suppose lead some sort of discussion. We can stop as long as we like, all expenses paid, and can have tickets free to all the events. I expect there will be a heat-wave and I shall leave early. Still it is something to look forward to, though not as much as I shall look forward to coming to Budapest in September.

My other bit of fun was to write an article in the *Sunday Express* last week attacking the metrication of everything, with which we are now threatened. I received an enormous fan mail, though of course my article will do no good. Do Hungarian peasants still buy food-stuffs by the pound as they do in France? One curious fact I learnt from one of the fan letters is that French ships still use nautical miles and knots for stating their speed. If we go over to metric measures, it will be impossible to obtain replacements for doors and therefore no house can ever be reconstructed. All tools will have to be replaced, to say nothing of beer mugs. All existing petrol pumps will have to be scrapped. And so on. It is a special bit of contemporary madness.

The most striking item of news is that Great Britain is technically bankrupt. The charges for interest on our vast debts, incurred since 1970, are too big to be met out of taxation, so we shall go on borrowing more and more until individuals and other countries refuse to lend. Then we shall have to repudiate just like the French in 1789 and most European countries after the First World War. I don't know whether capitalism is breaking down, but something certainly is. On top of this we have crisis throughout South Africa, a main source of British wealth. The last fragments of Empire are falling apart. So I may yet live to see the end of all things.

I have just read a very fine book by Elie Kedourie on the McMahon-Husayn correspondence of 1915 which first caused turmoil in the Near East. The Arabs claim we promised them all the Arab lands and then broke our promise by setting up the Jews in Palestine. I think they are wrong, but no one until now has examined the evidence in academic detachment. For one thing the British Foreign Office was always anti-semitic and therefore endorsed the Arab grievances. A wonderful tangle.

I broke off here because Daniel came to tea after all, though he was really not fit to do so. He said he could not remain solitary in the house any longer. He was in admirable political form, rejoicing at the crisis of capitalism and insisting that it could be all solved by more public spending. If he goes on like this he will soon find his way into Parliament or perhaps into revolution. He saw Crispin the other day and learnt that Crispin has firmly committed himself to Voluntary Service Overseas. So he will be off to Africa for two years, I hope not to Angola. Indeed his plans may be thwarted by an African civil war. It is a splendid thing to do, but I shall be sad to miss him for two whole years. I'm sure I shall never see Crispin again.

I am not looking forward to my birthday. Ten years ago I was at the top of my form and everyone praised me. Now I am almost a forgotten man who can't see any future work to do. The new *Festschrift* will be by young unknown men and, while it is well-meant of them to do it, I wish they hadn't. Ten years ago I was looking forward to writing Beaverbrook's life, and I enjoyed writing it. Now in retrospect it seems a waste of time: he really was not worth a book on that scale, and it only sold 4,000 copies. The Penguin edition of *English History 1914–45* sells twice that every year. Regretfully I have to admit it is my masterpiece, though I like *The Troublemakers* more. What consoles me in life is the thought of you and that we shall be together soon. Somehow we must arrange things well. No doubt I shall write again before you arrive. Don't forget that everything here is very expensive, and have plenty of English money. Your coach from the airport now costs, I think, 75p. Among other things you'll have to get used to decimal coinage which doubles the price of everything.

I am very impatient for your arrival and full of dreams of loving nights together that will probably not come up to expectations. Still, we shall be close to each other.

Lots of impatient love,

Alan
X

1976

29 February

Lovey Dovey,

    All fixed I hope for 18 March. As I told you I shall be at Gloucester Road one hour after the plane arrives. We will have dinner together that evening and can discuss plans. Goole was no great loss. It will be a dreary day for me. I am sorry you will miss Bournemouth. It would have been a convenient way for seeing Dorsetshire. On 19 March I go to the Historical Association at Wimbledon to talk on 'The General Strike'. I hope you'll come with me, perhaps by car. I thought vaguely that the following Monday, 22 March, we might go away together for the night, I don't know where. But you may feel you ought not to miss two working days so soon after you arrive. On 23 March I have to go to an office party given by my cousin Robin Thompson – hardly for you. But we will go to the little party that Alan Sked and others are giving for me on 25 March. My family wanted to give a party – again not for you – on 27 March, but I resisted this. I hate family parties.

    All is set for Manchester the following week. We will go up on 1 April and stay for nearly a week if that is not too much for you. I will make the television film most days and we can have the weekend off, probably in the Peak. On 29 April Pat and Mary are giving a little party and expect you. If you think it is too overwhelming to meet a lot of my old pupils and friends, I'll arrange for us to visit them some other time. You will have plans of your own, so I will not think ahead any further.

    I have had a misfortune. You remember the piece I wrote about myself for the *Journal of Modern History*. McNeill, the Editor, asked Donald Watt to write about me, which I thought all along was a mistake. When I opened the *Festschrift* Alan Sked and Chris Cook assembled for me, there was a piece by Watt on 'The Historiography of Appeasement', a repeat of an article he wrote years ago. It was very bad, condescending towards me and full of mistakes including crediting me with a book called *Britain 1914–1945* which clearly he can't have read. After some reflection I wrote to McNeill that I couldn't let my piece appear with Watt's. The simplest thing was to say that I had decided I was not a suitable person to represent English history writing. Alternatively McNeill might say to Watt that, as he had written about me so recently, it would be better to get someone else for the *JMH*. I don't know what he will reply, but I don't see what else I could do. I shall be sorry if my piece does not appear, but I should be even sorrier if it had appeared alongside Watt's. I hope you don't think I have done wrong.

    Apart from this, little has happened. Did I tell you I got a book in Russian by Cyril Vinogradov of Leningrad about English historians?

There is a lot in it about me, but I can't understand it. I shall ask Helen Szamuely who is now a pupil of mine to translate it, and you can translate more. I notice he does not mention *The Troublemakers*. Too frivolous for him no doubt. Still, it is agreeable to think that I am widely read in Soviet Russia.

Crispin has been accepted by Voluntary Service Overseas and will teach mathematics for two years in some Commonwealth country, presumably in black Africa. It is a noble gesture, much finer than any I could do. Daniel is so busy with the Young Socialists that I never see him. He has bought a motor-bike.

Paramour is a beautiful word by origin. It is old French for *pour amour*, two people who are together for love. But 'life-mate' is good too. That is what we are. I only hope nothing will happen while you are here to disturb it.

The *Guardian* is going to have an interview with me for my birthday. There are no interesting books at the moment. I am reading more about Engels in preparation for our visit to Manchester. But the house where he lived has been destroyed, like most of old Manchester.

And that's all I have to tell you except I am more and more impatient for you to come.

Many thoughts of Love,

Alan

5 March

Darling,

I have your letter of 28 February. This is just a hasty reply before I set off for Goole, a dreadful port on the Humber. I have settled we shall go to Canterbury or somewhere else for the night of 22 March. This will interrupt your work, but you will have plenty of time for more. Manchester is in order for the first week of April when we shall have a week together. After that you must settle down to serious work and not worry about seeing me! The Imperial War Museum is quite near here and I will take you down there. You had better plan to go to Birmingham at the beginning of May, when I am going to Bologna. As to books, you can become a temporary member of the London Library, which I can arrange for you, and then you can take out up to 10 books at a time. You

1976

will only need Volume III of Hankey. Where are the Chatfield papers? If at Cambridge, I might manage to be there too for part of the time.

Everything else seems difficult for me. In any case you are not free for another two years* and we cannot know what will happen by then. So let us do the best we can. It will be easier to judge the situation once you are here. At any rate I shall be at Gloucester Road around four o'clock and will wait patiently. The following evening I go to Wimbledon and hope you will come too.

I have told you the other dates. I told Pat Thompson the other evening that it would not do to plunge you straight into a party, so he suggested we should go for two nights – the first a quiet family evening and the next a party where you would feel at home. I must hurry off now to collect a new book on Stalin as a war lord. It will give me ideas for my television lectures. Though you tell me not to think ahead.

So with that sort of Love,

Alan

13 April

Darling,

I hope I didn't sound grumpy on the telephone yesterday. I did not hear very well, partly because there was a lot of noise on the line and partly because you speak so softly. Perhaps the real reason is that I am becoming deaf. However, I am sure you ought to stay in Yorkshire over the week-end in order to see as much of as many parts of England as possible. Leeds is like Manchester and yet different. The Dales are also like the Lake District and yet different. There is a Dales Way by which you can walk from, I think, Ilkley to Grasmere. We ought to do it some time.

I still have a cold in the head, but lemon is helping to clear it. I caused a sensation in *The Times* by giving my views on Irish affairs to Irish radio. *The Times* did me an injustice. They ran two sentences together and implied that I wanted all Protestants murdered. Whereas what I said was that both Protestants and Catholics should forget their religious differences, otherwise there would have to be a new partition or one or other would have to be driven out. However, what other people

* Eva wanted to secure the future of her sons in Budapest and finish her book for her Doctor of Sciences degree.

think of me does not worry me. Ulster television wanted to interview me, but they would not pay enough so that peril passed over.

I have one problem about next Tuesday evening. How shall we pass the time between half-past five and half-past seven when we can have dinner? I'll try to think of an answer. Perhaps the National Gallery will remain open. I shall try to arrange for us to go to Joanna's on 30 April, the day before your move. Chelsea is much nearer to Notting Hill Gate than it is to Islington. On the other hand the Shaw Theatre where *The Caretaker* is playing is much nearer Islington than Notting Hill Gate, so we can safely postpone our visit. There is a very good Italian restaurant where we can eat beforehand and even drink grappa. I haven't decided what we should do when I am due to go to Cambridge. We could spend the night at Ely or St Ives, but which night? You are sure to want to go on working to the last moment, but Friday would be a better night to be in the country. If you can get your visa extended and do not want to go on working, we would go to the Lake District or anywhere else you fancied from, say, 21 June, for a week or ten days. I must be in Oxford on 3 July and then go to the Isle of Wight on 5 July, and I expect you would like to go back to Hungary on 1 July or thereabouts.

Norman Stone came to see me yesterday. He writes on the Habsburg Monarchy in the twentieth century and has often been in Hungary. He even speaks Hungarian. Perhaps you have encountered him. He is an admirer of mine and has read, I think, all my books. We went on a walk round the City. By the way, there is a lunch-time concert next Tuesday, clarinet and piano works by Ravel and Brahms. If you want to go, you must make contact with me in the course of the morning.

No family news. Giles came to dinner last night and brought an enormous bunch of primroses that Alison had picked for me.

I hope this letter reaches you safely.

Love as in Manchester,

Alan
XXX

4 July

My Beloved Wife and Lovey,

It is very hard being without you. I walk through London and see all the places where we used to be together – Lincoln's Inn Fields, the Irish pub, the London Library. Never mind. We shall be together again soon and be sure to arrange everything efficiently (this is a show of bad temper on my part, eh?). This morning I tried to telephone you from Magdalen. The operator said he would call me back immediately. I waited an hour and nothing happened. Then he could not be traced, so I gave up in my usual impatient fashion and now I shall not ring you until I am in Magdalen on 20 July. Soon it will not be necessary for us to telephone each other at all.

I thought of you much of Thursday and hope that the arrangements at Heathrow were not too tiresome. The weather got hotter and hotter. I was glad indeed not to have gone to the British Academy dinner, though my dinner at the Beefsteak was pretty boring. I had an exceptionally busy time. Thursday I wrote a long review for a book on Mussolini by Mack Smith which did not deserve such length (*New York Review*). On Friday I invented captions for 280 photographs for *The Last of Old Europe*. Very laborious. I also wrote an article for the *Sunday Express* claiming that school holidays should be staggered – as in Germany, according to our German friends. On Saturday I went to Magdalen and attended the Gaudy dinner. It was again very hot. Dinner began at quarter-past seven. At ten o'clock we were only just finishing. I could stand no more and slipped out. Speeches, I hear, went on until after half-past eleven, and among them were kind remarks said about me. However, it could not be helped. Now I am again sweating preparatory to going down to the Isle of Wight tomorrow morning. I shall be more cheerful when the weather breaks, if it ever does.

It is no good repeating how miserable I am without you.

Please write to me. Please don't forget me. Oh, I do love you so.

Love to my Lovey,

I Love you,
Alan

9 July

Dearly Beloved,

I am worried that I shall not receive a letter from you for some time. Della is taking a week off and there is no one to forward letters from Fleet Street. However, I shall be back a week on Monday and perhaps shall find much to read then. My situation is worse than it has ever been before. After the happy weeks we spent together it is almost unbearable not to be with you. On top of that, Margaret is hysterical most of the time. This upsets me but does not affect my outlook in the slightest. I love you. I am going to marry you. And we are going to live together as soon as we can, unless the British economy collapses. So be full of confidence and hope.

Here is practical news. There is a new volume in the British history of the Second World War, *Grand Strategy*. This is volume I on the inter-war period by N. H. Gibbs. It is very heavy, so I cannot bring it with me. You must persuade your Institute to buy it, even though it costs £19. There is a chapter on the Rhineland showing that the British never contemplated military action. In fact they had no army at all, or so they said. This all comes from the Chiefs of Staffs' papers, so you may have it already. The same conclusion comes on the Czech crisis – war ruled out from the beginning. The naval side of the story is not done as well as in Roskill, partly because Gibbs has limited himself to the Chiefs of Staffs' papers and has not looked at the Admiralty records. The book would have been exciting if it had come out twenty years ago. Now most of the story has been told by others, though Gibbs of course pulls it together. I have written a long review for the *Observer* which I will try and keep for you.

My other activity is to write an introduction for the 21st volume of the *Bedside Guardian*. I can't think why I agreed to do this. Sentiment about Manchester, I suppose, though that has little to do with the *Guardian* nowadays. I am also reading a silly book of letters from Sir Desmond Morton about Churchill. He was Churchill's slave during the Second World War and had no high opinion of his master. I don't much care for these books about the great man, whoever he may be, seen from below. But I suppose I shall have to write something on it. I am also reading another book on the Bulgarian Horrors with great enjoyment. It will give me an alternative subject to offer to branches of the Historical Association if any invite me. So far only Norwich has. Perhaps they think I can only talk about the two World Wars, and perhaps they have lost interest in these.

It is a great relief to be in the Isle of Wight, even though I find Margaret excessively trying. Poor woman, she is driving herself into a nervous breakdown simply because she cannot show generosity to others. She is full of kindness and forethought towards others as long as they are in her power. But she is unyielding when I want something she can't offer. It is painful to say to her – 'I don't love you and I love someone else.' But that is the fact. However, I have been swimming every day in fresh, warm sea. Up at seven, swimming before breakfast, and then a longer swim in the early evening. Unfortunately the tide times are changing. High tide now at midday and therefore not good swimming

1976

either morning or evening. Daniel is here with his girl-friend and another friend who is very tiresome, always asking for things that we don't provide. Giles is coming down for the week-end to escape the heat in London. Probably the weather will turn cold and wet the moment he arrives. However, we can then go for a long walk on the Downs.

    I think constantly of our happy walks, even despite the worry about your leg. You must get it put right before next year. What a wonderful day we had on Crinkle Crags, I think the best walk I have ever done. You will be glad to hear that I have taken a wise precaution. I now carry spare keys to my car in my wallet, so that if I ever lock myself out again no problem will arise. Love and love and love. I am planning to come on 2 September which I will confirm later. So we only have a few weeks to wait. Then we shall snuggle up again. Margaret said to me: 'I know what is wrong with you, it is sex.' I thought of answering: 'By God it is.' But of course I love you for a thousand other things. What a lucky pair we are.

    Darling Lovey, never doubt me.

                        Alan

15 July

Best Beloved of My Heart,

    I am still feeling very cut off from you and shall be so until next Monday when I hope to find a letter from you in my room at Fleet Street. It is hateful to be without you. I need you very much. I am also cut off from others. Crispin has not written to me, even though he is back from Manchester or should be. Perhaps his mother has forbidden him to do so. And what is going on in the world? Here at Yarmouth the world might as well not exist. Today is St Swithin's Day and according to legend if it does not rain today it will not rain for forty days.* In that case there will be a real drought. Many towns, though not London, are already without water for much of the day. How is it in Budapest? I look at the temperature there each day and think of you lying in your garden. I hope you have gone to the Danube.

    Giles was here last weekend, Janet having allowed him to come on

---

   * The legend is, in fact, that if it rains on St Swithin's Day it will rain for the next forty days.

his own for once. He is a splendid companion, always gay and always keen for a walk or any other sort of adventure. We did fifteen miles one day and I am now so hardened against the sun that I suffered no ill-effects at all. The bathing has been wonderful, sometimes with high waves. But the wind blows here all the time and provides cool nights. All the same I shall be glad when this hot weather is over, particularly in London. I leave here on Monday. On Tuesday I have to explain to Chiefs of Police what is wrong with the world – as if I know. Then I shall be in Oxford for three days and after that say farewell to my rooms in Magdalen for ever. Margaret continues to be tiresome. She tries all the time to show how cooperative she is being, and every minute she looks at me like a spaniel who wants to receive attention. I am sorry for her, but there is nothing I can do. I have made up my mind, as you have, and nothing will make us change. We shall have troubles, but once we are together we shall always overcome them. I wonder whether you will really be happy with me. I know I shall be with you.

I have read a good deal. I finished Gibbs's book and reviewed it. I also reviewed the rather silly letters by Desmond Morton. Now I am labouring through a very long book in German about relations between Germany and Spain during the war. It is rather monotonous, always the same story. Franco was firmly anti-Communist and also determined not to be drawn into the war. He would have joined the German side if Germany had won. Otherwise he intended to keep out and somehow survive thereafter by exploiting anti-Communist feeling in England and America. He gambled on the Cold War and won, a very shrewd politician who beat all his rivals at home as well as abroad. Lastly, I am reading a book by David Irving which claims to produce much new German material but is really a smear on British policy. The most interesting part of the German-Spanish book is about Franco's attempts to secure a negotiated peace between Germany and the Western powers. There seems to be material about this in the PRO, which of course no English historian has thought of using. How unenterprising my colleagues are.

What are your boys up to? I shall be sad if I don't see Ferencz in September, but no doubt he will have other things to do. Have you cleaned the outflow of the sink lately? Have you sorted out all our legal problems? We shall have so much to talk about. And on top of that we shall have Aubrey to read. I'll bring Hašek and anything else you tell me, so long as it is not too heavy. Every night when I turn over I look for your curly head on the pillow beside me. As I have told you before, Coniston was the best time in my life and I think it was pretty good in yours. You will be glad to hear that I have found Real Ale in one pub on the Island, not as good though as Hartley's of Ulverston.

That's all for now. The sun is just coming through and I may be able to swim this afternoon.

My Dearest, I send you all the Love I have and for you that Love is limitless.

Alan
X

21 July

Darling,

Here I am writing a letter from Magdalen for the last time. I shall be sad to depart on Friday. This evening my colleagues are giving me a dinner, some thirty Fellows mostly with their wives. What a pity we are not married yet so that you could come too. After this I shall be in London until the end of August, when I go to Edinburgh. On 2 September I shall come to you. What clothes shall I bring? Will there be any formal occasions when I shall need a suit? I will bring heavy shoes but not boots. And shall I bring my shorts? Send detailed instructions about books you want. I shall not bring any that are too heavy.

I have your letters of 11 and 13 July. As to the certificate of no impediment, there is no such thing in England.* The authorities have no idea whether there is an impediment. It is up to me. If we were getting married in England, I should be asked if there were any impediment and if I falsely said 'No', the blame would lie on me. I will make a formal affirmation to a commissioner for oaths, and it will look like what your authorities want. I suppose at the ceremony we shall need an official interpreter. You must also arrange for the certificate to be officially translated into English afterwards. Next week, when I am back in Hungary, I will send you some money. Give it to Pisti at once and tell him to put it in the bank.

Here are two questions. First, where do you intend to live when I die? If you go back to Hungary you will not need a flat here. So I could borrow most of the money to buy it by getting a mortgage, and so we should have more free money to spend. Then the flat would be sold when

* Alan and Eva were preparing to marry.

I died and the money would pay off the mortgage. If you intend to remain in England, we shall have to make other arrangements.

Secondly, what do you expect me to leave you in my will? Anything I leave you will be tax-free, though there will be tax to pay when you die. I thought I might leave you the copyrights on my book for your lifetime. This will give you a good income, though there may be difficulty in moving it from England. It will also allow you to control the books through my agent and to publish my autobiography. You may have other ideas.

I have heard from Crispin, though I still have difficulty in communicating with him. He is going to a rain forest in Western Ghana where he will teach A-level maths. He will be on a course until the end of July, when I hope to see him and have some walks with him in August.

Margaret was in almost constant hysterics during the latter part of my time at Yarmouth. I shall have to move out if this goes on. She has also turned all the children against me. However, it is their loss.

I had an interesting time at the Police College, addressing Chief Constables. They were very sensible though rather heavy. One of them told me afterwards that he had nearly laughed at one of my jokes but a colleague had nudged him in time. They were quite ready to face mixed marriages as the solution to the problem of the coloureds, and agreed that coloureds of the second generation were as English as themselves. They were also ready to agree with me that the fear of revolution was a nonsense. Now I am lecturing to a summer school for three days on Britain and Europe.

The weather is cooler. Heavy rain yesterday. Cool sun today with north wind. It looks as though swimming days are over. Next week Andrew Snell is coming up for yet another recording. He says we jump too fast from the Town Hall in its great days to the Cotton Exchange and the end of Lancashire's greatness. 'The War Lords' begin on 3 August. The Penguin *Essays in English History* is out. I will bring a copy, though you know it all.

Despite my worries, much love.

Alan
xxx

1976

29 July

Darling,

It was miserable leaving my Oxford rooms for ever. I had lived there for twenty-three years. At one moment they were all around me. Then I closed the door and finished with them for ever. Fortunately they will provide us with a carpet, lots of rugs, a sofa and some chairs, so we shall have something to sit on. I have bought some frying pans and some cutlery. I have paid for the sheets and towels. I don't think I can do any more till you come. I will look at flats, but I would rather have your opinion as well. So probably we will take a furnished flat and live there for a little while getting our own flat in order. Oh, one other question. Are you sure you can stand Margaret's neurotic outbursts, which are sure to happen with her ringing up pitifully at all hours of the day and night? This broke Eve's spirit. You will be stronger.

I have set my lawyer the problem of a declaration of no impediment. He has solved it and I will get one soon. Of course he said no such thing existed in England, but he will consult others and ring up the Hungarian consulate. He was also emphatic that of course you would become a British citizen. But you must get dual nationality absolutely sure.

Amelia came to see me the other day. I have given them a great problem of course, because one of them will have to live with Margaret and none of them wants to. I said, 'I know, I understand. But this is the most important thing that has happened in my life. I love Eva and shall go on loving her until I die.' Amelia burst into tears and embraced me, so there is one who sympathizes. Giles and Sebastian are quite unconcerned, holding that it is nothing to do with them.

Andrew Snell is still being troublesome, wanting more about the cotton trade. The whole character of the programme is changing. He asked for a programme about Manchester, which I did. Now Manchester is fading into the background. He is a sweet boy but confused in his ideas. The lectures, however, are all set to start on Wednesday next and will run for six weeks. They will be published in the *Listener*. *Essays in English History* comes out tomorrow. I will collect the reviews. Michael Foot wrote a piece about me in the *Radio Times*, very ridiculous but heart-warming. There was also a full-page photograph in which my feet came out larger than anything else – perhaps a compliment to Michael.

I have found a prize-winning biography about Mrs Gaskell. Did you ever read any of her works? She was a marvellous character who has received the good biography she deserves.

It is still very fine and dry, but fortunately not so hot. I have swum at the Ponds where the water is now 68 degrees, which means 20 degrees to you – just right. I am sometimes shaky and a little upset, but the main thing I want is to see you again and I soon shall. Write to me soon, if only a postcard to say you remember me.

All the love I bear you,

Alan
X

1 August

Darling,

I got your letter of 26 July but had already found how to take out a certificate. I had to give your name etc., and perhaps got it wrong. I gave your second name as Anna. Should it be Hannah? I also said you were born in Budapest. Should it be Miskolc* or however it is spelt? I may telephone you, probably on Tuesday evening. If I fail to get you then, reply at once or, even better, ring Della at 353-8000, ext 3460. I shall receive the certificate on 24 August, so in plenty of time, and will bring it with me.

Also draft from the bank. I don't know why they sent it to me instead of straight to you. Also, maybe I have got your second name wrong again but I hope the bank in Hungary won't mind. If it does, keep the draft and I will exchange it for a new one.

Lots of love and eagerness.

Alan

11 August

My Dearest Love,

No letter from you since the one you wrote on 28 July. I hope this means you are on holiday, unworried by our problems. The certificate will be ready on 21 August and I will send it to you at once.

However, I'll tell you my news. *Essays in English History* made quite

---

* Where Eva was born.

1976

a splash. Alan Ryan in the *New Statesman* said I was the twentieth-century Macaulay. Robert Blake in the *Spectator* said I was the twentieth-century Dr Johnson, which I prefer. The *Listener* had my picture on the front, looking very academic and very old. The BBC are also going to bring the lectures out as a little book. Reading them, I don't think they are worth it. There is nothing new in them and I didn't intend that there should be. However, for the moment I am something of a public figure. Tonight I shall be on Hitler. Very annoyingly, ITV have put on a two-part feature on Hitler at the same time, and I fear that most people will switch to that.

Andrew Snell came up from Manchester yet again. This time he brought long passages from my remarks which he had cut down. He has in fact cut down many of the series in which I appear, and instead there will be other scenes with a recorded commentary by me. He is still pushing to reduce the amount on Manchester and increase the amount on the cotton trade. However, it is his programme to do what he likes with. I think he now repents that he allowed me to talk impromptu at all.

I have at last got the cheque from Lasky's and enclose it. If your bank will cash it, pay it in. If they will not, write on the back: Pay A. J. P. Taylor or Order, and sign it E. H. Haraszti. Then I can pay it into my bank.

I have done a second Diary for the *New Statesman*, full of fun. I am now desperate for ideas for next week, but no doubt they will turn up. You will also be fascinated to hear that I am seriously turning over ideas for 'British Destinies 1901–75'. I don't like the present title very much and will find a better one when I am with you.

I will leave a space now in case a letter comes from you later in the morning. Meanwhile, let me know anything you want me to bring. I don't promise to bring everything!

Later. No letter from you, though I hope to have one soon. I have just received the proofs of my introduction to *Ten Days That Shook the World* so I shall have plenty to do. It is again very hot and I am not going to Highgate Ponds.

Love and love and love,

Alan

17 August

Beloved,

I had your lovely letter of 7 August and am content that you are waiting for me happily. I shall collect the certificate next Monday, 23 August, and sent it to you at once. Otherwise I shall probably not write again. As you know I shall arrive at 19.25 on 2 September. I shall bring some money but not very much. We shall be all right with what you have already got.

Here the weather is still very hot. There has been no rain since May and now the drought has become almost a catastrophe. There are no vegetables in the shops. The grass and trees are dying. It is the worst drought for nine hundred years. There will be no recovery unless it rains not only throughout the autumn but all next year as well. However, there is no contending with nature.

Most critics said kind things about 'The War Lords'. Two however said I was showing my age and was not as lively – 'perky' was the word used – as I was. I think they are exaggerating the liveliness of my lectures all those years ago, but I was depressed all the same. It will make it more difficult for me to get a contract for another series. Oh no, they will say, he is too old. The lectures looked all right to me except that I was rather in a hurry, having too much to say in half an hour. But once people get an idea in their heads, they never get it out.

The *Essays in English History* had very good reviews. Robert Skidelsky (who sent his greetings to you) recognized that in them I was gloomy about England's future. And so I am. There will be another crisis in the autumn, when I tremble to think what will happen to sterling. Often I fear that you and I will not be able to manage financially. But I have gone on like this since we were in Paris in 1973 and we have come through all right so far. Meanwhile I have tried to begin my book on *British History in the Twentieth Century*, not very successfully up to now. Have plenty of quarto paper for me and I will work loyally in the mornings.

Daniel has gone to Heidelberg and is now I suppose in Poland. I hope he will not be too outspoken in his Marxism when he is there. Crispin is preparing for his departure. He is very enthusiastic about his new life. I dislike the thought of it very much, but he is right to do what he believes in. At the moment I have no troubles with Margaret except for the knowledge that she still hopes things will blow over if she is patient enough. They won't. We shall be together and that is that. But when? Do please get your plans defined before I come. I worry about the immediate future so much, wondering where we shall find a flat, how we shall arrange it and where the furniture will come from.

I have been writing the London Diary for the *New Statesman* for the last four weeks, very exhausting work but very rewarding (not financially).

Tom Driberg died suddenly. I gave him two paragraphs in the London Diary. He is said to have left memoirs, all about his homosexual doings and those of everyone else. He was a strange man, a really good Socialist and yet to conventional minds a very wicked man. Stephen Koss has written a rather pedestrian life of Asquith, which is at any rate better than Roy Jenkins's.

I have been to the Ponds nearly every day and shall go again this afternoon. As soon as I am with you I shall be more cheerful. Just now life is too much for me.

Love is all that matters.
So here is Love, lots of it.

> Alan

21 August

Darling,

Here it is, the precious certificate. Of course I realize it is too late to be of any use, but you had better have it all the same. We will discuss what to do next when we meet. The weather is again very hot, almost as hot as it was in June. I swim every day at the Ponds, which are not as good as Coniston. Now I must write my last London Diary for next week.

Do not lose this.
　　Much love and kisses,

> Alan

19 September

My beloved Wife,

Now I can really write that as a legal formula. How do you like having a husband even if he is far away?* The best thing I did in my life. However, no time for that. Here is my news. I had a wretched journey. The plane left reasonably on time. It was full with noisy young men speaking an unknown language, which sometimes sounded like German and where sometimes I seemed to hear French. Mysterious. Without warning we landed after an hour and a half. I thought perhaps we were going to crash and that my last hour had come. We came down on a deserted airfield, entered a deserted air station, and there we were in Luxembourg. Apparently there were few passengers for London, so our plane was commandeered as a charter flight back to Luxembourg. Of course we had to wait more than an hour as transit passengers, and then merely got into the plane that had brought us. We did not reach Heathrow until six.

I have been still pretty ill. My doctor said cheerfully that I had a virus and that it would take ten days to clear off whether he gave me any drugs or not. So he gave me no drugs. However, I am painting my mouth with a blue dye which lessens the pain. I am rather shaky all the time but am eating better and even drinking wine. I have started eating a boiled egg each day for breakfast, and maybe shall never return to bacon and eggs. We shall see. Margaret behaves well, except at intervals when she appears to have totally lost touch with life, when she wanders round not knowing what she is doing. Of course she is playing on my feelings. As long as we don't have rows I don't mind. In any case it will make no difference. She says she sent me a telegram to Budapest in answer to my letter. She did not say what was in it. Maybe she never sent it. She says there was an important message in it which she will tell me when I am better.** I am not curious to know. The less said the better.

Now here is really important news. The Zagreb academy has completed its edition of the Seton-Watson correspondence and it will be published on 15 October. There will be a banquet. Hugh and Christopher Seton-Watson are going, and the academy have asked me to go in order to strengthen the British party. I have agreed. I have also written to Neville Williams and have said that my wife is in Budapest where she

---

* Eva and Alan were married in Budapest on 15 September 1976.

** The telegram said: 'Living with Sophia next September. Sebastian organizing Barclay loan against St Marks cover rob. Margaret.'

is editing the Michael Károlyi letters. It would therefore be appropriate and also pleasant for me if the Yugoslavs would invite her to Zagreb for the celebrations. I have therefore asked him to suggest this. I'll let you know what he replies, but of course it all depends on the Yugoslavs. I'm pretty sure they will do anything for a good party, particularly as there really is a reason to invite you because of the Károlyi letters. You had better get your British passport ready so that you will be able to travel on it. I shall go to Zagreb on 14 October, attend the celebrations on 15 October, enjoy the following day in Zagreb and return on 17 October. It will be a wonderful and unexpected treat if we can meet.

I arrived home at seven o'clock on Thursday. At eight o'clock the Manchester programme began. Andrew Snell has made a fine mess of it. Great stretches of the programme were about the cotton trade and had nothing to do with Manchester. Then the switch would be the other way. Episodes were left hanging in the air because the sequel that should have gone with them had been cut out. Chetham's Library very wasted. Town Hall all right. Peterloo dead loss. The end was thrown away. There I was sitting by the Rochdale Canal. I got up to walk away, turned on my heel and – end of shot. None of that lovely walk down the towpath. However, it has been highly praised and I got a telegram of congratulation from Sir John Betjeman describing me as his old artiste friend.

Eddie Mirzoeff says we shall do the Prime Ministers in the spring. Daniel rang up while I was away and was surprised to hear I was not in England. He has not rung since I came back. Maybe I'll see him sometime on Sunday, and hope to be better by then.

Love to my two stepsons.
And of course to you.

xxx
Alan

21 September

Darling,
This is purely a business letter. Here is a copy of the report I have sent to Mrs Roth. You will see you have plenty of work to do. I also sent her the authorization about the money.

You are now my next of kin, so will you please sign the card about my kidneys and return to me. I ought to have done this long ago. I do hope you can arrange things about Zagreb. I will write to you again as soon as I hear from Neville Williams.

My fever has gone, though I still feel weak. My mouth is sore but improving. Life goes on in an empty way, made bearable only by the thought that we shall be together next year. Getting married was the best thing we ever did. I have at last had a letter from Crispin. He is living on a diet of yams, plantain and grease. The little boys shout after him in the street and ask his name. Daniel had a marvellous time in Poland, going to the best hotels because of zlotys at the unofficial rate. Cracow is full of rich Americans who have retired there after making their fortunes in America. Mary Taylor left her car unlocked while she was shopping in the market and it was stolen. Manchester has been a great success with the public, though I thought Andrew had ruined it.

I'll write again next week when I have more to say. Just now I am catching up on my work.

All my love to my wife,

Alan

X

25 September

Beloved,

A lot of news, most of it bad. I am slowly recovering, but am still very weak and go to bed most afternoons. I think my mouth will be all right some time next week, sore as it still is now. I hope I'll never be ill like this again.

I think I left my hairbrush and comb with you. Do not worry about this. I have two spares and can recover the other when I come to you or you to me.

Do not count much on Zagreb. I found that the arrangements are in the hands of Hugh Seton-Watson, not of the [British] Academy, and you know what a muddler he is. He has not yet told the Yugoslavs I am coming, and I certainly shall not go unless everything is firmly settled. When I proposed you, he said he would mention it to the Yugoslavs, but obviously did not like the idea. If anyone came from Hungary it ought, he said, to be Pach* or someone on that level. I said you were doing the

---

* P. Z. Pach, economic historian, at that time Director of the Institute for Historical Research in Budapest.

Károlyi letters but he did not listen. However, the Yugoslavs may write to you at the Institute. But I doubt whether they will offer to pay your fare. I hope you'll come even if you have to pay your own fare, but it is not very important just for a day or two. Let me know if there is any chance of your coming.

The real disaster is that Margaret turned down my suggestion of doing things in a friendly way flatly. In some ways this makes things easier for me. It means I need have no dealings with her once we are settled. Of course she is hysterical, poor woman, but that is no help. We must change our plans somewhat. I will find a flat early in the New Year and gradually furnish it. Then I suggest you come for a fortnight or so in September. You can see what I have done, and we will go to the Lake District or elsewhere for a holiday. Then you can go back to Hungary, clear everything up there and come for good at the beginning of 1978. Is this what suits you best? I hate every minute of our being apart, but I can't join you in England until you are definitely here for good.

I have started plans to go to Bologna next May. Then we can spend a week or ten days in Italy, or I will come to Budapest if you had rather. Sorry these plans are so complicated. Everything overwhelms me at the moment, especially when I am feeling so ill. But it will all come right in the end.

I rang Shirley and told her our good news. She was very pleased. How are you getting on with your British passport?

Your loving husband,

Alan

I love you just the same as before. You will always be my life-mate more than my Wife.

1 October

Lovey Dovey Wifey,

I received your letter of 24 September. I have sent my report on *Chartism* and have also signed the contract with the publisher. I had an invitation to dinner from Ernö Goldfinger. I told him I was busy until November and would love to come then. I also told him we were married, which surprised and pleased him.

Zagreb is cancelled for the time being. The date did not suit the

Yugoslavs. Hugh Seton-Watson is trying to arrange another one and of course I shall try to come. But my commitment to Bristol may make things difficult. I will tell you as soon as I have some firm news. Meanwhile, if you get an invitation (which as I told you I am not sure of) you must accept it and hope I will be there as well. In any case it will be fun for you. I hate this time when we do not see each other. The time seems endless, but we must accept our fate and think of a future which will come some day.

All flats are too small – one sitting room and two bedrooms. So I have switched to looking for a small house which will cost little more. This will give us two sitting rooms and three bedrooms. If I find one that suits I shall buy it and not wait for you to see it. Then I can put in gas central heating and perhaps knock the two sitting rooms into one. You know how bad I am at all this, but am doing my best.

Margaret continues to be very trying, constantly heaping abuse on you and lamenting her hard fate. I tremble to think how she will behave when we really settle down together. She can think of no one except herself and thinks all other people should be sacrificed to her. And of course whenever we get on a little better she imagines I have relented and will stay with her for good, which I shan't.

Cheerful news is that I have stirred things up at Bologna and hope we can both go there next May. The real nightmare is the fall of sterling. We are bound to have exchange control soon and then I may not be able to send you any money. Always be sure that the difficulties do not come from me but from circumstances. Maybe lots of public affairs will have changed in twelve months' time. Surely they cannot go on getting worse indefinitely. What I fear is a right-wing dictatorship. Certainly the Labour Party is incapable of providing a left-wing one.

Neville Williams is secretary of the British Academy, but unfortunately the arrangements with Zagreb are made by Hugh Seton-Watson, not by him. Sir John Betjeman is Poet Laureate and an old Oxford friend of mine. I am too weary to write London Diary at the moment but will get around to it later. I still insist that Neville Masterman is dead, but perhaps I am wrong.

Oh, Lovey, I need you so much and begin to think we shall never achieve permanent happiness together. I suppose we must be patient but it is very hard. By the way, I am nearly well again but not quite.

Love to my stepsons as before,
And a tiny bit of love for you.

XX
Alan

1976

7 October

Dearest Wife,

I have just received your letter of 28 September. My immediate news is that the celebration at Zagreb has been arranged for Friday 19 November. I shall be at Bristol on the Thursday and shall therefore fly to Zagreb on the Friday morning. The Yugoslavs have told Seton-Watson they will invite you but cannot pay your fare. Will you be able to go without their doing so? If you don't go, I may also call it off on the grounds that my visit would be too rushed, but I shall come if you go of course. Let me know. I can give you some money in Zagreb. That is all my important news. I am now recovered more or less completely. Instead my car is ill, behaving badly on the roads. I shall have to buy a new, smaller car next year if I can raise the money. But buying and equipping a house will cost a good deal. However, I do not mind that. All I want in life is to be with you, and each day I rejoice that one more day has gone by. It is agony to be without you. I miss you in the daytime and I miss you at night. I think of you with tousled hair in bed and the way you look at me when you wake up in the morning. It is a sad fate we are not together, but a good fate that one day we shall be.

I gave Shirley a ring and told her our news. Otherwise I have mentioned it to few, except of course to all the members of the family. Crispin wrote: 'I know you will both be happy.' He is having a tough time out in Ghana. His flat, though spacious, is infested with ants. The coloured teachers do not speak English very well and he is starting to learn Twi, the local language. He says it is like going to the university all over again, that is not knowing anybody. He is a good brave boy. As well as A-level maths he will teach physics and be head of the maths department. The truth is that VSO got in Crispin a boy of far greater abilities than their usual recruits, and he is wasted on Asankrangwa. I took Daniel to Leeds at the weekend. He is in for a pretty tough life too. His Hall of Residence is four miles from the University, and unless he gets a bicycle he will have to spend 50p a day on bus fares. Also he will have difficulty in playing a big part in local Labour politics when he is so far away. His room is smaller and worse furnished than a prison cell. However, he seemed not at all depressed by his surroundings whereas I was sunk in gloom. It seemed unfair that Crispin should have lived in such comfort at Cambridge, to say nothing of my stately apartments at Oxford. But this is how Daniel wanted it.

'Never turned a hair' means quite untroubled. Arthur Ransome wrote very good books for children a generation ago, all about imaginary adventures on Windermere. My first lot of children liked them very much, though I thought them rather boring. He wrote an autobiography shortly before he died and it has just come out. Very good. I'll keep it for you. He was in Russia all through the Bolshevik revolution and wrote I think the best account of it, particularly because he was entirely non-political. He married Trotsky's secretary.

I am hastily reading Volume V of Martin Gilbert's *Life of Churchill*, all on the inter-war period and very boring. But I have to review it. Otherwise life is dreary and with many difficulties. Margaret is quieter for the moment, but there will be more crises and complaints. I shall soon start looking at houses and will tell you when I find one.

Next week I start at Bristol on Tuesday. I shall go by train. The country is approaching a financial catastrophe. This will cause troubles for you and me as well as for everyone else.

Much love, Lovey,

Alan

11 October

Dearest Wife,

I have just got your letter of 5 October. I have found my hairbrush and comb. I am now quite well apart from being made a nervous wreck by Margaret's scenes and storms. I wish I could move out. My doctor merely said I have caught a virus and that it would go away, which it did.

Now as to our problems. Every flat I looked at was too small. For the same price or little more (£20,000) I can buy a little house and have found one. Ground floor: well-equipped kitchen, sitting room with alcove for dining room at one end. First floor: study for me, rather too large, and one for you a bit smaller. Second floor: big bedroom for us, smaller bedroom, and dressing room where we can keep clothes. No garden, but a little patio rather overlooked by other people. Parliament Hill Fields five minutes away. Highgate Ponds ten minutes away. There are fitted carpets and some cupboards. I will put in gas central heating. The people want to sell now, but would leave their furniture in until next autumn so that squatters will not break in. How does this sound to you? If you think it is too big I will cancel. But the only alternative is a three-room flat with much smaller rooms. I think it should be easy to clean with a Hoover. There is also a little room to keep brooms and a cellar where I can keep wine. So you see I have been active. It is better to buy now because money may have lost all value by next year.

The one problem will be the change-over. It is a catastrophe that you cannot come for another year, but it can't be helped. We shall have plenty of time to discuss our detailed plans.

Zagreb seems settled for 19 November. I think I shall have to fly in that morning and attend the dinner in the evening. Then I shall stop until the Monday morning, so we can have three nights together. The Yugoslavs will certainly invite you and, as you can pay the fare, all is well. I have started negotiations with the Johns Hopkins University at Bologna, so we can meet there early in May and then go on to Venice with what they pay me.

As to my other news, I am leaving for Bristol for the first time tomorrow and shall lecture on 'History in General'. The following week I lecture at University College London on 'The Bulgarian Horrors, 1876'. I thought that they should not pass unnoticed. No word from Daniel yet. Don't be disappointed if Crispin does not write to you. He is very busy and is settling into a new life. But remember the sweet words he wrote to me. I will send some money to Pisti next week. It would surely be better for him to come to London next year when he could live with us, but perhaps he would not like that! Will you need a visa to come to England on a Hungarian passport? You had better arrange this in good time.

I'll let you know more about Zagreb as soon as I can. I'll bring the marriage certificate if I remember.

All my love for now,

Alan

21 October

Beloved,

There is no soft word for husband. The post is being kinder to me than it is to you. I got your letter of 5 October last week and that of 18 October this morning. Only one practical matter. Let me know in English money how much you are paid per month, then perhaps I can get an addition to my pension.

I hope you approve of my buying a house. If you don't like it we can easily sell it. But any flat would be too small. I have heard nothing further from Zagreb. If and when I do, I will let you know at once, also the name of the hotel. Hugh Seton-Watson is such a muddler. We shall see.

As to news. I had a gay letter from Daniel. He says that Trotskyites under his leadership have already captured the University Socialist Society, though I do not think he knows what Trotskyites are. He is very happy at his Hall. If he moves from there he will get a flat with fat Anna, his girl-friend. He wrote to me that the standard of life at the Hall was much too luxurious, far above the standard most students had at home. I have begun well at Bristol. John Vincent is almost too kind to me. I gave very good lectures so far, and the Vice-Chancellor whom I met on the train told me they are anxious to have me again. Also my former pupil Roy Avery is headmaster of the Grammar School at Bristol, so I have another friend. In fact a dinner party of one sort or another is now arranged for all the evenings I am there. I also gave a good lecture at University College London on Tuesday on 'The Bulgarian Horrors'. I expect you have forgotten they ever took place.

Robert Rhodes James is a rather pretentious, youngish man who wrote the lives of Dilke, Rosebery etc. I have written two more pages of my first chapter, making five pages in all. Slow going. I am too busy reviewing books. Six hundred pages on *The Origins of the Morocco Question, 1880–1900*, twenty years in which nothing at all happened. A wonderful old-fashioned book of pure diplomatic history. Then I am expecting a huge book on Hitler by John Toland, an American or possibly Canadian writer. He did a very good book about Japan called *The Rising Sun*.

A very good idea that you should write your autobiography. You must write it in English and I will put it into good English. *I must rewrite my autobiography also, and you will have the pleasure of publishing it after I am dead.* I can't come to Hungary officially. I have been once, and it is quite wrong for a Fellow of the Academy to ask for these trips unless he has some genuine research to do. I will tell you as soon as I hear from Bologna. And I expect I will come for a weekend after Christmas. I have agreed to write the Diary in December, so you will have to wait a long time.

Greetings to my stepsons.
All Loving Thoughts,

Alan   xxx

1976

29 October

My Lovey Dovey,

    I am not especially expecting a letter from you, and write because I shall be rather busy next week. As I told you, I have asked the man in Zagreb to let both you and me know our hotel. I shall arrive on the Friday at 13.00, when either the Croats or the Seton-Watsons will meet me at the airport. Come too if you can. There is no morning plane on Monday, so I shall stay until the one at 17.45. Make your plans without thought of that. If there is a convenient train earlier, off you go and I will wave goodbye.

    I told you about the house I was negotiating for. A surveyor's report has revealed some defects which must be put right, so I shall wait for an estimate of the cost before I go further. If you think the house sounds too large, I can withdraw my offer without difficulty. But as I told you also, the alternative is a three-room flat probably in a less agreeable position. We shall probably have time to discuss this at Zagreb. It is very hard to foretell the financial future. If things get worse here, and I think they will, we shall be in difficulties. However, you have a wonderful way of managing things.

    Meanwhile Bristol is going well. My three lectures on 'History in General' were much applauded. 'The Twentieth Century' will not be so easy. I have a mad round of entertaining. Last week Roy Avery, headmaster of the Grammar School, had me to dinner. He is a very sweet character. It is strange that a good man like Roy should still be operating a private, fee-paying school in what is supposed to be an egalitarian society. I also did some sight-seeing, though I lost my way and got into an unnecessary panic that I should miss my train. Next week I am to have dinner with seven great university figures – Vice-Chancellor, Registrar and so on. My hotel has one disadvantage. It has no central heating in the bedrooms and the electric fire takes a long time to warm up.

    The *Daily Mail* rang up to say that they had received a letter telling them that I had married a Hungarian lady. I said (the conventional reply for saying nothing): 'No comment.' If, which is unlikely, they get on to you, say the same: 'No comment' and not another word. I do not mind, but would rather our marriage became generally known only when you are with me for good. However, I am not worrying. The *Daily Mail* has not so far published the story.

    Margaret goes up and down. Sometimes she is in tears and hardly human. At other times she seems to assume that she will go with me for good. She refuses to recognize that if she accepted you as one of the family, things would be much easier.

I think of you all the time and this alone keeps me going.

And love too,
XXXXXXXX
Alan

5 November

Dear Heart,

Your letter of 28 October took only four days to come. One from Daniel of the same date took three days, so you are not far away. As to the house, I got it through an estate agent. The owners are moving to a job in the North Country. But they do not want to move their furniture until next September. So they will put a friend in the house and pay all the expenses until then. The house has some structural defects and I am waiting for an estimate of what repairs will cost. If they cost too much, I shall abandon the house and start again. I shall also put in gas central heating, but not until next September. So the house will not be ready for us then. Perhaps you can go to Shirley's for a couple of days and then, after seeing the house, we can go on holiday. We will try to work out a time-table when we meet. If Margaret would cooperate, everything would be much simpler. At present she is unmanageable and I fear we shall have a terrible time when you come. She will ring up at all hours of the day and night and is quite capable of forcing herself into the house. She is like a wild savage, thinking only of herself and that in dramatic terms. All will come well in time, but I wish you were here to help me.

Daniel is deep in politics and, anticipating the revolution, threatens to leave the University in order to fling himself into politics full-time. I shall try to warn him, but I doubt whether he will take any notice. Crispin has at last written to me, after two previous letters had gone astray. He is very well and busy, sharing his flat with a black colleague. The headmaster, also black, objects to this on the grounds that a black teacher should not have as high a standard of life as a volunteer. So colour prejudice cuts both ways. I saw the review by Stone in the *Times Educational Supplement*, and very good it was. Now I am waiting for my picture book on Old Europe to come out. Maybe I shall be able to bring it to Zagreb. As to 'The Bulgarian Horrors' I am giving the lecture again at Bristol and am trying to persuade Eddie Mirzoeff to let me give it on BBC television. A single lecture should be easy to slip in without much planning.

I have just been elected an Honorary Fellow of Magdalen, a great and welcome honour. It means I can go there for a night whenever I feel like it and have the time. I shall also get free dinners. Bristol is a great success. My lectures have run well so far, though they are hard work. Last Wednesday I had dinner with seven professors. Strangely they called each other 'professor' instead of using Christian names which is what I am used to. I met Terry at a party the other night and told him our news, with instructions that he should tell Joanna and no one else. But Sebastian tells me everyone knows in Oxford. Probably Mary Thompson made a good guess and then gossiped.

Daniel is wrong to recommend the Duke of St Albans. The beer there is by no means good. We shall have to find somewhere better, though the area is not promising. I hear there will be fireworks, metaphorically, at a party next week. Antonia and Harold Pinter are to be there. Also Frank and Elizabeth, her parents, who have never met Harold. Elizabeth wants to to be reconciled, but Frank has said he will never be under the same roof as 'that man'. People are very strange.

Love to my stepsons for whom I will get Binham's book, and many loving kisses to you. I shall write again before Zagreb. Take care to be in good loving form!

X
Alan

9 November

Dearest One,

This is just a brief businesslike note to make sure we have got all arrangements right. Yugoslav Air Lines have got my ticket. Unfortunately Hugh Seton-Watson collected it and sent it to me, recorded delivery, and it has not arrived. However, I expect it will. I still do not know the name of the hotel where we are stopping. If you also do not know it, you should get in touch with the Croat Institute of Historical Studies in Zagreb who are looking after us. Probably it will be quite easy to telephone the Institute. The man responsible is called Boban or some such name. Probably I have told you all this before. At any rate, I am impatient to be with you.

The only event since Friday last is that I took Margaret to see John Wayne in *The Shootist*. This is a rather macabre film. Wayne recently had cancer and was cured, a rare achievement. Now he takes the part of a gunman who is dying of cancer and who at the end provokes a gun-fight in a saloon to ensure that he will die a sudden and painless death. Also in the film is Lauren Bacall whose husband, Humphrey Bogart, died of cancer, so it can't be a jolly subject for her. I wonder what I shall die of. Every year I put my affairs in order so that everything will be simple if I die. One year I shall forget to do this, and that will surely be the year I die.

I did a turn for Dutch television this morning, not very enlightening, and am off to Bristol early tomorrow. I shall not write again before we meet unless something critical happens.

Love with impatience,

Alan

26 November

Dearest Heart,

Here are the books for Ferencz and Pisti as a little Christmas present. I hope they do not go astray.

I spoke to Asprey just now on the telephone and he said that he had got everything under control. I hope so.

Monday was a grim day. It rained all the time and I did not go out except for lunch. Then I went to a restaurant near the station and had two hamburgers which cost 30 dinars. Others seemed to regard this as an adequate meal. However, my flight was very agreeable. Never before have I seen cities so clearly when we flew over them. I have written a letter of thanks to Mirjana. She was really very kind to us and made our visit a success. As usual we enjoyed every minute, and I feel more than ever that we shall have a happy life together.

Margaret was in bad shape. She declined your invitation to Budapest, at first violently, and then sent a grudging message of thanks. As you say, she will probably come round when you meet her. It is now clear that none of her children will have her to live with them and she is hysterically miserable at the thought of living alone. She suggested that her house should be converted into two self-contained flats, but I am pretty certain it would not work. We should have four rooms and a little bedroom as well. But we should always be conscious of Margaret downstairs. Also you would have no secure home if I died. So I will not pursue this idea further unless you think it might work after all. On the other hand, I have said that of course she could live with us, having the two rooms on the top floor. It was then her turn to say it would not work, and again I think she is right. But we must show we are cooperative even if she is not. I think she will stay on at St Mark's Crescent until we are settled, and God knows when that will be. We can only decide things when you are here.

I am having difficulties with the house. I had an estimate of £3,500 for necessary works, apart from the installation of gas central heating. This is far too much and I shall get another estimate as soon as I can. I am sure all will be arranged successfully in the end.

I have had a busy time as usual. At Bristol I had yet another dinner with the Vice-Chancellor and various professors. They are all very kind to me, but it gets rather wearisome. I told you, I think, that I had lost three ties in the hotel. I bought three smart new ones and then the hotel found the others after all. Still, I have three new ties. I tried British Airways both at the Zagreb office and at the airport, but there was no trace of the razors. I also bought at the airport a bottle of slivovic for 59 dinars, much cheaper than I could get it in England. I drank some of it on the plane and it is very good, though not like Serb slivovic.

At Bristol I also gave a lecture at the Polytechnic on 'The Bulgarian Horrors'. The audience had never heard of them and thought I was referring to the Bulgarian Politburo.

Lovely weather here, much better than in Zagreb. I had a five-page letter from Daniel, explaining why he was an unrepentant Marxist who expected the revolution very shortly. He will be disappointed. Now I must write the *New Statesman* Diary. At the moment I am short of ideas.

My love is unchanged,

Alan

X

7 December

Darling,

It is a long time since I heard from you. In fact the last I heard was your voice saying Goodbye. I feel so lost without you and my life seems to be passing in waste. However, things will soon be different. The problem over the house was all a misunderstanding. The estimate is only £600 and I shall soon complete the purchase. I hope we do not find the little yard too enclosed in hot weather, but we can easily picnic on the Heath. The actual move to the house, sorting my things out from Margaret's, will be agonizing, but I hope you will be there to help me. I still want you as badly as ever.

I sent the books for the boys by cheap printed rate and hope they have arrived. My razors have not been found and British Airways is refusing to pay for them, but I shall persist. Daniel, I suppose, will be coming home this week. Crispin remains silent, or else the post from Ghana is not working. Bologna does not want me next May. Apparently they get a grant from the Italian government for visiting lecturers, and this year the grant has been cut down. Now what shall we do? I have some money with Lucia in Rome, and plenty of German letters of credit which would give us ten days in Venice. Or I could come to Budapest for ten days. But I feel we may never be able to have a continental holiday together again if the economic situation here gets worse and I get poorer as my earning capacity declines. So I am in favour of meeting in Venice. I can send you £300 in the New Year and this will more than pay your fare. We can go to Ravenna by train for the day if we get up early enough, or we can spend the night there. Ravenna, though wonderful, is seen in quite a short time. The station restaurant where we change is the worst in Europe, an interesting experience in itself. Let me know what you think. I can't come to Budapest earlier, partly because I seem to have so much to do and partly because the fare is now so high in sterling.

Bristol has gone well. Tomorrow is my last visit and, though I have enjoyed my time there, I shall be glad when my journeying is over. I shall go from Bristol to Oxford and spend the night in College to assert my rights as an Honorary Fellow. I seem to have done nothing except read enormous books and review them on Canadian radio. First a frightful one by Toland on Hitler, and then one equally long but more interesting by Joseph Lash on Churchill and Roosevelt up to Pearl Harbor. I suppose that means another volume to come. Now I am deep in *The Hutchinson History of the World* by J. M. Roberts, eleven hundred pages very competent but very dull. Not up to the standard of H. G.

Wells's *Outline of History*. You will also see that I am writing the Diary for four weeks in the *New Statesman*. You will also have seen a long review by me of *The Morocco Question*, the most laborious work of diplomatic history I have ever read. Altogether a foolish way to spend one's life. Most of the time I am sunk in gloom and in worries about the future. I can't really believe that everything will come right in the end, but I shall go on preparing for the time when we are together. Think of me a lot and tell me all you are going. I expect you are too busy to write. I got on to the man at Wimpey's about Pisti, and he said all had been arranged satisfactorily.

It has been very cold and very wet, but I managed to walk all alone round the Heath last Sunday. Somehow I never seem to see any of my children. All, however, goes well with them.

Lots of love and longing,

Alan
xxx

Christmas Greetings

14 December

My Darling,

I got your letter last Friday (it is now Tuesday), but was too busy writing the *New Statesman* Diary and reading the eleven hundred pages of *The History of the World* by John Roberts of Merton. Very good and rather boring. However, here is my news. I got a second estimate for doing up the house and it came to £800, which is tolerable. So I have bought the house for £20,000, thus using up all the money that would otherwise have provided me with a pension. We must also put in gas heating, say £1,200. Otherwise the house is in good condition and any decorating must wait until I build up more money.

Now the great problem. Do not have delusions about Margaret. I do not love her. I am very sorry for her, even though she brought most of her troubles on herself. In the last few years I tried to make life easier for her because I had nothing better to do. She deliberately built up a picture that I had returned to her completely and that we were a loving couple, though she could often see that I was discontented and unsatisfied. She is a very wilful and determined woman and always has been.

Nothing will ever bring her to accept the future situation. She will work persistently to break up our relationship, as she did with Eve. She won't succeed: I love you. She insists that she hates you. I don't think she will change. I shall go on trying to make things easy for her, and shall even put up with her rages. But in the long run I don't think it will work. I shall break with her finally and shall be relieved to do so. But you will find we may have to do such things as refusing to answer the door, and having the telephone cut off or the number changed. Perhaps I paint too gloomy a picture, but I don't want you to come over thinking that everything will be solved without trouble. On top of this I am very impractical about household things and worry a great deal about the transition. I must try not to (sorry about this letter paper). Now forget it.

Let me know as soon as you can what you think about Venice. I am keen to go if you are. Bristol went on to a triumphant conclusion. They want me to go back next year if they can raise the money, and I am quite keen to go. Next term I shall have only University College London, which will be less fun. From Bristol I went to Oxford and spent the night in College. It was very agreeable but also nostalgic. I have lived there for twenty-five years and now it is my home no more. The food, however, is as good as ever. I rang Mary Thompson and told her our news. She sent you warm greetings but, knowing how hesitant I am, was a little surprised that I had acted so resolutely. Like others, she does not understand that love gives people courage.

I have been to three concerts where the Juillard Quartet played each evening a Mozart, a Bartók and a Schubert. I thought they were rather too romantic. I am also going to seven concerts where Brendel is playing all the sonatas of Beethoven, a marvellous experience. Still no word from Crispin, which may be all the fault of the post. Daniel should be coming back from Leeds soon, but he never writes to me and I shall expect him only when I see him. We are going to have five grandchildren for Christmas – Sebastian and his three, Amelia and her two. This is no doubt a calculated move by Margaret. Yet she realizes in her heart that my decision is final. She has fantasies because she is alone so much.

When I am alone I think only of you and of the life we shall have together. Love to my stepsons and to you one big kiss.

Alan

1976

17 December

Dear Heart,

I did not intend to write to you before Christmas, but the arrival of your presents has changed my mind. They were very welcome, though there is no need for presents between you and me. I shall drink the Tokay, but how do you suppose I shall be able to play the record with Margaret in the house? She flies into a tantrum at any mention of you, however remote, and is the more enraged now because I have completed the purchase of our house. In her sane moments she realizes that my decision has been made. At others she goes on dreaming about an imaginary future. However inevitable, the long interval has created a difficult situation.

Your card of greetings and that from my stepsons made me a little sad and apprehensive. You are so obviously a happy family enjoying life together that perhaps I am doing wrong and selfishly by taking you away from it. I fear that you will miss the boys and not be happy with me. After all, I am a poor substitute for them. However, you know best.

I am also depressed by public affairs. Healey's attempt to take stern measures has been a complete non-starter, no one is impressed by it and next year inflation will go from bad to worse. On top of this, oil prices are going up and I fear I shall have to give up my car before very long. I do not much mind for myself, but it is a convenience for Margaret and will be for you when you come. But our happiness does not depend on having a car.

To offset these worries, I have done another successful Diary for the *New Statesman*. Now I have one more which I must complete this weekend. Then I can forget about current affairs and shall not need to invent excursions with which to round off the Diary. I also wrote a laudatory review of John Roberts's *History of the World*, too laudatory for Terry who rang up and said, 'Surely you have praised it too much.' I stood firm and my praises will go into the *Observer* undiluted.

Crispin has been silent for two months. I rang the VSO office in London and they too had no news. They said Ghana was about the worst place in the world for correspondence and that I had no need to worry. As a general principle no news is good news, and I shall apply this principle now. I should like to hear from Crispin all the same. Daniel too has disappeared. His term is over and presumably he is back in London. But he gives no sign of life and I can't telephone him at home. So I wait for my phone which never rings. Perhaps he is in political trouble as a Militant and an infiltrator.

Here is another worry. Finbar* is eight years old. He is very good

---

* Alan's grandson by Sebastian and Mary Taylor.

at chess and mathematics. He can play the violin and the piano. But he cannot read or write and shows no sign of wanting to do so. If Sebastian approves, I shall go regularly and read to him in the hope that he will follow the text and want to read himself. Sebastian is too tired to read when he comes home and Mary is too harassed by the two little girls. I am told young people always manage to read in the end, but the longer they put it off the more difficult it is for them to start. I'd like to help if I could.

I think of you all the time. Indeed, without you I should have no interest in life, and I have little during this long period of waiting. You at any rate will have a Happy Christmas.

Love and longing impatiently,

Alan

31 December

My Darling,

I have put off writing to you in the hope that you might write to me first. But I am sure that you have been too busy with your boys over Christmas. I have been very distressed that I have not been able to telephone you. The truth is that Margaret never leaves me alone and, as she has her own extension to the telephone, she listens to all my conversations. I have no longer the refuge of Madgalen where I could telephone you in peace. So you must just do without hearing my voice until we are together.

This long period of waiting has been dreadful. I miss you all the time and grieve that we are not enjoying our life as we shall do next year. But do not doubt me. I shall not change in any way, however difficult things may be. One good piece of news: the house near Parliament Hill is now definitely ours. I shall get the repairs on it done in the spring and put gas central heating in during the autumn. By then I hope you will have seen it, and I am sure you will approve even though it may prove a bit big for us.

Margaret's main concern is to parade her misery and her loneliness. I merely count the days until the time when I have finished with her. But it is troublesome.

Be sure to tell me soon whether you would rather spend ten days in Venice or that I should come to Budapest. As you know, I should like to have a holiday in Venice together, but it is for you to decide. Apart from this I have no plans. For me it is a waste of time to go on holiday without you. I often think of our time in Coniston, which was the best holiday I ever had. But Manchester was good too. The Manchester piece has won a prize from the local society of architects as the most imaginative programme of the year. Eddie Mirzoeff has agreed to take six lectures on 'The World in the Twentieth Century'. I shall have to do some hard thinking about it.

I have finished my Diary in the *New Statesman* for the time being. It got better as it went on. Over Christmas I had time on my hands, so I began on my history of England and have written twenty pages. I can't say I am very pleased with it, but at least I have made a start. I have read a lot of rubbishy books, including one by Kay Summersby on her love affair with Eisenhower – she was his driver during the war. Surely most drivers and secretaries have harmless affairs with their bosses. Eisenhower soon ran off when she threatened to become serious. Like me, Eisenhower could not manage anything when it came to the point. Failure or success, I wish you were lying in my arms and that I were stroking you all over.

We have had very cold weather and I see you had the same in Budapest. Inflation is on the increase and will go up 14% at least next year. We shall be ruined. Perhaps you will regret having left the security of Hungary's economic system. I worry about the future, but worrying does not change things.

Love to my stepsons and even more to you.

X
Alan

1977

6 January

Beloved Wife,

Your letter of 15 December has just arrived, having been three weeks on the way. But of course this country has been dead for the last fortnight and is only just waking up. You must not be gloomy, indeed you mustn't. It only makes me still gloomier. Somehow we should never have made this arrangement, but what else could we do? My troubles were less over Christmas. Margaret flung herself into a family Christmas and was too busy to be unhappy. But I expect she will soon start saying that it was the last happy Christmas she will ever have, and I expect it is. I don't think it is practical to do any moving until I move altogether. Again Margaret will only complain. Whereas when the time comes she will organize the move. In fact it makes things easier for her if she feels she is wanted, and she certainly would be useful if she would only try.

It is wonderful news that you would like to come to Venice. As I told you, it may be our last continental holiday. I am tied here for part of April and after that we should avoid May Day, which will be a holiday in Italy. So I will make plans to come on Wednesday 4 May. I think if I plan early I can get a reduced fare on the aircraft and perhaps in the *pension* as well. I will enquire whether there is any way of finding furnished rooms for ten days or so. Then we can go out for our evening meal and do the rest ourselves. But I fear it will be impractical for so short a period. I will also see if I can get rail tickets here for Ravenna, and will investigate whether we can see it in a day or should go for a night. As I have told you, I have enough money in German travellers' cheques to pay our way. I look forward to it so much.

I have finished with the *New Statesman* Diary as you will see. I suppose I will do it again in the spring. I read a history of the RAF by Montgomery Hyde, from which I learnt the surprising fact that Inskip was responsible for the switch from bombers to fighters, so he was the man who made the Battle of Britain possible. I have also read a long American book about Bismarck and Bleichroeder which contained little of interest. I managed to write 12 pages of my book over Christmas, but have now decided they are all wrong and that I must write them again. But it is moving.

I have at last heard from Crispin, who is well apart from the damp heat. His school sounds like the one in *Decline and Fall*. One master was arrested for forgery and then released because the headmaster insisted the school could not go on without him. I had a terrible fright today. I saw a newspaper bill: 700,000 dead in Ghana earthquake. I was sure Crispin was among them. Getting nearer, I saw it was 'China earthquake' so did not worry.

All my worried anxious love,

Alan

14 January

Darling,
 Friday is a good day to write to you. I have cleared off a week's work and can relax while I write. I hope the fact that you have not written is evidence that you have had a busy and gay time over Christmas. I am only glad it is over. Here are some practical points.
 If we go to Venice for a fortnight I can get my air ticket at about half price – £72 instead of £130. Also, I might be able to find cheaper rooms. Ideally I'd like our own furnished flat, but this may be difficult for so short a time. Can you manage to be away for a fortnight? We can go to Ravenna and Verona, so will have plenty to do.
 Have you still got a driving licence, or can you get one shortly before you come to England? This will be valid for a limited period and then you will have to take a driving test for which I will train you, and perhaps you should have some formal lessons as well. Maybe you are too frightened to drive on the left and in English traffic. We shall see.
 As regards a British passport, you do not get this automatically. Thanks to the flood of black and brown immigrants, there are now strict rules. There has to be a legal claim and we shall have to pay £70. But it will be worth it to buy a wife, and such a wife too.
 My little book on British history has got moving and I shall soon carry it to 1914. What happens thereafter I do not know. I may also write a chapter on the National government of 1940–45 for a book on *Coalitions* that David Butler is editing. It is an interesting subject on which I shall have to ask Paul Addison to coach me. Then it should write itself, and it would be a useful exercise for me. However, I am not sure I know enough and I can't face reading, say, Dalton's diary, which I suppose I should.
 I have now completed the purchase of the house in Twisden Road.

The next thing is to get a builder to work on the roof and the damp course. I am bad at these things. There have been tiresome paragraphs about it in some papers, together with the information that I shall live in it with an Hungarian lady called Eva. Evidently they do not know your surname.

I will not weary you with my troubles with Margaret. She is proposing to move to a smaller house in a different area, where she will know nobody and will constantly complain of being lonely. She is hysterically hostile towards you, making out that you pursued me when it was the exact opposite. Or rather there was no pursuing one way or the other. We both wanted each other whatever the troubles involved, and they will be great. I worry a great deal and wish things were easier. But it is a price I have to pay and shall not worry once you are here. So do not worry on your side. I always recover my spirits when I think of our good times together, particularly in the Lake District. Every time I use my car keys I remember the occasion when I locked them inside the car at Cartmel. Never again.

No letter from Crispin. Daniel has disappeared, perhaps he has gone back to Leeds without telling me. Perhaps he has been thrown out and dare not tell me. There is no knowing.

Deep and lasting love,

Alan

21 January

Dearest,

I have your two letters of 12 January and 17 January (which arrived this morning). I answer your questions first. Barbara Betts is Barbara Castle. I am still waiting to hear from the BBC whether they would like 'The World in the Twentieth Century' or 'How Wars Begin'. We have abandoned 'The Prime Ministers' as too hackneyed. It is very distressing news that you fell and hurt yourself. Get well soon. I think of you as much as you think of me. You do not answer my questions about Venice. Is the first week in May all right? Can you get away for a fortnight in Venice? The last time we were there we were unhappy, and I sometimes fear we shall be again.

Now on my side I have bad news about the house. I duly bought it as I told you. The previous owner said he wanted to stay until

September, and that was fine by me. Then, after I had bought the house, he suddenly told me he had moved out and that the house was empty. There are two dangers. Squatters may move in and they are very difficult to get out. If the house remains empty for six months, the local council can issue a compulsory purchase order and take over the house at half-price. Do not say to me that I should put in some furniture. I have no furniture to move until Margaret moves to a smaller house, and I cannot get my furniture from Magdalen until September. Also, now that I look at the house I don't like it. It is too big for just you and me. Also it will cost £5,000 to put it in order. Now I am taking the following steps. I shall try to get the repairs put in hand at once. But I shall also look at the house again very carefully, and if I still decide I don't like it I shall sell it at once. This is a great setback, but I really think we would be better in a four-room flat where there are no stairs and no garden to worry about. One small bedroom for your boys to come to is enough, and if necessary we can work in the same room. But that is in the future. The important thing is to get the house secure or sold. I will report on this next week. If all else fails we will get a furnished flat when you come and start looking for something thereafter. Naturally I am very worried and anxious. Margaret rushed me into buying this house because she wants to move also. I always knew I should get things wrong. Now I am in despair and feel absolutely useless. By the time I write next Friday I shall have found a solution, but at the moment life is very bitter for me. Do not worry. We shall be all right when we meet.

End of my groaning. I have laid aside the book which I have come to dislike and am writing (a) a long piece on 'The Monarchy' for *Punch* and (b) a contribution on the National government of 1940 for a book edited by David Butler on *Coalitions*. This is more my sort of thing. I had a long letter from Crispin about his travels in Ghana. Daniel has gone back to Leeds. Finbar rang up the other night to say that he had just swum a mile – 66 lengths in the baths. I was delighted. It is more than I could do. He also won a chess championship.

I never answer letters in the *New Statesman*. There was a silly one about Michael. The editor, not me, got the date wrong. The sun is shining. Soon I shall be cheerful again.

Longing Love,

Alan

28 January

My Darling,

    I hope you have recovered from my distressful news about the house in Twisden Road. I was a nervous wreck for two days, unable to work or think. I am now clearer in the head. On looking at the house dispassionately, I was convinced that I had made a mistake. It is in a perfect position, but otherwise everything is wrong with it. It needs a great deal of money spent on it. It has seven rooms, most of them big, which are far more than we need. They would cost a lot to furnish and to heat and the last thing we want is to take a lodger, a frightful nuisance. So I have put it on the market and hope to sell it soon. This is a great setback, but better than being stuck with a house too big for us. Just to remind you, this is what it has. An enormous room on the ground floor running from front to back – big enough to be both our study and our sitting room. On the first floor a very big bedroom more than enough for us, and another room for a good bedroom. On the second floor two more big rooms, and a smaller one adequate for a bedroom. As well a laundry room and a kitchen. We should be lost in it. If you think otherwise, let me know and I'll call the sale off. But I'm sure it will not do. We need a flat or half a house with four rooms, don't you think? I mean to live modestly.

    I have just received your letter of 22 January and will try to answer all your questions. First Margaret: she is very difficult to talk to. Sometimes she is hysterical, and will get worse as time goes on. Maybe I shall make no plans and look only for a furnished flat, so that we can make arrangements only after you arrive. I will make plans for Venice as soon as I can, and enclose a little note. A yoke fellow is when two oxen are yoked to the same cart and have to pull it together. I shall not hear about Bristol until the late summer.

    It would be easy for Margaret if I were dead. But until then she will go on every minute thinking that I ought to be sitting with her in the evening or taking her to a concert. She also thinks everyone looks at her and thinks how badly she has been treated. I fear her children have all been influenced by this, and also feel I have betrayed her. All I know is that I want to be with you, and if she would help us we could give her friendship and an interest in life. Let us wait and see how things go when you come.

    As to work, I have written an introduction to Len Deighton's book on *The Battle of Britain* and an obituary of Sir Max Aitken, not that he is dead yet. Then I shall get down to the piece on the National government

1977

of 1940 for the volume on *Coalitions*. So my book on British history, which I don't enjoy, has slipped into the background.

I am hoping to see Daniel this weekend when he comes to London for a conference of Young Socialists. But perhaps he will be too busy. My telephone is out of order, so life has gone dead for which I am not sorry. This is a chaotic rushed letter, but I have to go off to the house, to guard it against squatters.

All my Love,

Alan
x

4 February

Darling,

Well, I have got one solid piece of news for you. I shall came to Venice on Sunday, 8 May, by charter plane, and stop a fortnight. This is much the cheapest way of doing it. I have also booked a double room at either the Dinesen, where we stopped before, or at the Alboretti in the next street where I stopped with the boys in 1974. Despite my insistence I am sure we shall get two beds, but it can't be helped. This is something really good to look forward to. We can certainly go to Ravenna, perhaps for a night, and can make day trips to Verona and Aquileia.

I have put the house in Twisden Road on the market. I regret this a little because it is in such an excellent position, just where we want it. But I can't face a house so big. If you think differently, I can still change my mind. But I am sure you would be condemned to endless housework and we should be worried about the house whenever we went away. I have no idea what I shall do next. Probably wait until the autumn and then search for a flat or half a house, what is called here a maisonette. If only Margaret would cooperate, things would be much easier. You could come to her house at first and we could look together, finding perhaps a house for her as well. At the moment she is behaving well, but I am sure she still dreams that everything will blow over and that she will go on just as she is. There will be violent scenes when she realizes that her hopes are in vain, but it can't be helped.

I go on busily, though most of the things I do are rather foolish. I wrote a piece on 'The Monarchy' for *Punch*, as I think I told you. I have also been persuaded by Jonathan Cape, the publisher, to write an introduction for a book of photographs of the Russian war which they got from Czechoslovakia. I don't want to get known as the man who writes introductions instead of getting on with his own books, but these photographs were so wonderful that I could not refuse. I have never seen such representations of the Russian people and of their life and sufferings in wartime.

However, I am also getting on well with my article on the making of Churchill's National government and how it worked thereafter. I keep rewriting so that I move slowly, but I have done 3,000 words out of 10,000. I also wrote an article for the *Sunday Express* for the Queen's anniversary, called 'Whatever Happened to the New Elizabethan Age?' It was good, but I am sure they won't use it.

Daniel was here last Sunday for a Young Socialists conference. Typically he gave no sign of life until 6.30 on the Sunday evening, when he rang up and asked whether he could come to dinner with Anna and a friend from Leeds. He was rather reserved and I wondered whether things were going wrong with him. But he said nothing and of course I did not ask.

David Marquand has produced 800 pages on Ramsay MacDonald. It is very good but also very boring. MacDonald gets less attractive, though also more pathetic, the more I read about him. Cynthia Kee wrote and urged us to visit her as soon as you were in England. It is nice that someone thinks of us. I think of you all the time. My life is empty without you, though I worry about the immediate future. Fortunately I am very well. My only misfortune is that I have nearly finished Pepys's *Diary*. What shall I read next at bedtime? I wish I were reading to you.

Love and love and love,

                                Alan
                                x

11 February

My Beloved Wife,

I got your letter of 3 February within four days and have been reading it ever since. Even more wonderful was our little conversation which cheered me greatly. Beforehand I was full of worries over everything. All day long I say to myself: it won't work, it won't work. A few words from you, and it is like the sun shining after rain and cold.

1977

I am glad you approve of my trying to sell the house. I am sure it is too big for us. But there is no certainty that it can be sold. So far no one has appeared for it. I shall go on patiently until June, hoping that no squatters will find the house. Then I shall have all the repairs and alterations done, with a recognition that we shall have to live there after all. The one thing in its favour is the situation, which is perfect. Otherwise everything is wrong. Of course, once it is sold there will be the trouble of finding somewhere else. I am hopeless at this, as I have told you. Also, Margaret insists on selling her house because she says she could not bear to live in it without me. So I shall end up with nowhere to live at all. I wish my life ran more smoothly. In some ways I hope she will persist in being hostile. Then I shall be free of her. On the other hand, if she is friendly I shall feel a duty to provide some life for her and it will be rather burdensome for us both.

I remember the passage in *Utopia* and also the account of Aubrey of More going into his daughters' bedroom with Roper, his future son-in-law, and pulling the bedclothes off them so that he could see them naked both front and back. We have carried out More's instruction. I love looking at you naked, and it always amuses me when you try to cover up or turn away.

Max Aitken is seriously ill and I have written his obituary, called 'His Father's Son'. But that does not mean he will die yet. There is scandal about the goings-on at Downing Street in Harold Wilson's time. It does not interest me except that it gets me lots of engagements on television. I have done one turn on Swiss radio about the monarchy, and am due to do two next week for German radio and television. Eddie Mirzoeff has fixed me definitely for six lectures on 'How Wars Begin' which I hope to record in June or July. The enjoyable thing I am doing is the essay on the National government of 1940. This is the sort of thing I do well.

Finbar is now playing chess in the London Junior chess tournament, and also learning the violin seriously. I heard the Bartók Quartet the other night. Their Haydn and Bartók were very good. Their Beethoven I did not like at all – too refined. I remember the time when we heard them together night after night.

The spring weather goes on and I walk a lot. Yesterday I met Skidelsky, who asked after you and is very unhappy with his life at the North London Polytechnic. I wish I could help him to a better job. He is really very able despite his interest in Sir Oswald Mosley.

Lots of love from far away,

Alan

21 February

Lovey Wife,

I had only just posted my letter to you on Friday last when I received your letter of 14 February. The post is certainly working at a fast rate. Yesterday I tried to telephone you but all international lines were engaged. I fear that at present telephoning is impossible and letters must make up for it.

There is no need for you to worry except over practical matters. Samuel Butler said: 'I don't mind the parting but I can't bear the leave-taking.' That is all that worries me: the turmoil when I actually move. But it does not alter my wish and my determination to have a life with you. As to the house, I shall keep it on the market until April or May. If no one buys it, I shall then have all the reconstruction done and gas heating put in, and we shall live there for good and all. But I would rather sell it and find somewhere smaller. There is no question of your coming here alone. If I have not found a smaller house or reconstructed the present one, we will take a small furnished flat, whatever the rent, and live there for a short time until we can get settled.

You need never worry that I shall cease to love you. But I sometimes worry that you may cease to love me, or at any rate decide that it is not worth while your moving from Hungary with all its troubles just for a few years. I really feel that I am getting older. I get wearier and I lack the capacity to do things I used to do. I drive my car with increasing reluctance and I find television more difficult. Maybe I imagine things, but so it is.

I had a good lecture at Norwich, but five hours in the train there and back were exhausting and I have not yet recovered. This week will be hard: a dinner at University College tomorrow night and a visit to Cambridge on Thursday. Meanwhile I am writing on Marquand's life of MacDonald, which is very good though very long. As you surmise, MacDonald's papers are now open and can be seen at the Public Record Office. His diary is a very important source. He was a well-meaning man but romantic and emotional, incapable of close reasoning and rational policies.

I shall not write again as soon as I have done this time.

This time I do not forget my stepsons. Love to them and very much love to you.

Alan

1977

3 March

Dearest Heart,

I got your letter of 24 February and write now as I shall be busy tomorrow. I have no news of importance to remark. As to the house, I have decided to do nothing until after Venice. If I have not sold it by then I shall have it repaired and made ready for us. I wish I had someone to advise me. I have always let Margaret arrange things and obviously I can't do that this time. She is in a bewildered state. She has looked at various little houses which never quite suit her, and of course she does not want to move until the end of the year. On the other hand, she does not want to be left in her present house without me. It is very sad for her and I understand her reproaches, but I just can't help it. If I thought she would cooperate fairly I would still urge her to divide a house with us, but she would give us no peace. Let us leave further discussion of this to Venice.

Now I answer your questions. Goak is merely a mis-spelling of joke. In the mid-nineteenth century there was an American humorous writer called Artemus Ward – not very funny, and I expect I am the only living person who read him, which I did when young. When he had made a joke, usually a bad one, he used to put in brackets (goak here). It was foolish for me to use this when no one knew the original. Marcia and Haines: The fuss has rather died down now. It was quite funny while it lasted, otherwise of no importance except to show what a miserable, petty man Wilson is. I do not know the reviewer in the *Financial Times* but he did a good piece. This week we are all writing on Marquand's life of Ramsay MacDonald. I got no letter from the Hausers. Amelia is very busy with her teacher-training course. Janet will shortly have to find some occupation when Alison goes to school full-time. All the children will remain friendly, but they will do nothing to help with their mother and begin to grow impatient with her. Of course they are a little cross with me for not looking after her, but they are also cross with her for wanting someone to look after her.

I had a gay time with the History Society at UCL. I told them about historians I had known and other frivolities. They gave me chicken with cream sauce and white wine. I also had an agreeable time with the National Trust dinner at Cambridge, though this time mostly middle-aged ladies in long dresses. They gave me chicken in cream sauce and white wine. I stopped in Magdalene which is even more old-fashioned than Magdalen at Oxford. They treated me very well. Now I have no more engagements except lectures four weeks running at UCL. At the moment there is a student sit-in against the latest increase in fees.

Crispin is now wearing native dress – a great cloth wrapped round him. It is alleged that St Crispin never existed, I don't know why. St George is also threatened. Now I have answered all your questions and must get back to writing about Russian war photographs.

Greetings to my stepsons who sound very grown-up.

And love to you who will never grow up,

Alan

9 March

Darling,

It was a stroke of luck last Saturday that I found you at home and that we had such a long talk. I hope it won't cost me too much. The situation is very difficult, but we shall be together before long, that is if my bookings come through in time. I have heard nothing so far, but there are still two months and CIT* has never let me down.

All has gone well with my new car. I pulled strings by writing to the former managing director of Fords, who was a friend of Max's, and he passed me on to the present head. So I was given princely treatment – a car to take me to the show-room and priority for delivery. I should have my Fiesta within the fortnight. It is white with darker trimmings, very smart. It will be far cheaper on insurance and on petrol. No doubt it will have a less luxurious air and be rather bumpier, but you will find it much easier to drive. So one thing has gone well and I am cheerful again. Everything else is much the same. I won't trouble you with further accounts unless the situation changes.

Meanwhile I have had plenty of work, some of it interesting. I have written a long introduction to the Soviet war photographs that Cape got from Czechoslovakia. They are less unknown than Maschler, the Cape director, imagined, some of them having been shown at exhibitions all over the world. Also they are rather ragged, giving out after the liberation of Soviet territory and moving almost at once to the last days in Berlin.

Next I have got a new radio series, excerpts from Churchill's war speeches with a commentary by me. The effect is rather scrappy, but this is how they wanted it. There will be three talks, of fourteen minutes

* Italian travel agency.

each. That is enough to get my name across but hardly more. After that will come 'How Wars Begin' in late May or early June.

As to books, there is a life of Erskine Childers, an upper-class Englishman who became converted to the Irish cause and was shot for opposing the Treaty in 1922, a strange story. There were also two more enormous books on Hitler by an American John Toland and by David Irving. Both worthless, but Terry wants me to write on them.

I met Arthur Marder yesterday. He has just completed a few weeks at the PRO and is returning to the States with over 2,000 xerox copies. As you probably know, he is writing a big book on the Royal Navy in the Japanese war. He tells me that virtually all Japanese war sources have been deliberately destroyed, and that the only Japanese evidence comes from interviews with aged admirals. Unsatisfactory.

Finally, the chairman of the City Music Society says he is weary of writing the annual report and has asked me to do it instead. So the position of President is not purely honorary. No goaks in this letter.

Sad about Pisti. My love to him and to Ferencz.

A bit of love to you also,

Alan
x

18 March

My Dearest Heart,

I find the long separation almost unbearable. I am very tired and very worried, and I need you to put me to rights. However, there is only a few weeks until we are together, unless Italy is by then in a state of civil war in which case I shall come to Budapest. Of course I'll let you know in good time.

Someone has made an offer to buy the house in Twisden Road. I am in two minds about this. If I keep it we shall have somewhere certain to go. But every time I visit it I feel that it is too big and that it would be a full-time job to look after it. So I think I shall sell it if I can get my money back, not otherwise. I can surely find a flat before the end of the year. I have always relied on others to advise me. Now I can't ask Margaret without her going into hysterics and there is no one else. I must struggle through somehow.

I have had an exhausting week. On Monday I went to the PRO

(which is moving to Kew in May and will then be shut until October – an excuse for not going any more). I looked at the Cabinet records for 1940. I don't think they will help me much, but I may try again. I met Roskill, who was also complaining. Tuesday I had a hard day at University College, and was told that there was no job for me next academic year because there is no money for special lecturers. So at last I am truly retired and unemployed. I don't like the feeling at all.

On Wednesday I went to the BBC and recorded three radio programmes to go along with passages from Churchill's wartime speeches. The producers liked it very much. I was less content. On Thursday I spent all morning until nearly two o'clock at the British Academy, choosing people who should receive grants. It was laborious, especially as Isaiah Berlin in the chair muttered very fast so that I could not hear what he said. Did I tell you that Neville Williams is dead – suddenly in Nairobi of all places? This morning I have been with Hamish Hamilton for two hours, choosing illustrations for the War Lords. Next week I shall have to devise captions for 150 pictures. That will take at least two days. So even though retired I have had plenty to do, indeed too much.

It looks as though Sir Max is dying. He has just had a second stroke. In which case I may lose my room in Fleet Street and my secretary as well. I shan't mind much, particularly when we are living together. Skidelsky wrote a very good review of Marquand's MacDonald in the *Spectator*, much better than mine. I am always too soft. I have also reviewed for the *New Statesman* the life of Erskine Childers, who was shot by the Free State as a republican rebel during the civil war of 1922. And now I have the 900 pages on Hitler by John Toland hanging over me. A dreary life indeed, but better than having nothing to do. You, I am sure, are working hard and contentedly. Are the boys also hard at work? Give them my greetings. My notecase collapsed, so I am now regularly using the one you gave me. It is very elegant and reminds me of you every time I pay a bill or buy coffee, now £2.50 a pound. Our economic troubles are as bad as ever. Perhaps you'll take fright at the prospect of living here. I hope not, very very much. Sorry this is such a boring letter, but nothing agreeable happens to me.

Much love, as you well know,

Alan

x

1977

25 March

Wife and Lover,

Just when I am feeling most depressed and despondent I get a wonderful letter from you, like that of 13 March, and it cheers me up. You ask lots of questions, some of which I have answered already. The house in Twisden Road is not sold yet. If it remains unsold until May I shall get Rob Howard, Sophia's life-mate and an architect, to advise me on reconstructing it, and shall decide we shall live there, though there are many things against it. But it is better we have somewhere to go to and we can overcome the difficulties. Certainly there is no difficulty about decorating it even when we are living there. But things like central heating and damp courses must be done beforehand.

I have just finished my lectures on 20th-century Europe at UCL. These will be my last lectures there. With the cuts in the government grant, UCL cannot afford me any more. I still hope Bristol will have me again. Otherwise I shall be truly retired and unemployed. I also have many things to do, not all of them important. For instance, the British Academy. Robert Blake, the chairman of the Recent History section, is going to Venice on holiday, so I have agreed to take the chair for him next Tuesday. This means among other things counting the ballot papers for new Fellows, a laborious task. Nowadays I go shopping on Friday afternoons, which are less crowded. You are right, there are no fresh green peas. But frozen peas are just as good and also cheaper. I have gone over to soft margarine instead of butter. It is healthier and only half the price. You will have to get used to it too.

I told you about my new car. There are always more delays than one expected and I have no news of it yet. But I must get it soon as my old car can't be used for long journeys. Also, I have heard nothing about Venice. I'll write to you at once when I do. If all else fails I will come to Budapest, but let's hope we can manage Venice somehow. With the student riots in Bologna it is perhaps a good thing we are not going there. I had a birthday card from Len Deighton, who is in Ravenna, but I suppose he will have left before we go there.

I have not been much on the Heath lately as the weather has been too cold and rainy. I see that you are already having a heat-wave in Budapest. Perhaps it is a good thing I am not there. Soon there will be a life of Parnell which I shall enjoy more. We have had a political crisis which came to nothing. The Liberals will be ruined by their new association with the Labour government, just as they were ruined when they entered the National government of 1931. I have sad news from

Martin Gilbert. His publisher refuses to spend any more money on the Churchill biography and he may never finish it.

I think about you a lot. Funny.

There is a truly loving thought.

Love from an old man of 71,

                              Alan

Belated birthday greetings to Pisti.
Also greetings to Ferencz.

31 March

Dearest Love,

Junor, editor of the *Sunday Express*, may want me to write something for his paper tomorrow, though this is unlikely, so I am writing to you a day early. Yesterday I received your letter of 22 March, full as ever of good cheer and thoughts about me. On one thing you are quite wrong. I am very bad at arranging things, very bad indeed. I can manage air or rail timetables, but I am hopeless at arranging a house. I have never done it and don't know how to begin. I can't choose wallpaper or colour wash for a room. I can't buy or arrange furniture. Our house when we have it will have to be entirely according to your taste. I don't think I can possibly put a house together before you come. Obviously I can't ask Margaret, and yet there is no one else. So I need you for this and other reasons.

However, I have news, some good, some less good. My car will be delivered early next week so I shall have it for Easter, though I shall not take it out much then. After Easter I shall get experience by long drives in the country. Someone has made an offer for the house in Twisden Road. I have accepted it, though I shall not make a profit out of it. But there is still a shadow ahead. The prospective buyer will now employ a surveyor who will discover the defects that must be put right. If he is faced as I was with a proposed bill for three or four thousand pounds, he may back out. If he does, I shall decide the house is unsaleable. I shall then spend all the money on it to put it right. If possible I shall ask Ernö Goldfinger to take charge of the reconstruction, though I fear he will be expensive. Also, I am rather shy of asking him. At any rate something will be decided about the present house quite soon. If I get rid of it I

1977

shall look for either a maisonette (half a house) or a flat. The problem is that most flats have three rooms and I suppose that ideally we need four. We can discuss this in Venice, from which no news so far.

I don't think I have any interesting reviews to show you. I did a long piece on Bleichroeder for the *New York Review of Books*, but it is of little interest. I have just done a review of a book on Oberdank for the *TLS* – a strange, sad story of a boy who insisted on being killed for the sake of irredentism. I have also read, as I may have told you, a very long book on Hitler by John Toland, and have written firmly in the *Observer* that it is not worth reading. I shall probably say the same on *Hitler* by David Irving, which is due out in June.

The War Lords will be out only in September. I have just chosen the pictures and the captions. Is it *The Last of Old Europe* you want to see? I'll bring it if I remember. Somehow I can't settle to work at the moment. I am worried about the future and apprehensive about the scenes Margaret will make when the time comes for me to leave. She is obviously still hoping it won't happen and is determined to harm you as much as she can. Never mind. It will pass over. Also it has suddenly become very cold, with snow and frost. I have had to go back to wearing a vest. Do you remember the trousers where you put in new elastic? They are again all too loose. Either I have become thinner or we did not make them tight enough in the first place. You can have another go in a year's time.

I don't think I want to meet Ránki. I did my duty by having him to dinner in Magdalen and we had nothing to say to each other. Do the boys go away for Easter?

Love to you all, but of course a special sort of love to you.

I may not write until after Easter.

Alan

2 April

Dearest prompt letter-writer,

Your letter of 1 April has already arrived yesterday and I feel I must keep up the same pace. But no more: I shan't write again for ten days. I rang on Saturday for no reason except to hear your voice and got Ferencz instead. I shall soon hear plenty of your voice. Now here is important news. Venice is fixed for 8 May. We shall be at the Pensione

Alboretti, Accademia 882. If you come by plane I shall not meet you. If by train, I may. Be sure not to get off at Mestre. Whichever you come by, take the *Expresso* or whatever it is called to the Accademia. Get off, bear slightly left and then straight along Accademia Via. The Pensione is about half-way up on the left. I shall enquire about Ravenna and also ask the Johns Hopkins University whether they would like me to come to Bologna with you for one night and one lecture.

You are not old at all, at any rate just right for me. I like a strong, well-matured body. I cannot imagine being attracted by the body of a young girl, though I like looking at them. There is no need to become ugly simply because you grow older. I too worry, particularly about the loose skin on my stomach, but you do not seem to mind or even to notice it.

I have a real worry. Margaret is having increasing trouble with her back passage. She will probably have to have yet another operation, which will make her an invalid for some time. I shall have to look after her, there is no one else. Perhaps it is not as bad as the doctors fear. But it gives me anxiety about the future. Of course, if she becomes really ill she will have to live with us. But she will fight against this and we shall find it difficult also. I shall see more clearly during the summer.

The fate of the house at Twisden Road is not yet settled. In some ways I shall be relieved to sell it as it is too big for us. On the other hand, I dread the thought of looking for a flat or maisonette. I am so useless at this. Shopping, however, will present no difficulties as long as we live near the districts I know – Kentish Town and Parliament Hill Fields. Janet and Mary will tell you how and where to shop. In the end I expect Margaret will also. As to margarine, we have now in England low-fat margarine which is half the price of butter, tastes just as good and does not harden the arteries. Everyone eats it now except for cooking! I was promised my car for today or tomorrow, but I expect it will not turn up until after Easter.

Little happened on my birthday, I am glad to say. No party of any kind, no letter from Crispin or Daniel. Mary Taylor gave me some flowers in a pot. Margaret gave me a gramophone record of Bach. Amelia gave me a kiss. The others forgot about it or knew that I do not like birthday celebrations.

Last night I met a BBC man who wants to make a television programme of me walking Offa's Dyke or the Pennine Way. I don't think this would be very interesting for viewers, but we shall see. Tomorrow I am going to make a radio talk on Bismarck. Not a novel subject for me. At the moment I am less depressed, though I shall not be happy until we are together. And that is not far off.

Lots of love and regards to the boys too,

Alan

15 April

My Dearest Love,

Ten days have gone since I last wrote, quite time enough for me to write again. One thing has gone right. I now have my new car. It looks very smart and is a delight to drive. The various knobs and switches are different from the Rover and I have trouble learning how to use them. I must drive the car slowly for the first 1,500 miles, so I shall go for a long trip in the country next week in order to get the car moving. You will have no trouble driving it unless you are worried by the right-hand drive. Of the house in Twisden Road, however, no news. I still fear that the sale will fall through.

Other good news. Bristol will have me as visiting professor next year. I will try to spread my lectures over two terms so that you will be here for some of them and can come to Bristol with me, at any rate once. It is strange to be planning for something that is still so far off. I think our visit to Venice should come off, but one can never be sure with the present industrial troubles. Robert Blake and family got there successfully but could not get back and finally had to come home by train, at British Airways' expense. He says there are now no restaurant cars, even on international trains. I shall try to get an invitation to Bologna for a night, but it is not important. We shall have plenty to do.

Daniel has altogether vanished from sight. He told me he would spend an extra week at Leeds, then silence. The Young Socialists have been having their annual conference at Blackpool and I suppose he has been there, making militant speeches. Probably he is back home and will turn up for dinner at a moment's notice. Crispin has also managed to write a letter now that his term is over. He went the two hundred miles to Accra in order to meet Prince Charles, and then was so busy drinking beer at the bar that the Prince failed to shake hands with him. He has also taught the staff at Asankrangwa to make fruit punch. The other family went away for Easter – Giles to Janet's parents in Sussex and the rest to the Isle of Wight. I stayed quietly at home and wrote a long review about a poor book on British political history by Rhodes James. This afternoon I shall address the annual meeting of the Historical Association on 'The War Lords'.

Alan Sked has now got a permanent appointment at LSE, so his troubles are over. He tells me that Donald Watt has actually written his piece on me for the *Journal of Modern History*, so if all goes well it and my piece will figure in the March number, delayed I expect until months afterwards. You will also see that I have been contributing to the *TLS*, though not on anything very exciting.

I often think about your shape and figure. Do you have favourite bits of me that you think about?

Lots of loving thoughts,

Alan
xx

22 April

Dear Heart,

If all goes well we shall be together in a fortnight's time. There will be trouble with Margaret before I leave, but this will somehow be overcome. She is still determined to go into mourning and announce the ruin of her life when I move out. But with the sale of the house still hanging fire, I have no idea where we shall go. This makes me gloomy.

It is of course possible that Italy will burst into revolution before we get there. In that case I will telephone to you in good time and come to Budapest, but I expect things will be all right. A funny thing has happened about the Pensione Alboretti. I chose it because the food is much better than at any other *pension* I have been to. Now the Pensione tells me that they are not opening their restaurant this summer, so we shall have to go out for our meals. I don't really mind this. There are cheap restaurants in the vicinity, I have plenty of money, and we have gone out every night in other places, such as Paris. We shall also be free to go away for the night if we want to. As the Pensione is not providing any food we can, I think, make our own lunch in our bedroom whenever we feel like it. I will bring knives and plates and we can buy food for a cold lunch in some neighbouring shop. This suits me better in any case than a cooked lunch in a restaurant. Among other things I have read that we should go to Burano, the island near Torcello, just for the pleasure of walking round it.

I took Margaret to Tewkesbury just to run the car in. The Fiesta is very easy to drive except that I cannot get as comfortable as I was in the Rover. Tomorrow I am taking Daniel and Anna to Leeds in order to clock up more miles. I shall stop the night at York with my friend Gerald Aylmer, who is professor of history there.

Prospects here are gloomy. Inflation is again roaring up. The unions are against any further limitation of wages. And now we have the panic that oil supplies are going to run out soon. Petrol will soon be £1 a gallon. Fortunately the Fiesta uses little of it. Apart from the thought of living with you, I do not like the future at all and I feel guilty at taking you away from Hungary where you would be better off and probably have a more interesting life. You must be crazy to want to live with me, but then I am crazy too. No family news of any interest. I shall write again next week and then need write no more.

Lots of love and good wishes to the boys,

Alan

24 April

My Darling Woman (if that is how you like being addressed),

I just got your letter of 19 April and hasten to answer it because you want to know when to arrive. I shall certainly arrive some time on the Sunday, though as it is a charter flight I don't yet know when. So please come on the Sunday. You will be alone most of the day, but we shall certainly be able to have the night together and we don't want to miss one. I have booked a room with a private bath (which in Italy means a shower) and toilet. I said firmly 'a double bed'. If they have given us twin beds, ask if they have a double bed. It is so much better to sleep together all night. If you are short of Italian money, borrow from the hotel and say I will pay them back when I arrive. If I learn when we are to arrive I will let you know, but do not attempt to meet me. There is sure to be confusion.

I had a good though rather exhausting drive up to Leeds with Daniel and Anna. The car is very easy to drive, but as the steering wheel is smaller than that of the Rover it has brought the rheumatism back to my thumbs. I must not overdo the driving until I am used to it. I went with Daniel and Anna to their flat. In fact they share a house with a businessman and a psychiatrist. There is a communal kitchen and sitting room. Then Daniel and Anna have a bed-sitting room, very untidy. He has given up the hostel altogether and just lives with Anna. I told him it was foolish not to share the communal life of the University, but he said he got plenty of it during the day-time. Incidentally they share a single bed.

I went on to York for the night with my friends Gerald and Ursula Aylmer. They made me very welcome. I walked round York before dinner and saw the Minster free from scaffolding for the first time in years. It has been so thoroughly restored that it looks as though it had just been built. I don't think I like it like this. I had nostalgic feelings about York, where I spent my youth and decided it was my favourite among English cities.

I went to the doctor this morning, mainly for fresh ointment for the irritation in and around my back passage.

I drove all the way back yesterday, hence the pain in my thumb. I don't expect I shall write again.

Much love, you Lovely Woman,

Alan

26 May

Lovey Mine,

I was distressed to hear that you were ill again. You must get really well, for my sake. We tried to be too clever with your train. We thought we could get on better if we met the train from Rome. If we had waited until 21.25 we should have discovered the sleeping car. In any case I should have stayed with you until the train left and then I should have found the sleeper. Moral: do not try to be too clever.

I made a sad farewell to the Alboretti and duly went to the Danieli. There I waited and waited, all in vain. Of course I should have made clearer arrangements beforehand, demanding to know what I should do if no one turned up. I only just caught the plane by taking a taxi. However, I have now asked for my L20,000 back. I am glad to report that I have received the cheque from Bologna, though as yet no razor. I don't think I shall see that again. Despite its loss and despite the rain it was a wonderful holiday, the best time we have had together. No, that is wrong. Each time we are together is the best. I can't get used to being without you. It seems so unnatural.

As I told you, Margaret is recovering very well. I had a talk with her doctor, who says the operation has been reasonably successful. He can't be sure. But a more serious operation is out of the question with a woman her age, so she must just hope it will be all right. I expect Margaret will come home on Saturday. Then my troubles will start. She is naturally very sorry for herself, complaining that she has been in hospital while I have been away enjoying myself. She has been 'abandoned', neglected and so on. Curiously enough, I have stopped feeling anything about her and she no longer upsets me. I am merely bored by her complaints and wait to get out of the room. Of course I'll look after her until she is well and take her into the country in my car. But she has been thoroughly unsympathetic to me, and I don't see why I should go on being sympathetic to her.

The house in Twisden Road is still unsold, though its fate is not yet decided. I have said I shall lose patience on 1 June. Actually I shan't be able to get men to work for some time after that, so things remain a little uncertain. I read every day of flats that would be more suitable, so it is worth waiting to see what will happen.

I have reviewed innumerable books. *Parnell* for the *New Statesman*, a very good piece. Three books on Lloyd George for the *Observer*, and I am now just settling down to deal with David Irving's ridiculous book on Hitler. Also I must make an index for *The War Lords*. I seem to have been hard at work every moment since I got back, and on top of all the work is Margaret to be visited, in Hackney of all places, and errands to be run for her.

Eddie has fixed my dates for late June and early July. I have chosen a hard subject, but it will be all right once I get going. The weather is better than it was in Venice, though not yet warm enough for me to go to the Ponds. I have no family news. Silence from Crispin and Daniel. Sophia and Rob went to Amsterdam for four days, which they much enjoyed. We must go there some time if I can ever face going abroad again.

Let me know when Pisti is coming to England and give me an address for him. My love to both of them.

I don't need to say love to you. You know it.

 Love,

    Alan

2 June 1977

My own sweet Darling,

No letter from you yet. I hope this does not mean you are ill. You are all I have in life, all I care about, and my need for you grows stronger all the time. Do not be ill or, if you are ill, get well. I have promised never to worry but sometimes it is hard.

Good news and bad. First good. I have got my Venice taxi fare back from the travel agency. Bad: I had not insured you so did not get back the doctor's fees. Also have not yet received my razor from Bologna and am beginning to fear that I never shall. Good: the memory of Venice which was our best time ever. Perhaps being married really makes a difference. At any rate I find being without you very strange.

I have plenty of troubles. 1 June has come and gone and the house in Twisden Road is still unsold. So I have got in touch with the builder and shall go round the house with him next week telling him what to do. The house is too big but we can make it very attractive. I think we shall have to take a lodger in the top-storey rooms. He will bring in money (or might be she), and will be someone as company for you in the house when I am not there. Perhaps we should have a study or work room separate from the sitting room. If anyone turns up in the next week or two who wants to buy the house, I shall agree. Otherwise I shall go ahead. This will make certain that we have somewhere to go by the end of the year. After all, if it proves much too big, we can sell it later or try to.

Margaret came out of hospital last Friday. She can walk about the house all right and even prepares most of the dinner. But she is in pain all the time and has never been out of the house except into the garden. I suppose she will move more in time, but things are hard at the moment. I have to do all the shopping, which cuts into my working time, and I have to be with her from tea-time on, otherwise she gets miserable and lonely. Sometimes she is brave, sometimes she is full of grievances. I shan't get much holiday this summer before you come, though I hope I shall get Margaret as far as the Isle of Wight. I shall also insist on going to Coniston with you in September. I have had a good idea for our first night after I meet you at Heathrow: we will go to Pat and Mary for the night. Oxford is not far and we shall then be well on our way.

I have been desperately busy ever since my return. So busy indeed that I have not had a moment for my own work and do not know when I shall have any. I reviewed Emmerson, perhaps too gently, for the *TLS*. I hesitated to say what a boring book it was. I have done *Parnell* for the *New Statesman*. I have attacked Irving's book on Hitler in next week's

Observer and three books on Lloyd George for the week after that. I am in danger of becoming a professional reviewer! I have also agreed to do the *New Statesman* Diary throughout August when there is nothing to write about. And I have received the official invitation from Bristol.

I have not heard at all from either Crispin or Daniel. Janet has glandular fever. Sebastian and his family are off to the Isle of Wight for ten days. Sophia is going to Cornwall. You can see I don't get much help from the family in looking after Margaret. I am very well but losing my memory. At any rate I lost my umbrella the other day. Let me know when Pisti comes. Love to them both.

Please do not be ill, my Lovey,

Alan

10 June

Lovey Mine,

I am very worried and anxious. No letter yet from you. I know I promised never to worry and not to bother if I had not heard from you. But when I spoke to you, you said you had been ill. If you are still not eager to write, let one of your boys send me the news. I came home in a state of euphoric happiness, exhilarated that I had found a real wife for the first time in my life. We shall have the most wonderful time together and it will last for many years. So get well and write me even a few lines.

One good bit of news. Margaret has found a house that suits her and she has made arrangements to buy it. She is also arranging to sell her present house by the end of the year. So there is no danger that she will make a scene over my leaving her: she will just not have room for me. She loves planning a house and is already thinking how to plan the new one. A great relief. The man who wanted to buy the Twisden Road house begged me to give him a little time longer to find the money, so I have not yet decided firmly to keep it. But I have spoken to the builder and he can do all the work in a few weeks if necessary. So I hope you do not mind my waiting.

Life with Margaret has its trials. She is still very weak and in constant pain, so she has hardly left the house except into the garden. I do all the shopping and look after her at home. No doubt she seeks to prolong this situation, but she is bound to recover however hard she tries to remain weak. I am not sure that I shall be able to take her to the Isle of Wight though she is anxious to go. I don't mind one way or the other for myself. My holiday will only happen in September. When would you like to come? I suggest 1 September, which is just after the summer Bank Holiday. Get your visa for a month. Then you will not have to rush back, though you do not need to stay the whole month. It will be easy to book a plane any time, except possibly at the week-end. Let me know as soon as you can and I will book our room at Coniston. We might even look for a house there!

I have been busy with trivialities. I have also had lots of reviews to write. Tom Driberg has left a posthumous biography, which is largely about his homosexual details which are very boring. One fuck is very like another and his were particularly sordid: most of them took place in public lavatories. Then I have had three books on Lloyd George, and am now waiting for the official life of Sam Hoare. I wonder how much it will reveal. Hoare suffered from being too clever. Apart from this I have been brooding over the topic: 'How Wars Begin.' The new lectures will be much more difficult than any I have done, very academic stuff, not popular anecdotes. I am doing Tom's book for the *New Statesman*, all the rest for the *Observer*. Oh yes, there is also a *Festschrift* for Arthur Marder for the *TLS*. I shall write glowingly about Arthur and critically about the essays. Roger Louis wants to establish a Taylor archive in Texas. I told him all my papers would go to Magdalen.

All my thoughts are with you. In imagination I still walk the streets of Venice and you are always with me. So please write as soon as you can. Love to the boys and send me news of them.

Your ever loving husband,

Alan

16 June

Oh, My Poor Darling,

How I wish I had been looking after you instead of looking after Margaret. But I am sure your boys looked after you well. Do not go back to work too soon. In fact, do not worry about work at all: the Institute, I am sure, will be patient and understanding. Re Bologna, I also got my razor back and today a cheque from Caruzanti, so all is well.

As to my own affairs, I am now so dominated by thoughts of you that Margaret's complaints do not upset me. I pity her, and pity is

1977

always a safeguard against any other feeling. I just want her to be quiet and accept what I can offer, which is care and attention. The Twisden Road house is not yet sold and I am beginning to think I had better keep it. At least we shall then be certain of somewhere to go. Running around for a flat would make me anxious all over again. Let me know as soon as you can when you propose to come exactly, whether on 1 or 2 September. I must be back by the middle of the month, when my Historical Association lectures will start.

Good news: not only has Bristol invited me for another year, but University College has renewed me after all. This will take nearly three days out of my week, but it keeps me in practice for lecturing. As well, some of those who used to attend seminars at the Library have now asked me to conduct a fortnightly seminar at the Institute of Historical Affairs* throughout the winter. Yet another demand on my time.

On top of this there are so many books to review that I have no time to write anything. Lloyd George: his nephew on his early life, showing how he made his brother keep him; Don Cregier, an American, with the first of a three-volume life, not particularly novel; and John Campbell on Lloyd George in the twenties when he was trying to make a comeback. Then there are two more books on Hitler: David Irving on *Hitler's War*, making out Hitler did not inspire the murder of the Jews (I confronted him on television over this and massacred him), and Waite on *Hitler the Psychopath*, which seems to be itself psychopathic. There is an official biography of Sam Hoare by Cross with great detail on Abyssinia; a *Festschrift* for Marder, mostly on naval affairs and very interesting; a comic book on the early Fabians, which made me laugh a lot; and some others I have forgotten. Garvin's *Chamberlain* is grotesquely long and I doubt whether you need to go through it. Judd is pedestrian but gets in all one needs to know. So you see I have too much work.

I hope to go to the Isle of Wight for the middle of July if Margaret is well enough. I shall be here throughout August and Pisti should ring me (353 8000, extension 3460) as soon as he arrives so that I can take him round the City churches.

The weather has been bitterly cold and we have had to turn on the central heating. As a result I have done no good walks. I need a companion and guess who it will be soon. My life will change completely when you are here and I only hope you will be happy with everything. One thing is certain: we shall never have misunderstandings or disputes,

---

* Affairs = correctly: research.

and we shall always say what we want to do. So get really well and stay well. I think of you and of everything we did.

   Much love,

Alan

---

28 June

Beloved Wife,

   It was delightful to get your letter of 23 June and to know that you are really well again. I have been following the hot weather at Budapest in *The Times* and see that it is now cooler. Here we have not had a single warm day this summer, and it looks as if we shall never have one. I send a little letter inviting you to come to England for a month. I have already reserved our rooms at The Sun* from 2 to 15 September. Let me know what airline you are coming on so that I know which terminal to meet you at. I will have my car at the Underground station not far away and we can go there by bus. I shall try to arrange that we go to Pat and Mary for the night. I am not quite sure where is the best place to meet, but I will be outside the Customs Exit.

   If I am not there do not be alarmed, I shall turn up. But if anything goes wrong, I will have you called over the tannoy as Mrs Taylor.

   As to my news, the house in Twisden Road is on the point of being sold and I am enormously relieved. I don't think anything will go wrong this time, but if it does I shall make the best of it and put the house in order. All this delay is rather troublesome. I can't look for a flat until the house is sold and I have got my money back. Also, I have no idea how to arrange or furnish a flat and get terribly worried over it. However, I can tell you all about this when we meet in September. Margaret, as I told you, has found a house, wonderfully equipped and in perfect condition. But she is lamenting that it has practically no garden, and is gloomy about the one she is leaving. I fear I have caused her great unhappiness, but it can't be helped. I want a few years of happiness myself before I die. She is also still very frail and in pain from her operation, but she is making a real effort to do things for herself. Once the transition is over she will make no trouble.

   My TV lectures have begun, very hard work but rewarding in more

---

* Sun Hotel in Coniston.

senses than one. Eddie's Margaret* left simply because she was feeling stale, and is now off on her own somewhere. Surely you know the Institute of Historical Research. It is in the Senate House. I rather regret that University College has invited me again. Bristol is quite enough for me to manage, and I have got bored with University College. Also it does not pay much. The truth is I am getting older, as I am sure you will notice. I am physically all right but my mind is not working well. I have stopped writing except for reviews and have no interest in ever writing a book again. Perhaps you will revive me. If not, we can go and live in Coniston. Cross's book on Hoare is about 400 pages. Most of the sources are FO and Cabinet records, but there is a certain amount from Hoare as well. Also good quotes from the private papers of others. The book is worthy but boring.

Of my young sons, Crispin has just finished the summer term and hopes to visit the former French colonies. There is famine in parts of Ghana, so I am anxious about him. Daniel has got a job in Leeds in order to earn money. With this money he proposes to motor to Poland with Anna in a little car he has bought. I don't think his work is getting on well, but there is nothing I can do. On the whole I am dispirited at present with my work and life, just as I used to be before we met. You will soon put me right. Do you remember that last good night at the Alboretti? It was very good, and a surprise too.

Not long now,

Alan

5 July

Darling,

I am going to the Isle of Wight for a fortnight, rushing up occasionally to make more television lectures, and thought I had better write before I went. I expect Daniel and Anna will be there for part of the time, and Margaret is now well enough to go. As the weather has now become fine and sunny I may get some sea bathing and good walks, but it won't be like being with you. Daniel has not done well in his exams. In fact he 'forgot' to take his exam in Politics, one of his best subjects. I fear he has lost interest in his work and in Leeds University.

* Wife of Alan's uncle.

He lives far away from the University in a flat with Anna, has no University friends and seems to have lost interest in political activity also. Maybe he would do better to leave Leeds and find some quite different activity. I am sorry of course, but he must make his own life as he thinks fit. In August he and Anna are going to Poland in his aged car. Rather risky.

The house in Twisden Road is still unsold, though there is someone who says he is eager to buy. If nothing has happened by the time I come back from the Isle of Wight, I shall accept the inevitable and have the house put in order. If we don't like it, we can try to sell it later. If on the other hand it is sold after all, I will at once look for a flat. Whatever we do we are in for a troublesome time, full of problems. But as you often say things will come right in the end. I hate my present life, particularly with Margaret pretending that our life will go on unchanged for ever. But at least she has found a house and is making plans for life on her own.

Otherwise things are going well with me, except that I am too busy and easily get tired. I have made three television lectures which were a great success. Eddie said he had no idea history lectures could be so exciting. The two World Wars will give me no trouble. The Cold War at the end will be more difficult and also more unusual. I fear it and yet welcome the challenge. You will find my review of Hoare in the *Observer* this week. I have also done Marder's *Festschrift* for the *TLS*. More importantly, I have had two splendid days at the Ponds and shall go there again this afternoon unless my work prevents it. I shall do a lot of writing in the Isle of Wight, perhaps even trying to go on with my little book on modern English history. It is difficult to find something fresh to say.

I miss you very much. Like you, I find happiness in thinking about you and about our times together, but it is not the same thing as being with you. Are you sure that your leg will not give trouble again? *And have you asked at the British consulate if you can get a British passport before you settle in England? The sooner you get one the better. You will then have no worries about a British visa.* But I expect you will have to be resident here first.

I did not go to the Academy dinner and so escaped a speech by Harold Macmillan, for which I was very glad. Instead I had dinner with my American former pupil, now a professor, Lance Farrar. I enjoyed this very much. I shall be in London when Pisti is here. Tell him I am expecting him.

All my love,

Alan

1977

12 July

Dearest Heart,

Your letter of 3 July was long in reaching me. It arrived in London after I had left for the Isle of Wight and Della sent it after me. I am sorry my depression made you depressed also. It is my nature to worry about the future and to imagine all kinds of difficulties which never occur. But you do not need to share these worries. Console yourself by thinking that whatever happens I shall always see the gloomy side of it beforehand and then be delighted how things work out. As you see, I am now at The Mill. In some ways it is a strain. Margaret is trying to do her best to make things attractive, with the constant implication that I ought to be pleased – which I am. Later on I shall reveal to her your intention of spending a month or so in Hungary during the summer, and then she will have every year a month in The Mill to look forward to. I don't know whether I am doing right. Maybe it would be better for us and kinder to Margaret in the long run if one day I simply walked out of her life. But we will discuss these things at leisure. I have a horrible presentiment that it will rain the entire fortnight we are at Coniston, so we shall have plenty of time for discussion!

I have now recorded four television lectures and have two more to go. The first three were very satisfactory. I looked forward to the fourth on the First World War, thinking it would be both easy and interesting. Perhaps it was too interesting. I got so involved that I went on too long and overran my stopping time. Instead of making a quick end I lost my nerve and broke off with an apology, a thing I have never done before. We made a reasonable end afterwards, but it was not the same thing. I was not so much depressed as angry with myself. I have always said there is one thing I can do well and without a mistake, and that is to lecture on television. Now I have slipped, I shall never be so confident again. Indeed, I came away resolving never to do another series of telelectures, but I expect I shall change my mind. Tomorrow, Wednesday, I go up to London for the day by train and shall give the fifth on the Second World War. I have taken more care this time, planning it out in my mind, and with safe places where to stop if the clock catches up on me. So I shall recover my confidence. Then on the following Monday I go up for a final lecture, and then on to Oxford for three days at a summer school. Then back to The Mill for a final week. The weather has been strange. Sea mist and rather cold east wind until the afternoon. Then the mist clears and there is warm but fresh sunshine. So I have been working or shopping during the morning, taking a siesta after lunch and then lying on the beach sun-bathing from four to seven. The open sea at Freshwater Bay has been very cold, much colder of course than last year, so I have been swimming in the Solent which has been delicious. If only the mornings were warm also, I should go swimming before breakfast, but there seems little change.

I got a write-up in yesterday's *Observer* as a telelecturer. The critics are suddenly expressing surprise that I lecture without notes, as though this were something new. They are also surprised that until last year I have not telelectured for ten years. Each time I say they will never ask me again, and in a way think they would be right. My review of Hoare was also in the *Observer*. And this coming week I hope my review of Waite on Hitler will appear. Now I have an enormous book on the revolution in Holland, 1781–1813, no doubt an extremely interesting subject but a bit remote from my own field. However, it keeps me occupied. Otherwise I have given up work, perhaps for good.

The house in Twisden Road is still unsold. The prospective purchaser is for ever making new difficulties. When I get back to London towards the end of July I shall finally make the decision. If the house is still unsold I will get my builder on it and make it attractive. There will be a chance for you to see it and say how we should arrange it. We might make a separate flat on the top floor and take in a friendly lodger to keep you company when I am away. I have stopped worrying about this. It is merely a nuisance.

Very much love and warm thoughts.

Lovey mine,

        Alan
        x

29 July

My Dearest Love,

 Your letter of 19 July arrived while I was still away and, as the post takes three days to the Isle of Wight, Della did not forward it. So I am writing the first day I am back. There was an enormous pile of correspondence, but I have now dealt with most of it. As for my news, the house in Twisden Road is sold at last, which is a great relief. As soon as I have time I shall look for a flat somewhere near Parliament Hill

Fields, and should have no difficulty in finding one. But there may be a little delay. The legal formalities over buying a house or flat take a long time – at least a month after the flat has been found and surveyed. So we must be patient.

The Isle of Wight was good and bad. After a few days of sunny weather when I had some good swimming, the clouds came up, the wind blew and I was usually very cold. I had some good walks and would have liked more. I have not written a word more about English history and am beginning to think I never shall. I have lost my enthusiasm for it. Indeed, I have lost all interest in writing except for reviews. My mind and my spirit have degenerated, and will not recover until the upheaval in my present life has taken place. I am nervous and worried all day long, though there is nothing I can do about it.

The bad side of the Isle of Wight is that Margaret would not rest and instead turned herself into a domestic slave. Apart from cooking elaborate meals, she cleaned up the entire house and carried off all the curtains, sheets and towels throughout the house to the launderette. We were there day after day. All the time she was secretly reproaching me for not appreciating all she was doing. I was exasperated that she was exhausting herself over a house that was no longer hers. I tried to persuade her that The Mill now belonged to the children and that they would have to look after it when she was gone. No good. It was very upsetting. I wish she would relax, but I suppose she is working herself into the ground as a way of escaping her unhappiness. Ah well, time will settle things.

I have not had Freddie Ayer's autobiography and am not anxious to acquire it. I shall however remember that you want to read about Mrs Gaskell. The television lectures got better and better, at least I think so. We shall have complaints over the Cold War one, and these will not worry me. My three days in Magdalen were enjoyable and also rather disturbing. I felt like a disembodied ghost, with no reason to be there and no place of my own. In some ways I regret that I did not spend more time in Oxford when I had my rooms there. They were my only real home, the only place that belonged to me, and I did not develop their character enough. However, I have no friends now in Oxford except for Pat and Mary and no way of making any, so it would be impossible to live there, much as I should like to escape from London. Returning to London gives me quite a shock after the peace and beauty of Yarmouth. Here at the *Express* all is in turmoil. All the Beaverbrook chiefs are being turned out, and new men are being brought in from the property company that has bought the papers. I have been promised that Della and I will stay where we are unless the *Standard* building is sold or pulled down, both of which are likely. This too is unsettling. In fact I shall not be happy until I see you. You do not say when your plane will arrive, but no doubt Pisti will know.

Love and longing,

Alan

Have your hair cut, I like it. I think my eyes are green.

5 August

Dearest Love,

I write now so that if you have any messages to send by Pisti you will have thought of them in good time. Tell me about any books you want. I have Mrs Gaskell in mind and have forgotten the others. Also tell Pisti when you are due to arrive. I don't need to tell you about clothes. To judge by the weather this summer we shall have plenty of rain, and you will also need strong shoes or boots. If it rains too much we will go sightseeing by car. Bring your driving licence and I will find out whether it is valid in England.

I am having a wearisome time, though I suppose it is inevitable. With the Twisden Road house securely sold, Margaret has flung herself into finding a flat for us and I have been going around every day, so far without much result. I have seen everything from luxury flats to tumbledown places that are cheap and need reconstruction. I think a glittering contemporary flat with every modern gadget is not really suited to our character, as well as being very expensive to run. On the other hand we don't want to be absolutely surrounded by noisy neighbours. I have had the idea of buying Amelia's house. She wants something rather bigger. Her present house is not all that small, but it would be easy to move into and we can be sure that everything will be in working order. However, her plans for another house may not come off. I keep telephoning her and at present her telephone is always engaged.

At this moment your letter of 3 August arrived. I send you at once the letter you need. I think the next time you should take your marriage certificate and point out that you are a wife going to meet her husband. However, everything will no doubt be all right.

Apart from looking at houses I have been very busy, though mostly with trivial things. I managed to turn out a satisfactory Diary for the

New Statesman and am not racking my brains for more. It is weary work. The truth is I shall have no real peace until this upheaval is over and we are safely settled together. Tomorrow I hope to go to Somerset House to see an exhibition of pictures on London's River through the ages. On Tuesday next I go to Oxford for three days in order to lecture once more, again to Americans. What an appetite they have for lectures. I don't believe it does them the slightest good.

I must get this letter off in a hurry.

Love just like yours,

Alan

8 August

Darling,

I have just had an enquiry from the Home Office people at Croydon about your visit. I have answered that you are my wife and that of course I shall maintain you while you are here. I am also trying to telephone them, but their line is always engaged. I think you ought to have told the British consul that you were my wife and then no questions would have been asked. The next time you go to the British consulate, take your marriage certificate with you and that should remove all difficulties. In fact I advise you to go at once without waiting to be summoned. I am much afraid that there may be delay and then all our plans will be ruined. In my opinion, as my wife you have an immediate right to a visa, but I may be wrong. However, try it and see what happens.

I am on the look-out again for a house or flat. I am also applying for a flat on the edge of the Heath. At the moment there is no vacancy. I have put my name on a waiting list and if a flat turns up I shall forget the house and take the flat instead. We shall see. It is all very tiring and I easily get worried. But I think something will come out of it all. I'll write again when I hear from you or when I am settled on a house. But it is essential you should arrive on 1 September.

I am just off to Oxford for a couple of days.

Much anxious love,

Alan

16 August

My Beloved,

Pisti has arrived safely, though I have not seen him yet. He rang me up yesterday and will come to see me on Friday, when I will take him round some Wren churches. I was occupied with the London Diary and with reviewing a study of Liddell Hart which I found rather difficult. Still, I expect he will find plenty to do. He tells me he is stopping with Shirley, so I will arrange to pick him up there when I come to meet you. Perhaps Shirley will come as well. She is much better at understanding Heathrow than I am. I have confirmed my night's visit with Mary Thompson. As they will want to lay a dinner on for us, we must move off from Heathrow as soon as we can.

The other piece of news is that I have found another house, again in Twisden Road. But this one is much better. It is only two floors instead of three, and is not threatened by noisy neighbours. Ground floor: two good rooms which can be turned into one by opening the folding doors. At the back another good room divided from the little kitchen only by a partition. I shall knock down the partition and then we shall have a kitchen-dining room big enough for eight people with built-in gas cooker, refrigerator and double sink. Under the stairs a little cellar for my wine. Upstairs: a big front bedroom and good second bedroom. At the back a smaller bedroom which I shall make into a big bathroom with airing cupboard and leave only the lavatory in the present bathroom. At the back of the house there is a big yard, a reasonably high wall and on its other side a large courtyard before flats begin. I hope you will like it. I saw lots and lots of other flats and houses and they were all horrible. Maybe you will be able to see it in September. But the legal procedure takes a long time here, and I doubt whether it will be completed within less than six weeks. After that my ingenious man has to get to work and that will take time. So we may not be together until after the New Year.

Margaret, after being difficult, has now become very cooperative and goes on almost as if the house were hers. She will want to choose the paint and the wallpaper, but I will try to see that there is nothing outrageous. I am sure all will be right. Apart from this I am still weary, partly from the strain of doing too much and partly from boredom. I have lost interest in history. Do not have illusions about me. There will never be a time when I shall work as I used to do. I have no longer any interesting subject, and I can't organize my life or my mind to go back to revising *English History 1914-1945*. I just do my journalism and let the days go by. That does not mean that I am unhappy. The thought of

1977

your arrival always makes me cheerful. Tell me, were you always as sensual as you are now or have I contributed something to it?

Bring your driving licence with you. I will find out if it is valid here. I don't expect I shall write again unless there is anything important to say.

I really get very impatient to see and feel you.

Love,

Alan

20 August

Dearest Lovey,

I said I should not write again, but there are a few things that cross my mind. When you come, be sure to bring my letter as well as your marriage certificate so that you can show them on immigration if necessary. Pisti has arrived and is stopping with Shirley. He came to see me yesterday afternoon and I took him for a walk round the City, showing him churches. We shall have another walk next week.

The main problem is solved as I told you. I have a house that will suit. I have decided to keep the small bathroom as it is and use the larger room next door as a laundry and store-room. Do you want a washing-machine as well as a spin-dryer? Do you want a deep-freeze? They are the fashion now, but I think unnecessary for a family of two persons. Would you like an electric grill and oven as well as a gas cooker? You see the sort of things I try to think of.

Pisti is very independent and adventurous, going round London on his own. But he has no acquaintances. Shirley is in Yorkshire and Pisti is alone with Shirley's son who sounds very strange. I have arranged to collect Pisti from Shirley's on the day you arrive and come with him to Heathrow. If there is any serious delay, send a message to Shirley's and I shall be waiting there to hear from you. But probably everything will be all right.

Did I answer your suggestion that we should go and live in Manchester? I have no friends there now, and have had none for more than thirty years past. I have no friends even in Oxford. So we must make the best of London for a few years. Perhaps later we might live in Yarmouth, Isle of Wight, but I suspect we should soon get bored.

No more now. I must write the Diary for the last time. Come out quickly from the Airport Control so that we can reach Mary's in good time.

Lots of love,

Alan
xx

17 September

My Beloved,

Just a little love letter to take you by surprise on, I hope, Monday morning. Each day we were in Coniston I loved you more and more and grew more confident that we shall have a good life together. I no longer worry whether I shall succeed in our sexual encounters and shall not mind what happens or when. We can be sure of the future.

I have had a terrible time since I got back, with Margaret in hysterics until midnight on Thursday and ringing me up more than once yesterday with suspicions that I was spending my time with you. I told her firmly that I was showing you our house on Monday and have no other plans, though of course we shall meet again. Please forgive me for being so weak, but existence is intolerable unless I keep Margaret in a better frame of mind. She has decided to take Amelia's house, which she knows and likes, and has already arranged to move out of this house soon after Christmas. So we shall have nothing to wait for except the alterations at Twisden Road. Unless of course you dislike the house and refuse to live in it!

I have found out about your naturalization. You simply apply to be registered as the wife of a British subject and this follows automatically. You will need your birth certificate, the death certificate of your late husband and of course our marriage certificate. You also have to make a declaration of allegiance! No problem I hope.

I was overwhelmed with work yesterday, including receiving cheques for £3,307, not bad. I shall need that and more to put our house right.

Deepest love until lunch time,

Alan

1977

26 September

Dearest Wifey,

You left only last Thursday, but it seems as though you have been away for years. Life is utterly empty without you. The only natural way of living is for us to be together all the time. Instead I am quite at a loss, with no one to talk to or to take interest in my doings. We must accept the situation with patience, but we can be absolutely sure that we shall not come to life again until we are together. Each time we are together is better than the one before, and this last time in Coniston was the best of all. Now I must spend no more time in complaining.

As I told you over the telephone, the news is fairly good though things will take a long time. The first stage in buying [the house in] Twisden Road will, I hope, be completed this week, and Mr Cox does not see why I need wait another month before actually getting the house. I agree with you about the bathroom. It will be much more agreeable to have space and light, and I am sure it can be arranged easily. Also I think we can keep the flower-bed on the left-hand side of the patio, though you will have to look after the flowers. Nothing else needs a decision now until I see what the house looks like after the alterations have been made. We can put two single beds in the spare bedroom, and there will thus be ample room for any guests we are likely to have.

Margaret has decided firmly on Amelia's house and is already making plans to change it for her own ideas. I do not see why so many changes are necessary, but with any luck she will have plenty of money when the present house is sold. It is already advertised and people are coming to see it. There should be no difficulty on that side.

I have done little of interest, partly because I have felt depressed and even ill. But I am all right inside because I keep thinking of you. It is fortunate that I read the book on rearmament while we were in Coniston. When I got back the *English Historical Review* sent it to me, so I could sit down and review it over the week-end. However, it will look strange if I review a book within a day of receiving it, so I have put my completed review away for a week or two. The most interesting fact is that Inskip comes out so well. Then I have been reading carefully Len Deighton's book on the Battle of Britain, too technical for me but very good.

On Friday I went to an Anglo-Bulgarian lunch. I sat next to the Bulgarian deputy ambassador, who was very boring. But I had a very interesting Bulgarian historian on the other side who told me that *The Struggle for Mastery*, Russian translation, was the standard textbook in Bulgarian universities. They are particularly pleased because I said that in 1878 Macedonia had a Bulgarian population, whatever it has now. Dickens made a very boring, pompous speech. I am glad my life is not spent among professional historians, who go on as though they were bishops or headmasters. Evans was there. I gave him your greetings and told him you would be here for good next year. He is an agreeable though not a very effective man. On Thursday night I went to the Beefsteak Club and had some fairly interesting company, though again on the pompous side. It rained throughout the weekend, but I managed to clean the car. Such are the activities of my life. I love you very much. I miss you. I send my love to my two stepsons and count the days until we shall be together.

Many kisses,

Alan

30 September

Much-missed Darling,

I have so much to do next week that I may not have time to write, so I send you an early letter now. The best news is that on Monday I shall sign the contract for the house in Twisden Road. In another month's time Kindleyside can start work on it, and everything should be ready some time in the New Year. I wrote to Janet, saying how much I appreciated her welcome to you and asking her to start buying kitchen things for us. Do you want a pressure cooker? I am terrified of them and have never used one, but they save a lot of time in cooking. Make any other suggestions that occur to you. I suppose a small portable vacuum cleaner, for instance.

Daniel has returned from Poland and I hope to see him tomorrow.

On Tuesday I went to Nuneaton, about eighty miles from London, where I gave a successful lecture on 'The Bulgarian Horrors'. The real horror was that at dinner there was only water to drink. On my return I tried to save money by waiting for a bus, and when I had waited in vain for half an hour had to take a taxi. This evening I am going to a party given by the Royal Television Society, whatever that is, and shall be received as one of the stars. I hope I shall get enough to eat. Malcolm Muggeridge is making yet another television film about Jesus Christ after which, he announces, he will make no more. About time too.

Next week I have a terrible time. Monday night: sleeper to

Edinburgh. Then a thesis examination and back to London by the afternoon train. Wednesday, John Vincent is giving a Raleigh lecture at the British Academy on Gladstone and Ireland, so I shall have to listen to him. Thursday I go north again to Grimsby, where I shall also visit Beverley where I have never seen the Minster, a great Gothic church. My contract with the *Sunday Express* has been renewed for another year. Christopher Falkus wants to publish my autobiography, which is impossible in present circumstances. I am so busy writing reviews that my *English History* book does not move.

I still cannot believe that soon we shall be sleeping together every night.

You can see my thoughts are on love, but there is much more to love than intercourse as we both know.

Lots of love, sexual and otherwise.

Alan
xxx

9 October

Dearest Lovey,

Here I am back in London after an exhausting week. So far as real news goes, I have little to say. The contract for the house in Twisden Road is settled, which means the property is certainly ours but there will still be some weeks before the deal is completed. English law over property has the most extraordinary delays. On the other hand Margaret has already found a buyer at the full price for St Mark's Crescent, so she will make a good profit and have to leave her present house some time in March. That means there is no chance of her delaying things. The only delay will come from practical problems, which I will write to you as they arise during the reconstruction of our house. Meanwhile write to me when you have ideas, such as the colour of the bath. Should it be a low one or the traditional height? Also ideas about the kitchen. I shall put two single beds in the spare room. Then both your boys can come at the same time, or Daniel and Anna. It occurs to me that if you come only in the spring you may not want to go back to Hungary in August. In that case one or both of your boys can come to England, and I can still keep my arrangement with Margaret to go to the Isle of Wight. All these things will be easy to arrange when you are here. At present I am desperately irritated and lonely because of the delays. It is interesting that our love grows more intense each time we meet. At any rate it does with me. The separation is now almost unbearable. I don't think I can come to Budapest because I have so many foolish engagements. If I do, we must somehow spend the nights together even in a single bed. I can no longer sleep without you.

Now for my activities. First, while I remember, my review of Newman's book on the Polish guarantee will come out some time in the *English Historical Review*. It is not very long, though long enough. I can't send it to you because it is not yet out. I'll tell you when to look for the appropriate number of the *EHR*. Last weekend I went to Edinburgh. Very agreeable sleeper on Monday night and rich breakfast provided by Paul* at the North British Hotel. Interesting thesis on the reactions of British academics to Germany during the First World War. I asked two questions which the candidate had not considered. Can academics be considered be as a single category? Why were the British academics so hysterical about Germany then? He tried to give lively answers. Good journey back in the afternoon, except that the train was an hour late at King's Cross.

Wednesday I heard John Vincent give a Raleigh lecture at the British Academy on Gladstone and Ireland, seeking to prove very perversely that Gladstone cared little for Ireland and knew less. Clever stuff all the same, but John read his lecture fast without expression and [with] his mouth almost closed. I only heard one sentence in ten. My lectures may be no good but people can hear me. Then on Thursday I went off to Beverley in East Yorkshire to see the two churches there and spent most of Friday looking at other churches around Hull. Then I crossed the Humber by ferry and so to Grimsby, where I gave 'The Bulgarian Horrors' for the tenth time, I think. Appreciative audience, but I think I shall have to close down on 'The Bulgarian Horrors' soon. Stopped at a new luxury hotel or motel which was very inferior to an old-fashioned one. Gadgets that did not work and service that was inadequate. I suppose all hotels except those run by a family, like The Sun at Coniston, are deteriorating. On Saturday I came back through Lincolnshire.

All this lecturing is rather absurd. It does not bring in any money and it does not add to my reputation, which is as high as it will ever get. I suppose I give these lectures from vanity, just to prove that I am still alive and can attract audiences. Tomorrow the shadow of Bristol looms over me. I am glad to report, however, that I have declined an invitation

---

* Paul Addison, a student of Alan's.

to an Anglo-German conference at Mannheim in December. I don't like conferences, I do not want to see Mannheim and I am still tied to Bristol. I am sure this is a boring letter, but I wanted to get something off to you before I go to Bristol. Many books to review including three volumes of Churchill documents. Deep and lasting love,

Alan
xx

20 October

Dearest Wifey,

    You can write 'Hubby' if you like, but it is only used as a joke. The younger generation are as conventional as we are, saying 'Darling' most of the time. In the North of England they say 'Love' which I prefer. I am still puzzled by the sexual reactions of the American women we have both been reading about. They seem to be saying that they get better feelings from other women or with masturbation than with a man. Surely this misses out the emotion that should go with sex. As well, I thought that real intercourse gave you a better orgasm but I may be wrong. In any case we do fine because, as you say, we can do anything and reveal anything. Believe me, I am just as interested in your doings as you are in mine except that I can't read what you write in Hungarian. I shall be with you in spirit during your visit to Turkey, not that I care about Ankara but Istanbul – Byzantine Istanbul – is fine. Don't bother about Topkapi. Spend as long as you can at Santa Sophia, and see also the church of the Karyia out in the suburbs. If you meet any history professor of the University give my greetings, though they won't remember me.

    I shall get the keys of Twisden Road tomorrow. Then I will get on to Kindleyside and he will, I hope, start to clear the patio at the back. I shall tell him to leave the flower-bed on the left-hand side, though clearing it of undergrowth, and I will also get him to pave the patio with coloured stones so that it will look quite elegant. After that he will assemble a team and get to work on the house, but I can't yet tell you when he will be finished.

    I am worried about the decorating. Some of the walls may need doing at once. The others I shall leave until you come. The ceilings, I suppose, should be a plain dull white, with restoration where necessary of the frieze. I shall also have to decide on the electric-light fittings and maybe order curtains. It will be wonderful to be together at night and equally wonderful to be together during the day. In daytime too you must tell me everything, including when you think I am doing anything wrong such as worrying about Margaret or not going out enough.

Answers to questions. Christopher Falkus is managing director of Weidenfeld & Nicolson, who are publishing Wilson's book through a subsidiary firm. I have no news of Cara, nor of anyone except Alan Sked who is still keen to work with you. By the way, do you propose to call yourself Eva Taylor in England or will you still be Eva Haraszti? I shall be happy either way, and you can of course use both names. I am glad you are in action about passports. On our side you can get British nationality for £25 as soon as you come to England and have two passports if that is all right on the Hungarian side. I am getting on well at Bristol. I have finished the Churchill documents. Last night I went to Winchester and lectured on Churchill's National government. Large audience and successful lecture. I am now reading a book on Monmouth's rebellion, the last rising of the English people, at any rate until Chartism. No family news of any interest, except that Daniel is living in a house with eight other students. The weather is warmer than it was in the Lake District. No more now except greetings to the boys from

Your loving hubby,

Alan

3 November

Lovey Mine,

Your letter of 28 October has just arrived. I answer at once so that you will get my letter before you set off for Ankara. Things at the house are moving, though only slowly. Kindleyside will clear the back-yard in the near future, leaving the flower-bed on the left. Otherwise he will cover the rest with paving stones. I will get him to colour-wash the back wall, in pink. We have had to sacrifice the outside lavatory which was in a very broken-down state. After all, you have only one lavatory at home and it creates no problems. As I told you, I will make the big back room into the bathroom, leaving a lavatory and basin in the smaller room. Shall I put a bidet in the smaller room?

I have passed on to Kindleyside your instructions about the colour on the walls. I have also suggested that we should have spot-lights in the sitting room and kitchen-dining room and ceiling lights upstairs. I shall keep the existing stair carpet as underlay for a new carpet I have bought. My big carpet from Magdalen will go in our bedroom. The existing sitting-room carpet is, I think, good enough for the kitchen. Janet says she will buy things for me and sweetly suggested that she should consult you as to various things you may want. So you will be hearing from her. I shall leave the washing-machine for you to choose. Kindleyside has to clear the back, put in a damp course, renew the drains and rewire the electricity. So he will not start reconstruction and decorating until the New Year.

Now as to my life. Good trip to Bristol. Agreeable dinner party, including a professor of archaeology who was interested in the monasteries of Macedonia. Too much to do, most of it trivial. I reviewed Wilson's very bad book on Prime Ministers. Now I am reading Roskill on *Churchill and the Admirals*, very funny, also David Irving on *Rommel*, not funny at all. Our industrial troubles have started again. We have staggered blackouts every night, and soon there may be another coal strike. I fear inflation will soon start moving again. Answers to questions: I knew Dorothy Woodman and liked her very much, which few did. I have had a visit from Hajdu and gave him a little assistance where to find things – mostly at LSE. I am interested to hear that my handbook on Hungary has survived. But your young colleague must be careful. After I had written it and it had been set up in proof, the FO deleted most of the history and politics and substituted versions written by Macartney. I suspect that your colleague found Macartney's version. I alone retained the original proof and now I have destroyed it.

I have had a very tiresome cold and cough which has made me ill. I also feel that I do too much, especially in the cold weather. Sometimes I feel I am becoming an old man. But I shan't feel that when I am with you. I shall certainly not choose your name in England. That is something you have to decide for yourself, though I think that you will find it easier as a matter of convenience to call yourself Mrs Taylor in shops and so on.

Much love from your Hubby and also from your lover,

Alan

xxx

11 November

Dearly Beloved and soon, I hope, House-mate,

This letter should reach you before you go to Ankara. If not, it will be all the more welcome when you get back. What news of your thesis and your doctorate? You tell me nothing about it, though I am sure it keeps you busy. I am busy too, but I must confess that I find this last period of waiting almost unbearable. I am so tied up that I cannot come to Budapest, and in the New Year I shall have to be constantly on hand in order to supervise the reconstruction. But it is agonizing. I am now so used to you that I miss you far more than I did at first. Then I think to myself: once this period is over we shall be together for good, not only at night but often throughout the day. I wish I had not been blackmailed into spending a night with Margaret each week, but perhaps she deserves it.

There is one thing I want to impress on you: from the moment we set up together you come first. If you ever feel neglected – and I daresay I am often careless – you have only to say so and we will arrange things. I don't care for anyone in the world except you, and shall never change on this. So never hesitate to complain when you feel like it. I had a long talk with Janet the other day. As you know, she is wholeheartedly in sympathy with us and will be of great use to us when you are here, advising you where to shop and going shopping with you. She will write to you about your needs and will buy cheaply during the winter sales. I will try to have the house inhabitable before you come, but you know how incompetent I am. I suppose you could go to Shirley, except that she is a long way off. These problems will solve themselves.

I started on the First World War at Bristol with great success – big audience and a good lecture. Then I went to Cheltenham and lectured to the local Historical Association in Cheltenham Ladies' College – one of the first public schools for girls and still very high class. I have had so many books to review that I have had no time for my own work. The Spears mission to Syria during the Second World War; Monmouth's rebellion in 1685, the last rising of the people of England; Enoch Powell on *Joseph Chamberlain*; David Irving on *Rommel*, arguing that Rommel was framed by Speidel. Now I am reading an enormous book on York Minster for the *Guardian*, this from piety and for pleasure. I wrote a devastating review of Wilson on Prime Ministers for the *Observer*, listing his mistakes and adding that if this had been the work of a student I should have marked it: Fail. The review gave universal pleasure.

The weather is as warm as summer. The power go-slow is over and we have electricity again. The next worry is a coal strike. In short, civilization is breaking down. Our love is not. Greetings to the boys.

Greater love than ever,

Alan
xxx

18 November

My own Darling,

It was good to speak to you on the telephone the other night, though I am always afraid that you will be angry with me or impatient over the long delay in our coming together. Often I wake up in the night and think – 'Suppose Eva changes her mind at the last minute and does not come. How shall I live?' Really I know the time will pass and that then we shall experience great happiness. At present, however, I am in great distress, wanting each day to go faster. I have a second cause of distress, a very silly one. A couple of days ago the 24 members of the Order of Merit, our highest award, were entertained by the Queen. There was a photograph of them, many of them undistinguished administrators or men who made a reputation by talking instead of by writing. I thought, 'Why not me? I am more distinguished than most of them and a better writer. So why not me?' and I felt I had wasted my life. In reality it is a compliment not to be asked to join such an Order.

I have seen your young girl-friend and talked to her at length about Macaulay. I also told her about our visit to Manchester. (Incidentally, Andrew Snell has left the BBC and is working for Weekend Television in London.) Will you tell her that the book on Engels and Manchester I mentioned to her is by Steven Marcus? I also said I would find out about illustrations for the industrial revolution. I expect you really know more about it than I do. She was a very intelligent girl. I told her she must translate Carlyle next.

No great news. I took Janet to see our house the other morning. She liked it very much and thought it could be made very pleasant. She said that I could trust Kindleyside completely. He is a very efficient man and will get the work going at a great pace once he starts on it. Janet passed on to me your instruction that you wanted fitted carpets. You can't have your wish completely. I am bringing my carpet from Oxford, which is very attractive and also of very good quality. It will go very easily into our bedroom, but there will be gaps at the edges which we can either cover with rugs or we can stain the surrounding floor. You see, I have to make the best use of what I possess already. Also, I have to share with Margaret the things from St Mark's Crescent when she moves to her smaller house at the same time as we move. There are two carpets in the basement which, if fitted together, will make a fitted carpet for our dining room-kitchen. Then I propose to use the carpet from the existing sitting room at Twisden Road (after cleaning) as a floor cover in the new bathroom. I have bought new stair carpets and will use the existing ones, again after cleaning, as the under-carpet. I know you would like me to have nothing to do with Margaret as far as our house goes. But I have to take what she has left over. If there is anything you don't like, we can change it after you come. Indeed, I am deliberately leaving lots of things to buy when you come. Do you approve of spot-lights in the sitting room? I keep thinking of things and have then forgotten about them when I come to write. Kindleyside begins this weekend to clear the back-yard and turn it into an attractive courtyard. What colour should the back wall be made?

Bristol continues to run well. Last Monday I was at dinner with the Vice-Chancellor, rather formal and boring. On Thursday I went to the Historical Association in North London and gave them a very good lecture on Churchill's government. There is a new very good book by Roskill on *Churchill and his Admirals*. Terry has now *five* reviews of mine not yet printed, so you can see I have been working hard, or even too hard. I am also editing the text of my TV lecture on 'How Wars Begin'. Altogether I am rather tired, but my cold has almost gone. The weather is unattractive and threatens to get worse. Fortunately it is warm both in the house and in my office.

Very much love,

Alan

xx

24 November

Beloved Wifey,

Your letter of 24 November arrived this morning, and I thought it would be nice to answer it at once. Outside it is very cold, and writing to you will keep me warm. Last Monday I took alarm that there would be snow, so I went to Bristol in my mountaineering boots. Instead it was sunny and bright. All the same, I had to walk up the lecture hall in my boots.

The students of University College London have invited me to give their Foundation Oration, which can be on anything I like. I think I must do it, but as usual I can't think of a subject. Any ideas? I have also agreed to visit the Historical Associations of Sheffield, Leeds and York on successive nights in March *1979*. Maybe I shan't be alive by then. I often reflect that we shall only have five years or so together, and that it is unfair to uproot you from Hungary for so short a time. We must make sure that it is worth it.

I have no news of the house except that Kindleyside has begun to knock things down. Janet says that the back bedroom is rather small for two beds. She suggested that we should turn it into the bathroom and put the bedroom at the back. I think this is impractical, if only because of the hot-water cistern and other things coming straight up from the kitchen. But we might put our own bed in the back room and the two beds in the front. I often think of how you turn away to slip off your clothes and what pleasure you get when I tell you to turn round. The thought alone is disturbing to me, that shows how much I want you. I am not sure about apple green for the back wall, but have seen a terracotta bath so know that that is possible.

Not much news. I have got through my heavy load of reviewing and am now preparing the text of *How Wars Begin* for publication. It reads quite well. *The War Lords* was published last Monday, rather gaudy. Now I have settled on *From Paris to Petrograd: Revolutions and Revolutionaries*. Eddie complained that there was not enough on the twentieth century, as I stopped at the Bolshevik revolution. I said – there have been no more European revolutions since then, and I don't know enough about revolutions elsewhere. Would he like a description of the glorious revolutions which put Gierek in power in Poland and Kadar in Hungary? Eddie took fright at this idea, so my original plan remains. I am not sure I know enough about the subject, or at least have forgotten it. But I have plenty of time to revive my memories.

No, I am not a sweet man except to you. I am inconsiderate. I don't spontaneously think of kind actions, though I try to make myself do them. I never put myself out for other people. If I had been a sweet man I should have had a less solitary life, or so I think. As long as you think me sweet, I don't care about anyone else.

See you soon!

Alan

3 December

Dearest Heart

Oh dear, how I do miss you. I miss you especially because my skin irritation has moved to my back and I need you to rub cream on it. Today has been exasperating. Here I am alone, with Margaret out at a meeting. I was looking forward to a telephone conversation with you, and then found that I had left my diary with your number in it down in Fleet Street. I tried to remember it, got as far as 850 and then must have guessed wrongly as I got a strange Hungarian voice. I also tried directory enquiries, who insisted that there was no Hudecz and no Haraszti in the Budapest directory. So I shall have to find an opportunity next week before you go to Ankara. I had so much to tell you and must remember it again now.

The back of the house is cleared and the annexe gone. It looks very spacious, and our neighbour whom I met is jealous that we have more space than she has. She is a friendly elderly lady who is looking forward to helping us. She has gas central heating and is very pleased with it. She also told me that when trains pass in the night the house shakes. So far neither hers nor ours has fallen down. Kindleyside has also transformed the kitchen-dining room, putting in new windows and moving everything around. He has also torn down the ceiling, preparatory to putting two water tanks in the roof. It looks utterly wild at present, but clearly he has nearly finished the heavy work already. I have bought a refrigerator, or rather Janet has bought one for me. Kindleyside will examine the gas cooker and report whether it can be made to work properly. I shall do nothing about a washing-machine until you arrive, as I cannot decide the size or indeed whether you want one. I shall take the gramophone I have here, but shall leave a television set for you to choose. I think we shall be fairly well equipped, except that we shall need some kitchen things in which I am reasonably expert.

I have been thinking about our money arrangements, which we must put on a business footing. More marriages break up in quarrels over money matters than over anything else. Our marriage will never break up, but we had better make sure. When you come I will explain to you how to open a bank account in England and how to use it. I will put £1,000 into your account and will repeat this each year. This money will be entirely yours to do as you like with. I will also give you £20 each week for the household shopping and for your everyday needs. Perhaps you should also have a Post Office savings account, which will enable you to draw money from the Post Office just across the road. Such an account earns interest of 5% tax-free. Please tell me if this is all right. If one or other of your boys comes, I will give him how much a week while he is in England? £15 a week while stopping with us and £30 a week when he is away? Perhaps that is not enough, but we can discuss it long before they come. As well, as soon as 1978 arrives I will send you £300 which is still the maximum I can send abroad in a year.

I am making no plans for the coming year after your arrival. I have got another TV series for July and a lecture at Edinburgh in August. Later in the spring of 1979 I have already arranged to visit the Historical Associations at Sheffield, Leeds and York all in the same week. This will give us a short holiday. So you see I have many plans in mind. The most important plan you can guess: just to be with you.

Crispin writes that electricity and water have gone off at his school. The boys have to carry water up from the town, and Crispin lives on tins of cold food or sometimes goes to the home of one of his coloured colleagues. He does not seem at all depressed by these conditions. I should go crazy. Daniel is silent.

I went to see *The Sting* for the second time and enjoyed it as much as I did at the first. The weather is very cold, but very good for walking. Bristol ended in a blaze of glory. I'll write again before you go away.

Very strong love and greetings to my stepsons.

Alan
x

12 December

Dearest Wifey,

I am still exhilarated by our telephone conversation. It made me feel so near you. It will probably be our last talk until after the New Year. So I send you a Christmas message: I never knew real love until I was with you. Now it is like a religious experience in the old days – something that makes us different from other people. We have complete intimacy of both mind and body.

Now for more practical news. Kindleyside is at work on the kitchen-dining room. He has made a good new door into the yard and a window beside it. At that end we shall have the boiler, the gas cooker and the refrigerator. When you come we can also put a washing-machine there if you want one. I have four dining-room chairs and can add more. Would you like a round table seating six or eight? I can buy one for £50. He is going to rewire the house this week, and I shall also discuss with him where to put the radiators in each room. In the sitting room there will be also a gas-fire which we may never need. I shall later put down as many carpets as I possess, and buy more later with you. The kitchen-dining room and the old bathroom will have cork tiles, which are very easy to keep clean. Kindleyside has produced a glamorous bidet in terracotta to go in the old bathroom, and has everything in the same colour in the new one. This will be the most expensive new equipment, but worth it. When you come I expect we will buy a desk for you and maybe other furniture. I have no idea when he will finish, but he says he will move fast in the New Year. After that I shall have to sort things out with Margaret. Before you come I shall get Janet to stock the house with essentials – cleaning materials, kitchen supplies and so on.

On Wednesday I went to a concert where Finbar and Claire* took part, having learnt the violin by the Suzuki method which I can't explain to you. In principle, they learn the violin just as children learn to talk. It is certainly very successful. Finbar has got a gold medal for his swimming, the highest award. Now he will start again on life-saving. He is also No. two Board in his school chess club and hopes soon to be No. one. No wonder he has no time for reading.

I told you something of my reviewing. I turn in my reviews and the *Observer* does not always use them, particularly when it loses an issue because of strikes in the production room. David Irving has now created a new sensation by alleging that Churchill cheated on his income tax. All nonsense I think, in any case Churchill deserved everything he could get.

Of the OMs** the scientists are the most distinguished though their subject is beyond me. The two historians are Veronica Wedgwood and Ronald Symes, who wrote a good book on *The Roman Republic* thirty years ago. I am not anxious to join such a mediocre collection.

Dearest one, let us rejoice in our love for ever and ever.

Alan
x

* Children of Sebastian and Mary Taylor.
** Holders of the Order of Merit.

1977

22 December

My Sweetheart,

I duly received your letter of 12 December. Also your Christmas present which you left with Shirley. You think of my every need. I feel all as you do, and this is a sure bond between us. You do not need to worry about money. We will try what I suggest, and if you find you can't manage the household on that you can have more. One of your needs is difficult to satisfy: a woman once a week is much more difficult to find than perhaps in Hungary. We can consult Janet and perhaps our friendly neighbour when the time comes. But a vacuum-cleaner, which we shall have, works wonders.

I had a long session with Kindleyside, deciding where the radiators and electric lights would go. I find to my delight that our bed will go against the chimney breast, with a hanging cupboard on one side and a cupboard with shelves on the other. This will leave plenty of room for two chests of drawers. We will get a dressing table for you when you come. In the back bedroom the bed will go along the wall behind the door. Would you like your little desk there, or with me in the back room downstairs? I don't think we should disturb each other if we were together. I shall also leave a gramophone and a television set until we are in. Bob Doyle will fix them for us. Kindleyside has got the kitchen nicely spaced out. First the cooker by the window, then the sink, then the refrigerator. Plenty of space for a round table at the far end, and lots of storage room. He will also provide an access to the roof so that we can stick our boxes up there. He says firmly that he will be finished by the end of February. Then the carpets will have to be made and fitted.

Daniel is back from Leeds. He has suddenly grown up. He has filled out and is now as handsome as Crispin (who, I hear, has grown a moustache). I tried to impress on Daniel that he is really clever and that he can get a First if he has confidence in himself. Even his tutors say that he writes with great distinction. I wrote a Christmas piece for the *Sunday Express* pleading for the release of Hess. It will do no good. Despite the holiday season I have as many books as ever to review: the Cold War by an American; Passchendaele by the Haig enthusiast John Terraine; an enormous book on Anglo-American relations in the Far East during the Second World War by Christopher Thorne. University College has announced my Foundation Lecture on 'My Place in History', a humble one I am glad to say.

I think of you in Ankara and hope you have not been seduced by a glamorous Turk.

Love as ever for the New Year and wishes also to the boys.

Alan

30 December

Oh, My Love,

What a delight to hear you. I was feeling depressed and that I should never cope with preparing the house all by myself. Your voice took away all my worries and I went out full of love, walking on air. Well, not quite all my worries. I am still worried about when you can come. When does your British permit expire, and can you get it prolonged by explaining that your incompetent academic husband has not got things ready in time? If not, I will find you somewhere for a few days. The Kees might take you, and though their house at Kew sounds a long way away you can be at Gospel Oak, our local station, in a quarter of an hour by the North London line. But it may not be necessary.

Here are the problems of our time-table. Kindleyside says he will be finished at mid-February, but as you know contractors are always a bit late. Carpet Care cannot cut and lay the carpets until Kindleyside is finished. Still, there should be plenty of time on our side. I should be much happier if your British permit gave you a few days in hand. Ask for an extra month. Also, do not forget your birth certificate and your husband's death certificate.

That is enough of my worries. I did all the buying of things yesterday and found it easier than I had expected. Now I have only to buy a gas cooker and a gas fire. I can't do this until Kindleyside is ready for it, but it presents no problem. Everything else we need, we can buy when you come.

Christmas Day was very exhausting. We had all the family except for Giles and Janet, but fortunately none of them stopped the night. The next evening Daniel and Anna turned up after spending Christmas Day with his mother. I gave him *The Spanish Civil War* by Hugh Thomas. That will occupy him for a long time.

I got my review of the Pemberton Billing affair into the Christmas number of the *New Statesman*, and the *Observer* will have a piece on Kitchener and Passchendaele this Sunday. Engel Janosi has asked me to write a long piece for an Austrian periodical on 'History and Biography'. I can write this in my sleep, at least I hope I can. I have also a long book on Guernica to review for the *English Historical Review*. So I have had plenty to read over the holiday.

I am revising my autobiography so that it will be all ready for you to publish when I die. I often think that we shall have only a few years together, but they will be good ones. Nothing is wrong with me except

1977

the irritation on my back, which I expect is due to nervous tension. Your coming will cure it automatically.

Let me have news of my stepsons and of your doctorate. I shall soon be going to Bristol again, and this term I have University College as well. This will make time go faster.

With all love for a wonderful New Year,

Alan

Strange that you will soon be know as Eva Taylor.

1978

9 January 1978

Dearest Love,

    I was delighted and relieved to reach you by telephone on Saturday night when I had almost despaired of doing so. I hope I explained that my worries were probably exaggerated, as they always are. What I really want to know is the latest date you must come to England if everything went wrong. Kindleyside is still confident he will finish in mid-February, but there may be bad weather to prevent work in the yard at the back. We are also threatened by a strike of electricity power workers which will mean electricity cuts, and one by tanker drivers which will cut off the supply of petrol. There is nothing secure about things nowadays.

    You must not get into the habit of believing that I am competent to arrange a house. I shall get Janet to help me in buying in supplies, but even so there will be many things missing. I have decided not to buy a dining table until you come, and leave it for you to decide. I think it is very unlikely that we shall ever have six people to dinner and ourselves as well, but you may have more ambitious plans. I shall also leave the washing-machine until you come. With the launderette just across the road you may not need one. I shall bring with me a drying rack which will be suspended above the bath and can be pulled up and down. I fear we shall have so many chairs that we shall not be able to pass between them. I cannot remember how many chairs are coming from Oxford. They are old-fashioned Victorian chairs which you may not like. In that case we can sell them and buy others. As you probably know I have no taste at all. Television and gramophone can also wait.

    As to my *Essays*, there are as you know two collections: *Europe, Grandeur and Decline* and *Essays in English History*. The first is the more suitable for Hungarian readers. There are also a few which can be picked out of my earlier collections, now out of print. Soon there will be 'The Historian' and 'The Biographer', which I am writing for an Austrian periodical, but it will take me some time. You had better leave the choice until you come here.

    I had a very amusing letter from Crispin, describing a festival in his town with the chiefs being carried, guns firing and special honours being paid to the VSO teachers. Daniel announced to me yesterday that he intended to become an electrical engineer. I said, 'But you are not good with your hands.' He said, 'That is true, I had never thought of that. My only intention was to become an official of their union.'

I really do no work nowadays except reviewing. I have lost interest in writing history. Also, I am too distracted with the coming move. I lie awake all night counting the number of hooks which will have to be unscrewed and then screwed in again. I start at UCL on Thursday and go to Bristol next Monday.

Love to you and greetings to the boys,

Alan

16 January

Dearest Love,

I received your little note. I am pretty sure the first week in April will be grand and suggest you decide on 5 April. If anything goes seriously wrong I will warn you in time, but I don't see why it should. Be patient and tolerant all the same.

I am having a mixed time. The bathroom equipment is stunning, all in terracotta. There will also be a built-in shower. Next week I shall buy a gas cooker with automatic lighting and a raised grill. You will find it quite easy to work. I am worried about storage room. Probably we shall need to install more shelves. I shall have the wine on racks in the kitchen-dining room. They make an attractive ornament to a wall. That is the extent of my worries at present.

I have just read an American book on the Cold War and written about it in the *New Statesman.* Now I have received an enormous book from Roger Louis on the Trusteeship system of the United Nations and its emergence from Anglo-American quarrels. Entertaining in its way, but too long. A neighbour called Mervyn Jones has also presented me with a novel centring on CND, with much sex as well. He is the son of Ernest Jones, so this is not surprising.

The only trouble that may throw us out is the threatened strike of power engineers in March which may cut off the electricity altogether. It seems that life will come to a halt.

My busy time is approaching. I gave my first lecture at University College last Thursday and was not pleased with it, perhaps because I am out of practice. Now I am off to Bristol for four lectures on the Second World War, when I must think of something new to say. We had a meeting of the British Academy last Friday. Our actual choices were not very exciting – Raymond Carr, expert on Spain; John Erikson, expert on the Soviet Army; and a rather dreary character called Gallagher who writes about the British Empire. I hope he falls through. When will the Hungarian Academy elect you, if ever?

Alison is now going to hospital every day. They find that her spleen is not over-working so her malady must lie elsewhere. Perhaps she creates her own antibodies, which apparently is bad. The whole thing harasses me and I am sure harasses Janet also. I hear Mary also wrote to you at Christmas.

In haste, lots of love,

Alan

20 January

Dearest Love,

Your letter to Janet arrived more quickly than your letter of the same date to me. This gives me the excuse to write to you again. My gloomy thoughts are solely over practical questions. I cannot believe that our house will be ready in time, but there are still two months to go. The house itself is also full of problems. I cannot see where we shall have enough storage room either for our clothes or for our kitchen supplies. However, you will solve these things. After a few days I shall send you off to Selfridge's with a credit card and you will be able to order everything we need. As I told you I shall wait for a washing-machine, a television set and gramophone until we are settled in.

Daniel: he has gone back to Leeds mainly, I think, for his political activities rather than his studies. He knows best what he wants to do. So far as I know he reads no serious books except the works of Trotsky, though I try to tell him that is dead stuff. But he is a fine boy. Crispin: he has been to the north of Ghana and seen wild animals, though no lions, for the first time. He proposes to return in July. It would be fine if we could take him to the Lakes, but I expect he will be too busy. In the autumn he is going to Bristol University for a year in order to take the Certificate of Education. Maybe I shall still be visiting professor there and shall see him often. I am sorry he is determined to become a school-teacher, but that is what he wants to do and there is no stopping him. Maybe he will become a headmaster in no time, or perhaps a powerful

1978

administrator. At any rate he has enjoyed his time in Ghana enormously. Hauser: I already have commitments in early October, so tell him how much we appreciate his invitation and are sorry we can't come. We must concentrate on our life in England.

I still do not know how Margaret and the others will behave towards us. I fear Margaret may want to interfere in our lives, telling you how you should do things. If so we can soon tell her to leave us alone. I should be glad to quarrel with her, which would relieve my conscience, but otherwise I must discharge my obligations to her. Do not imagine I love her in any way. Probably the others will all be friendly, though they will not concern themselves much with us except of course for Janet. Mary too will be a good friend.

I was amused that you were ashamed to write about some aspects of our life together. But you *must* write about them. I like it, just as I make you turn towards me when you try to turn away. You must have no shame in either writing or acting with me. Such writing will please us both. I know you want to write, but you need encouragement from me.

Cold weather, sleet and frost on the car. I get tired with both Bristol and University College, but manage some time. Margaret Morris came to my seminar and sent you her warmest greetings.

Love to all, especially to you,

Alan

2 February

Lovey Mine,

I have just received your letter of 26 January and enjoyed every word of it. At the moment I am not sparkling well. I have a boil or carbuncle at the base of my spine and this causes me much discomfort. However, I am now having it dressed daily by my doctor and taking pills as well. So I shall soon recover.

The house is progressing. Kindleyside has put so many cupboards and fixtures in the kitchen that we shall not need any open shelves. He says this is more modern. The walls of the sitting room will be so covered with book-shelves that we shall have little room for pictures, which does not worry me. What do you think about large wall mirrors, of which there are many at St Mark's Crescent? There is no point in having one over our bed except to look at each other, and we can do that anyway.

We might have one over a chest of drawers. But I mean to get a dressing table for you if we can fit it in. There will be room for one in the back bedroom. Then what about the sitting room? Would you like a mirror over the gas-fire, or shall we keep that space for a picture? The back room where we shall work might take a mirror, and maybe one in the hall for guests when they arrive. I will discuss this with Kindleyside. He has already put a full-length mirror in the bathroom, and we must have a small one over the hand-basin. The cupboards in the bathroom will take all our linen and perhaps our underwear, which will thus be aired and warm when we need it. I shall move the furniture just before Easter and so have time to arrange it over the holiday. I shall also get the books on the shelves, but I am sure we shall need more shelves. As to your typewriter, I have two good manuals if you want to type in English. Your own typewriter will be more useful if you want to type Hungarian. I have my own electric typewriter, so the two manuals will be all yours. I hope to get the carpets laid early in March, though I am still not sure when.

Do not be under the delusion that I work hard. I review books as they come in, and am now writing the *New Statesman* Diary for the next four weeks. But I have not attempted to write any book or part of one since 1976. Somehow I have lost interest or have nothing to write about. I have subscribed for the *TLS* until the end of March. Then we can have it delivered with the morning papers. We shall take only *The Times* and fight over which of us should read it first. Perhaps we shall quarrel and I will strike you, which is supposed to give women pleasure. Do not worry. It is unlikely to happen. However, I have learnt better this time. Unless Margaret accepts fully the place you hold in my life, she will see no more of me. However, I think things will work out, though she will be sometimes a burden.

I am now off to University College and after that to the Beefsteak Club. There is no danger that I shall stop loving you. You are more likely to change than I am.

No, no, both of us will love as long as life lasts.

Alan

1978

10 February

Dearest Love,

 I tried to ring you up the other night, but the lines to Hungary were all engaged and I could not get through. Now I do not see when I shall have an opportunity to ring you again. Soon however it will be unnecessary. We shall be able to talk to each other when we have anything to say. I wish I could reach out and touch you.

 News good and bad. Bristol is to give me an honorary degree in the summer. I attach no importance to these things, but it is pleasant that Bristol appreciates me and I also like to think of the pain that my honorary degree will cause to those who have slighted me. I must have some academic standing after all.

 The bad news is that Kindleyside cannot get the water pressure to make the showers work. As you will remember, the ceiling of the bathroom is low and the tank above it does not give enough weight of water. So no shower and no spray on the bidet. Perhaps we can consult Ernö Goldfinger and he will have some answer. Otherwise things are moving fast. The decorations are almost finished. I like the kitchen-dining room, which will be very easy to work. Kindleyside insisted that shelves are not 'modern', so we shall have lots of cupboards instead. I am not clear where we shall store all our clothes but no doubt some solution will present itself. How much luggage are you bringing? I should like to leave my car at Hatton Cross and come to Heathrow by Underground. But our return journey may prove difficult if we are overburdened. Perhaps I should consult Shirley, who is an expert in these things. Are you proposing to return to Hungary during the summer, or will Pisti bring more luggage for you? You do not need to bring a desk lamp. I have plenty.

 We are now having cold weather and the locks on my car door froze up. I solved the problem by opening the back and climbing in, but this is a somewhat undignified way of doing things. We are also having a petrol shortage due to a go-slow by the drivers of petrol tankers. But my garage keeps a supply for me in reserve, and I do not use the car except for short journeys in town. Life is moving peacefully on the whole. Margaret would like to plan our house as well as hers, but Kindleyside goes on his own way regardless. I look forward to the actual moving with some apprehension, but all these things will soon be over.

 Every weekend I contemplate the *New Statesman* Diary with anxiety, but it has worked out well each Sunday when I come to write it. You will be amused by my reflections, especially on my cornea and kidney cards. The only scandal is provided by Harold Wilson, who has clearly gone off his head. Did I tell you that I met Joanna the other night at a party? She embraced me excessively and said I smelled nice. I said it was merely man's smell. Is it? My boil or carbuncle is discharging satisfactorily and I now feel very well in myself. It was a strange thing to have, and still has to be dressed every day. But you don't need to worry that my cornea and kidney cards will be used before we meet. We shall need some time to get used to each other, but there will be increasing happiness every day. Of that I am sure.

Best wishes to my stepsons and to you,
Much, much love,

Alan

17 February

Dearest Love,

Whenever you start a letter 'dear Alan', I think it is an announcement that you cannot bear to leave Hungary and face a new life after all. But this always turns out a false alarm. You ask a lot of questions. I answer them first. My boil or carbuncle is getting better, though it is still discharging. I am very well now in myself and drink lemon juice every morning, though I doubt whether it does me much good. This morning I dispatched the mirrors and book-shelves to Twisden Road and will allot their places on Tuesday. I found I had five mirrors. One will go in the hall over the radiator and the little shelf for letters; one in the front sitting room over the gas-fire; one in the back bedroom over its mantelshelf; one in our bedroom between the two chests of drawers; one in the bathroom or the lavatory. I am worried that we shall not have enough room for our clothes. There are two hanging cupboards in our bedroom, but it will be a squeeze to get all my suits in one of them. Then at present I hang up most of my shirts, and shall have to get them all in a single drawer. The truth is that the house is too small and perhaps I should have kept the bigger one. But I did not like it. I think the cupboards will take all our stores and cooking things in the kitchen, and I shall have the wine in racks on the wall. We are going to have far too much bed-linen. There is a full stock waiting at Shirley's and now Margaret has produced a quantity of sheets and blankets she will never need. However, we must get it all in the airing cupboard somehow. It all depends how long I live. If I live ten years we shall get through this double supply. Otherwise you will have to marry again or else distribute the supplies between the two families. Until now I have always been spoilt by having too much space, especially when I had also my rooms in Oxford where I used to store my winter things during the summer and the other way round.

Family news. Margaret is in an increasingly hysterical state. I fear we shall have a difficult time at first, and you do not know how ruthless or persistent she can be. She is sure to develop some dangerous illness just to upset us and particularly me. Alison is very well at present, but the doctors have decided that she must have her spleen removed some time in May. Sophia is now, I think, a little overdue. During the half-term holiday Nolan and Milo* came for four nights. I read *Alice Through the Looking Glass* to Milo and *Treasure Island* to Nolan. We also played dominoes. Sebastian's address is Oak Village, London, NW5. He lives only across a couple of roads from us and Mary will always be eager to take you shopping. It will be more useful to go with Janet, who knows how to find the best and cheapest things around our district.

I wish we could arrange that you should come straight to the house. It depends partly what day and what time you arrive. If you come on a Saturday it will be difficult to buy food and so on, on Sunday morning. Otherwise I am sure I could provide for a single night. Also, it will be more difficult if you arrive late in the afternoon as there are no restaurants near us. We can decide nearer the time. Now I must again write the *New Statesman* Diary. It seems to come round with hardly a day's interval.

So still keep confident and faithful as I do.

Love,

Alan

26 February

My Sweetheart,

You must not expect many letters during the next few weeks. This is a very wearing time. It is bad enough that I have to go up nearly every day and argue with Kindleyside, who is an obstinate old man. Margaret is worse. She constantly tries to plan the house without going there,

---

* Alan's grandchildren by Amelia.

insisting that I must have this and that, producing things that I don't need and complaining from afar at what has been done. On top of this she is selling the larger articles of her furniture, and also for reasons that I don't understand is buying new furniture. As a result she is hysterical much of the time and I lead a harassed life. I close my eyes and think about the future when all, I hope, will be well. We shall have a fight at first, with Margaret constantly ringing up to say how lonely she is.

Otherwise the house is going well. Kindleyside has nearly finished for the time being. In May he will come back to deal with the outside of the house, so do not be disappointed if it looks rather shabby at the moment. Inside is splendid. I have moved my book-shelves and find that we have more shelf space than we can fill. As I told you before, I shall do nothing about a washing-machine until you come. There is a self-service launderette round the corner and perhaps that will be enough. We shall not have a television set or a gramophone at first.

I have at last heard from Daniel. But he told me no news about himself. Instead he sent me a long essay on Marx's attitude to the British Empire and India in particular. Sophia is still carrying her baby and appears very well. As she says, a baby is easier to manage inside you than outside. Alison will have her operation in May. This fills me with gloom.

I have just written my fourth and last Diary for the *New Statesman*. There is also a new editor, Bruce Page. I know nothing about him, so have no idea whether he will ever use me again. On Friday I go to Exeter. For the autumn I have arranged a four-day lecture tour of Stirling, St Andrews, Edinburgh and Glasgow, when I hope you will go with me. They agreed to pay your fare as well as mine. The other sensation is that there is to be a grand lunch in honour of the five-hundredth anniversary of the Oxford University Press, and I have been asked to propose the toast of the Press. There will be a glittering assembly of Lords and also Michael Foot, so I shall have to think of irresponsible things to say. Unfortunately it is before you come. Let me know your exact plans when you have them. It seems only a few days away.

The latest book to threaten me is a life of Portal, who was Chief of the Air Staff during the war. This does not sound very interesting. The *Observer* is running the diary of Goebbels during 1945, which is certainly not interesting. I cannot understand why it is expected to be a best-seller. Now I must read up the Congress of Berlin for my visit to Exeter on Friday. They say the snow has melted and the floods subsided.

My warm kisses on many places and much love,

Alan

1978

3 March

Dearly Beloved Ava,

Yes, I like the name very much. But I think you had better stick to Eva as your legal name. This will be on your passport and naturalization papers. You will have to sign that way in the bank and elsewhere when you use a credit card. We must train our friends to say Ava and all will be well. One other small thing I wanted to ask you: do you expect a wedding ring? I am much against this. It marks a woman as a man's property. I shall not give one to you unless you insist. I hope this does not disappoint you. You will be my wife just the same.

I think it is a very good idea for you to write to Kindleyside. This may encourage him to finish work. He has done all the big tasks and is, I suspect, now busy on some other job, leaving over the minor things that he dislikes. He has not yet put up the curtain rails or the towel rail in the bathroom. I will give him a push over the weekend. The carpets will go down on Monday. I have already moved all my books and shall move the clothes I don't need for immediate use. Then Kindleyside will come back in May to do the outside and the various other things that we have noticed by then. I think we now have plenty of cupboards, or rather as many as we can fit in. The little house is not as spacious as I have been used to, but we shall soon adapt. I am also fitting the lampshades. Later we can change any you don't like. There will be lots of other things to buy.

I enclose a little note to Pisti which I hope is in order. We can settle the date later. As to the rest of the family, Alison is to have her operation in May. We must hope for the best. Sophia is still waiting, by now a little impatiently. We shall see Mary Thompson when we go to Oxford at the beginning of May. I have also three days in Oxford during July, and we can have a double room in College if this amuses you. My next television series is fixed for June, two days a week, and you will be able to come to that too. I will give Shirley a ring one of these days and perhaps ask her to look at the house when the furniture is in.

Re appeasement and armament, did I show you the book by an American on the financial side of the problem, with Sir John Simon and the Treasury as the main obstacles? I have forgotten the name of the author and his book is now at Twisden Road, so I cannot look it up. However, it will be waiting for you if you have not got it already. It would be exciting to write on the beginnings of the Cold War, but of course the archives are only open to 1948 and perhaps you should wait a little longer. In any case you will be too busy housekeeping and buying things. If I were you I should keep clear of the Liddell-Hart papers, which are in great confusion. Here is a funny story. At the time of Suez, Eden consulted Hart about possible strategies. Hart outlined four courses, all of which he said would fail. Eden threw an inkpot at Hart, who rose up and crammed an upturned wastepaper basket on Eden's head. So the story is told. I am not sure I believe it.

Now I am off to Exeter. Hence the haste of this letter.

Lots of love,

Alan

14 March

Dearest Ava (if that is what you like),

Kindleyside has finished his work except for a little hut in the patio which he will make for us in the summer. The carpets are down. The central heating is working. I have moved the books and the suits I do not immediately want. The curtains are up, though I am not sure that all the runners are satisfactory. A little later I will ask Janet to stock the larder and buy household equipment. Would you like a trolley basket for the shopping? It is cumbersome, but you can carry more than if you used a hand basket. There are lots of mirrors and cupboards, but I am still worried whether we shall have space enough. Meanwhile Margaret is getting rid of all her accumulated stores of twenty-five years. It looks as though we shall get out all right on 31 March. I shall go with her for a week, during which time I shall also go to our own house most days. The telephone number is unchanged, 01–485–1507. You might find me in if you rang one day. In any case, I shall try to ring you some time after 3 April. If I have time I will ask Shirley over one day. Let me know soon precisely when you intend to come. If you arrive on a weekday, say 10 April, we can go straight home. At the weekend it will be more difficult. When does your entry permit expire?

My carbuncle subsided, but I have developed another which is very tiresome. It does not make me feel ill, but it is painful and I shall be glad to get rid of it. Otherwise you will have to dress it for me every day. I have made no plans for the summer and I don't suppose that you have. I wrote again to Hauser explaining that we could not go to Hamburg. I really have nothing to say on the subject he proposed.

Now for my life. I had a riotous time last night when I spoke to the students of University College on 'My Place in History'. I simply told them the more comic episodes in my public career. I can't say that I have ever taken myself seriously as a politician. I have been invited to Australia for five weeks, during which I should see everywhere and meet everybody. Nothing could be more horrible and of course I have refused. Last night Lord Annan, the Provost of University College, told me that he had pushed me hard for a high honour but that I had enemies in my profession. This did not surprise me. I am not at all sure that Annan pushed me as hard as he claimed. He is never one to be on the losing side. In introducing me, he said I was not interested in ideas. I replied that he had not mentioned my favourite brain-child, *The Troublemakers*, which is all about ideas. I don't suppose he has read it.

I am going to hear Charles Rosen, an American pianist, at the lunch-time concert. On Thursday I shall hear the La Salle Quartet play Webern and Schönberg, so I am having some relaxation. Crispin tells me the boys rioted the other day and the headmaster was so upset that he has gone to Accra to recover. Crispin is undisturbed. Daniel is attending a Young Socialist conference at Llandudno, so I do not expect to see him for some time. Do you intend to join the Labour Party? I am a member but never attend the meetings. Do not hope to turn me into a Communist, not even into a Titoite. Tito has just been here with universal acclaim.

Love to all,

Alan

20 March

Beloved Ava,

I have just received your letter of 12 March. It will almost be your last, as this is likely to be mine. It will be much better to talk than to write.

I have been very busy with the house in somewhat difficult circumstances. Margaret thrusts all sorts of things on me, many of which I don't want, and I cannot refuse for fear of a row. She has given me a great deal of linen and we may have too much with what you bought, but after all we shall use it in the end. There is more trouble with pictures, which often I do not like and which in any case I don't want to hang where she insists they must go. Fortunately, once you are here she will keep away, and does not need to know the changes we have made.

I have moved the linen to the airing cupboard and shall hang some of the pictures. Kindleyside has been rather elusive, agreeing to meet and then not turning up. I shall try again this afternoon. The remaining tasks are small – mainly adjusting cupboard doors. I took the vacuum cleaner to the passages and have made them reasonably clean. But I suppose they will be dirty again after the removal men have delivered the furniture on Wednesday. I am short of cutlery, but have eleven kitchen knives and most of the other cooking material we need. In the week before I move in, Janet will buy household stores for me so that we shall be able to start living straight away. I might even arrange for you to come to the house at once. We can go out for dinner the first night, or perhaps Janet will have us. She is very eager and sympathetic, confident that now she can carry Giles along with her. As she said to me yesterday, Giles is very hard underneath and will not respond to his mother's emotional blackmail. Sebastian is a different proposition, much more soft-hearted. My children must decide for themselves, but I shall not be prepared to see them unless you are welcome as well.

I went to a grand dinner at Magdalen, rather boring and very tiring. Now I am trying to have thoughts for the OUP lunch. Michael will be there and will be delighted at my irresponsible remarks if I make any. I might be serious for once, but this is unlikely.

My second carbuncle is improving rapidly. Though it is uncomfortable, it has never made me feel ill and I suppose I have got off lightly. Do not forget your papers which will turn you into a British citizen. You will have to make a declaration of allegiance, I suppose to the Queen. This is a harmless formality. I shall certainly arrange for us to go to Magdalen together. Double room, but not I fear double bed. We can try to fit into one. Many delightful things lie ahead. No sign of Daniel.

Love to all,

Alan

1978

The Mill
Yarmouth
Isle of Wight

3 August

Lovey Mine, Brightest Star in the Sky,

You do not need to feel lonely even though Pisti has gone and Ferencz not yet come, because I think of you all the time. You are with me in spirit when I go out for a walk or when I lie on the beach. It is a nuisance to have to talk to others because I want to think about you. I was reflecting that for thirty years or more I have had no companion, except of course my children who though satisfactory are not the same thing. It is quite strange to realize that from now on I have someone who goes with me on every sort of expedition from fell-climbing to exhibitions. With all the children more or less grown-up, I was desperately lost and lonely until you appeared.

I had a tiresome journey thanks to an incident, as it was called, on the Southampton line which delayed some trains and caused the cancellation of others. However, I was back at The Mill by six o'clock. Today has been wild and windy, but with sun again and no rain. Too windy to swim or sunbathe, so I went for a long walk alone on the Downs. A woman rang up from the German service of the BBC announcing that they were planning a series of profiles – as if that were a new idea! – and wanted to deal with me. I said I could do it, but only after 17 August. Such a trivial project is not worth a special trip. I also expressed a doubt whether I could do it in German. The prospect of a larger fee might have produced a more cooperative response, but I dislike this personal chitter-chat.

I have made some plans for the future. I shall abandon *English History in the Twentieth Century*, at any rate for the time being, though I will show the first chapter to you just to convince you that it is no good. I will attempt to rewrite chapter XI of my autobiography, because when that unpleasant story is over the rest is interesting and worth writing about. The end will have to be different. At present it ends by saying that I have had a frustrated and unhappy life. Now I shall have to end that everything has come right, so much so that I have almost forgotten that I was ever unhappy. It is hard to realize that our happiness will not last as long as my period of unhappiness did. Somehow it does not matter. My other resolution is that I shall go to Fleet Street on Tuesdays, when I go to the lunch-time concerts, and Thursdays, when I am available to write for the *Sunday Express*. The other days I shall have to find something else to do. In the early autumn we must go out for the day every Monday and every Wednesday, particularly as country houses on show are usually open only on Wednesdays. In this way you will see all the famous sights, though you will have to drive further and further in order to reach them.

I hope you manage to see some of your stepsons. Crispin should be in touch with you some time. Giles will be back again most of next week, and Sebastian also. I have an impression that Amelia and Bob will be back in Kentish Town early next week. I also have an idea that I will come back sooner or later, in fact on 17 August. I wish it would hurry up.

Much greater love than I used to send you in Hungary because I love you more and more. Very strange.

Alan
x x
xxxxx
x

Yarmouth Mill

10 August

Darling,

I am very distressed. I have received no letter from you, and get no answer when I telephone which I do two or three times a day. I have awful imaginings. Perhaps you are ill. Perhaps you are angry with me for leaving you alone. Perhaps – a more likely cause – the telephone is out of order. And of course the postal service has interminable delays, especially at this time of year. Here the London post does not come until midday, so I am restless and unable to work until it does and then there is no time left. So I must confess that chapter XI of my autobiography has hardly moved at all. I despair with what I have written and, like the future reader of it, find it an uninteresting story. You will have to give me some encouragement when I get back.

The weather has been very bad. Some days it rains all the time. Some days it is fine enough for me to get out on a walk and then, as on Tuesday, I am caught by a heavy shower which soaks all my clothes. Today there was sun. I went to the beach, whereupon it grew cold and rain began to fall. I pulled on my clothes and prepared to leave, only for the sun to come out again. I returned to the beach, waiting for a cloudless sky, and none came. So after lying in my clothes I stripped and plunged briefly into the sea which was very cold. For this and many other reasons I shall be glad when this last week is over. It has been a bitter experience, really too great a price for Margaret to exact. I fear you will get to hate the name of Yarmouth.

Daniel rang to say he is coming on Saturday. As his friend Michael Barnes cannot come too, I am apprehensive that Daniel will be bored. However, it is easy for him to return to London. I hope you get my note about future commitments. I shall go on trying to gèt a response from the telephone over the weekend. I have again missed the evening post and this letter will not start its journey until Friday morning. When you get this letter it will soon be time for our reunion. I'll arrive soon after tea.

      Love,
      Alan

Twisden Road
London NW5

10 December

My Lovey, my Darling,
  This is only Sunday morning and yet you seem to have been away for months. I miss you every moment. It is agony to be in this house without you, yet still more agonizing to be away from it. I wander from room to room looking for you. Believe that I shall love you for ever and ever, that the last eight months have been the happiest in my life and that our happiness will go on increasing as the years go by. I shan't write any more letters saying how miserable I am and how I miss you. But you know what I shall be feeling.
  I was alarmed to hear from Pisti that your plane had not even started. I realize how maddening it is for you that you could not communicate with me. However, in the end I got your message through Janet, though it did not reach me until this morning and by now, I hope, you are on your way. I have been very industrious. I have written a long review about Salisbury. I have moved all the books into the kitchen. I

did the full round of the Heath in beautiful weather. Today is less cheerful, but it is something to be sitting happily at my desk and thinking about you. At the moment there are no problems except that it is tedious for me to be so long with Margaret. Fortunately I was tired last night and went to bed early. I expect there will be an upheaval when the men lay the carpets, and whatever I tell them they are sure to get some things wrong. You will receive a full account. I'll leave further news until the post comes in tomorrow.

Monday: Nothing interesting in the post except a petition to sign in favour of the Authorized Version of the Bible. This I have signed with great pleasure. There are two things I want to say and ought to have said before. I realize and appreciate the difficulties you have in living in a foreign land and in having to use a foreign language all the time. You have been marvellous in overcoming these difficulties, and I ought to have given you greater praise. I also realize how tiresome it is for you that I am still burdened with Margaret. But the situation is inevitable. Incidentally, she was so bright when I arrived that I decided we were right to think her illness psychosomatic. However, she is feeling wretched again today so perhaps her maladies are real after all.

The other thing is that I wish you would rely on me more for practical advice. For instance, you could have paid for your excess luggage with a cheque backed by a cheque card. I also think that I could have advised you where to find a less resplendent mah-jongg set. I doubt whether your boys will ever master the game, and they will need a couple of friends to make up a four. However, the game may become all the rage in Budapest. Remember to try out all your ideas on me. I exist to make life easier and more enjoyable for you. Never fear that I shall disapprove of your ideas even if I laugh at them. After all, we live together to have lots of laughter even if we sometimes find other pleasures.

I shall be very anxious until I have heard your news about Ferencz. Give him my best wishes for a speedy recovery. Mary Thompson telephoned me to say how she appreciated our welcome to her offspring. She now has your address and will write appropriate words for Christmas. Tomorrow I shall go to the Beefsteak Club, which will be a merciful release. I shall not write again for a few days unless there is something I want to tell you. Of course I want to tell you of my love every day, but I expect you know about it already. Have a good time and come back to me as soon as you can.

Everlasting Love,

Alan xxxx
x

1978

Twisden Road
London NW5

14 December

Lovey Mine,

Here I am on Thursday with nearly a week over. Yet another three weeks seems like a century. I really do not think of anything or anybody except you, and what we shall do together when you are back. I have been up here every day, enjoying a solitary lunch and again thinking of how different they will be in three weeks' time. Your letters are piling up and I have stacked them in your room upstairs, not opening any of them. Tell me if I should look at them. I am sure they will keep and it is always nice to open one's own letters. There was a Christmas card from someone in Germany whose name I could not read.

Now, what have I done? I wrote a review of the Salisbury book on Tuesday and took it down to the *Observer*. It was strange to walk round the little City streets I used to haunt. It is much better up here. The Joplin concert was delightful but curious. Miss Davidov played Joplin as though she were playing Mozart on a harpsichord. She also gave little talks on Joplin between each piece. The Purcell Room was full of young people. Last night I went to the National Film Theatre and saw another Ben Travers piece with the great original masters Tom Walls and Ralph Lynn. It was nostalgic, though I had never seen it before. There was also a W. C. Fields short in which he used his classic expletive, 'Godfrey Daniels'. This evening I go to another Webern-Schubert concert. Margaret is now suffering from a bilious attack so severe that she cannot keep any food down. It is remarkable how she survives all these troubles.

I went to Modell, who almost complained that I was so fit. He gave me more ointments of many kinds but did not take my back seriously, merely remarking that it was one of those things. He sang your praises, saying what a delightful person you were. In this he is correct. He recommends that you should have an anti-influenza injection. He says that this only gives a 60% immunity, but even so it is useful for someone as inclined to pneumonia as you are. Perhaps you can get it done in Hungary. Otherwise, arrange it when you come home.

I shall be very glad to get more news of Ferencz. Perhaps you will ring me later today. If not, keep on trying round about lunch-time when I am usually here. But I also have concerns that take me down to London, and then I do not get here in time for lunch. I have read a short life of Balzac that did not tell me much, have started another Balzac novel and am pushing my way through the new book on Edward VII. It is full of mistakes, including William I described as Emperor of Germany and Peninsular used as a noun. As he is a history master at Eton, I shall abuse him for these mistakes.

Now I am off with the keys to the carpet people. I fear there will be turmoils tomorrow, and much trouble thereafter while I am getting the sitting room back to rights. I can't ask Pat to paint the kitchen until I have got the books back in here. But it will be something to do during Christmas week. The house is very warm and cosy. It only misses a human being in it.

I'll write again early next week, probably on Tuesday when I shall have more to report. There has been much rain and now it is cold. Perhaps things are better with you. Regards to both my stepsons and good wishes for their recovery.

All my love,

Alan

Twisden Road
London NW5

18 December

Lovey Mine,

Guess where I am typing this: in your little room upstairs. I have moved my typewriter there with some difficulty, and have got a flex long enough to reach the electric socket. The reason, as you no doubt realize, is that the carpet is being laid. On Friday only one man came and said he could not move the furniture all by himself. He had to send for another man, who was quite inexperienced. I left them to it. Of course they did not finish. By Friday evening the room was in chaos. Now, Monday morning, there is again only one man and much moving to do when he has finished with the carpet. I shall have to help him to move the safe. There is also the problem of where the rugs go. I cannot remember. I shall do my best and we can rearrange them when you get back. If necessary we can get Pat to help us. There has also been the problem of the gas-fire. The man laid the carpet right up to the fire. I told him, I hope rightly, that the hearthstone must be left open, otherwise there would be a fire risk. Meanwhile, he has spoilt the hearthstone by laying the carpet over it. I hope he will finish today. The present situation makes it impossible for me to do any proper work or to get at my things. The radio seems to be working all right. I am not so sure about the TV and, as I cannot remember where we bought it, I cannot get a man to attend to it. However, it can wait until you get back.

My situation is miserable. I am wretched without you and think about you all the time. To make things worse, I get on very badly with Margaret. Of course I sympathize with her illness and try to make life easier for her. But however ill she is, she persists in arranging things for me that I don't want to do. She has now committed me to an excursion to the Geffrye Museum with the more advanced grandchildren. The Museum will be swarming with children and the traffic will be building up for Christmas. The only hope for me is that my car may be taken to Zenith motors to have its door repaired. Christmas also is turning out badly.

Other news. I heard from David Kemp that, owing to his gastro-enteritis, the Liverpool programme has been cut down and will not have an historical introduction. I am not sorry. I have heard nothing from Eddie. I have agreed to address the annual meeting of the Pedestrians Association on 14 June, a rather silly commitment. I have also noticed that I have a commitment to some Americans early in June, so if we go to Coniston we must go for the last week of May. Yesterday Giles took me for a long walk, starting from his house and going all round the Heath. It was a lovely sunny day, rather cold but with no wind, so we could even sit in the sun for a little.

The posts are so bad now that it is a waste of time writing again before Christmas. So I shall not write until 26 or 27 December. Probably you will not receive any letter until after the New Year. But one will arrive sooner or later.

I don't need to send you my love. You have it all already. I worry a good deal about Ferencz. Let me have news of him.

Alan
x x x

Twisden Road
London NW5

21 December

Beloved of my Heart,

    Every day I miss you more. Every day I appreciate just how much you have sacrificed for me. I gave up nothing. For me your coming was pure gain. But you had to leave your children and come to live in a strange land. I see that in the packet I have not yet opened you describe me as the dearest man in the world. I can say more: for me there is not another woman in the world. There are female creatures I have to be responsible for, but they do not exist as women. Margaret is still very ill, hardly able to digest anything. I cannot believe that she can remain in this state. Despite her great toughness she must weaken eventually. Or perhaps it is true that old people need very little food and eat only from habit. At any rate she has been unable to leave the house, so I have not been able to take her to any concerts or on little excursions. It is a boring life, tolerable if not happy only when I am able to be here in Twisden Road.

    I have had a disturbed time. When I went out to post your letter the other day, I left my keys on the desk and locked myself out. I had to get a locksmith and it took four hours to break in. Evidently we are very secure. I got very cold and it cost me £30. You must throw away your present Yale key as soon as you get back. I have a plentiful supply of new ones. The carpet man took off the cupboard door in the sitting room and the carpenter has not yet arrived to shave it. So the sitting room is not in a presentable state. But at any rate it is warm with the gas-fire on.

    Here is some news which will make you laugh. The Administrator of the Polytechnic wrote that my employment there would require me to give 2 lectures or seminars a week for ten weeks each term. But I have only given four lectures this term and did not intend to give more next. So I replied that evidently there had been a misunderstanding, and that we had better forget about the whole thing. I don't mind having given the lectures for nothing, and am glad I shall give no more. I must look forward to better things with Norwich next year. I got £20 out of Thames for the damage they caused. The only thing that keeps me busy is a flow of books from Terry, but of course he had forgotten about the one I most wanted, Peter Clarke on the pre-war Liberals. No doubt it will turn up in time. The *Observer* is now coming out with three sections, just like the *Sunday Times* but on the whole better.

    I took my grandchildren to 'Frozen Tombs' at the British Museum.

Surprisingly they were interested in what they saw, though it meant nothing to them that the exhibits had been made three thousand years ago. The young have no sense of time. No news yet from Crispin or Daniel, but I live in hope they will appear some time.

I have not yet had any letter from you. Maybe you have not received mine. I am anxious for news about Ferencz, and greatly hope that things are going better with him. I spoke to Pisti the other day, but would have preferred to speak to you. I desperately want you back, although I am sure you are having a good time. It will be wonderful to see you again, to feel you, just to be with you. What a miracle our love has been and still is.

All my love now and always,

Alan

Twisden Road
London NW5

26 December

My Dearest Love,
Today is only Tuesday and there will be no collection of letters. But there will presumably be one tomorrow morning, so it should start my letter on its way then. I miss you very much. My sadness is far worse than when we used to part after a couple of weeks together. We were happy in Paris or Split, but I think we are far, far happier in our little house. I never imagined such bliss was possible in life. Now my only happy moments are when I am sitting here alone, but at least away from other people. The house is in good order, except that I cannot remember how the rugs should be put down and have left them for your return. Pat Denny has done a fine job on the kitchen, which is now dazzlingly white everywhere. My only bad news is that the double windows will not be fitted until the second half of January. They have already been very dilatory over this. At present, however, the weather is mild and the house deliciously warm.

I am still uncertain about your return. Come back on 7 January if you possibly can. I am here nearly every day at lunch-time and I shall try on my side to telephone you. Between us we ought to make contact somehow. If you are out, leave a message with Pisti as to when you return. I have had from you only a card dated 14 December, so there may be more definite news coming along in the post after Christmas.

Christmas Day was tiresome. There were twenty people to dinner at Amelia's – all my offspring, together with four Howards and Pat Denny. I observe that Rob Howard has taken over my place as head of the family. At any rate he carved the turkey, which I have done every year since my father died. I wish Giles had been there. Then, after a symbolic slice or two, I could have handed the job over to him. As it was, I had no choice. Rob Howard simply grasped carving knife and fork and handed out the portions. Sophia meanwhile told people where to sit. Bob Doyle was the only person who asked after you, which I thought was very kind of him. Of course Mary Taylor asks after you every day, but I take that for granted. Giles and Janet have gone to Brede, leaving warm messages for you. For the most part those present did not take any notice of me at all.

I am totally cut of from Crispin and Daniel. I saw Crispin last Friday, but only because Giles told me that he would call to see Alison. Daniel has given no sign of life and I am left with conjectures. Maybe he is staying in Leeds, and maybe Crispin is chasing some girl which naturally he would not want to confess. If you had been here, they would have been round at once. I guess they are fonder of you than of me, and quite right too. I share their taste.

Nothing interesting has happened. The Heath has been good for walking and was full of people even on Christmas afternoon when they ought to have been at home, listening to the Queen's Speech. There was a strike of tank drivers just before Christmas and so a shortage of petrol. I hope to replenish my supply in a day or two. *The Times* is still at a deadlock. As a result the *Observer* has sold over a million copies for the first time in its existence. No doubt it will lose all this if the *Sunday Times* ever comes back.

I think all international telephone lines are closed yesterday and today, but shall try tomorrow. End of story. Which reminds me that I have read two more Balzac novels. They are all about money.

Lots of impatient love,

Alan

xxxx

1979

The Mill
Yarmouth, IOW.

1 August 1979

My Love,

    I miss you very much. Indeed I do not understand how we ever managed to live apart. Every day without you is empty. So never worry. Most of my news is gloomy. Admittedly we drove down easily – just over two and a half hours, even though I never went faster than sixty mph. The Mill overcrowded as usual. The Sebastian Taylors surprisingly have no extras. The Doyles, however, have added Bob's daughter Tabitha and a Spanish girl of eighteen who cannot speak a word of any language other than her own. Also, briefly, an actress friend of Amelia's and two offspring. However, I retired to my room and read Len Deighton's book. It is strange. He is crazy on war machines just as someone else might be crazy on abbeys (that's me) or steam-engines. This greatly impresses me. I wonder whether it would impress an expert. The political background not very good, the technical very efficient. But the French campaign of 1940 won't make a book. For all practical purposes it lasted a single day: 13 to 14 May. After that it was simply a question of driving to the coast. However, it will make a book. I also told Terry I would do Thomas Pakenham's book on the Boer War.

    Yesterday was miserably cold. I worked in my anorak. In the afternoon I went for a walk on my own. Inland, there was less wind and even some sun. My skin is worse again, or perhaps I am more impatient. When I get back I must see a specialist, but that won't be until the middle of September and this provokes a gloomy vision of the next six weeks. Today is milder, and after a bright start is I think going to be wetter. However, three days are over. Soon there will be only a week to go. I see nothing of the other families except for occasional grumbles from Mary. I have not entered the sitting room and I don't suppose I shall.

    I have been thinking of my projected *Essays*. It will be useful if you look over the four old collections and the re-collections about Europe and England. This will give you some idea what we can't use. For instance Carlyle and Macaulay are out, so is Cobbett. I had an idea of grouping all the Socialists together and then remembered that I had done Keir Hardie already. Still we have Cole, Laski (too flattering, I think), Shaw, Wells. In the same section I can do other essays on Socialism, such as party pamphlets. On a brief survey it seemed I had not done the General Strike in book form. I favour the reminiscences I wrote for the *New Statesman* to the talk on 'The Twenties'. It will all give us some occupation during the winter evenings.

I am expecting Karen Brown and the producer tomorrow. I know exactly how they feel – that they would like a detailed programme settled in advance. Whereas I don't see how it can be done until we are on the spot.

I was glad to hear Pisti has had his tooth out and hope his fever has subsided. Avoid antibiotics. They are said to have after-effects. Get him well in time to do some sightseeing.

Margaret spent the entire day yesterday doing housework and never got dressed. She ate a boiled egg and a few potatoes for lunch, otherwise nothing. Very strange, I don't understand how she keeps going. I wish I had seen the last of her. It is not only that I want to be with you. I also want strongly not to be with her. This may be unkind, but so it is.

And here is a little bit of love for you, my beloved.

Alan
xxx

Yarmouth Mill

8 August

Dearest Love,
Your letter of 6 August came this morning with all its news and good cheer. As to our Granada plans, these had nothing to do with Karen Brown or anyone else. We made them and I think you may have forgotten the reason. You rightly said that you wanted to go back on Monday, 20 August, so as to be with Pisti before he left. Then it is not worth coming up for three days. Instead I shall come back on the evening of Friday, 24, and be with you over the weekend. On the Monday I shall go north again, and return on the Thursday. These arrangements were agreed by you and me before I left, and I have changed nothing with them. If you decided not to return for Pisti's departure, of course I should be pleased. But there will be difficulties

about hotel rooms, so we had better leave things as they are. The whole expedition is a purgatory to me and I am dreading it. I am not well. I have little idea what to say. And every town, especially Blackpool, will be swarming with people. After all I am an historian, not a travel agent. I have a ghastly feeling that I shall break down. There is one consolation. If I get through with the Granada show, I can postpone any BBC lectures until I am completely well, and that is going to take a long time. And here is a consolation for you. If the weather remains good, I thought we might go to the Yorkshire moors for a week towards the end of September. But don't be sure about it. The North London Polytechnic may make me prisoner.

Other news. I have told Jimmy Burns I will talk to the Beesly Society some time, but not until after I have talked to our seminar. I have written a long review of Thomas Pakenham's book on the Boer War and sent it off. The post from here is so bad that I don't know when the *Observer* will receive it. Also, I don't know how I shall get the copy of *How Wars Begin* back to Jenny Nicholson. She ought to have sent a stamped addressed envelope for its return. As it is, she will have to wait. The quote about the Establishment that you like comes from an essay on Cobbett which I have already published. But I am sure there are many others when I have time to go over them. I wonder whether I should let Harvester have them or stick to Hamish Hamilton. Probably I shall let David Higham* decide.

I have had some pretty grim weather. Two bathes so far, and I am sure they did me good. I have also been on one good walk, but otherwise it has rained and I have had only brief strolls. Meanwhile my scalp is worse than ever and my rash, having moved from my legs, has settled round my middle. The house is very cold and I cannot find a multiple plug, so I cannot have an electric fire when I am using my typewriter. Such are the penalties of modern inventions. There are too many people in the house, and I keep away from them in my cold room. Margaret in my opinion is not fit to be here, and it is a nuisance to look after her. How glad I shall be when all this is over.

Very good to hear from Crispin. Dilkes writes that Daniel can take his exam again if he can produce a medical certificate. This should be easy if he bestirs himself. If he is fooling about on an oil-rig, he may delay things too long. What a worry he is. All the same, I wish I had seen him.

I shan't write again – post too slow. I shall be back next Monday

---

* Alan's literary agent.

afternoon and then a rush to get off on Tuesday. I long to see you and miss you very much. Love to Pisti.

All my love,

Alan

Twisden Road
London NW5

24 November

My Precious Love,

I propose to write an account each day of what I have been doing. In the end there will be a letter, and with nothing left out. *Saturday*: not much of a day, mostly taken up with going to Heathrow and back again. After repeated attempts, I have managed to clean the windscreen from the anti-freeze liquid which is almost more trouble than the frost itself. Empty house, ghostlike and very agreeable. I walk round the deserted rooms occasionally to bid the ghosts of memory welcome. I wish I were staying here all the time instead of dragging to a strange house. I have finished the index. Now I face the problem how shall I get it to Hamish Hamilton. I cannot face the tedious journey to Long Acre, and HH are too mean to send a messenger or a taxi. The problem will no doubt solve itself next week. After lunch I went round to see Margaret and to do her shopping. She was in a very bad way, haggard, with pain in her bowels, and almost incoherent in her speech. I cannot believe she will last long, though she has great determination. I left her in bed and came home. I have explored the resources of the refrigerator and discovered the quantities of food you have left. I shall have a hard task to eat it all before you return. In another half hour I shall go for a drink with Sebastian, and then enjoy a lavish meal.

Sunday: A night alone in an empty bed. It was awful. I had no idea it would be so desolate. Last year when you went back for Christmas I noticed it less. I suppose then I had not got used to you. Now I depend on you for every minute of my life. The prospect of five weeks alone seems endless. However, no more laments. I ate some of the smoked salmon and some of the brisket. But there is plenty more. Then I played *Die Kunst der Fuge*, given on the organ. It was magical. I told Sebastian not to worry about the money I had lent him. He said his bank manager is raising difficulties. Either the money is a loan, in which case Sebastian must pay interest on it, or it is a gift, in which case I must pay capital gifts tax. Silly. I answered that the loan came out of income, not out of capital, so neither of us should pay anything. We shall see. Capitalism has its complications. Nothing much in the *Observer*. Book reviews boring. Blunt says his confession was incomplete and that he was still a Soviet agent in 1955. He must enjoy the limelight. He also proposes to resign from his other appointments. I wonder whether he will resign from the British Academy. It would give me an excuse for resigning from it also. There is to be a play on the BBC about Suez, with Eden as its hero. We shall be having one on Blunt next.

Your bag has just arrived. Evidently we are to have a Sunday post, at any rate a parcel post, from now until Christmas. The passport is missing. So is the cigarette lighter. Otherwise there seems to be everything: all your various membership cards, your cheque book and cheque card, your notebook, the guide to Amsterdam, even the hotel key. I have not attempted to sort the things out, merely put them on your desk for you to look through. I will write to the insurance company, and also to Hotel King. A curious end to an unpleasant story.

Daniel came round and we went for a walk. He could only manage as far as the foot of Parliament Hill. He is on drugs and he smokes a lot so this is, I suppose, not surprising. He is full of ambitions towards the future and then has flashes of sense. Also, as he now remarks, he has the support of his religious convictions behind him. I never thought I should have a Christian offspring. Perhaps he will come to his senses.

New television possibility: contributions to a Granada film being made for the 150th anniversary of the opening of the Liverpool to Manchester Railway. The producer who rang me up told me that the Liverpool Road station has been saved.

I have eaten an enormous dinner of brisket and pears. You have left me enough food almost to last for the five weeks you are away. Next year, if there is a next year, I shall not go to Margaret for my meals at all. Not that she provides me with meals even now. I buy my own food and she merely tells me how to cook it. By next year it will all be too much for her. I shall come back next weekend to eat the chops.

That's all for now,

Alan
xxx

Twisden Road
London NW5

27 November

My Dearly Beloved,
    Here I am now at Tuesday. Monday evening was a miserable time. I hated not being in my own bed. Margaret is wretchedly ill and it can't be pyschosomatic this time when she has to be in her house. Indeed she told me how she had been looking forward to it, and that now she could not enjoy it. I wish so much that you could help me to cheer her up without upsetting you. Of course you come first and I shan't do anything that doesn't work for you.
    Today I have done some things that I hope you will think profitable. I have taken your typewriter to Trills. I have also bought two cotton twill shirts and two briefs at Marks and Spencers. I have pushed on with the essays, and have begun writing round for permissions to publish. Pat was here yesterday evening and put the locks on the windows. But the bolt will not fit the door and we shall have to fit a key and lock instead. I'll get him to fix this before you return. You have certainly left me plenty to eat, and I don't know when I shall be able to eat it. Here is a complaint. You have turned the refrigerator too high and it is freezing solid food outside the deep-freeze. So I have turned the control from MAX to 5 and will see what will happen. I am in two minds whether to have the air-lock done on the boiler. I suppose we shall need it in the summer, but clearly all is working well as long as the heating is on. Perhaps I shall leave it until the milder weather next year.
    In a little while I shall set off for Ealing. There is a registered letter waiting for me at the Post Office which I shall collect on my way. I wonder what it can be. Kathy and her crew are coming tomorrow, so I may not have any time to write then, and Thursday of course will be chaos. But I shall hammer out a few sentences. I think of you all the time.
    Wednesday: Ealing was a very curious experience. I had an easy journey and a seat all the way despite the rush hour. I was met by the chairman, a strange gnome-like figure, whose possessions did not include a motor car. He walked me for a mile or so and then left me with two elderly ladies straight out of Jane Austen. One half-glass of sherry. Then I had tap-water with my dinner. One of the elderly ladies had broken her leg. Despite this she drove us to the meeting in a tiny car, disregarding all signs and warnings on the ground that she was a disabled driver. Very enjoyable meeting, I gave them a riotous account

1979

of what I tried to do as an historian. Most of the audience were over sixty and enjoyed my every word. The few members of the younger generation were rather shocked. Walk back to the Underground station, unfortunately accompanied. As it was, I had to wait for a drink until I got back to Camden Town some time after ten. I thought it too far to walk to the Spread Eagle.

 This morning I had my last seminar. It is a bad form of instruction. The young sit silent and I talk for an hour and a half. Surely it would be better simply to call it a lecture. However, it is all over now for this term. Later I had Kathy and her television crew. I recorded two fourteen-minute disquisitions on pre-war British policy, with lots of bright new ideas. Much confusion but no damage done. I am taking Len to the Beefsteak and then coming home for the night so as to welcome the gas men. I shall also spend Saturday night here in order to be available for Daniel. When I consider Margaret's state of health, I anticipate that the Christmas arrangements will break down altogether and that I shall be back here on my own with Margaret in hospital. But as you know she has a gift for recovery, though each time she sinks a bit lower and does not pull up so much. Pat has got a real job as a company secretary. I fear he will not be willing to put a lock on the door or to repair the fence, but we shall see.

 Lucia* wrote at last. She is much more cheerful. Alessandro has moved out of the family home and is living in his own flat taking a methadone maintenance programme, whatever that may mean. He has also taken his degree in psychology. Altogether a characteristic Lucia affair. I'll arrange for the money from Longanesi to be sent to here. No other problem that I can think of, except that I miss you. You told me you would be away five weeks and I have just realized that it will be eight weeks. Alas, alas.

XxXxXxXXxxXXXxxxXXXXxxxxXXXxxxXXxxXXxxXx
Alan

* Italian translator of *Origins of the Second World War*, also a friend of Alan's.

Twisden Road
London NW5

30 November

Dearest Heart,
    Yes, it's true. What with one thing and another, I missed Thursday. Now it is Friday. I don't know what happened – first a push to get on with my essays, and then a long and very boring book about Roosevelt's foreign policy from the *Observer*. It says what we know already – that Roosevelt took care never to get ahead of public opinion, perhaps shared the public opinion. For instance, was he deliberately working for war all along? Or did he, like so many Americans, hope that the Germans could be defeated without America actually getting in? We shall never know the answer for sure.

    The main event of Thursday was the coming of the gas man, the fitter who came in the first place. He found a much easier solution than he had imagined, merely to turn the pipe the other way round. Now our troubles will be over for good. All that remains is for Pat to put a lock on the kitchen door and we never need worry again. Today I have finished revising and preparing the essays. I must re-read them, write a preface and consider whether there are any more I can put in – or leave out. I have decided on *More Essays and Reviews*, an echo of a famous collection of theological essays published in 1860, but I think I can make the distinction between it and mine clear. I am also writing round for permission, some of it not easy. For instance, The Twentieth Century which published THE THING is dead. I have written to Philip Toynbee for advice. The *Saturday Review of Literature* is also, I think, dead, but I know no answer to that. Maybe Bob Silvers will know. I consulted Bruce Hunter of David Higham whether to offer the essays to Harvester or to Hamish Hamilton, and he said emphatically Hamish Hamilton. I am much relieved. It is so much easier to work with people one knows well. But of course Hamish Hamilton may not want them.

    I cannot describe how hard life is at Rochester Road. Margaret eats nothing. She lies in bed most of the day when she is not writing letters or cooking. She is unwittingly very short-tempered. She seems to get deafer all the time. After dinner she sits up 'to enjoy my company' and of course falls asleep. I feel very sorry for her, but it is not pleasant for me. I shall be glad to spend the night here and wish I could spend every night here.

    Saturday. Here I am for the best day of the week. I have just spoken to Ferencz and wish I could have spoken to you. But you always seem to be out. However shall I get through the next five weeks, particularly when there will be nothing to do over Christmas? This is a dreadful existence. However, there are some consolations. My skin is much better and I have decided to cancel my appointment at St George's on Tuesday. I can renew my visit later if need be. I can see that soon I shall have to start again on my autobiography for want of anything better to do. No post has come for you, and not even any telephone calls. Very little of interest for me except for a few cheques from the BBC.

I have just been out to East Finchley to see the Czech film about *The Crazy Movie Makers*. Very slow and very affected in a charming way, but rather pointless. Nothing to compare with his earlier film *Closely Observed Trains*. It would be worth your while visiting Bratislava just to see it. I walked all the way from here to East Finchley, quite interesting.

I don't think I told you about my evening at the Beefsteak with Len. He was as delightful as ever and enjoyed the experience. For me it was as bad as ever, and entirely convinced me that I should not go any more. I'd sooner go on my own to Edward's Bistro or Nontas, as I expect I shall have to do when Margaret is exhausted. I have just received a *Concise Oxford Dictionary* from Denniston of the Clarendon Press, and a *Boswell* from Roland Batty of Foyles, so all my problems are over. Now I'm going to the Dartmouth Arms and then shall prepare my meal – all cold except for the sprouts. After that a solitary bed but rich with memories of you, even of the floods. I love you.

Alan

Twisden Road
London NW5

3 December

My Far Away Lover,
Will you ever come back? I had a dreadful feeling when I spoke to you on Saturday that you were enjoying yourself much more than you do in England, and that perhaps you would decide to stop in Budapest. I fear I give you a dull life. However, don't forget me altogether. Oh, I do so wish you were here. The month of December will never come to an end. However, here is my latest news, such as it is.

Sunday: a dull day. Daniel did not turn up. Instead he telephoned from Militant that he had recovered £1,000 from them and that they would repay the rest if he needed it. Quite a triumph. He came round this morning and we went for a walk before he went back to Friern Barnet. His latest enthusiasm is as you know for religion, and now he wants to be baptized. The last member of the family to have this craze was Sebastian as a chorister. I said: 'Do as you like, but I won't pay the fee,' whereupon Sebastian dropped the idea. Daniel however has discovered that baptism is free, so he may go through with it. Terrible to have a child of mine anointed with holy water.

Big news today if it comes off. Next May is the 150th anniversary of the first railway in the world: the Liverpool to Manchester railway, propelled by the Rocket. Granada want a programme on it. I hesitated, not really knowing enough about it. However, I have been lent a book about it and will decide after reading it. If I can do it we will go to Manchester before Easter, preferably to the same hotel (can you remember its name?) and do the whole show in three or four days. That will leave us free to go to Rome after Easter. It will be something to look forward to. The Liverpool Road station is in process of being lavishly restored, and we can start the programme from there. Everything else is a blank to me.

I have cancelled my appointment at St George's tomorrow, I hope wisely. BBC Radio has just rung me to take part in a programme on Bertrand Russell, whom I don't think I admire all that much. The producer started to give me instructions concerning broadcasting over the phone. I said – 'I have broadcast before.' He was most surprised. Hotel King has sent 15 Gulden in refund of the deposit on the key. No word from the insurance company yet.

Tuesday: A very bad event. One of my teeth has broken off, leaving only a root. I don't know whether anything can be constructed on it, and must wait until 17 December to find out. Fortunately there is not a twinge of pain. I have finished a very long and very boring book on Roosevelt's foreign policy, and I suppose I must review it. However, I have plenty of time now that I have finished preparing the essays. I fear that we shall have to get the gas men again when you return. Both heat and water are getting far too hot. Maybe the very warm weather is the cause – even warmer than yours in Budapest. This morning I received your postcard written on the plane. A delightful surprise. And I have just done the round of the Heath in brilliant sunshine. This does me good. Tomorrow will be rather rushed, with a man from Thames in the morning and the seminar in the afternoon. So maybe I'll not finish this letter until Thursday.

Thursday: A brief summary of our commitments. Some time in April we will go to Manchester for the programme on the Railway. Next, David Kemp wants to get moving on the resorts. So I have agreed to a fortnight fairly early in June, nothing in July and a further week early in August. I hope this is all right. I can go to Yarmouth in July if you would like to go to Hungary for a fortnight. But keep the Granada dates for June and August clear. I hope I am not rushing you. The seminar by David Butler went very well: not a big attendance, but a discussion so prolonged that I had to close it just before seven. I wish you had been there. I miss you so much and will write again soon. Saturday will soon be here, when I can spend a night in our own bed.

Many kisses,
    Love, my Darling,

            Alan

Twisden Road
London NW5

7 December

Dear Mrs Taylor,
    What a wonderful thing that you are my wife and will go on being my wife for many years. In the eighteenth century a wife addressed her husband as Mr Taylor. I think that now I should address you as Mrs Taylor, even when we are in bed. Oh, I wish we were.
    Friday: I have finished Lord Raingo. The picture of Lloyd George and his War Cabinet is both entertaining and true to life. Lord Raingo is not Lord Rhondda or any other minister. He is Arnold Bennett, imagining what it would have been like if he had been a millionaire instead of a novelist, and Minister of Information instead of Deputy Director. Even so, the rise of Raingo to popularity is unconvincing. So are wife and mistress. If I had been either, I should have been greatly alarmed that both of them die in the book. Evidently Bennett wanted to get rid of them. However, he was the one who died. His last words to his mistress were 'It's all gone wrong, my girl.' The death is taken straight from *Clayhanger*, and is not as good.
    Review of *Roosevelt and Foreign Policy* written. Yet another book by Kenneth Morgan on Lloyd George, this time on the Coalition, I should have thought a dead subject. Ford Lectures by Leland Lyons on 'Culture

and Anarchy in Ireland', rather highbrow for me. Mary's ground-floor room is finished and the icons returned. I am going out to dinner with them tomorrow night. *TLS* has a long article by Noel Annan on the Blunt affair. Evidently Cambridge people take it more seriously than others do. Goronwy Rees, once so disapproved of, comes out as a hero.

Sunday: I had a busy day on Saturday. Worked steadily through the book by Kenneth Morgan, very well written but I think unconvincing as a vindication of Lloyd George. The weather was fine and I did the full round of Hampstead Heath, all alone and somewhat melancholy. I have just realized that I am only one-third through my solitude. Still, in another week I shall be half-way. At lunch-time an elderly woman called with a coat she said she had found for you. She wanted £22.50 and claimed it was worth £75. I hesitated what to do. Maybe you would like it as a Christmas present. Maybe it would not fit. So in the end I said I could not take it and that she must come again after 6 January. She made out she could not wait that long, but I think she will. In the evening Mary and Sebastian took me to a Chinese restaurant. They truly are good parents. At least they brought Finbar with them. He did not eat much of the food, but he drank two glasses of Coca Cola to his great satisfaction. It is very sensible to treat him as fit for grown-up company, and he certainly is. Of course it is easy for Finbar. He has his father's natural good manners and his own charm into the bargain. I always treated my sons as equals, and am glad Sebastian and Mary do the same. I paid half the bill, which I thought was only fair. The bitter had run out at the Dartmouth Arms, so I made do with Burtons.

No problems in our house except that one half of the bed is empty. I am trying to read *The Well Beloved* by Thomas Hardy. It is not very good, though it is revealing about his attitude to women. The Well Beloved is always the ideal woman until he meets her. Then it becomes someone else.

Monday: I thought I had finished the *Essays and Reviews*. But Chris has sent a very funny piece on Kingsley Martin which I shall put in. This makes the total exactly fifty, very satisfactory. Now I have only the preface to write. There is a strike of Shell drivers and consequently a petrol shortage. I hope it will be over before you come back. Otherwise I shall have to strain my back again. Marvellous to hear your voice, but don't think that I shall telephone every Sunday morning. I always spend Saturday night at home, the only good night of the week. I have so much Love I cannot express it.

My Darling,

Alan

1979

Twisden Road
London NW5

12 December

Dearest Love,
 Wednesday: I was too busy to write to you yesterday, as you will see. First I went to buy something I have wanted for a long time, a present for you and for me. You will like it very much, I hope. Then I went to the London Library and read many periodicals. Later I was at Broadcasting House, where I made a programme on Bertrand Russell with Tony Howard. I was less enthusiastic about Russell than Michael Foot apparently had been. I got home only at tea-time, and what did I find? Your letter of 3 December, the first you wrote no doubt. Oh, what an inestimable pleasure. I read every word again and again. And where did you find 300 people for Ferencz's wedding? I hope you did not have to entertain them all.
 I have finished Kenneth Morgan's book on the Lloyd George Coalition. And I have just received an extraordinary book by George Kennan on the making of the Franco-Russian alliance. He seems to think it was the sole cause of the First World War. How easy things would be if we had clung to Bismarck and his 'system'. The moral of the book is, never make an alliance with Russia. I think Kennan must be German by origin. The scholarship is slovenly. De Jongh has sent us a report from his Institute, covering seven years' work. The Dutch are certainly obsessed with the Second War. Here everyone has forgotten it except as material for best-selling thrillers.
 I got *Silas Marner* from the London Library and am not enjoying it very much. Very artificial compared to Balzac or even Hardy. Maybe it will improve. What a difference between Silas Marner the literary miser and Père Goriot the real one. I wish I had not read all the works of Balzac. If there were some left unread, I should have something to do during the long Christmas break.
 Thursday: I went down to the Festival Hall this morning and bought two tickets for a chamber concert on 8 January. So you will not be altogether without music when you come back. I meant to go to 'The Thirties' but it had taken me so long to get there and I had so much to do that I came home after buying coffee at I Camisa and chicory at the Algerian Coffee Shop. And what do you think I found when I got home? Nothing other than your letter of 6 December which only took a week to get here. It was enchanting in every word. It also worried me. You are much happier when you are busy. Here you become bored when you

have nothing to do. Unconsciously I am slowing down and fail to appreciate how much younger you are. Once upon a time I could write books and complete the first draft of my autobiography at the same time. Now I have not worked on my autobiography for months. Yet when I ask what I have done instead, I can only answer – put together a volume of essays that demanded virtually no writing at all. Very depressing.

I have had the proof of the Roosevelt book and thrown it away. But I will remember to cut the review out of the *Observer* on Sunday. This afternoon I went up to Waterlow Park, where I sat in the sun, and have hurried home to write the review on Morgan. That is now done and will go off tonight along with your letter. This will give me an excuse to drop into the Dartmouth Arms. I think there will be a further rise in beer prices. In that case we must go to the Dartmouth Arms on alternative days and thus save lots of money.

Yes, I miss you as much as ever. Even so, I would rather be alone during the day in our own house than in the society of others. I find Margaret very wearisome. Poor creature, she can't help her pains, her deafness or her short temper. But I wish her cooking menus were not so rigid – chop, steak, liver, mackerel; sprouts, lettuce, lettuce, sprouts. Every day pitta. I said I did not eat bread. She merely continued to hand out the pitta. I suppose she has to live in a routine to make her life bearable.

Thank goodness Saturday will soon be here and I shall be in my own bed. I don't suppose I shall send another letter until after the weekend. Daniel is now having 'industrial therapy', whatever that may mean, some kind of mechanical work I suppose. Love to your boys. The remark by Ferencz amused me. He is quite a philosopher.

Many Kisses,

Alan

1979

Twisden Road
London NW5

17 December

Beloved,

How strange it is that we mean all the world to each other and yet you are over there and I am here, both of us missing each other the whole time. No one will believe how much we love each other, especially me who has been waiting all my life for you. It seems silly to find the perfect mate only when I am over seventy, or at any rate over sixty when we first went to bed together. Perhaps when I am eighty we should go to Salzburg just to celebrate.

Now here is some good news. I went to my dentist this morning and he can build a new tooth where the other one fell out. I shall have to wait until the end of January to give the root of the tooth which is still there time to push up. The operation will take an hour, during which time he will take out the nerve and use its channel to implant the new tooth. This is nothing to me after spending every Friday afternoon for eighteen months at the Royal Dental Hospital.

Bad news. Amelia and Mary Taylor have agreed to combine for Christmas dinner after all. Or rather, Mary insisted that she would be bored merely with her children, and that everyone else must come to her. Amelia would have much preferred a quiet party at her house, but she has been overruled. Disadvantages for me: first, the dinner will start at six because Mary's children will be restless by then. Next, it will be very noisy. Worst of all, I shall have to take Margaret back to Rochester Road, which means no drink at dinner for me. It certainly was mad of me not to come to Budapest for Christmas.

I had Daniel to tea yesterday and who should come in but Giles, who had been for a walk on his own. He is keen to do a further stretch of the Lea Valley. So am I. Perhaps Daniel will be fit to do it also by then. Fortunately I had a good supply of crumpets, so we had a feast.

Tuesday: Unpleasant, wet day. I went on the Heath and had to run home again. I have finished chapter XIII of my autobiography and am not satisfied with it. However, I shall push on. I shall have more new stuff later on. Improved news about Christmas Day. Margaret says she will not be fit to come, and even if she does Sebastian will drive her home while I can go to Twisden Road. We shall see. I wonder whether Crispin will come to see me this weekend. I expect not.

I shall continue until just before Christmas. Then I shall stop. There will be no post between 24 and 27 December, and after that it will not be worth writing. Perhaps I will keep notes for you to read when you come back. We both know the arrangements for 6 January. We shall meet in the arrival lounge (not much of a lounge). Whoever gets there first will wait for the other. If there is a certainty of delay at Budapest, you might try to get the airline to give me a ring here before I leave for Heathrow at 9.15. Is there anything I should buy in the way of food? As you arranged, there are one dozen eggs, and we can buy some vegetables from the Continental. I will also stock in fruit. After we have met we come home, then we will take off all our clothes, look at each other and do nothing. What do you think of that?

I think I told you I strained my back. It continues agonizing in bed and gradually clears off during the day. I need you to massage me.

Love and Kisses,

Alan

Twisden Road
London NW5

16 December

Darling,

The letter heading does not mean I am in Oxford, merely that this is the last piece of College paper that I made off with. Last evening (Friday) I was with Giles and Janet, very good meal and good company. Alison of course asked after you. Here is today's news. I have recovered your typewriter from Trills, in perfect order I hope, at cost of £11.50. All it needed was cleaning and oiling, though I have not checked it. Hugh Trevor Roper has changed his name to Lord Dacre of Glantan and become Master of Peterhouse, Cambridge. As Professor he would have retired in two years' time; as Master he can go on for five. Also he does not need to bother about history any more, which will no doubt relieve him of doubts if any. Peterhouse is a small, very right-wing College where the Fellows wear black armbands on the anniversary of Franco's death.

Sunday: Breakfast cheered up by a call from you. Your absence is really too long. I am lonely beyond endurance, missing you all the time. Still, half the time has passed. The rest will go quicker, if only because I shall have plenty to do, beginning with the dentist tomorrow. I fear I shall have to have my mouth remodelled again, perhaps it is beyond it.

1979

There has been a catastrophe in the kitchen. Pat duly fitted a lock to the door, and in doing so cracked the glass in it. He thinks the crack can be disguised. I don't. We shall have to have it replaced at great expense. Otherwise the lock is a good job. I had a fine dinner last night, eating the first of the two chops from the deep-freeze, also pâté, Brussels sprouts and a pear, together with half a bottle of Chianti. Afterwards I played *Falstaff*, smoked a cigar and went to my solitary bed.

Christmas arrangements are again in turmoil. Mrs Linthwaite* is too frail to entertain the Sebastian Taylors, so they are stopping at home. But Amelia says that, with the boys away, she does not want to cook a big dinner. So as far as I can see I shall have a Christmas dinner with Bob and Amelia, with Margaret there as a non-eater. Sebastian and Mary will have some sort of dinner if their kitchen is ready in time. Giles and Janet will shiver with the Jenners down at Brede. The truth is that the grandparents, including Margaret, are beyond having Christmas visitors, while the young have never done them before. Maybe I shall come with you to Hungary another time, especially if Margaret is unable to cope with me. The strain makes her bad-tempered, though she does not mean to be.

I had a long letter from Paul, announcing his marriage four months ago and expressing his boredom with the *New Statesman*. Our plans for June and August in Lancashire have now been definitely fixed, and it only remains for me to think of something to say. We go to the British Academy on 7 January. The agenda for the Section meeting next day is so bad that I think I shall stay away. Giles thinks I should have an inch taken off my new trousers. What do you say? Have a good time and think sometimes of me.

     Love, Love, Love,

                        Alan

20 December

Dearest Distant Lover,

Thursday: I failed to write anything yesterday, mainly because I was finishing the *Essays* ready for delivery. Also, I tried to go for a walk and was driven home by the rain. Weather bad, and it makes my back ache. I have finished Alan Sked's book. Very interesting for me, with my old

---

* Mary Taylor's mother.

knowledge of North Italy in 1848; pretty unreadable for anyone else. However, I will write Alan a flattering note about it. I shall not however attempt to review it for the *Observer*. Now I am rather short of anything to read, and I shall not be able to borrow any Dickens with Janet at Brede. Maybe I'll try some Walter Scott. This morning I was rung by the BBC and invited to take part in 'Any Questions' at Cambridge. I refused, saying (a) I was not good at snap questions; (b) I did not like the Cambridge Union. Both true, but the producer did not believe me. Otherwise no one wants me over Christmas for television or anything else.

Chris* has sent me the Wendt review. I think it had better go in, if only because the subject has not been attempted by anyone else. Earlier today I have at last done an article for the *Sunday Express* on the old subject – let Hess out, and do it in defiance of the law. But it won't do any good. There have been some surprising Christmas cards, nearly all of them for you. Intimate friends of yours whom I have never heard of write long messages in the inside of the cards and send their greetings to me. Soon your room will be so piled with cards, magazines and books that it will be impossible to enter it. Here is a good bit of news for you. As you may remember, the Oxford Press gave me a *Concise Oxford Dictionary*. Now Foyle's have sent a second copy – secondhand but free, which you can have all for yourself. I have put it in your room. This evening Margaret is going to Sophia's, so I shall go out to dinner probably at Edward's Bistro, even if the proprietor is chairman of the local Conservative Party.

Friday: As foretold I went to Edward's Bistro. Very agreeable. I had pâté and a delicious pork chop, followed by home-made mince-pie. Not enough of a French meal to qualify for the title of Bistro. But satisfactory all the same. Waitresses also agreeable, even tasty though I did not taste. A further advantage that is within easy walking distance. However, I shall not have to go out for dinner much longer. This morning I did the weekend shopping, getting it over before the Christmas rush started. There is a flood of periodical literature, both the *Times Literary Supplement* and *Books and Bookmen*. The former shows how shoddy the second is. A very pompous article by Michael Howard on Kissinger in the *TLS*, half an article by the same author in *B and B* on me. I have to share with someone else. Each of the reviews raises a problem. I can understand everything in *Books* and it is dull and ordinary. The pieces in the *TLS* are always interesting, often fascinating, but I can rarely understand. There should be a Taylor Law stating that there is no greater waste of time than reading the weekly or monthly reviews. I wonder who reads either of them from cover to cover. You, I suppose, and sometimes me.

* Chris Wrigley, historian, Alan's pupil.

1979

I meant to walk round Waterlow Park this afternoon, but I had only got as far as Swain's Lane when there was a heavy snowstorm, so I took refuge in Cavour's and then came home again. Now I should like to take my car to be filled with petrol, but the windscreen is frozen over and I shrink from the labour of defreezing it. I think that instead I will wash my hair. The hot water is very hot, but the house takes all day to get warm after the cold nights. Last year, I remember, it was always warm, but perhaps that is my imagination.

Now I will catch the post before the weekend. As I told you in my last letter, I shall write one more letter next Tuesday. Then I shall not write any more except perhaps to keep a sort of diary recording anything sensational that may happen, though nothing will. At present I am very bored and very lonely and very unhappy. I do not think Christmas will cheer me up much.

Be sure to impress on the boys that they must clear the drain under the sink. I suppose Pisti as an architect is too proud to perform such a menial task. Only a fortnight now. The days must hurry, hurry.

Love, Kisses and more Love,

Alan

Twisden Road
London NW5

22 December

Longed-for Love,

Saturday: a dreadful day. Damp snow during the night and now soft rain all day long. I have not been able to go out at all. The only useful occupation would have been to go to bed, but I have no bed companion. As a result I feel heavy and my head aches. The only interlude will, I hope, be provided by Pat Denny who is coming to finish off the door. New glass must wait for your return. Pat has some idea for concealing the crack, but I don't think it will suit you.

Publishing activities are on the move. Roger Machell called this morning and carried off the *Essays and Reviews*. He does not like the title, and I agree with him. He left the final proofs of *Revolutions and Revolutionaries*, with the 's' left off Revolutions. Perhaps it is better so. There are a few misprints and some mistakes of mine, including wrong venue for the Chartist Convention of 1848 which you ought to have noticed. I have enjoyed the Cathedrals though the author, being I suspect Swiss, makes too much of Swiss and West German cathedrals and not enough of English. In my opinion English cathedrals are incomparably the best, though I admit Chartres has some merit. The Beaverbrook book is a rehashed version of *Success* but it is very funny. As to *The Comedians* I find it heavy going, as though Graham had become bored with the West Indies. And here is an interesting idea: Graham deliberately wrote *The Human Factor* to coincide with the explosion of the Blunt scandal. How cross Len must have been to miss it.

I shall eat the last chop today, and so next weekend must really cater for myself. Not that I bother to buy much. I keep myself well stocked for breakfast and lunch, and then have to add merely a chop and sprouts for dinner once a week. The house is still very cold. I wish Wilcox could get hold of his man and seal the sky-light, but now it will have to wait until after Christmas.

Sunday: Wonderful to hear your voice, a splendid opening to the day. I certainly need some cheer when I contemplate the weather – not all that cold but damp, with the rain turning into sleet and then back again into rain. However, I shall have some good reason to go out this afternoon if Daniel comes, as he usually does. He is a loyal son to me, partly because he gets bored and wants change of society. I have heard nothing from Crispin, although he must now be home for Christmas. As I think I told you, I shall write to him after Christmas to explain that I shall not continue my one-sided correspondence.

Mary Taylor's kitchen is now ready and very smart it is, despite her complaints against Kindleyside. It has everything – washer, refrigerator, enormous deep-freeze (not yet installed). But of course all the shelves are the wrong height, the doors to the various gadgets will not open properly and so on. It seems to me that the kitchen is so stuffed with equipment that there is no room for human beings, but Mary is confident she can get us all in on Christmas Day. She has an open grate for a fire, but does not know where she can get any coal.

Pat did not turn up yesterday. He is becoming unreliable now that he has got a job, but I suppose he will finish the door some time. The *Observer* has much speculation this morning as to who will be Regius Professor. They think it must be an early modern historian because Hugh was one. I think the opposite. More likely the mediaevalists will make a counter-revolution after being excluded last time. How this recalls the last occasion, with everyone asking what Macmillan would do, and me amused with the turmoil because I had already made up my mind to refuse. Though I have had some ambitions, to become a professor, Regius or otherwise, was not among them. Perhaps it was unfair on others for me to become an historian and yet not want the professional responsibilities that went with it.

No more letters and no more telephone calls. As I told you, I have had no letter from you for nearly a fortnight. You should have received at least three more of mine. It does not matter. I write them to relieve my loneliness. The calendar must hurry. The pages to 6 January must turn over fast.

Impatient Love,

Alan

JOURNAL*

1979 Xmas
December

Thursday: I was distressed at your distress when you left. You should never doubt me. I know I am often thoughtless and often forget how difficult it is for you to live in a foreign land. But when you are in trouble you must always tell me instead of bottling it up. The only thing I want in life is to make you happy. Confide in me and never hold your worries to yourself. After you had left I gave Finbar breakfast and took him across Highgate Road. Then I read Asa Briggs all the morning. The weather was terrible. Janet had a ward meeting and could not go to the National Film Theatre. I decided a second showing was too late for me, and the Beefsteak too far away. So I stayed for dinner with Margaret.
Friday: Two hours finishing Briggs. Then to collect my watch on Ludgate Hill. On to Soho for fish, and found a queue, so abandoned my quest and went to the Garrick Club, where I was early and Nico Henderson late. Nico was the complacent ambassador at his most condescending. I mentioned that I knew Maurice Oldfield, forgetting that Maurice must have cross-questioned Nico in 1951 after Burgess and MacLean defected. The mention was not well received. Robert Kee said we must go and have dinner with them. Afterwards I completed my shopping and spent the evening reading Telford Taylor.
Saturday: I wrote 900 words on Asa Briggs, condemning the book as

* Alan had promised to write Eva a diary while she was away.

inadequate and telling again the story of 'In The News'. Wanda Boothby has broken her knee, so they cannot come to dinner. In the afternoon a wonderful walk on the Heath, bright sunshine and clean snow. In the evening to the Queen Elizabeth Hall for a Mozart concert. Amelia and Bob with me for her birthday. She is 35. A boring early symphony, and later the Prague symphony which was enchanting.

Sunday: Revised my review of Briggs, read Telford Taylor, who is better as he gets nearer Munich. Took Finbar on the Heath. He walks too fast for me. Failing to contact Bill Webb, I took my review down myself.

Monday: Mild weather and soft rain. I am more cheerful that you may return on time. I miss you very much and think often of your trial today which will, I am sure, be a triumph for you. Fancy two D. Litts in one house. Early-morning panic. Philip Johnson rang up that they were already fully booked for the last week in May. However, I rang the Bridge Hotel in Buttermere and they have plenty of rooms. This means Nolan will get his way and ascend Scafell Pike, if the weather is better than it is now. Philip says they have twelve inches of snow in Coniston. After lunch I made an expedition to the City, where I sold Briggs and the book on Edward VII and bought a whistle.

Tuesday: Finished Telford Taylor. A curious mixture of good and less good. The diplomatic details are correct, though tedious. He knows, for instance, that Hitler was surprised over both Austria and Czechoslovakia. Weak on background. He says little about public opinion in either England or France. He does not mention the Far East, and therefore does not understand the attitude of the Admiralty. He passes over British distrust of Soviet Russia and misses economic appeasement. Finally, he tries to rewrite history by discussing what should have been done and how the Allies could have won in 1938. This will give me enough for 3,000 words. The snow has gone. We may even dare to venture to Bristol by car. In the evening I took Margaret to hear the Guarnieri Quartet playing Dvořak and Smetana, a very good quartet. I took in the laundry and forgot to tell him not to call next week. No need to keep any more journal.

Christmas 1979

Here is a continuation of my chronicle, since I cannot write a letter to you any more.*

Sunday: Daniel came to tea. He is full of plans for the future, mostly contradictory. He wants to return to Leeds either this autumn or in

---

* Eva was soon to be back in England.

1981. He also wants to get a flat in Camden Town and take a temporary job in a library. Rather distressingly, he tells me he has plenty of money, which he proposes to spend on a new car or on a holiday in the South of France. We spoke of Crispin, who seems set on ignoring me. I must take the same line. I shall lose a son, but I do not propose to run after him in vain. Perhaps you might write to him.

Monday: I have run out of quarto paper and am told it is now out of fashion. I am used to this size and shall miss it. I spent the afternoon with Sebastian, who also has ambitious plans. He tells me the Ministry of Defence expects war in the early Eighties, apparently on the ground that the Americans have recovered from their fright over Vietnam and want to try out their new weapons. This sounds plausible.

Tuesday: I gave Margaret your present and she cooed over it in her usual fashion. The evening was not too bad. I carved the turkey, not very well because Sebastian had not kept his knives sharp. The children behaved wildly, with Mary complaining but unable to control them. Afterwards Bob Doyle played jazz records which Mary had bought at a sale. This was not my form of entertainment, so I retired early to my own bed. This was a wonderful release, though I was lonely in it. Whatever should I do if for any reason I lost you? You have a good family to go to in Hungary. I have no one I care for except you. I read *The Comedians*. It is rather second-rate Greene, but even that is better than anyone else. I wonder what he wanted to convey – that Communisn and Catholicism are two different aspects of religion, or merely that America is always on the wrong side? The workings of Graham's mind are beyond conjecture. And the love story? A repetition surely of the same love story in all his other books, and a message to all the lovers he has had in real life. If one were to judge Graham by his novels, he must spend most of his time in bed, worrying about possible failures. What a blessing that failure does not matter with us, or more correctly even failure is a sort of success.

Wednesday: All day still happy in my own home, our home. I finished a foolish, pompous book by Kennan which I must review for the *TLS*. I also read that delightful little book about Scott that you gave me. I fear I must start reading Scott again. His novels are very good except for his rather stolid style. I note that this month I have read more than ten books for the first time for many years. This is the reward of loneliness.

Friday: Yesterday (Thursday) was a dreadful day, with heavy rain from morning to night. Somehow it depressed me. I could not work, I could not read, I could not write to you. However, it is now fine and sunny though cold. Maybe I shall have to come to Heathrow by tube and strain my back again with the luggage. Meanwhile, here are two important points before I forget. First, you must always buy granulated not caster sugar for general purposes, especially for people who take sugar in their tea or coffee. Second, what was the name of the hotel where we stopped in Manchester when I made that programme for Andrew Snell? I want to stay there again rather than at the Midland, and the name has gone from me. I am sure I could find it if only I were there. I have fixed for us to go on 26 March and to stay over the weekend, when we can make a visit to the Peak District and walk down Dove Dale or something like that.

Another instruction: I have bought some quarto paper. Please do not use it while the folio paper lasts. I have only too much of that. I have finished *Silas Marner*, a very sentimental tale typical of an old maid, except that George Eliot was far from being an old maid, unable to resist any man and yet priggish about sex. It is a mystery for me that she was ever ranked with the great novelists. Perhaps *Middlemarch* is better. I suspect she is numbered with The Great Unread.

Saturday: Another fine day. I went a long walk with Sebastian. I had on my soft shoes and it was hard work keeping up with him. By the end, though I could keep going by bending forward I could not stand upright when I stood still and nearly fell over, rather like High Crag. I don't think Sebastian noticed, but it was a warning that I must wear proper walking shoes when I go out on the Heath.

I began to worry that perhaps the dozen eggs you left have not kept fresh. So tonight I shall make myself an omelette to see whether they are all right. I have taken the precaution of buying a chop in case the eggs have gone off. If they are all right, I shall leave the chop in the deep-freeze for me to eat next and final Saturday. A further instruction: we must buy different toilet paper. This yellow kind breaks into thin strips unless one is careful. I am sure there are varieties which though soft are not fragile. As a matter of fact I regret the old hard-paper variety, much more efficient and not tearing into strips. But of course I do not suffer from piles.

I have written six pages on Kennan, which I hope will be almost enough. I must try to finish the review in the morning. What record shall I play after dinner? It cannot always be 'Oh, What a Lovely War'. I tried Beethoven's Third Symphony and thought it awful. I have lost all taste for music except chamber music, I suppose from lack of hearing.

Sunday: The eggs were fine and made a delicious omelette. I also treat myself every Saturday to rough pâté from Mrs Lever. Kennan is written and dispatched. Incidentally the post is still very slight – only letters posted in London are being delivered. Nothing from you since your letter of 6 December. I hope one or more will come soon. I am faced with a supplementary assessment for income tax, the result of bad addition and some omissions in previous years. I shall be worried until I know how much I have to pay. Fortunately, 1979 has been a good year for books though a bad one for television. Daniel has cried off a visit to me today because he wants to watch a television programme. I shall take a solitary walk on the Heath so as not to be hurried along by Sebastian. *Observer* very dreary today, all about the past year which is better forgotten except for our life together. Come back soon. Frost this morning. I worry about next Sunday. I worry too much and with no reward.

Monday: Nothing much to record. I wrote four pages of autobiography, not very satisfactorily. The second draft is worse, not better. Daniel came to tea, friendly but somehow listless, I suppose from the pills he is taking. He says the right things, but there is no spirit in them. Later I walked over to Janet's just to greet them on their return. Giles says he has walked twenty-five miles every day. They are the friendliest of my family, but very much turned in on themselves. I have just re-read Gibbon's autobiography with great pleasure, rather impersonal as you would expect from any historian. Strange fact: our greatest historian never saw an original document. He relied for everything on texts edited by Benedictines. Cold enough for me to put the radiator on in the kitchen. Oh, I wish you were here. The last days are the worst, they pass so slowly.

I lost all interest or zest for life. Everything except you seems pointless. Your letter of 18 December arrived only today. I have been worrying about the weather, frost and some snow. But I shall get to Heathrow somehow.

There is a good chance that Christopher Falkus will republish *The Course of German History* as a paperback when he goes to Methuen. I shall have to read the book again and write a new preface to it. From what people have said about the book, I thought it was too influenced by the war, but perhaps Germany really was like that. In any case the book was too clever. We shall see.

Friday: The typewriter man came yesterday and removed my big typewriter for a thorough overhaul. This will cost £75 and be worth it. As soon as you come back I want to change my will. Crispin is no longer concerned about my affairs, so I shall strike him out as an executor and put you in. Will this suit you? Will you be happy working with Giles, or shall I make you sole executor? You will need a second trusteee in any case, and Giles will be the best. The new *TLS* has a long review, rather late, of Seton Watson's correspondence. I have made a muddle about next Tuesday, when we are committed to both the Academy party and a concert at the Queen Elizabeth Hall. I think I see a way out.

1980

JOURNAL
1980
For My Lovey

Friday, 18 July: I made an easy exit from Heathrow, then inexplicably missed the turn on to the Great West Road and found myself taking the oldest route of all through Hounslow. I don't think it took more than ten minutes longer. I sat resolutely down and wrote a review of the three *Observer* books, presenting them as 'armchair travelling' – all the pleasures of travel without effort or leaving one's home. This made me too late for the City Music Society, regrettable but it was better to get the books out of the way.

Soft rain most of the day, which did not tempt me out on to the Heath. So I went down to Trills where I recovered your typewriter (no charge) and returned the visiting cards which they will replace, again free. On the way back I went into Margaret's house, which I may say had no emotional effect.* I hope to go with Daniel on Sunday and load all the records into my car. There are not more than a dozen books worth taking. Of course I should like some of the crockery and cutlery, but it is not worth making trouble over.

I have now discharged all my debts of correspondence, including a letter to Crispin. Soon I shall prepare to cook my dinner. I bought some raspberries, and also got some water biscuits in the blue packet from the self-service near Highgate Fisheries. I have read the *TLS*, not much in it.

Saturday, 19 July: A dreadful day, raining hard until three o'clock in the afternoon. As usual, having sent off a letter to Crispin yesterday, I received one from him this morning. He says mysteriously, 'I must begin thinking seriously about the future, which means equipping myself to do something better than teaching.' He also threatens to return to Ghana if Thatcherism continues to reign. I managed a further page on Napoleon III, though not with any great inspiration. In the afternoon I went in the rain to the Library and read the *New Statesman* – very dull and futile. On coming out I found bright sunshine, so pushed up through the cemetery to Waterlow Park where I sat in the sun for nearly an hour. Later I went to dinner with Giles and Janet. Giles is exhausted with the

---

* Margaret died in mid-July 1980.

family rows, which also involved him in drinking a lot of sweet white wine. Apparently there is to be both an address by Jock Stallard and hymns. I should like to stay away, but it makes a bad impression on strangers who know nothing of the background. So I shall put on my best suit and a black tie. After all, it is the last funeral I shall attend except my own. Giles is very reliable but he is also very soft, following his rule, 'Decorum at all times'. I slept badly. Do I miss you, or is something wrong with me? Either way it is tiresome. The bed is miserably empty. Both Mary and Sophia want us to go to The Mill, a risky undertaking.

Sunday, 20 July: Dreary weather. I tried to read the *Observer* and found nothing in it. Daniel's arrival was a welcome relief. He was in splendid form, cutting down his food intake at last. This leaves me with the embarrassing legacy of a whole brown loaf for myself to eat. We went to Rochester Road after lunch and carried off such gramophone records as I wanted, which were fewer than I had supposed. I could not see anything else worth removing, but we must pay a visit together when you come back. Daniel and I set off for Waterlow Park until the rain drove us back just when we were within earshot of the band. Busy evening doing the housework I should have done in the day-time.

Monday, 21 July: Margaret's funeral. I was glad about it for her sake, otherwise unaffected. I certainly did not feel sad about her spoilt life and mine. She was now freed from life and I had found perfect happiness, so why worry? A fair number of Margaret's friends and some of her relatives. I left Giles to play the part of principal mourner which he did very well, but inevitably some people made more fuss of me. Amelia sobbed loudly throughout the Bach record and the reading of a poem by Thomas Hardy. Daniel attended and looked very distinguished. Then everyone except me went off to a party at Amelia's. I returned home and got in my first good walk on the Heath since you left. I am still trying to consume the brisket. It would feed an army, and I expect I shall still be eating it when you return. The prospect of ten more empty days is not consoling. But I am learning how to get through them. Book of *Essays* to be definitely published on 25 October.

    I hope this will be my last literary adventure, though I suppose something will turn up. In the evening I met Sebastian, who told me that Amelia's funeral wake went on until early evening. I am glad I was not there.

Twisden Road
London NW5

21 July

My Lovey,
 I was firmly resolved not to write to you and to keep a diary of events instead. But I can't refrain from writing any longer. Also, I thought you might be interested to hear about Margaret's funeral. It was fancier than I would have liked, but not too bad. Bob Doyle put on a restrained Bach record. Jock Stallard made a short speech paying tribute to Margaret's work in the Labour Party etc. No mention of me, I am glad to say. I read a short poem by Hardy, more because I liked it than she did. All the relatives including ex-husbands – Robert Mac-Gibbon and Tim Fell, Mrs Benstead very prominent. Daniel came and looked very distinguished. Afterwards they all went to a wake or party at Amelia's house. I did not go: there had been enough hypocrisy already. I felt no twinge of sorrow, only happy relief for Margaret's sake. And of course gratitude: not to her, but to the life-mate who has brought me such complete happiness.
 Daniel and I went to the house in Rochester Road and removed about half the records. The others I did not want. The record cabinet will not, I think, fit under the sitting-room window, so the records are at present dumped under the television table. There is no immediate intention of selling the house so Giles suggests that, when I have removed all my property – and I think I have – every member of the family, including you and me, should go round with stick-on labels, indicating what we would like. Then the executors will sort it out.
 I went to Janet's for dinner on Saturday, mainly meat risotto, and to Mary's last night, roast lamb badly carved by Sebastian. On the other hand, Robert MacGibbon assured me that there is no need to remove a prostate gland merely because it is enlarged. Both Mary and Sophia want us to go to The Mill for a few days, or as long as we want. Of course we could go in September, but there will be no one else there and The Mill needs people even if one fights with them.
 No letters today, and no phone calls except one from my old friend Freddie Hurdis Jones. Now I shall try to write a little more on Napoleon. With any luck I should finish it tomorrow and then I can return to my autobiography. The house seems very empty without you. I want to call out, 'Anyone in?' whenever I come home.
 Many kisses and loving embraces,

Your Man

JOURNAL

Tuesday, 22 July: The first warm day since May. In the morning I finished off Napoleon and Eugenie and dispatched it through Fitzgerald junior. In the afternoon I went to the Ponds and had a marvellous time in the sun, finishing with a swim in fairly cold water. I have begun re-reading my autobiography as preparation to write the next chapter. Of course something else will intervene just when I start to write. I talked to Mary about The Mill. The problem is that the half in which my rooms are has been let from the middle of August. No one can be blamed for this: I had projected to go to The Mill while you were away. We could perhaps go for the day just for you to see it, either on your own or with your children. Then we will make a firm plan for next summer, going down for a fortnight in July when The Mill is free from tenants.

Wednesday, 23 July: This ridiculous fuss about the Act of Settlement raised its head again, carrying me down to Bush House where I made a broadcast chat about it, trivial stuff. However, I combined it with a visit to Gaston where I sold books for £27. Also, I spent some time sitting in Lincoln's Inn Fields and thinking of the meetings which decided our marriage. But this year there are no deck-chairs, I can't think why. Very fine sun in the afternoon and the water much warmer, altogether delectable. Walked over to Janet's for a dinner. We should have whole chickens sometimes instead of chicken legs. Roasted, they are much better and can be eaten cold the next evening. After dinner I played backgammon with Giles and won. I suppose they will be going to Brede by the end of the week. Janet's father sounds in a bad way, perhaps her mother also. I told Giles that he was always welcome for dinner when we are at home, but of course we shall be away immediately after you come back.

Thursday, 24 July: Another warm day, with good sunshine at the Ponds and the water really good enough to swim in for a long time. The rain earlier in the year has made the water beautifully fresh even in late July. In the middle of the morning I broke off my work to go to Friern Barnet to sell the books we had decided to throw out. On the way back I spent the money on another case of Chianti. It was strange to go to Friern Barnet without visiting Daniel. I am increasingly worried about him. Why has he not heard from Leeds? I must try to get the truth out of him, which is not easy. I am also depressed about my draft autobiography. I wrote it before we came together and it is full of self-pity. Who cares now why my marriage with Margaret broke up, and what right had I to go on being miserable for years just because of that? If my marriage to

Margaret was not working, surely I should have simply walked out of it. I fear I shall appear a contemptible figure. Maybe I had better not write after all. I slept very badly. Hot nights? Missing you? Too much food? At any rate it is a nuisance.

Friday, 25 July: Good news: Brookfield Garage have at last found the cause of the leak in our car. There was a crack under the bonnet which must have been there when I bought the car and should have been found by Zenith long ago. A great treat in the afternoon. Finbar came with me to the Ponds. It is true it meant a shorter time lying in the sun. On the other hand, it was a great pleasure to see him swim and dive. The Sebastian Taylors are off to the Island this evening, leaving at eight o'clock and hoping to catch the last ferry at midnight. Better them than me.

My gloom over my autobiography deepens as I approach the point where I have two broken marriages lying in fragments around me. Once, I cared about this. Now, what does it matter? I am so happy that I don't care in the slightest what happened to me in the past. I think I shall have to cut out all the personal part. You must advise me when you get back.

Saturday, 26 July: All is arranged for our journey to the north next Sunday. We shall take train to Preston, though I hope not stop there. I had a busy morning shopping. Unlike you, I allow only one vegetable and am lucky that I can have broad beans one day, peas the next. Mrs Lever is on holiday for a fortnight. The warm weather came to an end with thunderstorms and heavy rain. I was not sorry. Every member of the family except me has gone to The Mill, and I feel very much alone. Not that I care. Many things occupy my mind, not necessarily fruitfully. In the afternoon I walked over to the Spread Eagle and met my former pupil Freddy Hurdis Jones. He told me that he had spent yesterday with Michael Howard. I had no idea Freddy was Michael's contemporary. Freddy is now an official interpreter for the Common Market at Brussels. He left Magdalen under a cloud as someone totally useless, and now his career is highly rated. He has a holiday flat on the Giudecca. We might borrow it, or at any rate see him.

Sunday, 27 July: The *Observer* is on the point of committing suicide, very worrying for my income. Daniel came for lunch as usual. He says he has not heard from Leeds. He was good company, but not so far as to come to the Ponds. Daniel tells me Crispin is in London. Of course none of them has an obligation to visit me, but I am a little hurt all the same. Crispin is repeatedly in London. He knows how I should like to see him and to hear his news. Perhaps you should write to him. And yet I don't know. Moral pressure on him is the last thing he would welcome. I must just resign myself to losing him for some reason I don't understand.

Monday, 28 July: A wasted day. Visit from an American scientist who is writing a book or an article about Michael Polanyi. I know too little, especially about the Polanyi family. Karl Polanyi was a close follower of Michael Károlyi's, the sister was a Communist. Perhaps you know about them. For me it is all guesswork. Very good afternoon at the Ponds. All the same, I wish I could have been at The Island in this fine weather. There is something I wish much more. I need you desperately. I have no life without you. And I can't go on with my autobiography. It is all dead stuff. I don't care any more about my life before I met you. Now I feel I have been living with you for ever.

Tuesday, 29 July: Despite my doubts about my autobiography, I sat down this morning and began a fresh chapter. I think I see my way, writing mainly about my books in the early Sixties. Still very hot, though not absolutely bright sun. As a result there was hardly anyone at the Ponds, though the water was warmer than ever. They are certainly sun worshippers. In the evening I went to dinner with Giles and Sebastian, supplying the wine. We have settled the problem of The Mill for next summer when you and I, plus any of your boys who care to come, will go in July.

Wednesday, 30 July: Another profitable day. I wrote a good deal and see my way to complete chapter XVI. Whether I shall also find the time is a different matter. It is characteristic of my life that I get to work just when I shall have to break off. Weather dull, so I walked down to Kentish Town. The main road is closed for three or four weeks because of a burst water main. To my delight, Crispin came to tea. He is a splendid boy, a real credit to me, or is he a credit to his mother? He tells me he will probably be a candidate at the local elections in the autumn. No doubt Giles is right in foretelling that Crispin will end as an MP, or perhaps even a Cabinet Minister. Certainly he will be more Left-wing than his uncle. Curiously, he started moderate and has moved Left consistently. Crispin is just off to Scandinavia and may call on his return or even before he goes.

1981

THOUGHTS IN SOLITUDE
1981

24 July: Truly an easy journey back. Post uninteresting, except for a biography of Castlereagh, not a subject of great interest for me. Telegram from Bob Silvers, that David Carlton's book on Eden has not yet been published in the United States so it looks as though I am going to miss it. I fear I am getting lazy. Telephone from Bristol BBC asking me to take part in a series on school examinations. Would I assess the O-level History papers? Answer: No. Telephone call from La Couriere della Siera, Milan: Would I write an article surveying the wave of violence all over the world? Answer: No. Two thoughts occur to me as I grow older: first, the world is such a bloody awful place that the universal violence is not surprising, there is no inspiration, no hope for the future, no beauty. Second, perhaps the more prosaic explanation is that we have not had a world war for forty years and people everywhere are bored. Think how much more interesting the world was when we were all united against Hitler. It looked as though something real was going to happen. And what have we got? Thatcher instead of Baldwin, Mitterand instead of Laval, Reagan instead of Hoover, Brezhnev instead of Stalin. Not an inspiring thought.

After reading *The Times* and the *TLS* (very boring), I went upstairs and started on *An English Husband*.* Here are some first impressions. The subtitle is misleading. What is the Catch–22, which means you are trapped both ways? It may mean something to you but you do not make this clear. Yes, it is clear later. The English is perfectly coherent and does not need much correction, though I see I have made corrections already. I don't feel that you have made up your mind clearly as to what you are writing about, whether your relations with me or your life in general. Sometimes you seem to wander off on to subjects which are not connected with me, or somewhat remotely. I think, for instance, that there is too much about my relations with Michael. Of course I understand that this will appeal to Hungarian readers, but in so far as I am the central figure of the book it implies that my friendship with Michael was of special influence on me. No, it was fun and inspiring, it evoked personal love, but Michael was not a

---
* Eva's mss.

central figure in my life. Hubert Ripka taught me as much about Central Europe.

Small points. You do not reveal that you went to Vienna in 1965 specifically in the hope of meeting me, and you do not make it clear that you did not do so. Instead you tell a long story about Fritz Fischer, whom you never met. When you get to Königswinter, you imply that our relationship was purely friendly. You even say we never kissed. Quite the contrary, we embraced violently on a bench in a dark corner near the river as Hauser observed. I remember, too, a passionate parting. As to Salzburg, you do not relate how you almost refused to come because I told you to bring your contraceptive device, and in retaliation I nearly refused to come. Also, you do not make clear that my expression of a wish to come to your bedroom was a total surprise to you, and that even when I came you had not expected me to step briskly into your bed. Your surprise makes the story much funnier.

I have already had to rewrite my autobiography, so do not be depressed if you have to do the same. It is terribly difficult for an historian writing an autobiography to remember that the book, unlike a work of history, is not a narrative of events, it is an account of what happened to whoever is writing it – what he or she felt and thought, how things turned out. But let the world go by unless it has a special impact on you. *An English Husband* is about you and me, everyone else is an auxiliary. I'll write more on this later.

Rain all afternoon. I did not get out until four o'clock. Then I took the dreary road to Kentish Town, summoned by the Owl Bookshop which had a book for you. I collected it, paying £1.25. Much amused that it is about Old Age: Which of us is threatened by this tiresome complaint, you or me? In my opinion you are a young middle-aged and I am not very different, a little unsteady on my feet but otherwise with not a trace of old age now that the exercises have restored my youth. Maybe I appear old to others, maybe my sexual powers have declined, though that may be psychological. But I don't feel old except when I have slight trouble with my eyes or skin. In one way today has been very strange: I have never passed so much water in my life, every half-hour an outpouring. Where does it come from? Normally when I drink beer it has little effect, and what there is passes over by the morning. Perhaps getting up at five-thirty upset my rhythm. Odd.

See you tomorrow if I have time. Otherwise I'll write about Crispin on Sunday.

25 July: I went off to the Market in excellent time. I think I have bought too much – quantities of peaches, grapes, peas, broad beans.

No doubt they will all get consumed in time. Pisti has gone to Norwich and will not be back for dinner, so I shall eat brisket all on my own, leaving plenty for another night. Output of water normal, I am glad to say.

I pushed on with *An English Husband*, chapter I. It gets more on the subject as you go on, especially when we start meeting in earnest. I think I was right to delay our marriage, though it looked strange to you. In my opinion you could not leave your boys until they had graduated, and it would also have been wrong for me to leave Crispin and Daniel until they could stand on their own feet. By 1976 Crispin did not need me. Perhaps Daniel did, as witness his breakdown, but we could not realize that. You seem to have regarded Köszeg as a farewell, I regarded it as a pledge of eternal love. At any rate, in my roundabout way I meant to marry you all along and how wonderfully it has turned out, at any rate for me.

Crispin and Lynn arrived for lunch, rather late. He has become more authoritarian than ever, perhaps at the prospect of becoming a husband. Lynn has straight yellow hair coming down nearly to her waist. Face like a Victorian doll, except that it is very alive. They give the impression that Crispin dictates everything, e.g. their camping in the Lake District. But maybe she has always wanted to be emancipated and Crispin has been her liberator. I conveyed your regrets at not coming to the lunch and assured Crispin that you would send Wainwright as soon as you came back. Meanwhile, he has carried off my set.

Giles and Janet came round to inspect the love-birds. Giles remarked, not unreasonably, that they had not seen Crispin for a long time. Crispin was rather embarrassed and said it was not a sign that he had ceased to be fond of them. Giles gave the love-birds a chopping board, a sensible present. Then they departed for Southend and the Giles Taylors to Brede. By bad planning The Mill is empty all week. We could have stayed on indefinitely, but in this weather it would not have been much fun.

Not much rain today but very cold this morning, almost enough to need the central heating. This afternoon, once left alone, I did the full round of the Heath and felt much better for it. Now I shall pod the peas and eat the brisket.

26 July: My loneliness has really begun today. Pisti left early for Norwich and I suspect that he will not be back until ten o'clock or so. You can imagine how lonely I was last night when I tell you that I played two Bartók quartets and two Beethoven trios. No sun today but rather warm, and I was foolish to go a long walk round the Heath instead of visiting the Ponds. I am feeling very well, which must be the result of my exercises, walking more steadily and a good deal faster. But oh, I feel so sad. More of *An English Husband*. In regard to Margaret, common memories had nothing to do with my continuing to see her. After all, the common memories were of Robert and Dylan.* She was lonely, she was declining physically. I wanted to make her last years easier, and it worked. I am not sorry I went on seeing her, though this hurt you more than I appreciated. But throughout she was a burden to me, not a pleasure. I loved you as I had never loved anyone, and still do. If you had told me your troubles frankly and freely, I should have tried to put them right. Instead, I thought selfishly that we were having a perfect life.

This evening we shall have brisket again, at least I shall. We shall also have corn on the cob, broad beans and what is left of the gooseberries. I cannot imagine when we shall get through the raspberries and the peaches, a riot of luxury. I think I am foolish to keep these notes till you come back. You will then be so pleased to see me that you will not bother to read them. So tomorrow or the day after I will post them to you. But maybe I shall not write enough to send any more.

27 July: A foolish, wasted day. I took the car round to Regent's Park Garage, which will do a better job than Brookfield. Then I returned Khrushchev to the London Library, had a pork pie on the way home and then found my way to the Ponds. Warm air, no sun. Stone ground very hard to lie on, and made me ache. Water just acceptable. Most of the day I puzzle how I shall pass the time for over a fortnight. You can't imagine how lonely I am. Pisti is very sweet and cooperative, but he is out for most of the day and I spend much time worrying how I shall feed him. I am not a bad cook, but I am a hopeless caterer. This must be the longest time we have been separated since we were married. It is too long.** You have friends in Budapest even if you are sometimes lonely. I have no friends in London. My children long ceased to be friends, though they are quite friendly. But think of it. Day after day with no one to talk to except Pisti when we play backgammon.

Here are items of news. I have booked for us to go to Dieppe on 2 September, a Wednesday, and to return on Sunday. We could take a train from Victoria at either 7.50 or 11.10. I decided for the later one, I hope rightly. It is possible that Giles and Janet may come as well. Giles's

---
  * Robert Kee and Dylan Thomas.
  ** Alan did not wish to go to Hungary during the summer because of the heat.

plan for a day in Boulogne has not worked out: all the ferries are fully booked, so not everyone is staying at home to watch television.

Marjorie Taylor is organizing a Taylor lunch at Ross-on-Wye on 19 September. I said we would both go – after all I am the head of the family, though no one is likely to acknowledge it.

The Queen is coming to the Historical Association reception at midday Wednesday 25 November. A pretty grim ceremony.

The house in Grove Terrace with a dilapidated red front door has had its door renovated and painted green. The grass has also been cut. I shall now post this letter, having it weighed so as to pay the excess postage. Two packages of labels came addressed to you. Pisti claimed them, and has I think carried them off. He is a very good boy.

I love you and miss you so much.

Laundry £14.32!

x

Alan

28 July: Not a rewarding day. I finished *An English Husband*. It did not distress me at all. I knew your difficulties and tried to put them right, which I have now done (I hope). It was all a mixture of carelessness on my part and misunderstanding on yours. Your account is unfair to me here and there. You do not mention that I told Margaret that I should never see her again, and that I passed on to Giles all the papers dealing with her affairs. I relented on your encouragement when she went into hospital. I read it all as a message of love, and I certainly need one. There is no love in my life at the moment, indeed there is nothing of any kind.

In the evening I went to the Primrose with Sebastian. Very good, cheap meal. The restaurant was deserted. I am sure we shall lose it soon. Sebastian and I talked about The Mill. He emphasized how anxious The Others are that you and I should use it fully. Good news: planning permission for the garage extension has been refused without discussion. Reason: enlargement of Mill Lane impossible without ruining the estuary. Sebastian very triumphant. On the other hand, he is very dissatisfied with the work of the Southern Water Board. By moving all those rocks, they have made it impossible to moor either on our side or the Kitteridges. Fascinating question: who appoints the Water Board, and who is it responsible to? Also, the flood in front of the garage has not disappeared. Sebastian is very cross with Amelia for bringing down the TV set. Result: the children sit indoors all day watching it instead of being out playing games, swimming or sailing. I said perhaps the parents could ban the watching of TV until, say, seven o'clock in the evening. Apparently it is impossible to lay down rules for children, no 'Go to your rooms'. That is where I am going now.

30 July: This page is out of order: I ought to have written on it yesterday, but forgot that Library writing papers will take typescript on both sides. Another very dull day. Weather rather better, so I had a good afternoon in the sun and the Ponds. Otherwise nothing and nobody except the window-cleaner. He certainly does not earn his money. He was in and out before I could discuss what he should do. Pisti is going to the circus tonight with Lizzie, so I shall be on my own all evening. Sebastian has gone back to the Island and is not returning next week. Giles might be here one evening, but I shall arrange a meeting only if Pisti has an engagement. Otherwise, I must keep him company and he me.

Characteristic anecdote of your husband, the great historian. I read chapter XVIII of my autobiography and saw my way clear how to rewrite it. I planned to start today. Then two books arrived for review: a life of Castlereagh, very commonplace, and the first and now the only volume of Arthur Marder on Anglo-Japanese naval relations, very long and obviously fascinating. So the revision of my autobiography is put off again and probably never will be achieved. You see, once you are back here I shall be so happy that I shan't want to write anything. Incidentally, an objection to *An English Husband* occurs to me. You were proposing to leave me before Margaret died. The whole situation makes me very unhappy. I appear so utterly inconsiderate and selfish. It really is a wonder that you put up with me for so long.

I have unearthed in the deep-freeze two bits of meat which look like stewing beef. However, I do not propose to stew them. I shall grill them and see what happens. Also I shall have an avocado, now very soft, and finish off the raspberries. There are still the chicken pieces and, I suppose, the belly of pork. I shall have to spend tomorrow morning shopping, as I shall be away on Saturday. It is difficult catering in advance, as I do not know until the last moment whether Pisti is going out for the evening. Finale: Geoffrey Thomas, who runs the Oxford lectures, writes with thanks and adds that next year he will insist that I bring you with me. I shall insist too, though it must be dreary for you.

29 July: Maybe you would like a description of the royal wedding from me, as seen on TV. I expect you can guess my difficulty. I did not watch it at all. I spent the morning reading David Carlton on Anthony Eden to the end. The later part lacks any access to new documentation and so contains little new. We all know that Eden arranged the Suez aggression with the Israelis and then denied it. Carlton becomes perverse in the extreme towards the end, arguing that Chamberlain was right to seek a greater Germany as a barrier against Russia, and that Eden has brought all our present troubles upon us by his enthusiasm for the Soviet alliance. I expect this will become the new orthodoxy.

Pisti went out vaguely to see the wedding crowds from afar. I went to the Ponds in the afternoon, though there was little sun. Water rather warmer than yesterday. In the evening we both went to the Goldfingers. Pisti showed Ursula how to use the sieve for making dumplings. Ernö wanted to know how Lady Diana Spencer, now the Princess of Wales, is related to Genghis Khan. I could not help him. Ernö's mother was in splendid form, alert and almost talkative until she came round to her son. Then she became utterly blank. The two exchanged looks of hatred, which I suppose has become a habit. It is clear that Ernö is still totally baffled by his mother's attitude to him. Pisti loyally held back on the drink and so was able to drive us back. He drives very much as you do, very fast and with some impatience. It makes me realize how cautious I am in comparison.

I am in despair with my solitude. Day after day goes by without exchanging a word with anyone except the shopkeepers and the company at the Ponds. And I am not through the first week yet. More than two weeks to go, and soon even Pisti will have gone. Somehow I must arrange to go to The Mill next time, though I shall be equally unhappy there. I do not enjoy the company of my children or grandchildren unless you are there. I have difficulties even with making the bed, which insists on sliding to my side, and I am not strong enough to pull it back. In other words, I need you. But how boring life must be for you with only me for company.

31 July: The fine weather has gone quickly enough just when I was getting used to it; rain every now and then as well. I duly went shopping this morning, though I made do with Kentish Town Road and did not go near Inverness Street Market. Perhaps this is the sensible thing to do. Carter's is as good as Talbys, and perhaps Walton is as good as the Market. I have stocked up for the weekend and see my way clear until Pisti's departure. How I shall survive thereafter I do not know. I also went up to Davison's in the car and returned loaded with bottled beer.

If you happen to see today's *Times*, you will find me in the Diary classified along with Isaiah and E. P. Thompson as the 'Brains of England'. A very funny paragraph which will cause pain in many quarters. E.g. Hugh Trevor Roper is not mentioned even as an 'also ran'. It is strange to me how people fall for Isaiah. He is entertaining, he has an impressive manner, he implies that everything he says is profound, but what does it all amount to? As for E. P. Thompson, I see no sign of brains at all. I have just had the reprint of an address he gave on 'Exterminationism', which seemed to me sheer gibberish. I will duly add it to the pile of printed stuff that I am hoarding for you. I suppose it is more the air with which you say things rather than what you say which impresses you. Freddy Ayer, also mentioned in the list of 'Brains', is another of the same sort.

The Taylor party at Ross-on-Wye gets bigger and bigger. There will be not only my cousins and their wives, if still alive, but their children and their grandchildren. If I produced as many, I should add a total of ten children and wives and eight grandchildren. It would need a barracks to accommodate them all. At any rate, I have arranged for you and me to stay at the hotel for two nights, one before and one after. I also said to Marjorie Taylor, 'Of course I shall preside as the head of the family,' to which she agreed.

Now I must move off to simmer the haddock in milk and water, boil the broad beans (already podded) and offer Pisti the alternative of raspberries, pears or greengages. One of these days I shall become a good housekeeper, though never a good cook.

1 August: Further to our telephone conversation of a few minutes ago. I could not help thinking that my two sons were the best-dressed people in the room. I thought pretty highly of my daughters-in-law as well. As to the in-laws, I promised we would go down to see them at Southend some time. Mr Levy is by no means the Jewish trader we had surmised. He works at the Post Office headquarters on Tower Hill – what a delightful spot for an office. Mrs Levy works part-time organizing a multiple store in Southend.

When the best man read out a message* which suddenly mentioned Budapest I was staggered, and even more when he concluded with Eva pronounced correctly Ava. Crispin has certainly made it clear to all and sundry, including his mother, how he loves you. We shall have trouble, I fear. I wish you were here to protect me.

Did I tell you that my memory was going? I sat down the other night to play the patience called St Helena, which I used to play every night, and I could not remember a thing about it. Piquet, yes; backgammon, yes. But St Helena, no. Old age, old age.

The Civil Service strike is over. So there will be no further anxiety about the time of your return. I suppose, too, that I shall get my tax

* Eva's congratulations for Crispin's wedding.

demand. Other financial news: the age limit is removed for inflation-free bonds. You can invest up to £3,000 in them. I wonder whether you should. If inflation roars up again, you will benefit. If it declines, of which I see no sign at present, you will be stuck with money which is not growing and yet not earning. I think perhaps that you should consult David Reoch about all your investment policy. My stockbroker would also advise you. But he would be keen to put you into ordinary shares, otherwise called equities. Of course there is always Sebastian, but he is a gambler and also changes his opinion from day to day. Still, I should like you to be both happy and secure in your financial affairs. I am not at all sure that it is right for you to stay in building societies for any length of time. I use them as a home for cash that I shall need within the year. Now I am off to clean a lettuce and make an omelette.

2 August: A dull day. Sunday is the worst of days because it is certain that the telephone will not ring. Daniel told me yesterday that he had no plans for today, and sure enough he did not come round or even ring. The cure for boredom is to work, and I did quite a lot. The *Observer* is still on about the royal wedding (remember it?), which I did not read. The section on English culture this week is about the Normans, not well done I thought. Too flattering to the Normans, who were crude conquerors. We have seen most of the buildings listed, though I suppose we should go to Copley in Essex – frescoes over-restored. Weather very fine and sunny but with rather a cold wind. I had a good session at the Ponds where the water is now 67 Fahrenheit.

I have written a lively review of the life of Castlereagh which was sent to me by both the publisher and the *Observer*. A dull man, though his policy is interesting. I made some light-hearted remarks. I am also reading Arthur Marder's book on Anglo-Japanese naval relations from 1936 to 1941 – end of the naval treaties to the sinking of the *Repulse* and the *Prince of Wales*. Not new, but marvellously done. In the introduction he thanks me specifically for 'encouragement', as if he needed any. This moved me. Here is a problem. The Chiefs of Staff said over and over again that England had three potential enemies – Germany, Italy and Japan – and could not fight all three at once. Right. Then why on earth did they not recommend that England must make a deal with one or other of them? Instead, they drifted on until they were at war with all three and then merely said, 'There you are. We told you it could not be done.' A helpless drift to disaster. The one satisfactory thing about it is that Chamberlain emerges more discredited than ever. I think Max's policy of detachment from Europe was the wisest, though the least moral, not that there was much moral in opposing Japan. These are questions without an answer.

Pisti is going to the Vanburgh Theatre with your friends whose name I can never remember. I am going to eat a chop, accompanied by cabbage, and conclude with eating some of the peaches which are going rotten.

Only one more Sunday without you. I am beginning to count the days impatiently. Don't forget me by any chance.

3 August: This is just to finish off the record so that Pisti can take it with him. A hot day, though nothing like as hot as it is with you, the very thought of which makes me blench. I went to the Ponds and had to take shelter underneath the trees. I worry about swimming, which I now find much harder than in the sea. I find I can't hold my head up for long and so go back to port in anxiety. I fear my swimming days are over unless we go to The Mill again. In the evening I went out to dinner with Giles. Giles is only concerned to make The Mill pay, hence he is always seeking new tenants and keeping The Others who want to use The Mill at bay. He is very keen that we should go there more often. We shall see.

4 August: I finished my review of Castlereagh and sent it off. The *TLS* has already sent David's book elsewhere, so I am safe from having to review it. The day started cool with mist, but is now as hot as yesterday. However, I shall probably venture out. This evening Pisti and I will have a last meal together. One piece of advice: in future when you leave me you must label the various packages in the refrigerator. As it is, I don't know whether we shall be eating belly, chicken or cod tonight. Whatever remains will keep me going for some days. As to myself, I can only tell you that I think of you from morning to night. Each day I miss you more. It seems a long and weary time before you are here. Do not doubt that I shall be waiting for you as full of love as I waited at Salzburg, or when you arrived at Heathrow in 1978, or perhaps more because I love you more each day.

5 August: I was up at half-past six to rouse Pisti. So we were off in good time. I took him to Euston, where we could reach the Victoria line without rush or trouble. Now, I suppose, he is on his last stretch home. Daniel and Luke* are proposing to have a day in Vienna, so they may not arrive in time to see you. By the time they arrive you will be locked in my arms.

* A friend of Daniel's.

I had a date for two o'clock at the far end of King's Road – the World's End pub, in fact. Knowing me, you can guess that I left home at half-past nine, but I had an excuse – I had my hair cut, very smartly, on the way. Even so, I had to sit for more than an hour in the pub, eating a pork pie and drinking a pint of rather questionable Real Ale. My talk to the Americans went off quite well, though I had a feeling that they had never heard of Lloyd George before. These summer schools are a mere excuse for a jaunt to England or the continent at the expense of university funds. However, I received £125, the first bit of income for a long time, which worries me quite a lot. Returned very easily on the 137. I notice that Oxford Street is now jammed with private cars, though they are in theory banned: another sign that civilization is breaking down. There is to be a rail strike on 1 September. It will include the ferries and be the end of our trip to Dieppe.

Next, I undid the parcel which I had got out of the deep-freeze and unfrozen. I thought it was two cod steaks that I had bought late last week. Horror. It was a huge piece of brains. I had no idea what to do with it. I soaked it well and then fried it in oil. The brains were tender, otherwise not a success. There was far too much of it and even I could not finish it. So it went into the bin. Not an enjoyable dinner. I bought some fresh taramasalata, and ate some of it last night. Daniel is going to Gill on Sunday, so I have far too much bread in the house. I have to consume it myself. Perhaps this is why I am no longer constipated.

6 August: This was a really startling day, with the worst storms London has known for years. I had just got my breakfast out on the patio when heavy drops of rain fell. I retreated indoors just in time. After that we had torrential rain and great claps of thunder, to say nothing of vivid lightning, for two or three hours. There was nothing to be done except read patiently, as a result of which I have nearly finished Arthur Marder's book. There is nothing startlingly new in it. That is, we know why the Japanese went to war and why the two British ships were sent out to Singapore. Arthur somehow makes sense of it all. That is, he shows that both sides were mad and yet explains why they were mad. What happened in December 1941 sealed the fates of both Empires, all to the profit of the United States – and maybe Germany. In the afternoon I managed to walk as far as Swain's Lane, but it was risky and not very inspiring. I loaded up with biscuits and scones in preparation for Roger Louis, only for the telephone to ring at half-past four with the news from Roger that the railway lines were flooded so no trains running to Gospel Oak, nor for that matter on the Piccadilly line into town. This proves what a mistake it was to shift the Record Office out to Kew. If it had still been in Chancery Lane, Roger could have come by bus. Instead, I read that the entire office in Chancery Lane will be closed soon. Other news: one of the greatest art collections of recent times has been bequeathed to the Courtauld Institute. We must go and see it as soon as you come back.

This evening I revealed the two cod steaks, cooking one for tonight and the other to be eaten tomorrow, cold. Not a great success. The cod steak was rather tough and quite tasteless. It proves I am no cook. At the Dartmouth Arms, a young couple spoke to me on the ground that they had heard me at Rugby. Did I really go to Rugby? If I did, I must have spoken badly or at least not well. The young man said I gave a rambling talk on my experiences as an historian. Did I have any such experiences? I only seduced one historian as far as I can recollect, and it was certainly a pretty good experience. But it is all long ago. More heavy rain in the evening. I listened to Brahms No. 4. Set not working well. We must consult someone, but with Bob Doyle unobtainable I do not know whom.

7 August: Now my story begins to be really drab. I have not spoken to a soul. I have not been out. I read, I went upstairs and lay on our bed. My only thought was that in a week's time you would be with me again. In the afternoon I went to Swain's Lane in search of *pâté de campagne*, only to find that Mrs Lever had closed for a fortnight. As a result I had a terrible meal in the evening, the cod cold and tasteless, the rest not worth recording. I think we will forget about today.

8 August: At least I was more energetic. I went to the market, rather without purpose. At any rate I stocked up with peas. When I opened the last packet in the deep-freeze, believing it would be chicken, it turned out to be cod. So the chicken never existed except in your imagination. I could not face more cod, so I put it in the bin and bought a pork chop which turned out to be little better. In the afternoon I did the whole round of the Heath, including Kenwood House. Do you remember the old man who had strained his Achilles tendon? He too was doing the whole round. In the meantime he has had a stroke and a prostate operation. Now he has shingles. Yet he still marches stalwartly on, an example to me. In the evening I telephoned Németvölgyi, only to learn from Pisti that you were in hospital with pneumonia. I was shattered. Shall I even see you again? How can I go on without you, day after day of complete emptiness? I don't see how I can manage my life at all. I must ring you early next week in the hope of some better news. I can never risk your leaving me again. I am too much in the dark and too miserable to write any more. I got the documents for Dieppe, but with the rail strike hanging over us I doubt whether we shall ever see Dieppe.

9 August: Today was a little better. I applied my usual doctrine that it is no good worrying about something if you can't do anything about it. Maybe you are very ill, maybe you are dying. There is nothing I can do except wait until Monday when, as far as I can understand, Pisti will have more news about you. I filled my morning as much as I could by reading every page of the *Observer*, even the fashion pages which I could not understand. After lunch, I again did a pretty energetic stride round the Heath. Tiresome weather. Not warm enough to sit out, and then sun just when I am not near a seat. I did a bigger swing round, getting lost on the way, in order to visit the men's lavatory just near the entrance to Kenwood, or rather quite a long way from it. When I got there I found a man, first washing himself, then washing his trousers which had got into the mud, and finally washing two thermos flasks. This quite put me off my stroke and I left without passing water, particularly when he said he had seen me on television. What is that? I had almost forgotten. Now I had to calculate whether I could hold out to the next station of relief near the tennis courts, or should I slip behind a bush. I tried many a bush and always, just as I had taken position, there were voices from afar. In the end I reached the tennis courts without an accident. Desperately cold. There was a band playing and a small audience, some of whom had rugs over their knees. Surprise appearance of Daniel at tea-time. A human being at last. I gave him the address of Henrietta* in Vienna, though I expect she will be away. It seems mad to stop overnight in a strange town. But these are wild boys. Daniel has found a bed-and-breakfast room in Bristol, which means unfortunately that he will always go out for his evening meal. I gave him the Avery address also, and told him to rely on them if he had any difficulty. I shan't be happy until he has settled down. Pork chop again for dinner. Tasteless and not at all interesting. Rather silly concert in the evening. But I have finished Marder and will review him tomorrow. Where am I to fit in his book? The shelves are already full. For this, if for no other reason, I need you back badly.

10 August: I wrote my review of Marder in the morning. As I think I told you, it has all been said before but Arthur says it better. I praised the book to the skies. It deserves it for making the story so exciting. Weather still tiresome, no more rain but cloud every time I thought of going to

* Friend of Alan's who came to live with him and Margaret for a time.

the Ponds. So I went to the Heath and stayed waiting for the sun which always escaped me. Every day the post brings Hungarian newspapers for you and nothing for me except an occasional bill from John Lewis. In the evening I went to dinner with the Carriers, her sister and brother-in-law from Australia, also Sebastian. He has now finished with The Mill, and I think they are off to somewhere in France. A very enjoyable evening. John Carrier is rather pompous, but Sarah is very sweet and the more so because of her deafness. I came home too late to ring you up (actually it wasn't, I had forgotten the time difference). I must wait for news tomorrow. House empty. My life empty. Everything empty.

11 August: I must run things together a bit, having been too engaged though not happily. Tuesday I went down to the London Library in order to return a work by Wilkie Collins, *Armadale*, which I read somewhere was his best work. It isn't. In fact it is unreadable. Half-way through the first volume I decided it would not do and returned volume 2 unread. Very good weather for the Ponds in the afternoon. I kept counting the minutes until I could ring you up. Then something like half an hour before I could get the ringing tone with you. I don't think you realized how distressed and anxious I had been. I still think you are being too optimistic, but we shall soon see.

12 and 13 August: Trip to Oxford. Two gay lectures, which were much appreciated. Dinner at St John's with the summer school – very inferior food and lots of whisky. No sign, I am glad to say, of Michael Hurst. Ron Pacey* is dead: went on a visit to his son in Southampton, felt unwell and died. I wrote a letter to Mrs Pacey, saying how it was a great loss for me. Other personal news which has made me laugh. There is a great outcry because the BBC Director-General has rejected first E. P. Thompson and then Edward Heath as Dimbleby Lecturer on BBC Radio (not even television). And guess who engaged first one and then the second: Mr Edward Mirzoeff, as *The Times* refers to him. What is said or not said on sound radio is not of the slightest importance except for the pompous heads of the BBC. If I were asked to give six radio lectures, I should turn it down out of hand. However, the embarrassment of all concerned is very funny. I went to Oxford by motorway. Time: one hour forty minutes. I returned over the Chilterns. Time: one hour forty-five minutes, and a more agreeable journey. But maybe I drive faster than my mate. Or rather I drive slower on the motorway and faster on ordinary roads. Average speed: 60 miles per hour in each case. I got

* Alan's manservant at Magdalen. He was a dear friend to him.

back too late to go to the Ponds. Instead I loyally put all the laundry to soak. Next time, if there is a next time, you must teach me how to wash clothes before you go. Maybe there won't be a next time. We shall see. Now I don't need to write any more. I'll go shopping tomorrow morning and arrive in Heathrow after lunch. So this wretched period has its end.

1982

Twisden Rd.
London NW5

1 July 1982

Darling

I had resolved not to write to you but to keep my diary record waiting for you. However, there is an urgent reason I must write even though I may catch you on the telephone. I wrote to Karl Miller that I could not do the Diary for him at present, and instead lightheartedly offered him the Romanes Lecture. He has just rung up and said he will take it without cutting it at all. I am very glad to get it in print. But where is it? I went up to your room, but cannot find my way about at all. Also your cupboard is locked. I really ought to know where my archive is, so much more precious than Kossuth's.* Ring me up as soon as you can so that I can get it to Karl. I am going to Janet on Saturday, and one evening Sophia will come over. Next week I suppose I might go to Amelia, but have heard nothing. At any rate, try any night after eight o'clock. I am always busy over my dinner by then.

Last night I went to Mary's, a rushed supper composed mainly of spaghetti bolognese, not very digestible. Then they rushed off to Acland Burghley. Mary is all on Claire's side, so I did not argue. Still, if she really wants to move I suppose it is best for her to do so.

It has been raining heavily all morning. However, I am going to brave the weather in order to buy a 19½p stamp. Karl Miller was very surprised to learn that I was not in bed. As a matter of fact, I continue to feel very fit. Still a little shaky when shaving, and my legs aching when I walk too far. But no headaches, and water flowing free. Indeed, I feel very trapped by having ever agreed to this Ultrasound examination. Once a doctor sees a chance of cutting and slashing, nothing can stop him.

Now I must rush out and then return to Keegan's boring book. I shall deliver the autobiography to Roger Machell this afternoon.

Much love and kisses. Two days gone, nineteen to go.

X X X
Alan

* Eva's work on Kossuth as an English journalist.

Twisden Rd.
London NW5

5 July

Sweetheart, My Love,

I had resolved not to write to you but to keep all my news for the diary, awaiting you when you come home. But I am so lonely and miserable that I have to write if only to feel you near me.

Food: I have been out twice to Janet's, once very troublesome to Mary Taylor's. As a result, I have hardly started on the brisket and shall finish the minced-meat only this evening. I have had some bad days with my health, others very fit and able to walk to Janet's within a quarter of an hour. What really worries me is that I am making no money. Karl wanted me for all August, but I had to tell him that I should probably be in hospital and certainly could not commit myself. He, on the other hand, had already engaged someone for July. On top of this the *Observer* has become totally silent. I shall ring Terry tomorrow. But for the time being no money. The alarm that Curtis Brown had paid me £8,000 in 1980 turned out completely false. They paid me £2,000, which was what I said. Some muddle by the Tax Inspector.

It has been very cold, so much so that Amelia, with whom I am going to have supper on Wednesday, turned on her central heating. Bill Cane had an operation and nothing wrong was found – certainly not the wart he thought he had on his bladder.

Two Hungarian newspapers arrive for you every day. Shall I destroy them? Otherwise the house will gradually sink under their weight. There are also some letters that seem to be fairly urgent. But I suppose they are in Hungarian, so I will not open them.

Don't bother to answer this letter. I shall not write again, if only because I am so depressed. I feel I have no future, nothing but getting steadily worse and less effective in life. All my life is wrapped up in you, and it seems pointless to go on living when you are not here. However, I have now worked off my unhappiness and am off to the Continental.

All my love,

                     x   Alan   x
                               x

1982

JOURNAL

Tuesday, 29 June: A miraculous change has come over me – no headache, no lassitude, no discomfort. I don't suppose it will last, but it is very agreeable while it does. I was able to work all morning and to do practically the whole round of the Heath in the afternoon. I have not felt so well since last year. I am not very happy with the end of my autobiography, but there really is not much more to say except that I am very happy and I don't think I shall have any sensations to record in the future. At any rate we must see what Roger Machell and others at Hamish Hamilton have to say about it. I can see that they will think it trivial, but then I am a trivial person. Most people take themselves too seriously. I might say this in a preface.

The house seems very empty with you not in it. I keep expecting to hear your key in the front door and no key turns. Nothing much has happened. Some sun and some rain. Giles has asked me to dinner on Saturday. This evening I shall eat half the soup, leaving the rest in a jug in the refrigerator, and shall cook half the cauliflower, leaving the rest for tomorrow. Around seven o'clock I shall call in at the Continental and buy some broad beans for one night. I shall also buy a pork pie for tomorrow when I go to Mr Tombs and Mr Johnson. Then on Thursday I shall deliver the autobiography to Roger Machell. I shall have a bath tonight and cut my toenails with my left-handed scissors. I miss you very much.

Wednesday, 30 June: The left-handed scissors are totally useless for the cutting of toenails. Next time I go into town I shall buy a pair of folding scissors at Clements. Today was a wasted and exhausting day. I delivered your bracelet to Fish – it will cost around £2. Then I went down to the bank and collected my prescriptions from Tombs. After this I went to the Health Centre to have a pee (no other relief station in range). No result. I developed a panic that my prostate had caused a complete blockage, but after drinking a pint of Young's Ordinary all was well. Mr Johnson tells me that the worst thing about being in hospital is having to use a bed-pan. It will be particularly humiliating for me because I shall be unable to use it. After lunch, I had my hair cut and collected five boxes of headed notepaper. That will last our time. Going out to Mary Taylor's this evening. This will leave me with too much food, but it can't be helped. I shall struggle on with Keegan before I go – very bad and pretentious. I hope to listen to Asa* on Marx and Engels in London. Then I shall retire to my lonely bed. How often during the night I turn towards you, and there is no one to turn to.

* Asa Briggs.

Perhaps I should deliberately go to hospital so that you would have to come back and look after me. I have stuffed everything into the bin, which is now back to normal.

Thursday, 1 July: As I expected, supper with the Sebastian Taylors was not entertaining. We talked interminably about the problem of Claire. I think it is a mistake to fuss too much about children. At any rate, there is no vacant place at Acland Burghley so the problem has to be postponed. Today I had a busy day. I worked hard on Keegan all morning and wrote four pages – 1,200 words. I should finish it tomorrow. The book is I think worthless, but just the sort of thing Bob Silvers likes. I packed the typescript of *An Uninteresting Story* in my briefcase and set off for Covent Garden. Roger Machell likes the title, which I was rather ashamed of. They are reprinting *The Origins*, which I must reread even though the benefit goes to the second Mrs Taylor. You will I hope have received my letter by now, so you will know about the Romanes which I must deliver to Karl as soon as possible. I am in a terrible puzzle about my prostate operation. I feel totally well. Shall I cancel the operation or go through with it all the same? I wish you were here to help me.

Friday, 2 July: An unexciting day. I worked hard all morning at the book about the Normandy campaign, getting more and more impatient with its worthlessness and therefore more outrageous in my judgements. I hope it will amuse Bob Silvers, maybe he will be merely shocked by it. At any rate, I finished it and it will go off to New York tomorrow. Two invitations to speak – from the Cambridge Social Democrats and from the H. G. Wells Society. They both got a card of refusal. The weather was difficult: quite warm and yet threatening rain. After lunch I went off with a rug to the Heath and lay in our favourite place for about half an hour. Then the clouds gathered and I returned home just in time to escape the rain. Same again later: hot enough to read in the patio, then not only rain but cold enough to tempt me to put the central heating on, which I didn't. My life is full of preparations: podding the peas for this evening and cooking the porridge for tomorrow morning. I shall have the brisket again this evening. It seems to me I shall be still eating it when you come back. Tomorrow will mark the end of the first week when you have been away. Also the first day when I have seen nobody and hardly been out of the house. To complete my empty life, the *TLS* was delayed and I shall have to wait for it until tomorrow. It looks like another railway strike on Sunday. The NUR and the ASLEF are now openly at war. What a sad end to the great British trade union movement. I am glad to see Clive Jenkins is in trouble. I think I'll now slip out for a drink.

Saturday, 3 July: Off to Inverness Street Market as usual, but my purchases sadly reduced. Even so, I think I have bought far too much. Raspberries still go on and I can't resist buying them. Then I came back and wrote to Crispin, just to remind him that I was still alive. Of course, how long I shall stay alive is a different matter. Having finished with Keegan, I am now back with the volume on British Intelligence, which I don't think I shall finish if I survive for years. After lunch Sophia arrived all alone. We walked up Parliament Hill and sat on a seat at the top in agreeable sunshine. Sophia is so absorbed in her job that she is really not very interesting. Her political enthusiasms are all forgotten. In the evening I went to Giles and Janet. The kitchen is wonderfully improved. More space, more room and equipment much more up-to-date. I can't describe it, you must go and see it. I miss you very much. Also, my recovery is at an end and I am back in bed much of the time.

Sunday, 4 July: An empty day. It took me two hours to read the *Observer* and I did not find a single point of interest in it, quite enough of itself to send me back to bed. I had the gas-fire on in the sitting room. I went on the Heath in order to listen to the band, a better one than we heard last Sunday. But it was too cold to lie on the grass, so I struggled up to the top of Parliament Hill again. This made me much better and I went to Torriano Cottages at a great rate, as fast as I used to walk before I was ill. There we had roast beef, and afterwards I refreshed Giles's memory of cribbage. Nothing else to report except emptiness.

Monday, 5 July: Another bad day. I struggled along with the history on British Intelligence, too difficult for me to understand. Very distressed by General Sir Somebody Hackett, aged seventy-four, remarking that he regarded any age above seventy as a bonus which one should accept as a gift from Providence. I had thought I was safe until eighty. Now I count every day as precious and am not safe for survival. Daniel to tea, so charming and so sane. He also regretted having upset you by his remarks. Then I had a wonderful telephone conversation with you. I found the Romanes and have sent it to Karl Miller. Let us hope you won't leave me again. After all, shan't be here this time next year. One week of loneliness over.

Tuesday, 6 July: A wasted day, or at any rate morning. Two VAT inspectors came and spent three hours going over my records. They caught me out on a few things, but I didn't think they earned their salary. They started a wild idea which they are now trying to enforce on me. Lectures etc. to universities and colleges are exempt from VAT, but services, such as driving to the Lecture Hall, are liable to VAT and they want me to go through three years of VAT, collecting it. I have never had a more exasperating morning. But when they had gone I finished reading the book on British Intelligence. I must also tell you that I ate half the brisket without heating it, and what is more I am going to eat the rest tomorrow. So I still have two haddock cutlets and one chicken piece in the fridge, which incidentally has started to leak, and without you I do not know how to stop it. Slept very badly. I kept turning to you and you weren't there.

Wednesday, 7 July: I shall not eat the rest of the brisket tonight. I shall eat it on Friday instead, and tonight I shall go to Amelia's. I went and had a very agreeable evening. Bill painted a horrific picture of University College Hospital. He said the noise was so great that he could not sleep and advised me to get ear-plugs. It is really urgent that I should go to hospital. Difficulty with water now beginning. I am frightened and do not know what to do without you. We have ruined our summer, and maybe I have ruined my physical state. Only bit of good news is that I wrote the review of Hinsley's book on British Intelligence and got some fun out of it. I wanted to go to the Ponds but it was too far for me. I can only walk any distance when you are there. How I wish we could have the good life we had when I was younger. Now you are tied to a decaying, forgotten old man. Things will never go right with me again.

Thursday, 8 July: I went to my dentist in the morning. My teeth are working loose in their sockets and the bridges have cracked. However, we must wait for the whole structure to fall apart and then the dentist will make some artificial substitute. Fortunately I have no pain and am not likely to have – the roots are out already. Then a trip down to Gaston's to sell Keegan's book. The Stationery Office does not allow its books to be sold second-hand. Hence I am stuck with Hinsley, which I must take to the History Book Shop. I went to Mary Taylor's for supper, a rather tough Stroganoff and not much else. Mary and Sebastian have started going to Hampstead mixed Pond before dinner. What a loyal, good husband he is. I suppose he loves Mary, but it takes a lot of patience to do so.

Friday, 9 July: At last I came back to life, or perhaps life came to me in the shape of the Canadian Broadcasting Corporation, complete with

1982

attractive interviewer and crew. Topic: foolish. Should the War Room – Churchill's shelter under the Admiralty building – be turned into a tour for sightseers? Everything will be made smart, a second underground corridor will be inserted in order to enable the sightseers to get out again. I took the romantic view that we should keep the shelter just as it was, even if not very many people could visit it. It did not matter one way or the other, but it brought me back to the cameras.

Troublesome afternoon: rain-clouds and threat of rain, so I could neither go for a walk nor stay happily at home. Bright stroke: Terry had already allotted Elizabeth's book on the Jameson Raid, but I got Bill Webb interested. Something to write about. In the evening I finished off the brisket, still not heated up again. It was delicious. In the night, worried that my prostate was now blocking my water. It cleared in the morning, but still alarming. A new worry. There is a nurses' strike. How can I get taken in by UCH? Frightening.

Saturday, 10 July: Usual routine. Off early to Inverness St Market. Even then it was very crowded. Bought most of the usual things, though less of them. Returned to find that the lesser Frigidaire had flooded and turned itself off. Spent most of the morning wiping up and emptying the fridge. Thought I should have to send for a man. Then found that the frig, once wiped dry, was working again and I shall have to move all the contents back again. In the evening went to Giles and Janet. After rich meal, Giles and I played dominoes for Alison's delectation.

Sunday, 11 July: Truly nothing in the *Observer*. However, corrected the proofs of Keegan's review from the *NY Review of Books*. Good to have some employment. In the afternoon went out and listened to the band on the Heath. Sophia, Rob and offspring came to tea without warning. They ate all the gingerbread. Later went to Giles and Janet. They are the most welcoming of my family. This evening we played cribbage, with Alison herself playing under Giles's instructions. Then home to a delectable telephone call. We shall soon meet unless I have a car accident.

Monday, 12 July: First letter from you: it has taken a fortnight to arrive. I was wise not to write a letter at all, merely think of you all the time. I went off to the Bishopsgate Institute to attend a City Music Society concert. There I was told that this was not a Society concert but a Festival of London concert, and that my green ticket was no good. I was furious. I said, 'I am the President of this bloody Society and you say I have to pay. Well, I shan't pay, I am leaving.' Ivan Sutton came out very apologetically and I entered without paying. Concert not worth all the fuss: Chopin played very loudly, which I did not enjoy at all. I came back by 214 direct from Finsbury Square to Gordon House Road, a delightful journey. If we want to visit the Bunhill cemetery, the 214 is the way to do it.

Evening, went to Amelia's. Very good lasagne cooked by Bill Cane. He improves with time, or perhaps mellows a little. Very depressed. My work is at an end. I have nothing to read, nothing to review. I have said I couldn't write the Diary for the *London Review of Books*, whereas it looks as though my operation will never take place. My life has come to a complete stop. I am dreading driving to Oxford all on my own. No one, not even you, realizes that I am very ill. My decline over the last six months has been frightening, though no one except me seems to notice it.

Tuesday, 13 July: I finished reading Elizabeth's book about the Jameson Raid and got Bill Webb to let me review it for the *Guardian*. Not a very good review. I had very little to say that I hadn't written for the *Manchester Guardian* thirty years ago. Still, it gave me something to do. But there is a problem. My Parkinson's disease, if that is what I am suffering from, makes me hit the wrong keys and my typing gets worse and worse. In the afternoon I lay on The Heath. I really ought to make the effort to go to the Ponds, but I am afraid there will be too many people there and I hate stumbling before a crowd. Evening dinner with Michèle* and family. Agreeable company, but food rather spartan and of course no drink. So I slipped home for a bottle which her husband and I drank. He is all right, she is very enlivening. Still, I was glad to get off home. Then Australia rang up wanting my opinion about the War Room, but the line got lost before I said anything. I expect they'll try again. Very black and hopeless feeling. You must somehow make a new man of me.

Wednesday, 14 August: Nothing much to record. Thunderstorm in the morning. Cleared up enough for me to go a little walk in the afternoon. I bought ear-plugs in preparation for going into hospital. Oh dear, I wish all this time of solitary misery were over, and the wretched illness also. I count over and over again the days until next Wednesday. Our telephone conversation cheered me up. Nothing else worth writing. I ate the chicken leg from the deep-freeze.

* A neighbour in Twisden Road.

Thursday, 15 July: This was the worst day physically of while you have been away. I got up feeling very shaky, and was not improved by a rich breakfast. I spent most of the morning lying on my bed. Then there came to lunch John Midgeley, whom I once knew as a reporter on the *Manchester Guardian* – in fact, I got him on to the paper. He was in love then with a good-looking student of mine called Hilda Bristow. She was not in love with him, but he persuaded her that if she went to bed with him she would fall in love. This is a very old trick which I thought no longer was effective. However, we invited them out to Three Gates for more than one weekend when they tried his remedy. No good. Hilda Bristow went out of my life. John Midgeley went to the London office of the *Guardian*, and then moved to New York where he is now head of the *Economist* Office. He also has a wife and children, more or less grown up, so his remedy must have worked in the end. He was boring when I knew him fifty years ago and is boring now. However, he brought a huge piece of Double Gloucester and, what I had never heard of, Shropshire Blue also. When he left, there followed the heaviest fall of rain I have ever seen. Bad for St Swithin's Day. In the evening I cooked two haddock fillets and a small red cabbage, the latter very soggy. Altogether a very empty, unhappy evening until I spoke to you. That made me quite fit again.

Friday, 16 July: This day was quite the reverse. I felt quite fit and went up to Waterlow Park, where I sat on a bench for quite a time. On the way home I bought a croissant at the expensive shop. In the evening I took Daniel and Gill to the Primrose. It was nice, they were nice, the weather was nice. But misfortune followed. I woke not at six but at two, and had to get up every quarter of an hour during the night to have relief. Robert* tells me this is an advanced stage of prostate trouble. I am again in great distress. Shall I go to Oxford or cancel? I am really not fit for it, especially with the traffic problem. I wish you were here. And that is the end of my Diary. I must somehow survive until next Tuesday.

* Sophia's first husband, who is a doctor.

1983

3 July 1983

Darling Love,

    I miss you very much, all day long and much of the night. I turn towards you and you are not there. I go up to your room. You are not there. I can't imagine how I am going to get through the next three weeks. To make things worse, my illness has suddenly become worse. My left hand now shakes as badly as my right. I shall not be able to shave much longer with an old-fashioned razor. I am also less steady on my feet. All this came quite suddenly in the middle of the night and won't go away. Also, my nausea is with me all the time. I should like to consult Michael, but I suppose he is away and I must just go on with the pills. If the trouble gets worse, I shall go back to five pills a day instead of six.

    I have not done much. Friday morning I sat indoors and read about the French war of 1814, a very solid book by Housseau. I don't suppose it will be of much use to me, but it is better to have some idea of what I shall say if I say anything at all. I am very frightened at the prospect of lecturing in Oxford. If things get worse I must call it off. Friday afternoon I walked up past the Lido and then back by the tennis courts, calling in at the Bull and Last.* Saturday I did an abbreviated round of shopping, driving the car without difficulty. I read all morning. After lunch I mounted the Throne** and remained there until tea-time. I thought that if I had a really long lie, I might recover somewhat. And so I did. About half-past six I walked all the way to Janet's, a distance I thought beyond me. It did not tire me at all and I was very pleased with myself. But today is very different. I feel that I have slipped back permanently and that I shall soon be permanently in a chair. I need you very badly, but I must somehow manage and not ask you to come back early. I wish some member of the family could look after me, but they are all busy in their own affairs and I must drag out this dreary existence. It is terrible to feel that day after day is ahead when I shall see no one. Probably I shall be unable to look after myself, and then what on earth am I to do?

    Janet was much impressed by Jill Craigie. She also said that Joanna

---

* A pub.
** A reclining chair on the patio.

was very drunk, and Terry by no means sober. I hear that Sophia has already moved into Rochester Road. She has bought her flat in Warrington Crescent and is now having much of it changed. Sebastian started back at work on Friday, and will be working regularly from tomorrow. The weather has been much the same – sunnier, but quite cold at the same time. I can't decide whether to go to bed for the afternoon or to try for a walk and a lie-down on the grass. I will add something to this letter tomorrow.

Later on Sunday afternoon: I have decided to finish this letter now. That will leave me free to write again in the middle of the week. I spent the afternoon on the Heath, warm sun and rather cold wind. I lay on what seemed to be dry grass. When I got up, I found my bottom all damp. A brisk walk – with stick – soon dried it off. I am very worried how I am to get to Gaston. I can't take a stick to Central London, yet I can't walk steadily without one. I feel very gloomy about the future. I am threatened with the life of an invalid any time now. I don't want to leave, yet I may go on for years as you sometimes imply. Perhaps nuclear warfare would be an improvement to that. It is maddening to face a future of permanent feebleness for which there is no remedy. When you come back, everything will feel better even if not perfect. But three weeks is a terrible long time.

Lots of love to you and the family,

Alan

6 July

My Sweet Heart,

I have hesitated to write or ring you up during the last few days. Most of the time I have felt pretty ill, and then recover when I take my next lot of pills. The last couple of days have been very hot, and I have got as far as the Heath to lie in the shade. But to walk as far as the Ponds has been quite beyond me. A waste of very fine days. Yesterday, Tuesday, I was just beginning to hope that I might reach the Ponds when Mr Lewis rang up and asked me to go round at once so that he could take a further impression of my mouth – a waste of a good morning.

I am surviving. On Sunday evening I was with Sebastian and Mary. Sebastian is recovering fast, though he really needs six months off which he will never get. Claire was in fine fighting form, challenging any rule that Mary laid down. Monday I was all alone and finished the brisket. Last night, Tuesday, I ate an enormous quantity of broad beans and scrapped the casserole which had contained the brisket. Something adequate was revealed. I now look forward to a round of entertainments. This evening I am going to Amelia's. Tomorrow I shall have to look after myself, and this will be a good opportunity to eat the Finnan haddock. Friday I go to the Quinns for dinner. I was also there yesterday for tea, which was far from being luxurious. She is a lively creature, but not much in touch with life. Saturday I shall be with Giles and Janet, Sunday I shall be with Sophia at Rochester Road. It has just been sold for I think seventy-four thousand pounds, so all ends well with the legacy of Margaret's. Giles's patience has at last been justified. My plans for next week have not yet been formed, but I hope to stir up some invitations. The Primrose restaurant is too far. I'd rather cook for myself at home.

Margaret* has just rung up to say that she has a sore throat. Maybe she will be recovered by next week.

It is terrible to think that you have not yet been away for a week. It seems more like a year. Next year there will be no problem. I shall not be fit to be left, if indeed I am here at all. I am also dreading my time in Oxford, but I can't see any way of escaping it. I hope we shall manage Buxton on 27 and 28 July. At any rate, I have told them we are coming.

The prospects for the Diary of 29 July are cheering up. At any rate, I have decided to run nudism hard. One paragraph on Parson's Pleasure. Another on Highgate Ponds. After that, I can discuss the spread of nude beaches. Finally, I shall have to think of some other topic and that will not be easy. I hope you are having a good time and not too hot. Yesterday was really hot, though with some cold wind. Today has turned cooler, though one can't say for how long. I foresee a difficult problem the day you return. We shan't be home until eight o'clock at the earliest, and there will be nothing to eat in the house. I suppose omelettes will have to do. Instructions, please.

Oh dear, lots of love but I wish you were here. I am all alone. I have nothing to read and shall have to rely on *The Good Soldier Schwejk* for all my reading from now until you get back. Are you missing me as much as I am missing you? Love and love and love.

Alan

* Weekly help.

1983

9 July

My sweetheart

I have just received a letter from you dated 2 July, but as it referred to events here later than that, such as Daniel and Gill calling on Monday, 4 July, your historian's precision for dating must have gone astray. Do not imagine for a moment that I am happy or content with the society of the family when I can get it, which is rare. I am alone for days on end. Most mornings I feel pretty down and have to rest most of the morning, thinking I shall never be fit again. Then around lunch-time I recover and am fit to walk to the Heath, though not to the Ponds. Somehow I manage to make a dinner of some sort. Then I play Beethoven sonatas, not very interesting.

Here is my schedule. Tuesday, 5 June, I had to go to Lewis for a further model of my mouth. Hence I missed the laundry and shall have to wait in for it this Tuesday without fail. Somehow I cooked my own dinner, mainly by having a further portion of the brisket. Wednesday, Margaret rang up to say she could not come. Luckily I stayed in until after lunch, when a man whom I had forgotten came to see me about Lord Berners. I fear I had not a great deal to tell him. The *English Historical Review* arrived. It has an article for you on 'Chartism and the Trades', a bit remote for me. Incidentally, all the letters for you appear to be from one or other of these firms whom you deal with by post. They are all loyally piled in your room, together with a proof of *George V* and one of the Diary. I am in bad trouble with the next Diary. I have done two pages on nudism at Parson's Pleasure and in the Highgate Ponds, but I can think of absolutely nothing with which to fill the remaining three pages, and time is getting short. Here is a little item of news which will amuse you. The local authorities at Torbay have decided not to interfere with girls going topless. The police say they can find no law against it. Enlightenment at last. Thursday I went to the London Library and had a very useful morning, principally with the *Historical Journal*. A very funny article about the discussions during the war [as to] how much they could reveal afterwards from the Foreign Office files. Apparently not much.

I forgot to mention that I went to Amelia's on Wednesday evening, very agreeable. Nolan is now very tall and very thin, I'd say over six feet. Thursday, I cleared up nearly everything left in the refrigerator. All that remains is the haddock, which I shall eat on Tuesday. Last night, Friday, I went to the Quinns which was delightful, particularly as Quinn produced a bottle of champagne. After that we had first white wine and then claret, so after leaving their house apparently steady I had some difficulty in getting home. I have just read in *The Times* that it is quite usual for an elderly man to waken up around three or four in order to make water, and then not to be able to go to sleep again. It is a mistake to take a pill. The correct course is to get up and go for a walk. Certainly brandy does not make any difference.

I am now beginning to worry how I shall manage in Oxford, particularly to lecture standing for an hour. I think I am mad to go, but I can't see any way out. Life looks very rough ahead. Tonight I shall be with Giles and Janet, tomorrow evening with Sophia. Oh dear, I wish it was with you instead.

More love than ever before.

                Love,
                  Alan

Epilogue

There was no need to write more letters to Eva. They went everywhere together as long as Alan was able.

Alan bravely fought against his illness, his frightful Parkinson's disease, at first at home and later in a rest home, where he died on the 7th of September 1990.

Index

Where, in the text, a book has been mentioned but no title has been given, the author only has been listed.

Abyssinia, crisis in 17–18, 33, 60–1, 187, 190, 209, 279–80, 349
  article 17
  in Crozier papers 69
  seminar 60–1
Addison, Paul 230, 364 & n.
  The Road to 1945 260
Aigner, Dietrich: *Das Ringen um England* 5
Aitken, Max 24, 29, 118
  and *Beaverbrook* 20, 34, 50, 51
  and Beaverbrook Library 204–5, 209, 210, 212, 214, 273
    see further under Beaverbrook Library: closure of
  dinner for Lord Thompson 81
  illness and death 331, 336
    AJP's obituary 328, 331
  policy on *Sunday Express* 76
  style of criticism 90
Alexander, Field Marshal 121
All Quiet on the Western Front 193
Allen and Unwin (publishers) 113
America: AJP and moving to 14, 189, 193, 205
  Eva invited to 260
American Historical Review, article 17
American Book Club: publish *Beaverbrook* 73 & n.
Anderson Tapes, The (film) 58
Andrews, Henry 226
Anglo-Bulgarian lunch 361–2
Anglo-German naval pact 2, 4, 8, 69, 180–1
  AJP's views on 3–4, 69
  Eva and 8, 9, 14
    see further under Haraszti, Eva: works
  originators 33–4
Anglo-German payments agreement 47, 50–1
Anglo-Soviet trade agreement 141

Annan, Lord 389
Annan, Noel 412
Anti-Corn Law League 1
Anti-Corn Laws: AJP on 285
anti-Fascists 47
appeasement 30, 47, 177, 182, 280, 289, 387
  AJP's views on 26, 33
architecture, Romanesque 261
Arday, Lajos 139
Armistice Day 98
Armstrong, William: photograph collection 272, 274, 293
Arnhem, battle of 198
Asankrangwa *see* Taylor, C.: voluntary work
Asprey 316
Astor, Lady 93, 95
Atlas Mountains 86
atomic bomb 237
  U.S. reasons for using 169
Aubrey, John: *Brief Lives* 296
  on Thomas More 331
Austen, Jane: *Emma* 195
Australia: invitation to AJP 389
Austria: Putsch 33
  see also Vienna
Austro-Hungarian foreign policy 108
Avery, Roy 312, 313
Ayer, Freddie: autobiography 355
Ayerst, David: *Manchester Guardian* 30, 33
Aylmer, Gerald and Ursula 344

Bacall, Lauren 316
Bach, J. S.: *St Matthew Passion* 215
Bagehot II, Walter 232
Baldwin, Stanley: AJP's attempt to discredit 277
  biography 2, 150
  source of material on 60
Balkans crisis 250

462

INDEX

ballet, AJP and 58
Balzac, Honoré de: AJP reads 167, 400, 413
    life of 395
Bangor lecture 100
Barcsay, Jenö 74
Barnes, Michael 393, 432–3, 456
Barnett, Corelli: AJP's criticism of 90
    The Collapse of British Power 90
Barrington-Ward (editor of *The Times*) 30
Bartók, Béla 68
    music 57, 58, 72, 104, 434
Bartók Quartet 104, 217, 223, 224, 331
Bates, H. E. 7
Battle of Britain 70, 255, 324, 361
battles 18
    see also individual names
Batty, Roland, book from 409
BBC: Dimbleby Lecture 445
    opening of new premises 285
Beaverbrook, Lady (second) 205
    and AJP 177
    approval for husband's biography 34
    on husband's mistresses 37
Beaverbrook, Jennifer 219
Beaverbrook, Lord 12, 31, 84, 111, 420
    AJP and 20
        biography *see under* Taylor, A. J. P.: works
        lectures on 6
        photographed with 17
    on Bonar Law and Churchill 159
    character 72
    Crozier material on 67, 70
    historical significance of 87
    love-life 36–7
        and sex talk 271
    on his son 15
    on writing books 12
Beaverbrook Foundation *see* Beaverbrook Library
Beaverbrook Library: AJP working in 15, 34, 40, 44, 52, 54, 56, 60, 61, 74, 89, 93, 95, 103, 110, 120, 130, 143, 144, 146, 160, 162, 200, 202
    responsible for running 64
    archivist *see* Wheeler, Katherine
    bomb alert 121
    closure of 118, 204–5, 208, 210, 212, 214, 216, 221, 228, 230, 233–6, 238, 262
    effect on AJP 118, 208–9, 224, 232, 242, 243, 264
    for holidays 64, 134, 140
    reason for 273
    guide to 176
    magazine subscriptions 216
    U.S. researchers at 81

Beaverbrook Newspapers: cutbacks 252
    see further Beaverbrook Library: closure of
    losses 212
    1975 profit 267
Bedford, Duke of 83
Bedside Guardian: AJP's introduction 294
Beefsteak Club 56, 147, 231, 248, 261, 293, 362, 382, 394, 421
    with Deighton 409
Beesly Society talk 403
Beethoven, Ludwig van: *Fidelio* 215
    Third Symphony 424
    other music 434, 459
Bennett, Arnold 411
Benstead, Mrs 428
Bergmann. Ingmar 217
Berlin, Isaiah 336
    AJP and: opinion of 438–9
        shows autobiography to 158
    Times mention of 438
Berlioz, Hector: *Grande Messe des Mortes* 223, 227
    other music 189
Berners, Lord 459
Bethell, Nicholas: *The War Hitler Won* 97, 110
Betjeman, Sir John 66, 308
    telegram from 305
Betts, Barbara *see* Castle, Barbara
Beverley Minster 363, 364
Bible: language of James I translation 12
    petition on Authorized Version 394
    quoted 7–8
Big Sleep, The (film) 58
Binham 315
Biocca, Lucia (friend and translator) 13–14
    children 188
        daughter at university 63, 198
        son on drugs 407
Biocca family: politics 71, 198
Birmingham lecture 46
Bismarck, Otto von 76, 324
    'system' 413
Bizet, Georges: *Carmen* 110
Blackshirts 124, 239
Blackwell (booksellers), Oxford 10
Blake, Robert: reviews *Beaverbrook* 82, 84, 341
    on AJP 301
Bleichroeder 324, 339
Blomberg, General 198
Blue Train, The 91
Blunt, Anthony 405, 412
    see also Greene, G.: *Human Factor, The*
Boer War 401, 403
Bogart, Humphrey 65, 316
Bogidar (historian) 192

INDEX

Bologna: meeting in 290, 307, 308
   University at *see* Johns Hopkins University
Bolshevik revolution 92, 185, 310
Bond, James 58
Bond, Maurice 216
Bonar Law, Andrew 82, 159
   son *see* Colraine, Lord
Book of the Month Club: effect on royalties 98
Books and Bookmen 418
Boothby, Lord 8, 82–3, 192
   Eva's interest in 84–5
Boothby, Wanda 422
Bootham School, York 120
   AJP visits 164
Borley, John 268
Boswell, James 112
   Journal 58
Boulez, Pierre 58
Bournemouth lectures 280, 281, 285, 289
Bradbury, Malcolm: *The History Man* 274–5, 283
Brahms, Johannes: Symphony No. 4 443
Brandt, Willy 102, 106–7, 179, 183, 186
Brassey, Thomas 268
Braun, Eva: home movies 165
Brecht, Berthold: *Threepenny Opera* 63
Brendel, Alfred 215, 320
Briggs, Asa 421–2, 449
   party for 20
Bright, John 4
Brighton 62
Bristol: with Eva in 341, 377, 381
Bristol Polytechnic lectures 317
   number each term 398
   AJP as visiting professor 341, 349
Bristol University lectures 312, 313, 315, 318, 366, 367, 368, 370, 379
   entertaining at 313, 317
   honorary degree from 383
Bristow, Hilda 455
British Academy 380, 417
   AJP and: takes Chair at 337
     excuse or resigning from 405
     and grant candidates 336
     dinners 237, 242, 293
       Eva at 425
       President's speech 73
     Raleigh lecture 363, 364
     reception at 57
     Poland and 51
   secretary *see* Williams, Neville
British Council 2, 18
British Museum: and Beaverbrook Library 205, 208, 209, 214
   'Frozen Tombs' exhibition 398–9

Keeper of Manuscripts *see* Waley, Arthur
Brooks, Rosemary (AJP's archivist) 40
   death 40, 42
   as proof-reader 46
Broszat 65
Brougham, Lord 228
Brown, George 250
   see also George-Brown, Lord
Brown, Karen 402
Brown, W. J. 192
Brussels 27
Budapest: AJP declines to go 435
   Eva in 393 *ad fin*
     address in 202 and n.
     behaviour in 262
   meetings in 29, 184, 189, 191, 194, 202, 217–22, 223–4, 231, 141, 194, 201, 202, 220, 244, 246, 257, 258–9, 260, 302, 304
   and Eva's friends 192
   Eva's worries about 199
   marriage 304 and n.
   see also Hungarian Academy of Sciences
Bukharin, analysis of 187–8
Bulgaria: 1876 Horrors 294, 311
Buñuel, Luis: *The Discreet Charm of the Bourgeoisie* 118
Bunyan, John: *Pilgrim's Progress* 88, 216
Burgess, Guy 58, 421
Burns, Jimmy 403
Butler, David (ed.): *Coalition* 325, 327, 328–9, 330, 331
   AJP's articles for 325, 327–8, 330, 331
   seminar 411
Butler, R. A. B.: autobiography 45
Butler, Samuel: quoted 332
Butow 275
Buxton: with Eva in 458
Byron, Lord 7, 228

Ca'Oro, Venice 176
Cabaret (film) 126
Cadogan, Sir Alec: diaries published 47
Cambridge: invitation from Social Democrats 450
   National Trust dinner 333
Cambridge University: Christ's College *see* Taylor, C.
   commemoration of benefactors 151
   Churchill College: AJP at 2
     lectures 99, 280, 332
   Peterhouse: Master *see* Trevor Roper, Hugh
     students and Christianity 170
Campaign for Nuclear Disarmament 13
Campbell, John 349

464

INDEX

Campbell-Bannerman, Sir Henry: biography 257
Canada: invitation to 260
Canary Islands 217
Cane, Bill 448, 454
Canterbury: with Eva in 290
  see further Kent, University of
capitalism 19
  effect of Depression on 183
  failure of Liberal 97
  perceived collapse of 154, 156, 163, 200, 202, 287
  recovery of 184
Captain Swing 171
Cara 366
Carlton, David: book reviewed 432, 437
Carlyle, Thomas 369
car industry collapse 220
Carpaccio, Vittorio 176
Carr, Raymond 380
Carrier, John and Sarah 445
Casement, Roger 125
Castle, Barbara 326
Castlereagh: biography review 432, 437, 440, 441
'Cat' *see* Churchill, Clementine
Cavour, Count 93
chamber music 19, 424
Chamberlain, Neville 26, 65, 78–9, 90, 187
  policies 126, 440
  on appeasement 280
  on Russia 438
Chandler, Raymond 58
Channel Islands, German occupation of 233
Channon, Sir Henry 19
  Diaries of . . . 18 and n
Chaplin, Charlie: *The Great Dictator* 110
Charles, Prince 341
Chartist movement 8, 10, 14, 82, 459
  AJP on 2, 285
  Charterville allotments 10
  1848 Convention 420
  see further Haraszti, Eva: works
Chartres, meeting in 134, 138, 159, 164, 169, 420
Chatfield Papers 291
Cheltenham Historical Society lecture 368
Cheltenham Ladies' College 368
Childers, Erskine: biography 335, 336
Chichester Cathedral 120
China: earthquake 325
  recognition of 109
Churchill, Clementine: nickname 114
Churchill, Winston 23, 33, 62, 70, 159, 187, 190, 209, 213, 318, 374
  AJP and: declines to write on 192
  lecture on 275
  review of book on 47
  on Baldwin 150
  on Beaverbrook 90
  book of letters from 294
  character 187
  foreign policy 56, 233, 240, 270
  National government *see* Butler, David: Coalition
  on Gamelin 237
  grave 244
  source of material on 60
  War Room 453, 454
  war speeches 334–5, 336, 243, 244, 247
Citrine, Walter 70
City Music Society 426, 453–4
  annual report 335
Civil Service strike 426, 439–40, 453–4
Clarke, Peter 398
Clazy, Bob 178–9
Clazy, Michael 179
Clazy, George 178
Cleland, John: *Fanny Hill* 115, 119
climate, changes in 114
  approach of Ice Age 213
  effect of 66
  heat-wave 254, 256
Cliveden set 181–2
Closely Observed Trains (film) 137, 409
Cobb, Richard 208
Cobbett, William, essay on 4 101
  quoted 403
Cockburn, Claud 181
Cohen 187
Colchester oyster feast 20
Cold War 141, 203, 296, 375, 379, 387
  AJP's worries on origins 169
Cole, G. D. H. 44–5
Coleraine, Lord 185
Collins, Wilkie: *Armadale* 445
Cologne, Germany 20
Colvin, Ian: *Chamberlain's Cabinet* 26
Common Market 63, 72, 89, 106, 126
  effect of Britain joining 247
  on inflation/unemployment 97
  interpreter at *see* Jones, Freddie
Communism: effect of moderation of 187
  fears about 185
Communist Manifesto: AJP's introduction 6
concerts 157, 215, 320, 395, 413, 422, 425
  lunch-time 292, 389, 391
  see also individual composers, groups, works
Congress of Berlin 192
Conscience of the Rich, The 224, 226
Constable, Kathleen *see* Tillotson, Kathleen

INDEX

Cook, Chris 251
   and *Festschrift* 289
Courtauld Institute art collection 443
Covent Garden (opera house) 100
Cowling 252
Cracow, Poland 51, 71
Craigie, Jill 456
Crazy Movie Makers, The 409
Cregier, Don 349
Cromwell, Oliver 4, 190
   film about 16
Crosland, Anthony 49
Crosland, Eve 19 n.
Cross, Colin 126, 348, 349, 351
Crossman, Richard (Dick) 16
   AJP on television with 109, 111
   Diary 272, 274
   interviews AJP 115
   leaves politics 49
   review of *Beaverbrook* 84
Crozier, Mary 67
Crouzet reception, Eva at 150
Crozier, W. P. 33
   interview records 59, 60, 62, 65, 67, 68–70, 73, 76
      AJP as editor: anxiety over 80, 95, 125, 130
      problems in reading 70
      publisher for 94
      publication date 130, 138
      reviews of 143
      serial rights 95
Crusades, modern 150
Curzon, Lord 141
Cyprus war 193
Czechoslovakia, crisis in 11, 69, 294

Dacre of Glantan, Lord 416
Dahlerus 97
Daily Express 53
   articles for 160, 200, 202
   emancipation of 271–2
   management changes 355–6
Daily Mail: on AJP's marriage 313
Dales Way 291
Dalton diary 325
Danish Resistance 233
Dardanelles, the 209
David and Charles (publishers) 111, 113
Davidov, Miss 395
Davin, Dan 240
de Gaulle, Charles 179
De Jongh, report from 413
decimal coinage 28
Deighton, Len 11, 154, 337, 409, 420
   The Battle of Britain 328, 361

AJP's opinion of 401
   and *The Second World War* 166
   seminar with 287
Della (secretary) 118, 196, 216, 232, 233, 235, 236, 237, 271, 284, 293, 353, 354, 355
   court fine 283
   present for 160
Denmark: invitations to lecture in 34, 35, 39, 42
Denniston, book from 409
Denny, Pat 396, 399, 400, 406, 408, 417, 419
Depression, the Great 104, 156, 186
Deutsch, H. C. 198
Dickens, Arthur G (director of Institute of Historical Research) 242
   speech by 362
Dickens, Charles: *Dombey and Son* 228
   Little Dorrit 112
Die Kunst der Fuge 404
Die Welt, article for 252
Dieppe, with Eva in 435–6
Dill, John 182
Dirksen 51
Disley, Manchester 163, 174
Documents on British Foreign Policy 150, 154, 156
Doherty 177, 179
Doncaster, Girls' High School 17
Dorset 270
   see also Hardy, Thomas
Dostoevski, Fëdor: *The Brothers Karamazov* 167
Doyle, Bob 375, 400, 423, 428, 443
Driberg, Tom 78, 267
   biography 348
   death 303
   heart attack 273
   review of *Beaverbrook* 82
Dunhill 44, 45
Dunn, Lady 20
   see also Beaverbrook, Lady
Durham Cathedral 218
Durham lecture 218
DV 223, 227
Dvořák: American quartet 97

Ealing lecture 406–7
Eastbourne 232
Easy Rider (film) 58
Economist: articles in AJP's style 101
   head of U.S. office *see* Midgeley, John
   reviews for 23, 237
   used as archive 50
Ede, JR (at PRO) 209, 210
Eden, Anthony 156, 181, 187, 388, 405, 432, 437–8
Edinburgh Festival: 'Meet the Writer' 250

INDEX

seminar at 287
Edinburgh University 234
  lectures at 229-30, 373
  thesis examinations 363, 364
Edward I, King 86
Edward VII, King 232, 422
  review of biography 395-6
Edward VIII, King 198, 203, 214
  see also Windsor, Duke of
Eisenhower, Dwight D. 323
El Alamein 147
Elgar, Edward 58
Eliot, George: *Middlemarch* 424
  Silas Marner 413, 424
Emmerson, RW review of 346
Empire Crusade 72
encyclopaedia, Italian, articles for 80, 103
  rewriting 88
Engels, Friedrich 203, 268
  AJP on 285
English Historical Review 49, 187
  'Chartism and the Trades' 459
  reviews in 177, 361, 364, 376
Epstein (author) 177
Erikson, John 243, 245, 380
Esler (carpenter) 2
Eulenburg and Lichnowsky 139
Europe: attitude of historians to 28
Exeter 386

Fabian Society 349
Falkus, Christopher 366, 425
  and AJP's autobiography 363
'Fanfare for Europe' 106
Farrar, Lance 352
Farrer, David: review of *Beaverbrook* 82
Fascism 102, 104
  AJP's stand on 236
  future historians and 96
  probability of return of 97, 124, 183, 191-2
Faulkner: *The Sorrow and the Fury* 179
Fell, Tim 428
Fields, W. C. 395
Fiesole 123-4
films, AJP and 19
  subjects of 104
  sex 27-8
  see also individual titles
Financial News: used as archive 50
Financial Times: reviews in 333
  used as archive 50
First World War 126
  AJP and: lectures on 368
    starting date for 102
    anniversary of outbreak 139
    Eastern Front 260, 292

Italian army conditions in 74
  revival of interest in 190
Fischer, Fritz 4190, 433
  AJP's lecture on (*Festschrift*) 177 and n,
    227, 288, 289
  essay by Eva 251
  pupil *see* Wendt
Fisher, Jackie: biography of 165
Fisher, Warren 156
Fitzgerald jun. 429
Flaybert, Gustav 34
Florence 83, 123
  German tourists in 124
Foot, Michael 72, 179, 192, 386, 390
  on AJP 299
  and Beaverbrook 78-80
  and Russell 413
France: Communist-Socialist Coalition 179
  and economic crisis 170
  foreign policy 187
  president: election of (1974) 179
    lack of 183
Francis I, Emperor 94
Franco: foreign policy 296
Franz Joseph, Emperor 40
'Free Speech' 192, 195, 197, 200, 241
Fritsch, General 198
Frost, David 109
Fuller, Roy: review of *Beaverbrook* 84

Gallagher, William 380
Gallipoli 44
Gamelin, Maurice 237
Garibaldi, Giuseppe 93
Garrick Club 421
Garvin: *Chamberlain* 349
Gaskell, Mrs 299, 355, 356
Gaston (booksellers) 452, 457
Genghis Khan 438
Genoa conference 143
George III, King 12
George-Brown, Lord 188
Germany: economic crisis 169
  as economic partner 47
  foreign policy (1933-36) 4, 33-4, 181, 182,
    194-5, 296
  see also Anglo-German naval pact
  Imperialism 4
  inter-war problem s 62, 78, 79
  Nazis 185
    debate on sociology of 65
    recognition of East 109
  Soviet spy ring *see* Rote Kapelle
  West: historical conference 8
  as world power 102
Germany's First Bid for Colonies 159

467

INDEX

Gibbon, Edward: AJP reading works 167
  autobiography 425
Gibbs, N. H. 294, 296
Gilbert, Martin 32, 338
  Churchill 239-40, 251, 259, 310
  review of 44
Girl, 20 (book) 261, 271, 279
Gladstone, William: Ireland policy 363, 364
Glasgow 208
Glastonbury Historical Society lecture 223, 224
Gloucester Cathedral 216
Goebbels: diary serialization 386
Goering, Hermann 51, 97
Goldfinger, Ernö 307, 383
  AJP asks his help 338
  mother's attitude to 438
  and wife 217, 438
Good Soldier Schwejk, The 458
Goodman, Lord 29
Goole lectures 270, 280, 281, 289, 290
Gordon Riots 60
Grantham 51
Graves, Robert: *I, Claudius* 261, 271
Great Britain: cathedrals 420
  class war 87
  economic crisis/inflation, AJP's fears: 76, 97, 99, 110, 114, 136, 143, 156, 159, 160, 166, 169, 179, 183, 184, 186, 189, 191, 197, 198, 201, 204, 207, 215-16, 220, 223, 229, 235, 238, 273, 288, 289, 343
  bankruptcy 287
  capitalist remedy 246-7
  examples of 195-6
  Labour government and 321
  reaction to 170, 243
  talks on 200
  and unemployment 110, 154, 201, 273
  free land in 14
  fears of dictatorship 308
  foreign policy, inter-war 2, 4, 33-4, 50-1, 56, 65, 81, 139, 156, 182, 187, 294, 361, 437, 440-1, 442
    see also Anglo-German naval pact
  General Election (1974): prospects 200-3
    talk on 206
  government: Cabinet papers *see* Public Records Office
  government: Conservative 27
    and bankruptcies 220
    AJP's criticism of 29, 76, 83, 162-3
    loss of control 117, 154, 159
    policy on workers 62
    rebels in 32-3
    scandals 143, 183
    see also Profumo Affair
    Socialist policies 114
  government, Labour: and cause of strikes 79
    clinging to power 179
    Lib/Lab pact 337
  government: National *see* Butler, David: Coalition
  heat-waves 293, 295, 298, 299-300
  Hungarian legation party 95
  industrial disputes 367, 368-9
    AJP's answer to 117
  intervention in Greece 160
  Labour Party 72, 203, 247
    deputy leader *see* Foot, Michael
  Liberal Party 121, 125
  possible revolution in 185, 191, 197, 247
    street fighting 200
  state of politics in 87
  as Socialist community 97, 165
  'Splendid Isolation' of 125-6
  strikes/go-slows/shortages 27, 29, 30, 61-2, 70, 72, 75, 79, 87, 117-18, 121, 123, 148, 150, 153, 154, 157, 160, 162, 165, 166, 169, 183, 192, 194, 378, 379, 400, 412, 450-1
Great Men: AJP's essays in 49, 59, 60
Great Unread, the 424
Greene, Graham 142
  AJP's opinion of books 142
  The Comedians 420, 423
  The Human Factor 420
Gretton, Peter: *Former Naval Person* 23
Grey: as Prisoner in Russia 11, 156
Griffith (President of Magdalen) 132, 137
Grimsby lectures 17, 364
Grigg, John 132
Guardian, The: articles on AJP 75
  birthday interview 290
  editor 33
  AJP's reviews 368, 454
Guarnieri Quartet 422
Guernica: book review 376
Guinness, Alec 126
Gumshoe (film) 58, 65
Guy Fawkes Day 269

H. G. Wells Society: invitation from 450
Hackett, General Sir John 451
Hadfield, Alice 10, 14
Hair (show) 110
Hajdu 367
Halifax, Lord 26, 65, 181
Hamish Hamilton (publisher) 82, 336, 403, 404, 408, 449
  and *Beaverbrook* 81

INDEX

Dictionary of World History 161
  see also Machell, Roger
Handel: *Messiah* 215
Hankey, Maurice: biography of 23, 56, 291
  papers 2
Hansard 156
Haraszti Taylor, Eva: and AJP: age
    difference 43 and n., 45, 340, 433
  asks about Lloyd George 193
  breaking with 210, 215, 263, 437
  Christmas presents 54, 161, 209-10, 274, 321, 375
  as executor 425
  first meeting vii, 429
  gifts 90, 104, 151, 167, 336
  hero-worship of 272
  leaves copyrights to 135, 162, 222
  as 'life-mate' 202, 290
  as next of kin 305-6
  on his nature 210
  photograph of 257
  telephone calls 147 *passim*
  upset by/unhappiness at 221, 270, 265
  academic position 98 and n.
    doctorate 377, 422
  books from/to 82, 101, 103, 108, 110, 138, 140-1, 150, 159, 176, 202, 206-8, 213, 214, 222, 224, 226, 228, 230, 242, 246, 261, 271, 282, 423, 433
    Beaverbrook 81
    Venice guidebook 134, 136
  citizenship 299, 360, 390
  coat for 412
  driving 66, 70, 74
    accident 103
    licence 325, 359
  in England 292, 266, 281, 285, , 286, 288, 297-8, 299, 307, 346, 348, 363, 378, 383, 385, 393
    AJP's engagements during 282-3
    Home Office enquiry 357
    money for 285, 300, 301, 308, 309, 318
    name in 280, 350, 366, 367, 387
    not a good place to live 136
    passport 311, 325
    at PRO 1 n.
    research subjects in 270
    return to 399-400, 405, 416
    scholarships to vii, viii
    shopping with Janet 385
    unhappiness in 421
    visa/permit for 270, 280, 376
  finance: advice on investments 440
    AJP's settlement on 372-3, 375
    problems with 98-9
    royalties given to 73 and n., 95, 104

  scholarship money 261
  security of 43
  health: accidents/illnesses 51-2, 55, 236, 326, 344, 347, 352
    operation 96, 104
    pneumonia 443, 444
  invitations: to Ranke conferences 22, 38, 40
    see also Ranke Gesellschaft
    to Zagreb 305
  joins Labour Party 389
  and lecturing 112
    on Hungarian rising 203
  letters: AJP destroys Eva's 201
    limiting 45, 48, 59, 113
    from Crispin 311
    from Mary 380
    on keeping AJP's viii-ix
  marriage 226, 230, 269, 304 and n.
    first viii
    death of husband vii, 3 and n.
    name after 411
    worries about the future 258
  nationality: after marriage 153, 165, 175
    legal problems 296
    owning property in England 162
  present for Margaret 423
  records 68, 261, 262, 274
    Crispin borrows 72
    and Royal wedding 437
  sons viii
    acceptance of AJP 250, 266
    AJP and 28-9, 71, 133, 142-3, 170, 189, 206, 227, 296
    books for 206, 315, 316, 318
    in Bulgaria 192
    in England 79, 363
    holidays with 40
    need for secure future 291 and n.
    problems of leaving 321, 398, 434
    see also Hudecz, Ferencz; Hudecz, Pisti
  and stepsons 392
  visits Turkey 365, 366, 368, 375
  typewriter 406, 416, 426
Haraszti Taylor, Eva, works: AJP and:
    advice on sources 387-8
    corrects mss. 432-3
    proposed introduction for 113
    and translations of 21, 28, 111, 242
  Anglo-German naval pact 51, 69
    AJP as translator 70, 95
    AJP's opinion of 73
    copy for Marder 183-4
    finishes for Doctorate 291 and n.
    publication of 28
    reviews of 264
  The Appeasers: AJP suggests revising 251

469

INDEX

article on Kossuth 447 and n.
autobiography (*An English Husband*) 273, 312
  AJP reads 432 and n., 433–6
  Chartism 21 and n., 112
  AJP sends book on 82
  AJP's report on 307
  British publication of 110–11, 113
  as editor: Károlyi letters 305, 307
  essay for Fischer *Festschrift* 251
  George V: proofs for 459
  problems with 94
  The Treaty Breakers: AJP reads 180 and n, 181–2
  AJP's criticisms of 181–2
Hardie, Frank 190–1, 280
Hardy, Thomas 270
  birthplace 270, 281
  novels 172
    The Well Beloved 412
  poem 427, 428
Harlow lectures 135, 148
Harpers: review in 225
Harrison, Rex 265
Harrison and Best 29
Hartley, L. P.: *The Go-Between* 58, 151
Hartwell 108
Harvester (publishers) 403, 408
Hašek, Janslav 296
Hatvani, Baroness ('Lotsi') 168, 189, 237, 254
Hatvanyv, Baron 230 and n.
Hauser, Oswald 38, 40, 46, 82, 136, 198
  on Anglo-German relations 96, 100, 152, 177–8
  invitations to AJP 135, 381
    declined 388
  sends AJP copies of lectures 167
  sends Eva copy of paper 176
  review by 264
Haydn, Joseph 68
Hazelhurst, Cameron: review of *Beaverbrook* 84
Healey, Denis 321
Heath, Edward 62
  AJP's criticism of 160
  and Dimbleby lecture 445
  and miners 169
Heller, Joseph: *Catch-22* 255
Hemingway, Ernest: *Across the River and into the Trees* 89
  Farewell to Arms 88
Henderson, Nico 421
Henrietta (friend) 444 and n.
Henley lecture 252–3
Hess, Rudolf 237, 418

Higham, David 403, 408
Hildebrand, Klaus: *Vom Reich zum Weltreich* 5
Hillgruber 132
Himmler, Heinrich 51
Hingley 176
Hinsley 451
  AJP's review of 452
historians: English 289–90
  how they work 113
Historical Journal 459
Historical Association 270
  branches 17
  see also individual branches
  Eva's interest in 285
  lectures to 281
    alternative subject for 294
    at annual meeting 342
    future lectures 371, 373
    the Queen visits 436
histories/biographies, AJP's: in Russian 92–3
History: reviews in 232
History Book Shop 452
Hitler, Adolf 2, 30, 50–1, 65–6, 78, 100, 104, 181, 206, 239
  ability as military commander 145
  elimination of military commanders 198
  aims 93, 102
  AJP's view of 23, 96 and n., 236–7
  approach to in *Origins . . .* 126
  lecture on 275, 301
  biographies on 147, 150, 312, 318, 335, 336, 339, 349
  films/ TV series about 96, 109, 110
  personality 109
  policies 4, 33, 102, 132, 177, 178, 185–6
    AJP on strategy 138
  religion 65
  revival of interest in 126
Hoare, Sir Samuel 26, 69, 181
  official life of 348, 349, 351, 354
Hoare-Laval plan 61, 181, 187, 277
Hobsbawm, Eric: *The Age of Capital* 268
  (ed.): history of British Society 29
Horowitz 215
hotels, English 86
House of Lords: comtempt of 186
  Record Office: and Beaverbrook Library 216, 224, 233
Housseau 456
Howard, Michael 125, 418, 430
  on AJP 418
  and *The Second World War* 166, 169
Howard, Rob 179, 345, 400, 422, 453, 455
Howard, Rosa (granddaughter): illness 243
  present for 179
Howard, Sophia 66, 457, 458, 460

accident 66
living expenses 99
politics 66
pregnancies 385-7
  birth of daughter 176, 179
  see further Howard, Rosa; McGibbon, Robert
Howard, Tony 413
Hudecz, Ferencz (son) 408
  books from AJP 147, 161, 167
  in England 252, 253, 257, 296, 391
  illness 394, 395, 397
  wedding 413
Hudecz, Pisti 206, 227, 393, 402
  AJP talks to 399, 443
  books from AJP 194, 199
  in England 311, 345, 347, 349, 352, 357, 359, 383, 391, 434, 435, 436, 438, 439, 441
  leaves for home 441
  with Lizzie 437
  note to 387
  tooth extraction 402
  and Ursula 438
Hugo, Victor 34
Hungary 239, 254
  economic situation 184
    devaluation of currency 210
    Lake Balaton 246
  Institute of Historical Research vii, 351
    copies of AJP's books for 1
    Eva at 98 and n.
    lecture/seminars at 246, 250, 252, 254, 349
    official trips to 312
    see also Budapest
  photographs of old 272
Hunter, Bruce 408
Hurst, Michael 445
Hyde, Montgomery: biography of Baldwin 150
  History of the RAF 324

Ignotus: review by 256
Igoe, Della and Bill: Bill at *New Statesman* 44-5
In Their Wisdom 224, 226
Imperial General Staff: Chief of *see* Wilson, Sir Henry
'Impressionists in England exhibition 112
'In the News' 192
India, British Army in 198
Industrial Revolution, collected essays on 108
Inglis, Brian: review of *Beaverbrook* 84
Inskip, Thomas 324

International Socialists 66
International Telegraph and Telephone 27
IRA 44, 87
  bombing campaign 120-1, 260
  British attempts to infiltrate 143
  denunciation of 63
  Sunday Express and 76
Ireland: AJP visits 83, 87, 89, 91, 134, 140, 144
  British campaign in 277
  irredentism 339
Irving, David 296, 374
  Hitler's War 335, 339, 345, 349
  Rommel 367, 368
Ischl 203
Isle of Wight:
  The Mill 39 and n., 146, 192, 196, 197, 241, 248, 249, 252, 253, 254, 255, 256, 258, 293, 294, 295-6, 349, 351, 353-4, 355, 391, 392-3, 401, 438
  local authority problems 436
  with Eva in 429, 434
  Historical Association 206, 208
Ischerwood, Christopher: *Salkly Bowles* 126
Israel, war in 148
Italy: economic crisis 169
  German alliance 33-4
  political chaos 124, 183
  Vienna files on 196
  see also First World War; Ravenna; Rome; Venice

James, Robert Rhodes 312, 342
Churchill. A Study in Failure 8
Jameson Raid 453, 454
Janácek, music by 97, 224-5, 227
Janosi, Engel: article for 376
Japan: and Anglo-German naval pact 69, 150, 156
  loss of fleet 181
  war: with America 178
    documentary sources destroyed 335
Jenkins, Clive 451
Jenkins, Roy: biography of Asquith 303
Jenner family 417
Jesus Christ 12
  see also Muggeridge, Malcolm
Joll, James 23, 101
Johnson, Mr 449
Johnson, Paul 78
  History of England 89
  review of *Beaverbrook* 82
Johnson, Philip 422
Johns Hopkins University, Bologna 340
  invitation from 271
    cancelled 318

INDEX

negotiations with 311
Jonathan Cape (publishers): book for 329–30, 334
Jones, Freddie Hurdis 428
　career 430
Jones, Mervyn 379
Joplin, Scott, 257, 261, 262, 274, 395
Joseph II, Emperor 94
Joseph of Aramathea 224
Journal of Modern History 177 and n.
　articles for 190, 244, 268, 342
　Brandel number 259
　intellectual autobiography for *see* Taylor, A. J. P.: works
Judd 349
Juillard Quartet 320

Károlyi, Catherine (Katus) 50, 129, 168
　AJP's suspicion of 192, 211
Károlyi, Michael 1 and n., 84, 112, 129
　letters 305, 307
　　destroyed by Katus 50
　　to AJP 129
　　see further Haraszti, Eva: works
　research on 18
Kassa, bombing of 119
Kathy (television producer) 406, 407
Katus *see* Károlyi, Catherine
Kee, Robert 376, 421, 435
Kedourie, Elie 287
Keegan 447, 449, 451, 452
　review of book 449, 450
Kemp, Betty 75
　takes AJP to dinner 149
Kemp, David 397, 410
Kent, University of: and Beaverbrook Library 224, 228
　opening of cartoon exhibition 267
　lectures t 62, 65, 266
Kennan, George 413, 423, 424
Khrushchev, Nikita 435
Kierkegaard 283–4
Kilmartin, Joanna 285, 384, 456–7
Kilmartin, Terry 285, 398, 448, 453, 457
　reviews from AJP 370
Kindleside (builder) 366–7, 369, 371, 372, 376, 378, 381–2, 383, 385, 386, 388, 390, 420
Kissinger, Henry 106
Knox, John 182
Königswinter: meeting in 9, 15, 20, 21, 198, 433
　reason for AJP leaving 22
Kopov 94
Koss, Stephen 252, 265, 303
Kossuth, Lajos 447 and n.

Krasin (diplomat) 141
Kyle, Keith 75

La Couriere della Siera 432
La Salle Quartet 389
Lady from Patiola, the 207 and n.
Lake/Peak Districts, holidays in 39, 40, 41, 97, 133, 135, 136, 138, 192, 194, 235, 241, 248, 249
　with Eva 273, 275, 281, 283, 286, 292, 296–7, 323, 326, 350,, 360, 361, 397, 422, 424, 430
　problems in 195
　The Sun, Coniston 350 and n., 364
Lancaster lecture 253
Larousse 161
Lash, Joseph 318
Last Ten Days of Hitler, The (film) 126
Latvia, Eva in 70
Laval 187
　see also Hoare-Laval plan
Lawrence, D. H. 118
　Lady Chatterly's Lover 116
Lawrence, T. E. 231
La Vien, Jack 243, 247
Leach: *German Srategy Towards Russia 1939–41* 132
Leamington lecture 205–6
Leeds University: centenary oration 192
　lectures 213
League of Nations *see* Abyssinia, crisis in; Anglo-German naval pact
Lehar, Franz: *The Merry Widow* 100
Lehrer, Tom 261
Lenin 92–3, 243
Levellers 8
Lever, Mrs (shopkeeper) 424, 430, 443
Levy, Mr and Mrs 439
Lewis, Pete (dentist) 457, 459
Lewis, Michael 134, 136–7
Liddell-Hart: *History of the Second World* 18
　papers 387–8
Lillie, Beatrice 90
Lincoln, Abraham 281
Linthwaite, Mrs 417
Linz 32
Listener, The: and Beaverbrook 84
　lectures in 299
'Little Dolly' (Mrs Doris Fell) 267, 273
Liverpool, Lord 29
Liverpool University lectures 135, 148
Liverpool to Manchester Railway anniversary 405, 410, 411
Ljubljana, meeting in 22, 43, 46, 94, 118, 120, 122, 123
　clothing for 121

472

INDEX

Grand Hotel Union 117
Lloyd George, David 14, 132, 141, 156, 161, 239, 270
  Bennett on 411
  books on 132, 137, 281, 345, 348, 349, 411, 412, 413
  and Churchill 270
  diary 49
  essay on 49, 59, 60
  love letters 111–12, 114, 132, 139, 168
    copyright dispute 225, 262
    use of Welsh in 170
    see also Taylor, A. J. P.: television; works
  Second World War papers 118
Lloyd-George, Lady Frances (Pussy) 14–15, 49 and n., 114, 167, 168
  diaries 80
Lloyd George, Jennifer (daughter) 275
  and parents' love letters 82, 112, 132
Locarno, Pact of 2
Lockhart, Bruce: diaries published 147–8
London: AJP's daily routine in 53
  Barbican flats 18, 53
  bombs in 260
    at Old Bailey 120–1
  Geffrye Museum 397
  Highgate Ponds 89, 91, 238, 254, 299–300, 301, 303, 352, 429, 431, 435, 437, 438, 440, 441, 445, 446, 452, 454, 457
  Imperial War Museum 290
  Kenwood House 443
  Lord Mayor's Banquet 244–5, 246
  National Film Theatre 395, 421
  National Gallery 292
  the Ritz 17, 19
  Sadlers Wells 58
  Somerset House exhibition 357
  storms 442
  World's End pub 442
London Junior chess tournament 331
London Historical Association lectures 276, 370
London Library 413, 435, 445
  Eva enrolled at 290–1
  loses book from 62
London Review of Books: Diary 454, 458, 459
London School of Economics: demonstration at 25
London University: classes at 135
  Creighton Lecture 119, 154, 160
Longford, Elizabeth 453(?)
  AJP's review of book 454(?)
  Wellington 95–6
Lopokova, Lydia 152
Lord Raingo *see* Bennett, Arnold
Losey, Joseph 58

Louis, Roger 93, 442
  and AJP's autobiography 257
  book from 379
Lubbe, van der 2
Luxembourg, Rosa 179
Lynn, Ralph 395
Lyons, Leland: Ford Lectures 411–12

Macaulay, AJP and: opinion of 369
  reading works of 167
  biography of 130, 131, 137
MacDonald, Ramsay: biography of 330, 332, 333
Macell (in Royal Navy) 2
McGibbon, Rob (Robert) 179, 400, 428, 453, 455
  AJP asks his advice 337
Machell, Roger 419, 447, 449
MacLachlan, Donald 30
MacLean, Donald 421
Macmillan, Harold 352
mah-jongg 394
Mahler, Gustav 63
Manchester: with Eva 289, 290, 424
  Cotton Exchange and trade 132, 298, 299
Manchester Guardian 454
  AJP's editing and use of records 60
  and Muggeridge 101
Manchuria 181
Mannheim: invitation declined 365
Mao Tse-tung 17
Marcus, Steven 369
Marder, Arthur J. 19, 184, 187, 213, 335
  article 17–18
  books 274, 281, 283, 400–1, 442
    AJP's review 444–5
  essays 209
  Festschrift for 348, 349
    AJP's review of 352
Margaret (weekly help) 458 and n., 459
Margaret, Princess 49
Maria Theresa, Empress 94
Marquand, David 330, 332, 333
  review of book 336
Marshall, Peter: *The Raging Moon* 7, 27
Martin, Kingsley 16
  article on 412
  biography of(?) 131
Marwick, Arthur: review of *Beaverbrook* 84
Marx, Karl 268
  AJP on 6
Maser 147
Maschler (Cape director) 334
Mashkin, M. N. 251 and n.
Massingham (editor): biography of 198
Masterman, Neville 139

473

disapproval of AJP 126
review of *Chartism* 21 and n.
Masters, The 211
Magdalen College, Oxford: AJP at: elected Honorary Fellow 315, 318, 320, 333, 355
  manservant *see* Pacey, Ron
  re-elected Fellow 97
  retirement from 211
  rooms at 274, 282, 296, 297, 299
  campaign to admit women 48, 76, 81, 99–100
  candidates for research fellowship 274
  dinner at 390
    Gaudy dinner 293
    Restoration Dinner 149
  feast at 208
  financial problems 206, 208
  founder 6
  President: election of 211
    illness of 132
  Old Boys' party 137
  sit-in protest 170
McMahon-Husayn correspondence 287
Medici family 123
Mendelssohn, music by 104
Mercer, Lucy 239
Merman, Ethel 109
Methuen (publishers) 425
Metternich, Prince 76
Michel, Henri, in translation 259
Michèle, and family (neighbour) 454 and n.
Middlemas, Keith: *The Diplomacy of Illusion* 78–9, 82, 101
  (with Barnes): life of Baldwin 2
Midgeley, John 455
Milan 238
Mill, James 228
Miller, Karl 447, 448, 451
Minelli, Liza 126
Mirzoeff, Eddie 315, 323, 331, 345, 352, 372, 397
  and Dimbleby lecture 445
  wife leaves 351
Modell, Dr Michael: and Eva 395
Mold lecture 275–6
Monet, London paintings 112
Monmouth's rebellion 366, 368
Montgomery, Field Marshal 145
Moon, manned flights to 28, 107
More, Thomas: *Utopia* 331
  see also Aubrey, John
Morgan, Kenneth 411, 412
  AJP's review of book 413, 414
Morton, Sir Desmond 294, 296
Moscow 141

British attitude to visiting 10–11
Eva in 9, 22, 26
invitatiion to conference in 8
AJP's reasond for not visiting 11
Mosely, Sir Oswald 17, 235, 239, 242, 331
  autobiography 236
  AJP and 19
  biography of 230
  see also Blackshirts
motor industry, possible collapse of 179
Mozart: *Entfuhring...* 29
  Cosi Fan Tutti 203, 209
  other music 97, 422
'Mrs Simpson' 160
Muggeridge, Kitty 102, 255
Muggeridge, Malcolm 250, 255
  AJP renews friendship with 197
  autobiography 277
  AJP's criticisms of 101
  marriage 101–2
  on 'Free Speech' programme 195
  on Jesus Christ 362
  and Kirkegaard 283
  opinion of Greene 142
  politics 101
  review of *Beaverbrook* 82, 84
Munich to Dunkirk 56
Mussolini, Benito 33, 65, 187, 293
  film on 110
  lecture on 275
  see also Abyssinia, crisis in

Namier, Julia and Clara 251
Namier, Lewis: book on 251–2
  tribute to 159
Napoleon I, Emperor: AJP's review of book on 47
Napoleon III, Emperor 40
Nation: editor *see* Massingham
National Trust properties 161
Nationalist sentiment 63
Nelson: launch of *Dictionary of World History* 149–50
New Brunswick, University of: and Beaverbrook Library 224
New Hungarian Quarterly reviews in 213, 249, 252, 263–4
New Statesman 323, 324, 358, 359, 383, 385, 417
  AJP and letters in 327
  AJP's opinion of 426
  articles in 301, 317, 319, 321, 347, 356–7, 382, 386
    London Diary 301, 303, 308, 317, 319, 321, 323, 324, 356–7, 358, 359, 382, 383, 385, 386, 447

INDEX

and *Beaverbrook* 78, 82
   and cartoon exhibition 267
   editor 16, 49
   see also Page, Bruce
   reviews in 44–5, 132, 137, 150, 228, 233, 301, 336, 348, 376, 379
New Testament: authorship of 12
   Paul's Epistles 12
New York Review of Books: article in 339
   reviews for 56, 58–9, 125, 293
Newman 364
Newport 8
newspapers, books on 30
Nicholson, Jenny: book for 403
Nicolson, Harold 8, 150
Nicolson, Nigel: *Portrait of a Marriage* 150, 152, 228
Nightingale, Florence 157
Nineteen Thirties, The 29
Nixon, Richard 9, 183
   in Peking 63
   policy 106
Nonconformists 252
North Africa: Allied landings 147
North of England tours 17
North Shields lecture 239
Northcliffe, life of 31
North-West Frontier 86
Northern Ireland: AJP's policy for 186
   killings in 59–60, 87
   sectarianism in 188
Norwich Historical Association lectures 107, 109, 294, 332, 398
novels: contemporary 7
   best of 1975 *see* Bradbury, Malcolm
nuclear weapons crisis 150
Nuneaton lecture 362

O'Connor, Feargus 14
Oberdank 339
Observer 427, 444, 448
   Beaverbrook serialization 51
   closure rumour 256, 259, 430
   colour supplement 102–3
   effect of *Times* strike 400
   literary editor *see* Kilmartin, Terry
   on Normans 440
   reviews for 76, 82, 89, 137, 140, 150, 177, 228, 230, 233, 236, 274, 339, 345, 347, 348, 352, 354, 374, 376, 395, 398, 403, 408, 414, 418, 426, 440–1
Oder-Neisse line 106
Offa, King 36
Offa's Dyke 34, 36, 39, 40, 80, 82, 85, 86, 100
   BBC programme on 340
Offenbach, Jacques: *La Belle Hélène* 259

Orpheus in the Underworld 58
Oh, Calcutta (show) 16
Oh, What a Lovely War! (show) 11, 257, 424
Ohrid (Okhrid?) 10
   meeting in 197, 203, 205, 207, 209–10, 212, 213, 214, 231
Old Testament: David 12
Oldfield, Maurice 421
opera 19, 29, 58
   audiences in Budapest and Moscow 203
   in Salzburg 38
   see also individual composers
Oran, sinking of fleet at 209
Order of Merit 369, 374 and n.
Origins of the Morocco Question 1880–1900, The 312, 319
Osborne, John: plays by 217
Ovendale 280
Owen, Robert 253
Owl Bookshop 433
Oxfam 258
Oxford History of Modern Europe 211–12
Oxford town: wartime 163
   with Eva at 387, 390
Oxford University 208
   AJP trys for post 13
   AJP up at 125, 174
   AJP's lectures at 6, 112, 134, 135, 149, 165, 230, 265–6, 267–8, 281, 445
   starts lecturing at again 79
   worries over 456, 460
   eating in Hall 240
   film on 58
   Ford lectures 125–6
   lecture organizer *see* Thomas, Geoffrey
   lunch toast 390
   Magdalen: AJP at *see* Magdalen College, Oxford
   news of AJP's marriage in 315
   party for AJP 284
   Regius professor 420–1
   St. Antony's: Bulgarian lecture 10
   seminar in 185
   students demand on meetings 67
   summer school, AJP teaches at 353, 442
      paid for 442
   tutor in politics 246
   University College 23
   Waynflete lectures 6
Oxford University Press 116
   Anniversary lunch toast 386
   Concise Oxford Dictionary 409
      copy for Eva 418
   head of *see* Davin, Dan

Pacey, Ron: death 445
Pach, P. Z. 306 and n., 307

Page, Bruce 386
Paine, Tom 4
Pakenham, Thomas 401, 403
Palmer, Alan 76
Paris: holidays in 29, 30, 34
    meetings in 133-40, 142-4, 146-7, 149, 151, 152, 155, 158, 159, 164, 168-9, 183, 185, 201, 231, 241, 399
    clothes for 148
    threat to 157-8
    Eva in 148, 150, 153, 154
    Hotel de la Bretonnerie 152, 153, 167
    Hotel Mont Blanc 134, 145-6, 148, 149, 231
    Restaurant Vagenerde 152
    strikes in 154
Parker, Alistair 65-6, 187, 190209
    seminar by 60-1
Parnell, life of 337, 346
Parvus 243
Passchendaele 375, 376
Past and Present: 'Chartism in London' 2
peace ballot 2
Peace Pledge Union 161
Peacock, Thomas Love: novels 230
    satirical portraits 228
Pearl Harbor 141
Pearson, Michael: *The Sealed Train* 243
Pedestrian Association address 397
Pelling, Henry 190
Pemberton Billing affair, review of book 376
Pembroke 15
Penguin paperbacks 163, 224, 255, 288, 298
    Communist Manifesto 6
    English History 1914-1945 6, 14
        see further Taylor, A.J.P.: works
    English history essays 226, 229, 235, 237
    rights to illustrated book of Second World War 246
    room at Foyle's 230-1
Pennine Way: BBC programme on 340
Penny (editorial assistant) 195
Pepys, Samuel: AJP reading diary 112, 330
Pevensey Castle 137
Peterloo massacre 2
    AJP on 285
Pilgrim's Way 47-8, 100
Pinter, Harold: and Antonia 315
    The Birthday Party 223, 225
    The Caretaker 65, 217, 223, 225, 292
Place Beaverbrook, France 17
Poet Laureate see Betjeman, Sir John
Poland 47, 97, 239
    invitation to AJP 51, 70, 73
    proposed lectures 68
    visit cancelled 71

Polanyi, Michael, and family 431
poppy, tall: alluded to 48-9
Populists 92
Porec: meeting in 91, 94, 123, 126, 159
Portal, Air Chief Marshal 386
Portsmouth lectures 280, 286
Post Office: blacks out AJP's show 195, 197
    see also Great Britain: strikes
Potsdam 225
Powell, Enoch 188
    Joseph Chamberlain 368
Prague Quartet 97, 100
prime ministers 233
    see also individual names
Princess of Wales, ancestry 438
Profumo Affair 130-1, 143
Proust, Marcel 167
psychology of politicians 202-3
Public Record Office (PRO) 64 and n.
    and Beaverbrook Library 209, 210, 214
    Cabinet papers 26, 78, 82, 97, 272, 296, 336
    closure of Chancery Lane 442-3
    Eva at 1 n.
publications, sponsored 264
Punch: articles for 327, 329
Pursuit of Love, The 261
Pussy see Lloyd-George, Lady Frances

Quinn family 458-60

Raeburn, Sir Henry 145
Ranke Gesellshaft conferences vii, 9, 42, 45, 203, 224, 235
    AJP at 167
    declines invitation 82, 135, 136
    plans for future 22
    proposed subjects 15, 203, 224
    Eva invited to 9, 10, 13, 196, 198
    contribution on naval pact 14
    proposed talk at 203
    1971 speaker 32
Ránki, György 116, 125, 129, 151, 246, 339
    book for review 249, 251
    wife (Elizabeth) 275 and n.
Ransome, Arthur 309-10
    autobiography 310
Ravenna: meeting in 43, 83, 175, 318, 340
Real Ale 297
Reading Historical Association lecture 271
rearmament 65, 182, 361, 387
Reed, John: *Ten Days that Shook the World*: introduction 255, 256
Rees, Goronwy 412
    A Chapter of Accidents 58
Reformers, the 182
Reichstag fire 2

INDEX

Reoch, David 440
Review of Modern History AJP's autobiography for *see* Taylor, A.J.P.: works: intellectual biography
revolutions of 1848 28
Rhineland, occupation 30, 100, 294
Ribbentrop, Joachim von 33, 51
Ripka, Hubert 433
Roberts, J. M. (ed.): *The Hutchinson History of The World* 318–19, 321
Robertson, Esmonde (ed.): *Origins of the Second World War, The* 26
Robertson, James 280
Rome: AJP in 2, 71
   Hotel Inghilterra 7, 9, 70
   lectures in 9
   strikes in 9
Roosevelt, Theodore 275
   biography 239
   on Churchill 187
   foreign policy 408, 410
   Roosevelt and Foreign Policy: review of 318, 411, 414
Rosen, Charles 389
Rosenberg, Alfred 33
Roskill, SW 23, 216, 294, 336
   article by 213
   Churchill and the Admirals 367, 370
Rote Kapelle 59
Roth, Edith 305
Rowland, Peter 281
Royal romances 198
   see also 'Mrs. Simpson'
Royal Televesion Society party 362
Royal United Services Institution Journal 213
Rugby talk 443
Russell, Bertrand 413
   programme on 410
   (with Whitehead) *Principia Methematica* 91
Russia: Cold War policy 169
   German invasion of 140–1
   invitation to Eva 155, 159
   Kulak war 187
   as Utopia 101
   see also Anglo-German naval pact
Ryan, Alan 301

Sackville-West, Vita 8
   biography 150
St Andrews University: lectures 176, 177, 182
   journey to 178
   students' questions 178
St Crispin and St George 334
St Denis 138, 169
St Helena patience 439
St Stephen's crown 102–3

St Swithin's Day 295 and n., 455
Salzburg: meeting in viii, 35, 36, 39, 40, 42, 44, 55, 68, 77, 120, 134, 198, 202, 224, 433
   difficulties with hotels 37–8
   Hotel Traube 41, 42
Salzburg Festival 38
Saturday Review of Literature 408
Schacht, Hjalmar 51
Schoenberg, Arnold 58, 63
Schubert, Franz: music by 58
Scott, Sir Walter 418, 423
   biography of 145
security, collective 187
   Eva and 277
Servant, The (film) 58
Seton-Watson, Christopher 304, 313
Seton-Watson, Hugh 304, 306, 308, 312, 313
Seton-Watson correspondence 304–5
   launch of 304–5
   review of 425
Severn river 86
Second World War 47, 100, 126
   AJP and: approach to researching 30–1
   changing ideas about 74
   on outbreak of 65
   Crozier interviews and 69–70
   greatest English novel of *see* Waugh, E.: *Sword of Honour*
   help for Finland 69–70
   lack of infornation on 118
   market for books about 28
   navy v. Air Force argument 56
   origins of real 178
   Official History of . . .: Grand Strategy 56, 294
   size of fleets 181
   see also individual battles, people, places
shadow cabinet 48–9
Shakespeare: *Hamlet* 29
Shandy, Tristram, father of 113
Shaw, G. B.: *Black Girl* 263
   Man and Superman 227
   Misalliance 126
   Pygmalion 190
Shelley, Percy B. 228
Shootist, The (film) 316
Sieberg, Else 190
Silvers, Bob 408, 450
   telegram from 432
Simon, Sir John 181, 187, 387
Simpson, Mrs. 160, 198
Shirley (Hadi, Eva's friend) 307, 309, 314, 359, 375, 387
Sked, Alan 196, 198, 203, 232, 366
   AJP asks for report on 198
   at LSE 342

INDEX

Crisis . . . essays in honour of A. J. P. Taylor 217 and n, 417–18
  doctorate 217
  and *Festschrift* 289
  party for AJP 289
Skidelsky, Robert 230, 233, 271, 302, 331
  review by 336
Skinners' Company dinner 103–4
Slansky, Peter 265
Smetana Quartet 116, 223, 224–5, 257
Smith, Mack 293
Snell, Andrew 298, 299, 301, 369, 424
South Africa, crisis in 287
South Downs Way 232, 234
Spain: AJP's reasons for not visiting 11
  in Second World War 281
Spanish Civil War 33, 65, 376
  symphony on 58
Spanish History of the War: articles for 255, 258, 262, 274
Spear, mission to Syria 368
Split: meeting in 151, 163, 164, 166, 167, 169, 171, 172–3, 174, 175, 183, 188, 399
Spectator: reviews for 301
Speer, Albert: Memoirs 23
Stalin, Joseph 275
  books on 176, 177, 185
  character 176
  and his generals 243
  and Roosevelt 239
Stalingrad 147, 243
Stallard, Jock 427, 428
statesmen, 1930s 62
  see also individual names
Stegerwaldhaus 17
Stendhal 34
Stevenson, Frances: love letters 111–12, 114, 132, 139
  see also Lloyg-George, Lady Frances
Sting, The (film) 373
Stockhausen, karlheinz 58
Stone, Norman 260, 292
  review by 314
Storia Illustrata: article for 225
Stoye, John 206, 211
Strachey, Lytton 242
Stravinsky, Igor 58
Stresa front 180
Struggle for Mastery in Europe 206
Suez crisis 388, 405, 437–8
Summersby, Kay 323
Summers, Sir John: 'Building London in the Eighteen-Sixties' 121
Sunday Express 76, 191, 229
  AJP and: articles for 23, 200, 287, 293, 330, 338, 375, 418
  contract renewed 363
  loses contract with 99, 101, 109–10
Sunday Times, The 229
  on AJP's 67th Birthday 123
  Beaverbrook serialization 51, 68
Sussex University lecture 62
Sutton, Ivan 454
Sutton lecture 93
Swift, Jonathan: *The Tale of a Tub* 24, 229, 282
Swing, Captain 4, 5
Switzerland: Third Reich and 185
Sykes, Christopher 101
Symes, Ronald: *The Roman Republic* 374
Szamuely, Helen 290
Szamuely, Tibor: memorial prize 116
  The Russian Tradition 256 and n.

Taylor Alan John Percivale (AJP):
  abusive letter to 190
  accused of being appeaser 26
  activities: mountain climbing *see* Lake/Peak District
    swimming *see* London: Highgate Ponds
    walking *see* Offa's Dyke etc.
  ambition, lack of 177
  appearance 20
    doubts about 74
    self-description 73–4
  approach to history viii
  archivist *see* Brooks, Rosemary
  birthdays 29, 68–9, 121, 122, 337, 338
    AJP on 288
    interview on 290
    presents 340
    Sked and 70th 217 and n.
    mentioned in the Press 123
  brother-in-law *see* Crosland, Anthony
  cardgames 439
  character 55–6
  children: acceptance of Eva 299, 333, 380, 381
    attitude towards 5, 15
    in autobiography 84
    Christmas with 53, 105, 161, 216, 221, 320, 376, 400, 415, 417, 420
    as companions 237, 391, 438
    daughter staying with 256–7
    as friends 435
    holidays with 7, 29 *passim*, 203
    see also individual places
    and living with Margaret 299
    outings with 47–8 *passim*
    paying for 211
    reads Bible to 12
    in school play 29

478

INDEX

sorrow at their growing up 144
tells about Eva 129, 309
see also individual names
and Christmas 53-4, 276
collapse of private life 174
dinner from admirers 284
domestic queries/criticisms of Eva 405 *passim*
driving 38, 66, 70, 74, 103, 117, 230, 343-4, 383
　new car 334, 337, 341, 343, 430
　problems from 111
on dying 265
effect of lack of work 264-5
on end of career 242
on Eva's grasp of English 59, 77, 90, 205
family home 39 and n.
　see further Isle of Wight, The Mill
and family parties 289
fear of having to leaving England 189, 261
films and operas seen *see* individual composers and titles
finances 110, 200, 204
　fees 241, 338, 448
　income tax assessment 425
　lack of earnings 211, 442, 448
　money for Eva *see* Haraszti Taylor, Eva
　pension/insurance worries 191
　problems 98-9, 101, 118, 184, 207, 229, 336
　share speculation 130, 156, 198, 247
　travel expenses 171, 172, 191, 194, 201, 212, 214, 220, 241, 244, 246, 254-5, 318, 346, 360
　VAT inspection 451-2
　worries over 136, 166
on friends/young people 16-17, 22, 113
　telling about Eva 211
on his faults 19
on French authors 34
German, improving 14
　see also Haraszti Taylor, Eva works
girlfriends: first *see* Tillotson, Kathleen
　reviving friendships 75
godson *see* Clazy, Michael
grandchildren 176, 320
　first 67, 72
　more expected 172
　outings with 397, 398-9, 430
　stay with 385
　and TV 436-7
　see also individual names
health 85-6, 92, 93, 102, 103, 395, 435, 449, 450, 452
　bowels 217-18, 234, 276, 344
　carbuncles on spine 381, 384, 388, 390

depression and its causes 22, 39, 57, 44, 105, 106, 115, 118, 134, 141, 155, 157, 158, 177, 186, 224, 266, 269, 270, 319, 353, 438, 454
　deterioration in 127, 201, 242-3, 261, 272, 376-7, 414, 416, 454
　dizzy spells 114
　donor cards 305-6, 384
　on future as invalid 457
　head colds/coughs 34, 77, 80, 117, 124, 279, 281, 291, 367
　informing Eva of 51-2, 55
　loss of memory 220, 439
　Parkinson's disease 447, 448, 454, 455
　prostate fears 217-18, 234, 276, 344, 449 *passim*
　rheumatism 106, 108, 111, 113, 117, 120, 124, 126, 153, 165, 255, 258
　skin problems 39, 85, 129-30, 131, 133, 134, 137-8, 197, 401, 403, 409-10
　teeth 96, 410, 415, 416, 452
　viral illness 304, 306
　views on 96
on himself as historian 52
honorary degree 14
house-hunting 41, 308 *passim*
　alterations/furnishings 365-6 *passim*
　local shops 438
　moves into 393-4
and just causes 13
keeps diary for Eva 404 *passim*
letters: on Eva's handwriting 167-8
　noting subjects in 114
　on problems 174-5
　on styles of address 168
literary agent *see* Higham, David
love for Eva 2, 52 *passim*
　and being together 117
　effect of 45
　lack of communication 95
　language barrier 127
　reasons for 36, 41
　worries over future with 57
and Magyar governing class 172
marriage, first two 168
　cost of 99, 101
　divorce from Margaret 127-8, 153, 154, 155
　resentment over first two 56, 64, 68
　unhappiness in 142, 155
marriage, to Eva 101, 108, 207, 217, 220, 1281, 297 and n., 304 and n., 306, 319
　accommodation after 41, 198, 270
　certificate 300, 302, 303, 306
　'declaration of no impediment' 297, 299
　practical difficulties 43 and n., 99, 156-7, 204

479

Press and 313
reasons for 92
ring 387
self-doubts about 64
settling problems 266
tells daughter about 129
and material possessions 201
meets pre-war colleague 148
mentioned in Russian book 289-90
modelling 102
and music 57-8, 100
   loses taste for 424
   see further City Music Society; individual composers
on nudism 459
on old age 451
as only child 36
at Oxford *see* Magdalen College, Oxford
parents: on his father 13
   father's girl-friend *see* 'Little Dolly'
   on his mother 211
   politics 108
photographs 54, 100
   in *Listener* 301
   in *Radio Times* 299
politics: on being a left-winger 73-4
   opinion on 179
   as pro-Russian propagandist 239
professorship 99, 209
priority in marriage 368
on researching pointless topics 254
reading tastes 112, 167, 172
   see also individual authors
on retirement: pension for 25, 121, 125, 157
   unemployed after 337
and reputation in Hungary 250
school *see* Bootham School
secretaries *see* Della; Veronica
self-pity 28
selling books 228, 230, 279, 282, 422, 429, 452
on sex 113, 115-16, 118, 295, 365
   homosexual 348
   and magazine questionnaire 119
   lesbian 152
social life 13
students/pupils: speaking on behalf of 24, 67
teaching, views on 205
on his treatment of women 15
typewriter 111, 129, 152, 425
   learning to use 17
way of life 13
   cure for boredom 440
   daily routine 52-3, 56, 391-2

eating/drinking habits 11, 19, 46, 129, 194, 197, 257
sleeping habits 65
wardrobe 17
will: contents of new 135, 162, 222
   in Eva's favour 298
   removes Crispin as executor 425
on worldwide violence 432
written about 7
Taylor, A. J. P.: works 312
on absurdity of 364
on choosing approach to 51
loses interet in writing 379
method of indexing 46
no ideas for 205
opinions of 244, 279
out of touch with new historical work 269-70
to be remembered by 177
autobiography 44, 55, 67-8, 84, 88, 108, 113, 119, 158, 163, 165, 174, 177, 205, 222, 224, 228-9, 247, 259, 415, 431
   delay in starting 73
   Eva's suggestions for 147
   finishes 253
   political beliefs in 111
   publisher for 363, 449
   rewriting/revising 312, 376, 391, 392, 425, 428, 433, 437, 447, 449
   stops work on 100, 241, 431
   subjects covered 147, 192, 197
   title 450
Beaverbrook 4, 6-7, 8, 12, 15-16, 18, 20, 26-7, 30, 64, 78, 93, 177, 247
   completes first draft 14, 34, 39
   criticisms of 77-8
   Eva's questions about 90
   faults in 72
   fee for 35
   finishes 42
   index for 44, 49, 51, 55, 59
   introduction for 34
   M. Aitken's approval/censorship 24, 34
   opinion of 24
   proof-reading 46, 49, 51, 54, 163
   publication of 73, 75, 77, 81, 82-3, 95
   publicity for 80
   reviews of 84, 86, 98, 104
   revising mss. 15-16, 31
   royalties given to Eva 73 and n., 76-7, 211
   sales 87, 98, 104
   serial rights 51, 68, 77, 99
   talk on 189
   as waste of time 288
Bismarck 206, 244

INDEX

German translation 1
lesson learned from 28
The Course of German History 24
  new preface for 425
  opinion of 24
  paperback edition 425
English History 1914-1945, new edition 6, 11, 14, 116, 133, 177
  bibliography update 116-17, 125, 130, 133, 222, 259
  rewriting 16, 24, 56, 243, 259, 279, 281
  no progress on 358, 363
  sales figures 288
Essays in English History 226, 229, 237, 298, 378, 417
  for Hungarian publication 378
  new piece for 412
  proof-reading 282
  publisher for 408
  publication of 299, 419, 427
  repackaging *see More Essays and Reviews, below*
  reviews of 300-1, 302
  title chosen 235, 241
Europe, Grandeur and Decline 378
From Paris to Petrograd: Revolutions and Revolutionaries 371, 419-20
The Habsburg Monarchy: copy sent to Eva 202
  mistakes in 6
  payment for Slovene translation 121
  rereads 244
How Wars Begin (from lectures) 403
intellectual biography 232, 242, 244, 247-8, 250, 259, 289, 342
  finishes 254
  with publishers 268
Life of Aitken see Beaverbrook, above
More Essays and Reviews 401-2, 408
  adds General Strike to 402
  problems with publisher's permissions 408
Napoleon III and Eugene 426, 428, 429
Origins of the Second World War 1, 105, 126
  AJP's opinion of 24, 178
  captions and index 200
  criticisms of 26
  Italian translator *see* Biocca, Lucia
  not profitable 211
  preface to 1
  reprint of 450
  title used by Macmillan 26
  trouble over 236
  viewpoint in 93
  wrong title for 178
The Second World War: an Illustrated History, The 59, 67, 74, 87, 96, 108-9, 111, 113, 116, 118, 119, 125, 134, 139, 141, 143, 147, , 147, 153, 154, 158, 159, 160, 164, 169, 228, 251
  adding more ideas 120
  advance copies 226
  approach to 81, 87, 93, 96, 102, 145, 160, 163
  as pro-Russian 160
  doubts about 62-3, 169
  excuse for postponing 70, 95
  international praise for 193
  maps/illustrations 166, 195
  proofs/index 166, 197
  problems with 72, 94-5
  publication 213, 235
  publicity for 233-4, 244
  reviews 237, 239, 242, 246, 254
  sells rights 246
  starts 102, 104, 105-6
  translated 251
The Struggle for Mastery in Europe 14
  AJP's opinion of 24
  rereads 244
  Russian introduction 251 n.
  as standard text 361-2
  supplementary bibliography 16
The Troublemakers 177, 288, 290, 389
  AJP's opinion of 24
The War Lords 339
  chooses pictures 339
  index 345
  publication 371
Taylor, A. J. P.: works as editor and introductions:
Bedside Guardian introduction 294
Communist Manefesto introduction 6
Cozier interviews *see under* Cozier
Crossman's *Diary* 273
Diary of Lady Lloyd-George 14-15
  poor sales 80
Dictionary of World History 149-50
  introduction for 49
The Last of Old Europe 274, 314, 339
  captions for 293
  introduction 272
Lloyd George love letters 111-12, 139, 164-5, 166-7, 183, 189, 193, 194, 198, 200, 208, 229, 247
  copyright claims 262, 275
  criticisms/reviews 270-1, 275
  idea for approach to 186, 193
  index 250
  at printers 229, 235, 237
  proofs 238, 259
  published 260

INDEX

publisher for 198, 213, 214
serial rights 229, 260
success of 266, 275
title (*Darling Pussy*) 143
Ten Days that Shock The World introduction 255, 256, 301
series on English Prime Ministers 95
Taylor, A. J. P.: projected works:
'British Destinies 1901–75' 301
Great Britain in the Twentieth Century 205, 268, 302
abandons 391
Cold War 387
English History (illustrated) 76, 125, 275, 312, 322, 324, 325
stops work on 327, 329
introduction to Russian war photographs 330, 334
post-war history 225
Taylor, A.J.P.: articles 23, 103, 110, 213, 301
see also New Statesman: London Diary
subjects covered: attack on British politicians 11
attack on metrication 287
Battle of Britain 255
the Biographer 378
Casement 125
democracy in Western Europe 252
English history 80
fiction and history 113
Fritz Fischer *Festschrift* 190, 289
General Strike 262
the Historian 378
Hitler's strategy 138
Labour history 2
Monarcy 327, 329
nudism 458
Oberdank 339
public opinion polls 200
release of Hess 375, 418
rival marches 200
school holidays 293
Second World War 258, 274
Tom Driberg 303
whatever happened to the New Elizabethan Age 330
Yalta conference 225
see also New Statesman: London Diary
Taylor, A. J. P.: broadcasting: on German Radio 268
profile of on German Service 391
subjects covered: abdication of Edward VIII 79
Act of Settlement 429
Beaverbrook 49, 823
Bertrand Russell 410, 413
Bismarck 340–1
Churchill 344–5, 366
his own reviews 318
How Wars Begin 335
Irish affairs 291–2
Monarchy 331
school examinations 432
Second World War 232, 235
Taylor, A. J. P.: lectures 208, 280, 447
chairman at 65
to Chiefs of Police 296, 298
Creighton lecture 119, 154
University plan to publish 160
during Eva's stay in England 282–3
falling attendances 269–70
fees due 22
future plans 230
general comments on 178
Neale lecture 119
Romanes lecture 450, 451
Scottish tour 386
televised *see below*
see also Ranke Gesellschaft
subjects covered: 1914–1945 230
Beaverbrook 4, 5
Beaverbrook as a historian 62, 65, 100
The British Left in the thirties 62, 252, 254, 266, 303
Bulgarian Horrors 1876 311, 312, 314–15, 317, 362, 364
Churchill 62, 213, 218
Churchill Oration 192
Churchill's National Government 366, 370
Cold War 27, 352
the coming of the war 28, 176, 229–30, 252, 254, 271
Congress of Berlin 386
decline of Europe 62
England and France 1933–35 9
Europe in the twentieth century 79
First World War 190, 368
the General Strike 289
governing élite of Austria-Hungary 46
Great Britain in the twentieth century 93
Half in, Half Out 241
history in general 230, 267–8, 311, 313
Hitler 239
how wars begin 268, 326, 331, 348
Lloyd George 253
My Place in History 375, 388–9
Nazi foreign policy and German society 99
origins of the Second World War 34, 100, 178, 227, 275–6
the Prime Minister 326

482

INDEX

Roosevelt 275
Second Front 65
Second World War 112, 120, 148, 165, 379
   the Soviet problem in British policy 185
   Stalin 97-8, 100, 102, 275
   state of the nation 200
   Suez crisis 203
   the twentieth century 313
   twentieth-century Europe 337
   the two World Wars 352
   on war 287
   the world in the twentieth century 323, 326
   see also individual countries/venues
Taylor, A. J. P.: reviews *see* individual authors/books
   lose of money over 125
   method of working 382
Taylor, A. J. P.: television appearances 1, 28, 76, 194, 202, 206, 231, 235, 253, 274, 284, 316, 402-3, 405, 410, 411
   lack of work 99
   lectures on 241, 326, 351, 353, 354
   Heroes series 4, 350-1
   new series 373, 387
   refuses 'Any Questions' 418
   self-opinion on 285
   The War Lords 275, 285, 298, 301, 342, 336
   reviews of 302
   weekly discussion programmes 188, 192-3, 250
   see further 'Free Speech'; 'In the News'
   subjects covered: *Beaverbrook* 80, 189
   Churchill in wartime 243, 244, 247, 250
   class struggle 165
   democracy in Great Britain 195
   devolution 274
   economic crisis 170, 252
   Election results 206
   Hitler and the Duke of Windsor 206
   Hitler boom in England 96
   how historians work 111, 115
   how wars begin 370, 371
   Lloyd George 275
   Manchester 285, 305, 306, 323
   monarchy 170
   Moon landings 11-12
   most political history is fiction 109
   pre-war British policy 407
   programme contents 28
   survey of year's events (1972) 106-7, 109
   walking 340
   War Room 452-3, 454

Taylor, Alison (granddaughter) 77, 292 *passim*
   health 385
   hospital visits 380
   operation 386, 387
Taylor, Amelia (daughter) 128 and n, 129, 299 *passim*
   financial troubles 152
   son (Milo) 385
   teacher-training 333
   birthday 422
Taylor, Crispin (son) 19 and n., 63, 83, 134, 135, 144, 148, 179 *passim*
   career 268
   doubts over 259
   future prospects 276, 280, 288, 426
   voluntary work 280 *passim*
   at Christ's College, Cambridge 63, 83, 262 *passim*
   AJP paying for 99
   AJP visits 152
   examinations 72, 80, 83 189
   Clerk of School Parliament 77
   driving 114, 120, 129, 133, 137. 140
   letters to/from AJP 295, 324-5, 426, 451
   and Lynn 434
   wedding 439 and n.
   and music 63, 68
   no contact with AJP 221, 318, 320, 430-1
   politics 174, 203
   as party candidate 431
   religious views 151
   in Russia 197
   vacation job 258
Taylor, Daniel (son) 29 *passim*
   AJP and: advice to 66-7
   fears for 429
   book for 376
   in Bristol 444
   career 269, 378-9
   decides on University 144, 259
   and dictatorship 114
   driving 192, 200, 209, 219, 225, 256
   essay on Marx 386
   gambling 225
   girlfriends: Anna 174, 312, 330, 343-4, 351, 352
   Gill 442, 455, 459
   hears AJP lecture 154
   health 287-8, 427
   drug problem 405
   interests 148, 179, 223, 257-8
   at Leeds University 277, 282, 309, 327, 366, 380, 422-3
   AJP paying for 99
   'forgets' to take exams 351

prospects 375
   threatens to leve 314
and Luke (friend) 441
and Manchester University 269, 273, 277, 280
in Poland 302, 306, 351
politics 66–7, 223, 229, 239, 258, 263, 273, 276, 288, 290, 312, 314, 317, 389
   canvassing 203, 227
   takes *Militant* 262, 409–10
and religion 405, 410
school: leads strike 77, 78, 80
   passes exams 144, 217, 245, 257
vacation job 256
Taylor, Eve (wife) 56
   Margaret's effect on 299
Taylor, Giles (son) 39 and n. *passim*
   canvassing 203
   Daniel and 223
   as Margaret's executor 436
   and The Mill 441
Taylor, Janet 39, 367, 368
   and AJP's new house 390
   expecting first child 67, 72, 74
   see further Taylor, Alison
   letter from Eva 380
Taylor, James (grandfather) 132
Taylor, Marjorie: Taylor lunch 436, 439
Taylor, Margaret (wife) 56, 155, 279 *passim*
   AJP and: determined to leave 296, 307, 382
      feelings for 348–9
      relations with 221–2
   behaviour over Eva 319–20, 327 *passim*
   death 426
      funeral 427, 428
   in Eva's autobiography 435
   ex-husbands 428
   health breakdown 293–4, 304
      operation 340, 345–6
   house-hunting 350 *passim*
      AJP lives with 260 and n., 388
   meets Eva 316, 317
   shares belongings 370, 426–8
Taylor, Mary 161 *passim*
   children (Finbar, Claire and Tilly) 320, 321 and n., 322 327, 374, 412, 421, 422, 430
   interests 331, 374
   and Eva 400
Taylor, Sebastian 161, 183 *passim*
   financial problems 404–5
   and religion 410
   and use of The Mill 436
Taylor, Sophia 51 and n, 52
   see further Howard, Sophia
Taylor, Telford: review of book 421, 422

Taylor Law on reading 418
Terraine, John 375, 376
Tewkesbury 221, 343
Thatcher, Margaret 260
   election as Party leader 228
theatre 19
   see also individual plays
Thomas, Dylan 276, 435
Thomas, Geoffrey: invitation to Eva 437
Thomas, Hugh: *The Spanish Civil War* 376
Thomson, George Malcolm: review by 275
Thomson, Lord: dinner for 81
Thompson, E. P.: AJP's opinion of 439
   and Dimbleby lecture 445
   'Exterminationism' address 439
   The Making of the British Working Class 214
   Times mention 438
Thompson, Mary and Pat 266, 284–5, 286, 387, 394
   AJP and Eva stay with 284, 291
   and AJP's marriage 315, 320
   and AJP's autobiography 273
   party 289
   warned of Eva's arrival 284
Thompson, Robin 289
Thompson, V.: *The Anti-Appeasers* 32–3
Thorne, Christopher 375
Tillotson, Professor Kathleen 57, 75, 121, 154, 228
   Novelists of the Eighteen Forties 75
Time-Life luncheon talk 200
Times, The 53, 432
   AJP's letter to 62
   and *Beaverbrook* 84
   articles on AJP 36, 75, 242, 438
   'Brains of England' 438
   editors 30
   owner *see* Thomson, Lord
   report of broadcast 291–2
   strike at 400
Times Educational Supplement: reviews in 314
Times Literary Supplement 216, 412, 418, 426, 450
   AJP and: articles for 113, 339
      sent to Eva 125, 130, 131
      opinion of 172
      reviews in 95, 96, 124, 125, 208, 254, 256 and n., 346, 348, 352, 423, 425
   Eva and 230, 246, 250
   subscriptions to 172, 382
Tito 103
Tojo, lecture on 275
Toland, John 318, 335, 336, 339
   The Rising Sun 312
Tolstoy, Leon: *War and Peace* 114, 167
Tombs, Mr 449

INDEX

Toscanini, Arturo 38
Toynbee, Philip 408
Travers, Ben 395
Treaty-Breakers or Realpolitikers 213
Trefusis, Violet 150
Trevor Roper, Hugh 130, 438
   AJP's joke on 139
   see further Dacre of Glantan, Lord
Trier 20
Trieste 91, 123
   British and 160
Trill (printers and stationers) 406, 416, 425, 426
Trotsky, Leon 66, 92
Trotskyites *see* International Socialists
Trottel, Ferdinand der 12
Turin 92, 93
Turkish embassy dinner 95, 151

Ulam 176
Ullman, Richard, H 141
Ulm 32, 35, 42
United Nations Trusteeship system 379
United States: anti-Communist feelings in 185
   attitude to Japan 30–1
   drug-taking in 9
   joint economic campaign against 49
   see also
universities, freedom in 13
   see also undividual universities
University College London: AJP and: last seminar 407
   lectures 79, 97–8, 100, 119, 227, 230, 268, 311, 312, 320, 337, 379
   renewal of lectureship 228, 349, 351
   retired from 336
   success of lectures 102
   and Beaverbrook Library 205
   dinners 332
      History Department 245
   Foundation Oration 371, 375, 388–9
   History Society 333
   Provost *see* Annan, Lord
   student sit-in 333
University College Hospital 452
Ustachi, denunciation of 63

Vansittart, Sir R. G. 47, 182, 280
Vaughan Williams, Ralph 58
Venice: meeting in 7, 22, 32–5, 43, 46, 49, 60, 64–5, 70, 71–2, 74, 76, 79, 81, 87–8, 91, 92, 94, 118–19, 151, 164, 175–6, 188, 199, 241, 318, 322–3, 324–6, 328, 329, 343, 344
   AJP's route to 91
   AJP takes start of autobiography 84, 88

AJP on Eva driving to 83
clothes, drink and food 88
Companion Guide to 136
Hemingway in 88–9
Hitler in 33
holiday flat 430
Lido 93, 95, 159
misunderstandings in 110
Pensione Alboretti 330–40, 342–3
Pensione Dinesen 80, 88, 92, 111, 122
waterbus 88
Venturi, Professor 92–3
   in Oxford 150–1
Verdi: *Falstaff* 38, 417
   Te Deum 189
   Traviata 19
Veronica (AJP's secretary) 38 and n., 39, 40, 44, 53, 54, 70, 74, 83, 90, 93, 95, 151, 183, 231, 241, 271, 374
   AJP kisses 122
   and *Beaverbrook* proofs 46
   leaves AJP 112 and n, 118
   new job 121
   on holiday 89
Versailles 134
   Treaty of 30
      Anglo-German naval pact and 4
      disarmament clauses 182
Victor Emmanuel 93, 94
Vienna 1
   AJP's first intentions in 21
   international conference 11
   meeting in 218, 433
Vierteljahres heft für Zeitgeschichte 2
Vietnam War: end of 106
   U.S. involvement in 9, 11
      policy, novel about 142
   Sunday Express and 76
Vincent, John 312
   lecture 363, 364
Vinogradov, Cyril 289–90
Voluntary Servide Overseas (VSO) 280, 288, 290
Vom Politik zu Weltpolitik 4

Wagner: Ring cycle: AJP's opinion of 277
   in English 58
   Reingold 58, 68–9
   Siegfried 277
   Valkyrie 276, 277
   Tristan and Isolde 100
Wainwright walking books 434
Waite: *Hitler the Psychopath* 349, 354
Wales: castles and other sites 86, 253
   devolution question 276
Waley, Arthur 279

INDEX

British Public Opinion and Abyssinia 276–7
Walls, Tom 395
Walmsley: *Peterloo* 2
Ward, Artemus 333
wars 18
   AJP's expectation of 423
   see also individual wars
Watt, Donald: 'The Historiography of
      Appeasement' 268(?), 289
Watt, Donald: on Ferrari 342
Waugh, Evelyn 112
   Brideshead Revisited 217
   Decline and Fall 324
   Sword of Honour 217, 222, 224, 226, 228, 282
Wayne, John 316
Webb, Bill 422, 453, 454
Webern, Anton von 58
Week, The 181 and n.
Weidenfeld and Nicolson (publishers):
   managing director *see* Falkus,
      Christopher
Weinberg, G. L. 33
Wellingtopn, Duke of 47
   AJP's assessment of 96–7
Wells, H. G. 131
   biography of 130, 137
   Outline of History 319
   Rebecca West and 226, 228
   see also H. G. Wells Society
Wendt, Bernd Jürgen 171
   Economic Appeasement . . . 47, 49, 52, 97,
      110
      copy returned to AJP 122
      details for Eva 50
      review of 418
      sources 49, 50–1
West, Rebecca 223
   Black Lamb and Grey Falcon 226
   and Wells *see* Wells, H. G.
Wheeler, Katherine Bligh 121, 160
   present for 160
Wilcox 420
Wilde, Oscar 7
William of Waynflete 6
Williams, Neville 304, 306, 308
   death 336
Wilson, Angus 112, 367
   AJP's review of book 368

Wilson, Harold: AJP's criticism of 160
   Crossman on 272
   and election 203
   elevation of secretary 186
   Eva's quieries on 333
   going downhill 201
   publisher for 366
   scandal over 331, 383–4
Wilson, Sir Henry 141
Wilson, John 257
Wilson, T. W. 51
Wimbledon Historical Association talk 289
Winchester lecture 366
Windsor, Duke of: as head of government 206
   death of 79
Wohltat, Helmuth 51
Wolverhampton lecture 65, 67
   country house stay after 67
Woodford 62
Woodman, Dorothy 367
Worcester Cathedral 216, 221
working classes, assertion of 121
   see also Thompson, E. P.
world economic slump 186
world markets, pre-war 50–1
Worsthorne, Peregrine 250
Wrigley, Chris 418
Wroclaw, Poland 68
Wyatt, Woodrow 188

Yamamoto (battleship) 181
yoke fellow 328
York 161, 163, 164, 281, 344
   enforced stay in 162
York Historical Association 120
York Minster 368
York University 14, 164
Yorkshire, Eva in 291

Zagreb Academy *see* Seton-Watson
   correspondence: launch of
   Croat Institute of Historical Studies 315
   invitation to Eva 306–7
      cancelled 307–8
   meeting in 309, 311, 312, 313, 315–16
Zeldin (former pupil): articles by 211–12
Zhikova, Mme 10
Zhukov, Marshal 145
Zola, Emile: *Nana* 279, 283